FROM ONE WAR TO ANOTHER

FROM ONE WAR TO ANOTHER

*Powerful leaders start wars but citizens
fight them and experience the horror*

John W. Lanza

Bright
Spot
BOOKS

Bright Spot BOOKS

Caldwell, NJ 07006

Cover Art by Jim Ryan
Book Layout and Drawings by Todd Slater
Chapter Silhouettes and Maps by Author
Photo Credits appear in Photo Captions

Visit website at www.FromOneWarToAnother.com

Library of Congress Control Number: 2023923641

ISBN: 978-0-9827529-1-3

Printed in the United States of America

First Edition: June 2024

The seed for this book was planted in 2011 when a World War II veteran airman, John J. Cooney, sought me out at a book talk to tell me about his experience in going down over Italy in a B-24 heavy bomber. This book includes his experiences in World War II as well as those of his crewmates and other crews in his bomb group, but it includes much more such as his father's experiences in World War I and my experiences in trying to understand World Wars I and II.

John's father was in the Medical Department in World War I which was tasked with keeping the troops fit for service and restoring them to health when they were wounded or became sick. John was in the Army Air Forces in World War II flying strategic bombing missions with a far different task— destroying the enemy's ability to wage war by bombing the factories that made their weapons; the oil fields that fueled them; the airports, harbors, and marshalling yards that stored their respective planes, ships, and trains; and the transportation facilities that delivered firepower and manpower to the battlefront.

World War I was so awful that it was supposed to be the war to end all wars, yet twenty years later World War II was far worse because countries kept developing more destructive weapons between wars. While I spent years researching both wars, I only had the pleasure of spending time with two of the airmen in the book—John and one of his crewmates, Meyer Osofsky. I am grateful for those experiences and would like to dedicate this book to them and the other veterans I wrote about. Each one of them deserves our everlasting respect and gratitude.

Contents

Exhibits

Preface

On Sunday, February 27, 2011, I gave a book talk at the Long Island State Veterans Home on the campus of Stony Brook University in Stony Brook, New York. The veterans' home was at the end of an aptly-named road—Patriots Road—which was lined with banners describing its veterans—bravery, honor, duty, valor, courage, spirit, caring, dignity, respect, and pride. This was my seventh book talk, but my first at a veterans' home. I was looking forward to it because my book—*Shot Down Over Italy: A true story of courage and survival in Nazi-occupied Italy*—pays tribute to veterans.

In 2006, I formed a small publishing company, Bright Spot Books LLC, because I wanted to write stories about bright spots in our society, and who are brighter spots than the veterans of World War II? Many lost their money in the Great Depression and loved ones in World War II, but emerged from those tough times with goodness, grace, and humility. Tom Brokaw got it right when he called them the Greatest Generation.

My wife Diana accompanied me on the eighty-mile trek from our home in New Jersey to the veterans' home on Long Island. The talk was sponsored jointly by the Center for Italian Studies at Stony Brook University and the Long Island State Veterans Home. We decided to have it at the Veterans Home instead of the Italian Studies Center so as not to inconvenience the veterans. Arriving early, I noticed that the chairs were set up a good distance from the lectern. As the veterans filtered in, I quickly saw why—many of them were in wheelchairs.

Thanks to Lee Grace Cannella of the Veterans Home and Josephine Fusco of the Italian Studies Center, we had an impressive turnout. Dr. Mario Mignone, Director of the Center, got the ball rolling with a brief history of the war in Italy and nice comments about my book. I had a captive audience, and the talk went well.

I was told beforehand that two veterans—John Cooney and John Blankenship—wanted to see me. After the talk, I met with each of them. Cooney had flown thirty-five missions as a ball-turret gunner in a B-24 Liberator during World War II, and Blankenship had flown 84 missions as a fighter pilot in an A-26 Invader during the Korean War. I had a nice chat with each of them.

I kept in touch with John and noticed that he was a caring "can do" person who was appreciated by the staff and residents of the Long Island

FROM ONE WAR TO ANOTHER

State Veterans Home. He was featured in a television program called *Heroes on Our Island* which sought out Long Island residents who did extraordinary things to make the world a better place.[1] He was also featured on the cover of the brochure of the Long Island State Veterans Home (Exhibit 0.1).[2]

I learned that he wrote a letter on behalf of interested residents, employees, and volunteers to the executive director of his veterans' home, Fred S. Sganga, to initiate a "Butterfly Project" to plant bushes with flowers that attract butterflies and offered $200.00 for the first purchase of bushes.[3] Butterflies were once caterpillars that made silk and one wonders if he initiated the project because the parachute that saved his life during the war was made of silk?

I also learned that he was recruited by Mr. Sganga, President of the National Association of State Veterans Homes, to speak on behalf of veterans like himself on the importance of the Senior Crimestoppers Program which protected the 30,000 veterans in our nation's 160 state veterans' homes. In his speech, John pointed out that veterans entered the service, went to war, did the job, and were proud of their service. Now they are vulnerable as senior citizens and needed this program to help protect them against petty crime.[4]

Two years later, on May 19, 2013, I was invited back for another talk, and John and I got together again. Like my uncle, with whom I bonded on my book, he had to parachute out of a plane that went down over Italy, but unlike my uncle, who landed in enemy territory in Nazi-occupied Italy and left his parachute behind, John landed in friendly territory south of Nazi-occupied territory in Italy and kept his parachute. Later, he had a tailor shop in Italy make a silk wedding dress out of it. I found this fascinating.

John and I continued to correspond and share information. I visited him on March 12, 2014, at which time I gave him a binder with my research findings. Three months later, I visited him again, but he was feeling his age, so we didn't spend much time together. That night I sent him a letter mentioning that I was thinking of writing an article about him and publishing it in the Long Island State Veterans Home newsletter around Veterans Day (November 11, 2014). He liked the idea, so I began to work on the article.

While writing the article, I connected with Meyer Osofsky who lived and trained with John in the States and lived with and flew with him on combat missions in Italy. In fact, he was on the plane with John that went down over Italy. He had nice things to say about John and even visited him at the Long Island State Veterans Home with his son Alan. Unfortunately, John's health had taken a turn for the worse and he and Meyer were unable to share wartime stories.

Exhibit 0.1
Veteran John J. Cooney

Courtesy of the Long Island State Veterans Home

FROM ONE WAR TO ANOTHER

John died on September 21, 2014, ten days before the article was published in his in-house newsletter. Prior to his passing, however, I sent him a letter giving him a rough idea about what I was writing, so he left us aware of what I was going to say about him. I sent the article to the Long Island State Veterans Home for publication in its October newsletter (Exhibit 0.2).[5]

John was laid to rest at the Calverton National Cemetery on Long Island. His daughter Mary asked me to say a few words at his burial service. As I started to speak, Taps began to play at a nearby burial service, making an emotional experience even more emotional. After the honor guard folded the flag and presented it to Mary, she and her brother Kevin said they wanted me to have it. I was deeply moved and honored. It is now in a display case in my home, a daily reminder of John and veterans like him and Meyer.

In November 1914, Mary also arranged a Remembrance Celebration for her father at which family members and friends, some of whom traveled from afar, paid tribute to him. I was asked to talk about his wartime experiences. It was evident from the speeches that he touched many, including me, in an incredibly positive way. One of his nieces, Nancy Leo, reminisced that he would introduce the kids in his family as "America's future" and that when he called her the first thing she always heard was "Hollywood calling!" He was a positive influence in their family so when a family member referred to me as his biographer, I felt an obligation to learn more about him, with the thought of writing a longer article or maybe even a book paying tribute to him and the veterans he served with during World War II.

My thoughts turned to action, and I began doing research to determine the feasibility of writing another book. Because I was able to find the "loading list" for each of my uncle's twenty-eight missions in a B-25 medium bomber, I just assumed I would be able to find the "loading list" for each of John's thirty-five missions in a B-24 heavy bomber. After considerable time and effort, I learned that John's bomb group did not pass down the "loading lists."[6] This development, along with John's passing, significantly hampered my ability to obtain the amount of information I thought I needed for a book.

Determined to carry on, I learned that John's father, John Sr., served in World War I, which made me consider writing about two wars and the service of a father in one and the son in the other. I began to read about World War I and the more I read the more interested I became in that so-called Great War. At one point when I was finding it more difficult to obtain information on World War I than on World War II at the National Archives, I asked an archivist why and was told because it wasn't our war.

A Resident's Story by John Lanza

John J. Cooney grew up during the tough times of the Great Depression in North Bergen, New Jersey, as the oldest of five children. In 1939, at the age of sixteen, things got even tougher when he lost his father and he and his fourteen-year old brother Robert became the main breadwinners of the family.

Cooney remained in school, but he worked several jobs. He worked for a tailor during the week, an A&P on Saturdays, and a deli on Sundays. Often, he brought home unsold food for the family. At the age of twenty he answered the call and entered the Army Air Forces. He trained hard to become a ball-turret gunner on a B-24 Liberator, a four-engine heavy bomber with a ten-man crew. They were being trained to defend against enemy cannons on the ground and enemy fighters in the air while flying missions to bomb precise targets from four miles up. After training for seventeen months, Cooney and the crew headed for Europe. They were assigned to the 725th Bomb Squadron of the 451st Bomb Group in Castelluccio dei Sauri, Italy.

Cooney entered into combat in October 1944 and flew thirty-five missions over the last seven months of the war. He had many harrowing experiences, but one in particular stood out in his mind, his fourth mission on October 23, 1944. On that fateful day seventy years ago, his plane was flying over the Adriatic Sea to bomb a target in Germany. About 150 miles from the home base, it lost number one engine when a cylinder head blew and number two engine because of an excessive oil leak.

They were forced to abort the mission and drop out of the formation. His pilot Bob Cookman and his co-pilot Russ Flint acted quickly to prevent the aircraft from going into a spin, and struggled to fly it back to the Italian mainland on two engines.

Cooney recalls that the aircraft was descending rapidly and gradually getting out of control despite the heroic efforts of Cookman and Flint. With no suitable place in sight for a crash landing, Cookman ordered his crew to abandon ship. Flint jumped at about 1,000 feet, but Cookman bailed too low for his chute to open properly and save his life. Thanks to the heroics of his pilot and to his trusty parachute, Cooney survived the war. He attended Haverford College on the GI Bill, married and raised five children. When he was in Italy, he had an Italian tailor make his parachute into a silk wedding dress. Having worked for a tailor, he knew the value of silk, especially the silk that saved his life. The significance of the dress has never been lost on his daughter Mary. She has worn it on Veterans Day to educate her class about veterans like her father whose service and sacrifice preserved our precious freedoms.

Exhibit 0.2
Article on John J. Cooney
Courtesy of Long Island State Veterans Home

FROM ONE WAR TO ANOTHER

The Americans were in World War I for about a year and a half compared with the British and French who were in it for almost four and a half years. General Pershing, the leader of the American forces in World War I, understood this and said, "The struggle of the Allies was much longer, their sacrifices much greater than ours."[7] Nevertheless, the entry of the United States into that world war provided the manpower necessary to turn the tide in favor of the Allied Powers to outlast the Central Powers and end the war.

In wartime, there are fighting forces and there are support forces to support the fighting forces. John Sr. served with one of the support forces in World War I. He was an enlisted man in the Medical Department which cared for the sick and wounded during World War I. His son John served with the fighting forces in World War II as an enlisted man in the Army Air Forces who flew combat missions. While this book discusses two wars and how they were started, fought, supported, and ended, it also has a strong bent toward the Medical Department John Sr. served with during World War I and the Army Air Forces John and Meyer served with during World War II.

While John Sr. did not use the senior designation, it is used throughout this book for the sake of clarity. By some standards, both father and son were ordinary people called upon to serve their country. From my vantage point, they, and others like them, are far more than ordinary. In many respects, this book is a tribute to men like John and his father plus Meyer and others who were called upon to serve their country in time of war and did so honorably. It also pays tribute to some of the leaders of our armed forces and some of the leaders of our industries who supported the troops during both wars.

World Wars I and II forced countries to go from producing goods and services that improve the quality of lives to producing goods and services that destroy lives. These wars were horrible in so many ways, but when they reared their ugly heads and posed threats to our way of life, we needed men and women like those in this book.

Chapter 1

THE ROAD TO WORLD WAR I

John Joseph Cooney was born on Friday, May 4, 1923, almost four years after his father, John Joseph Cooney Sr., returned from serving overseas in France during World War I. He was born in New York City to John Sr. and Anna Millon Cooney. When John was born, America and the rest of the world, particularly Europe, were recovering from World War I, the deadliest conflict the world had ever known up to that point. During that war, his father served with the United States Army Medical Department in three evacuation hospitals in France that provided medical support for soldiers of the American Expeditionary Forces fighting in France on the Western Front.[1]

World War I was so big and so awful that many felt it would be the war to end all wars. It involved over thirty countries[2] and sixty-five million people.[3] Over nine million military personnel were killed and over twenty-one million were wounded.[4] In addition, almost eight million military personnel were either missing in action or prisoners of war.[5] One would think that the high number of casualties would be incentive enough to prevent future wars. Who could have known then that four-out-of-every-five men born in the United States during the 1920s, when John and his brother Robert were born, would twenty years later serve in a war that was far worse?[6] But there were hints after WWI that problems lie ahead.

During the same year John was born, inconceivable inflation was taking place in Germany, the result of the Allies socking it to Germany after World War I. The terms Germany was forced to accept in defeat were harsh and ruined its economy.[7] The strain on the German economy contributed to the German mark becoming almost worthless. For example, 62 billion marks were worth only one U.S. dollar in October 1923.[8] The people were losing faith in their government and that same year a young man attempted a coup in Munich to seize power from the government for himself and his political party. The coup was unsuccessful, and he was sent to prison, but the power-grab made the young man a national figure. While in prison, he put his thoughts in a book describing his political philosophy and his planned conquest of Europe.[9] That man, of course, was Adolf Hitler, and his party was the Nazi party.

Both of John's parents were the children of immigrants and both were born in the metropolitan New York City area—his father on March 27, 1890, in New York City and his mother just across the Hudson River in Jersey City on March 24, 1899.[10] Interestingly, John's grandparents had migrated from countries that were on different sides in both World War I and World War II. On his father's side, both grandparents came from Ireland. On his mother's side, his grandmother came from Austria and his grandfather from Hungary.[11]

America was the land of opportunity, and John's grandparents on both sides came to America to improve their lot in life. Many other families came to America for the same reason, making its population multi-ethnic. According to the 1910 census report, 13.5 million of the 92 million Americans were born in a foreign country. The most were born in Germany (2.5 million) followed by Russia (1.6 million), Ireland (1.3 million), Italy (1.3 million), Great Britain (1.2 million) and Austria (1.2 million).[12]

Immigrants were drawn to the United States because it had a government founded on the principal that all men are created equal. The desire of the American colonists to be free and independent from British rule resulted in the American Revolution. The 1776 Declaration of Independence drafted by Thomas Jefferson stated that "all men are created equal, that they are endowed by their Creator with certain unalienable rights, that among these are Life, Liberty and the Pursuit of happiness."[13] The founding fathers of America created a government that allowed people to participate in governing themselves. Immigrants came to American to get away from the monarchies and autocracies of Europe that viewed them as subservient, not in any way equal to their leaders.

Interestingly, Jefferson helped his friend Lafayette (Gilbert de Motier the Marquis de Lafayette) draft the 1789 French Declaration of the Rights of Man and of the Citizen that inspired the French Revolution. Like the Declaration of Independence, its basic principle was that "all men are born and remain free and equal in rights,"[14] The desire of people to be free from the Old Order of monarchies and autocracies and to have a voice in government was growing in Europe before World War I. Influenced by the American Revolution and the French Revolution, the people were causing the Old Order to break down in favor of a New Order with more power for the people. More people wanted a more democratic form of government and were willing to fight for it.

Freedom is not free and American citizens were expected to serve their country in times of war. They were expected to protect and preserve America's four precious freedoms expressed eloquently years later by President Franklin Delano Roosevelt in his speech to Congress on January 6, 1942, after the bombing of Pearl Harbor—freedom of speech, freedom of religion, freedom from want, and freedom from fear. In his notes preparing the speech, he wrote: [15]

"The first is freedom of speech and expression everywhere in the world. The second is freedom of every person to worship God in his own way everywhere in the world. The third is freedom from want—which translated into international terms means economic understandings which will secure to every nation everywhere a healthy peace time life for its inhabitants. The fourth is freedom from fear—which translated into international terms means a world-wide reduction in armaments to such a point and in such a thorough fashion that no nation anywhere will be in a position to commit an act of physical aggression against any neighbor."

The fear of war was ever present because nations were increasing their armaments, not reducing them. As one might guess, those citizens born in countries that America was at war against came under increased scrutiny during World War I and later during World War II. To prove their loyalty, many of them enlisted in the military or supported the military in other ways such as purchasing war bonds. The great majority of German foreign-born American citizens proved to be loyal during World War I and World War II. In fact, General Pershing, the Commander-in-Chief of the American Expeditionary Forces in World War I, was of German heritage, and so was General Eisenhower, the Supreme Commander of the Allied Forces in World War II.[16] On the other hand, a small minority of German Americans were not loyal to America. Of those, some returned to Germany while others became spies in America, and some even engaged in espionage.[17]

FROM ONE WAR TO ANOTHER

The Seeds of Discord

World War I was called the Great War because of its enormous scale. There had been other wars, but none had the scope and impact of this global conflict. It brought new ways to kill such as poisonous gases that caused slow, painful deaths; tanks that brought significant destructive power to the battlefield; machine guns that wrought much more havoc than rifles; flamethrowers that brought hellfire to the troops; more powerful and accurate artillery that could obliterate soldiers from miles away; and airplanes dropping bombs on soldiers for the first time.[18]

The Industrial Revolution had its pluses and minuses and the ability to create weapons of destruction that did way more than just kill was a big minus for the soldiers in the trenches of World War I. This was the first war in which many soldiers who were killed in action couldn't even be identified, leading to unknown soldier monuments in countries that honor the war dead. There were of course many technological advancements that enabled people to be more productive and live longer, but the big minus was the creation of more powerful weapons of destruction. By World War II, we had weapons that could destroy cities and today we have weapons that could destroy much more. Let's hope we never have a third world war.

World War I didn't just happen overnight. The seeds of discord were planted many years before in the middle of the 19th Century when Otto von Bismarck of Prussia, one of the thirty-nine independent states of Germany, became a powerful leader with a vision of uniting the German states into a superpower. Bismarck grew up in a household that subscribed to the Prussian way of life, namely a well-ordered, military-like, disciplined life. It was believed that such a life involved being on time, dressing neatly, obeying the rules, and following orders.[19]

Bismarck was a respected leader. With his diplomatic and persuasive skills, he won over Wilhelm I, the King of Prussia. In 1861, Wilhelm I chose Bismarck to be his prime minister and allowed him to guide policy and become the de facto leader of Prussia. On his watch, Bismarck adopted a strategy to grow through war. He forced two wars—one against Denmark in 1864 and another against Austria in 1866—which doubled the size and wealth of Prussia. Both wars demonstrated that militarism and autocracy could benefit the state. Consequently, Prussians who had opposed war began to embrace and even applaud it. Put in other terms, Bismarck transformed a peace-loving people into a war-loving people.[20]

The Road To World War I

With Bismarck in the driver's seat, Prussia became the most powerful of the German states, none of which were free states. They were mostly monarchies supported by divine-right aristocracies in both rural areas and urban areas. The country aristocrats were landowners who lived in castles and ruled over the peasants in the villages; they wanted war to escape taxes that peace brings. Bismarck's father was one of them. The city aristocrats were the manufacturing capitalists who ran the factories that grew out of the industrial revolution and contributed to a significant increase in the populations of German cities; they wanted war because it was good for business.[21] Even the German universities promoted war, teaching that war is beautiful, noble, desirable, and right—the final measure of a nation's worth. They taught that "Germany is stronger, wiser, better than 'decaying' England, 'decadent and licentious' France, 'uncouth and anarchic' Russia, and 'money-serving' America."[22]

In 1870, Bismarck provoked a third war, with France this time. Prussia again emerged victorious, giving Bismarck the power in 1871 to unite the thirty-nine German states into a new German Empire under Kaiser Wilhelm I. Kaiser is the German word for emperor. Bismarck became the chancellor, which is the equivalent of a prime minister. From his new position, Bismarck continued to promote a policy of war to make Germany a military and economic power in Europe.[23] Bismarck didn't just defeat France—he embarrassed the proud nation on the world stage and planted seeds of hate which took root and grew over the next forty years.[24] When the French tried to negotiate favorable terms for ending the war, he called them an envious and jealous people who would not show gratitude for more favorable terms and socked it to them.[25] He took their land—Alsace and Lorraine with five thousand square miles of territory, one million five hundred thousand people, and valuable iron and ore deposits. He took their money—a billion dollars in reparations. And he kept a German army in Alsace and Lorraine until the debt was paid.[26]

Things changed for Bismarck in the year 1888 which is known in Germany as "the year of the three emperors." His mentor, Kaiser Wilhelm I, died on March 9 at the age of ninety. He was replaced by his son, Frederick III, who was sick with throat cancer and died ninety-nine days later, on June 15 at the age of fifty-six. This resulted in Kaiser Frederick III's son, Wilhelm II, inheriting the crown at the age of twenty-nine. Wilhelm II had been brought up to respect the abilities of Bismarck, but he was strong-minded like Bismarck and started to usurp some of his powers. undermining him in the process. This lack of respect prompted Bismarck to resign. While Kaiser

Wilhelm II was a militarist like Bismarck, he lacked the experience, skill, and diplomacy of Bismarck.[27]

Kaiser Wilhelm II dreamed of building Germany into a major naval, colonial, and economic power, and Great Britain was aware of this threat to their power on all three fronts.[28] He admired the British Empire and the Royal Navy and set out to plant colonies around the world and build a rival German navy.[29] To have a reserve of manpower to draw from in case of war, Kaiser Wilhelm II pushed through a military requirement that each man, when he reached the age of twenty, had to serve for two years.[30] In pursuing his dream, however, he was unable to maintain the carefully manipulated balance of international rivalries as had master-strategist Bismarck. For example. Bismarck considered it important to have a good relationship with Russia to prevent Germany from having to fight a two-front war.[31] Wilhelm II, on the other hand, broke the alliance Bismarck had forged with Russia and this break eventually led to Germany fighting a two-front war during World War I which was not in Germany's best interests.[32]

With Kaiser Wilhelm II arming his country, other European nations became worried about the intentions of Germany, especially France on its western border and Russia on its eastern border. And of course, Great Britain recognized Germany's threat to its world power. This unrest prompted European nations to arm themselves for protection.[33] Some of the larger nations entered into treaties and alliances to help each other in case of war. Some of the smaller nations aligned themselves with some of the larger nations for protection.[34] The irony of all this is that, while these diplomatic alliances were formed to prevent war, they had the opposite effect. They created dependencies that not only paved the way to war but led to a world war with a level of destruction that few could have imagined beforehand.

The Balkans

Whenever major change occurs among nations, stability is often at risk, and this was the case in Europe leading up to World War I. As the German states of the German Empire united into a formidable independent Germany, three major empires that lacked such unity—the Austro-Hungarian, Ottoman, and Russian Empires—were crumbling as individual states in each empire sought independence. In time, the fall of the Austro-Hungarian Empire would result in the independent states of Austria, Czechoslovakia, Hungary, and Yugoslavia. The fall of the Russian Empire would result in the creation of the independent states of Poland and some of the Baltic states—Finland, Estonia, Latvia, and Lithuania. And the fall of the Ottoman Empire would result in the independent state of Turkey and some of the Balkan states— Serbia, Montenegro, and Bulgaria.

With Germany growing in strength and with France, Russia and Great Britain worried about Germany's belligerence, alliances continued to be formed for protection and security. These alliances resulted in dependencies that enabled a regional conflict to escalate into a world war that took everyone by surprise. Since the turn of the century, the European alliances had tilted against Berlin and its militaristic posture.[35] The two large alliances before war broke out in Europe were the Triple Alliance between Germany, Austria-Hungary, and Italy, and the Triple Entente between Great Britain, France, and Russia. An entente is like an alliance in that countries agree to help each other in affairs of international concern. The Turks of the Ottoman Empire jumped on the bandwagon by aligning with the Triple Alliance. Some of the Balkan states, such as Bulgaria, aligned with Austria-Hungary in the Triple Alliance while others, such as Serbia, aligned with Russia in the Triple Entente.[36]

As countries built up their armies, an arms race developed and tensions grew in Europe (Exhibit 1.1), which was becoming a powder keg ready to blow.[37] Germany was being aggressive and worrying other countries and did not care about losing "face." It cared about losing the arms race.[38] War was becoming inevitable and all that was needed was a spark. The large industrial countries were reaching beyond their borders for more land and resources. Great Britain and France had each established an empire of colonies, and Germany and Italy wanted to follow suit.[39] At the same time, militarism and nationalism were growing in each country with patriots able and willing to fight for their independence. Consequently, if one country had a problem with another country, the growing alliances would draw in more countries and escalate the problem.

Another source of European tension was the instability in the Balkans, which had a multitude of ethnicities that traditionally hated and clashed with each other.[40] The Balkans included Greece, Serbia, Bulgaria, Macedonia, and Bosnia (Bosnia-Herzegovina), and were surrounded by four important seas—the Black, Mediterranean, Adriatic, and Aegean Seas—that were vital for cultural and mercantile exchange. The Balkans were also sandwiched between three major empires—the Ottoman, Russian, and Austro-Hungarian Empires—that wanted a piece of the Balkans and were in decline.[41]

Exhibit 1.1
Europe Before World War 1

Before World War I, much of Europe was governed by powerful autocrats who ruled empires with absolute power over the people and built armies to expand their power. There were the German Empire ruled by Kaiser Wilhelm I, the Russian Empire ruled by Tsar Nicholas II, the Austro-Hungarian Empire ruled by a dual monarchy 1n which Franz Joseph was Emperor of Austria and King of Hungary, and the Ottoman Empire ruled by Sultan Mehmed V. The people were subservient, democracy and freedom were absent, and civil unrest was high. When the Prussian autocracy and militarism led to a united German Empire that posed a threat to the rest of Europe, tensions ran high, and alliances were formed to keep peace and provide protection in case of war because there was no international forum in which to debate disputes between nations. Consequently, when Archduke Franz Ferdinand, heir to the Austria-Hungary crown, was assassinated by a Serbian nationalist, a dispute between Austria-Hungary and Serbia escalated into a world war in which eight of every nine men in the world were drawn into a war that cost nine million lives and 200 billion dollars. World War I would end these empires and prove to be a war for democracy and peace, but the way peace was handled would only lead to another world war before a forum was developed to resolve international disputes in a diplomatic way instead of a militaristic way.

The Road To World War I

With a melting pot of ethnicities and significant change taking place, the Balkans became a restless region of Southeast Europe. It derived its name from the Balkan Mountains that stretched from the Serbian-Bulgarian border to the Black Sea. As far back as 1888—the year of three emperors in the German Empire—Otto von Bismarck, who united the independent German states into a superpower, predicted that a future European war would probably "start with some damn foolish thing in the Balkans." Twenty-six years later, his prediction would come true.[42]

The Balkans were part of the Ottoman Empire for centuries and had a multitude of ethnicities known as the Slavs. Slavs were people who spoke the Slavic languages and included the southern Slavs (Serbs, Croats, Bosnians, Slovenes, Macedonians, and Montenegrins), western Slavs (Poles, Czechs, Slovaks, and Sorbs), and eastern Slavs (Russians, Ukrainians, and Belarusians). Bulgarians speak a Slavic language and are often associated with the southern Slavs.[43]

The Balkan countries had a frightful amount of illiteracy and little wealth.[44] Even though they fought with each other, they had one thing in common. They were all tired of having been ruled by non-Slavic people for centuries. They were all united in that they wanted to be independent of the Turks of the Ottoman Empire. In the 1912 Balkan War, Bulgaria, Serbia, Montenegro, and Greece joined to drive the Turks of the Ottoman Empire out of Europe. When Bulgaria ended up with most of the land acquired from Turkey in Europe, the other Balkan states demanded their share which led to a second Balkan War in 1913 that was lost by Bulgaria.[45]

These regional disputes in the Balkans would eventually spin out of control and lead to a European war—just as Bismarck predicted a quarter-century earlier. What Bismarck never envisioned, as few did, was that it would escalate into a global war. A regional dispute arose when Austria-Hungary annexed (i.e., took over by force) Bosnia and Herzegovina in 1908. Serbia was upset because it had been trying to unite the southern Slavs into a new Serbian nation and wanted the Serbs in Bosnia-Herzegovina to be part of the new nation. Consequently, when Austria-Hungary annexed Bosnia-Herzegovina in 1908, Serbian nationalists were up in arms, most notably those who were members of an organization known as the Black Hand.[46] The Black Hand was a secret Serbian society that used terrorist methods to promote the liberation of Serbs outside Serbia. To strike a blow against the Austro-Hungarian Empire for annexing Bosnia-Herzegovina, these terrorists formulated a plan to assassinate Archduke Franz Ferdinand, heir to the Austria-Hungary crown.[47]

FROM ONE WAR TO ANOTHER

Assassinations were not unusual at that time. In the two decades before World War I, the presidents of six countries (the United States, France, Mexico, Guatemala, Uruguay, and the Dominican Republic) had been assassinated, as had been the prime ministers of another six countries (Russia, Spain, Greece, Bulgaria, Persia, and Egypt). What's more, kings and queens or empresses of five more countries (Austria, Italy, Serbia, Portugal, and Greece) had been the victims of assassins.[48]

The Black Hand operatives planned to assassinate Ferdinand when he visited Sarajevo, the capital of Bosnia. Danilo Ilić, a Bosnia Serb who was a member of the Black Hand living in Sarajevo, was tasked with coordinating the plan. He recruited six teenage Bosnian Serbs to train for the assassination—Vaso Čubrilović, Nedeljko Čabrinović, Trifun Grabež, Muhamed Mehmedbašić, Gavrilo Princip, and Cvjetko Popović. He equipped them with hand-thrown bombs, pistols, and cyanide pills to commit suicide if threatened with capture. The cyanide pills would later prove not to be fatal—the poison was old.[49]

The opportunity for the assassination arose on June 28, 1914. General Oskar Potoirek, Bosnia's governor, invited Franz Ferdinand, the inspector general of the imperial army, to inspect maneuvers of the imperial forces in the Austro-Hungarian provinces of Bosnia and Herzegovina. After that, Ferdinand was scheduled to be in a motorcade through Sarajevo to meet the mayor at town hall. Nedeljko Čabrinović, one of the operatives, learned from a friend of his father, an officer in the Sarajevo police department, the exact date Ferdinand would be visiting Sarajevo.[50] By coincidence, the date coincided with Ferdinand's fourteenth wedding anniversary, so he decided to bring along his wife, Sophie.[51]

It is noteworthy that June 28 was a dark date in the history of Serbia. On June 28, 1389, the medieval Serbian Kingdom lost the bloody Battle of Kosovo against the invading Turks of the Ottoman Empire. The loss was devastating to the Serbs because they became subject to Turkish rule for six centuries.[52] The Serbs were now trying to break from the Ottoman Empire and form a new southern Slavic state to include Bosnia-Herzegovina and the Serbs were determined to strike back. On the other hand, June 28 was a bright date for Ferdinand because he married his wife Sophie Chotek on that date in 1900. He loved his wife, and they had a contented family life. His marriage did not meet with the approval of the emperor and the court because Sophie was considered of lesser birth and rank in the context of royalty. Nevertheless, Ferdinand went ahead with the marriage even though their children would not inherit his titles and privileges.[53]

Ferdinand was warned to cancel his trip because 40 percent of Bosnia-Herzegovina's population were Serbs and riding in a motorcade with open-topped car was a blueprint for disaster.[54] We will see the June 28 date again because the Treaty of Versailles which officially ended World War I was signed on June 28, 1919, exactly five years after the war started on June 28, 1914.

The assassins were positioned along the motorcade route and when Ferdinand's car drove by Čabrinović, he threw a bomb at it, and missed! The bomb bounced off the back of the car and blew up behind it, injuring those in the car behind them and some bystanders.[55] When Ferdinand got to the next stop, town hall, he decided to change the planned route and visit the wounded at the hospital. On his way to the hospital, a wrong turn was made and when the driver of his car stopped to turn around, he was close to another assassin, nineteen-year-old Gavrilo Princip, who acted quickly and shot Ferdinand and Sophie. She had insisted to be allowed to remain by his side during their anniversary day.[56] In the ensuing chaos, Ferdinand's focus was on his wife. He said his wound was nothing and called for Sophie not to die for the sake of their children. Minutes later, they were both dead.[57]

The Spark

The assassination of Franz Ferdinand, on June 28, 1914, was the spark that unleashed all the European tensions that had been building up as the European nations armed themselves for protection in case of war. Before the assassination, Germany, Austria-Hungary, and Italy formed the Triple Alliance and Great Britain, France, and Russia formed the Triple Entente.[58]After the assassination, a chain of events was ignited that led to more European countries being pulled into the war which escalated to become a global war pitting two major alliances against each other—the Central Powers, formerly the Triple Alliance, and the Allied Powers, formerly the Triple Entente. After Franz Ferdinand was assassinated on June 28, the Central Powers consisted of Germany and Hungary-Austria (Italy decided to remain neutral) while the Allied Powers consisted of Great Britain, France, and Russia (Exhibit 1.2).[59]

Austria-Hungary felt Serbia was a destabilizing force in the Balkans and that its government was behind the assassination.[60] The Serbian government said they had nothing to do with the assassination and was willing to punish any one of its subjects who was proved to have anything to do with it.[61] Nevertheless, the ambassador of the Austro-Hungarian Empire delivered an ultimatum of ten demands for Serbia to meet to avert war. The demands

Exhibit 1.2: Alliances Before World War I

TRIPLE ALLIANCE

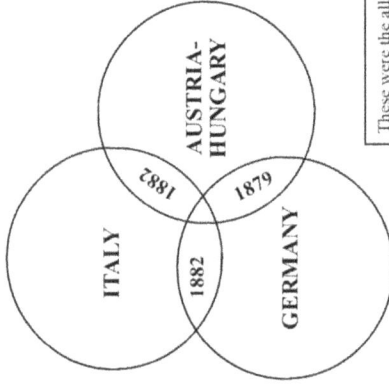

TRIPLE ENTENTE

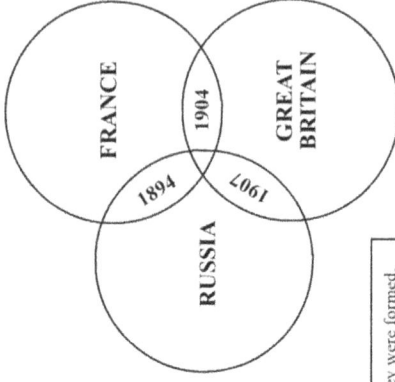

ITALY

AUSTRIA-HUNGARY

GERMANY

1882

1882

1879

SERBIA

FRANCE

RUSSIA

GREAT BRITAIN

1904

1894

1907

These were the alliances between the major European nations, and the dates they were formed, before the assassination of the archduke of Austria-Hungary on June 28, 1914. The assassination prompted Austria-Hungary to issue an ultimatum to Serbia with ten unconditional demands for Serbia to meet to avert war. Serbia was able to agree to most but not all of the demands which resulted in Austria-Hungary declaring war on Serbia on July 28, 1919. With Russia supporting Serbia and Germany supporting Austria-Hungary, their alliances with other nations drew more nations into the war which escalated into World War I.

included some they felt Serbia would not agree to such as ordering its news-papers and schools not to criticize Austria; dismissing army officers, teachers, or officials whom Austria might object to; and allowing Austrian officials to sit in the Serbian courts to judge Serbians accused of assassinating Franz Ferdinand and his wife Sophie.[62] When Serbia as expected did not agree with all of Austria's demands, both sides began to mobilize for war.[63]

The house of cards soon began to fall. On July 28, 1914, Austria-Hungary declared war on Serbia which was aligned for protection with Russia. On August 1, Germany and Russia declared war on each other. On August 3, Germany and France declared war on each other. On August 4, Germany invaded Belgium and Great Britain declared war on Germany. On August 6, Austria-Hungary declared war on Russia and Serbia declared war on Germany. On August 12, Great Britain and France declared war on Austria-Hungary.[64] It didn't take long before the war in Europe pitted the Central Powers of Germany and Austria-Hungary against the Allied Powers of Russia, France, Great Britain, Belgium, and Serbia.

Great Britain all along was concerned with Germany's becoming a naval power. On August 7, it asked Japan for help in dealing with combat raids of the German Imperial Navy against its colonies in the Far East. Japan responded by declaring war on Germany on August 23. Two days later, Japan declared war on Austria-Hungary to further help the Allied cause.[65]

The Ottoman Empire was coming apart because the Balkan nations wanted to be free of Turkish domination. Turkey wanted to avoid this im-minent disintegration and chose to align with Germany because it thought that Germany would win the war. This suited Germany, because it's aim was to keep Turkey from joining the Allied powers and to encourage Romania and Bulgaria to enter the war on the side of the Central Powers.[66] Bulgaria eventually did join the Central Powers, but Romania joined the Allied Powers.

In 1915, the cards continued to fall. On May 23, Italy, which had for years been an ally of Austria-Hungary, changed its allegiance and declared war on Austria-Hungary. Switching sides promised to give it control over the territory on its border with Austria-Hungary from Trentino to Trieste.[67] On October 14, Bulgaria declared war on Serbia prompting Great Britain and France to declare war on Bulgaria on October 15 and 16, respectively. On October 19, Russia and Italy also declared war on Bulgaria.[68]

In 1916, the cards kept falling as Portugal and Romania entered the war on the side of the Allied Powers. As the war escalated, the dominions and colonies of the warring nations, located around the globe, were drawn into the fray.[69]

FROM ONE WAR TO ANOTHER

World War I was not America's war. It was Europe's war. Early on, the United States adopted a policy of neutrality because President Woodrow Wilson and most Americans wanted peace not war.[70] Wilson was a thoughtful man who wanted America to act as a force to instill peace in the world.[71] His position and the position of most Americans of neutrality took a hit on May 7, 1915, when a German U-boat sank the *Lusitania*, a British passenger ship carrying American civilians.[72] The term U-boat comes from the German word "Unterseeboot" meaning "undersea boat."[73] Americans referred to their undersea boats as submarines. Of the 1,959 passengers and crew on board the *Lusitania* on that unlucky day, 1,198 were killed, including 125 Americans.[74]

American public opinion began to change after the disaster, but Wilson and most Americans still favored peace over war.[75] Even though the Germans contended that the *Lusitania* was carrying war materiel (e.g., the equipment and supplies of a military force), the fact that a war ship sunk a commercial ship with innocent women and children aboard didn't sit well with the American public or President Wilson.[76] He responded with paper instead of guns. He sent three notes to Germany known as the "First, Second, and Third Lusitania Notes."[77]

In the first note, he urged Germany to cease its policy of unrestricted submarine warfare against commercial ships of any nation. Germany responded that it had a right to sink the *Lusitania* because it was carrying munitions. In the second note, he denied that the *Lusitania* was carrying munitions, and added that even if it were, sinking a passenger ship with women and children without a challenge or a warning is against a principle of humanity. This prompted his Secretary of State, William Jennings Bryan, to resign saying Wilson was being too provocative which wasn't appropriate for the leader of a neutral country. This did not stop Wilson from sending a third note warning Germany that if it sank another merchant ship with Americans on board this will be regarded by the Government of the United States as being a deliberately unfriendly act.[78]

On August 6, 1915, the Germans U-boat sunk the *Arabic*, a British passenger ship traveling from Liverpool to New York, killing forty-four passengers.[79] This prompted President Wilson to warn Germany that if it was determined they sunk the ship without cause, the United States may cut diplomatic ties and enter the war.[80] Germany responded that they had instructed their U-boat commanders in June 1915 not to torpedo passenger ships without warning and that the U-boat commander who torpedoed the *Arabic* thought he was being attacked by the *Arabic*. Apparently, the *Arabic* was zigzagging, as many passenger ships did for safety when crossing the

Atlantic.[81] In any case, on September 1, 1915, Germany curtailed their U-boat activities to appease Wilson and prevent America from entering the war.[82]

There followed a period of relative calm until a German U-boat torpedoed the French passenger ferry *Sussex* on March 24, 1916, resulting in eighty deaths and injuring several American civilians.[83] The *Sussex* ferried passengers across the English Channel between England and France. This angered Wilson and prompted him to address Congress on April 19, 1916, and say the United States has "no choice but to sever diplomatic relations with the Government of the German Empire altogether."[84] In response to Wilson's warning, the German Government issued what is known as the "Sussex Pledge" on May 4, 1916, by agreeing not to sink any more passenger ships and that merchant ships would not be sunk until the presence of weapons had been established and provisions made for the safety of passengers and crew.[85]

In 1917, the Germans reneged on their pledge. The German navy felt that resuming unrestricted submarine warfare against the British could result in a German victory and end the war by the fall of 1917. They first convinced the German army of this and together they convinced Kaiser Wilhelm on January 8, 1917. The German Chancellor, Theobold von Bethman-Hollweg, didn't agree with them, fearing that it would bring the United States into the war and turn the tide in favor of the Allies. Nevertheless, he supported the Kaiser's decision and unrestricted submarine warfare resumed on February 1, 1917.[86]

The End of Neutrality

On February 3, 1917, President Wilson met with Congress to announce that diplomatic relations with Germany had been severed because Germany had violated its pledge to suspend unrestricted submarine warfare in the North Atlantic and the Mediterranean. He didn't ask for a declaration of war because at that time he didn't think the American public would support him.[87]

When a telegram from the German Foreign Secretary, Arthur Zimmermann, was intercepted by the British naval intelligence and found its way into the American press on March 1, 1917, public opinion toward war started to change in favor of war. The telegram was an implicit attack on the United States because Germany asked Mexico to align with Germany against the United States and in return offered to help Mexico regain territory lost to Texas, New Mexico, and Arizona.[88] It was now crystal clear that Germany posed a real threat to the United States.

FROM ONE WAR TO ANOTHER

Sensing public support for war, Wilson met with Congress again on April 2, and requested a declaration of war against Germany. He said:[89]

> *"Neutrality is no longer feasible or desirable where the peace of the world is involved and the freedom of its peoples, and the menace to that peace and freedom lies in the existence of autocratic governments backed by organized force which is controlled wholly by their will, not by the will of its people."*

He also pointed out that the United States did not have a problem with the German people but with the Imperial German Government that led them to war. He said that the United States will be fighting "for democracy, for the right of those who submit to authority to have a voice in their own governments, for the rights and liberties of small nations, for a universal dominion of right by such concert of free peoples as shall bring peace and safety to all nations and make the world itself at last free."[90] On April 4, the Senate gave its support of war by a vote of 82-6 and on April 6 so did the House by a vote of 373-50.[91]

Germany did not want the United States to enter the war against them. The resumption of unrestricted submarine warfare was a gamble that German Chancellor Theobald von Bethmann-Hollweg argued against, and he was right. The gamble didn't pay off. When the United States entered the war, many German officers and politicians knew the war was lost because the United States brought fresh troops to the battlefront at a time when troops from both sides were worn out from living and fighting in the trenches for three years.[92]

Chapter 2

AMERICA MOBILIZES FOR WORLD WAR I

When the United States entered World War I in April 1917, it was not prepared to fight a war in a foreign land and faced an uphill battle to mobilize for a war that had been raging for three years. After Germany invaded and occupied Luxembourg and Belgium in 1914, it positioned its army to invade and occupy French territory. In the ensuing three years, Germany pushed its western border into French territory creating what became known as the Western Front. By the time the United States entered the war, Germany occupied French territory with about 7 percent of the French population and about 75 percent of France's coal and iron.[1]

A lot of blood had been shed by British, French, and Belgian troops resisting German troops who invaded Belgium, France, and Luxembourg. In addition, a lot of soldiers had been injured by poison gas as biological warfare raised its ugly head during World War I. By the end of the war, more than 100,000 tons of chemical weapons had injured some 500,000 troops, killing almost 30,000 soldiers, including 2,000 Americans.[2]

When the Americans entered the war, the Germans were dug in along the Western Front which extended from Nieuport (now Nieuwpoort) in the region of Flanders in Belgium on the North Sea southward through Belgium, past Luxembourg and through France down to the Swiss border. The length of the Western Front kept changing during the war as battles raged along it. It went from 432 miles in October 1914 to 392 miles when the war ended on Armistice Day, November 11, 1918. It was at its longest, 532 miles, in July 1918 after the last German offensive before the last Allied offensive reduced it to 392 miles by war's end. The most miles held by American forces were 101 miles in October 1918 during the last Allied offensive that ended the war.[3]

FROM ONE WAR TO ANOTHER

At the beginning of the war, the Germans invaded and occupied Belgium and Luxembourg, and then pushed into France, taking slices of land as it advanced. Some of these slices were called salients and included the St. Mihiel salient that American troops would recapture for France near the end of the war. The entry of America into the war brought with it fresh troops and the promise to not only prevent further losses of French land but to turn the tide and recapture the land occupied by or lost by France, Belgium, and Luxembourg to Germany.

For the first three years of World War I, the prime focus of British and Belgian forces had been on the northern part of the Western Front to, among other things, prevent the Germans from seizing ports on the English Channel. The prime focus of French forces had been on the central part of the Western Front to prevent the Germans from seizing Paris. It would take a while to prepare American forces for combat, but when they were prepared, they would focus on the southern part of the Western Front.[4]

After three years of war, the German Army and the Allied Armies were stalemated in trench warfare along the Western Front. It was a war of attrition, and the Allies were hopeful that the Americans would enter the war and provide the manpower necessary to wage offensive battles to drive the Germans from the land they were occupying in France, Belgium, and Luxembourg. This line of thinking was very much in line with the thinking of the general who would lead the American troops into World War I.

The American Military Leader

In May 1917, the American Expeditionary Forces was formed and Major General John Joseph "Black Jack" Pershing was designated as its Commander-in-Chief with responsibility for organizing and leading the United States Army into World War I. An expeditionary force is a military force dispatched to fight in a foreign country, in this case France where the British Expeditionary Force and the Canadian Expeditionary Force were already engaged in war. This was the first time in the history of the United States that a major fighting force was sent overseas in an international effort.[5]

Pershing had been on a fast track for years. He was a leader who proved his mettle in the American Indian Wars, the Spanish-American War, the Philippine Insurrection, and the Mexican Punitive Expedition. He exhibited leadership skills early. At West Point, he rose to first captain, the highest possible rank for a cadet, and after graduation continued to perform well over the years in both line and staff positions. His first assignment after he graduated from West Point in 1886 was with the 6th Calvary Regiment fighting in the Southwest against Apache Indians and in the Dakotas against Sioux Indians.[6]

In 1891, he was assigned as a professor of military science for four years at the University of Nebraska at Lincoln while also attending its law school.[7] He believed in discipline, cracked the whip, and turned a failed military program at that university into one that won a national military drill competition. When he left the program, he left behind a strong legacy—a drill team that was renamed Pershing Rifles in his honor and which spread to other universities over the years. Today, it is a coed military fraternal organization which instills the qualities Pershing stood for—leadership, integrity, discipline, and military vigor.[8] Pershing also left the university with a law degree.[9]

In 1895, Pershing was assigned as a young lieutenant to command the 10th Calvary Regiment consisting of African American soldiers who patrolled the western regions of the United States.[10] This was when some sources say he picked up the nickname "Black Jack." Two years later, in 1897, he returned to West Point as an instructor where he was unpopular with the cadets because he was such a strict disciplinarian. Other sources say this is where he picked up the nickname "Black Jack" from cadets who didn't appreciate him and used the name in a derogatory manner. Pershing was never discouraged by such use, often praising the African American soldiers who served under him, an unpopular thing to do at that time.[11]

In May 1898, Pershing was assigned to command the 10th Calvary Regiment again and two months later led the regiment in an assault on San Juan Hill in Cuba, one of the bloodiest battles of the Spanish-American War. This was the battle in which Lieutenant Colonel Theodore Roosevelt led a charge of the "Rough Riders," a regiment of volunteer cowboys and college students, for which he posthumously received the Medal of Honor in 2001. The citation read, "His leadership and valor turned the tide in the Battle of San Juan Hill."[12] When Pershing was singled out in that battle by his commander, Lieutenant Colonel T. A. Baldwin, as the "coolest man he ever saw under fire," he came to the attention of Roosevelt as a leader with a bright future.[13]

The Spanish-America war started when Cuba wanted to be free of Spanish rule. The United States entered the war to help Cuba and ended up helping itself as well because at the end of the war Spain freed Cuba and ceded Puerto Rico and Guam to the United States. In addition, Spain sold the Philippine Islands to the United States for $20 million.[14] The Filipinos did not want to be an American possession any more than it wanted to be a Spanish possession and this situation resulted in the Philippine Insurrection.[15]

FROM ONE WAR TO ANOTHER

When Theodore Roosevelt became President in 1901, he pushed to have Pershing promoted from captain to colonel, but the Army declined, citing its policy of promotion based on seniority rather than merit.[16] Five years later, Roosevelt would again push Pershing for rapid advancement and get his way against the Army brass. During peacetime, a promotion policy based on seniority often leads to a bureaucracy which gets streamlined during wartime when merit out of necessity becomes more important than seniority in selecting the best commanders to lead the troops into battle.

In 1903, Pershing returned to the States and was assigned to the War Department in Washington, D.C. during which time he met Helen Frances "Frankie" Warren, the daughter of powerful Wyoming Senator Frances E. Warren, who was chairman of the Senate Committee on Military Affairs.[17] That year he also studied at the Army War College and became a member of the General Staff of the Army. In 1905, he married Frankie, with President Theodore Roosevelt in attendance, and the young couple started a family.

In 1906, Roosevelt again pushed to have Pershing promoted three ranks from captain to brigadier general. This time merit and connections trumped seniority because Pershing received the promotion, jumping over 862 officers who were senior to him.[18] Pershing never lacked confidence in his ability to lead and handled the three jumps by continuing to demonstrate the leadership qualities that prompted the jump. A brigadier general is a one-star general, the lowest rank of the generals of the Army. Subsequent ranks are major general (two stars), lieutenant general (three stars) and general (four-stars). Few get to the next level, General of the Army (five stars), and Pershing would be one of only two to reach the highest military rank. Pershing would become General of the Armies (equivalent to six stars), a rank held by only him and George Washington.[19]

Pershing's first assignment as a brigadier general was to return to the Philippines and become the military governor of the Moros Province. The Moros were Muslims. His family joined him, and they all remained in the Philippines for seven years until 1913. During this time, Pershing made a concerted effort to understand the Moros culture which had many factions and tribes.[20] His family was with him, and this turned out to be a very pleasant period of their family life. The wife of an aide to Pershing, Anne Orr Boswell, was a longtime close friend of Frankie. She was the maid of honor at Frankie's wedding, and Frankie named her second daughter, Anne Orr Pershing, after her.[21] They were friends and met at Wellesley College (Frankie '03 and Annie '04), married military men, and enjoyed each other's company.[22]

America Mobilizes For World War I

In January 1914, the same month that the Panama Canal was completed, Pershing took command of the Eighth Infantry Brigade at the Presidio in San Francisco. At that time, the city was hosting the 1915 Panama-Pacific International Exposition which would attract almost nineteen million visitors. Soldiers from the Presidio supported the Expedition with parades, honor guards and artillery demonstrations.[23] The Presidio was a major military installation in San Francisco that was a base for American troops deploying to the Philippines and other military installations in the Pacific. It was established in 1776 as "a symbol of United States authority in the Pacific" and was a major command post in the Mexican, Civil, and Spanish-American Wars. It was still a command post when Pershing arrived there, and it would continue to be so during World War II and the Korean War.[24]

When Pershing was assigned to the Presidio, he and Frankie were the proud parents of four children—Helen, age 8, born in Japan; Anne, age 7, born in the Philippines; Warren, age 5, born in Cheyenne, Wyoming (Frankie's hometown); and Mary Margaret, age 3, born in the Philippines.[25] He moved his family into a two-story house at the Presidio. The houses at the base were old wooden structures that had become fire hazards.[26]

In April 1913, one of the small wooden houses caught fire and Mrs. George H. Schall and her three small children, ages 8, 6 and 3, were burned to death. Another tragic fire occurred in November 1914 and Mrs. Michael Sanderson burned to death in her wooden quarters. Both their husbands were sergeants on duty at the Presidio.[27] While the Pershing home was no doubt one of the best of the old frame buildings, it was also an antiquated wooden structure.[28]

In 1915, the instability in Mexico caused by the Mexican Revolution was beginning to affect the states bordering Mexico. Pershing was ordered from the Presidio to Fort Bliss in El Paso, Texas where he was assigned as second-in-command to Major General Frederick "Fighting Fred" Funston of the Eighth Infantry Brigade. General Funston was best known for his leadership in the Spanish-American War and for his valor in the Philippines for which he received the Medal of Honor.[29] Once again, Pershing had to move his family.

On August 27, 1915, a week before his family was to join Pershing at Fort Bliss, a fire broke out in their house at the Presidio.[30] At the time, Frankie's good friend, Anne Boswell, was visiting with her two sons, James, age 5 and Philip, age 2½.[31] At about 4:30 am, Anne was aroused by smoke, woke her sons and her nurse maid, and called to Frankie. When she opened her door on the second floor there were flames in the staircase, so she went back into her room, and they all went out the window onto the roof over the porch and started screaming for help. Three soldiers heard them and rushed to the scene. Her nursemaid jumped into the arms of the men. By that time, the Pershing's longtime orderly, William J. Johnson, was on the scene, and Anne dropped her two sons into his arms and then jumped into a flower bed, wrenching her back badly.[32]

Johnson retrieved a ladder and he and the soldiers climbed onto the roof and through a window into Warren's room and found him unconscious. Later, it was surmised that Frankie got into the room of her daughters but was unable to get into Warren's room. Tragically, Frankie and her three daughters perished in the fire. Warren survived the fire thanks to Mr. Johnson. The loss was the worst catastrophe in Pershing's personal life.[33]

After the funeral, Pershing brought Warren to Fort Bliss along with his sister, May, to look after the youngster. When Pershing arrived at Fort Bliss, there was a letter waiting for him from Frankie, his deceased wife. She wrote, "Do you think there can be many people in the world as happy as we are?"[34]

One can only imagine how heartbreaking and difficult this tragedy was for Pershing, but he resumed his duties at Fort Bliss as the situation at the border worsened. In March 1916, Pancho Villa raided Columbus, New Mexico, killing eight American soldiers and wounding nine civilians. President Wilson reacted by deploying troops to Mexico. Pershing was tasked with capturing Villa and led nearly ten thousand troops, including his 10th Calvary, into Mexico in what is known as the Mexican Punitive Expedition.[35]

Only two years earlier, Pancho Villa had been the provisional governor of Chihuahua and had cordial relations with the United States and with Pershing himself.[36] In fact, on August 26, 1914, a photograph was taken of General Villa at Fort Bliss with a smiling General Pershing. In the photograph was Pershing's aide, George S. Patton, Jr., a young lieutenant with great potential.[37] Villa no doubt respected Pershing because he sent him a telegram in 1915 expressing his sincere condolences for the loss of his wife and three daughters.[38] But times had changed. Now, it was Pershing's duty to hunt him down because he turned on the United States when President Wilson supported his rival, General Venustiano Carranza, for the presidency of Mexico after the former president, Victoriano Huerta, was forced into exile.[39]

The manhunt into Mexico to capture Villa was the largest manhunt in United States military history. The two top candidates to lead the expedition were Major General Funston and Brigadier General Pershing. It was a tough decision, but President Woodrow Wilson and Secretary of War Newton D. Baker chose Pershing over Funston because he was more diplomatic.[40] Because the Germans had infiltrated Mexico promoting anti-American sentiment to provoke a war with the United States, diplomacy was important. This was the second time that Pershing was chosen for greater responsibility over someone senior in rank to him.

Pershing spent two years looking for Pancho Villa. While he did not capture him, he gained valuable field experience in leading an Army of ten thousand troops and the expedition was considered a success because talks with the new Mexican President Carranza eased tensions between the United States and Mexico.[41] The experience would prepare Pershing and his valuable aide, First Lieutenant Patton, for greater responsibilities in the world war they were about to enter.

In 1917, with the United States on the cusp of World War I, President Wilson had been thinking of who should command the American Expeditionary Forces in Europe and his first choice was Funston. While diplomacy was important in the Mexican Punitive Expedition, it was not an issue here because World War I was already in play and a decisive leader like Funston was a front-runner because he had commanded troops and proved he could think strategically and handle the details of an army to implement a strategy. However, when Funston died of a heart attack on February 19, 1917, Pershing entered the picture. The United States entered the war in April 1917 and Wilson gave the command of the American Expeditionary Forces to Pershing in May 1917.[42]

Pershing had many attributes that made Wilson's decision easy. He looked the part—he emanated strength and had the bearing of a true leader. He expressed his views frankly and respectfully, could be diplomatic, showed no interest in politics, was fluent in French and could read and write the language well, and was the only commander to have led over twelve thousand men into battles during his military career.[43]

The American Expeditionary Forces

May 1917 was a busy month as the United States began to mobilize for war. Manpower was needed for the military because at that time the Regular Army and the National Guard lacked the manpower to fight a war. To obtain the manpower, Congress passed the Selective Service Act which President Wilson signed into law on May 18, 1917, granting him the authority to draft civilians into military service for what was called the National Army.

The Act required three registrations for the draft. The first registration required all men between the ages of 21 and 31 to register on June 5, 1917.

FROM ONE WAR TO ANOTHER

The second registration required all men who had turned twenty-one after June 5, 1917, to register on June 5, 1918. (A supplemental registration was held on August 24, 1918, for those who became 21 years old after June 5, 1918. This was included in the second registration.) The third registration required all men 18 to 45 years old to register who hadn't yet registered.[44]

As we will see much later, John Cooney trained in the States with a crew that included Bob Cookman, Russ Flint, Ted Cylkowski, Ray Goodson, Calvin Chin, David Orkin, Kirk Mosher, Meyer Osofsky, and Chuck Muth. It is noteworthy that all of their fathers had registered for the World War I draft as noted below (their ages are in parentheses):[45]

The fathers of Flint, Cylkowski, Cooney, Mosher, Osofsky, and Muth (all 21 before June 5, 1917) registered in the first registration on June 5, 1917. A total of 9,587,000 men registered in this first registration.

The father of Cookman (21 after June 5, 1918) registered in the supplemental registration on August 24, 1918. This was considered part of the second registration. A total of 736,000 men registered on June 5, 1918, and 158,000 on August 24, 1918.

The fathers of Goodson, Chin, and Orkin registered in the third registration on September 12, 1918. A total of 13,228,000 men registered in this third registration.

Overall, 23,709,000 men registered for the World War I draft.[46] Like the drafts for the Revolutionary War and the Civil War, the World War I draft was a wartime draft. All three drafts were signed into law after the nation was at war. The draft for World War II, however, was the first peacetime draft in the nation's history. The nation wasn't at war when President Franklin Delano Roosevelt signed it into law on September 16, 1940, as the Selective Training and Service Act, but war was on the horizon and Roosevelt wanted to get an early start. There were still many isolationists against war but that all changed with the surprise attack on Pearl Harbor on December 7, 1941.[47]

When the United States went to war in April 1917, it had a big job ahead to build up the Army because, at that time, there were only 190,000 military personnel in the Regular Army and National Guard.[48] By the time the draft was instituted in June 1917, this total had increased to only 213,000.[49] The purpose of the draft was to create a National Army to supplement the Regular Army and National Guard. All three—the Regular Army, National Guard, and National Army—formed the United States Army.

Since the Army only had room in existing forts, camps, and stations to house 124,000 military personnel, new facilities had to be organized and constructed in less than six months to provide shelter for an Army projected initially at 1.5 million men, but which reached over 3.6 million men by the end of the war. To meet this need, Secretary of War Newton D. Baker ordered the construction of sixteen tent camps in the south and southeast for housing and training National Guard troops and sixteen wooded cantonments in other regions for housing and training National Army troops.[50]

The existing Regular Army troops and National Guard troops would be the first to go overseas because they had already received military training even though more training and experience would be needed overseas to prepare them for combat. To train new recruits and draftees of the National Army and National Guard presented a formidable challenge. The Army hired contractors who in turn hired over 200,000 civilian employees to build the tent camps and wooden cantonments and by September 1917 the Army was housing and training troops in these facilities.[51]

Preparing to Manage the War

In May 1917, Pershing went to England and France with a contingent of about a hundred officers who would comprise his General Staff to study the general staff systems of the British and French and to become familiar with the leaders he would be working with and the conditions under which he would be working.[52] He was received by both countries with gratitude for entering the war and with the hope that America would provide the manpower necessary to turn the tide of war in favor of the Allies.

For Pershing, gratitude was a two-way street. The French government asked him to march his soldiers through Paris as a morale booster for the locals, after which he and his staff visited the tomb of the Marquis de Lafayette just outside Paris and placed a wreath on his tomb as a token of America's gratitude for his support during the American Revolution.[53] Lafayette believed in the equality of mankind and the right of the American colonists to rule themselves. He later drafted the Declaration of the Rights of Man for his country.[54] Pershing appreciated Lafayette's support during America's time of need and was glad to return the favor.

Pershing knew that a well-organized General Staff was essential to coordinate the activities necessary to build and run a successful modern army in a foreign land. He needed such a staff to help him implement policy and handle the details of administration, supply, preparation, and operation of the American Expeditionary Forces.[55] After evaluating his options, he organized his General

Staff with five groups and numbered them with a "G" for General Staff preceding each number. G-1 section was responsible for administration in charge of organizing and equipping the troops; G-2 section was responsible for gathering intelligence on the enemy and producing useful information including maps; G-3 section was responsible for strategy, planning, and execution of combat operations; G-4 section was responsible for coordinating services to support combat operations such as supply, construction, transportation, and evacuation and hospitalization of the sick and wounded; and G-5 was responsible for the education and training of the American Expeditionary Forces.[56]

Pershing would initially set up his General Staff in Paris, and then move it to Chaumont which was closer to the Western Front. Later, he would move those members of his staff responsible for supporting combat operations from Chaumont to Tours, France, so that he could work more closely with those members of his staff focused on combat operations. It was up to the members of the General Staff located in Chaumont to coordinate the many activities that went into organizing, training, and deploying troops for combat operations, and it was up to the members of the General Staff in Tours to coordinate the many operational, logistical, and administrative activities that were needed to support combat operations.[57] Coordinating the buildup and development of a modern army from 190,000 men on April 6, 1914, when the United States entered the war, to 3,665,000 on November 11, 1918, when the fighting stopped, was a herculean task, especially since over 2,000,000 of them were in France.[58]

Preparing to Fight the War

The Americans were trained in divisions. There were Regular Army divisions, National Guard divisions, and National Army divisions. The American infantry division was a key fighting unit during World War I, small enough to have mobility and large enough to fight a prolonged battle. Pershing also wanted larger divisions than the French, British, and Germans to wage open warfare as he was no fan of trench warfare that was waged along the Western Front for the past three years between the Allied French and British divisions and the German divisions. He felt larger divisions provided the manpower to break out of the trenches and engage in prolonged open warfare to recapture land lost to the Germans during the war.[59] The approximate average strength of the British, French, and German divisions in 1918 was 11,800, 11,400, and 12,300, respectively.[60] Pershing opted for divisions twice the size of any of them to provide greater driving power.[61]

Pershing formed infantry divisions of 28,000 personnel to include about 1,000 officers and 27,000 enlisted men to be commanded by a major general. In addition to leading this fighting force, the division commander would also lead about 12,000 non-combat personnel responsible for services to support combat operations such as medical care, communications, engineering, transportation, and other support services. In fighting a battle, the division commander could therefore be leading as many as 40,000 people, 28,000 engaged in combat operations and 12,000 engaged in supporting the combat operations.[62] Pershing believed that a larger division of 28,000 troops would "conserve the limited supply of trained officers, maximize firepower, and sustain itself effectively in combat." [63]

In June 1917, the first American troops arrived in France where Pershing and his General Staff had established facilities to train them for combat. He wanted to be sure they were prepared for battle before placing them in harm's way.[64] He set up a school in Langres to train officers in general staff work and to select those with leadership potential for further training; in Saumur to train officers in the use of modern artillery; and in Issoudin to train officers in aviation (Exhibit 2.1).[65] He knew it would take time to train American officers as well as the enlisted men serving under them.

President Wilson, Secretary Baker, and General Pershing were concerned with the heavy casualties of trench warfare and did not want American troops under the command of British and French commanders who seemed to be wed to this type of warfare. While Pershing was no fan of trench warfare, he nevertheless had his troops exposed to and trained in trench warfare with British and French divisions to gain combat experience. His preference was for his troops to be engaged in more open warfare. Wilson, Baker, and Pershing also wanted American troops to serve under an American commander, not a British or French commander, and on a distinctly American sector of the Western Front.

During World War I, the American Expeditionary Forces sent 2,057,675 military personnel to Europe. Of that total, 1,078,222 or 52 percent were combat personnel and 979,453 or 48 percent were support personnel.[66] The 1,078,222 combat personnel were in 43 divisions averaging a combat strength of 25,075 in each division, which was more than twice the average combat strength of British (11,800), French (11,400) or German (12,300) divisions.[67] Pershing was devoted to his goal of having American divisions with twice the manpower of European divisions and he achieved that goal.

Of the combat force of 1,078,222 in 43 divisions, about 5 percent, or 52,944, were killed in battle or died from their wounds and about 19 percent,

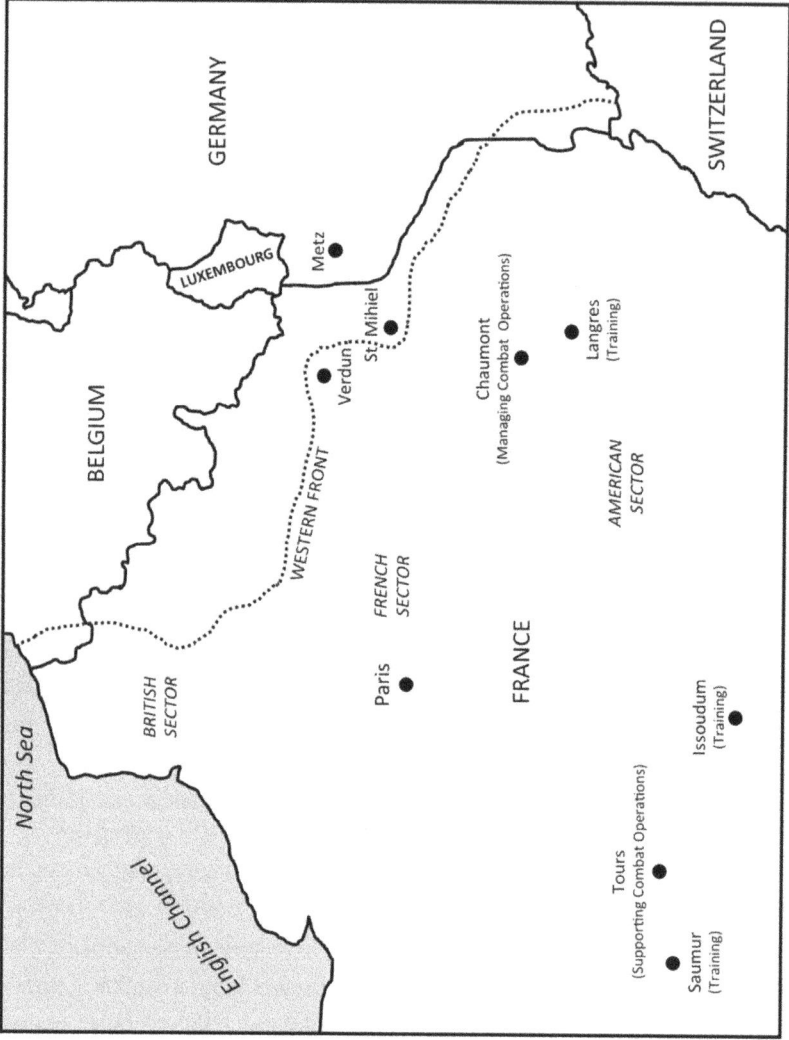

Exhibit 2.1: Sites for Managing, Supporting, and Training American Troops

or 202,628, were wounded and pulled through. Together, about 24 percent, or 255,572 Americans who saw combat in European theater during World War I, were casualties of war.[68] To that total, you can add over 4,000 Americans who were prisoners of war or were missing in action in World War I.[69]

The 43 divisions of combat personnel consisted of eight Regular Army divisions, seventeen National Guard divisions, and eighteen National Army divisions (Exhibit 2.2). The Regular Army divisions sustained a greater percentage of casualties (42 percent) than the National Guard divisions (24 percent) or National Army divisions (15 percent) because they were the best trained and saw the most action. Likewise, the National Guard divisions were next because they had been reserve units receiving training whereas the National Army recruits and draftees had no military training when they entered the service.[70]

The total number of Americans mobilized for military service during World War I was 4,734,991 (Army, 4,057,101; Navy, 599,051; and Marines, 78,839).[71] Thus, about 47 percent of those mobilized, or 2,057,675, served overseas in the American Expeditionary Forces while the other 53 percent, or 2,297,325, served in the States. To manage and control a military force of this magnitude, the President needed a workable chain of command and Pershing needed an effective and efficient staff to coordinate the many activities to build and operate a modern army to fight a war far from home.

It took a while to establish the Chain of Command for the American Expeditionary Forces in World War I, but once established it served its purpose well (Exhibit 2.3). It provided an infrastructure for giving and executing orders downward throughout the organization and for providing feedback back up the chain. Responsibility was delegated at every level in the chain so that instructions flowed downward along the chain and accountability flowed upward along the chain. Each commander in the chain received orders from above, implemented them, and provided feedback on the results.

Preparing to Support the War

In May 1916, almost a year before the United States entered World War I in April 1917, Congress passed the National Defense Act which expanded the size and scope of the National Guard for the purpose of mobilizing sufficient manpower in case of war.[72] In August 1916, Congress passed the Army Appropriation Act which authorized the establishment of the Council of National Defense for the purpose of coordinating the mobilization of industries and resources for the national security and welfare.[73] In October

Exhibit 2.2
American Divisions Sent to Europe in World War I

Types of Divisions	Number of Divisions (Personnel)	Killed in Battle or Died from Wounds (% Personnel)	Wounded (% Personnel)	Casualties (% Personnel)
Regular Army Divisions	8 (200,640)	18,927 (9%)	66,057 (33%)	84,984 (42%)
National Guard Divisions	17 (426,360)	19,557 (5%)	81,048 19%	100,605 (24%)
National Army Divisions	18 (451,440)	14,460 (3%)	55,523 (12%)	69,983 (15%)
Total Army Divisions	**43 (1,078,440)**	**52,944 (5%)**	**202,628 (19%)**	**255,572 (24%)**

Exhibit 2.3
Chain of Command
American Expeditionary Forces
World War I

President
Woodrow Wilson

Secretary of War
Newton D. Baker

Army Chief of Staff
General Peyton C. March

March oversaw America at war, not just AEF at war.

AEF Commander
General John J. Pershing

Pershing oversaw First, Second and Third Armies.

TYPE OF GENERAL	STARS
General of the Armies	5
General of the Army	4
Lieutenant General	3
Major General	2
Brigadier General	1

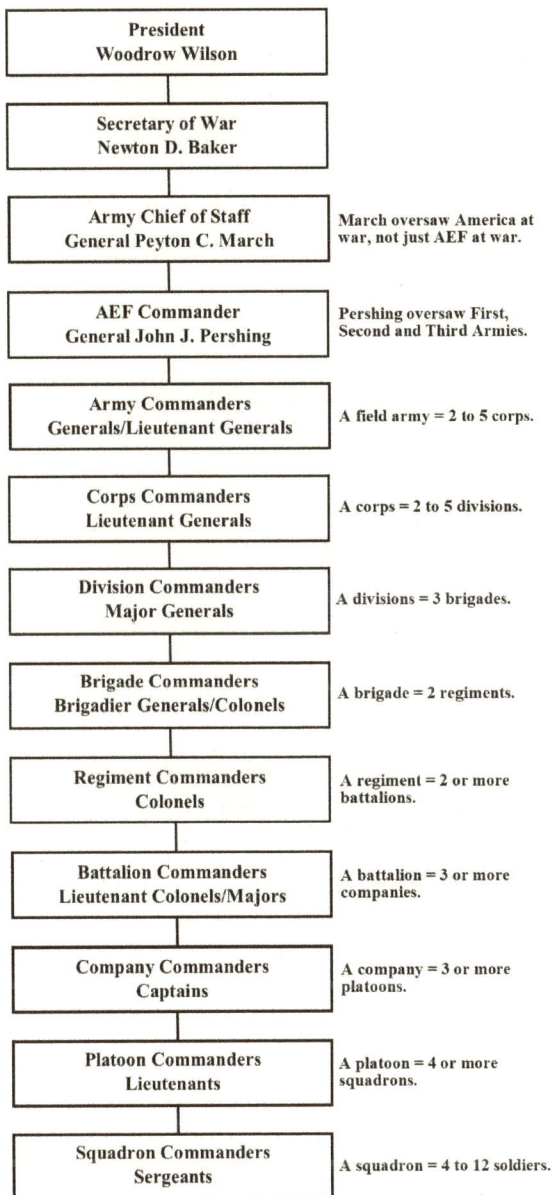

Army Commanders
Generals/Lieutenant Generals

A field army = 2 to 5 corps.

Corps Commanders
Lieutenant Generals

A corps = 2 to 5 divisions.

Division Commanders
Major Generals

A divisions = 3 brigades.

Brigade Commanders
Brigadier Generals/Colonels

A brigade = 2 regiments.

Regiment Commanders
Colonels

A regiment = 2 or more battalions.

Battalion Commanders
Lieutenant Colonels/Majors

A battalion = 3 or more companies.

Company Commanders
Captains

A company = 3 or more platoons.

Platoon Commanders
Lieutenants

A platoon = 4 or more squadrons.

Squadron Commanders
Sergeants

A squadron = 4 to 12 soldiers.

FROM ONE WAR TO ANOTHER

1916, President Wilson established an advisory group of industry executives called the National Defense Advisory Commission to collaborate with the Council of National Defense and advise it of the tasks needed to mobilize for war and to coordinate the nation's military, industrial, and economic resources toward that end. These initiatives recognized the importance of having leaders in industry, labor, science, and finance work with government and military leaders to be prepared in case of war.[74]

The six members of the Council of National Defense were the six Cabinet members responsible for coordinating the means to meet the military, industrial, and commercial needs of the nation; and for determining how to adapt our present manufacturing and production facilities to provide the materiel required for warfare. Materiel is different from material. Material that ends with an "al" relates to many things in everyday life but materiel that end with an "el" relates to things used by the military such as tanks, planes, ships, guns, and ammunition to fight a war; and food, shelter, and medical products to support those fighting the war. The military produced the manpower to fight the war and industry produced the materiel to support the troops.

The seven members of the National Defense Advisory Commission were six executives of industries that would be needed to produce war materiel to support the troops, plus a labor leader to help resolve labor disputes and prevent costly strikes. The Commission members were responsible for using their specialized knowledge to help determine the allocation of the nation's resources to satisfy the needs of the military in case of war while still satisfying the needs of civilians on the home front for these resources.[75] The Council was expected to inform President Wilson of what was needed to mobilize so that plans could be made to inform American manufacturers of the part they must play to support the nation in case of a national emergency (Exhibit 2.4).[76] It is noteworthy that twenty-three years later the Council of National Defense and National Defense Advisory Commission would be revived to assess the mobilization needs for World War II.

The Council and Commission did its job in analyzing the abilities of the nation's major industries to meet the military needs in case of war but ran up against an Army bureaucracy that was unable to purchase materiel quickly and efficiently and was competing with the Navy for materiel. Recognizing that both materiel and manpower would have to be coordinated to support the nation's war effort, President Wilson established a War Industries Board within the Council of National Defense on July 28, 1917.[77] The War Industries Board was tasked with coordinating the mobilization of

Exhibit 2.4
Initiatives to Prepare for World War I

Council of National Defense
Created Aug. 29, 1916, to coordinate the mobilization of industries and resources for national security and welfare.

Newton Baker	Secretary of War
David F. Houston	Secretary of Agriculture
William C. Redfield	Secretary of Commerce
Franklin K. Lane	Secretary of the Interior
William B. Wilson	Secretary of Labor
Josephus Daniels	Secretary of the Navy

National Defense Advisory Commission
Created Oct. 11, 1916, with industry experts to advise the Council on mobilization issues involving their respective fields of expertise.

Executive	Background	Field of Expertise
Bernard M. Baruch	Financier	Raw Materials
Howard E. Coffin	Vice President Hudson Motor Co.	Munitions and Manufacturing
Dr. Hollis Godfrey	President Drexel Institute	Engineering and Education
Samuel Gompers	President American Federation of Labor	Labor
Dr. Franklin H. Martin	Secretary-General American College of Surgeons	Medicine and Surgery
Julius Rosenwald	President Sears, Roebuck & Co.	Supplies
Daniel Willard	President Baltimore & Ohio Railroad	Transportation

the nation's industry to produce the materiel needed by the nation's fighting forces to win the war.[78]

The War Industries Board was created by executive order and not by legislation and therefore lacked the political and legal clout of the Council of National Defense. This situation resulted in the Board's first chairman, Frank A. Scott, having a nervous breakdown and the second, Daniel Willard, quitting in frustration.[79] War materiel included all items, such as ships, planes, tanks, vehicles, guns, ammunition, and protective gear which are necessary to equip, operate, maintain, and support military activities. It also included the raw materials necessary to build these items such as iron, steel, rubber, and other necessities. In sum, its mission was to coordinate the effort to arm America during World War I.[80]

It seemed to Wilson that a superman was needed to head the War Industries Board and thought of Bernard Baruch, a member of the War Industries Board, who knew a great deal about the country's economic resources and how to cut through red tape to get things done. Wilson knew that Baruch had been a loyal supporter and served on the National Defense Advisory Commission where he demonstrated his leadership abilities. However, he was not sure Congress or businessmen would support Baruch because of his reputation as a ruthless speculator.[81]

Baruch had been passed over for chairman despite performing well as a member of the War Industries Board. When Secretary of War Baker, who felt Baruch was not qualified to be chairman of the Board, asked Baruch to ask John F. Ryan if he wanted him to be chairman, Baruch felt humiliated by being asked to be an errand boy for Baker. He refused and never forgave Baker. Years later, for example, he refused to accept a Distinguished Service Medal from Baker, receiving it later from President Wilson.[82]

After being passed over, Baruch complained to a friend, William G. McAdoo, who went to see Wilson. McAdoo was a strong supporter of Wilson, as well as being his Secretary of the Treasury and his son-in-law. Other powerful voices spoke up for Baruch and convinced Wilson that members of Congress would just have to learn to accept Baruch. Still not sure of Congress supporting Baruch, Wilson requested the cooperation of each of his Cabinet members in supporting him.[83] He got the support, and he got his superman.

On March 4, 1918, Wilson appointed Baruch to head the War Industries Board and Baruch restored order to the mobilization effort (Exhibit 2.5).[84] He understood that wars were won not only by those fighting on the battlefront but also by those civilian forces behind the battlefront providing the

Exhibit 2.5
War Industries Board

Created March 4, 1918, to coordinate the mobilization of industrial production to support the American fighting forces.

Board Member	Responsibility
Bernard M. Baruch	Chairman
Alex Legge	Vice Chairman
Edwin B. Parker Houston Attorney	Priorities Commissioner
Robert S. Brookings Cupples & Marston	Price-Fixing Committee Chairman
George N. Peek Deere & Company	Finished Products Commissioner
Rear Admiral Frank F. Fletcher Navy Department	Navy Representative
Maj. Gen. George W. Goethals War Department	Army Representative
Hugh A. Frayne American Federation of Labor	Labor Representative
Jacob L. Replogle Replogle Steel Company	Steel Administrator
Leland L. Summers Consulting Engineer	Technical Advisor
Albert C. Ritchie Attorney General of Maryland	General Counsel
Howard P. Ingles Milton Manufacturing Co.	Secretary

materiel needed to fight on the battlefront. While Baruch brought order to the process, there simply was not enough lead time for American industry to produce the number of planes, artillery, vehicles, tanks, ships, trains, and other necessities to support the American Expeditionary Forces in France.[85] The members of the Board would change going forward but Baruch would remain its chairman during the war.

America would learn from this experience and be better prepared to produce war materiel for World War II. For World War I, America had to obtain much of the necessary war armaments from French and British suppliers. Nevertheless, there was hidden value in the War Industries Board national planning process to obtain war materiel through the business-government cooperation fostered by Bernard Baruch. It brought to light how such cooperation could solve economic problems and deal with crises, and President Franklin D. Roosevelt would later seek such cooperation in his New Deal programs and projects implemented to dig out of the Great Depression.[86] Moreover, when World War II was on the horizon, Roosevelt would seek the advice of Baruch in preparing for it and Baruch would lead him to William Knudsen who knew how to produce war materiel in an efficient and effective manner, namely through mass production.[87]

It was primarily American manpower that helped secure an Allied victory in World War I, not American materiel. American materiel would play a bigger role in defeating the enemy in World War II, most notably in the production of aircraft to support significant airpower. In World War I, heavy artillery did most of the damage and John Cooney Sr. served with three evacuation hospitals that treated the victims of that war. In World War II, heavy bombers did most of the damage and John Sr.'s son John would fly thirty-five missions in B-24 heavy bombers that inflicted much of the damage on the enemy.

The United States had never fought in a war of the magnitude of World War I, and to complicate matters it was fought far away across an ocean. The nation was starting from a weak position because it only had a small Regular Army that was scattered all over the nation and in outlying possessions.[88] But action was quick. The 1st Division was formed from the existing Regular Army and arrived in France in June 1917. The 2nd Division was soon formed in France from the Regular Army and included a brigade of Marines.[89] In July 1917, it was decided that the American army would need at least one million soldiers by May 1918.[90]

Three more divisions formed from National Guard units arrived in France in 1917. The 26th Division was formed from units in New England and arrived in October. The 42nd Division was formed from units in twenty-six states and the District of Columbia and arrived in November.[91] Douglas MacArthur, then a colonel in the 42nd Division, noted that the units that made up this division stretched across the nation like a rainbow, and it became known as the Rainbow Division.[92] The 41st Division was formed from units in nine states from Washington to New Mexico, and the District of Columbia arrived in December.[93] By year-end 1917, five American divisions were in France, but only the 1st Division had served at the front.[94]

Gaining Respect

The first battle Pershing had to fight when he got to France was with his fellow French and British commanders who expected his troops to be assimilated into their armies under their control. However, he was faithful to his instructions from Wilson and Baker, namely that "the United States are a separate and distinct component of the combined forces, the identity of which must be preserved."[95] He negotiated with French and British commanders and worked out a compromise whereby some American troops served with small British and French units such as companies but took orders from American officers reporting to French officers at higher levels who were providing overall strategic direction.[96] This arrangement enabled American soldiers to obtain valuable combat experience while ensuring that they remained under American command whose ultimate purpose was to engage in offensive warfare under American command when they were ready for such warfare.[97]

British forces were focused mainly on the northern sector of the Western Front to protect the English Channel port and French forces were focused mainly on the central sector of the Western Front to protect Paris. Consequently, it was decided that American forces would focus on the southern sector of the Western Front near the Lorraine and Alsace regions of France.[98] France bordered Belgium in the north, Luxembourg in the center, and the regions of Lorraine and Alsace in the south. France and Germany had fought over Lorraine and Alsace for centuries. Since Germany won the last war between them—the Franco-Prussia War of 1870—it now occupied Lorraine and Alsace.

It made sense to have American forces focus on the southern sector for three reasons. First, the Americans needed to transport additional forces and supplies to the front and the roads and railways in the southern sector were considerably less crowded than the roads and railways in the other two sectors. Second, the Lorraine and Alsace regions were strategically important to Germany because they served as buffer zones between the Allies and Germany's Rhineland, considered the industrial heart of Germany and the source of its military power. And third, it positioned the Americans to strike Germany in a vital, strategic area and deliver a mortal blow to its military strength.[99]

By the end of 1917, there were only 176,665 American troops in Europe of which the 1st Division was the only one that had served at the front and gained combat experience.[100] It served with the French 18th Division along the Western Front near Parroy, about thirty-two miles west of Toul, one of the fortified towns of France where a large American hospital center—Justice Hospital Center—was being set up to support American troops. The Center was being set up to provide support for the first major battle led by an American commander. Toul was also where the American Second Army would set up its headquarters when it was organized for the second major battle led by an American commander.[101]

In 1918, Pershing began the process of moving troops toward the southern end of the Western Front. His goal was to have American troops gain valuable combat experience. In January, the 1st Division relieved a French division at the front just north of Toul. In February, the 42nd entered the front southeast of Toul near Lunéville and the 26th Division entered the front northeast of Toul near Soissons. In March, the 2nd Division also entered the front with the French further northeast of Toul near Verdun.[102] With the 1st Division and 42nd Divisions entering the front line near Toul, medical support was set up to support them, and John Sr. would serve with two evacuation hospitals that provided this support (Exhibit 2.6).

Pershing was training his troops to act on their own, and their first challenge was to retake the town of Cantigny.[103] By May 1918, the 1st Division of 26,500 soldiers, below its desired complement of 28,000 soldiers, was the only fully trained American division in France.[104] On May 28, it went into action and in three days of battle retook Cantigny. While the price was high—one out of every three of the four thousand Americans in the battle were casualties—the victory demonstrated the mettle of the American soldier.[105] This was important because the British and French Armies did not think the American Army could get up to snuff quickly enough to act on its own, preferring American troops to be assimilated into the experienced British and French Armies. Wilson and Pershing were adamantly wed to the objective of having the Americans act on their own in their own sector of the Western Front. The actions of the American troops at Cantigny went a long way toward gaining the respect of British and French military leaders.

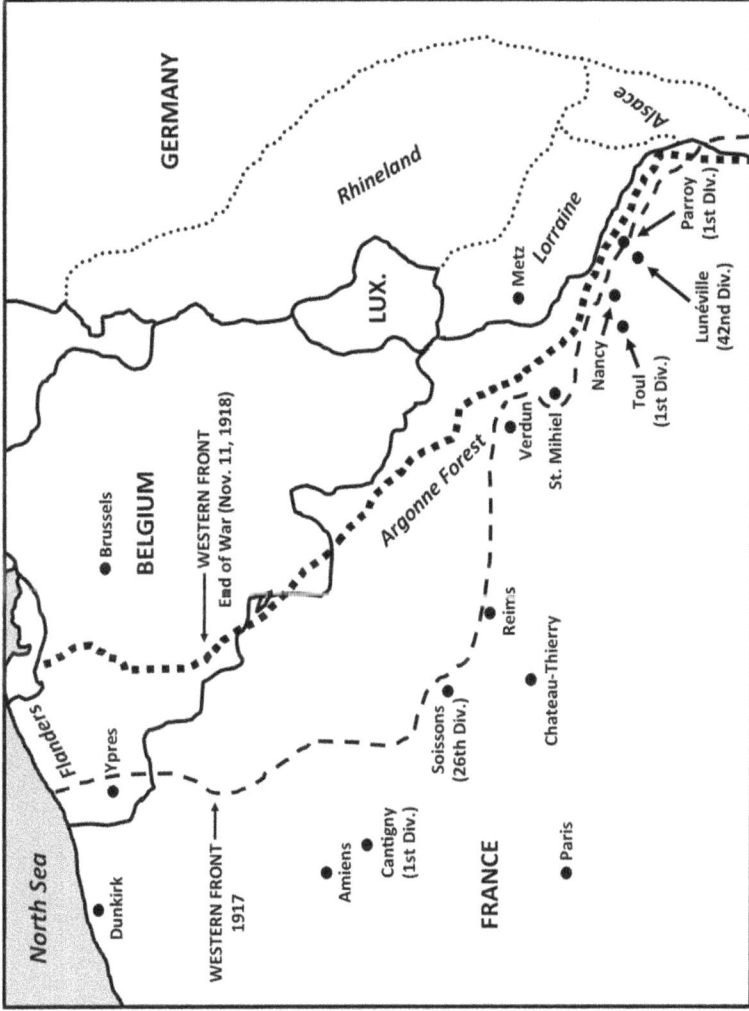

Exhibit 2.6: American Divisions Gaining Combat Experience

Chapter 3

THE IMPORTANCE OF MEDICAL SUPPORT

The United States was entering a war being fought with more destructive weapons than ever before making medical care more important than ever before. General Pershing had many critical needs. The enormity of building and operating a modern army across an ocean in a foreign land was a great challenge. Pershing knew he had to develop an infrastructure for the fighting forces to operate within and an infrastructure for the service forces to support the fighting forces. The military mobilized over 4.7 personnel in World War I to serve in the Army, the Navy, and the Marines.[1] The Army was under the War Department with Newton D. Baker as Secretary of War and the Navy and Marines were under the Navy Department with Josephus Daniels as Secretary of the Navy.[2] Pershing was responsible for the operations of the American Expeditionary Forces (A.E.F.) of the Army. The Army had by far the most military personnel and sustained the most casualties during the war (Exhibit 3.1). John Cooney Sr. was one of over 4.7 million who served during World War I and each contributed to the war effort.

Pershing initially set up his headquarters in Paris then moved it to Chaumont to be closer to the Western Front. Next, he decided to separate the two infrastructures, leaving those focused on combat operations in Chaumont and moving those focused on supporting combat operations to Tours. The support forces were originally called Lines of Communication and later took on the name Services of Supply (S.O.S.).[3] The S.O.S. became the lifeblood of the A.E.F. supplying it with the manpower and firepower to fight a war in a foreign land.[4]

When a nation goes to war, especially a war fought far away, logistics are important and support services involve logistics. It is said that an amateur talks tactics, the serious student talks strategy, but the professional talks logistics.

47

Exhibit 3.1
World War I Casualties

Branch of Service	Mobilized	Killed	% Killed	Wounded	% Wounded
Army	4,057,101	115,516	2.8%	204,002	4.5%
Navy	599,051	7,287	1.2%	819	0.1%
Marines	78,839	2,851	3.6%	9,520	1.2%
Totals	**4,734,991**	**116,516**	**2.5%**	**204,002**	**4.3%**

In addition, 4,500 Americans were prisoners of war in World War I.

The Importance Of Medical Support

Warfare consists of three elements—strategy, tactics, and logistics. Strategy involves the planning of warfare, tactics involves the carrying out of those plans, and logistics involves providing everything necessary to support the strategy and tactics. Ideally. logistics involves the right amount of support in the right place at the right time.[5]

Pershing was a professional soldier of the highest order.[6] He knew that to create, train, and transport troops, and to design, build and transport war materiel, he needed to focus on the support services as well as the fighting forces. Not only was it important to get troops, planes, and ships to where they could do their jobs, but it was important to keep them supplied. An army needs to be fed, trained, armed, cared for when soldiers are sick or wounded, and it needs to have reinforcements ready to replace those sick or wounded. It needs to supply and maintain not only its troops, but its ships, planes, trains, tanks, cars, trucks, jeeps, ambulances, horses, and mules. The S.O.S. was a vast supply system that supported the fighting forces.[7]

The S.O.S. included transportation support (to get ships, trains, planes, tanks, cars, trucks, jeeps, ambulances, horses, and mules to where they could do their jobs); communications support (to enable the fighting forces to communicate with each other); engineering support (to build and maintain roads, bridges, railways, bases, docks, depots, and other facilities); ordnance support (to supply weapons and ammunition); and medical support (to help prevent sickness and to care for the sick and wounded). Each support service was faced with formidable challenges to build and organize a system to support the war effort.[8]

The medical support of the A.E.F. during World War I was the responsibility of the Medical Department of the United States Army. The Medical Department was the part of the S.O.S. that provided medical services to support the combat operations of the A.E.F. The S.O.S. dealt with the procurement and distribution of materiel and would learn from its experience in World War I the importance of lead time in mobilizing for World War II. In fact, two important lessons learned from World War I were the importance of war materiel in fighting a modern war and the importance of lead time in producing war materiel.[9] When the United States entered World War I, they were behind the eight ball in terms of producing war materiel, but its manpower mobilization was impressive and proved to be decisive in contributing to an Allied victory. In fact, its vast manpower turned the tide in favor of the Allies in World War I. As we shall see years later in World War II, it was its vast airpower that turned the tide in favor of the Allies.

FROM ONE WAR TO ANOTHER

John Cooney Sr. served in the Medical Department during World War I. The Department had three objectives—to be sure those selected for service were fit for the rigors of war, to keep them fit for service, and to restore them to health if they became sick or wounded.[10] It did background checks and conducted physical examinations of new recruits; it oversaw sanitary conditions to encourage good hygiene to prevent disease; and it provided medical care for the sick and wounded. It also furnished all medical and hospital supplies and protected the health of animals in the Army.[11] Succinctly stated, the Medical Department was the service of the Army that "maintained its health, treated its sick, and healed its wounded."[12] The scope and complexity of the responsibilities of the Medical Department is evidenced by the fact that its official history required fifteen volumes and 16,573 pages (Exhibit 3.2).[13]

From its experiences in the Civil War and the Spanish-American War, the Medical Department learned how critical it was to have enough physicians and nurses to care for the sick and wounded and of having battlefield evacuation procedures to get those who needed medical treatment to those who could provide it as soon as possible. At the end of the nineteenth century, the United States Army and the medical profession realized the importance of being prepared for a war and entered the twentieth century with a conviction to do something about it.

Preparing for Medical Support

In the seventeen years leading up to the United States entry into World War I, the Medical Department worked with the civilian medical community to develop a reserve system of physicians and medical supplies that could be mobilized in case of war. To help this cause, a law was passed by Congress in 1908 that authorized a Medical Reserve Corps—a peacetime pool of trained physicians which grew from 180 in 1909 to 1,757 in 1916.[14] Additionally, the Defense Act of 1916 enhanced medical preparedness for war by authorizing Congress to appropriate funds to procure equipment for projected field hospitals, evacuation hospitals, base hospitals, ambulance companies, and regimental infirmaries.[15]

General Pershing knew from his battlefield experience in Mexico the importance of medical support. As commander of the Mexican Expedition, he developed a good working relationship with three surgeons who would become key leaders in the Medical Department in World War I—Colonel Merritte W. Ireland, Colonel Walter D. McCaw, and Colonel James Glen-

Exhibit 3.2
Official History of the Medical Department World War I

Vol.	Contents	Pages
I	The Surgeon General's Office	1,402
II	Administration American Expeditionary Forces	1,137
III	Finance and Supply	948
IV	Activities Concerning Mobilization and Ports of Embarkation	512
V	Military Hospitals in the United States	870
VI	Sanitation	1,152
VII	Training	1,234
VIII	Field Operations	1,220
IX	Communicable and Other Diseases	636
X	Neuropsychiatry	570
XI	Surgery Part 1: General Surgery, Orthopedic Surgery, and Neurosurgery	1,386
	Surgery Part 2: Empyema, Maxillofacial Surgery, U.S. Ophthalmology, A.E.F. Ophthalmology, U.S. Otolaryngology, A.E.F. Otolaryngology	886
XII	Pathology of the Acute Respiratory Diseases and of Gas Gangrene Following War Wounds	660
XIII	Part 1: Physical Reconstruction and Vocational Education; and Part 2: Army Nurse Corps	1,022
XIV	Medical Aspects of Gas Warfare	918
XV	Statistics Part 1: Army Anthropology	648
	Statistics Part 2: Medical and Casualty Statistics	1,396
Total		16,597

This Official History of the Medical Department of the U.S. Army was prepared under the direction of Major General M. W. Ireland, M.D., Surgeon General of the United States Army.

nan. Ireland would become the Chief Surgeon of the A.E.F., McCaw would become his assistant, and Glennan would become the Chief of the Hospitalization Division. The close working relationship Pershing developed with these physicians in Mexico would serve him well in World War I.[16] Ireland would also succeed the Surgeon General William C. Gorgas when Gorgas reached the mandatory retirement age, at that time 64, during the Meuse-Argonne Offensive, the largest and most decisive American-led operation of World War I.[17]

Pershing had an eye for talent and wanted Ireland for Surgeon General when the war started but had to settle for the more-experienced Gorgas. When Gorgas retired and Ireland succeeded him, he not only did his job exceptionally well during World War I but after the war was reappointed as Surgeon General in 1922, 1926 and 1930 by Presidents Harding, Coolidge, and Hoover, respectively. As an item of interest, in 1890, Ireland roomed with George D. De Shon, who had been Pershing's roommate during their senior year at West Point. De Shon later decided to go to medical school with the idea of entering the Medical Corps of the Army. In a memoir Ireland wrote after the war, he said De Shon was the person who got him interested in becoming an Army doctor.[18]

While Pershing was preparing his combat troops for battle overseas, the Medical Department was preparing medical personnel to support his troops. Since the Medical Department had limited experience with the types of battle wounds being inflicted upon the troops engaged in trench and gas warfare, its personnel received training in the French and English medical systems that had already been providing medical care to the victims of trench and gas warfare.[19]

There was a greater need for medical support in World War I than in any previous war. The sheer size and intensity of the Great War brought more deadly weapons with more destructive power resulting in more and worse casualties. Not only this, but it also had more disease to contend with because the trenches during World War I were breeding grounds for disease. Rats infested the trenches—disturbing soldiers' sleep, spoiling their food, and carrying disease. Trench warfare provided ideal unsanitary conditions for rats to multiply and grow as big as cats. Blood-sucking lice were also a problem, breeding in the seams of the soldiers' filthy clothing. Trench fever, trench mouth, trench foot and trench nephritis were all dreaded diseases that became a harsh reality of life in the trenches.[20] Nephritis was one of the diseases that reared its ugly head during World War I, mostly with soldiers who fought for years in the trenches. John Sr. may have been exposed to the disease because he contracted it, and it may have contributed to his untimely death over twenty years later at the relatively young age of forty-five, but the Army felt otherwise.[21]

One infectious disease that was understood and controlled during World War I was yellow fever. In 1891 Carlos Finlay and Walter Reed, for whom the Walter Reed National Medical Center in Bethesda, Maryland is named, discovered that yellow fever was transmitted by mosquitos. Following this discovery, William C. Gorgas, a young Army surgeon at that time, directed a strategy to control the disease by eliminating stagnant pools of water that bred mosquitoes and by putting screens on barrack windows to keep the mosquitos out. He became an expert in preventative medicine, and this is one reason he was appointed by President Wilson as the Surgeon General responsible for the Medical Department in World War I.[22]

Another infectious disease that was not understood during World War I was a deadly influenza that spread like wildfire and resulted in a worldwide influenza pandemic. It struck in January 1918 and lasted for the rest of the war and into 1919. Despite his expertise, Gorgas was unable to prevent the spread of the influenza among the troops, and neither could anybody else prevent it from spreading around the world. Estimates of the number of people it killed worldwide ranged from 50 to 100 million people including some 675,000 Americans.[23] A hundred years later, it raised its ugly head again.

The war with its concentrations of soldiers living, training, and fighting together under often unsanitary conditions contributed to the spread of influenza in the military. Statistics from the Medical Department show that diseases were among the leading causes of deaths in the Army during World War I (Exhibit 3.3). In fact, more U.S. military personnel in World War I died from diseases and non-combat injuries than were killed or wounded in combat. The statistics show that 3.5 million of the 4.0 million personnel in the Army contracted diseases, most notably the influenza, and that 58,119 of them died from these diseases.[24] One reason for so many deaths from diseases is because antibiotics to treat infectious diseases were not yet available during World War I. It would be another ten years before penicillin was discovered in 1928.[25]

Exhibit 3.3 shows the leading causes of U.S. deaths during World War 1. These figures do not include the deaths of Navy, Marines, and Coast Guard personnel. If they did, they would total 63,114 non-combat deaths and 53,402 combat deaths for a total of 115,116 deaths, the figure stated by the Department of Veterans Affairs, the National World War I Museum, and the United States Military Academy at West Point.[26]

Exhibit 3.3
Leading Causes of Deaths
United States Army in World War I (April 1, 1917, to December 31, 1919)

Cause	Admissions	Deaths	Combat vs. Non-Combat Deaths
Diseases	3,515,464	58,119	Non-Combat: 63,710
Non-Combat Injuries	299,069	5,591	
Wounded in Action	224,089	13,694	Combat: 50,385
Killed in Action	36,691	36,691	
Totals	**4,075,316**	**114,095**	**114,095**

This table does not include admissions and deaths in the Navy, Marines, and Coast Guard. If they were included, the total United States deaths in World War I would be 116,516.

The Importance Of Medical Support

Never Enough Medical Personnel

There were never enough medical personnel during World War I. One reason is because German offensives in March and April 1918 prompted the Army to slow down shipping support units, including medical support units, to speed up shipping combat units to France. The fact that German U-boats were sinking ships at an alarming rate contributed to the Army's decision to expedite the shipping of combat units. While this change was intended to be temporary, the medical support units never caught up with the combat units.[27] In May 1918, the Medical Department had a personnel shortage of 13,671 personnel. By September 1918, the shortage had increased to 26,497.[28] By the end of November 1918, the shortage had grown to 38,552.[29]

The Medical Department planned to have field hospitals, evacuation hospitals, and base hospitals in France. The evacuation hospitals were said to be the backbone of all combat hospitalization but there were never enough of them.[30] The original plan was to have two evacuation hospitals for every Army division.[31] Since only thirty-seven evacuation hospitals reached France, with seven of them arriving after the Armistice, the plan for having two for every division fell far short because forty-three divisions were sent to France during World War I (Exhibit 3.4).[32] Of the thirty evacuation hospitals in France before the Armistice, two were assigned to the S.O.S. and two others were assigned to an area that did not see action. Of the remaining twenty-six, four were broken up leaving twenty-two evacuation hospitals in the combat zone to support twenty-nine divisions which were engaged in combat.[33] John Cooney Sr. would serve with two of the evacuation hospitals in the combat zone—Evacuation Hospitals No. 12 and 1—and later with one of the evacuation hospitals that reached France after the Armistice—Evacuation Hospital No. 37.

Even though there were never enough medical personnel during World War I, the numbers were large as was the case with most numbers in the Great War. In his 1918 Annual Report to President Wilson, dated December 5, 1918, Secretary of War Baker said the Medical Department increased from about 8,000 personnel on April 6, 1917, when the United States entered the war against Germany, to almost 327,000 when the war ended on November 11, 1918.[34] This was a remarkable increase considering how long it takes to educate and train physicians and other medical professionals. Of the approximately 146,000 qualified physicians and surgeons in the United States, 34,837, or about 24 percent of them, served during World War I.[35]

Exhibit 3.4		
American Divisions (43) Sent to France in WWI		
(Regular Army) [National Guard] {National Army}		

Month	#	Divisions
Jun. 1917	1	(1st Fighting First)
Aug. 1918		FIRST ARMY ORGANIZED
Oct. 1917	2	(2nd Indianhead) [26th Yankee]
Nov. 1917	1	[42nd Rainbow]
Dec. 1917	1	[41st Sunset]
Feb. 1918	1	[32nd Red Arrow]
Mar. 1918	1	{93rd Blue Helmuts}
Apr. 1918	2	(3rd Marne) {77th Statue of Liberty}
May 1918	9	(5th Red Diamond) (4th Ivy) [27th New York] [28th Keystone] [30th Old Hickory] [33rd Prairie] [35th Santa Fe] {80th Blue Ridge} {82nd All American}
Jun. 1918	6	[29th Blue and Gray] [37th Buckeye] {78th Lightning} {83rd Ohio} {89th Middle West} {92nd Buffalo}
Jul. 1918	6	(6th Sightseeing Sixth) [36th Texas] {76th Onaway} {79th Liberty} {90th Tough 'Ombres} {91st Wild West}
Aug. 1918	5	(7th Hourglass) [39th Delta] [40th Sunshine] {81st Stonewall} {85th Custer}
Sep. 1918	4	{84th Railsplitters} {86th Blackhawk} {87th Acorn} {88th Cloverleaf}
Oct. 1918		SECOND ARMY ORGANIZED
Oct. 1918	3	[31st Dixie] [34th Sandstorm] [38th Cyclone}
Nov. 1918	1	(8th Pathfinder)

The Importance Of Medical Support

Baker wrote: "Probably no working force has ever been organized which contained more distinguished men of a single profession than are today enrolled in the Medical Department of the United States Army." He also praised the work of the American nurses who watched over and cared for the troops in splendid fashion.[36] While he did not single out the enlisted men for praise, they also served well and sacrificed much. For example, 4,711 enlisted men in the Medical Department died in the service of their country along with 524 doctors and 271 nurses.[37]

The mortality rates of those who were hospitalized for both battle injuries and their non-battle injuries and sicknesses were lower than in any previous war, indicating that the understaffed Medical Department did a better job of caring for the wounded and sick than in any previous American war.[38] This prompted Major General Johnson Hagood, who served as the president of the board that created the S.O.S., to say: "I am absolutely certain that they (our soldiers) had better medical attention (than any other soldiers in Europe)."[39]

John Sr. Goes to War

John Joseph Cooney Sr. registered for the draft in June 1917, the same month that American troops arrived in France for the first time.[40] He registered in Jersey City, New Jersey, not far from the Statue of Liberty, the foremost symbol of the land of the free that he was going to war to defend.[41] About a year later, on June 28, 1918, he was ordered to report to Camp Dix (now Fort Dix) in Wrightstown, New Jersey, to begin his military training.[42] By coincidence, June 28 was also the date on which four years earlier Bosnian Serb Gavrilo Princip shot Austrian Archduke Franz Ferdinand and his wife Sophie to spark the chain of events that led to World War I.

Camp Dix was established to train men to become soldiers for the battlefields of Europe. It was named for John Adams Dix who was a veteran of the War of 1812, a U.S. Senator, and the Secretary of the Treasury just before the Civil War when Southern rebels were threatening to seize a sailing vessel, called a cutter, that was federal property. Its captain sympathized with the rebels which prompted Dix to send a letter to the lieutenant of the cutter ordering him to arrest the captain and said: "If anyone attempts to haul down the American flag, shoot him on the spot." While the cutter was captured and fell into Confederate hands, his quote was a rallying cry for the North during the Civil War. Five years after the war, Dix became the Governor of New York.[43]

FROM ONE WAR TO ANOTHER

At the time, women were not permitted to participate in armed conflict.[44] Therefore. Camp Dix was only training enlisted men in the National Army who were, like John Sr., assigned to depot brigades for their basic training.[45] The depot brigades were set up to receive and organize recruits, provide them with uniforms and equipment, and train them for overseas duty.[46] John Sr. was assigned to the 153rd Depot Brigade for his basic training (Exhibit 3.5)[47]

Evacuation Hospitals

On July 17, 1918, after almost three weeks of basic training, John Sr. was assigned to Evacuation Hospital No. 12 in the Medical Department of the United States Army. The Army Medical Department had been mobilized by President Wilson only nine months earlier on April 28, 1917, to support the American Expeditionary Forces in France, assisted by the American National Red Cross which provided the nurses.[48] An evacuation hospital operated between a field hospital close to the battlefront and a base hospital further from harm's way where more extensive medical care was provided for war casualties. A field hospital was a small medical unit, a mini hospital if you will, close to the front to temporarily take care of battle wounds before the victims could be transported to evacuation hospitals for more extensive medical care.[49] The highly acclaimed 2018 documentary film, *They Shall Not Grow Old*, depicted life in the trenches on the Western Front in World War I. It showed the extent of the casualties of war and the challenges of providing medical care to soldiers in dire straits.

Evacuation hospitals were an important part of the Medical Department evacuation and hospitalization system of the American Expeditionary Forces (Exhibit 3.6). The system consisted of first aid stations close to the front line backed up by dressing stations and ambulances to transport the wounded to field hospitals where the patients were triaged, or sorted into categories based on their condition, such as those who required surgery, those who were gassed, and those who were sick in other ways.[50]

The field hospitals had limited equipment and could only treat the less serious cases. Ambulances were used to move the more serious cases to evacuation hospitals for surgical care. The evacuation hospitals were usually located about five to ten miles behind the lines out of the range of enemy artillery. They were located at railheads so that hospital trains could transport patients to base hospitals which were better equipped to help then make a full recovery.[51]

Exhibit 3.5
Private First Class John J. Cooney, Sr.
Courtesy of Cooney Family

Exhibit 3.6
Medical Department
Evacuation and Hospitalization System
World War I

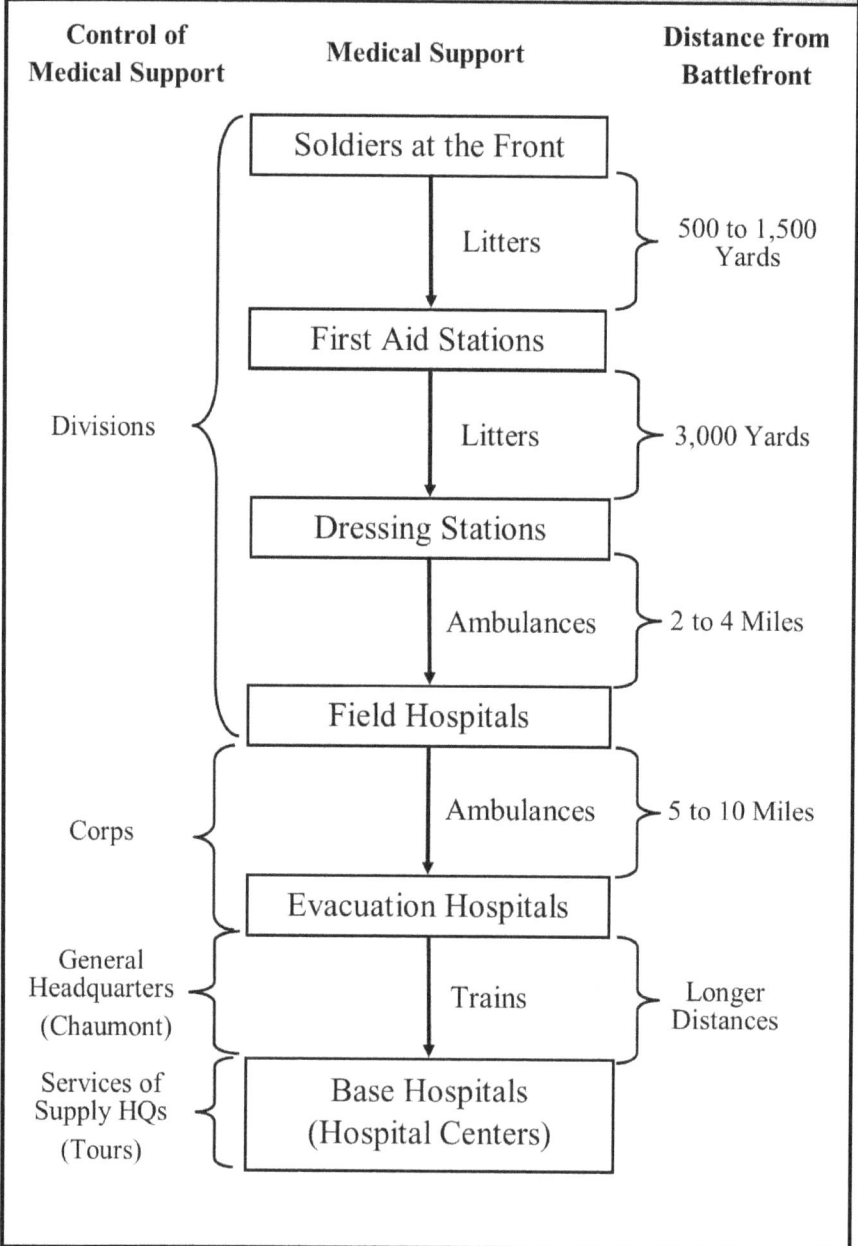

Control of Medical Support	Medical Support	Distance from Battlefront
	Soldiers at the Front	
	Litters	500 to 1,500 Yards
	First Aid Stations	
Divisions	Litters	3,000 Yards
	Dressing Stations	
	Ambulances	2 to 4 Miles
	Field Hospitals	
Corps	Ambulances	5 to 10 Miles
	Evacuation Hospitals	
General Headquarters (Chaumont)	Trains	Longer Distances
Services of Supply HQs (Tours)	**Base Hospitals (Hospital Centers)**	

The Importance Of Medical Support

The division commanders had control of the medical personnel up to the field hospitals to ensure that their soldiers were being cared for close to the battlefield. The corps commanders oversaw and controlled the evacuation of the soldiers from the field hospitals to the evacuation hospitals. The evacuations of soldiers from the evacuation hospitals to the base hospitals involved railroads and came under the control of General Headquarters in Chaumont, where Pershing relied on William H. Atterbury, Director General of Transportation, to oversee the railroads.[52]

Pershing always sought the best and Atterbury was considered one of the best railroad men in the United States with vast experience in running railroads. Because his expertise was sorely needed, he entered the Army at the high rank of brigadier general.[53] Pershing made a good choice because at war's end, Atterbury received his country's Distinguished Service Medal along with similar honors bestowed upon him by the Allied countries with whom he coordinated wartime railway travel—France, Great Britain, Belgium, Serbia, and Romania.[54]

Railroads were important because the base hospitals were farther behind the lines and many of them tended to be grouped into large hospital centers. As previously mentioned, and worth repeating, oversight and control of the base hospitals and hospital centers themselves were transferred by Pershing from Chaumont to Tours, which was farther away from the front, to allow Pershing and his commanders to focus on the fighting forces at the front while officers in Services of Supply focused on support units in the rear which included the base hospitals and hospital centers.

The Medical Department was made up of male doctors, female nurses, and enlisted men. All the military doctors were men even though American women doctors also wanted to serve during World War I. In fact, one-third of practicing U.S. female physicians registered for war service, but the door was not open for women doctors in the military at that time. Some who wanted to serve close to the action overseas found ways to do so.

Dr. Caroline Sandford Findley of the New York Infirmary for Women and Children led an all-female U.S. hospital that served in France under the auspices of the Women's Overseas Hospitals and earned the rank of lieutenant in the Medical Corps of the French army. Dr. Rosalie Slaughter Morton of Columbia University College of Physicians and Surgeons and other U.S. women doctors went overseas under the auspices of the American Women's Hospitals to serve in France and Serbia, a country which appreciated female doctors because male doctors could not provide care to Muslim women. Dr.

FROM ONE WAR TO ANOTHER

Anna Tjomsland of Bellevue Hospital in New York City went to Vichy as a contract surgeon and later served with the U.S. Army but as a civilian doctor not a commissioned military doctor.[55]

Some women doctors were honored for their service. Dr. Morton was decorated by the French, Serbian, and Yugoslav governments for her service. Dr. Olga Stastny of Boston's New England Hospital for Women and Children, who went to France under the auspices of the American Committee for Devastated France, was awarded the French Medaille de Reconnaissance for her service. Dr. Alice Weld Tallant of the Women's Medical College of Pennsylvania, who served with the Smith College Relief Unit in France, received the French Croix de Guerre for her service.[56]

Despite the good work of these pioneering women, the door was still closed to female physicians at the start of World War II. The door didn't open until President Franklin D. Roosevelt signed into law the Sparkman-Johnson Bill on April 16, 1943, allowing women to enter the Army and Navy Medical Corps as commissioned medical officers. The first female physician through the door was Dr. Margaret Craighill of the Women's Medical College of Pennsylvania. She was a third-generation military officer. Both her father and grandfather were graduates of the United States Military Academy at West Point. Dr. Craighill was a graduate of the University of Wisconsin and the Johns Hopkins University School of Medicine. She retired from the military as a lieutenant colonel and was the recipient of the Legion of Merit in recognition of her exemplary wartime service.[57]

Enlisted men such as John Sr. could be trained to provide direct help to the doctors and nurses by performing duties such as carrying litters (i.e., stretchers for evacuating the sick and wounded), or they could be assigned to do other work indispensable to their medical units. For example, some might bring useful skills to the military and be assigned to perform them as a tinsmith, mechanic, plumber, electrician, barber, or tailor. Others might simply be assigned to police, mess hall, orderly, telephone, quartermaster, or office duties.[58] A quartermaster is responsible for providing quarters, rations, clothing, and other supplies to soldiers.[59] Private Harry B. Rodcay was an enlisted man in an evacuation hospital in France during World War I. In one of his letters to home, he wrote they had all kinds of workmen in their outfit so that when they wanted something done, it got done.[60]

As previously mentioned, John Sr. would serve in France with three evacuation hospitals during World War I—Evacuation Hospital No. 12, Evacuation Hospital No. 1, and Evacuation Hospital No. 37. First, he would ship out

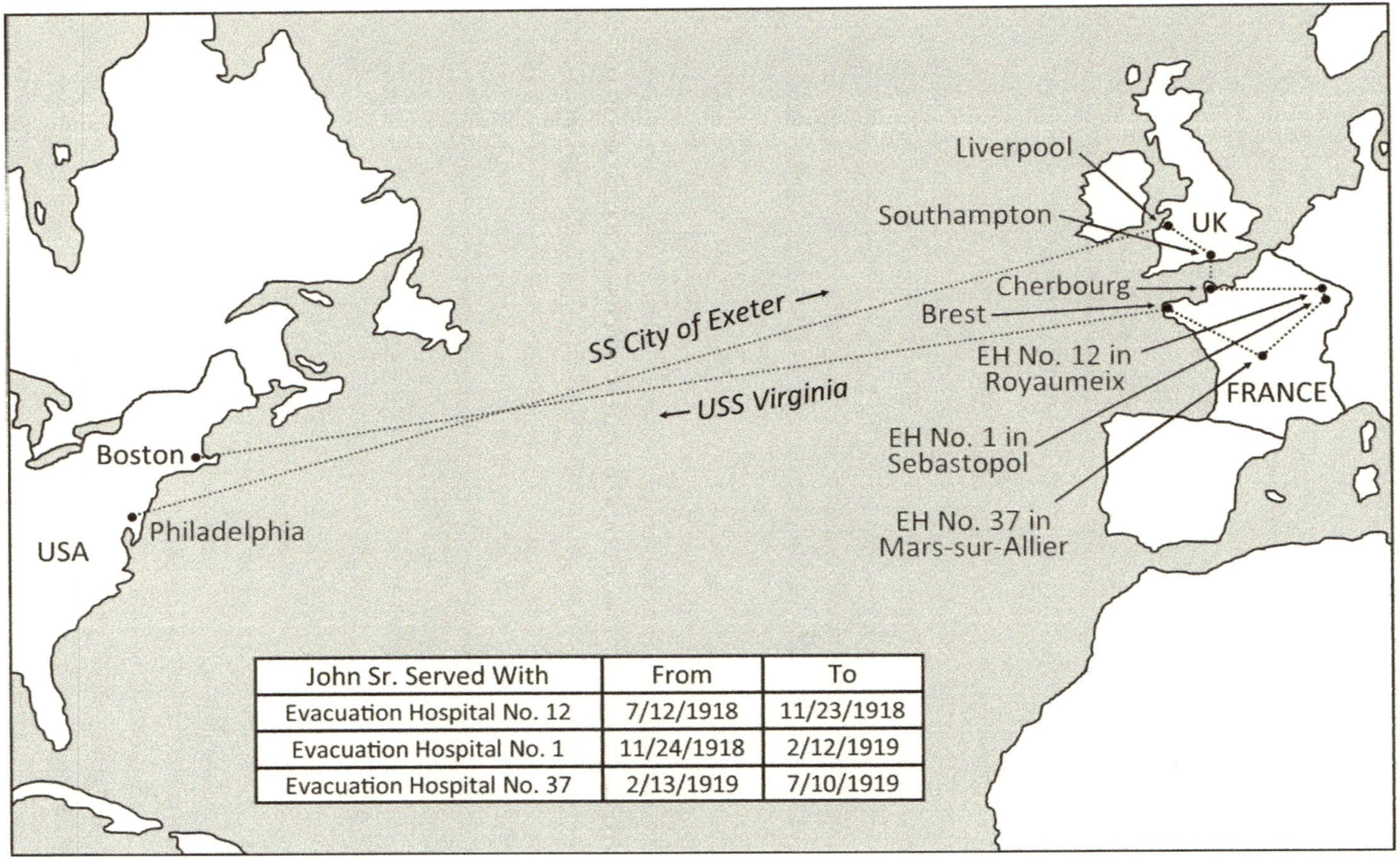
Liverpool
Southampton
UK
Cherbourg
Brest
EH No. 12 in Royaumeix
FRANCE
EH No. 1 in Sebastopol
EH No. 37 in Mars-sur-Allier
SS City of Exeter →
← USS Virginia
Boston
Philadelphia
USA

John Sr. Served With	From	To
Evacuation Hospital No. 12	7/12/1918	11/23/1918
Evacuation Hospital No. 1	11/24/1918	2/12/1919
Evacuation Hospital No. 37	2/13/1919	7/10/1919

Exhibit 3.7: John Sr.'s Trip Over and Back and Evacuation Hospitals He Served With

from the United States on August 16, 1918, with Evacuation Hospital No. 12 and serve with it in France until November 23. Second, he would serve with Evacuation Hospital No. 1 until February 12, 1919. Third, he would serve with Evacuation Hospital No. 37 until it returned to the States where he would be honorably discharged from military service on July 10, 1919 (Exhibit 3.7).[61]

Evacuation Hospital No. 12

Evacuation Hospital No. 12 is where John Sr. served from July 17, 1918, to November 23, 1918. About six months after he enlisted in the Army, Evacuation Hospital No. 12 was organized at Fort Riley, Kansas, on January 3, 1918, with one officer and 181 enlisted men. On June 1, it left Fort Riley for Camp Dix to prepare for overseas duty with intensive classwork and hospital training. At Camp Dix, a request was made for additional personnel and the authorized strength of Evacuation Hospital No.12 was increased accordingly. John Sr. was one of the fifty-four enlisted men added to the hospital along with thirty-three officers, bringing the total to thirty-four officers and 235 enlisted men by the time they were ready for overseas duty.[62]

On August 14, 1918, they took a train to Philadelphia where they sailed for Europe on August 16 on the SS *City of Exeter*, a troopship built in Belfast in Northern Ireland.[63] They arrived in Liverpool, England, fourteen days later on August 28, and were towed through the Manchester Ship Canal to Manchester where they took a train to a rest camp at Southampton but didn't get much of an opportunity to rest. On August 30, they sailed across the English Channel on the SS *Archangel*, a troopship built in Clydebank, Scotland, to Cherbourg, France, arriving on August 31.[64] From there they traveled by train for three days and two nights, arriving at Pagny-sur-Meuse on September 3.[65]

They spent only ten days at Pagny-sur-Meuse, a small village located about eight miles southwest of Evacuation Hospital No. 1, where John Sr. would later be assigned. Pagny-sur-Meuse was swampy and full of flies, not conducive to caring for medical cases. Consequently, the hospital handled only a few cases of slightly wounded soldiers before moving to more permanent quarters at a more suitable location only nine miles northwest in an old French hospital near Royaumeix, which was about four miles north of Evacuation Hospital No. 1.[66]

Evacuation Hospitals No. 12 and 1 were both close to the front lines and would be busy during the major American battles of World War I—the Battle of St. Mihiel and the follow-up Meuse-Argonne Offensive. Evacuation Hospital No. 12 would treat 2,700 patients before the Armistice, with over a thousand of them being seriously wounded. After the Armistice, it would treat another 200 before moving to another location in early December.[67]

By coincidence, John Sr.'s son John would marry a young lady whose father, Thomas M. Dalton, was serving in Royaumeix during World War I when John Sr. was serving nearby with Evacuation Hospital No. 12. Dalton was a corporal in the 11th Platoon of Company B of the 56th Engineers, known as the Searchlight Regiment. Company B's headquarters were established in Royaumeix on September 8, 1944.[68] The 56th Engineers operated 36-inch and 60-inch searchlights to help artillery units protect American troops on the front line from night air raids by illuminating the skies for the anti-aircraft batteries to shoot down the attacking aircraft.[69] They set up their searchlights about four miles behind the front and provided this support for the Battle of St. Mihiel and the Meuse-Argonne Offensive.[70] It's a shame that John Sr. passed away in 1939 before his son John married Dalton's daughter Phyllis in 1950. As World War I veterans serving in the same area of France at the same time, they no doubt would have had a deep respect for each other and may have even shared war stories at the wedding.

John Sr. served with Evacuation Hospital No. 12 until November 23, 1918, a little more than a week after the Armistice, at which time he was reassigned to Evacuation Hospital No. 1, which was only four miles to the south. A week after he left Evacuation Hospital No. 12, his former hospital was ordered to provide medical support to the newly formed Third Army as it advanced into Germany toward Berlin.[71]

Evacuation Hospital No. 1

John Sr. served with Evacuation Hospital No. 1 from November 24, 1918, to February 12, 1919. Evacuation Hospital No. 1 was the first evacuation hospital formed by the Medical Department. It was organized at Fort Riley in Kansas, on October 10, 1917, the same camp at which Evacuation Hospital No. 12 was later formed on January 3, 1918. The officers and enlisted men of Evacuation Hospital No. 1 were selected from those on duty at Fort Riley and received careful military training.[72] It was called into active service two months later, on December 17, 1917. The unit traveled from Fort Riley to Camp Merritt in New Jersey, then to Portland, Maine where it boarded the British steamship SS *Canada* on December 27 for Halifax, Nova Scotia and on the next day sailed for Europe with 17 officers and 181 enlisted men, arriving in Liverpool on January 7, 1918.[73]

FROM ONE WAR TO ANOTHER

From Liverpool, Evacuation Hospital No. 1 was ordered to Toul and occupied a group of unfinished buildings just three months north of Toul which were called the Sebastopol Barracks and became the permanent home of Evacuation Hospital No. 1 for the rest of the war. The American 1st Division had moved just north of Toul to relieve a French division on the front line and needed medical support, and Evacuation Hospital No. 1 was one of the medical units to provide this support. It was located seven miles south of the battle line held by American troops.[74]

The French turned over the unfinished buildings to the Americans for use in caring for its sick and wounded soldiers. Evacuation Hospital No. 1 was initially set up with an initial bed capacity of 900 beds.[75] It was the first American front-line hospitalization unit installed near the Western Front.[76] Not only this, but it was responsible for training many surgical teams, nurses, adjutants, quartermasters, and even commanding officers of hospital units who arrived in France after them.[77]

Evacuation Hospital No. 1 was doing double-duty in preparing itself for handling an increased volume of patients while training medical personnel from other hospitals. To prepare for the major American battles ahead, it increased its bed capacity from 900 to 2,800 and its personnel to 97 officers, 92 nurses, and 674 enlisted men. Its orders were to prepare to serve, with help from Mobile Hospital No. 3, as one of the principal evacuation hospitals for wounded soldiers from the south face of the St. Mihiel salient that the Americans were planning to retake from the Germans.[78] From February 1918 to August 1918, it treated on average up to 200 patients a day, gaining valuable experience in handling battle wounds. From September to the Armistice on November 11, 1918, it treated on average about 450 patients a day. After the Armistice, it began treating the sick as well as the wounded and from that time until February 1919, it treated on average about 550 patients a day.[79]

Evacuation Hospital No. 1 was where Major Raoul Lufbery was taken when he was fatally shot down over the Toul sector on May 19, 1918. Lufbery was at that time America's most revered fighter pilot. Born in France to a French mother and American father, he came to America when he was six-years old and grew up in Wallingford, Connecticut. He was one of the American pilots who volunteered in 1916 to fight with the French in World War I. He served with a squadron of American fighter pilots that was known as the Lafayette Escadrille and had more confirmed victories than any other American in the squadron. A memorial plaque in the Wallingford Historical Society states that he was officially credited with sixteen confirmed victories.[80] However, his citation in the

National Aviation Hall of Fame states his official kill record as seventeen and notes that it was unofficially much higher.[81] Fighter pilots were not credited with a victory (an enemy plane shot down) unless it could be verified by a witness.

When the American Air Service was formed in 1918, Lufbery was recruited to train American pilots of the 94th Aero Squadron in combat techniques. One of the pilots he trained was Eddie Rickenbacker, who went on to become America's greatest ace of World War I with twenty-six confirmed victories.[82] Rickenbacker revered Lufbery, saying everything he learned about combat flying he learned from him.[83] In his book, *Fighting the Flying Circus*, he said Lufbery was the leading American Ace with eighteen victories.[84] Lufbery was buried with full military honors on May 20 at the American Cemetery for Evacuation Hospital No. 1. Colonel William "Billy" Mitchell, commander of the American Air Service, attended the ceremony and Eddie Rickenbacker led a flyover with six of his fellow flyers and dropped red roses over the cemetery.[85] Both men would become aviation legends.

Lufbery's remains were later moved to a place of honor at the Lafayette Escadrille Memorial Cemetery near Paris. The cemetery was cared for by the French until the American Battle Monuments Commission assumed responsibility for it in 2017. Since the Lafayette Escadrille squadron is considered the birthplace of American combat aviation, it was fitting for the Americans to care for it.[86] It was also fitting that the chairman of the American Battle Monuments Commission—from its inception in 1923 until his death in 1948—was General Pershing who had a deep respect for those who gave their lives in the service of their country. He made sure that their service and sacrifice would be preserved with dignity and honor in those hallowed grounds.[87]

Evacuation Hospital No. 1 treated patients from the two major American battles of World War I—the Battle of St. Mihiel and the Meuse-Argonne Offensive. It treated 3,410 cases before the Armistice and another 505 cases after the Armistice. At its peak, it treated patients on twenty-eight operating tables in eight operating rooms supported by two sterilization rooms. It was a hectic time for keeping accurate records and it was thought that the hospital probably treated more cases and that many of the cases involved multiple wounds.[88]

Since John Sr. arrived at Evacuation Hospital No. 1 eleven days after the Armistice, he was not there during its peak period. He arrived after the shooting stopped and things had calmed down a bit, and he remained there until February 12, 1919, when he was ordered to Evacuation Hospital No. 37, which didn't even get to France until after the Armistice.[89]

FROM ONE WAR TO ANOTHER

Evacuation Hospital No. 37

John Sr. served with Evacuation Hospital No. 37 from February 13, 1919, until he was honorably discharged from the Army on July 10, 1919.[90] Evacuation Hospital No. 37 was organized at Camp Greenleaf, Georgia on September 1, 1918, with two medical officers and 100 enlisted men. On the same day, it left for Camp Grant, Illinois, where additional personnel were added to the hospital. By the Armistice on November 11, 1918, it had a complement of sixteen officers and 237 enlisted men but was still in the United States. The next day, all but seven officers boarded the USS *Northern Pacific* in Hoboken, New Jersey, for overseas duty. It arrived at Brest, France, on November 22, 1918, ten days after the Armistice, and was joined by the other seven officers who traveled overseas on another transport. Brest was a port city where military troops were dropped off in World War I.[91]

When Evacuation Hospital No. 37 arrived at Brest, it was ordered to proceed to a medical concentration area in Joinville, located 440 miles west of Brest.[92] Joinville had been designated by the Medical Department in October 1918 for the exclusive use of sanitary operations, the purpose of which was to educate soldiers on the importance of proper personal hygiene habits and keeping their surroundings clean to stay healthy and protect against disease.[93]

Joinville was located twenty-five miles west of Domrémy-la-Pucelle, the village where Joan of Arc was born 500 years earlier in 1412.[94] The area contained nine villages and was about twenty-five square miles so there was plenty of room to build living quarters for many doctors, nurses, and enlisted men, plus the area had good roads to all parts of the American front and was near several railroads.[95] Evacuation Hospital No. 37 arrived in Joinville on December 1, 1918. It remained there for a month while being equipped and trained in preparation for further duty.[96]

On January 1, 1919, Evacuation Hospital No. 37 was ordered to proceed to the Mars-sur-Allier Hospital Center (Mars Hospital Center) near Mars-sur-Allier in the eastern center of France. It arrived at the Mars Hospital Center on January 10 and two days later relieved Base Hospital No. 48.[97] Base Hospital No. 48 had arrived at the Mars Hospital Center on July 25, 1918.[98] It was busy with a continual stream of wounded soldiers during August, September, October, and November."[99] It treated 4,822 cases in a little more than six months before it was relieved by Evacuation Hospital No. 37. Of those cases, 2,960 were surgical cases and 1,862 were medical cases.[100]

The Importance Of Medical Support

As previously noted, there were never enough medical personnel in France during the war nor were there enough evacuation hospitals. Ambulances and trains were also in short supply. Because the United States did not have sufficient lead time to produce ambulances and trains for World War I, it had to borrow them from the Allies, and planes as well. This would change in World War II. America would learn from the World War I experience the importance of lead time in mobilizing for war efficiently and effectively to produce the vehicles, trains, tanks, ships, and planes needed for World War II.

Base hospitals were also in short supply during World War I, prompting a decision to group them together into large hospital centers to share support personnel, services, and medical equipment.[101] The Medical Department planned twenty base hospitals at the Mars Hospital Center, but ended up with only nine, two of which arrived after the Armistice, as did two Evacuation Hospitals (Nos. 30 and 37).[102] Even though the war had ended, these base hospitals were busy caring for war casualties up to the time that the patients were well enough to be sent home to the States.

The Mars Hospital Center was authorized in 1917.[103] The site on which it was built was a farming field outside the village of Moiry near Mars-sur-Allier. Rebecca Goethe was a teenager watching her cows in the field when the first soldiers arrived to pitch a tent in the middle of the field and informed her family of their plan to build a hospital center. She watched as the American liberators built the small city, forcing her family to find lodging in the village. The railway linking the evacuation hospitals to the hospital center went through part of what had been their garden. When hospital personnel arrived, followed by trainloads of wounded soldiers, she saw firsthand the suffering war brings to its combatants, and came to appreciate the Americans who fought and died for France.[104]

The Mars Hospital Center was originally planned to house 60,000 people—43,000 patients and 17,000 personnel and laborers. It never reached that level. Nevertheless, at its peak it was like a small city with about 23,000 people—16,000 patients and a work force of 7,000 people that included 500 doctors, 700 nurses, 2,400 enlisted men, and 3,400 laborers.[105] It had 700 buildings on thirty-three acres with roads, water, sewerage, and lighting facilities.[106] It also had its own fire department, railroad system, theaters, vaudeville houses and many more features of a small city. During the war, 37,774 patients were treated at the Mars Hospital Center, and 438 of those who died there were buried in the Mars Cemetery. This low death rate of 1.16 percent reflected the efficiency of the hospital center in caring for its patients.[107]

FROM ONE WAR TO ANOTHER

When Evacuation Hospital No. 37 reported for duty at the Mars Hospital Center to take over for Base Hospital No. 48, it had twenty-one officers and 222 enlisted men.[108] Evacuation Hospital No. 37 operated at the Mars Hospital Center for a little over a month before being relieved by Base Hospital No. 80 on February 25, 1919 which took over its duties of handling patients with battle injuries as well as non-battle medical conditions such as gas inhalation, influenza, pneumonia, diarrhea, rheumatism, nephritis, neurosis, pulmonary tuberculosis, measles, mumps, scarlet fever, diphtheria, and cerebrospinal meningitis.[109]

As the operations in the Mars Hospital Center were scaling down, one of the medics in Base Hospital 80, Charles DeVries, decided to take French lessons. He walked into the village of Moiry to find a teacher and the person he asked to teach him French, Rebecca's foster mother, said her daughter would teach him. Four years later, Charles and Rebecca, after falling and love and three years of correspondence, were man and wife. They had a daughter, Lucy DeVries Duffy, who grew up in America with a mother who never lost her love for France.

In 1968, on the 50th Anniversary of the Armistice, Rebecca wrote a letter to *La Montagne*, a newspaper in Nevers, France. The Mars Hospital Center was in Nevers, a department of France which is divided into regions which are then divided into departments. Rebecca's letter spoke of the warm relations between the Americans at the Mars Hospital Center and the people of her village.[110] This warmth was never lost by the citizens who every year remember the 438 men and women of Mars Hospital Center who died there. In 2008, on the 90th Anniversary of the Armistice, Lucy, a resident of Brewster, Massachusetts, traveled to Saint Parize-le-Châtel, France, to be part of a ceremony at the monument honoring Americans who died at the Mars Hospital Center. The inscription on the monument states (translated into English): "To the Americans Who Died for France, for Right and for Liberty."[111]

Evacuation Hospital No. 37 personnel remained in France for a few months until they received their orders to head for home. In June, they were ordered to Brest, one of the three main embarkation ports in France—the other two being St. Nazaire and Bordeaux. Railroads led to these embarkation camps where soldiers went through "the mill," a process in which their service records and their pay were brought up to date, followed by a thorough medical examination. They were stripped and examined by doctors. If no disease was found, they were directed to the clothing department where they received new clothes from head to foot. Before donning their new clothes, they took a shower and had a haircut and a shave. After they made it through "the mill," they were brought to billets, temporary lodging places, where they waited for their ship to come in.[112] Twenty-six years later, two crewmates of John Sr.'s son John, would, after being liberated from a prisoner of war camp, go through a similar process in France and then wait for their ship to come into the embarkation port of LeHavre to take them home.

On June 23, 1919, John Sr. and his Evacuation Hospital No. 37 mates boarded their ship, the USS *Virginia*, and set sail for Boston, Massachusetts. At that time, their unit was comprised of twenty-three officers and 236 enlisted men. They arrived in Boston ten days later, on July 5, 1919.[113] Ironically, after returning from the most brutal war in history, the big news on the home front was that Jack Dempsey defeated Jess Willard for the Heavyweight Championship of the World in one of the most brutal fights in boxing history.[114] Evacuation Hospital No. 37 was demobilized in July 1919 at Camp Devens in Ayer, Massachusetts.[115] From there, John Cooney Sr. went home to New Jersey. Like many other veterans, he never spoke to his family about his wartime experiences.

Chapter 4

DECISIVE BATTLES

Ever since General Pershing arrived in France in June 1917, he had been preparing to lead American troops in a major offensive in an American sector of the Western Front. His plans included strategically locating American depots, hospitals, training areas, and other installations with this goal in mind. By the end of the summer of 1918, he felt his divisions were ready to be grouped into corps to form an American army under an American commander. Not only did he have confidence in his fighting forces, but he also had confidence in his support forces. The American Expeditionary Forces under his command had constructed quarters to house and train troops; depots to store materiel; roads and railroads to transport troops and materiel to the battlefronts; hospitals to treat the sick and wounded; and other installations to support an American army in France. After a year of preparing his fighting and support forces for war, Pershing formed the American First Army on August 10, 1918, with him as its Commander in Chief. He was now wearing two hats as he was still Commander in Chief of the American Expeditionary Forces.[1]

With the entrance of the United States into the war, there was a need to channel this infusion of significant manpower into an overall strategy in a coordinated way to achieve success against Germany. This led to the establishment of a Supreme War Council in November 1917 to synchronize the war effort of all the Allied armies. The Council was tasked with the responsibility of overseeing the conduct of the war and approving all military actions carried out by the Allies armies fighting along the Western Front.[2]

On March 21, 1918, German General Erich Ludendorff launched a major offensive with the objective of defeating the British and French forces before the Americans could reinforce them. Ludendorff recognized that the British and French forces didn't work together well and planned to take advantage of this situation by attacking the seam between them to split them where they were most vulnerable. At that time, the British forces under Field Marshal Douglas Haig viewed as their essential task to protect the English Channel ports while the French forces under General Philippe Pétain viewed as their essential task to protect Paris. In other words, each was focused on protecting his own nation's interests rather than in working together to defeat the enemy.[3]

On March 26, British and French government and military leaders met and charged French Marshal (General) Ferdinand Foch with coordinating the actions of the Allied armies on the Western Front. In his memoirs, Foch wrote, "Instead of a British battle to cover the Channel ports and a French battle to cover Paris, we would fight an Anglo-French battle to cover Amiens, the connecting link between the two armies."[4] During April, however, while coordination of the armies improved, it was determined that both armies needed manpower immediately, and they looked to the Americans for help.

In April, there were only five American divisions trained for combat (1st, 2nd, 26th, 42nd, and 32nd) in addition to the African American troops of the 369th Infantry Regiment that were serving with the French infantry.[5] Pershing had pledged his support to the French which led to the 369th Infantry Regiment being added to the fully-integrated African colonial troops of the 16th Division of the French Fourth Army in March 1918. The 369th Infantry Regiment would go on to serve in combat at the front for 191 days, longer than any other U.S. unit. The Germans gave the unit the name Hellfighters, and it came to be known as the Harlem Hellfighters because it was initially formed as a National Guard unit in Harlem.[6]

General Pershing was all for getting more American troops to France faster. Consequently, a priority was established in early May to transport American infantryman and machine gunners to France as soon as possible, and the British chipped in with transport ships to speed American manpower to France. As a result of this cooperative effort, the number of American troops in France increased from 60,000 in March to 93,000 in April, 240,000 in May, and 280,000 in June.[7]

With Foch's efforts to coordinate the actions of the British and French armies paying dividends and with an infusion of American manpower on the horizon, the advantages of a unity of command was recognized and Foch was appointed the Commander in Chief of the Allied armies on May 14, 1918.[8] He was given responsibility for overseeing the operations of all the Allied armies while providing strategic direction and making sure that the Allied armies, along with their logistics and supporting resources, were in sync to achieve strategic Allied objectives.[9] The process which led to Foch being given this responsibility was gradual and began in February 1917 when British Prime Minister David Lloyd George voiced his concern that there was a lack of unity among the different Allied armies.[10]

The Allied leaders now felt that this unified command would best position the Allies to counterpunch Ludendorff's German offensive and then deliver a knockout blow to end the war.[11] Foch organized a centralized reserve to provide logistical support for each of the Allied armies and created an environment that fostered teamwork.[12] By working together under a unified command structure, the Allies were able to stop the last strong German offensive and, with an infusion of American manpower, turn the tide and position itself to mount a strong Allied offensive.[13]

Foch, working with the commanders of the Allied armies, designed a series of coordinated attacks along the Western Front to deliver the knockout punch. The different Allied armies were to attack different parts of the Western Front at different times but in a coordinated manner. This came to be known as The Hundred Days Offensive because it began on August 8 and ended with the Armistice on November 11, 1918.[14] It was a series of battles along the Western Front with a concentrated and unified strategy involving a coalition of British, French, American and Belgian forces to drive the Germans from their fortified positions and cut their supply lines to make it difficult for them to continue to fight and, therefore, surrender to end the war.[15]

In July 1918, the Allies had an advantage with its aviation, its tanks, its artillery, and its manpower due in good part to the infusion of American manpower. It was time for the Allies to abandon its general defensive attitude characteristic of trench warfare and adopt a strong offensive attitude.[16] On July 24, Marshal Foch brought together at his headquarters in Bombon, France, Field Marshall Douglas Haig (Commander in Chief of the British Expeditionary Force), General Philippe Pétain (Commander in Chief of the French Army), and General John J. Pershing (Commander in Chief of the American Expeditionary Forces), to plan a succession of coordinated attacks for The Hundred Days Offensive.[17] The British forces included the armed forces of its Dominions such as Canada and Australia, and the offensive included the Belgian forces as well.

The initial objectives were to mount attacks in August to free the Paris-Avricourt railway line and the Paris-Amiens railway line which the Germans were using to supply their front lines and to also clear the mining region in the north and drive the enemy from the vicinity of Dunkirk and Calais.[18] On August 8, British forces attacked the northern part of the Western Front around the city of Amiens and in three days Amiens and the Paris-Amiens railway line was cleared.[19] Ludendorff later described the battle as the "black day of the German army."[20] This battle was followed by more August battles as British and French forces waged coordinated attacks against enemy forces.[21] In the six weeks from August 8 to September 4, the Germans lost the ground they gained from their spring offensive as the Allied troops achieved the objectives mapped out for them by Foch.[22]

These accomplishments were a prelude to Foch's "Grand Offensive" to utilize all the Allied forces in an all-out effort along the Western Front to end the war. The effort would include coordinated attacks, one after another, along the northern, central, and southern parts of the Western Front, designed to create chaos for the German forces, push them out of France and Belgium, and end the war. Foch's plans for the use of the American forces, however, changed and were at odds with what Pershing had been planning all along.

On August 30, 1918, Foch surprised Pershing with different plans for using American divisions. Foch wanted to restrict Pershing's plans and place his divisions under French command to reinforce the French Second Army attack between the Meuse River and the Argonne Forrest in a major battle that would become known as the Meuse-Argonne Offensive.[23] Pershing felt that dispersing his divisions in this way would decimate the American Army he was preparing for war since he came to France. He pointed out to Foch that President Wilson wanted the American Army to fight together under American command and that the Allies understood this while providing opportunities to help prepare them to realize his goal.[24]

Pershing followed up by visiting General Philippe Pétain. He explained how his First Army would capture the St. Mihiel salient and regroup to attack at the Argonne Forest in the Meuse-Argonne Offensive as part of Foch's Grand Offensive. He convinced Pétain, and they met together with Foch and convinced him too.[25] Pershing was confident in his First Army because he had an impressive group of military leaders under his command, some of whom would go on to become historic figures such as Captain George S. Patton, Jr., Major Douglas MacArthur, Colonel George C. Marshall, Major General John A. Lejeune, Colonel Billy Mitchell, Major Eddie Rickenbacker, Major William Donovan, and Captain Harry S. Truman.[26] He also had faith in his fellow soldiers and was always grateful to them, so much so that, when he died fifty years later in 1968, he asked to be buried next to his troops in Arlington National Cemetery with the same simple white marker on his grave that was on their graves.[27]

Decisive Battles

With Pershing's plans in sync with Foch's plans, the Grand Offensive began on September 12 with the Americans going to battle in the southern part of the Western Front while battles by the other Allied armies followed in the central and northern parts of the Western Front. On September 28, Belgian forces (with help from British and French forces) attacked second in the northern part of the Front near Ypres in Flanders, Belgium. On September 29, British forces (with help of Australian and American forces) attacked third in the central part of the Front. They attacked German fortifications in St. Quentin and French forces attacked German fortifications outside St. Quentin.[28] According to plan, the Allied armies kept up the pressure on the Germans—day after day and battle after battle—in a relentless manner. The result was the end of World War I.

The following sections describe the contribution of Pershing and his forces in the Grand Offensive. Haig and his British Empire forces, Pétain and his French forces, and King Albert and his Belgian forces also contributed honorably in the Grand Offensive to end the war. At war's end, the Belgian, British, French, and American forces were in control of the Western Front from top (north) to bottom (south).

The Battle of St. Mihiel

When the war began in 1914, the Germans seized and occupied more than 150 square miles of French land referred to as the St. Mihiel salient. Pershing knew that the Germans depended on the iron mines in Briey, just north of Metz, as well as the railroads out of Metz.[29] The salient protected the strategic centers of the Briey iron basin and Metz railroad supply lines.[30] He was determined to recapture the salient for France and disrupt these critical German supply lines. He felt that advancing to Metz would have "a tremendous morale and material effect on Germany."[31] The St. Mihiel salient was in the shape of a triangle formed with its points near three French towns—Verdun, Pont-à-Mousson, and St. Mihiel. The salient extended about twenty-five miles from Verdun to Pont-à-Mousson along what had been the border between France and Germany and then extended about sixteen miles deep into France to the town of St. Mihiel.[32]

When Pershing got the green light to lead American troops in the Battle of St. Mihiel (Exhibit 4.1), and then follow that up by leading them in the Meuse-Argonne Offensive, his Chief of Staff, General James McAndrew, and his Chief of Operations, Colonel Fox Conner, began planning the details of these major back-to-back battles. It was a gigantic task to figure out how best to concentrate troops in one battle and then move them and their

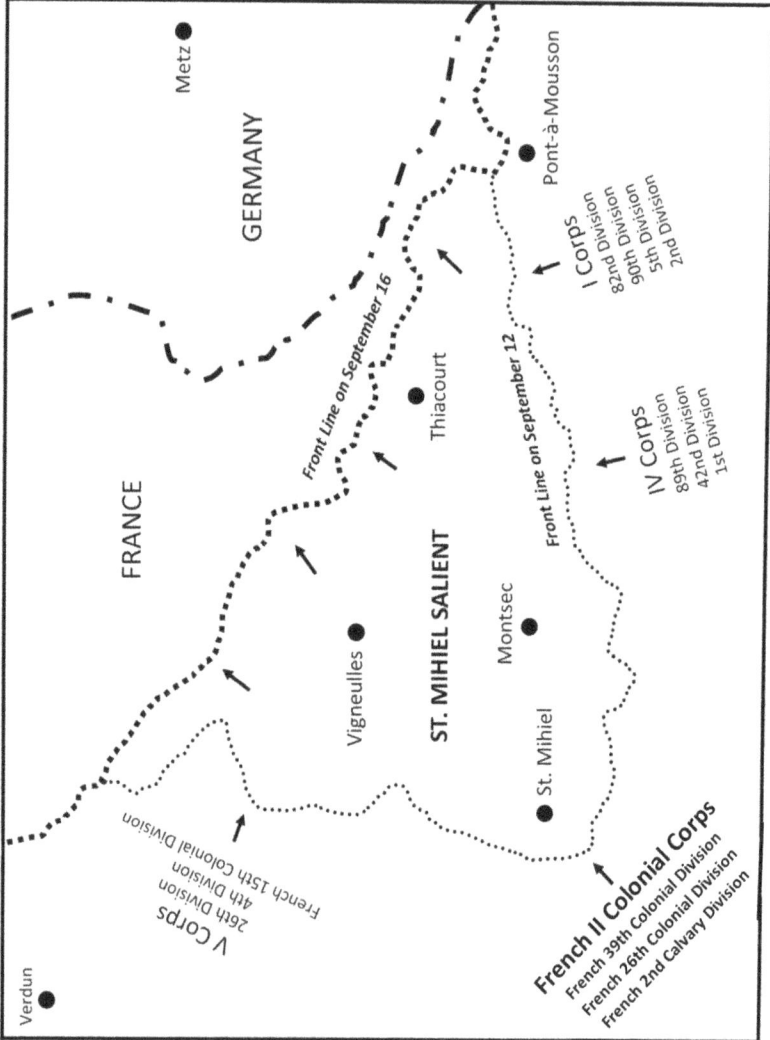

Exhibit 4.1: Battle of St. Mihiel

firepower to a second battle sixty miles away soon thereafter.[33] Conner was a talented military man who recognized other talented military men. It was he who selected the zone of attack and it was he who brought Colonel George A. Marshall aboard to help him with planning the tactics and logistics for the critical American battles ahead. And it was he who would later become an important mentor for Dwight D. Eisenhower.[34]

Marshall set about planning for the Battle of St. Mihiel and the follow-up Meuse-Argonne Offensive.[35] The plan was for General Pershing to lead nine American divisions (1st, 2nd, 4th, and 5th of Regular Army; 26th and 42nd of National Guard; and 82nd, 89th, and 90th of National Army) totaling 550,000 troops and four French divisions totaling 110,000 troops into the Battle of St. Mihiel with the objective of driving the Germans out of the salient.[36] This was at the time the largest offensive operation ever undertaken by the United States.[37] After recapturing the French land in the salient, the plan was for the Americans to regroup and move sixty miles northeast to fight in the Meuse-Argonne Offensive scheduled to begin on September 26, 1918.[38]

Pershing felt that surprise was essential for a successful St. Mihiel attack. He also felt that a surprise attack was a challenge because he thought the Germans were expecting an American attack. Consequently, he didn't want the preliminary artillery bombing by 3,000 cannons to be prolonged (some bombings lasted for days), so he limited the shelling to four hours before the infantry attack.[39] He also had at his disposal a large, combined air force led by another American—Major William "Billy" Mitchell. Mitchell was commanding air forces of three nations—American, French, and British—acting together to support the ground forces and to attack enemy supply lines.[40]

Pershing led the St. Mihiel attack on September 12, 1918. The First Army's I Corps with its 2nd, 5th, 82nd, 90th Infantry Divisions and IV Corps with its 1st, 42nd, and 89th Infantry Divisions attacked from east to west. The V Corps with its 26th Infantry Division, part of its 4th Infantry Division, and the French 15th Colonial Infantry Division attacked from west to east. Between them the French II Colonial Corps, with its 2nd Dismounted Calvary Division, 26th Colonial Infantry Division, and 39th Colonial Infantry Division, attacked from southwest to northeast.[41] Four days later, on September 16, they achieved their objective of driving the Germans out of the St. Mihiel salient and recapturing the French land that was lost to the Germans in 1914.[42]

Pershing was pleased because his troops had recaptured 200 square miles of French territory and placed his First Army in a favorable position for the Meuse-Argonne Offensive.[43] The First Army had also captured 16,000 prisoners and 443 guns, liberated many villages from enemy domination, and put the Allies in a position to threaten Metz, a key city in the support of the German army.[44] A German report of the attack was complimentary of the American artillery for being flexible and accurate and felt that "the masses of infantry assured the victory."[45] The victory, however, was costly to the "masses of infantry" who sustained 7,000 casualties in the battle.[46]

King George of England sent President Wilson a congratulatory message: "On behalf of the British Empire, I heartily congratulate you on the brilliant achievement of the Americans and Allied troops under the leadership of General Pershing in the St. Mihiel salient."[47] President Wilson also appreciated the effort and sent General Pershing a congratulatory message: "Please accept my warmest congratulations on the brilliant achievements of the Army under your command. The boys have done what we expected of them and done it in a way we most admire. We are deeply proud of them and of their Chief. Please convey to all concerned my grateful and affectionate thanks."[48]

Pershing also received similar messages from Supreme Allied Commander Foch and British Commander Field Marshall Sir Douglas Haig. Foch wrote: "The American First Army, under your command, on this first day has won a magnificent victory by a maneuver as skillfully prepared as it was valiantly executed. I extend to you as well as to the officers and to the troops under your command my warmest congratulations!"[49] Haig wrote: "All ranks of the British Armies in France welcome with unbounded admiration and pleasure the victory which has attended the initial offensive of the great American Army under your personal command. I beg you to accept and to convey to all ranks my best congratulations and those of all ranks of the British under my command."[50] Pershing's patience, persistence, perseverance, and faith in the American armed forces to perform well in battle as a separate and distinct component of the Allied forces had at last been recognized and applauded by his French and British Allies.

Billy Mitchell and Airpower

The Battle of St. Mihiel was the first battle in World War I led by an American. It was also the first time a large, combined Allied air force was led by an American, Billy Mitchell, who would become the leading proponent of the use of airpower in war, and its effective use in World War II would one day be attributed to his influence. However, before his influence was appreciated, he would be court-martialed for promoting airpower in a non-tactful manner that ruffled the feathers of military leaders. Undeterred, he kept on preaching the merits of airpower. His persistence and the efforts of his disciples would result in the United States becoming the leading builder of military aircraft in World War II and this airpower would be a decisive factor in ending that war. His story is worth telling because he is known today as "the Father of the United States Air Force."[51] While American manpower helped to turn the tide in World War I, American airpower was a key factor in turning the tide in World War II.

Billy Mitchell was born in Nice, France in 1879. After his parents married, they went to France for a long stay during which time he was born. As a small boy, he spoke French better than English. Three and a half years later, his family returned to the States.[52] Billy's fluency in French would serve him well when he was fighting with the French in World War I.[53]

Billy's grandfather and father had been favorite sons and pillars of the community in Milwaukee, Wisconsin. His grandfather, Alexander, was a successful banking and railroad executive. He was also a congressman who was active in state and national politics.[54] His father, John, was a congressman as well as a senator and had a wide range of interests including military history, world affairs, and linguistics. His father spoke five languages—English, French, German, Italian and Spanish—and Billy also mastered all of them. In addition, he learned to speak two Philippine languages and a little Russian and Japanese.[55] His father loved military history and Billy loved visiting the old battlefields in Europe with him.[56] He grew up to be a well-traveled, well-informed, and well-spoken young man who had strong views but was not always tactful in presenting them.[57]

In 1898, when Billy was an eighteen-year-old college student, the Spanish-American War broke out and he enlisted immediately, and served his country in Cuba, the Philippines, and Alaska. His interest in scientific matters led him to the Army Signal Corps, where he was assigned to construct telegraph lines in Cuba. He and his men built 138 miles of telegraph line through the tropics that had boa constrictors twelve feet long or longer.[58] After that, he was assigned to construct telegraph lines in the Philippines, where he had to contend with disease, wild boar, alligators, lizards up to five-feet long, snakes of all sizes, and insects of all sizes.[59] In a year and a half, he supervised the building of the longest stretch of telegraph mileage in the Army's 16,000 miles of wire and cables.[60]

Impressed by Mitchell's leadership and organizational skills, the commander of the Signal Corps, General Adolphus Greely, talked him out of leaving the service for the challenges of civilian life by presenting him with an overwhelming challenge—to construct telegraph lines across Alaska. Greely said it was "the toughest job I've asked a man to do."[61] Two previous attempts were unsuccessful.[62]

In 1901, at the age of 21, Billy accepted the challenge. He formulated a plan to deal with the extreme weather conditions and began to implement it by assembling tough men and tough dogs to brave the tough winters (temperatures as low as seventy degrees below zero) in the Alaskan wilderness for what some felt was an impossible job.[63] Billy was a "hands-on" leader who developed good relationships with his men, his dogs, and even with native Alaskan Indians, some of whom hated white men and others of whom had never seen a white man. [64]

During the winter months, he blazed trails through the wilderness with his dog teams, charting the route of the communication line and laying out the equipment so that the poles could be installed and strung with wire during the summer months when the ground wasn't frozen. In so doing, his ingenuity and inventiveness overcame many obstacles such as the frigid temperatures, snow as deep as eighty-five feet, suspicious Native Indians, and wolves. The equipment was delivered during the winter months because mud also made the roads tough to transport equipment during the summer months.[65]

During the summer months, he overcame obstacles such as hordes of mosquitos and difficult ground conditions. While the ground was not frozen, it almost never thawed out deeply.[66] His crews laid out from five to ten miles of wire a day and working parties followed erecting the poles and putting insulators on the wire.[67] In the two years from 1901 to 1903, he built the Washington-Alaska Military Cable and Telegraph System (WAMCATS), a 1,467-mile communication line that linked Alaska to the rest of the world. He did the impossible job which reaffirmed Greely's confidence in him to perform well against heavy odds.[68]

With his inquisitive mind and "can do" attitude, the Army Signal Corps was a good place for Billy to be at that time. The Signal Corps was not only responsible for military communications; it was also responsible for military aviation. When he was building telegraph lines across Alaska, he became interested in aeronautics while studying for the exam he would have to take for his next promotion to captain.[69] The same year that Billy finished his assignment in Alaska, the Wright Brothers were preparing for the first successful airplane flight which took place on December 17, 1903, at Kitty Hawk, North Carolina.[70]

In 1907, the Army Signal Corps established an Aeronautical Division.[71] In 1908, Mitchell saw Orville Wright give a flying demonstration at Fort

Decisive Battles

Myer, Virginia.[72] In 1909, the Army commissioned the Wright Brothers to develop an airplane for the military.[73] In 1911, Congress approved funds to expand aeronautical developments and the early pilots were flying Wright and Curtiss aircraft.[74] The head of Curtiss was Glen Curtiss, an aviation pioneer like the Wright Brothers. Like them, he started out building bicycles and his penchant for going fast led him to building motorcycles and then airplanes.[75] In 1914, Congress approved the creation of the Aviation Section in the Signal Corps to replace the Aeronautical Division, thereby giving official status to the Army's air force.[76] In 1916, Mitchell was promoted to major, headed the Aviation Section, and learned to fly at his own expense.[77] In his new assignment, he became involved with the first use of aircraft in a military operation—the Punitive Mexican Expedition.[78]

General Pershing was the commander of the Punitive Mexican Expedition. In 1916, he and Mitchell were among the first to be involved with the use of American-built aircraft in a military operation—eight Curtiss JN-3 airplanes, known as Jennies. The Jenny was the first mass-produced American aircraft and was used to look for Pancho Villa. Only ten pilots were used in this aerial operation, and for observation only, so the Americans had little experience in the use of airpower when they entered World War I, and even less experience in combat flying.[79]

By coincidence, the unit of a young Corporal Nathan Twining was part of Pershing's expedition into Mexico in pursuit of Pancho Villa. This was Twining's first exposure to aviation.[80] It no doubt had a lasting effect on him. He later attended West Point and then, as an infantry officer, he applied to be trained to be a pilot every year for four years until he was accepted into the program.[81] He never looked back and had a long and distinguished career in military aviation. Twenty-eight years later, he would be General Twining, the commander of the Fifteenth Air Force that John Cooney flew with during World War II.

When America entered World War I, the only American flyers with combat experience were thirty-eight courageous pilots who volunteered to fly with the French in an outfit called the Lafayette Escadrille, and eleven of them did not survive the war.[82] Fortunately, Pershing and Mitchell had some aviation experience, recognized its merit, and put it to good use in World War I.[83] Raoul Lufbery, mentioned in the previous chapter, was one of the Lafayette Escadrille pilots. He was a highly regarded fighter pilot, and was recruited to train the American fighter pilots when the United States entered World War I.

FROM ONE WAR TO ANOTHER

When the United States entered the war in 1917, it had only a fledgling air force and no aircraft industry. All it had was several shops, such as that of the Wright brothers, which hand-built aircraft, and the Curtiss shop, which produced the Curtiss JN-4 that was useful in training American pilots but could not stack up against the British and French aircraft and therefore were not used in combat during the war.[84] While the United States provided raw materials for its European Allies to produce combat aircraft, it needed to start producing its own combat aircraft when it entered the war in April 1917.[85] Since planes were needed in a hurry and because it took time to design and build them, the Americans decided to produce the British DH-4 (DH stands for de Havilland) because of its relatively simple design and because it was well-suited to the new American 400-horsepower Liberty v-12 engine. The DH-4s that were built in America by the Dayton-Wright Airplane Company were called "Liberty Planes."[86] The Liberty engine was said to be America's greatest mechanical contribution to World War I.[87]

For the Battle of St. Mihiel, Billy Mitchell commanded a force of 1,481 airplanes.[88] The force included 742 French planes, 609 American planes, and 130 British planes. Most of them were pursuit planes (701) followed by observation planes (366), day bombers (323), and night bombers (91).[89] Mitchell also had twenty observation balloons under his command.[90] His task was threefold: (1) to provide accurate information to the infantry for their artillery barrages; (2) to prevent the enemy from interfering with Allied air or ground forces; and (3) to bomb the enemy supply routes.[91]

Airplanes and observation balloons greatly influenced the way World War I was fought in the trenches. Their use for aerial observation enabled both sides to see the positions of the enemy, forcing combatants into fixed positions along the Western Front. If either side broke out of a trench to advance, the observer would see them and call in an artillery barrage to stop them. Artillery was a key weapon in trench warfare and to use it effectively the infantry, the artillery, and the aerial observers had to be in sync.[92]

The Western Front stretched about 440 miles along the western side of Germany from the North Sea through the battlefields of Belgium and France down to the northwest corner of Switzerland. Parallel trenches were dug on both sides along this Front by the Allies and the Germans. Between them was a wasteland of barbed wire and desolation called No Man's Land, the result of artillery shelling whenever one side decided to leave their trenches to attack the other side.

The soldiers on both sides had more firepower than in any previous war and used it to bombard one another. As a result, the war became one of prolonged deadly encounters as the Allies and the Germans took turns blasting each other from both sides of No Man's Land. Each bombardment was followed by a stalemate of picking up the pieces before another deadly encounter and another stalemate of picking up more pieces.

The horrible conditions in the trenches made World War I become a war of attrition in which manpower became important because it involved wearing down the enemy. This type of warfare kept on keeping on until the last man standing won, making manpower a key factor. When the United States entered the war in 1917, bringing to the front Pershing's fresh troops and Mitchell's airpower, the Germans were in trouble. As the Lord of the Admiralty, Britain's top naval official during World War I, Winston Churchill knew the Germans would be overwhelmed if the United States entered the war. In fact, he previously encouraged England's Board of Trade to attract neutral shipping to Britain's shores, thinking this would increase the possibility of German U-boats sinking ships with American passengers and pull America into the war.[93] When the *Lusitania* and *Sussex* were sunk with American casualties, however, President Wilson was still more interested in fostering a peace between European nations than in going to war. It took the German resumption of unrestricted U-boat warfare and the Zimmermann telegram (in which Germany was proposing an alliance with Mexico against the United States) to convince President Wilson to enter the war.[94]

Pershing didn't believe in trench warfare. He viewed it as a defensive strategy. He was a proponent of open warfare, an offensive strategy.[95] Thanks to significant manpower, supported by significant artillery and airpower in addition to larger infantry divisions, he was able to pursue his preferred offensive strategy in the Battle of St. Mihiel. When the Germans withdrew from the St. Mihiel salient, Pershing drew the praise of Allied leaders, and he thanked Colonel Billy Mitchell and his men for their supporting airpower in a letter: "Please accept my sincere congratulations on the successful and very important part taken by the Air Force under your command in the first offensive of the 1st American Army."[96] Pershing followed up on this battle by leading more than a million American and French troops into an even larger battle.

The Meuse-Argonne Offensive

When the Americans drove the Germans out of the St. Mihiel salient, they not only boosted their own morale, but they gained the respect of their French and British peers for a job well done.[97] Next, they faced an even greater challenge in the Meuse-Argonne Offensive. Foch did not think the Americans could regroup and move most of their battle-tested troops from the Battle of St. Mihiel to the Meuse-Argonne Offensive in a timely manner. Pershing contended that they could and was afforded the opportunity to prove it.[98]

Colonel George C. Marshall was given the responsibility for planning to move about 600,000 personnel, 2,700 guns, 93,000 horses, and 900,000 tons of supplies and ammunition sixty miles northwest to the Meuse-Argonne area. To complicate matters, this had to be done in less than ten days and in secrecy because the success of the offensive depended on surprise and speed.[99] The task was formidable because it also included moving evacuation hospitals, field kitchens, oil and gas tanks, supply depots, and other support for the troops engaged in battle.[100] To do this in secrecy, Marshall worked out the logistics to move the personnel, equipment, and supplies by night.[101]

When Pershing wrote his memoir, *My Experiences in the World War*, and thought about Marshall's gigantic task of moving so many troops and millions of tons and munitions sixty miles under the cover of darkness in such a short time, he wrote, "When viewed as a whole, it is believed that history gives no parallel of such an undertaking with so large an army."[102] This task of course would be trumped twenty-six years later with the Normandy Invasion.

Marshall's logistical plan was important to the overall strategy of the Grand Offensive because the Meuse-Argonne Offensive was designed to destroy the German supply system. Its main objective was to cut the railroad lines that ran parallel to the Western Front on the German side from Metz to Sedan.[103] This railroad was the main line of support for Germany to supply manpower, supplies, and equipment for its fighting forces. Cutting this supply line would hamper Germany's ability to continue fighting the war.[104]

Marshall came through. On September 26, 1918, the date to mount the first attacks of the Meuse-Argonne Offensive, the fighting forces and support forces were ready to go. At 2:30 am, the American artillery began shelling the German lines and at 5:30 am the American infantry divisions left their trenches to engage in open warfare with the enemy. The attacks were a surprise because the Germans thought the Americans had been preparing to attack Metz.[105]

At the end of the first day, the American First Army had pushed the Germans back about five miles and outran its artillery support. On the second day, they kept up the pressure with infantry assaults and captured more ground but not as much as on the first day. On the third day, with good artillery and tank support, they pushed the Germans back about a mile and a half. By the fourth day, the First Army had advanced eight miles.[106] The Germans brought in fresh troops and the Americans went on the defense. However, by then the Allied pressure on other parts of the Western Front along with the advances in the Meuse-Argonne Offensive caused the German Generals Ludendorff and Hindenburg to urge the German government to ask for an armistice.[107]

The Meuse-Argonne Offensive lasted forty-seven days from September 26 to November 11, 1918 (Exhibit 4.2). It involved 1.2 million American troops and was costly.[108] It resulted in the deaths of half the Americans who died in combat during World War I.[109] According to the National World War I Museum and Memorial, it was "the bloodiest battle the United States military has ever fought, with over 26,000 (Americans) killed and 95,000 wounded.[110] Overall, the Allies and the Germans each suffered over a million casualties. [111]

While United States entered the war late, it was able to produce considerable manpower rather quickly and this infusion of manpower helped to end the war. It was not, however, able to produce considerable war materiel with the same speed. Twenty-two years later in 1940, with the threat of another war on the horizon, President Franklin D. Roosevelt would seek Bernard Baruch's advice on how to mobilize for the inevitable war, and Baruch would educate the President on the importance of lead time in producing war materiel and recommended William S. Knudsen to lead the mobilization to produce war materiel, especially aircraft.[112] While American manpower would be key in helping the Allies to turn the tide in World War I, American airpower would be key in helping to turn the tide in World War II.

It would take another forty-three days before a peace settlement was attained on November 11, 1918. Meanwhile, the fighting of the Meuse-Argonne Offensive would continue, more lives would be lost, a second American army would be formed, and more acts of courage would occur. In his memoir, General Pershing would recognize three heroic acts of courage that occurred in October 1918, and they involved Major Charles White Whittlesey of Pittsfield, Massachusetts; Sergeant Alvin Cullum York of Pall Mall, Tennessee; and First Lieutenant Samuel Woodfill of Bryantsburg, Indiana.[113] All three of them received the Congressional Medal of Honor, and all three of them were chosen by General Pershing to serve as pall bearers for the Unknown Soldier of World War I.[114]

From October 2 to 7, Major Whittlesey's battalion, known as "The Lost Battalion," was cut off from his division, the 77th Division, and was surrounded by Germans who killed or wounded half his battalion of 550 soldiers. On the fourth day, the enemy offered him a proposition to surrender, and he treated it with contempt. The battalion had some carrier pigeons to send messages in case of trouble and the first two released to bring a message to division head-

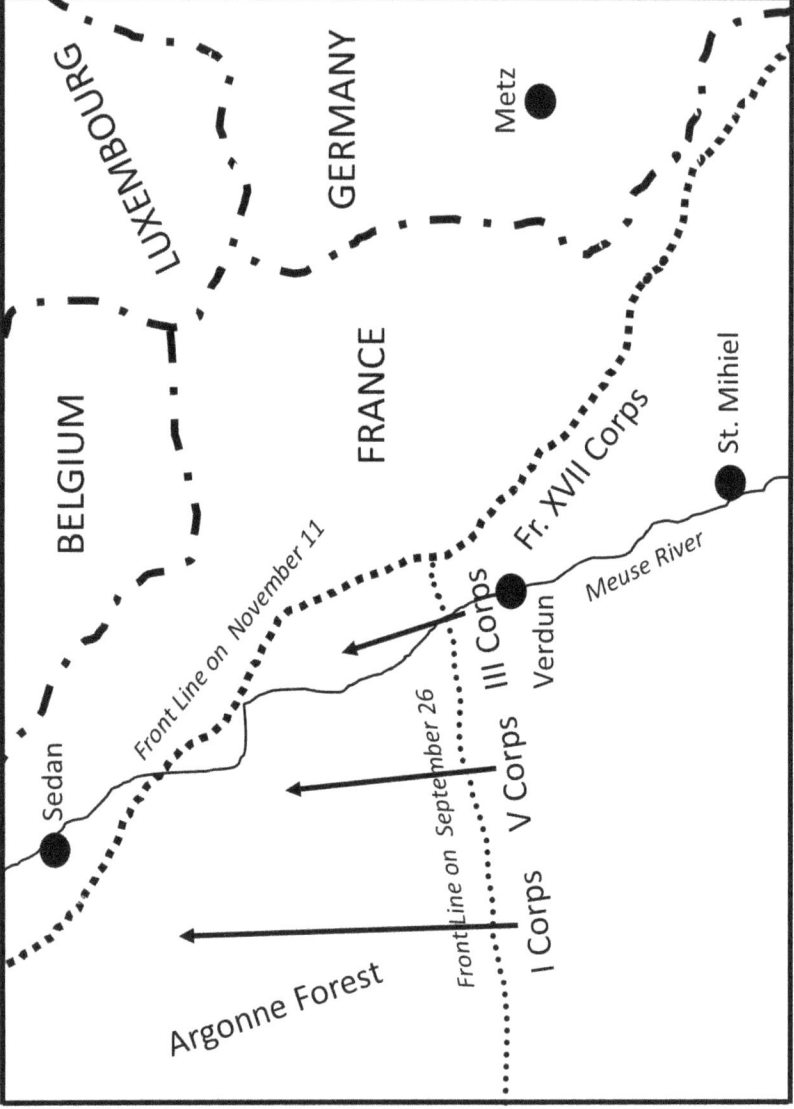

Exhibit 4.2: Meuse-Argonne Offensive

quarters were shot down but the third one got through despite being wounded in the eye and leg. As a result, the Lost Battalion was saved on October 8.[115]

On October 8, Sergeant York's platoon in the 82nd Division had suffered heavy casualties which included the three other noncommissioned officers, so he took command of the platoon and led seven men in charging a machine gun nest that was firing at them and he not only took the nest but captured four officers and 128 enemy soldiers. The irony of York's deed is that he was a staunch pacifist who felt violence was a sin, but when confronted with a wartime situation of either them or us, he mustered up extraordinary courage to perform one of the bravest acts of World War I.[116]

On October 12, when First Lieutenant Woodfill's company in the 5th Division came under heavy machine gun fire, he led his men in attacking not one but three machine gun nests. He got to the first nest and shot three of the gunners. A fourth enemy soldier tried to club him with his rifle but in a hand-to-hand struggle Woodfill shot him with his pistol. Shortly thereafter, he led his men in attacking a second machine gun nest where he shot several men and captured another three. Minutes later, he and his men charged a third machine gun nest where he shot five men in the nest with his rifle and killed two others with a pickaxe. Inspired by their courageous leader, his men pressed on.[117] It is noteworthy that Woodfill's mother was the daughter of a German immigrant who came to America in the 1840s to avoid fighting with the Germans and years later her grandson went back to fight against the Germans and emerged as an America hero.[118]

By the end of October 1918, the German military leaders realized they did not have the strength to continue the war. Generals Ludendorff and Hindenburg proposed that the German government ask for an armistice. As a result, Prince Max of Baden, a German political moderate thought suitable to deliberate with the Allies, reached out to President Wilson to negotiate a peace settlement based on Wilson's Fourteen Points (Exhibit 4.3).[119]

Wilson's Fourteen Points were his attempt to form a general association of nations to provide "mutual guarantees of political independence and territorial integrity to both large and small States alike."[120] Throughout the war, Wilson's objective was simply to end the war and create a League of Nations as a forum to deal with problems between nations in a diplomatic rather than militaristic way. Britain, on the other hand, "desired imperialistic gains after the war and France was vengeful and sought political gains and territorial security."[121] This is why Prince Max reached out to President Wilson instead of the British and French leaders.

Exhibit 4.3

President Wilson's Fourteen Points

1. Open covenants of peace, openly arrived at, after which there shall be no private international understandings of any kind but diplomacy shall proceed always frankly and in the public view.

2. Absolute freedom of navigation upon the seas, outside territorial waters, alike in peace and in war, except as the seas may be closed in whole or in part by international action for the enforcement of international covenants.

3. The removal, so far as possible, of all economic barriers and the establishment of an equality of trade conditions among all the nations consenting to the peace and associating themselves for its maintenance.

4. Adequate guarantees given and taken that national armaments will be reduced to the lowest point consistent with domestic safety.

5. A free, open-minded, and absolutely impartial adjustment of all colonial claims, based upon a strict observance of the principle that in determining all such questions of sovereignty the interests of the populations concerned must have equal weight with the equitable claims of the government whose title is to be determined.

6. The evacuation of all Russian territory and such a settlement of all questions affecting Russia as will secure the best and freest cooperation of the other nations of the world in obtaining for her an unhampered and unembarrassed opportunity for the independent determination of her own political development and national policy and assure her of a sincere welcome into the society of free nations under institutions of her own choosing; and, more than a welcome, assistance also of every kind that she may need and may herself desire. The treatment accorded Russia by her sister nations in the months to come will be the acid test of their good will, of their comprehension of her needs as distinguished from their own interests, and of their intelligent and unselfish sympathy.

7. Belgium, the whole world will agree, must be evacuated and restored, without any attempt to limit the sovereignty which she enjoys in common with all other free nations. No other single act will serve as this will serve to restore confidence among the nations in the laws which they have themselves set and determined for the government of their relations with one another. Without this healing act the whole structure and validity of international law is forever impaired.

8. All French territory should be freed and the invaded portions restored, and the wrong done to France by Prussia in 1871 in the matter of Alsace-Lorraine, which has unsettled the peace of the world for nearly fifty years, should be righted, in order that peace may once more be made secure in the interest of all.

9. A readjustment of the frontiers of Italy should be effected along clearly recognizable lines of nationality.

10. The peoples of Austria-Hungary, whose place among the nations we wish to see safeguarded and assured, should be accorded the freest opportunity to autonomous development.

11. Rumania, Serbia, and Montenegro should be evacuated; occupied territories restored; Serbia accorded free and secure access to the sea; and the relations of the several Balkan states to one another determined by friendly counsel along historically established lines of allegiance and nationality; and international guarantees of the political and economic independence and territorial integrity of the several Balkan states should be entered into.

12. The Turkish portion of the present Ottoman Empire should be assured a secure sovereignty, but the other nationalities which are now under Turkish rule should be assured an undoubted security of life and an absolutely unmolested opportunity of autonomous development, and the Dardanelles should be permanently opened as a free passage to the ships and commerce of all nations under international guarantees.

13. An independent Polish state should be erected which should include the territories inhabited by indisputably Polish populations, which should be assured a free and secure access to the sea, and whose political and economic independence and territorial integrity should be guaranteed by international covenant.

14. A general association of nations must be formed under specific covenants for the purpose of affording mutual guarantees of political independence and territorial integrity to great and small states alike.

Decisive Battles

The Armistice to End the War

The Armistice to end the war involved the German government in Berlin, the Allied Supreme Council in Paris, and President Wilson in Washington, D.C. The Germans sought the Armistice based on Wilson's Fourteen Points without modifications, the French sought modifications to prevent Germany from invading them again and to be compensated for the destruction in France caused by Germany, and the British sought modifications to maintain its naval leadership by limiting Germany's ability to threaten its leadership position.[122] Foch and his French commanders created a list of military demands and Haig and his commanders followed suit and the Supreme War Council began pre-Armistice negotiations in late October 1919. Colonel Edward House, Wilson's most trusted advisor, represented Wilson at the negotiations in Paris at which the final terms of the Armistice were completed in early November and arrangements were made to present it to the German government for signing.[123]

Representatives of France, Britain and Germany met in French Marshal Ferdinand Foch's railroad car in the Forest of Compiegne, France to sign the Armistice to end World War I on the 11th hour of the 11th day of the 11th month of 1918. The Armistice was an agreement to end fighting as a prelude to peace negotiations. The date became a national holiday in many Allied nations including the United States. In November 1919, President Wilson proclaimed November 11 as the first commemoration of Armistice Day in the United States with the following words:[124]

"To us in America, the reflections of Armistice Day will be filled with solemn pride in the heroism of those who died in the country's service and with gratitude for the victory, both because of the thing from which it has freed us and because of the opportunity it has given America to show her sympathy with peace and justice in the councils of the nations..."

In 1938, Armistice Day became a federal holiday. After World War II and the Korean War, veterans of those wars lobbied to also be recognized for their wartime service. In 1954, Congress passed a bill to honor veterans of every war on November 11, and President Dwight D. Eisenhower signed it into law, changing Armistice Day to Veterans Day.[125]

Chapter 5

BETWEEN WORLD WARS

When the fighting ended with the Armistice, John Cooney Sr. was among the many medical support personnel who remained in France to care for war casualties. Medical support was still needed in France because about 10 percent of the soldiers who fought for the American Expeditionary Forces were convalescing in hospitals.[1] The terms of the treaty to formally end World War I still needed to be formalized, agreed to, and signed off on. While medical care was being administered to war casualties, military and political leaders were hammering out the details of the treaty to formally end the war.

John Sr. would not get home until July 5, 1919, twelve days after the signing of the Treaty of Versailles on June 28, 1919.[2] The signing was exactly five years after the day (June 28, 1914) on which an angry teenage Serbian nationalist, Gavrilo Princip, assassinated Franz Ferdinand, heir to the Austro-Hungarian crown, to spark World War I. John Sr. would resume his life as a civilian while the Treaty of Versailles would get mired in controversy for years and eventually be used by Hitler in his quest to take over Germany and lead it into World War II.

While Hitler was creating a path to World War II during the 1930s, John Sr. was raising a family during the Great Depression. He had experienced the hardships of war in France and was now experiencing the hardships of economic turmoil at home. He worked hard and was fortunate to have a good wife, a good job, and a good home. But he didn't have good health, and in 1939 with another war brewing overseas, he died, and his family fell upon hard times.[3]

While John's family was adjusting to life after World War I and dealing with the Great Depression and while Hitler was paving his way on to the world stage, significant advances were being made in the aviation industry that increased the importance of airpower in war.[4] Hitler would be the first to take advantage of airpower in war, but the United States would trump him in World War II.

The Treaty of Versailles

The Treaty of Versailles (Treaty) was controversial when it was formulated, and it's still controversial. It changed the landscape of Europe. From the old Austro-Hungarian Empire came three independent countries—Austria, Czechoslovakia, and Hungary. Poland was formed from Austrian, German, and Russian territory. Yugoslavia came from Serbia and large portions of Austrian-Hungary, Bulgaria, and Montenegro. Additional territory was added to Greece and Italy, and Estonia, Finland, Latvia, and Lithuania gained their independence from Russia (Exhibit 5.1).[5]

The Paris Peace Conference that produced the treaty that changed Europe was said to be full of politicians making self-serving decisions that resulted in a treaty with terrible consequences. It became fodder for Hitler in his rise to power. He felt that the injustice of the Treaty wrecked the German economy, a sentiment shared by the German people. When he gained the power, which he strongly sought, he denounced the Treaty and led Germany down the path to World War II.[6]

While thirty-two Allied countries participated in formulating the terms of the Treaty of Versailles, the Big Three who led the effort were Georges Clemenceau, the Prime Minister of France; David Lloyd George, the Prime Minister of Britain; and Woodrow Wilson, the President of the United States.[7] All of them wanted to prevent Germany from starting another war. However, they didn't see eye to eye on how best to accomplish this and took different positions as regards the harshness of the Treaty.[8]

Clemenceau wanted revenge by punishing the Germans and making them pay for the war damages. This was the way it always had been—to the victors went the spoils.[9] Lloyd George said he would go along with making Germany pay dearly because he knew the British people also wanted to punish the Germans. His main concern, however, was justice, not revenge. He felt a harsh treaty would lead to another war. Another concern of his was to ensure that the British Empire continued to maintain control of the seas.[10] Wilson all along wanted to make the world safe and promoted his League of Nations as an organization to resolve international disputes at the table in a diplomatic way rather than on the battlefield in a belligerent way.[11]

Exhibit 5.1: Europe After World War I

After World War I, the four authoritarian empires—the German, Russian, Austro-Hungarian, and Ottoman Empires—had fallen, and the borders of Europe were redrawn. The German Empire lost territory to Poland, which had reconstituted itself, and to France; and East Prussia was isolated from the rest of Germany. The Russian Empire also lost territory to Poland and to the newly-created Baltic countries of Estonia, Latvia, and Lithuanian, along with Finland. The Austro-Hungarian Empire was split up into Austria and Hungary and lost territory to Czechoslovakia which was created for the Northern Slavs (Czechs and Slovaks) and to Yugoslavia which was created for the Southern Slavs (Slovenians, Croats, and Serbs). Yugoslavia also absorbed the Balkan countries of Serbia and Montenegro. Italy and Romania gained territory while Bulgaria and Turkey lost territory to Greece, and the Ottoman Empire lost its hold on the Slavic people. While it appeared that democracy had triumphed over autocracy, the way Germany was treated in the Versailles Treaty sowed the seeds for trouble ahead and the creation of new nations still didn't resolve the difficulties of minorities in those countries.

FROM ONE WAR TO ANOTHER

The peace negotiations opened in Paris on January 12, 1919.[12] Wilson went in wed to his Fourteen Points and his priority was to have his fourteenth point, the League of Nations, adopted to guarantee the political independence and territorial integrity of great and small states alike.[13] He was an idealist who thought you could trust nations, including Germany, to work together for the common good.[14] Clemenceau and Lloyd George thought otherwise. Bismarck put Germany on a path to unite the German race and fight for more territory to become a dominant world power, and the way the Germans handled a peace settlement with Russia less than a year earlier demonstrated to Clemenceau and Lloyd George that they were still on this path.

On March 3, 1918, the Central Powers (Germany, Austria-Hungary, Ottoman Empire, and Bulgaria), led by Germany, entered into a peace agreement with Russia to stop the slaughter of its people.[15] The Russian Empire was crumbling after 300 years of autocratic rule by the family of Czar Nicholas II, and the war exposed its lack of sufficient economic and industrial strength to fight a war, resulting in the loss of a million men. This led to a social revolution with workers and soldiers protesting against the czarist regime and killing the Czar and his family. The Germans took advantage of this crisis by arranging for Vladimir Lenin, the exiled leader of the revolutionary Bolshevik party, to return and appeal to the Russians for a peace settlement. Lenin and his party seized power in November 1917 and four months later entered a peace agreement with the Central Powers called the Treaty of Brest-Litovsk.[16]

It is a largely-forgotten treaty that was named for the city in Russia where it was signed, which happens to be where Meyer Osofsky's father Harry was born.[17] The treaty was neither fair nor just.[18] It forced Russia to give up 34 percent of its people, 32 percent of its farmland, 50 percent of its industrial holdings, and 90 percent of its coal mines.[19] Lenin called the it an "abyss of defeat, dismemberment, enslavement, and humiliation."[20]

Germany shot itself in the foot with such harsh terms because it brought the Allied Powers together with a unity of purpose to defeat Germany in its quest to be a dominant world power.[21] It was difficult for Wilson argue for a fair and just treaty for Germany considering how the Germans treated the Russians in the Treaty of Brest-Litovsk. In fact, the treaty was so unfair that it was later nullified in the Treaty of Versailles.[22] It was short-lived which is probably why it is largely forgotten,

Clemenceau and Lloyd George wanted Germany to pay for what it had done in reparations, territory, and colonies. Even so, in the first month of negotiations, Wilson felt he had established his priorities and secured accommodation on major issues.[23] He then returned home to garner support for his League of Nations and left his trusted adviser Colonel House in charge of negotiations with instructions to deal only with military and naval clauses of the peace agreement. House did not follow Wilson's instructions and approved compromises on basic issues of peace and the Covenant of the League of Nations. The Covenant defined the main function of the league to promote international cooperation and achieve international peace and security. [24]

When Wilson returned to Paris and met with House, he was shocked and felt that House had given away everything he thought he had won before he left Paris. His wife Edith wrote in her memoir that her husband emerged from the meeting looking as though he had aged ten years. House had compromised Wilson's ideals and even agreed with the idea of a preliminary peace agreement without the League of Nations which would be taken up separately.[25]

Clemenceau and Lloyd George got what they wanted when Wilson was away, and the treatment of Russia by Germany supported their position. Thus, instead of a fair and just peace settlement, the Treaty of Versailles became another peace agreement where the victors got the spoils, humiliating Germany on the world stage, ruining its economy, and planting the seeds of hate that led to another war twenty years later.

At that time, Franklin Delano Roosevelt was the Assistant Secretary of the Navy to Josephus Daniels, who was the Secretary of the Navy. In that position, Roosevelt had administrative responsibilities that included working on the budget, accounting, purchasing supplies, and dealing with legal and policy matters, so he was picking up knowledge that would come in handy during World War II when he was President. He sailed to France on the same ship that brought members of the preparatory commission for the Versailles Peace Conference, and in France he had an opportunity to talk with Clemenceau, Lloyd George, King Albert of Belgium, Supreme Allied Commander Ferdinand Foch, and others involved in the peace negotiations. He saw and appreciated the work of Wilson regarding his League of Nations which influenced his own support of the United Nations years later. More importantly, he saw the dark clouds gathering over Europe for a first world war which years later would enable him to recognize the dark clouds gathering over Europe again for a second world war.[26]

Respected by Roosevelt and many others, Wilson was a hard-working man of principle and worked himself to death. The war, the post-war Treaty of Versailles negotiations, the promotion of his League of Nations, the lack of support for it by his Congress, and the influenza pandemic all took its toll on him. During the first half of 1919, he spent most of his time in Europe negotiating the Treaty and planning the League of Nations for which he received the Nobel Peace Prize in 1919.[27]

During this time, he worked extremely hard, didn't have time to relax or exercise, and fell victim to the flu which was part of the worst pandemic in history. The flu weakened him, but he was on a mission and didn't curb his workaholic ways. The fact that Congress didn't support ratification of the Treaty, or his League of Nations, weighed heavily on him, and he was determined to do something about it.[28]

When he returned from Europe, instead of resting, he picked up the pace to convince his skeptics in Congress and the American public of the importance of ratifying the Treaty and joining the League of Nations. This included a presidential train tour across the country to bring his case to the people. This wore him out and he had a stroke in October 1919, which left him unable to discharge the powers and duties of his office.[29] Lloyd George felt Wilson was "as much a victim of the war as any soldier who died in the trenches."[30]

While hard to believe now, Wilson's condition was kept secret. His wife Edith shielded her husband, and basically decided what was important for him to see and what was not.[31] It wasn't until February 1920 that the president's stroke began to appear in the press, but the details of his disability and his wife's management of affairs still wasn't known by the American public. Edith helped him with the routine duties and details of government until the end of his term in 1921. He died three years later in 1924.[32] Edith lived long enough to ride in President Kennedy's inaugural parade.[33]

War Reparations

Clemenceau, who wanted to punish the Germans, prevailed and the Treaty was harsh. Germany had socked it to France in 1871 and France got its revenge by socking it to Germany in 1918—an eye for an eye and a tooth for a tooth. Its impact on Germany was devastating and, in the end, ineffective because it was eventually used by Hitler to his advantage to gain power. It required Germany to cede land to France, Belgium, Poland, and Italy; its coal mines to France; and all its colonies and war materiel to the Allies. All its properties in foreign countries were to be confiscated, and it was required to abolish compulsory military service and limit the size of its army and navy as well as its general staff and officers. Germany was not allowed to have tanks, planes, submarines, large warships, and poison gas, and could not take part in Wilson's League of Nations.[34]

To England's advantage, Germany was also required to cede to the Allies all seagoing ships with a carrying capacity exceeding a specified tonnage, half of all ships carrying another specified tonnage, one-fourth of its fishing fleet, and two-fifths of its inland navigation fleet. In addition, it was required to cede large amounts of machinery, building materials, trains and trucks, and its sub-ocean cables were to be confiscated.[35]

Finally, Germany was required to pay reparations of 132 billion gold marks (about $33 billion dollars).[36] To make its first war-reparations payment of $500 million in August 1921, the Germans had to print money and kept on printing money, devaluing its currency to make its war-reparation payments in worthless currency. It defaulted on a payment in January 1923 prompting France and Belgium to occupy the Ruhr to force the payment, but the value of the German currency had collapsed, and the result was hyperinflation.[37] It got to the point in 1923 where a loaf of bread cost 428 billion marks.[38] Simply stated, the harshness of the Treaty of Versailles ruined the German economy. It was a treaty that was difficult to enforce, one reason it was ineffective.

In 1924, an American banker named Charles Dawes came up with a plan for the U.S. to lend money to Germany to pay the reparations so the countries which received the reparations could use the money to pay off its U.S. war loans. Germany agreed to pay back its U.S. loans when they came due.[39] The Dawes Plan resulted in Dawes receiving a Nobel Peace Prize in 1925. When the bonds came due, however, the Germans defaulted, and the American investors lost a lot of money.

In 1929, an American named Owen D. Young, the head of General Electric, came up with what became known as the Young Plan to reduce Germany's reparations payments to 121 billion gold marks (about $29 billion) payable over fifty-eight years.[40] Germany ended up paying about 22 billion gold marks (about $4.5 billion dollars) from 1918 to 1932 before Adolph Hitler took over Germany.

The harshness of the Treaty of Versailles in punishing Germany did not prevent another world war—it paved the way to another one. Its harshness wiped out the life savings of many citizens who no longer trusted their government and set the stage for Hitler to rise to power. He promised to undo the injustice of the war reparations, tear up the Treaty of Versailles, and restore Germany to its old greatness.[41] When he rose to power in 1933, he cancelled all reparation payments. Again, American investors lost a lot of money.

FROM ONE WAR TO ANOTHER

Many years later in 1953, West Germany offered to slowly pay back some of the bonds it defaulted on during the 1920s, saying it wouldn't pay off everything until the country was reunified again. With the Reunification of Germany on October 3, 1990, the Germans began to pay off everything, an amount which had been adjusted downward many times. Twenty years later, on October 3, 2010, Germany made its last interest payment, finally settling its World War I war reparation obligations ninety-two years after the end of World War I.[42]

In her book, *Paris 1919: Six Months That Changed the World*, published in the United Kingdom as *Peacemakers*, Margaret MacMillan, great granddaughter of David Lloyd George, stated, "Reparations helped to poison relations between Germany and the Allies, and among the Allies themselves, for much of the 1920s and 1930s."[43] The spoils of war were divided among the Allied nations at the expense of the German people, many of whom never subscribed to the Nazi menace but were powerless to do anything about it because in a dictatorship the power is with the dictator and not with the people.[44] In hindsight, maybe the Allies should have concentrated more on getting Europe back on its feet and less on making Germany pay for everything.[45]

Germany was embarrassed on the world stage by the Treaty of Versailles. Even though the Germans ended up paying far less than originally called for in the Treaty, its currency, economy, and political stability were destroyed, and its pride took a major hit. As British Prime Minister Lloyd George feared, a harsh treaty did lead to another war.[46]

It is noteworthy that the United States took a different approach after the surrenders of Germany and Japan in World War II. It focused on helping those countries to rebuild their infrastructures. The Marshall Plan, promoted by Secretary of State George C. Marshall, provided funds for the recovery of Europe, and helped to halt the spread of communism on the European continent. West Germany was a major beneficiary of this aid.[47] As regards Japan, General Douglas A. MacArthur led an effort to provide widespread military, economic, and social reforms to help that country recover from the war.[48] These efforts resulted in Germany and Japan becoming important U.S. allies, allowing the United States to have a military presence in their countries.[49]

John Sr. Comes Home

When John Sr. came home from World War I in 1919, he returned to his trade as a plumber.[50] He got into the plumbing business because his uncle,

John W. Cooney, the brother of his father Peter, was in the business in a big way.[51] Peter died in 1904 at the age of forty-two when John Sr. was only twelve years old, and John W. was there to help him become a plumber.[52] Immigrant families lived by a code of helping each other.

John W. was a successful man in the plumbing business. He invented and patented an automatic sewer ejection system that was installed in the Blair Building at the corner of Broad Street and Exchange Street in the heart of Manhattan's Financial District. The system removed liquid waste in an efficient, sanitary, and dependable manner to the street sewers.[53]

The Blair Building, home of the investment banking firm of Blair & Co., was next to the New York Stock Exchange. During the Roaring Twenties, the New York Stock Exchange achieved new highs which led to it buying the Blair Building for expansion in 1928 before the stock market crashed in 1929 and opened the door to the Great Depression, the deepest and longest-lasting economic downturn in the history of the Western industrialized world.[54]

Nancy Leo, the daughter of John's sister Kathleen, recalled that John W. was an immigrant who realized the American dream. She mentioned that his automatic ejection system was also installed in the Ansonia Hotel, a residential hotel where Jack Dempsey and Babe Ruth lived; the Flatiron Building, one of the first skyscrapers in New York City and now a national historic landmark; Madison Square Garden, the most famous sports arena in the world; and in numerous mansions along Long's Island's Gold Coast.[55] The Gold Coast, brought to light by the publication of *The Great Gatsby*, probably had the greatest concentration of wealth during the first half of the 20th century.[56]

The Roaring Twenties were good to many, including John Sr. and his family. In the early twenties, he met and fell in love with Anna Millon. Both their parents were immigrants, and both came from large families, he from a family of six children and she from a family of seven children. They were married on October 16, 1922, at St. Patrick's Cathedral in New York City, presumably, according to their son Peter, at one of the smaller chapels.[57]

Their first home was in Brooklyn, where John and his brother Robert were born in 1923 and 1925, respectively. Then they moved across the Hudson River to North Bergen, New Jersey, where Kathleen was born in 1927, the same year that Babe Ruth hit sixty home runs. Joan was born in 1930 at the beginning of the Great Depression, and Peter was born in 1937 near its end in 1939, also the beginning of World War II.[58] Large families suited them and many other immigrant families. The bigger the family the better because families were strong units that stuck together and helped each other out, and help was needed to get through tough times.[59]

John grew up in North Bergen, just across the Hudson River from the Upper West Side of Manhattan. He lived in a neighborhood of immigrants who, like his grandparents, came to America for a better way of life. America was the land of opportunity where hard work paid off. He recalled: "I grew up with neighbors who worked hard to become doctors, lawyers, teachers..."[60] Early on, he picked up the strong work ethic of his neighborhood.

He grew up during the Great Depression, always working. Times were so tough that many youngsters had to drop out of school to work full-time to help provide for their families. As a teenager, John worked for a tailor during the week, an A&P on Saturdays, and a deli on Sundays. Often, he brought home unsold food to the family.[61] Everyone chipped in to help the family during those tough times, making the family unit a strong one.

In 1939, when John was only sixteen years old, things got even tougher for his family. His father passed away at the age of forty-five, causing John and his fourteen-year-old brother Robert to go from childhood to manhood in a hurry. They were thrust into the roles of being breadwinners for the family.[62] Four years later, both would go from the frying pan into the fire. They would go to war.[63]

John's sister Joan seemed to think their father, John Sr., suffered from complications stemming from his having had his appendix out when he was in the service in France. She also seemed to recall that her father needed intensive care at home before he passed away.[64] John's sister Kathleen, however, doesn't recall anything about complications from appendix surgery. She thought he was the victim of poison gas, causing him to have kidney problems.[65]

Kathleen said her father was a quiet man who, like many veterans, never talked about his wartime experiences.[66] Annelise Cooney Mora, the daughter of John's brother Robert, seemed to recall that her mother, Bente, told her that her father thought his father died from a botched surgery he needed after some incident in World War I and could never talk about it because it made him too upset.[67] Peter said some family members thought his father had an appendix operation in Europe during the war that connected two organs accidentally.[68]

The death certificate stated that John Sr. suffered from chronic nephritis, but that the principal cause of his death was lobar pneumonia.[69] Nephritis was a new disease that reared its ugly head during World War I. It had many labels including war nephritis, but the one most widely used was trench nephritis even though many of the soldiers affected by it had never been in the trenches. There was no consensus on what caused it and no effective way of preventing or treating it, but it was a harsh reality of World War I that led to many deaths.[70]

John Sr. was exposed to soldiers with nephritis and conditions that caused it, so it's conceivable that he picked up the disease in the service. Nephritis was among the diseases for which British soldiers received disability pensions. According to Neil Clark, a British journalist, nephritis was listed as the cause of death for many British officers who served in World War I.[71]

John Sr. died on May 13, 1939, about four months before the start of World War II on September 1, 1939, the day when Germany invaded Poland.[72] The invasion was a first step toward Hitler's goal of making Germany a world power. As far back as when John Sr.'s son John was born in 1923, Hitler wanted to make Germany a world power again. That was the year when the German currency had become worthless and wiped out the life savings of the middle and working classes, opening the door for a power-hungry dictator to rise to prominence.[73]

Buildup to World War II

The rise of Hitler was related to the debasement of the mark, the German currency. From 1921 to 1923, the mark was significantly debased. As it declined in value, Germany found it difficult to pay its debts. When it defaulted on deliveries of timber to France, France occupied the Ruhr in January 1923. The Ruhr was the industrial heart of Germany that furnished Germany with four-fifths of its coal and steel production. This occupation strangled the German economy and the mark really plunged in value. By November 1923, it took 4 billion marks to buy a dollar. In other words, the German currency had become utterly worthless, reducing the purchasing power of salaries and wages to zero. Since the life savings of the middle classes and the working classes were wiped out, the people lost faith in the German government.[74]

The big industrialists and landlords, who stood to gain though the masses were ruined, goaded the government to deliberately let the mark fall to free the government of its public debts, to escape from paying reparations, and to sabotage the French in the Ruhr. The destruction of the currency enabled German industrialists to wipe out its indebtedness by refunding its obligations in worthless marks. The industrial tycoons, the Army and the State benefited from the ruin of the currency, while the masses suffered. This was the environment in which Hitler saw an opportunity to gain power in Germany.[75]

Early on, Hitler tried to take advantage of the situation. Inspired by Benito Mussolini's march on Rome in October 1922 to install the Fascist government in Italy, Hitler planned a march on Berlin to install the Nazi government in Germany.[76] Before the march, however, he attempted a coup in Munich in November 1923.[77] The German people didn't realize how much the industrial elite, the Army, and the State were benefiting from the debasement of the currency, and Hitler planned to inform them in dramatic fashion.[78] Faraway in America, John was only six months old when this coup took place. Little did he know that twenty years later he, like his father before him, would go to war as a young man against the same enemy.

Hitler put his plan into action when leaders in the Bavarian government held a rally in Munich. He and his storm troopers disrupted the rally to gain support for his revolution. The plan backfired because the local population wasn't behind him, and he ended up in prison.[79] While behind bars, he began writing *Mein Kamp (My Fight)*, the book in which he formulated his Nazi philosophy and his planned conquest of Europe. Among other things, he wrote that he would one day repudiate the military restrictions of Germany by the Treaty of Versailles.[80] After prison, he finished the book and spent years implementing his plan to conquer Europe by rising to power in a country that felt a need for a strong leader who could make Germany a world power again. In his quest for more power on the world stage, he led Germany into World War II.

While Hitler was busy paving the way to World War II during the thirties, John Sr. was busy working hard to support his family during the Great Depression. When John Sr. died on May 13, 1939, following an illness, the Cooney family was heartbroken, especially young John who revered his father—his hero if you will. To throw fuel on the flames, he lost his hero just as times were going to get a lot tougher with another world war on the horizon.[81]

Heroes in Peacetime

John grew up around heroes. Baseball and boxing were big when he was a kid, and he had something in common with legends in both sports. He went to the same high school as Lou Gehrig, the Iron Horse, and he lived in the same town as Jim Braddock, the Cinderella Man. Gehrig was one of the greatest baseball players of all time, and Braddock pulled off one of the most stunning upsets in boxing history.

During the thirties when John was growing up, Gehrig was a hero to many, including young George H. W. Bush. The future president looked up to him not only because he was such a good ballplayer, but because he played the game with dignity and grace.[82] He also handled adversity with the same virtues.

In 1938, Gehrig became seriously ill with amyotrophic lateral sclerosis (ALS), a debilitating disease with no cure. Around the time of his thirty-fifth birthday on June 19, his wife noticed that he was having trouble with his balance.[83] ALS is a disease that works up and down the spinal cord, killing nerve cells. Its effect on Gehrig was to sap his strength because the disease causes the muscles to waste away.[84] For a man known as the Iron Horse, this was devastating. It was the beginning of the end of one of the greatest careers in baseball history.

On July 4, 1939, two months after Cooney lost his father, Gehrig gave one of the most memorable speeches in the history of sports. Even though he was very sick, he told a Yankee Stadium crowd of 60,000 people that he was "the luckiest man on the face of the earth."[85] He chose to focus not on his unfortunate personal circumstance but instead on his good fortune of having played with great Yankee teammates and before great Yankee fans for seventeen years. Two years later, he passed away on June 2, 1941, at the age of thirty-seven from the disease which is now referred to as Lou Gehrig's disease. He handled his unlucky fate with the same virtues that framed his life—dignity and grace (Exhibit 5.2).[86]

It is worth noting that Lou Gehrig, one of the most-respected Americans ever, was of German heritage. Both his parents were born in Germany, and both immigrated to America at a young age—his father Heinrich at twenty and his mother Christina at eighteen.[87] Both came to America for a better way of life, found each other, and started a family in a German neighborhood in a northern section of Manhattan called Yorkville, not far from Yankee Stadium.[88]

Lou was born on June 19, 1903, before vaccinations and antibiotics were available to prevent and treat diseases such as tuberculosis, diphtheria, cholera, pneumonia, scarlet fever, measles, and whooping cough.[89] Because the Gehrigs were poor, they lived in a crowded tenement building that was a breeding ground for disease, and this didn't bode well for the Gehrig children. Lou was lucky to escape disease but his two sisters and only brother weren't so lucky. His older sister, Anna, died at three and a half months old on September 5, 1902. A local doctor said the cause was convulsions.[90] His younger sister, Sophie, died at one year and eight months old on March 22,

Exhibit 5.2
Lou Gehrig, Baseball Hero
Drawing by Gregory Stone

1906, after having been diagnosed with measles, diphtheria, and broncho-pneumonia. His brother, the fourth child, died at birth.[91] As a result of these tragic losses, Lou became an only child and grew up close to his mother.[92]

Lou was in high school when the United States entered World War I. By coincidence, he attended the High School of Commerce in Manhattan, the same high school that John would attend after his father died four months before the beginning of World War II.[93] After high school, Lou earned an Ivy League education at Columbia, and went on to become a Yankee captain and legend and an inspiration to many. One can see why he felt he was the "the luckiest man on the face of the earth."[94] By another coincidence, John's family knew Columbia well. After college when John worked in the finance industry, he took post-graduate courses in economics and statistics at Columbia. Many years later, his daughter Mary and son Kevin received post-graduate degrees from Columbia.[95] In addition, his brother Peter is a Columbia graduate.

Like Gehrig, Jim Braddock was also an inspiration to many during the hard times of the thirties. He went from being a prominent boxer during the late twenties, able to provide well for his family, to an oft-injured, out-of-work boxer during the early thirties, unable to support his family on part-time work as a longshoreman on the New Jersey docks, even resorting to welfare relief. He became an inspiration to millions when his injuries healed, and he not only gave back the relief money but went on to reach the pinnacle of boxing by becoming the heavyweight champion of the world.[96]

Braddock was a heavy underdog in 1935, but he was injury-free and in good shape for the first time in years, the result of the physical work he did as a longshoreman.[97] Encouraged by his good health, he trained harder than his opponent, Max Baer, a large imposing boxer with a devastating punch that had killed a man in the ring. Braddock's training paid off big. In a bout for the ages, he beat the formidable Max Baer at the Madison Square Garden Bowl in Queens, New York to win the heavyweight crown. He went from destitution to respectability during hard times, and was given the name "Cinderella Man."[98]

Cooney recalls delivering clothes from the tailor shop to Braddock's house when he was a teenager. As famous as Braddock was, Cooney was impressed that he lived modestly and was a family man.[99] Braddock lived in North Bergen for the rest of his life, and North Bergen is rightly proud of him. Today, a large, beautiful county park in North Bergen, with an amazing view of the Manhattan skyline, bears his name—James J. Braddock North

Hudson County Park. On September 26, 2018, the 100-year anniversary of the park, a 10-foot statue of Braddock was unveiled in the park to honor the local hero (Exhibit 5.3).[100] Previously, in 2005, a terrific movie of his rags-to-riches story, *Cinderella Man*, was released that was directed by Ron Howard and starred Russell Crowe as Braddock and Renee Zellweger as his wife Mae.[101] The movie nicely captured Braddock's inspirational story.

Young Cooney, like other kids, appreciated the Iron Horse and the Cinderella Man, but his biggest hero was closer to home—his father, John Sr. Just nine days after his sixteenth birthday, John lost his hero.

When John Sr. died at the age of forty-five, his wife Anna was left widowed with five children—John (16), Robert (14), Kathleen (12), Joan (9), and Peter (1 1/2). John not only lost his hero, but he was thrust into the role of being the man of the family. His sister Kathleen said he had to quit his daytime school to work full-time.[102]

While the Depression forced many youngsters to drop out of school, Cooney's mother knew the value of an education and encouraged him to remain in school despite taking on a heavier workload to help the family. The only way he could do this was to work during the day and attend high school at night, and to his credit he followed that route.

Every day, he rode the ferry across the Hudson River to Manhattan to work as a messenger at Sherman & Sterling, one of the first major U.S. law firms to develop a global presence.[103] During the thirties and throughout the war, the firm helped its clients venture outside U.S. borders. John probably learned a thing or two from working for such a prestigious and far-reaching firm.[104]

Every evening, he attended the High School of Commerce on West 65th Street in Manhattan, a school whose mission was to prepare young men for careers in business in New York City. It was a unique and specialized high school. Its aim was "to provide a training which shall be broad and liberal in its character, and at the same time acquaint the students with the principles and techniques of commercial transactions."[105]

John probably also learned a thing or two from his high school because he ended up as a successful businessman in the finance industry in New York City. One can only conclude that he applied himself in his job and in his studies. You must tip your hat to this charter member of the Greatest Generation.

When Anna became a widow, her husband's veteran benefits helped some, but not much. The benefits consisted of payments of $46 a month from May 1939 to July 1939, $54 from July 1939 to May 1941, $50 from May 1941 to January 1943, $46 from January 1943 to September 1945, $42

Exhibit 5.3
Jim Braddock, Boxing Hero
Photograph by John Lanza

from September 1945 to July 1948, $38 from July 1948 to September 1955, and $30 from September 1955 onward.[106]

At the time of John Sr.'s passing, the family lived in the Woodcliff section of North Bergen, one of the nicest sections, but with his passing, paying the mortgage and putting food on the table became a problem. Anna needed help, and help was on the way, thanks to President Franklin Delano Roosevelt.

As Governor of New York, Roosevelt was interested in housing issues, and as President of the United States he made affordable housing a priority. He supported legislation to provide low-rent public housing for American families who had been hit hard by the Great Depression.[107] As part of his New Deal, he supported legislation such as the Wagner-Steagall Housing Act of 1937, which created the United States Housing Authority that shifted control of public housing to local communities to address local housing needs. Anna had the good fortune of living in a town that addressed these needs by establishing the North Bergen Housing Authority, which initiated a project to create a low-rent, federally funded housing complex in North Bergen called Meadowview Village.[108]

Meadowview was built to accommodate 172 families in eight buildings overlooking a vast meadow called the Meadowlands, a piece of land that many years later would be developed to include Giants Stadium (now MetLife Stadium, home of the New York Giants and the New York Jets), the Meadowlands Arena (later the Brendan Byrne Arena and then the Izod Center), and the Meadowlands Racetrack. Meadowview was developed with trees and spacious lawns, along with play areas and free outdoor parking spaces. In sum, it was a desirable place to live, and 1,100 families, including Anna's, submitted applications for the 172 apartments.[109]

As the widow of a veteran with five children, Anna was selected to be the "first" tenant of Meadowview Village. Because it was a high-profile project, her family entered the Village amidst notable fanfare on June 28, 1940. Hard to believe, but here is that June 28 date again. On that date in 1389, the Serbs lost the Battle of Kosovo that led to six centuries of being subject to Turkish rule. On that date in 1900, Archduke Franz Ferdinand married his wife, Sophie. On that date in 1914, Ferdinand was assassinated (and Sophie was also killed by the assassin) to start World War I. On that date in 1919, the Versailles Treaty was signed to officially end World War I. And here we have the Cooney family entering Meadowview Village on that date in 1940.

The Cooney family was welcomed into Meadowview Village by the mayor of North Bergen; the vice chairman, executive director, and comptroller of the North Bergen Housing Authority; the architect of Meadowview Village; a representative of the United States Housing Authority; and the former heavyweight champion of the world, James J. Braddock.[110] Anna was quoted in a local newspaper as saying that she was honored to be the first to move into the new housing development and was thrilled to be there. So were her kids.

Her daughters Kathleen and Joan celebrated the move by carving their initials in the fresh cement.[111] Kathleen remembered Meadowview Village as being a nice place to live, where people took care of their property.[112] Peter never forgot the day they moved in because Braddock picked him up and held him in his arms. He was too young at the time to remember it, but it was later burned into his memory because someone snapped a photograph that appeared in the now defunct *Hudson Dispatch,* a local paper serving Hudson County. He had the news clip for years. He wishes he still had it.[113]

Airpower

The period between World War I and World War II has been called the Golden Age of Aviation. During this period, there were many advances in aviation that paved the way to the airpower produced by the United States for World War II. During the 1920s, airplane racing was popular in the United States and Europe, and this competition led to many advancements in planes to make them faster and more powerful. An aircraft industry was developing which replaced biplanes constructed of wood and fabric with monoplanes constructed of more durable aluminum.[114] Interest in aviation was growing and when Charles Lindbergh made his one-man flight across the Atlantic Ocean in 1927, he became a worldwide celebrity and gave the aviation industry an incredible boost.[115]

During the 1930s, airplane designs improved, and engines became more powerful along with the fuel to power them. High octane gasoline was developed to improve the performance of aircraft. Other improvements were Turbo superchargers which enabled aircraft to provide sea-level pressure at high altitudes and oxygen systems which enabled airmen to breathe at these high altitudes. Technology was developed to enable pilots to rely on their instruments to fly when they could not see where they were going such as during the night or in overcast weather.[116]

The Great Depression of the 1930s was not good for commercial aviation, but the ongoing need of preparing for war to preserve peace was good for military aviation. Consequently, from 1931 to 1937, the major American aircraft companies did more than half their business with the military.[117]

FROM ONE WAR TO ANOTHER

Through the 1920s and 1930s, General Henry Hartley "Hap" Arnold was one of a few young officers who promoted airpower in the military. In 1938, he became the head of the Army Air Corps and had the good fortune of having the support of President Roosevelt. When Roosevelt saw the effectiveness of German airpower in the early days of World War II, he agreed that the United States needed more planes, lots of them. Therefore, the United States embarked on a program to enhance military aviation and Arnold, a disciple of Billy Mitchell, was able to command an air force that increased forty-fold during the war and became the largest air force in the world by war's end.[118] It took an incredible mobilization effort to make this happen.

Chapter 6

AMERICA MOBILIZES FOR WORLD WAR II

The United States didn't enter World War II until Pearl Harbor was attacked on December 7, 1941, over two years after the war started on September 1, 1939, when Germany invaded Poland. A lot happened during those two years to help the United States prepare for war. President Roosevelt sensed that Hitler's thirst for power was not going to end in Europe, and that he was a threat to the entire free world.[1] When Germany overtook France and threatened to overtake Britain, Roosevelt realized he had to act to protect the United States from Hitler who was building a military powerhouse, especially as regards airpower. Hitler wasn't his only concern—Mussolini in Italy and Hirohito in Japan were fascist leaders with totalitarian regimes who were increasing their military power. It would soon become evident that Nazism and fascism were serious threats to the free world.

When Army Chief of Staff George C. Marshall told Roosevelt that the United States did not have enough soldiers, guns, tanks, artillery, or planes to fight a war with Germany or these other fascist regimes, he sought the advice of Bernard Baruch, who led the mobilization effort for World War I. Baruch's advice was to put William Knudsen in charge of the mobilization effort for World War II.[2] At that time, Knudsen was the president of General Motors and was widely recognized as a production genius.[3] Roosevelt reached out to Knudsen in May 1940 for his help in putting together an organization to prepare for the possibility of entering World War II.

FROM ONE WAR TO ANOTHER

Mobilizing for Another World War

The term mobilization was first used in the 1850s to describe the way the Prussian army prepared for war.[4] From 1862 to 1890, Bismarck mobilized his Prussian troops in wars that changed Germany from a peace-loving people to a war-loving people.[5] When the United States mobilized for the Civil War, it established the first wartime draft and the same was true in every war through World War I. However, the experience in World War I made it evident that mobilization issues were more than simply acquiring manpower to fight a war. It also required a buildup of support forces with equipment and supplies (i.e., war materiel) to support the fighting forces and lead time was important in this process. Military leaders needed time to obtain, prepare, and equip the fighting forces for battle, and industry leaders needed time to adjust from a peacetime economy to a wartime economy.

To address the need for war manpower, the government instituted in September 1940 the first peacetime draft in U.S. history to prepare for the possibility of war.[6] To address the need for war materiel, the government instituted a Munitions Program in June 1940 which, despite obstacles such as political isolationism, pacifism, and opposition to preparing for war, was adopted and ratified by Congress to launch a program of industrial mobilization.[7] The military needed to define its needs, industry needed to produce the goods to satisfy those needs, and the government needed to manage the process. This was no easy task, and President Roosevelt knew it.

In the two decades after World War I, the United States had become an isolationist country more focused on domestic affairs than foreign affairs and for good reason—it was dealing with the Great Depression.[8] However, there was more focus on how to be better prepared for a future war than there was in preparing for World War I. After the end of World War I, Congress passed the National Defense Act of 1920 which put the Assistant Secretary of War in charge of planning for a future industrial mobilization.[9] In 1921, he formed a Procurement Division with a Planning Branch and in 1922 the Army and Navy Munitions Board was established to provide a unified procurement program for both services.[10] The Planning Branch created an Industrial Mobilization Plan in 1924 which was updated in 1930, 1933, 1936, and finally in 1939 after Germany invaded Poland to start World War II.[11] The Plan was never used because it had no real depth of understanding of the industries that needed to be mobilized for war. The Plan was also a political issue for

Roosevelt because organized labor, agricultural spokesmen, influential New Dealers, and industry leaders were opposed to it.[12]

Roosevelt had to deal with this situation while Germany, Japan, and Italy were pursuing policies of imperial expansion in 1939 and 1940 that were a threat to the free world.[13] He did so by establishing a War Resources Board in August 1939 as a civilian group to collaborate with the Army and Navy Munitions Board in formulating economic mobilization policies. Politics played a part in that Roosevelt wasn't comfortable with the makeup of the Board and its loyalty to him, nor was he comfortable with the fact that it did not have a representative from labor or agriculture. As a result, the War Resources Board was abolished three months later in November 1939.[14]

In May 1940, Roosevelt established the Office of Emergency Management as an executive branch office to coordinate defense activities for all government agencies except the War and Navy Departments. Also in May 1940, he revived, under the Office of Emergency Management, the Council of National Defense, and the National Defense Advisory Commission. The revival of the Council of National Defense was an initiative to coordinate the mobilization of industries, resources, and people for national defense and preparedness for war. The revival of the National Defense Advisory Commission was an initiative to assemble experts to advise the Council of National Defense on mobilization issues involving their respective fields of expertise (Exhibit 6.1).[15]

At that time, he reached out to William S. Knudsen and convinced him to leave his job as the head of General Motors to take a position on the National Defense Advisory Commission with responsibility for industrial production including the production of planes.[16]

Knudsen was the first dollar-a-year man appointed by President Roosevelt in the mobilization for World War II and Bernard Baruch was the first dollar-a-year man appointed by President Woodrow Wilson in the mobilization for World War I. Both presidents turned to leaders from business and industry to head agencies formed to prepare to defend the nation from the threat of war.[17] Both were willing to work for the government at a dollar-a-year to serve their country in time of war.

Knudsen was an immigrant from Denmark who viewed himself as an ordinary man who worked hard and became rich in the process.[18] He arrived in this country with the name of Signius Wilhelm Poul Knudsen. Early on he got a job in a shipyard and when he was sent to the person who kept track of his time and gave his name, the timekeeper let him have it: "What the hell! Give me something I can write!" That is when Signius Wilhelm Poul

Exhibit 6.1
Initiatives to Prepare for World War II

Council of National Defense	
Revived May 29, 1940, to coordinate the mobilization of industries, resources, and people for national defense and preparedness for war.	
Harry H. Woodring	Secretary of War
Charles Edison	Secretary of Navy
Henry A. Wallace	Secretary of Agriculture
Harry L. Hopkins	Secretary of Commerce
Harold L. Ickes	Secretary of the Interior
Frances Perkins	Secretary of Labor

National Defense Advisory Commission		
Revived May 29, 1940, to advise Council of National Defense on mobilization issues involving their respective fields of expertise.		
Executive	Background	Field of Expertise
William H. Knudsen	President General Motors Corporation	Industrial Production
Edward R. Stettinius, Jr.	Chairman United States Steel	Industrial Materials
Sidney Hillman	President Amalgamated Clothing Workers of America	Labor
Chester C. Davis	Governor Federal Reserve Board	Agriculture
Ralph Budd	Chairman Chicago, Burlington & Quincy Railroads	Transportation
Leon Henderson	Director Office of Price Administration	Prices
Dr. Harriet Elliott	Dean of Women University of North Carolina	Consumer Protection

Knudsen in Denmark became William S. Knudsen in America, known by many simply as Bill Knudsen.[19]

Knudsen had a gift for making things out of metal, lots of things, and he could make them in an efficient manner.[20] He worked on bicycles in Denmark that led him to a bicycle manufacturer in Buffalo where he used his skill for building bicycles which eventually led to his building cars and trucks in Detroit.[21] By coincidence, the Wright Brothers started out working on bicycles. They opened their own bicycle shop in 1893 and in 1899 began building their first aircraft in a room above the bicycle shop.[22]

Knudsen was a driven man who appreciated the opportunities the United States afforded him to build things.[23] He helped Ford mass-produce cars and later did the same for General Motors, rising to become its president. He understood the assembly line and how to set it up to deliver the goods.[24] He also liked people and got along with them. Roosevelt, a Democrat, took Baruch's advice and asked Knudsen, a Republican, to lead the effort to mobilize for war by building lots of guns, tanks, planes, and other weapons of destruction.[25]

Roosevelt wasn't the only president who reached across the aisle for the good of the nation. Abraham Lincoln did the same to help keep the nation united in the face of a war that was tearing it apart.[26] Both Roosevelt and Lincoln were considered great presidents who respected and had faith in their fellow Americans on both sides of the aisle. While Knudsen and Roosevelt had different political views, they both put aside their partisan views to work together for the common good of the country.[27]

Knudsen was glad to help. The country had been good to him, and he welcomed an opportunity to pay it back.[28] He appreciated his adopted country so much that he traded in his high-paying job ($300,000 with bonus) as the president of the General Motors, at that time the largest corporation in history, for a government job with a salary of a dollar a year.[29] He understood as well as anyone the importance of lead time in changing from a peacetime economy to a wartime economy, and he hit the ground running.[30]

The idea of car companies building weapons of war such as bombers can be traced to Knudsen who was confident that the automobile industry, the nation's biggest employer, could lead a production effort to make this happen. Knudsen was a force behind the phrase "the arsenal of democracy" which characterized the transition of America from a peacetime economy to a wartime economy.[31] Roosevelt made the phrase famous when he used it in a radio broadcast on December 29, 1940.[32]

FROM ONE WAR TO ANOTHER

When Roosevelt called upon Knudsen for help, he understood the importance of beefing up the nation's airpower. According to Hap Arnold, who became the head of the Army Air Corps on September 28, 1938, it took a tough up-and-down battle with jurisdictional troubles and headaches about appropriations to produce the B-17 Flying Fortress, the first strategic heavy bomber.[33] The B-17 was introduced in 1938 in response to an Army Air Corps request for a large, multi-engine bomber. It had been put out for bids in 1934 and was built by Boeing. By the time Arnold took over the Army Air Corps, President Roosevelt was sold on the importance of airpower.[34]

Hap Arnold, like Billy Mitchell before him, promoted the importance of airpower in war. However, Arnold used more tact than Mitchell ever did and with President Roosevelt's support was able to garner the support he needed to produce a second strategic heavy bomber, the B-24 Liberator. Designing another heavy bomber to satisfy Arnold's requirements—to fly faster (300 miles per hour), farther (3,000 miles), higher (35,000 feet), and to carry a bigger bomb load than the B-17—was no easy task, but Consolidated Aircraft in San Diego took on the project and began producing B-24 models by the end of 1939.[35]

It was the intention of Arnold to fight fire with fire. Hitler was fortifying his airpower and Arnold and his longtime colleagues and friends—Carl "Tooey" Spaatz and Ira C. Eaker—felt America needed to follow suit. The three of them had long careers in military aviation and had been lobbying for an increase in airpower for years. Arnold was the acknowledged leader of the three with Spaatz as his trusted deputy and Eaker as the third musketeer. For thirty years, they formed a close-knit partnership to promote airpower that was beginning to pay dividends.[36]

War Production Challenges

The National Defense Advisory Commission was formed after history repeated itself when Germany, just as it did in World War I, invaded the three countries that stood between Germany and France—the Netherlands, Belgium, and Luxembourg—to get to France once again. In so doing, German troops pushed over 338,000 British, French, and Belgian resistance troops onto the beaches of Dunkirk, a French seaport, with the intention of driving them into the English Channel. The British reacted with an evacuation operation called Operation Dynamo which was dramatically brought to life in the popular film *Dunkirk* that was released in 2017 and grossed $526 million worldwide. The British mobilized an armada of 665 civilian vessels and 222 naval vessels to evacuate troops in a nine-day operation from May 26 to June 3, 1940. The operation came to be known as the Miracle of Dunkirk.[37]

With these Allied troops driven off the European continent, Germany invaded France which led to the fall of France in which it signed an armistice agreement with Germany in June 1940.[38] The invasion prompted President Roosevelt to order the production of 50,000 warplanes.[39] Hitler was building a fortress—a wall around Europe—and Arnold was on his way to producing heavy bombers to fly over the fortress to drop bombs over Germany and countries aligned with or occupied by Germany.

Since producing 50,000 new warplanes was a priority of the President, he looked to his Secretary of the Treasury, Henry Morgenthau, Jr., a trusted and loyal colleague, to help coordinate aircraft production. Morgenthau needed help in determining what planes and engines to build and recruited George Jackson Mead to advise him. Morgenthau called Mead "the greatest living authority on airplane engines." [40] Mead had retired from United Aircraft Corporation in 1939 and President Roosevelt appointed him as a member of the National Advisory Committee for Aeronautics.[41]

The Committee was founded in 1915 when the United States was trying to catch up with Europe's rapid technological advancements in aviation. It was an independent government agency reporting directly to the President who at that time was Woodrow Wilson. Through the years, it played a major role in the research and growth of the aviation industry. It consisted of experts who advised on all aspects of aviation from designing planes to testing them for use. It was akin to a think tank on aviation.[42] When Mead joined the Committee (Exhibit 6.2), he was elected as its vice chairman.[43]

Mead knew aircraft engines. He had spent his life designing them and was one of the founders of the Pratt and Whitney Aircraft Company which later became part of the United Aircraft Corporation.[44] He was the head of aeronautical engineering at both companies and led the teams that developed the Wasp and Hornet engines which gave rise to a family of engines that powered military aircraft during World War II.[45]

While Mead could provide advice on the types of engines and planes to build, it became clear that a production expert was needed to produce the necessary planes and engines and other war materiel, and Knudsen was that expert. Roosevelt had revived the National Defense Advisory Committee with Knudsen and experts representing industry, labor, agriculture, and public consumers to assess the nation's ability to mobilize for war.[46]

Exhibit 6.2
National Advisory Committee for Aeronautics

Member	Background
Dr. Jerome C. Hunsaker (Chmn.)	Chief of Design, U.S. Bureau of Aeronautics
Dr. George J. Mead (Vice Chmn.)	Co-Founder of Pratt & Whitney Aircraft Co.
John F. Victory (Exec. Secy.)	NACA's First Employee
Dr. Charles G. Abbott	Secretary, Smithsonian Institution
Lt. Gen. Henry H. Arnold	Commanding General, Army Air Forces, War Department
Maj. Gen. George H. Brett	Acting Chief of the Air Corps, War Department
Dr. Lyman J. Briggs	Director, National Bureau of Standards
W. A. M. Burden	Special Assistant to the Secretary of Commerce
Dr. Vannevar Bush	Director, Office of Scientific Research and Development
Smith J. De France	Engineer in Charge, Ames Aeronautical Laboratory
Dr. Robert E. Doherty	President, Carnegie Institute of Technology
Dr. William F. Durand	Aerodynamics Pioneer and Professor, Stanford University
Maj. Gen. Oliver P. Echols	Commanding General, Materiel Command, Army Air Forces
Clinton M. Hester	Administrator, Civil Aeronautics Authority
Robert H. Hinckley	Chairman, Civil Aeronautics Authority
S. Paul Johnston	Editor, Aviation Week Magazine
Rear Adm. Sydney M. Kraus	Bureau of Aeronautics, Navy Department
Dr. George W. Lewis	Director of Aeronautical Research for NACA
Rear Adm. John S. McCain	Bureau of Aeronautics, Navy Department, 1942
Dr. F. W. Reichelderfer	Chief, United States Weather Bureau
Henry J. E. Reid	Engineer in Charge, Langley Memorial Aeronautical Lab
Edward R. Sharp	Administrative Officer, Aircraft Engine Research Laboratory
Rear Adm. John H. Towers	Chief, Bureau of Aeronautics, Navy Department
Dr. Edward Warner	Civil Aeronautics Board, Washington, D.C.
Dr. Orville Wright	Aviation Pioneer
Dr. Theodore P. Wright	Assistant Chief, Aircraft Branch, War Production Board

America Mobilizes For World War II

With his Administration recruiting big businessmen like Knudsen and Mead for his mobilization team, Roosevelt was walking a political tightrope because he was elected on campaigns attacking big business. In his 1932 campaign, he attacked big business for becoming too powerful and rich while forsaking the consumer.[47] In his 1936 campaign, he continued to attack big business for its concentration of wealth and power "built upon other people's money, other people's business, other people's labor."[48] Now he was seeking the help of big businessmen on the eve of another election. As one would surmise, his selections for the National Defense Advisory Commission were carefully made with politics in mind.

While each member of the National Defense Advisory Commission had a mobilization task to focus on, only three of them (Knudsen, Stettinius, and Budd) were from big business while four of them (Hillman, Davis, Henderson, and Elliott) were New Dealers. Of the three from big business, Knudsen was tasked with industrial production regarding airplanes, engines, tanks, and other war materiel. Edward R. Stettinius Jr., chairman of U.S. Steel, was tasked with supervising the flow of raw materials to the factories. Ralph Budd, chairman of the Chicago, Burlington & Quincy Railroads, was put in charge of transportation problems to prevent bottlenecks which might threaten quick deliveries of war materiel.[49]

Of the four New Dealers, Sidney Hillman, president of the Amalgamated Clothing Workers of America, was tasked with coordinating employment policies for the war industry including training of those for noncombat duties and dealing with labor issues. Chester C. Davis, a governor of the Federal Reserve Board, who was an agriculture advocate, was tasked with preventing conflicts of national agricultural policy regarding the feeding of civilians as well as those engaged in the defense program. Leon Henderson, director of the Office of Price Administration, was tasked with stabilizing prices of raw materials required for war materiel and with rationing raw materials which were desired by civilians but required for national defense. Harriett Elliott, Dean of Women at the University of North Carolina, who was a consumer advocate, was tasked with advising on consumer protection during the mobilization effort.[50]

The National Defense Advisory Commission was not the answer for the industrial mobilization effort. It did not have a formal leader and it did not have the authority to get things done that needed to be done. Also, the members didn't work well together as a team. The three businessmen argued that industries should work freely under the profit system, and the New Dealers countered that a more democratic approach with government, business, and labor working together as patriots, not for the almighty buck, was best. In her book, *No Ordinary Time: Franklin and Eleanor Roosevelt: The Home Front in World War II*, Doris Kearns Goodwin quotes Secretary of War Stimson as saying, "If you are going to war in a capitalist country, you have to let business make money out of the process or business won't work."

In reaching out to Knudsen, Roosevelt no doubt understood this, but he also understood the political ramifications of giving Knudsen, a businessman and a Republican, too much power. While Knudsen did what he could to influence the leaders of the automobile industry to convert from making cars to making weapons of war, he did not have the power to get things done his way, but he had the respect of the leaders of the automobile industry and his influence started them thinking about mobilizing for war. While he and the National Defense Advisory Commission were widely criticized for not getting things done, his influence was being felt by the automobile industry which he was preparing to get things done.[51]

Knudsen met with General Marshall of the Army who told him his responsibility was to produce war materiel. The following day, he was told the same thing by the Navy. After thinking long and hard, he assembled a group of automobile industry experts to help plan an infrastructure to produce war materiel which included aircraft; tanks, trucks, and tractors; machine tools and heavy ordnance; ammunition and light ordnance; ships; food and food products; and miscellaneous equipment. The experts, their background, and the war materiel each was tasked with planning for appear in Exhibit 6.3.[52]

Mead, who had a knack for evaluating planes and engines, was put in charge of aircraft.[53] Like Knudsen, he was also a patriot glad to help his country in time of need, and his federal government salary for 1940 as a special advisor was only five cents.[54] In addition to being viewed as a creative genius of aircraft engines, Mead was, like Knudsen, a team player who appreciated every member of the team. When interviewed by Louis M. Lyons of the Boston Globe in 1935 while he was at United Aircraft, he was quoted as saying:[55]

> *"The way you do anything as complicated as aviation is through a team. We've got a group over in our plant—boy they're great. If anything makes me provoked, it is to see someone claim credit for anything. Nothing worthwhile is done without a team to do it."*

When Knudsen was appointed to the National Defense Advisory Committee in June 1940, he met with the Assistant Secretary of War, Louis A.

Exhibit 6.3
Industry Experts Recruited by Knudsen to Help Produce War Materiel

Industry Executive	Background	War Materiel
Dr. George Jackson Mead	Aeronautical Engineer and Co-Founder Pratt & Whitney Aircraft Company	Aircraft
John D. Biggers	President Libbey-Owens-Ford Glass Company	Tanks, Trucks, and Tractors
Harold S. Vance	Chairman Studebaker Corporation	Machine Tools and Heavy Ordnance
E. F. Johnson	Expert in Parts and Accessories General Motors	Small Arms and Ammunition
Rear Admiral Emory S. Land	Chairman Maritime Commission	Shipbuilding
William H. Harrison	Vice President and Chief Engineer A.T.& T	Construction
George M. Moffett	President Corn Products Refining Company	Food and Chemicals
J. C. Nichols	Kansas Businessman Instrumental in Building WWI Museum	Miscellaneous equipment

FROM ONE WAR TO ANOTHER

Johnson, and asked how much munitions productive capacity the Army needed and how fast it would need the materiel. These questions resulted in the Munitions Program of June 30, 1940, which was approved by Roosevelt and by Congress which appropriated the funds. The Munitions Program was a major development in the preparedness policy of the United States because its purpose was to put American industry to work in a big way as soon as possible to produce essentials such as airplanes.[56] With the passage of the Selective Service Act three months later, this mobilization of the nation's materiel was matched by the mobilization of its manpower.

Knudsen did not waste any time in letting the leaders in the automotive industry know how important it was for their companies to help the country mobilize for war. The United States automotive industry was a production juggernaut. In 1939, it produced 78 percent of the passenger cars made in the world, and 63 percent of the trucks and buses. On October 24, 1940, Knudsen had an informal meeting with the automotive leaders including the heads of Ford, General Motors, Chrysler, and Studebaker and told them the safety of the country was threatened and that planes, tanks, guns, and munitions were needed to defend it. He stressed above all else the need for heavy bombers and left his aide, Major James H, "Jimmy" Doolittle, to help bring these rival car companies together to help produce them.[57] The Army Air Corps (name changed to Army Air Forces in 1941) stationed Major Doolittle in Detroit as a liaison officer to assist the automotive industry in its planning for its contribution to the mobilization effort.[58]

Doolittle was a legendary pilot who not only knew planes from flying them but also knew how they worked from having received a PhD in aeronautical engineering from the Massachusetts Institute of Technology. In addition, he also had industrial experience in the aviation industry. When Shell decided to get into the business of providing aviation fuel and lubricants in America as it had been doing in Europe, Doolittle was hired as the head of Shell's aviation department.[59] Like Arnold, Doolittle was a diplomatic "can do" person and was a leader. Like Knudsen, he liked people and got along with them. Like Mead, he had a knack for evaluating planes and engines. Like all three, he was a patriot who loved his country.

Ten years earlier in February 1930, Doolittle had resigned from the service, where he was a test pilot, to take the job at Shell. When Roosevelt addressed Congress in May 1940 and called for a program that would produce at least 50,000 planes a year, he left his high-paying job and returned to the service as a major. Arnold's executive officer, Ira Eaker, reached out to him to take a job as an Army Air Corps representative helping to produce lots of planes for war.

124

His job, as he saw it, "was to effect a shotgun marriage between the aircraft industry and the automotive industry."[60] He would later in the war put his life on the line in leading the Doolittle Tokyo Raid on April 18, 1942, which was immortalized in the book and movie, *Thirty Seconds Over Tokyo*.[61] He would receive the Congressional Medal of Honor for his courage and leadership.

The groundwork laid by Knudsen and Doolittle in the automotive industry led to the formation of an Automotive Committee of Air Defense and three weeks after Pearl Harbor the industry formed the Automotive Council for War Production representing almost 500 manufactures to oversee the transition of the automobile industry from a competitive industry which mass-produced cars and trucks during peacetime to a cooperative industry which mass-produced weapons of war during wartime such as planes and tanks.[62]

Knudsen recruited industry leaders to not only build lots of weapons, but to help put in place an infrastructure for building them in an effective and efficient manner.[63] Knudsen knew that it would take time for the automobile industry to retool and build new facilities so it could mass produce weapons of war. He also knew the importance of accuracy in retooling and recruited skilled craftsmen who knew that he appreciated their skills. He also believed that there isn't anything America cannot do if everyone works together.[64]

Teamwork was the key and as previously noted teamwork was missing from the National Defense Advisory Commission in part because it did not have a leader and in part because of the makeup of its members. The businessmen were used to operating to make money and were against government control, military officials were used to operating to protect the nation and fight its wars and wanted to be in control, and government officials were used to operating in a political environment for the welfare of the nation and wanted to be in control. Senior government officials and military officers had the authority but did not have relevant technical and industry knowledge, and business leaders had the technical and industry knowledge but lacked the authority of the military or the government.[65] Consequently, it was challenging to control the mobilization process.

As a result of the control problems encountered by the National Defense Advisory Commission, it was integrated in January 1941 into a new agency, the Office of Production Management. Knudsen, whose expertise was production, served as the director general and Sidney Hillman, founder of the Amalgamated Clothing Workers whose expertise was labor, served as the associate general director. Its divisions and directors appear in Exhibit 6.4.[66] The purpose of Office of Production Management was to develop and execute

Exhibit 6.4
Office of Production Management
Created January 7, 1941, to manage war production.

Board Member	Responsibility
William S. Knudsen	Director General
Sidney Hillman	Associate Director General
W. H. Harrison	Director Production Division
Douglas C. MacKeachie	Director Purchases Division
J. S. Knowlson	Acting Director Priorities Division
William L. Batt	Director Materials Division
Leon Henderson	Director Civilian Supply Division
Floyd B. Odium	Director Contract Distribution Division
Sidney Hillman	Director Labor Division
Herbert Emmerich	Secretary
John Lord O'Brian	General Counsel

policies relating to the production of defense materials, but again Knudsen still did not have the power to get things done the way he would do them if he were fully in charge without the military and government bureaucracies.

In March 1941, a Senate Special Committee to Investigate the National Defense Program was formed with Senator Harry S. Truman as its chairman. When in 1940 President Roosevelt requested $10.5 billion to bolster the national defense and Congress appropriated the funds, Truman expressed a concern that the awarding of defense contracts would favor big business over small business and proposed an oversight committee to investigate the national defense program and the handling of contracts. The committee consisted of seven members—five Democrats and two Republicans—and came to be known as the Truman Committee. Truman wanted his committee to be a "benevolent policeman" investigating a broad agenda including problems such as wartime shortages, cost overruns, and labor strikes.[67] Truman had a reputation for being a fair man and told his staff that he did not want them grandstanding for headlines or going on witch-hunts.[68] He said their primary job was to get the facts.

It was no secret that Truman was no fan of big business with its concentration of power. He did not like big banks, big insurance companies, and big corporations.[69] He thought the national defense program would make big men bigger and hurt the little men, which he could appreciate having been a small businessman.[70] He was also suspicious of the "dollar-a-year" men, the powerful and wealthy corporate executives who went to work for the government. He felt they may be inclined to make decisions to benefit their companies.[71]

Knudsen was one of the "dollar-a-year" men, but he was also the production genius Roosevelt reached out to for help, especially for the production of big bombers. On May 4, 1941, Roosevelt sent a letter to Knudsen saying, "I know of no single item of our defense today that is more important than a larger four-engine bomber capacity."[72] Thus, Truman needed to temper his criticism of big businessmen like Knudsen who were key to the mobilization effort. Nevertheless, Truman and was determined to be a "watchdog" over government defense spending and to get the facts to be sure government defense contracts were handed out fairly and that contracted corporations provided the goods in accordance with their contracts.[73]

The Victory Program

Knudsen had been trying to nail down the requirements of the military for war supplies, and Colonel Henry S. Aurand, an expert of logistics serving under General Marshall, got the ball rolling. He sent a memorandum to Marshall saying there was a need for a program to determine the total war supplies required by the Army, the Navy, the British agencies requesting war supplies under the Lend-Lease Act, and the Maritime Commission that shipped the war supplies. The Lend-Lease Act set up a system that would allow the United States to lend or lease war supplies to any nation deemed vital to the defense of the United States.[74] Aurand felt the program needed to coordinate the production and distribution of the war supplies required to meet the demands. Knudsen and his fellow industrialists who produced the war supplies had been asking for something like this for months.[75]

Aurand's memorandum made sense to the Under Secretary of War Robert P. Patterson who took the ball and ran with it by recommending a joint committee with representatives of the Army, Navy, Maritime Commission, and the Office of Production Management to determine the ultimate production needs of the United States to win the war should the United States enter it. President Roosevelt got on this bandwagon and agreed that it was important to determine the munitions needs for an ultimate victory over Hitler and penned a letter on July 9, 1941, that began a process that led to the Victory Program.[76]

Roosevelt knew that he would at some point have to ask civilians and the industries that supplied them with consumer goods to make sacrifices for the welfare of the nation at war, but he did not have a good handle on the extent of the sacrifices because he did not have a good handle on the overall production needs to meet the overall military needs in the event of war.[77] Consequently, in that letter, he directed the War Department and the Navy Department to give him a report on the overall production requirements needed to defeat our potential enemies.[78]

The War Department responded by assigning Major Albert C. Wedemeyer to prepare estimates of the manpower requirements for the Army, and Colonel Aurand to prepare estimates of the materiel requirements of the Army.[79] Aurand had worked on the Munitions Program of June 30, 1940, which was essentially a defensive program not an offensive program because the country wasn't at war. When the Lend-Lease Act was enacted on March 11, 1941, it became another draw on the country's productive capacity that needed to be dealt with and he was given that task to deal with it.[80]

Wedemeyer and Aurand were both West Point graduates who became generals and were best known for their work on the Victory Program. Wedemeyer was a skilled strategist and Aurand was a skilled logistician. Both served under the wing of Army Chief of Staff George C. Marshall and made major contributions to the mobilization effort of the United States to produce the manpower and materiel needed to fight World War II.

The fourteen-page report produced under Major Wedemeyer was entitled "Ultimate Requirements Study: Estimate of Army Ground Forces." It pointed out the way to victory by stressing the importance of creating a productive capacity to produce "the most modern equipment designed to give mobility and destructive power to our striking forces."[81] The report estimated the manpower the Army would need to supply with arms to win the war, namely 8.7 million Army personnel (6.7 million for the Army Ground Forces and 2.0 million for the Army Air Forces). These estimates were remarkable considering that three-and-a-half years later, on May 31, 1945, the Army had 8.3 million personnel (6.0 million Army Ground Forces and 2.3 million Army Air Forces). The report also estimated a need for 215 divisions that would later be significantly paired down to 90 divisions.[82]

The report produced under Colonel Aurand was entitled "Ultimate Munitions Production Essential to the Safety of America" and became the basis of Army estimates of its materiel needs for civilian production authorities to satisfy. Aurand's estimates were shared with Admiral Stark, Chief of Naval Operations.[83] They were also reviewed and updated as Aurand worked with colleagues such as Knudsen, who was brought into the Army at the high rank of Lieutenant General; Stacy May, who became the head of the Statistics Division of the War Production Board; and Robert R. Nathan, who became the head of the Planning Division of the War Production Board. These collaborations enabled the Munitions Program to be tweaked to define the ongoing material needs of the Army and Navy for industries to mobilize for war. There has been so much written about who was responsible for the Victory Program, but the fact of the matter is that it was a collaborative effort.

The reports of Wedemeyer and Aurand were a big step in helping Marshall, the Chief of Staff of the Army, to determine what was needed to win the war, but he also needed input from Army Air Forces of what they needed to wage an effective air war. Therefore, he ordered General Henry A. Arnold, Chief of the Army Air Forces, to come to Washington, D.C. on August 2, 1941, at which time he told him he needed a plan from the Army Air Forces to respond to the President's July 9 letter estimating its needs to wage a winning air campaign.[84]

On August 3, Arnold met with his Chief of Staff, Brigadier General Carl "Tooey" Spaatz, who put four colleagues of his Air War Plans Division

(AWPD) to work on the task—Lieutenant Colonel Harold L. George (division chief), Major Haywood S. Hansell, Major Laurence S. Kuter, and Lieutenant Kenneth N. Walker. He had known and appreciated them for years and knew they believed in the supremacy of airpower. He told them to come up with a plan by August 12 to guide American airpower though World War II to include "strategy, timing, targeting, production, manpower, training, organization, and support."[85]

They came up with the plan in nine days against heavy odds. In 1995, Richard Overy, who published extensively on the history of World War II, said in his book, *Why the Allies Won*, that the greatest single advantage enjoyed by the Allies during the war was airpower and that a small group of airmen led by Colonel Hal George was given the impossible task of drafting the American air plan in nine days and produced a plan that was approved and implemented to begin the work of "establishing massive American airpower even before America entered the war."[86]

Wedemeyer had the chief responsibility of putting together the ultimate requirements of the Army, Navy, and Army Air Forces into a report dated September 10, 1941, which came to be known as the Victory Program. It laid out a program of what was needed for American to win a war and it was produced three months before the bombing of Pearl Harbor launched us into the war. The Victory Program was never static—it kept changing during the war.[87]

While the Wedemeyer report estimated a need for 215 divisions to win the war, this estimate was significantly changed after Pearl Harbor. Through the first half of 1942, the mobilization planners believed they would need to activate only 200 Army divisions and 115 air combat groups to defeat the enemy.[88] During the second half of 1942 and through the summer of 1943, modest success in bombing missions led Marshall to appreciate airpower, prompting him to expand the number of air combat groups from 115 to 273. Meanwhile, economists working on the War Production Board produced a report claiming it was not feasible for the American economy to supply an Army of more than 100 divisions by the end of 1943.[89] Marshall, believing he could rely on the Army Air Forces to gain air superiority, reduced the Army divisions needed for victory from 200 to 90 and by August 1943 the Army reached its combat strength of 90 divisions which got the job done during the war.[90]

While the United States was not at war in September 1941 when the Wedemeyer report came out, it helped to give industry a better idea of what to expect if it entered the war. At the time, big business was still focused on the bottom line and producing goods for a peacetime economy, not a war-time economy. Nevertheless, the government was planning to be prepared for the possibility of war with the resultant problem of allocating resources between the American consumers and the military. To prepare to deal with this possibility which was trending toward a reality, Roosevelt established the Supply Priorities and Allocations Board in August 1941. While Knudsen was on this Board, his subordinate in the Office of Production Management, Donald M. Nelson, who had been a senior executive of Sears Roebuck, was put in charge of the Board in setting priorities and allocating resources. As the chief merchandising executive of Sears, the world's largest distributing firm, he probably knew more about where almost everything in the United States was manufactured than anyone else in the country.[91]

In October 1941, there were issues involving industry shortcomings in meeting the demands of war, even though America was not yet at war. These shortcomings brought the Office of Production Management under the microscope of the Truman Committee. In its first annual report prepared in the final months of 1941, the Truman Committee concluded that the fact that the Office of Production Management had two leaders—Knudsen and Hillman—instead of one, was a problem that needed resolution.[92] Roosevelt had appointed two leaders because he wanted the power of leadership shared on the Office of Production Management. Roosevelt always tried to make sure no one person got too much control—he wanted to be in control.[93] After Pearl Harbor was attacked on December 7, 1941, however, Roosevelt responded to the Truman Committee's criticism by disbanding the Office of Production Management and creating the War Production Board on January 6, 1942, with one leader, Donald M. Nelson.[94]

Nelson was not opposed to the dollar-a-year men and, in fact, was one of them when he left Sears to serve with the Office of Production Management. He felt these business leaders were critically needed by our country because they ran the industries which needed to provide the goods to win the war. Roosevelt felt the same way. When testifying before the Truman Committee as the head of the War Production Board, Nelson said the experience and knowledge of the dollar-a-year men was essential for the success of the war production program. He estimated that there were about 300 dollar-a-year men serving full-time and about 200 serving part-time.[95]

Nelson told the Committee that it would not help the economy to have small business companies competing with big business companies to produce weapons and arms in such a short period of time. He also pointed out that they follow four strict rules in appointing dollar-a-year men: (1) they must have outstanding business or technical ability, an unimpeachable integrity, and be especially qualified in the work for which they are chosen to perform; (2) there must be, after a reasonable effort to find out, no person of equal ability willing to serve on a regular government salary; (3) they are not to make decisions directly affecting the affairs of their own companies; and (4) they must pass a thorough investigation by one of the government investigatory agencies.[96] As a result of Nelson's defense of the dollar-a-year men, Truman said if that's what it took to win the war then his Committee would not stand in the way.[97] One imagines that Nelson's being a fellow Missourian did not hurt Nelson's chances of getting Truman to back off. Nevertheless, the Truman Committee would go on to be an able "watchdog" of defense spending and save the American taxpayers billions of dollars.[98] The greatest legacy of the Committee was probably the positive effect it had on the career of Harry Truman.[99]

Most dollar-a-year men were Republicans, prompting Roosevelt say to Knudsen, "Bill, couldn't you find a Democrat to go on this dollar-a-year list?" Knudsen replied, "There's no Democrat rich enough to take a job at a dollar a year."[100] It was good that they could engage in an exchange like this. It reflected the mutual respect they had for each other and the importance of humor in getting leaders with different political beliefs to work together.

Nelson was given the authority to exercise general direction over the war procurement and production program and to determine the policies, plans, procedures, and methods of the Federal departments, establishments, and agencies. He also had the authority to supervise and make changes to the Office of Production Management which was folded into the War Production Board (Exhibit 6.5). He viewed his job as making enough war materiel to lick Germany and Japan in the shortest possible time, and he was prepared to make whatever organizational changes had to be made to accomplish that job.[101] He also had words of praise for Knudsen, saying that even though he "was invested with only the shadow of actual authority" he "moved mountains through his own prestige, persuasiveness, and strength of character."[102]

Knudsen was a member of the new War Production Board but in a more focused role. He was appointed by President Roosevelt as a Lieutenant General (three-star general) of the U.S. Army and the Director of Production for the War Department with special emphasis on the production of airplanes, tanks, guns, and ammunition. He was the only civilian to enter the U.S. Army at such a high rank.[103] In making the appointment, Roosevelt said, "Bill Knudsen is one of the greatest production men in the world and

Exhibit 6.5
War Production Board
Created January 16, 1942, to direct the production of war materiel.

Board Member	Responsibility
Donald M. Nelson	Chairman
Henry L. Stimson	Secretary of War
Frank Knox	Secretary of Navy
Jesse H. Jones	Federal Loan Administrator
William S. Knudsen	Director General of the Office of Product Management
Sidney Hillman	Associate General of the Office of Product Management
Leon Henderson	Administrator of the Office of Price Administration
Henry A. Wallace	Chairman of the Board of Economic Warfare
Harry Hopkins	Special Assistant to the President Supervising the Defense Aid Program

his acceptance of this new post means that he can give his entire time to the direction and expediting of production, a field in which he has no equal."[104]

Knudsen would keep on working the magic he had been responsible for since Roosevelt reached out to him in 1940, even though it was not always appreciated by those who were adversaries of big business. His job was to go to factories producing war materiel in which bottlenecks developed that slowed production and figure out ways to overcome the bottlenecks. During the last three years of the war, he flew 250,000 miles to inspect 1,200 factories to improve production.[105] Edward A. Guest, Detroit's poet, once said: "Bill Knudsen is the greatest immigrant in the history of this country."[106]

The War Production Board operated until the end of the war. It directed war production and the procurement of materials and in its three years supervised the production of $185 billion worth of weapons and supplies. It changed frequently and faced many challenges such as disputes with the armed services and criticism from the Truman Committee and others who found it difficult to believe that the major automobile companies that competed so fiercely with each other could put away the hatchet and cooperate with the government to do what it took to support the troops.[107]

The War Production Board, like those agencies that preceded it—War Resources Board, Office of Emergency Management, National Defense Advisory Commission, Office of Production Management, and Supply Priorities and Allocations Board—was formed under great stress to deal with a national emergency—how to mobilize to defend the country in case of war. One of its Board members, J. S. Knowlson, put things in perspective when he wrote that the War Production Board "operated on a democratic basis, and had all the weaknesses of our system."[108] It also had all the strengths of our system. None of these organizations were perfect, but taken as a whole, they moved the mobilization process along and helped to get the job done in converting the United States from a peacetime economy to a wartime economy.

The Spark

The attack on Pearl Harbor was the spark that pulled the United States into World War II. The surprise attack on December 7, 1941, stunned the nation and ended any thoughts of remaining a neutral nation. The United States had powerful allies in Great Britain and the Soviet Union that would form a triumvirate to lead the Allied nations into a global war against the Axis nations led by the triumvirate of Germany, Italy, and Japan.

America Mobilizes For World War II

Congress responded quickly and unanimously to the Pearl Harbor attack by declaring war against Japan on December 8, 1941. And when Germany declared war on the United States in the wake of the Pearl Harbor attack, Congress again acted quickly by declaring war against Germany on December 11, 1941.[109] Knudsen had already been working his magic for over a year and a half, and this lead time produced impressive results. The mobilization effort was by no means a one-man effort. Knudsen was part of a large team of patriots that rallied to produce the materiel necessary to support our troops at war.

Thanks to Billy Mitchell and his disciples like Hap Arnold, all of whom believed in and promoted the value of airpower in war, the United States was better prepared for World War II than it ever was for World War I. Hap Arnold understood that airpower was more than just a lot of planes. It did of course depend on a large aircraft industry, but it also depended on an infrastructure to train crews to operate the planes and mechanics to keep them flying. It needed airfields to maximize their use along with pipelines through which to provide replacement planes and parts as well as replacement airmen to maintain a constant fighting strength.[110] With Knudsen's industrial genius and the support of President Roosevelt, Arnold was able to lead a program to develop the airpower Mitchell and his disciples had been promoting for years and the manpower with skills to effectively utilize this airpower.[111]

Before the United States entered the war, air superiority belonged to the feared German Luftwaffe. However, when the Americans entered the war, it brought with it a formidable production capability to produce weapons of war. When the United States entered the war at the end of 1941, an infrastructure was already in place to produce military aircraft for its Allies. Consequently, when it entered the war, it was positioned to mobilize and outpace other countries in producing military aircraft of all types and sizes. During World War II, the United States became the leading producer of military aircraft in the world. Its output of aircraft was impressive and outpaced the military aircraft produced by its enemies Japan and Germany and by its ally Great Britain.[112] As a result, air superiority shifted from the Germans to the Americans (Exhibit 6.6).

From July 1940 to August 1945, American aircraft factories built 97,810 bombers and 99,950 fighters for a total of 197,760 combat aircraft that were accepted by the Army Air Forces during World War II. This was an arsenal of bombers and fighters capable of inflicting considerable damage on the enemy. Aircraft factories also built 101,533 non-combat aircraft for reconnaissance (3,918), transport (23,929), training (57,623), communications (13,643) and special purposes (2,424). Overall, the United States built

Exhibit 6.6

USA Leading Producer of Military Aircraft in WWII

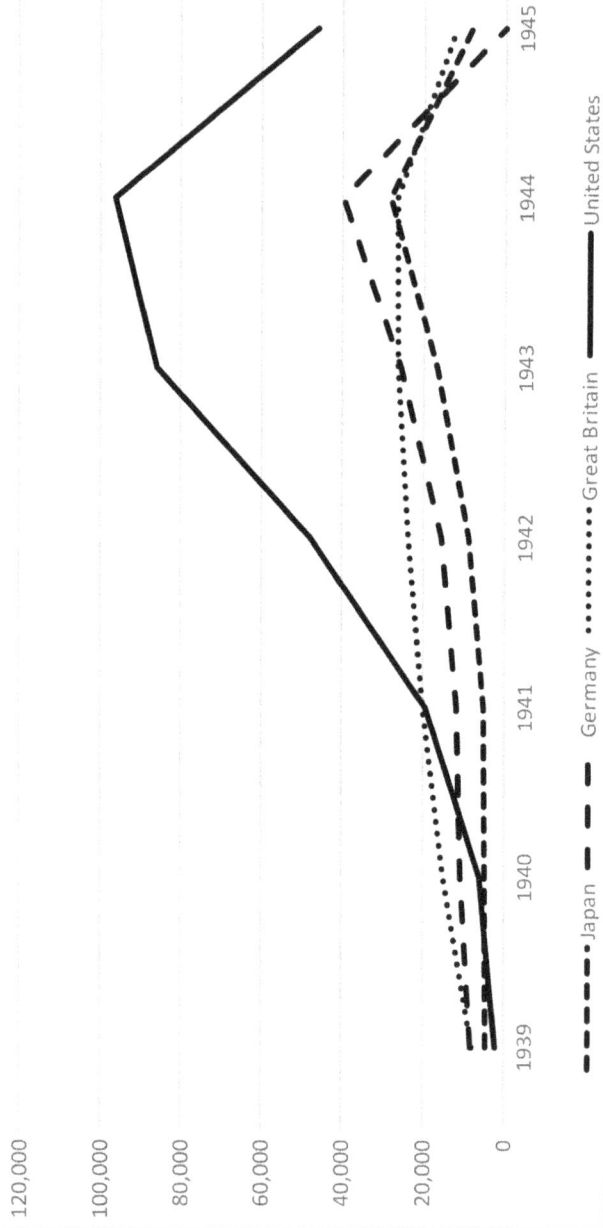

120,000

100,000

80,000

60,000

40,000

20,000

0

1939 1940 1941 1942 1943 1944 1945

Japan — — —   Germany ••••••   Great Britain ──── United States

299,293 aircraft for the war.[113] Of the planes built, 33 percent were bombers and 33 percent were fighters. They were sophisticated flying machines that required well-trained individuals and crews to get the most out of them, and John Cooney and Meyer Osofsky would be members of crews trained to fly them in combat during World War II.

In a message to Congress on the progress of the war on September 17, 1943, President Roosevelt spoke of the importance of airpower:[114]

> *"When Hitler was forced to the conclusion that his offensive was broken, and he must go on the defensive, he started boasting that he had converted Europe into an impregnable fortress. But he neglected to provide that fortress with a roof."*

With the support of Roosevelt, the United States had mobilized and was well on its way to producing the airpower needed to drop bombs over Hitler's supposedly impenetrable fortress of Europe.

Willow Run

Willow Run was one of the great mobilization stories of World War II. In December 1940, Jimmy Doolittle and George Mead approached Edsel Ford, the president of Ford, and Charles Sorensen, Ford's wizard of mass production, about helping Consolidated Aircraft to build B-24 heavy bombers. Sorensen was a tough, no-nonsense production expert known as "Cast-Iron Charlie." Sorensen wanted to check out how Consolidated was building the B-24 before Ford Motor Company committed to help.[115]

When he visited the Consolidated plant in January 1941, he learned that it wanted to tool up to build a B-24 heavy bomber a day. He said Ford could build one every hour, but only if Ford could make the complete plane, not simply parts of the plane which was what Consolidated had in mind. Edsel Ford was on board with Sorensen's assessment.[116] As a result, Ford Motor Company contracted with the Army Air Corps on February 25, 1941, to build the B-24 Liberator four-engine bombers at a new Ford factory to be constructed at Willow Run near Ypsilanti, Michigan, which was outside of Detroit.[117]

Sorensen, like Knudsen, was born in Denmark, immigrated to the United States, and became a key executive for Henry Ford, but they had different personalities. Knudsen knew the business but wanted to run it his way. For ten years, Henry Ford's way and his way were in sync. When he disagreed with the direction Ford was going in, he moved on. At the time, Ford said: "I consider Mr. Knudsen the best production man in the United States." He also said that Knudsen was too strong for him to handle because it was his business and he wanted to run it his way. Knudsen said he left because he did not want to quarrel with Mr. Ford, who he had a great deal of respect for, and because he wanted to keep his self-respect by finding another job in which he could do things his way.[118]

It is noteworthy that Knudsen felt he had an obligation to his stockholders who owned the company and to his employees who worked for the company. He aimed to protect the savings of the stockholders who were invested in the company and to protect the jobs of the employees who invested their skill in the company. In his ten years at Ford, the company's stock was tightly held by the Ford family, but employees increased from 15,000 to 100,000. In his nineteen years at General Motors, stockholders increased from 3,931 to 249,386 and employees increased from 65,665 to 393,493.[119] During his time with General Motors, it became the largest corporation in the world, and he became its president. Thus, Knudsen's way worked out very well for both Ford and General Motors.

Sorenson, while abrasive in personality, did things Ford's way. He did what Ford told him to do and continued to be a key executive at Ford. He was competitive and he was smart, and he laid out in one night his vision for the Ford plant to build B-24s and was a prime mover in making his vision a reality. With war on the horizon, he was given responsibility for Ford's defense contracts. Even though the two Danish-Americans did not get along personally, they both wanted to succeed in destroying Hitler's war machine, especially after Hitler invaded their birth country in 1940.[120]

Because the demand for heavy bombers was so great, the Army Air Corps decided in 1941 to form a pool of manufacturers to produce the B-24 Liberators. While Consolidated Aircraft designed it, Ford, North American Aircraft, and Douglas Aircraft were recruited to help build it.[121] They took a page out of the B-17 production experience in which Boeing designed and built the bomber, but Douglas Aircraft and Lockheed (Vega) also chipped in to help build enough of them to satisfy the demand.[122]

General Arnold's tactful lobbying on the importance of airpower paid off. On June 20, 1941, the Army Air Corps became the Army Air Forces. This organizational change put the Army Air Forces on a par with the Army Ground Forces, allowing Arnold to report directly to General Marshall. Even though the Army Air Corps became the Army Air Forces in 1941, many veterans still refer to it as the Army Air Corps. In any case, this organizational change was a real boost for the program to enhance airpower.[123]

According to Secretary of War Stimson, the purpose of the Army Air Forces was "to place our air arm under one responsible head...to provide the ground forces with essential aircraft...and to permit Air Force autonomy to the degree needed."[124] Hap Arnold now had the authority and support to enhance the airpower needed for World War II. The Germans ruled the skies early in the war, but this started to change with the support of Roosevelt and the development of American airpower.

The Willow Run bomber plant made history. It began operation in 1942 as the largest factory in the world, creating many jobs and mass-producing many B-24s, including the one that John Cooney and Meyer Osofsky would go down in over Italy three years later. By that time, the plant would be employing 42,500 people, only 10,000 of whom had been Ford employees with mass production experience before the war. The others had to be trained to work on an assembly line, just as many civilians had to be trained to become soldiers, sailors, and airmen.[125] Once again, teamwork was the key.

Many of the workers at Willow Run were women. The increase in the demand for aircraft and the decrease in the supply of men, who went to war, created opportunities for women in industrial jobs. Between 1940 and 1945, the female percentage of women in the U.S. workforce increased from 27 percent to nearly 37 percent and gave rise to the popular "Rosie the Riveter" icon of a female worker flexing her arm with the slogan "We can do it!" And, indeed, they could do it, and do it well.[126] And it's a good thing that they could do it well because 5 to 7 million women worked in defense industry jobs during World War II.[127]

Willow Run also provided opportunities for little people whose small stature and strong arms enabled them to do riveting and assembly work in tight spaces.[128] For example, on the wing assembly line they were small enough to get inside the wings to hold the steel plates in place so that rivet gun operators on the outside could attach the aluminum skin of the wing to the steel plates in a secure and proper manner. Ford personnel searched all over the country to find little people to help build planes and recruited about 350 of them.[129]

The Ford Motor Company had a history of hiring African Americans going back to the late 1920s.[130] However, they worked in Ford's city operations in Detroit where many of them lived. Willow Run was built in a rural area, about forty miles from Detroit, where housing was an issue. The Federal Public Housing Administration built Willow Run Village to deal with this issue, but mostly white families moved in at a time when integration was a big issue. While many blacks worked with whites, not many lived in the same neighborhoods as whites. Consequently, while black women and men worked at Willow Run, not as high a percentage of them were represented there as in Ford's city operations.[131] Nevertheless, the war brought together diverse employees such as women, little people, and African Americans to work for the common purpose of producing war materiel to support the troops. Diversity was a by-product of the war.

The B-24 made history as the most-produced aircraft of World War II. It is difficult to determine the exact number of B-24s built during World War II, but most estimates are that almost 18,500 were built and accepted for use by the military.[132] Most went to the Army Air Forces, but some went to the Navy. While the B-24 was designed by Consolidated Aircraft in San Diego, the Willow Run factory produced more B-24s than any other factory. It built 6,792 complete Liberators and made what were called "knock-down kits" with parts for 1,893 others to be assembled at other factories. Consolidated Aircraft's two factories in San Diego and Fort Worth produced 6,725 and 3,034, respectively. North American Aircraft's Dallas factory and Douglas Aircraft's Tulsa factory produced 966 and 964, respectively (Exhibit 6.7).[133]

The original B-24 design was modified many times based on feedback from its users—the air crews who flew them in combat and the ground crews who kept them running. The most-produced model was the B-24J (6,678) that John Cooney and Meyer Osofsky went down in over Italy followed by the B-24H (3,100), the B-25D (2,728) that Louie Zamperini went down in over the Pacific Ocean, the B-25M (2,593), and the B-25L (1,677). Other models (A, E and G) were produced in smaller numbers.[134] Russell J. Flint, the co-pilot of the B-24J that Cooney and Osofsky went down in over Italy, flew 27 combat mission during World War II—12 in a B-24H, 12 in a B-24J, and 3 in a B-24M.[135] The fact that the B-24 was the most produced American military aircraft during World War II reflects its usefulness as a weapon of war.[136]

The Cooney Family

John Cooney was one of the many Americans who provided the manpower behind the airpower for World War II, and every one of them has a story to tell but most never got to tell their story. When John entered the service in May 1943, he was working for the Western Electric Company in Kearny, New Jersey, one of the many companies contributing to the war effort.[137] College was not an option for John because his family couldn't afford it. After the

Exhibit 6.7
B-24 Liberators Built and Accepted by the Military During World War II

Year	Consolidated San Diego, CA	Consolidated Fort Worth, TX	Ford Ypsilanti, MI (Willow Run)	North American Dallas, TX	Douglas Tulsa, TX	Total
1940	7	0	0	0	0	7
1941	169	0	0	0	0	169
1942	1,123	50	24	8	0	1,205
1943	2,345	1,233	1,291	394	61	5,324
1944	2,450	1,751	3,991	562	905	9,659
1945	631	0	1,486	0	0	2,117
Total	6,725	3,034	6,792	964	966	18,481

war, he and many other men and women, including minorities, who could not afford college before the war, would be able to attend college, thanks to the GI Bill. The official name of the GI Bill is the Servicemen's Readjustment Act of 1944. It was passed by Congress to help veterans of World War II adjust to a civilian life in peacetime after a military life in wartime.[138]

During the first three decades of the twentieth century, Western Electric was one of the largest distributors of electrical equipment in the United States. During the third decade, however, it lost some business because its biggest customer, the Bell System, was adversely affected by the Great Depression. In fact, the 1930s was the only decade of the twentieth century in which the number of telephones produced in the United States went down.[139]

World War II turned things around for Western Electric because the federal government, in mobilizing for war, became its biggest customer. The company ended up providing more than 30 percent of all electronic gear for the war.[140] John joined the company just as the tide turned and became a job setter.[141] When he left for the service, he was a foreman responsible for readying and adjusting the machinery for tooling on a production line.[142] It wouldn't be long before he would be readying and adjusting a different type of machinery—machine guns and bomb mechanisms—for overseas combat missions in a B-24 heavy bomber.

When the United States entered World War II, John and his brother Robert were two of the many young men called into service to defend their country against dictators—Hitler, Mussolini, and Hirohito—who posed a threat to America's precious freedoms. These threats united America for a common purpose in a way that has not been seen since. Young men everywhere wanted to go overseas to join the fight, and family members at home wanted to help support them. Many young women also wanted to join the fight, and many did but were not yet allowed to bear arms on the battlefield. The country had not yet been diversified to allow women to fight alongside men on the battlefield.

Three famous people were born in the same month as John—Joseph Heller, James Arness, and Prince Rainier III of Monaco. All three, like him, would serve in World War II—Heller as a bombardier for the 340th Bomb Group of the Army Air Forces, Arness as an infantryman for the Third Infantry Division of the U.S. Army, and Rainier as an officer with the French Free Army.[143]

After the war, Heller would write *Catch-22*, a classic American novel;[144] Arness would star in *Gunsmoke*, the longest, prime-time television series of the 20th century;[145] and Prince Rainier III would rule the Principality of Monaco for almost fifty-six years.[146] War engages people from all walks and stations of life, and no war engaged more people than World War II.

John had something in common with Prince Rainier—Grace Kelly. After the war, John, a handsome and always resourceful young man, would, while attending college, take advantage of his good looks and do some modeling. One of the models he worked with was Grace Kelly.[147] Years later, after a successful career as a model and movie actress, Kelly would leave Hollywood to marry Prince Rainier III and become the beautiful Princess of Monaco.

John also had something in common with five other famous men—Jimmy Stewart, George McGovern, Joseph P. Kennedy, Jr., Chuck Bednarik, and Louis Zamperini. They all flew combat missions during World War II in a B-24 heavy bomber. Stewart the actor and McGovern the politician were B-24 pilots. Kennedy, the older brother of President John F. Kennedy, was a pilot of the Navy version of the B-24 called the PB4Y patrol bomber and was killed while flying on a secret mission. Bednarik the pro football player was a waist gunner in a B-24 and Zamperini, whose life was the subject of three biographies and a movie, was a bombardier in a B-24.[148] Again, war draws people from all walks of life together for a common purpose—in this case to defend the United States from countries ruled by dictators who posed a threat to the American way of life.

John signed up with the Army Air Forces, and his path led to the Mediterranean Theater of War (Exhibit 6.8). His brother, Robert, called Bob, signed up with the Army and his path led to the Marines in the Pacific Theater of War. According to Bob's son Brendan, his father started in the Army but was promoted to the Marines because he knew shorthand.[149] Brendan said he served with the Marines in Hawaii, the Marianas, and Guam. He also said his father once wrote his mother Anna a letter when he was in the Marianas and had to have a tooth pulled without an anesthetic.[150] Ouch! He would serve in the Pacific until the end of the war.

Their mother Anna was unable to follow them abroad, but she did her part at home. World War II was an "all-in" war in which everyone chipped in to help support the troops. Families were strong units that came together to help each other, and this type of support became invaluable when the country went to war. It brought out the best on the home front as mothers, fathers, sisters, brothers, wives, and others chipped in to help those in harm's way. Anna became a driver in a motor pool for the Newark Signal Corps.[151] Women were needed for non-combat jobs to free up men for combat duty, prompting Congress to pass a bill on May 15, 1942, to create the Women's Army Auxiliary Corps (WAAC).[152]

Because Anna had a family to support and could not travel, she was unable to join the WAAC, so she did the next best thing in becoming a civilian

Exhibit 6.8
Staff Sergeant John J. Cooney
Courtesy of Cooney Family

"woman in uniform." She drove Army personnel in Army vehicles. With a husband having served in the last war and two sons serving in the current war, she qualified for the job. While she wasn't a WAAC, it can be said that this excerpt from a chapter entitled "Women in Uniform" in the book *American Home Front in World War II* by Richard Clay Hanes surely applied to her:[153]

> *"Patriotism was the main reason women volunteered to serve in the WAAC. Sometimes they volunteered because there were no men of fighting age in their family; in other cases, they wanted to show support for a male family member in the service. Several of the first group of volunteers were widows from the Pearl Harbor attack. Many volunteers saw the WAAC as a chance to combine adventure and patriotic service. WAAC volunteers came from all over the country."*

Anna was called a "chauffeurette" and was assigned to a motor pool for the Newark Signal Corps.[154] She drove inspection officers around in a drab, olive-green 1941 Ford Army staff car (Exhibit 6.9).[155] Her son Peter said she was popular in the neighborhood because she had gas at a time when gas was being rationed, as were many other products that were needed for the war.[156]

The Army Signal Corps had a huge responsibility to develop the communications equipment needed for World War II. During World War I, wire communications was the modus operandi, and was supplemented by runners, motorcycles, messengers, and even carrier pigeons. [157] In World War II, with more mobile ground forces as well as significantly more air forces, laying wire no longer cut it.[158] Radio communications became critical in World War II, and the Signal Corps was responsible for developing, procuring, and furnishing dependable radios and other mobile communications equipment.[159]

The radio was one of the wonders of the early twentieth century as it freed long-distance communication from the constraints of wires.[160] An offshoot of radio was radar (radio detection and ranging) which was used for "detecting, locating, and recognizing objects at considerable distances." [161] Radar is in essence seeing with radio waves and was put into airplanes to locate bombing targets when darkness or overcast conditions made the targets difficult to sight by eye.[162] In 1944, when John was overseas flying bombing missions, his former employer, Western Electric, was the largest manufacturer of radar in the United States, supplying more than one-half

145

Exhibit 6.9: Anna Cooney - Driver for the Newark Signal Corps.
Courtesy of Cooney Family

of all the airborne and shipborne radar sets. It was doing its part to support the war effort by producing communications equipment for the military.[163]

Since the Signal Corps contracted and subcontracted with many companies that developed and supplied communications equipment to the military, quality control was an important issue which led to the creation of the Signal Corps Inspection Agency.[164] Its national headquarters was in Dayton, Ohio, with five zone headquarters in San Francisco, Chicago, Newark, Philadelphia, and Dayton. Each zone conducted inspections to ensure the quality of the communications equipment being produced for the military.[165]

At that time, Lieutenant Colonel Frank Prina was the commanding officer of the Newark Signal Corps Inspection Zone, and Anna was one of the chauffeurettes who drove inspectors to their inspections. She was proud to support the military, and did her job well, prompting Prina to recommend her for an Efficiency Award. The citation commended her for "outstanding efficiency in the performance of duty during the six-month period ending January 15, 1944."[166]

Western Electric, her son's former employer, was so large that in the month of April 1942 forty Signal Corps Inspectors from the Philadelphia, Chicago, San Francisco, and Wright Field districts, along with inspectors from the Army Air Forces' Aircraft Radio Laboratory at Wright Field, were focused on inspecting the work it was doing for the military.[167] The Aircraft Radio Laboratory was "responsible for the research, development, and inspection of aircraft and radar equipment."[168]

While Anna became a chauffeurette to help support the war, her son John went to war for a specific reason he mentioned in a 2010 interview for a television show called *Heroes on Our Island.* The show profiled ordinary people living on Long Island who had done extraordinary things to make the world a better place. John, then a resident of the Long Island State Veterans Home, was featured on one of the shows. When asked why he went to war, he said he objected to all the Jewish people being killed.[169]

John entered the service at Fort Dix, New Jersey, the same place where his father entered the service twenty-six years earlier when it was called Camp Dix. It was renamed Fort Dix on March 8, 1939, when it became a permanent Army post.[170] As did his father before him, John went through basic training there for three months. After that, he trained to be an aerial gunner at Lowry Field Gunnery School in Colorado and Tyndall Field Gunnery School in Florida.[171]

This training prepared him for further training as a ball-turret gunner on a B-24 Liberator, a four-engine heavy bomber. It had a ten-man crew and could carry a heavy bomb load a long way. John would become well acquainted with the aircraft while training with his crew in the States and would put his training to good use in Europe flying thirty-five combat missions on a B-24 during World War II.[172]

Chapter 7

TRAINING FOR COMBAT MISSIONS

There were many challenges to be met in going from a peacetime economy to a wartime economy. Building B-24s was one of them because they were sophisticated flying machines with lots of parts. Manpower was required to put the parts together and this had to be done in a timely manner because they were needed to fight a war. Each B-24 had 550,000 parts and required 700,000 rivets to connect the parts. With the war draining the supply of manpower, a door was opened for women to fill the gap, and they did so admirably, as symbolized by the iconic Rosie the Riveter. Considering that almost 18,500 B-24s were manufactured during the war and that each required 700,000 rivets, it took almost 1.3 billion rivets to build the B-24s. Since the job of riveting fell mostly to women with a handful of little people helping, one can see how Rosie the Riveter became an icon of the war.[1]

Training crews to fly B-24s in combat was another challenge. Crew members had to be thoroughly trained in different disciplines in addition to learning to operate as a team to achieve the precision necessary to find targets in enemy territory thousands of miles away and drop bombs on them from as high as five miles.[2] It took time to train crews to develop the skills necessary to operate these sophisticated flying machines in combat. Consequently, as soon as they rolled the B-24s off the assembly lines, they were flown to Army airfields set up around the country to train crews for combat missions.

The Beast

The B-24 was a beast. It was big and foreboding and could inflict a lot of damage. It was rugged, it lacked grace and beauty, and its high wing and soft underbelly made it unsafe to ditch at sea.[3] The popular 2010 book and 2014 movie, *Unbroken*, shows how tragic ditching a B-24 at sea could be. The beast was hard to get into, uncomfortable to be in, and hard to fly. The only crew members with seat belts were the pilot and co-pilot. It flew at high altitudes in extremely cold weather with the bomb bay open on bombing runs, requiring the crew to wear bulky fleece-lined clothing for warmth, oxygen masks for breathing, and flak suits for protection.[4]

It flew long distances yet didn't have a bathroom or even a toilet. It had a relief tube in the front and back of the plane, but it was difficult to use under freezing conditions with bulky clothing. It also had a receptacle with a wax paper bag that was even more difficult to use.[5] If someone in the front of the plane used the tube, the ball-turret gunner wanted to know so he could turn his turret around to avoid his window from being sprayed by urine which could freeze on his window and obstruct his view.[6]

The beast was built for destruction, not comfort or safety.[7] While it was originally designed to fly 3,000 miles at 300 miles per hour at an altitude of 35,000 feet,[8] it's range, speed, and altitude depended on factors such as the weight of its armaments and the weight of its bomb load. For example, a B-25J model, the plane that John went down in over Italy, could fly 3,300 miles as a ferry without armaments or bombs, but could only fly 1,700 miles carrying a bomb load of 5,000 pounds and additional defense armaments found on the later J model. Its maximum speed was 290 miles an hour at an altitude of 25,000 feet with a maximum service ceiling of 28,000 feet, or five and a half miles.[9]

The B-24 Liberator also had the firepower to wreak havoc on attacking fighters with its ten fifty-caliber machine guns—two each in its nose, top turret, ball turret, and tail, and one on each side of its waist. It was tailor-made to suit its purpose—to fly high and deep into enemy territory to destroy the ability of the enemy to wage war by bombing the factories that made the weapons of war, the oil refineries that fueled them, and the supply lines that delivered them to the battlefront. Its name, the Liberator, also suited its purpose—to liberate millions of people from Nazism and fascism. The fact that more B-24s were built than any other American airplane during the war is a testimony to its key role in helping to win the war.[10]

Crew Responsibilities

The B-24 was typically staffed by a crew of ten—four officers and six enlisted men. The four officers were the pilot, co-pilot, navigator, and bombardier. The six enlisted men were the nose-turret gunner, the flight engineer who was also the top-turret gunner, the radio operator who was also a waist gunner, the ball-turret gunner, a second waist gunner, and the tail-turret gunner. The bombardier, navigator and nose-turret gunner were in the nose compartment. The pilot and co-pilot were on the flight deck, and the radio operator and the flight engineer were behind them. On bomb runs, the flight engineer manned the top-turret machine guns, the radio operator manned one of the waist machine guns while another waist gunner manned the other waist machine gun. The ball-turret gunner was behind the bomb bay in the ball turret, which he climbed into, was lowered, and manned his machine guns during combat. The tail-turret gunner was in the back of the plane manning his machine guns. On some missions, a photographer came as an eleventh crew member and was situated between the waist gunners and tail-turret gunner by the camera hatch and the camera installation used to film the bombing results.

The pilot was responsible for commanding the crew and flying the aircraft, and the co-pilot helped him. They had to ensure that the aircraft was properly inspected by crew members before every mission and they had to be prepared to fly the aircraft in hazardous conditions such as adverse weather, enemy attack, and at night. They had to maintain flight records and report observations made during missions and, like all members of the crew, they had to be able to fly at high altitudes and use the oxygen and the interphone equipment.[11]

The navigator was responsible for getting the aircraft to the target area at a predetermined time and needed to know different techniques of navigation to get there such as dead reckoning (using a past known position and mathematical calculations of time, speed, distance, and direction), pilotage (using visual markers such as roads, rivers, and railroads and using maps or charts), celestial navigation (using the stars, moon, sun, and horizon to calculate positions), and radio navigation (using radio waves from locations with known positions). He also needed to test and inspect all navigation equipment prior to the flight and to furnish crew members in flight with data such as wind direction and velocity, ground speed, and drift on any heading.[12]

The bombardier was responsible for sighting and hitting the target with the plane's bombs. He had to inspect and test the bombing equipment prior to the flight and be proficient in sighting the target during a bomb run by adjusting the bombsight for specific conditions such as groundspeed, altitude, and drift. By transposing these conditions into the bombsight in accordance with mathematical tables and adjusting the bombsight as he neared the target, he had to determine the point in space at which to release the bombs to hit the target.[13]

The six enlisted personnel were all aerial gunners during combat trained to protect the aircraft from enemy attack. They had to inspect their machine guns before each mission; load, aim, fire, and reload their machine guns during missions; and inspect their weapons after missions. Those firing from a turret were also responsible for maintaining the turret including preflight and postflight inspections.[14]

The top-turret gunner was also the flight engineer, or aircraft mechanic, responsible for maintaining a constant check on the aircraft's mechanical functioning and making limited repairs and mechanical adjustments while in flight. He was also responsible for transferring fuel from one tank to another to maintain a balance of the aircraft, and after each mission he had to report any needed repairs to the ground maintenance crew.[15]

One of the waist gunners was also the radio operator responsible for the aircraft's transmitting and receiving equipment used to communicate within the aircraft, with other aircraft, and with ground personnel. He had to have a thorough working knowledge of combined radiotelephone and radiotelegraph procedures and authentication. He had to be able to tune the radio equipment accurately and quickly to any required frequency and to maintain calibration charts, revising transmitter tuning data as necessary. He also had to inspect the radio equipment and keep it operational by making minor repairs if necessary.[16]

In addition to being an aerial gunner, the plane's armorer had to inspect, repair, and maintain equipment such as bomb racks, bomb shackles, and bomb release mechanisms and make sure the bombs were correctly loaded on the bomb racks so that they would release properly and be armed to detonate at a specified time such as when they hit the target or some specified time after impact.[17]

Bombs were delivered to the aircraft by ordnance, the branch of the armed forces that stored and supplied weapons and ammunition. Typically, ordnance personnel inserted a fuze in each bomb and added an arming wire. The fuze was a device that caused the detonation of an explosive charge at a specified time which could be upon impact or sometime after impact. The arming wire was a long wire strung from the nose of the bomb through two lugs on the bomb to the tail of the bomb with a swivel loop in the middle of the wire that would be attached to the shackle and used later to pull the arming wire from the bomb when it was released to arm the bomb for detonation. Bombs were also checked upon delivery to be sure they were fuzed with an arming wire intact and were not damaged in any way.[18]

Before the bombs were loaded on the aircraft, the plane's armorer removed the shackles on the bomb racks that would hold the bombs on the racks. Each bomb would be attached to a shackle on the ground. The swivel loop on the arming wire of each bomb also had to be carefully attached to each shackle before the shackle with the bomb attached was lifted and slid back into its position on the bomb rack. Thus, each bomb was connected to the bomb rack at three points—the two releasable hooks on the shackle that held each bomb in place and the swivel loop of the arming wire. When each bomb was released by the bombardier, it would fall away from the two hooks. The arming wire that kept a small propeller in the bomb from spinning would be ripped from the bomb, causing a propeller to begin spinning as the bomb fell. After so many revolutions, the spinning propeller would arm the fuze of the bomb so that the bomb's explosive charge would detonate when it hit the target or afterwards if it had been armed in that manner.[19]

Dale Satterthwaite, a B-25 pilot with the 340th Bomb Group who flew combat missions over Italy, tells a story in his memoirs of an instance on May 12, 1944, when a fragmentation bomb dropped by one plane hit another plane below it in the same formation. A fragmentation bomb is used to bomb smaller targets such as troops or parked planes. When it explodes, it scatters fragments of steel called shrapnel which can be as deadly as bullets. At thirty pounds, fragmentation bombs are a lot smaller than general-purpose, high-explosive 500- or 1,000-pound bombs which are used to destroy larger targets such as buildings. A fragmentation bomb landed in the cockpit between the pilot and the co-pilot and didn't explode because it hadn't fallen far enough to arm itself for detonation. The co-pilot, who was on his first mission, panicked and bailed out while the more-experienced pilot picked up the bomb and tossed it out the same hatch the co-pilot bailed through, then flew the plane back to the base. This was an embarrassing experience for the co-pilot.[20]

Even if a bomb, which had not fallen far enough to arm itself, hit a plane, it could still destroy the plane if it ignited its gasoline tanks. This happened on January 14, 1944, to a B-24H Liberator flown by Second Lieutenant Harold E. Pickard on a mission from Grottaglie Airfield, near Taranto on the foot of Italy, to bomb the town of Mostar, Yugoslavia. According to the tail-turret gunner, Staff Sergeant Robert O. Hansen, their plane was hit by three bombs dropped from another plane in their formation. The bombs landed in the front of the aircraft.[21]

Hansen figured one of the bombs hit near the upper turret and ignited the gasoline tanks, causing an explosion that broke the plane in half. The only survivors were Hansen and a photographer, Sgt. Charles LaMarca, who was near him in the back of the plane. The other nine members of the crew weren't so lucky. Hansen and LaMarca ended up in a prisoner of war camp with some crew members of other planes on the mission.[22]

Bombs aboard an aircraft always had to be handled with care. If for some reason a mission were aborted, and the crew didn't want to land with live bombs in the bomb bay, they could disarm the bombs by making sure the arming wire wouldn't be pulled from the bombs and then salvo the bombs, which means release them. By disarming a bomb, the propeller would not be activated and begin spinning, and the bomb would not be armed to explode when it landed or when it was set up to explode before it was disarmed.[23]

Many bombs dropped during World War II never detonated because they weren't armed for various reasons. To this day, many remain a threat to explode. An estimated 2.7 million tons of bombs were dropped over Europe during World War II. Half of them were estimated to have been dropped over Germany, and as many as 10 percent of them are still in danger of exploding someday.[24] The threat of live bombs is something Germany must still live with over seventy-nine years after World War II.

To deal with this ongoing threat, Germany requires a certification that the ground is free of unexploded bombs before any construction project can begin. As expected, the certification process is dangerous. More than 500 tons of bombs are defused every year in Germany. Since 2000, eleven bomb technicians have been killed trying to defuse live bombs.[25] In 2010, three members of a bomb squad were killed trying to defuse a bomb dropped on the town of Göttingen during World War II, and two others were seriously injured.[26] In 2015, 20,000 people in the city of Cologne had to be evacuated so that a bomb squad could defuse a bomb.[27] In 2016, 54,000 people in Augsburg had to be evacuated for the same reason.[28] In 2017, 50,000 people in Hanover had to evacuated so that three unexploded World War II bombs could be removed from a construction site.[29] In 2019, about 600 nearby residents were evacuated so a 500-pound bomb in the Main River in Frankfurt, which was too volatile to be transported to shore, could be detonated. The explosion "sent a gush of water shooting 70 feet high" and could be heard miles away.[30]

John Cooney recalled one occasion when, after the bombs were released, one of them was still hanging in the bomb bay. Because it was dangerous to land with a live bomb swinging in the bomb bay, he had to walk to the bomb on a narrow catwalk with the bomb bay doors open to release the bomb from its shackle. Years later he told his brother Peter that he attached a lifeline to his belt and used a sludge hammer to free the bomb. This was a part of his job that was precarious because he had to do this without a parachute and the catwalk was less than a foot wide. One slip and he could have been swinging in the open bomb bay in a speeding plane miles above the ground.[31]

John was rather large for a ball-turret gunner. The turret was small to reduce drag when lowered into position below the belly of the aircraft, and so it was typically operated by a small man. John was six feet tall and weighed one-hundred and fifty pounds, so it was a tight squeeze for him. The ball turret was a metal and plexiglass ball with twin-fifty machine guns and an eighteen-inch window for sighting a target. It was lowered beneath the plane for combat, but otherwise was retracted into the fuselage for take-offs and landings.[32]

When entering enemy territory, John would climb into the ball turret through a door, so his back would be to the door and the guns would be pointed down. He placed his feet in footrests, crouched down so that his knees were almost up to his head, and gripped the two handles that would allow him to operate the turret and shoot the guns. Since there was no room for his parachute in the turret, he had to leave it in the fuselage. When secured inside the turret, he would lower the turret beneath the aircraft using electro-hydraulic controls.[33]

The ball-turret gunner sometimes needed help in getting lowered into position. Meyer Osofsky, a waist-gunner who was a crewmate and a tent-mate of John, recalls one instance during the war when he was flying with another crew. He was the right waist gunner helping to lower another ball-turret gunner into position and recalled: "There was a (i.e., hydraulic) valve with a red handle that needed to be opened (i.e., hand cranked) to lower the turret. I opened it and nothing happened. I closed it and opened it again and still nothing. When I closed it and opened it a third time, the ball dropped suddenly, jolting the gunner, and he called me a son-of-a-bitch. I figured that there must have been an air bubble to prevent the hydraulic fluid from activating the release mechanism the first couple of times."[34]

After the turret was in position beneath the aircraft, John would rotate it so that the guns were parallel to the ground. He would be curled up like a fetus in a womb with his hands on the guns and his feet in position to activate the intercom and sight the target. His thumbs would be used, as if he were playing a video game, to move the turret and fire the guns.[35] His headphones would be in his helmet and a microphone would be in his oxygen mask. He would test his guns to be sure they were ready for combat and, to keep warm in the sub-zero temperatures at high altitudes, he would plug in his flight suit. Once in his combat position in tight quarters with no room for his parachute, he would look for enemy aircraft and pray.[36]

FROM ONE WAR TO ANOTHER

George McGovern, who ran for President of the United States in 1972, was a B-24 pilot during World War II. Like John, he flew thirty-five combat missions to complete a tour of duty. McGovern had a deep respect for the ball-turret gunner. He felt it was the most terrifying position on the plane. The gunner was cramped in a ball suspended below the plane in an uncomfortable position in more ways than one. He thought it took a special kind of courage to man the ball-turret position.[37]

Paul M. Stevens was a chaplain with the 450th Bomb Group. He flew twenty-nine missions and was wounded on his last one, but his most heart-wrenching experience involved a B-24 ball-turret gunner who was stuck in his turret. The mechanism that lifted the turret had been shot away and the wheels could not be lowered because they lost their hydraulic system. The plane was running out of gas and needed to do a belly landing which meant the ball-turret gunner could not be saved. A colonel summoned Stephens and said the gunner wanted to talk to him. Over the interphone system, the gunner asked that his parents not be told how he was going to die, only to be told that he died in combat. He also asked the chaplain to pray for him as his plane hit the runway and destroyed the turret with him in it. Stephens sent his personal effects to his parents with a letter saying their son died bravely serving his country.[38] McGovern was right—it did take a special kind of courage to man the ball turret position.

John had the courage to fly as a ball-turret gunner, and he also had the nightmares that went with the position. He was isolated from the rest of the crew in a bubble below the plane without a parachute. In his cramped quarters, he had a bird's-eye view of enemy fighters attacking and anti-aircraft batteries firing shells at them. He could see enemy shells explode and disburse deadly flak in their direction, and he could see their bombs hitting their targets with devastating effect. Meyer said John had awful nightmares that prompted him to volunteer for missions to get through his requisite thirty-five missions as soon as possible.[39]

The Crew

John was twenty-one years old in 1944 when he was a staff sergeant engaged in training with his B-24 crew in the States for overseas duty. His crew ranged in age from eighteen to twenty-seven and came from different parts of the country. John and four others were from the Northeast, four were from the Midwest, and one was from the Southwest. They had varying backgrounds and interests but were now being trained to come together as an efficient and effective flight crew of a heavy bomber (Exhibits 7.1 and 7.2).

Exhibit 7.1: Crew in States: Front row are officers Cylkowski, Goodson, Flint and Cookman. Back row are enlisted men Muth, Chin, Mosher, Osofsky, Orkin and Cooney. *Courtesy of David Chin*

Exhibit 7.2

Cookman's Crew Who Trained Together in the States

Crew Member	Position	Hometown
2nd Lt. Robert G. "Bob" Cookman	Pilot	Mason City, IA
2nd Lt. Russell J. "Russ" Flint	Co-Pilot	Chicago, IL
2nd Lt. Thaddeus "Ted" Cylkowski	Navigator	Simsbury, CT
2nd Lt Ray M. Goodson	Bombardier	Joliet, IL
S/Sgt. Hong Sing "Calvin" Chin	Nose-Turret Gunner	Hempstead, Long Island, NY
T/Sgt. David Orkin	Engineer/ Top-Turret Gunner	Forest Hills, Queens, NY
S/Sgt. Kirk G. Mosher	Radio Operator/Right Waist Gunner	Albuquerque, NM
T/Sgt. Meyer "Mike" Osofsky	Left Waist Gunner	Brooklyn, NY
S/Sgt. John J. Cooney, Jr.	Ball-Turret Gunner	North Bergen, NJ
T/Sgt. Charles J. "Chuck" Muth	Tail-Turret Gunner	Indianapolis, IN

Training For Combat Missions

The pilot was Second Lieutenant Robert "Bob" Cookman from Mason City, Iowa. Bob was twenty-four years old. He had two brothers and two sisters. He was raised in a close-knit, athletic family with cousins that lived within six blocks of each other and played sports together growing up. His cousin, Willie Cookman, was the oldest of the group. Willie's brother, Jim, was the same age as Bob. Jim played end for the 1938 Mason City High School state champion football team, and Bob was the quarterback who threw passes to him, as he had done numerous times in neighborhood games. Their yearbook said Bob was an expert field general and Jim was an excellent pass receiver.[40]

Bob also played high school baseball with his younger brother Richard, who was called "Mickey."[41] One summer, Bob, Jim, and Mickey (Richard) played together on the Mason City American Legion Junior baseball team. Dan Cookman, the younger brother of Willie and Jim, was the batboy. That summer, the four of them had their picture taken with Tom Mix, the cowboy film star who was in town with his circus and wild west show. They all had fun growing up together.[42]

After high school, Bob and Jim continued playing football together at Mason City Junior College, where Willie had played before them.[43] After junior college, Bob, Jim, and Mickey (Richard) played baseball together in the Mason City Industrial League.[44] Bob worked for Jacob E. Decker & Sons, a meat-packing plant that was a major employer in the community. A cousin, Harry, who went by his middle name Joe, said many family members worked at Decker & Sons at one time or another.[45]

When the war came, Bob and his cousins Willie, Jim, Dan, and Harry (Joe) left Mason City to serve their country. Bob and Dan joined the Army Air Forces. Willie and Harry (Joe) joined the Army, and Jim joined the Navy.[46] They were all now engaged in the serious business of war. Their fun together had come to an end—for some, a while, and for others, forever.

The co-pilot was Second Lieutenant Russell "Russ" John Flint from Chicago, Illinois. He was twenty-two years old, and Flint was not his birth name. His father, John Kravesky, was born in Allentown, Pennsylvania in 1893 to parents who came to America from Czechoslovakia. When John was a young man, World War I broke out and he served in France with G Company, 145th Infantry Regiment, 37th Division (Buckeye Division) and was wounded in action. He was shot in the right foot in the Baccarat sector of the Lorraine Front on July 31, 1918.[47] Years later, his son Russ would also serve his country honorably.

After the war, John became a fireman in Braddock, Pennsylvania where he met and married Selma Frohlich, who had immigrated to America from

Czechoslovakia in 1902 with her parents and her sister Margaret. Margaret attended the Palmer School of Chiropractic where she met and married Albert Kabana. She and her husband both graduated as a Doctor of Chiropractic in July 1920.[48]

Russ was born in Braddock on July 25, 1922, after which John decided to become a chiropractor like Margaret and Albert. He moved his family to Davenport, Iowa, to attend the Palmer School of Chiropractic, the first school of chiropractic in the world. Daniel David Palmer, considered to be the founder of this science of healing, started the school. John Kravesky studied there and received his Doctor of Chiropractic degree in April 1925.[49]

John's time in Davenport was bittersweet. It was sweet because he was pleased with his chiropractic experience. He loved the school as did his wife's sister Margaret and her husband Albert. In fact, Margaret and Albert loved the school so much that when they had a daughter, they named her Palmera after the school's founder. Twenty years later in 1942, Palmera also received a Doctor of Chiropractic degree from Palmer and went on to become a Fellow of the Palmer Academy of Chiropractic and the first woman to speak at a Palmer graduation. John's time in Davenport was bitter because they had a daughter Geraldine while he was attending Palmer, and she died at the age of four.[50] It was very bitter because a family never gets over the loss of a child.

After graduating from Palmer with his Doctor of Chiropractic degree in 1925, John decided to move to Chicago to set up a general chiropractic practice. He also decided to change his family name from Kravesky to Flint. It was a time when many people changed their names to sound less ethnic. Young Russ had lost his sister and now he had lost his birth name as well, but he was always resilient with a positive attitude.

Russ Flint attended Austin High School in Chicago and graduated in 1940. His yearbook listed his nickname as "Duck." He listed as his ambition to be as handsome as McNellis and must have been friends with Jim McNellis because McNellis's ambition was to be as handsome as Flint. His yearbook also characterized Russ as "Lucky, Loose, Happy."[51] He and McNellis clearly enjoyed their tongue-in-cheek humor and Russ would enjoy this type of humor with his friends for the rest of his life and beyond.

Russ was in the Army Junior Reserve Officers Training Corps (JROTC) in high school. The JROTC was established by the National Defense Act of 1919 to "instill in students in the United States secondary educational institutions the values of citizenship, service to the United States, personal responsibility, and a sense of accomplishment." Another purpose was to raise awareness of military service and encourage college-bound students to pursue a commission through ROTC in college.[52]

After high school, Russ attended the Aeronautical University of Chicago to study engineering and took courses such as mathematics, physics, and airplane theory.[53] Aeronautical University was established in 1929 as the Curtiss-Wright Aeronautical University. Its purpose was to provide formal ground instruction for the pilots of the Curtiss Flying Service. It was reorganized in 1933 as the Aeronautical University of Chicago to provide formal ground instruction for pilots as well as courses in the study of aviation mechanics, aviation administration, and aviation welding.[54]

Aeronautical University was the first accredited flight school in the Midwest to admit African American students and served as the entry point of some of the country's African American pioneering pilots such as Cornelius Coffey and his wife, Willa Brown. Cornelius founded the Coffey School of Aeronautics, the first African American-owned and operated private flight training academy in the United States. Willa Brown became the first African American woman to have both a mechanic's and a commercial pilot's license in the United States. They were both involved in the training of about 200 African American pilots who became Tuskegee Airmen, some of whom may have even flown escort missions for Russ's crew during World War II.[55]

After a year at Aeronautical University, Russ enlisted in the Army Air Forces on September 28, 1942.[56] He became an aviation cadet to become a pilot and received thirty-six weeks of training divided into four courses of nine weeks each. The first course consisted of general military training and preliminary groundwork prior to a flight program that involved three levels of training—primary, basic, and advanced. During nine-weeks of primary training (PT), cadets flew sixty to sixty-five hours in Stearman PT-17s, Fairchild PT-19s, or Ryan PT-22s. During nine weeks of basic training (BT), cadets flew seventy hours in Vultee BT-13s. During nine weeks of advanced training (AT), cadets flew eighty hours in the North American AT-6. During advanced training, each cadet was assigned to bombardment training to fly bombers or pursuit training to fly fighters depending on his temperament and physique.[57]

Russ was assigned to fly bombers. He received his wings and was commissioned as a second lieutenant in the Army Air Forces on April 11, 1944, at Spence Field in Moultrie, Georgia. His class consisted of forty-three students.[58] Back in June 1941, the site of Spence Field, which was six miles southeast of Moultrie, consisted of swamp and tobacco farms. That month, it was selected to be a training field for aviation cadets. The field was officially built and named Spence Field on January 21, 1942, and the training of cadets began on February 22, 1942, with the first class graduating on April 29, 1942.[59]

Russ was well-suited to be a pilot. He had a knowledge of mathematics and some experience in the field of applied sciences, was in good shape with good reflexes, and could make rapid decisions. As previously mentioned, his yearbook characterized him as lucky, loose, and happy. He was preparing for war where luck is a good thing to have even though happiness is a tough emotion to feel when flying in harm's way. On the other hand, being able to stay loose in stressful situations is an asset when engaged in the dangerous business of war, and Russ had that ability.

The navigator was Second Lieutenant Thaddeus "Ted" Cylkowski from Simsbury, Connecticut. He was at twenty-six (soon to be twenty-seven), married, and the second oldest member of the crew. His grandparents on his father's side and his mother emigrated from Poland, but his father was born in Collinsville, Connecticut, about five miles from Simsbury where Ted grew up. Ted was the oldest of six children—four boys and two girls.[60] He loved music. As a youngster, he studied piano under R. Augustus Lawson, a talented, classically trained musician who was the dean of music teachers in the Hartford, Connecticut area.[61] At the age of sixteen, Ted was giving piano recitals of music composed by renowned Polish composer Frederic Chopin.[62]

Ted went on to study at the Juilliard School of Music, a prestigious school in New York City for musically gifted students. He studied piano and in May 1940 earned his diploma, the equivalent of a bachelor's college degree, after which he became a full-time musician until he entered military service on October 15, 1942.[63] While at Juilliard, he met and fell in love with one of its talented students, Doris Markus, who also studied piano and earned her diploma a year earlier than him in May 1939.[64] They married in 1943 in New York City when Ted was on leave from the service and had their wedding reception at the iconic Essex House on 59th Street overlooking Central Park.[65] When he returned to duty and went to crew training at Mountain Home Airfield in Idaho, Doris went with him.[66]

Two of Ted's brothers also served during World War II—Henry with the Marines and Edward, also called Kenny, with the Army's 69th Infantry in Belgium and Leipzig, Germany. His youngest brother Conrad would serve later with the Army during the Korean War.[67] His parents and his two sisters—Wanda and Irene—had plenty to worry about during World War II with Ted, Henry, and Kenny (Edward) serving in the military.

Training For Combat Missions

The bombardier was Second Lieutenant Ray M. Goodson from Joliet, Illinois. Ray was twenty years old. He had an older brother Glenn, who was also in the service, and two older sisters Aileen and Lila.[68] He graduated from Joliet Township High School in 1942 from which Glenn graduated in 1939. According to Ray's high school yearbook, he was active in several clubs, including the art and dramatic clubs. He also sang in a cappella choir and ran track.[69] In Ray's senior year of high school, Pearl Harbor was attacked, his brother Glenn enlisted, and a tragedy related to the war rocked his hometown.

Joliet Township was one of the towns selected to produce ammunition and explosives for the U.S. Army. Joliet was in Will County which had the highest unemployment in Illinois prompting the Chamber of Commerce to lobby hard for the facility.[70] It was selected because it had a suitable labor supply, access to main highways and rail lines, raw materials nearby, adequate electrical power, and large tracks of land to provide room for separation of facilities and expansion.[71] The government purchased thirty-six square miles of land from local farmers for $8 million and spent $81 million building the plants.[72] A fourteen-square mile area was used to build an operation to make explosives called the Kankakee Ordnance Works and a twenty-two square mile area was used to build an operation to pack the explosives into bombs, shells, and mines called the Elwood Ordnance Plant. Both plants were together referred to as the Joliet Army Ammunition Plant.[73]

Sanderson and Porter, a New York engineering firm, was hired in 1941 to build and operate the Elmwood plant and Du Pont was hired to build and operate the Kankakee plant.[74] The two plants were said to be the most sophisticated munitions operations in the world. During the war, the Elwood plant handled over 926 million bombs, shells, mines, and other munitions and the Kankakee plant produced over one billion pounds of TNT (trinitrotoluene, a powerful explosive chemical compound).[75]

On June 5, 1942, a month after Ray graduated from high school, a terrific explosion occurred in the Elwood Ordnance Plant at 2:41 am when workers on the night shift were loading anti-tank mines onto railroad cars. Something went terribly wrong and forty-eight people were killed, and many others were injured. What caused the explosion was never exactly determined despite an investigation. The blast shattered windows for miles around and was said to be heard as far away as Waukegan, Illinois, about sixty miles north of Joliet. It was one of the deadliest accidents in the history of Illinois.[76]

After high school, Ray went to work for Sanderson and Porter, the firm hired to build and operate the Elwood Ordnance Plant. It was a large facility and while the explosion put one of the twelve production units out of action, operations continued in the other units because the war was still going on and the military depended on the Joliet Army Ammunition Plant to provide ammunition for their weapons. The Elwood and Kankakee plants were government-owned, contractor-operator industrial (GOCO) facilities and were part of the "first wave" of GOCO facilities authorized in September 1940 to support the war as the United States geared up for war.[77]

Ray's brother Glenn was in the Army Air Forces as a liaison pilot with the Tenth Air Force in Burma and Ray soon followed him into the Army Air Forces as a bombardier in the Fifteenth Air Force in Italy. Ray went from a place that built bombs to a place that dropped them. He was trained to sight and bomb targets in enemy territory.[78] The explosion at the Elmwood plant gave him an appreciation of the dangerous work being done on the home front. He would soon gain an appreciation of the dangerous work being done on the battlefront.

The nose-turret gunner was Staff Sergeant Hong Sing "Calvin" Chin from Hempstead on Long Island, New York. He was nineteen years old. His son David doesn't know when he picked up the nickname Calvin but that's what the crew called him and that's what he was called after the war, along with simply "Cal." He was born in Canton, China in 1925 as Hong Suey Chin and came to America in 1938 when he was almost thirteen years old.[79] His parents, like most parents, wanted him to have a better life and the United States was the land of opportunity. Things have changed in China since then as China is now a rising world power challenging the United States as a world leader on many fronts.[80]

Long Island was known as "the cradle of aviation" because hundreds of civil, commercial, and military aircraft were built there during the 1920s and 1930s.[81] Calvin was in the middle of the cradle. He grew up near the Grumman Aircraft Engineering Corporation that would build Navy aircraft such as Wildcats, Hellcats, and Avengers for World War II. He also lived near the Republic Aviation Corporation that would build over 15,000 P-47 Thunderbolts for the war, some of which escorted his crew on combat missions to protect them from enemy fighters. In addition, he lived only three miles from Roosevelt Field where Charles Lindbergh took off on May 20, 1927, for his historic flight across the Atlantic Ocean.[82]

By the time Calvin arrived on Long Island, Roosevelt Field was "the largest and busiest civilian airfield in America with over 150 aviation businesses and 450 planes based there."[83] He was no doubt influenced by his environment because he became a student at the Roosevelt Aviation School which prepared students for careers in aviation. Consequently, when his country came calling, he entered the service in the Army Air Forces on December 15, 1943. He was activated for duty on January 5, 1944.[84]

The engineer and top-turret gunner was Technical Sergeant David Orkin from Forest Hills, a residential neighborhood in the borough of Queens in New York City. He was nineteen, eight months younger than Chin and the youngest member of the crew. He grew up not far from another member of the crew, Meyer Osofsky, who grew up in Brooklyn, another borough of New York City. He would befriend Meyer in the service and be in his wedding party after the war.[85]

David was an only child. He was born in New York City, where both of his parents were also born. His grandparents on both sides were immigrants. Both his father's parents came from Russia while his mother's father came from Austria and her mother from Hungary. According to the 1930 and 1940 Census reports, his father was a salesman for a haberdashery in 1930 and a life insurance agent in 1940.[86]

When David registered for the draft in 1943, he was working as a shipping clerk for the Henry Hudson Hotel in Manhattan, another borough of New York City.[87] The hotel had an interesting history. It was originally built by Anne Morgan, daughter of J.P. Morgan, as a clubhouse for the American Women's Association. It opened in 1929 and became a residence for unmarried professional women who were looking to get ahead in a man's world but were excluded from the men's clubs and corporate offices. Anne built it with her huge inheritance.[88]

In 1941, the American Women's Association went bankrupt, and the building became the Henry Hudson Hotel open to both sexes.[89] It was located on 57th Street and had 1,250 rooms and a swimming pool. During the war it was used to house military personnel being trained for overseas duty. For example, Naval Intelligence personnel lived there occupying several floors while learning codes. After the war in September 1945, historic chess matches took place in the hotel ballroom where ten leading chess masters of the United States played ten leading chess masters of the Soviet Union over the radio. Almost twenty years later in 1963-1964, the United States Chess Championship took place in the Henry Hudson Ballroom and was won by Bobby Fischer.[90]

David went to work at the Henry Hudson Hotel after high school and was working there when the United States Government took over several floors. He saw firsthand the impact of war on his hotel. He registered for the draft in 1943 at the age of eighteen.[91] After he was activated for duty and underwent intensive training in the States for combat duty overseas, he was on his way to experiencing the impact of the war on him personally.

The radio operator and right waist gunner was Sergeant Kirk G. Mosher from Albuquerque, New Mexico. Kirk was twenty-one years old. His father Frank emigrated from Canada to Lansing, Michigan where he met his wife Ruth and where she gave birth to five children. Kirk was the oldest and had two younger brothers, Dan and Jerry, and two younger sisters, Ruth and Jackie.[92] Frank was an accomplished musician when he moved his family to Albuquerque in 1932. He played the drums and banjo and helped form a Musician's Union in Albuquerque.[93] He also formed his own orchestra and raised his sons to love music.

Kirk took to music early. At the age of thirteen in 1936 he sang and played guitar at a Parent-Teacher Association meeting.[94] In 1937, he and his brother Dan, age twelve, played in a hillbilly band at a music and dance school.[95] In 1938, he played banjo in a popular hillbilly band composed of students from Albuquerque High School.[96] After high school, he devoted his career to music but had a day job.[97]

When Kirk signed up for the service at the age of nineteen, he was working for the U.S. Army Corps of Engineers in Albuquerque while pursuing his career in music.[98] In 1941, the U.S. Army Corps of Engineers in Albuquerque was assigned a military construction mission to support the U.S. Army and Army Air Forces which were preparing for the possibility of war. They got involved with the construction in 1941 of the Albuquerque Army Air Base which became a training center for bombardiers of B-17s and B-24s.[99] In 1942, it was renamed the Kirkland Army Air Base for Colonel Roy C. Kirkland, who died in 1941. He was a military aviation pioneer who learned to fly with the Wright brothers and in 1912 was the pilot of the first plane to fire a machine gun.[100]

In 1942, the United States was changing from a peacetime economy to a wartime economy and the U.S. Army Corps of Engineers embarked on a secret project to build an atomic bomb before the Nazis. Colonel Leslie Groves, a strong leader who supervised the construction of the Pentagon, was put in charge of the project called the Manhattan Project. Groves, who would have preferred to command soldiers in battle rather than civilian scientists on a project, was told that the bomb could win the war and was elevated to general to lead and manage the project.[101] To start with, he sought a scientist who understood what needed to be done to build such a bomb and J. Robert Oppenheimer was his choice.[102] Oppenheimer needed a laboratory to build the bomb and suggested a desert site in Los Alamos, New Mexico, an area he knew well as he and his brother had a ranch in the nearby Sangre de Cristo Mountains.[103] Among the projects of the Albuquerque District of the U.S. Army Corps of Engineers where Kirk worked was to build the infrastructure needed to build the bomb in the desert.[104] If Kirk had not gone into the service, he may have been involved in some way with the secret project to build the atomic bomb.

Kirk joined the Army Air Forces on May 3, 1943. He did his basic training at Sheppard Field in Texas, his radio training in Sioux Falls, South Dakota, and his gunnery training in Yuma, Arizona.[105] His two brothers followed him into the service. Dan and Jerry both served in the Marines during World War II.[106] Were it not for the war, the Mosher family would no doubt have played a lot of music together because their father Frank had his own orchestra and played the drums; Kirk played the guitar, banjo, mandolin and a mean lead guitar; Dan played the steel guitar; and Jerry played the banjo.[107] But Uncle Sam came calling, and Frank's band of sons heeded the call as he did in World War I.[108]

The left waist gunner was Technical Sergeant Meyer Osofsky from Brooklyn, New York. He was twenty years old. Meyer's parents were immigrants—his father Harry came from Russia and his mother Jennie from Romania.[109] Harry had experienced hard times in Europe and was a refugee who came to America by himself in steerage—a large open area in the lower part of a ship where immigrants of little means traveled en masse to America. He was sponsored by his aunt, who had previously immigrated to America. She met and helped him pass through Ellis Island, the gateway through which immigrants entered the United States for more than sixty years from 1892 to 1952.[110] As their ships entered New York Harbor, immigrants were greeted by the Statue of Liberty, the foremost American symbol of the freedom they were seeking for a better way of life.

Many immigrants, when they came to America, changed their names to sound less ethnic. Meyer's father's name in the old country was Herschel Osowski, but his aunt felt he needed to change it to assimilate better in the new country. She said that the "w" in his name sounded like an "f" in English so why not make it an f? So, just like that, "Herschel Osowski" from the old country became "Harry Osofsky" in the new country.[111]

Harry didn't speak English, but with the help of relatives was able to get a job in the textile industry and became a hard-working American citizen. When the United States entered World War I, Harry was working in the knitting business and registered for the draft. On his draft registration card, he listed his birthplace as Brest-Litovsk, Grodno, Russia.[112] Brest-Litovsk was a border city in Europe at a time when borders weren't stable. A border city might become part of a different country with a different culture at a different time. While Brest-Litovsk was Polish in character, it had been annexed to Russia when Harry was born but he grew up in a family that spoke Yiddish (to each other) and Polish (to the landowners), not Russian.[113] On March 3, 1918, Russia signed the Treaty of Brest-Litovsk with the Central Powers (Germany, Austria-Hungary, Ottoman Empire, and Bulgaria), ending its participation in World War I.[114]

When America entered World War I, so did Harry. He entered the Army on May 29, 1918, and served overseas with Company K of the 316th Infantry Regiment from July 9, 1918, to May 29, 1919.[115] The 316th Infantry Regiment was assigned to the 79th Infantry Division in France and saw plenty of action during the war. Meyer said his father Harry served as an interpreter. Because Yiddish grew from German dialects, he was able to learn to speak German, a useful skill in a war against Germany.[116]

The 79th Division entered the front line for the first time on September 26, 1918, and had its share of hard fighting. It took part in the Meuse-Argonne Offensive, capturing the strong position of Montfaucon on September 30.[117] In that Offensive, the 316th Infantry Regiment sustained 1,936 casualties (299 killed, 1,351 wounded, 233 missing in action, and 53 prisoners of war).[118] The 79th Division was then relieved before entering the battle again on October 29 and from that time until the Armistice on November 11, 1918, was almost constantly in action.[119]

After the war, General Pershing reviewed the 79th Division on April 12, 1919, the climax to its service in France. Pershing had high standards and they all knew it. After galloping around the entire division on his horse, he dismounted and the 316th was the first infantry regiment he inspected. As Lieutenant Charles M. Sincell, commander of Company K (Harry Osofsky's unit), fell into step, Pershing remarked: "Lieutenant, your personal appearance is a splendid example of your men."[120] Harry must have been proud to be in a unit that drew the praise of General Pershing.

The day after the review, Pershing sent a letter to the Commander of the 79th Division, Major General Joseph E. Kuhn, giving the 79th credit for the capture of Montfaucon and commending the 79th Division for its record of service.[121] He wrote: "This is a fine record for any division, and I want the officers and men to know this, and to realize how much they have contributed to the success of our arms. They may return home justly proud of themselves and of the part they have played in the American Expeditionary Forces."

Soon after the review, the 79th headed for home. They traveled by train to the port of St. Nazaire, France, arriving on May 15. They were deloused (i.e., disinfected to remove germs) before going through a final rigorous inspection prior to boarding the USS *Texas* for the trip home, arriving in Philadelphia on May 29.[122] Harry had been overseas for almost a year. He was honorably discharged June 7, 1919, at Camp Dix in New Jersey.[123] He was happy to be home and proud to have served his country.

After the war, Harry reentered the workforce in the knitting business, got married, and started a family. He and his wife Jennie raised a large family of seven children. Meyer was the second-oldest child. He had four brothers—Abraham (his older brother), Herman, Gerald, and Stephen—and three sisters—Annette, Estelle, and Frances.[124]

Meyer always appreciated his parents. They came to America from a broken Europe, worked hard, were resourceful, and set a good example for their children. He said his mother could make a meal out of nothing and his father provided them with a business acumen that would one day pay off for him and his older brother Abe. Meyer said today people feel entitled, but in those days, there were no free lunches. You had to work hard to get ahead.[125]

Meyer met his future wife, Aileen Bryant, when she was at Cunningham Junior High School and he was at James Madison High School in Brooklyn. Meyer was a good student and played basketball. He was once a class president and in his senior year was selected by this class as the "All-Around Boy." Aileen was a better student and was also a class secretary.[126] Two years younger than him, she skipped grades and graduated with him in June 1942 at the age of fifteen.[127] Aileen's father, Harry Bryant, was an architect and builder who was commissioned to build military barracks around the country and Aileen skipped a grade with each move.[128]

After high school, Meyer worked in the Brooklyn Navy Yard, where he was called "Mike," a familiar name, instead of "Meyer," an unfamiliar name. He was a welder of destroyers, hoping to make some money so he could go to college.[129] His older brother Abe was a student at the City College of New York (CCNY), and the caption under Meyer's picture in his yearbook said he was headed to CCNY as well.[130]

When his country went to war, Meyer and Abe did what many young men did at that time and what their father did before them—they entered the service. Meyer entered the Army Air Forces and would serve in the Mediterranean Theater. Abe entered the Signal Corps and would serve in the Pacific Theater.[131] Aileen would have to wait until after the war to marry Meyer. She was familiar with the military because her father, also named Harry, built military barracks in the United States.[132] Also, in addition to Meyer serving overseas, her brother Albert was a fighter pilot in the Pacific Theater. In fact, her brother flew cover for the Enola Gay when the B-29 heavy bomber dropped the atomic bomb on Hiroshima.[133] She had two loved ones to worry about during the war.

The tail-turret gunner was Technical Sergeant Charles J. "Chuck" Muth from Indianapolis, Indiana. At twenty-seven, Chuck was the oldest member of the crew and the only one with a child—James Robert Muth, who was six years old.[134] Muth was not Chuck's birth name, but that of his stepfather, Henry Robert Muth. His mother Victoria married Charles J. Shea in 1916 when she was fifteen and gave birth to Chuck in 1917 when she was sixteen.[135] Shea went off to World War I in 1918 and returned in 1919.[136] By 1920, he and Victoria had separated, and she changed Chuck's last name to Kershaw, the surname of her mother's second husband, Walter J. Kershaw. During the 1920s, Victoria hitched up with Henry and in 1930 the three of them were living together in Barrington, Illinois, but Chuck was still going under the name Charles Joseph Kershaw. [137]

By the mid-1930s, the family was living in Indianapolis and Chuck took his stepfather's surname and became Charles Joseph Muth for the rest of his life, a long one.[138] In 1935, he attended the Tennessee Military Institute in Sweetwater, Tennessee, a college preparatory school where he was on the basketball and track teams. He was a guard on the basketball team and did well on the track team, coming in first once in the javelin, the 40-yard dash, and the 220-yard dash.[139]

Like his mother, Chuck also married young. In 1937, back in Indianapolis, he married Mildred Eckerty, who grew up on a farm in Eckerty, Indiana, and they soon had a son, James Robert Muth. At the time, Chuck was working at the Apollo Theater, one of the leading movie theaters in downtown India-napolis.[140] In April 1940, he, Mildred, and James were living in Indianapolis and Chuck was working in retail automating, but not for long.[141]

At that time, William Knudsen was recruiting industry leaders to put in place an infrastructure to change from a peacetime economy to a wartime economy and the International Harvester Company was one of the companies to make this change. During the war, International Harvester plants made steel; armaments such as anti-tank guns, torpedoes, and cannon shells;

vehicles such as tractors and bulldozers; and truck engines.[142] Its plant in Indianapolis made the truck engines, and Chuck got a job there as a welder. He was working there when he registered for the draft in October 1940.[143] The Indianapolis plant provided top-notch support for the military during World War II and was the recipient of three Army-Navy "E" Awards. The "E" Award was granted to plants which achieved excellence in the quality and quantity of their work for the War Department or the Navy Department.[144]

Chuck was helping the war effort on the home front and would soon be helping it on the battlefront, just like his biological father Charles Shea and his stepfather Henry Muth—both World War I veterans. Henry had even been the commander of the American Legion post in Barrington, Illinois. Chuck was called into service for World War II on November 6, 1943, despite having a son who was almost six years old.[145] The day before he entered the service, a force of a thousand American planes, including B-17 and B-24 heavy bombers, escorted by P-38 and P-47 fighter escorts, flew into Nazi Germany and bombed three synthetic oil works as well as vital railway yards.[146] It wouldn't be long before Chuck would also be flying combat missions.

Chapter 8

THE COMBAT TEAM

Each member of a B-24 Liberator combat crew had to train hard to acquire the individual skills needed to be a productive member of the crew. Each also needed to work together closely with the other members of the crew to prepare to defend against enemy cannons on the ground and enemy fighters in the air while on missions to bomb precise targets from four or five miles up.[1] To be successful, all members of the crew had to be vigilant in performing their jobs because they were operating a sophisticated weapon of war and their lives depended on them all doing their jobs.[2] Their objective was to develop into an efficient and effective combat crew.

Each crew member—Cookman, Flint, Cylkowski, Goodson, Chin, Orkin, Mosher, Cooney, Osofsky, and Muth—trained in his individual specialty, usually at different training facilities, before coming together to train as a combat team at Mountain Home Army Air Field located about ten miles southwest of Mountain Home, Idaho.[3] In his individual training to become a radio operator, Kirk Mosher had to certify in writing that he read the *Radio Operators' Information File* which stressed the importance of teamwork and stated what he could do to be a good team player:[4]

> *"Crew teamwork is the foundation of successful air operations. Strive for good teamwork in training and it will come easy in combat where it pays off the dividends. Personal proficiency is part of teamwork. Know your duties, know your equipment, and keep abreast of new techniques and procedures."*

FROM ONE WAR TO ANOTHER

Each member of the crew had to likewise know their duties and their equipment and keep abreast of new techniques and procedures.

The Importance of Teamwork

At Mountain Home, the crew was brought together to use their individual skills by practicing flying in formation, shooting their machine guns (both air to air and air to ground), bombing from various altitudes, flying cross country (day and night), flying at different altitudes (high and low), and flying by instruments. They also cross-trained to back each other up for contingencies, such as situations in which one or more crew members are wounded or worse.[5]

It was not all business at Mountain Home. The four officers lived together and got to know each other, and the six enlisted men lived together and got to know each other. Crew members also found time to pal around together. Meyer and Chuck, both of whom were welders when they enlisted, got along well, and would take a bus to Boise, about fifty miles away, to let off steam. Meyer fondly recalls that they would hang out at the B-24 Club which sold pitchers of beer for a quarter and hard-boiled eggs for a nickel. The girls in the place would plug the eggs, telling them that they would put lead in their pencils. Meyer said it was a nice diversion from the training they were undergoing.[6] Meyer also recalled that Chuck's wife Mildred visited once and the three of them went out to dinner together at the B-24 Club.[7]

Combat training was intense. It was precise, challenging, dangerous, and could result in tragic accidents. One mistake on the part of any crew member and it could be curtains for the entire crew. They depended on each other for safety. There were so many dangerous aspects to combat training. Even if you mastered most of them, you could still become a fatality if you were not careful. Just after Cookman's crew left Mountain Home, a B-24 bomber with a crew of seven crashed in mid-air with an A-23 bomber with a crew of two, killing all the crew members of both planes. The A-23 was a modified B-26 Marauder bomber. At that time there was a need for a plane to tow a target for high-altitude gunnery training, and over two-hundred B-26s were modified for use as target tugs to satisfy the need for B-24 aerial gunners to aim at moving targets.[8]

There were 1,713 accidents during Army Air Forces training in the States, resulting in the loss of 2,796 airmen and 746 airplanes.[9] Add to this the challenge of flying in combat with the enemy shooting at you, and it is no wonder that twice as many Army air officers were killed than Army ground officers during World War II, even though the ground forces had significantly more officers than the air forces.[10]

Calvin Chin kept his certificate from Mountain Home Army Air Field which stated that he satisfactorily completed the course on combat crew training on August 8, 1944.[11] He also kept photos of his crew who he always appreciated. Exhibit 8.1 is a collage of photos of three of his officers—Cookman, Flint and Goodson—and him arm in arm with Kirk Mosher who would both fly on the same dangerous mission on Friday the 13th in different planes and with different results. The collage also includes a photo of him in his combat gear in front of his nose-gunner position on the B-24.

The crew went next to Topeka Army Air Field in Topeka, Kansas, for combat assignment.[12] Topeka was a holding area where crew members continued to get to know each other as work partners and comrades. As a fan of Chinese food, Meyer recalls how a Chinese restaurant in Topeka rolled out the red carpet for them. He said the owner loved Calvin, who would open a Chinese restaurant of his own after the war at which Meyer would throw a party to celebrate the occasion.[13] Teamwork didn't end with the war.

It was at Topeka Army Air Field that Kirk Mosher decided to tie the knot with his hometown sweetheart, Carmelita "Carmie" Smallridge. On Friday, August 25, 1944, they married in the chapel at the airfield. Thinking ahead, Kirk took out a life insurance policy with Carmie as beneficiary. He knew the risks of war and wanted to leave his young wife something in the event he didn't make it back. Carmie was only eighteen years old and returned to Albuquerque to stay with her mother while Kirk served overseas.[14]

When the crew was ready for overseas duty, they traveled to Camp Patrick Henry to wait for their ship to come in. Camp Patrick Henry was a staging area for military personnel heading overseas via the Hampton Roads Port of Embarkation in Newport News, Virginia. The port had a post office, hospital, chapel, several theaters, a bank, a general store, two libraries, recreation facilities including a boxing ring, and a rail system to allow troops to travel to downtown Newport News.[15]

Hampton Roads was one of eight major ports of embarkation in the United States for the movement of troops and cargo to overseas theaters of war. The seven others were Boston, New York, Charleston, New Orleans, Los Angeles, San Francisco, and Seattle. Each port was assigned primary responsibility for one or a few overseas theaters of operations. Hampton Roads shipped chiefly to the Mediterranean Theater of Operations. During

Cookman

Flint

Goodson

Chin and Mosher

Chin in Front of his Nose Gunner Station

Exhibit 8.1
Snapshots of Combat Team Members
Courtesy of David Chin

World War II, more than 1.6 million military personnel and about 15 million tons of war materiel passed through Hampton Roads.[16]

The commander of the Hampton Roads, Brigadier General John R. Kilpatrick, had been a two-time consensus All-America football player at Yale University who received the Distinguished Service Medal in World War I and went on to become the president of Madison Square Garden. He was recalled to active duty in World War II. He compared the tactics of football to the tactics of battle: "Each man has a duty to carry out on the football field as well as on the battlefield. Each man must aid the fellow next to him besides doing his own job and must keep going when tired and hurt. It's the team with the most spirit that wins."[17] John and his crewmates could relate to this as they had just completed intense combat training that stressed the importance of teamwork.

On September 1, 1944, exactly five years after the beginning of World War II, John's crew boarded a ship at the Hampton Roads Port of Embarkation in Newport News, Virginia, and headed for Naples, Italy.[18] George McGovern's crew mirrored the training and travel experience of John's crew. They also trained at Mountain Home Army Air Field and had a short stay at Topeka Army Air Field before moving on to Camp Patrick Henry to wait for their ship to come in.[19] And like John's crew, they were aware of the danger of formation flying because of training accidents. McGovern's wife Eleanor thought planes collided because they were training the crews too fast.[20]

John's ship had tight quarters for the enlisted men. Meyer said they were packed into four-deep bunks in the hull of the ship that smelled like hell. He dreaded sleeping under those conditions, so he searched for and found alternate sleeping arrangements in a 6 x 6 truck that was bolted down on the deck. The 6 x 6 was a rugged six-cylinder truck with six wheels that could carry a cargo of six tons. He located some blankets and told the other five enlisted men who were his crewmates to do the same and follow him, and they did. As a result, instead of bunking down in smelly, cramped quarters below deck, they crossed the Atlantic in relative comfort of a truck on the deck under the stars and had in Meyer's own words "a beautiful crossing."[21]

The trip overseas provided some memorable times for Meyer. Some evenings, Ted Cylkowski, an officer and their navigator, would visit them in their truck. Meyer thought he was brilliant and well-spoken and knew a lot about the stars.[22] As navigator, he of course was trained in celestial navigation, the skill of navigating by observing the positions of celestial bodies, such as the stars. Years later, his son David said he was interested in astronomy and kept star charts, so he did indeed know a lot about the stars.[23] Meyer also remembered that he had a talent for capturing the attention of an audience.[24]

Cylkowski's ability to hold an audience was later put to good use in Italy when he was grounded due to air sickness. He was assigned to headquarters of the 450th Bomb Group as the Group Orientation Officer giving lectures to airmen arriving at the base in the village of Mandurian on the heel of Italy to welcome them to the bomb group and provide them with guidelines for becoming familiar with and adjusting to their new surroundings.[25]

The 450th Bomb Group was known as the "Cottontails" and would fly 265 accredited missions against a variety of targets throughout Nazi-occupied Europe. They picked up the nickname "Cottontails" after a mission in which they attacked the Prufening Aircraft Factory in Regensburg, Germany on February 25, 1944. It was one of the two missions for which the 450th received a Distinguished Unit Citation (the other was a mission to the Ploesti Marshalling Yards in Romania on April 5, 1944). The German Luftwaffe spotted their white rudders and called them "White-Tailed Liberators." Axis Sally, an American who did propaganda broadcasts for Nazi Germany during World War II, used the term in her broadcasts which led to the nickname "Cottontails."[26]

As the Orientation Officer of the 450th Bomb Group, Cylkowski introduced the United States Armed Forces Institute Program to the men assigned to the group because it would benefit them in the long run.[27] The Institute was founded in 1942 as the Army Institute and its purpose was to provide educational opportunities for members of the Armed Forces to prepare them for civilian life after the war. It was expanded to the Navy allowing members of the Armed Forces in their spare time to continue or begin a high school or college education. They were provided an opportunity to receive instruction in "business, scientific, technical, mechanical, industrial, liberal arts, and engineering fields—anything from accounting and aviation to trigonometry and welding." Those interested were given the *Catalog of the United States Armed Forces Institute* that was filled with "a whole parade of educational opportunities."[28]

President Roosevelt wanted to do more to help veterans returning from World War II than was done for veterans returning from World War I.[29] He wanted to help them make their transition from wartime to peacetime as smooth as possible.[30] During the war, the Department of Labor estimated that fifteen million men and women serving their country would return to the work force. To prepare for this reality, the National Resources Planning Board, a White House agency, was formed and, after careful study, recommended a series of training and education programs. The American Legion was involved in the process and the result of this collaboration was the Servicemen's Readjustment Act of 1944, known as the GI Bill of Rights or simply the GI Bill, which Roosevelt signed into law on June 22, 1944, just sixteen days after the June 6 Normandy Invasion.[31]

The GI Bill "offered Federal aid to help veterans adjust to civilian life in the areas of hospitalization, purchase of homes and businesses, and especially, education." It helped veterans to further their education in colleges or on-the-job training programs and to buy homes, farms, or businesses. About eight million veterans took advantage of the GI Bill.[32] It was an investment in the veterans of World War II that helped to expand the middle class and led to a generation of veterans that came to be known as the Greatest Generation.

President Roosevelt knew the importance of supporting veterans because his support of the veterans of World War I helped to get him elected. After World War I, Congress passed the World War Adjusted Compensation Act of 1924 over the veto of President Calvin Coolidge. It was called the Bonus Act because it promised the veterans of World War I compensation for their sacrifices in serving in war that took them away from their jobs in the United States. It promised veterans a bonus of $1 per day for serving stateside and $1.25 per day for serving overseas.[33]

The problem was that wrangling over the budget deferred these payments until the birthdays of the veterans in 1945. This did not sit well with the veterans. In 1929, Congressman Wright Patman of Texas, a veteran, sponsored a bill to make these payments immediately, but the bill went nowhere. In 1932, a jobless veteran named Walter W. Waters proposed that veterans head to Washington, D.C. in protest to get their bonuses now instead of in 1945 because the country was experiencing the Great Depression and the veterans needed money now. His proposal developed legs and veterans started to flock to the nation's capital, which prompted Patman to resurrect his cash-now bill.[34]

Waters was smart and demanded military discipline of the veterans. In much the same way that Allied leaders in prison camps demanded military discipline of prisoners of war to obtain unity and one voice in representing the prisoners, Waters was determined to organize a disciplined army of veterans to support their cause.[35] The veterans who came to Washington, D.C. were called the Bonus Army and/or the Bonus Expeditionary Forces.[36] They lived together in camps near the U.S. Capitol. The largest camp was in Anacostia Park across the Anacostia River from the Washington Navy Yard located just south of the Capitol. Even though it was a time when school buses and schools remained segregated, blacks and whites in the Bonus Army lived and protested together for a common cause. This prompted Roy Wilkins, a prominent civil rights activist from the 1930s to the 1970s, to write in his NAACP monthly in 1932 that "there was one absentee (in the Bonus Army): James Crow."[37]

When the Bonus Army grew to over 20,000, there were incidents involving the police and President Herbert Hoover called in the Army to ensure crowd control. The Army group called in was led by men who would become legends in World War II—Douglas MacArthur, his principal aide Dwight D. Eisenhower, and his executive officer George S. Patton. At one point, MacArthur disregarded a presidential directive not to enter a large camp of veterans. He took matters into his own hands and led five tanks and 300 armed and helmeted infantrymen into the camp in Anacostia Park, dispersing the protesters with weapons drawn and clouds of tear gas. This incident did not sit well with the media or the general public.[38]

Roosevelt, who was a savvy politician, took advantage of the situation. Even though he had also been against the immediate payment of the bonuses because he felt it favored a special class of citizens at a time when everyone was suffering, he changed his position to get votes and told an aide, "this will elect me." He was right. People wanted change, and Roosevelt was elected in November 1932 as the first Democratic President since Woodrow Wilson who had served from 1913 to 1921.[39]

After he was elected, however, Roosevelt did not push Patman's cash-now bill. He compromised and started a new public works program called the Civilian Conservation Corps which created "veterans' rehabilitation camps" in South Carolina and Florida that put veterans to work even though the pay was low at $1 a day that some called slave wages.[40] In 1935, however, a tragic event took the lives of a group of veterans in the Civilian Conservation Corps. A hurricane in the Florida Keys stranded veteran workers building a highway from Miami to Key West, and at least 256 of them were killed by the storm.[41]

This tragic incident prompted Patman to once again reintroduce his cash-now bonus act which finally became law.[42] In 1936, the Bonus Army finally got their bonuses.[43] When the United States went to war again, the importance of compensating veterans for their service was recognized, and the GI Bill was the result. It became one of the most important pieces of social legislation in American history and members of Cookman's crew would benefit from it after the war.[44]

As Cookman's crew sailed to Italy, Meyer also recalled that co-pilot Flint, another officer, would also pay them visits in their truck. Enlisted men seldom called officers by their first names, but Meyer said he felt comfortable in calling Flint by his first name, Russ. This was the guy who was characterized in his high school yearbook as "happy-go-lucky." Meyer thought he was a terrific person to be around and developed a high regard for him as his co-pilot.[45]

Boxing was the second most popular sport at that time, baseball being the most popular. You couldn't play baseball on a ship, but you could box. Meyer, a lefty, liked to box and so did one of his crewmates, Ray Goodson, so they went at it on the high seas on the way to Europe. The enlisted men usually boxed each other, but once Meyer faced off against an officer other than Ray and floored him. He apologized saying it was "just a lucky punch," but the officer said he was fine and that's what you're supposed to do in a boxing match.[46] As the troops crossed the Atlantic to fight for their country, boxing was a sport that fit right in.

After weeks of seeing nothing but ocean and sky, they sailed through the Straits of Gibraltar sighting the Rock of Gibraltar on their left as they entered the Mediterranean Sea. It was an impressive sight. It was a heavily guarded British fortress overseeing ships entering the Mediterranean Sea. It had been the headquarters for General Dwight D. Eisenhower and Admiral Sir Andrew Browne Cunningham in November 1943 when they directed the American-British invasion to liberate French North Africa, the first of many major combat operations in which American and British forces teamed up to work together with the soldiers, sailors, and airmen operating under a combined offensive command.[47] It is noteworthy that Germany and the Axis nations never teamed up to work together like the Allied nations.

It is also noteworthy that teamwork was missing from the leaders of the Luftwaffe as compared to the leaders of the United States Army Air Forces in Europe when Cookman and his crew arrived in Italy on September 27, 1944. The top Army Air Forces leader was Henry "Hap" Arnold in Washington, D.C. with Carl "Tooey" Spaatz in London commanding the United States Strategic Air Forces in Europe under which Jimmie Doolittle commanded the Eighth Air Force in England and Ira Eaker commanded the Twelfth and Fifteenth Air Forces in Italy.[48] Cookman and his crew would fly strategic bombing missions for the Fifteenth Air Force.

Arnold, Spaatz, and Eaker had known each other for years, had been involved with the growth of aviation, and had a high regard for each other. In fact, Arnold, Spaatz, and Eaker got along so well that Eaker's biographer, James Parton, wrote, "The trio's teamwork, like that of the three musketeers, remained constant."[49] Jimmy Doolittle already had legendary status for having put together a team of eighty aircrew members to fly a dangerous mission that produced the first strike against Japan after the bombing of Pearl Harbor. For leading the Doolittle Tokyo Raid on April 18, 1942, he received the Congressional Medal of Honor on May 19, 1942.[50] It was the first U.S. victory of World War II.[51]

One of the reasons the Luftwaffe failed to keep pace with the Allied air forces during the war was that it had been designed for blitzkrieg operations flying tactical missions to support the Wehrmacht, the German army.[52] Blitzkrieg is a German term meaning to attack the enemy by surprise, with speed, and with superior firepower.[53] It was designed for a short war, not a long war. Hitler underestimated the resolve of the British on the western front and the Russians on the eastern front.[54] This gave America more time to mobilize and when it entered the war and started bombing German targets the tide turned in favor of the Allies.[55] Also, the Luftwaffe was led by young and inexperienced commanders some of whom flew fighters and dive bombers on tactical missions to support invading troops and had little experience with and appreciation for four-engine bombers that flew strategic missions that bombed larger targets such as the factories that built weapons and oil fields that fueled them. They failed to envision the impact that four-engine bombers (B-17s and B-24s) being developed by the United States would have in the war.[56] In 1937, for example, Goering stopped all work on the development of a four-engine bomber for the Luftwaffe.[57]

There were significant differences in leadership at the very top of the Allies and the Axis. While Roosevelt left tactical matters to his generals and reserved himself for political and strategic matters, Hitler thought he knew more than his generals and was meddlesome, and his word was law.[58] Hermann Goering, his top air force commander, was more interested in doing what Hitler wanted than what his subordinates told him should be done. As a result, high-ranking generals in the Luftwaffe had little influence in changing decisions made by Hitler that they didn't feel were sound, and this reality was reflected in the turnover among his generals.[59]

Reporting to Goering was the Chief of the Luftwaffe Staff, but the Chief kept changing. His first Chief, Walther Wever, died in an air crash in May 1936. His second, Albert Kesselring, requested reassignment in May 1937. His third, Hans Jurgen Stumpff, requested reassignment in January 1939. His fourth, Hans Jeschonnek, committed suicide in August 1943. His fifth, Gunther Korten, was killed in July 1944 by the bomb intended for Hitler that was planted by Claus Schenk von Stauffenberg who was portrayed by Tom

Cruise in the 2008 movie *Valkyrie*. His sixth, Werner Kreipe, had to submit his resignation after he got into a heated argument with Hitler. His seventh, Karl Koller, served until the end of the war.[60]

In addition to Jeschonnek, who was Chief of the Luftwaffe Staff from February 1939 to August 1943, Goering also had under him Erhard Milch, the Secretary of Aviation, and Ernst Udet, the Chief of Luftwaffe Supply and Procurement. While Jeschonnek, Milch, and Udet were the designated commanders with the most to say about the air defense of Germany, they didn't get along and never worked together as a team.[61] Udet had been one of the most famous combat pilots during World War I with sixty-two aerial victories, second only to the eighty of the legendary Red Baron, Manfred Freiherr von Richthofen. Even though Udet was a national war hero, he was unable to cope with Hitler and Goering and killed himself in November 1941. A frustrated Jeschonnek also killed himself two years later.

Suicides also occurred at the very top. When the war ended, Hitler killed himself on April 30, 1945.[62] After he was found guilty at the Nuremberg war trials, Goering killed himself on October 15, 1946.[63] Milch was also found guilty at Nuremberg. He was sentenced to life imprisonment but was released in 1954 and wrote a book entitled *The Rise and Fall of the Luftwaffe*.[64] He had been director of Lufthansa before he became Secretary of Aviation, was the real architect of German air power during the 1930s, but Goering was jealous of him, excluded him from technical development and production, and gave the work to Udet, who didn't have the experience and organizational skills of Milch to succeed in the position.[65] The camaraderie you find in a team was missing from the Luftwaffe.

City in Ruins

Three weeks after Cookman and his crew departed from Hampton Roads, their ship arrived in Naples, Italy, where Meyer was surprised to see youngsters in little skiffs begging and diving for money and other items that were thrown into the water for them.[66] When McGovern's ship came into Naples later that month, he was also surprised to see dozens of youngsters on the wharf begging for candy and gum, but the ship's captain wouldn't let them throw any in the water because a couple of days earlier some children had drowned diving for candy in the water.[67]

Naples had fallen on tough times—the fate of many cities in war-torn Europe. It had once been one of the wealthiest and most industrialized centers of Italy, which gave rise to the term "Vedi Napoli e poi muori ("See Napoli and then die"). In other words, one must experience the beauty and magnificence of Naples before dying.[68] Now this beautiful city was in ruins, and depravity and death were all around. Its infrastructure was decimated by Allied bombs that started to fall in 1940, and continued to fall for the next four years, making Naples the most bombed Italian city of World War II. The targets were Naples' port, rail, industrial, and petroleum facilities as well as its steel mills.[69]

Naples was an important port for the Allies, and the Germans knew it. A year earlier when the U.S. Fifth Army landed at Salerno in September 1943 and British Eighth Army landed at the foot of Italy, the Allies had three objectives. The first was to set up Allied airfields on the Foggia plain for heavy bombers so that they could bomb Axis targets which were out of the range of the heavy bombers at Allied airfields in England. The second was to capture Naples because the Allies needed an important port through which to supply these Allied airfields. The third, of course, was to land troops to liberate Rome which would be the first Axis capital to be liberated—the other two being Berlin and Tokyo. [70]

When the Allies threatened to capture and occupy Naples, the Germans decided to destroy what the bombs didn't so that the Allies wouldn't be able to use Naples to their advantage. They blew up the port facilities, sunk the ships in the harbor, destroyed key rail facilities, blocked rail and highway tunnels, and removed all vehicles that might be of use to the Allies. Furthermore, they destroyed water, sewer, and electric power utilities. [71] The Germans continued to leave a path of destruction as they pushed ever so slowly up the Italian peninsula during the war in Italy.[72] This mindset was employed by Hitler himself. When he was told by Albert Speer, his chief architect and minister for armaments and war production, that the war was lost, he ordered the destruction the German infrastructure (factories, bridges, railroads, mines and more) rather than have it fall into the hands of the Allies. Speer did what he could to prevent these orders from being carried out before Hitler committed suicide.[73]

As the third largest city in Italy after Rome and Milan, Naples employed many laborers whose lives, homes, and livelihoods were destroyed when the city became a battleground. The devastation killed many civilians and left many others scraping for food and money. About a year before Cookman's crew arrived in Italy, Italy surrendered on September 3, 1943. Germany responded by occupying Italy, and many Italian men were carted off to Germany to be slave labor, leaving behind women and children to fare for themselves as they were pushed to the edge by widespread poverty. Moral decay set in as women turned to the streets to sell themselves. The children, especially orphans, also turned to the streets to beg and steal to survive.[74]

One author called Naples at that time "the prostitution capital of the world."[75] Consequently, venereal diseases, such as gonorrhea and syphilis, were a big concern for the military personnel in Naples. Members of the armed forces were repeatedly shown educational films of what could happen to them if they forgot "to put it on before they put it in."[76] Despite these repeated warnings during the war, air forces personnel serving in Western Europe during the war had 31,156 cases of gonorrhea, 3,842 cases of syphilis and 479 cases of other venereal diseases for a total of 35,477 cases of venereal diseases.[77]

Meyer remembered that before they received their pay, they had to be checked for venereal disease. They called the medics who checked them "pecker checkers."[78] They got paid at the end of the month and they called payday "the day the eagle shits," a reference to the bald eagle, a symbol of America, dropping money in their pockets.[79] Meyer recalled that his monthly pay was $144 which included a 20 percent increase for overseas duty and a 50 percent increase for combat duty.[80]

During the war, American troops in Italy were paid in Allied military currency, also known as invasion currency. Whenever the United States invaded a country during the war, it would pay the troops with Allied military currency that was pegged to the currency of the country being invaded. In this case, the dollar was pegged to the lira, whereby a hundred lire were equal to one U.S. dollar, or one lira was equal to one U.S. cent. Meyer said a haircut cost five lire. Stephen Ambrose in his book *The Wild Blue* said skilled laborers were paid seventy-five lire a day and unskilled laborers fifty lire a day. A hot bath cost twenty-five lire.[81]

Over fifty years later, on January 1, 1999, the Italian lira ceased to be the official currency of Italy when it was replaced by the euro, the official new currency of the European Union which in November 2022 had twenty-seven European states as members. The euro was a step in the direction of uniting the European countries, which had a long history of fighting each other.[82] It was a long time coming. As far back as 1897, Senator John Mitchell of Wisconsin, Billy Mitchell's father, said in a speech to the graduating class of Columbia College in Washington, D.C. (later George Washington University) that he had a dream that the nations of Europe might one day federate themselves to form a union which would be "more beneficial and more stable than the forms of government under which they now live."[83] His dream was for peace in the world, but rather than come together the European nations came apart in World Wars I and II. It would take almost a hundred years from Senator Mitchell's speech to the founding of the European Union in 1993.[84] The irony of it all is that Germany is a heavyweight member state and has acted in tandem with France, a country it invaded in both World War I and World War II.[85]

When Cookman's crew arrived in Italy, they stayed at a "repo depot," or "replacement depot," in Naples, awaiting further orders. They were there to "replace" other airmen. Soon, they were assigned to the 725th Bomb Squadron, 451st Bomb Group, 49th Bomb Wing of the Fifteenth Air Force in the Mediterranean Theater of Operations. The 451st Bomb Group was located on the other side of Italy at Castelluccio Airfield in Castelluccio dei Sauri, a small town in southeastern Italy. Italy is shaped like a boot, and this town is on the part of Italy that looks like a spur on the boot. They crossed Italy by train and truck, arriving at Castelluccio Airfield on Wednesday, September 27, 1944.[86]

Castelluccio Airfield began operations on March 15, 1944, as the home base of the 451st Bomb Group flying B-24 Liberators. It had extensive taxiways for its four bomb squadrons, parking spaces called revetments for its planes, and a steel control tower.[87] It was one of many Army Air Forces airfields serving as home bases for the bomb groups and fighter groups of the Fifteenth Air Force. Some were built by the Army Corps of Engineers. Others were built earlier by British engineers, taken over by the Germans when they occupied Italy, and taken back by the Allies when they invaded Italy. All of them were located within a twenty-five-mile radius of Foggia and were collectively referred to as the Foggia Airfield Complex. The Complex was an important part of the strategic bombardment campaign against Nazi Germany during 1944 and 1945.[88] The headquarters of the Fifteenth Air Force was in Bari, Italy, about seventy-five miles southeast of Castelluccio Airfield.

George McGovern's crew was assigned to the 741st Bomb Squadron, 455th Bomb Group, 304th Bomb Wing of the Fifteenth Air Force. It was also located on the spur of Italy at San Giovanni Airfield, about five miles outside the town of Cerignola and about twenty-five miles from Cookman's bomb group at Castelluccio Airfield.[89] Cookman's and McGovern's crews were among many crews stationed on the spur of Italy. At that time, the number of missions required for a tour of duty in the 451st Bomb Group had increased from twenty-five to thirty-five.[90]

Before April 1, 1944, only twenty-five missions were required for a tour of duty because of the physical and mental strain of flying strategic combat missions far into enemy territory without long-range fighter escorts. When the long-range P-51 Mustang became available for long-range missions, the length of a tour increased to thirty missions from April 1 to June 5, and then to thirty-five missions on D-Day, June 6, 1944. By the time John's and McGovern's crews arrived in Italy, they and each of their crewmates were expected to fly thirty-five combat missions. The odds of completing this many combat missions, even with long-range fighter escorts, were not high, and they knew it.

Chapter 9

FLYING COMBAT MISSIONS

The Fifteenth Air Force, to which John's 451st Bomb Group was assigned, was an offshoot of the Twelfth Air Force that was split up in late 1943. It was decided that the Twelfth Air Force would fly tactical missions utilizing medium bombers, such as the two-engine B-25 Mitchell and B-26 Marauder, while the Fifteenth Air Force would fly strategic missions utilizing heavy bombers such as the four-engine B-17 Flying Fortress and B-24 Liberator.[1]

Tactical missions were flown to support Allied ground troops by bombing enemy troops and their means of transportation—trains, ships, and vehicles—that brought more troops and more equipment and supplies to the battlefront. Strategic missions, on the other hand, were flown to destroy the enemy's ability to wage war by bombing their factories that made the weapons; their oil fields that fueled the weapons; their airports, harbors and marshalling yards where planes, ships and trains were respectively kept and maintained; and their railroad lines, motorways, bridges, and viaducts used by trains and vehicles to deliver the troops and weapons to the battlefront.[2]

Organizing for Combat

The Fifteenth Air Force was organized into five bomb wings (5th, 47th, 49th, 55th and 304th) and two fighter wings (305th and 306th) located in about thirty airfields within a radius of twenty-five miles around Foggia on the spur of Italy.[3] Cookman's crew was in the 49th Bomb Wing that consisted of three bomb groups—the 451st, 461st and 484th. His crew was in the 451st Bomb Group based at Castelluccio Airfield in Castelluccio dei Sauri, about

189

twelve miles southwest of Foggia. The 461st and 484th Bomb Groups were both based at Torretta Airfield, about twenty miles southeast of Castelluccio Airfield. The 451st Bomb Group had four bomb squadrons—the 724th, 725th, 726th and 727th—and Cookman's crew was in the 725th Bomb Squadron.[4] Each bomb squadron had a complement of B-24s and pilots to fly them on combat missions. The orders for the combat missions came down the chain of command from the top and the results of the missions went back up the chain of command to the top. The pilots and their crews followed orders and routinely flew into harm's way.

General Ira C. Eaker was commander of the Mediterranean Allied Air Forces (Exhibit 9.1). Under his command was the Twelfth Air Force which flew the tactical missions with medium bombers and the Fifteenth Air Force which flew the strategic missions with heavy bombers. Eaker had grown up with military aviation. He received his wings in 1918 and was an air commander on every level during his long career. He had recently commanded the Eight Air Force in England before becoming the commander of the Twelfth and Fifteenth Air Forces in Italy.[5]

Eaker was stationed at the Royal Palace of Caserta, the largest royal residence in the world, which was the Headquarters for the Allied American and British Forces in Italy during World War II.[6] Caserta was about twenty miles north of Naples on the west coast of Italy. The headquarters of General John K. Cannon, commander of the Twelfth Air Force, was also in Caserta. The headquarters of General Nathan F. Twining, commander of the Fifteenth Air Force, was in Bari on the east coast of Italy nearer Eastern Europe where it flew many of its missions. As previously mentioned, Bari was about seventy-five miles southeast of Castelluccio Airfield from where John Cooney flew thirty-five combat missions during the war.

Like General Eaker, General Twining had also grown up with military aviation and could never have imagined this level of responsibility twenty-eight years earlier when he was a corporal in a unit looking for Pancho Villa in Mexico where he was exposed to military aviation for the first time.[7] At its peak in May 1944, the Fifteenth Air Force had twenty-one bomb groups and John's 451st Bomb Group was one of them.[8] Twining, along with legendary airmen Billy Mitchell, Hap Arnold, Ira Eaker, Tooey Spaatz, and Jimmy Doolittle, had experienced the growth of American combat aviation from its inception.[9]

By the time the United States entered World War II, Twining had come a long way, and was prepared for greater responsibility at a time when there

Exhibit 9.1
Chain of Command
Mediterranean Allied Air Force
October 1944

Mediterranean Allied Air Force (MAAF) Lt. Gen. Ira C. Eaker (Caserta, Italy)

Fifteenth Air Force Mediterranean Allied <u>Strategic</u> Air Force (MASAF) Maj. Gen. Nathan F. Twining (Bari, Italy)

Eaker also commanded the Twelfth Air Force's Mediterranean Allied <u>Tactical</u> Air Force (MATAF) under the command of Lt. Gen.General John K. Cannon (Caserta, Italy).

49th Bomb Wing Brig. Gen. William L. Lee (Castelluccio dei Sauri, Italy)

Twining also commanded the Fifteenth Air Force's four other Bomb Wings (5th, 47th, 55th and 304th) and two Fighter Wings (305th and 306th).

451st Bomb Group Col. James B. Knapp Castelluccio Airfield

There were two other Bomb Groups in the 49th Bomb Wing—the 461st and the 484th—and both were stationed at Torretta Airfield.

725th Bomb Squadron Capt. John P. Janensch Castelluccio Airfield

There were three other Bomb Squadrons in the 451st Bomb Group—the 724th, 726th, and 727th—and were also stationed at Castelluccio Airfield.

B-24 Liberators Pilots Who Flew Them Castelluccio Airfield

The pilots were the commanders of the B-24s who led their crews into harm's way on combat missions.

was a dire need for military leadership. In January 1943, he became commander of the Thirteenth Air Force.[10] In November 1943, the Fifteenth Air Force was established, and he was put in command by General Eisenhower.[11] The same month, he moved the Fifteenth Air Force and its bombers from North Africa to bases on the east coast of Italy around Foggia to be closer to strategic bombing targets in eastern Europe.

In December 1943, General Arnold, the head of the Army Air Forces, gave Twining four objectives: (1) destroy the German Air Force; (2) support the Italian ground campaign; (3) participate in the Combined Bomber Offensive; and (4) weaken the German presence in the Balkans.[12] The Combined Bomber Offensive alluded to the strategic bombing of Germany by British airmen, who bombed at night with Lancaster and Halifax bombers from 7,000 to 17,000 feet, and by American airmen, who bombed during the day with B-17 Flying Fortresses and B-24 Liberators from 15,000 to 25,000 feet.[13] The objective of the Combined Bomber Offensive was to destroy "vital centers" that supported the German war machine such as the factories that made the planes; the oil fields, refineries, and storage depot areas that fueled the planes and other weapons; and other factories such as those that made ball-bearings which were vital components for weapons such as planes and tanks.[14]

Arnold was asking Twining to destroy German military, industrial, and transportation targets to undermine the morale of the German people to support the war. He would achieve those objectives. By the end of the war in Europe, he had commanded 1,900 planes and 89,000 personnel.[15] And he didn't stop there. After the war in Europe, he was ordered to take command of the Twentieth Air Force in the war in Japan and directed the final strikes against Japan which included the dropping of the atomic bombs on Hiroshima and Nagasaki that ended the war with Japan.[16]

Teamwork in Combat

The West Point class of 1915, consisting of 164 students, produced fifty-nine generals, the most of any graduating class. The book *West Point 1915: Eisenhower, Bradley and the Class the Stars Fell On* by Michael E. Haskew provides a history of this class which produced two five-star generals—Dwight D. Eisenhower and Omar Bradley—who were football teammates. For the rest of their lives, they and some other members of the class felt their athletic experiences had been essential in building character and teamwork.[17]

Flying Combat Missions

Teamwork was important during wartime. It was especially important for bombing crews who typically operated a sophisticated weapon of war with a goal of bombing a target about five miles below. Major Paul R. Nugent, a bombardier in the 47th Bomb Wing, used the game of football to stress and clarify the importance of teamwork on bombing missions. He wrote about Teamwork in Bombing Missions (Exhibit 9.2).[18]

A football team has four tries to get a first down and it may take several first downs to score a touchdown. A bombing crew, on the other hand, has only one try to score a hit on the target. It isn't easy to score a touchdown in football, and it's a whole lot harder to score a hit on a target of war from a plane speeding along five miles above the target. Yet, this was the objective of the many heavy bombers based on military airfields on the spur of Italy. This location placed them within the range of key strategic bombing targets in Germany, Austria, and Eastern European countries that were out of range for the Eighth Air Force based in England. For example, it placed the Fifteenth Air Force much closer to the Romanian oil fields that powered the Nazi Germany war machine. Weather conditions were also better in this part of Italy than in England.

The Weather Factor

Hap Arnold recognized the need to carry out bombing missions in poor weather, and the harsh winters of 1942 and 1943 convinced him that it was a high-priority need.[19] Many missions could not be completed during those winters because overcast conditions made it impossible for lead bombardiers to find their targets using their Norden bombsight. Consequently, Arnold decided that radar was needed to fly daylight bombing missions during overcast weather conditions when the target could not be sighted. In mid-1943, the task of developing a capability to bomb under overcast conditions fell to Lt. Colonel William S. Cowart of the Eighth Air Force, assisted by Major Fred A. Rabo.[20]

The term RADAR is an acronym for Radio Detection and Ranging. Simply said, it was a system with a transmitter that emitted radio waves that were reflected off a target back to a receiver in the system. The radio signals received were amplified enabling the radar operator to detect objects on the ground that were targets.[21] The human eye uses light waves to see and has trouble seeing through fog, rain, snow, clouds, and darkness. Radar, however, uses radio waves that can see through these obstacles.[22]

Exhibit 9.2
Teamwork on Bombing Missions

In bombing, as in any other game, certain fundamental principles must be organized, studied, and mastered. A good football team must be able to tackle, block, pass, kick and run. A good bombing team must be able to FLY FORMATION, NAVIGATE PRECISELY, AND BOMB ACCURATELY. As is true in team sports, coordination is the most vital factor in successful bombing. It is not enough for the pilot to fly formation and the navigator to navigate. These two men must work closely together to insure the bombardier maximum coordination at the most critical moment of the entire mission—THE BOMB RUN.

Just as football games can be won in the locker room, a successful bombing mission is often "flown" in the briefing room. Proper mission planning, adequate target materials, and their proper presentation and study do much to insure maximum destruction of the target. A successful rendezvous, proper spacing, adherence to the briefed course, and adequate flight check of all bombing equipment also are essential. But execution of these preliminary steps does not guarantee the target will be destroyed any more than well-memorized signals and proper lineup guarantee victory to a football team prior to the kickoff.

In the bombing business, the "kickoff" occurs at the control point. The bombardier has checked his equipment, has taken a dry run, and has pre-set all possible data in his bombsight. The pilot has attained the briefed altitude and air speed and proceeds to move into trail and becomes properly spaced. The navigator picks up the I.P. (Initial Point) and begins to swing the formation so it will pass over the I.P. squared away on the correct heading. The bombardier now takes the ball. Success or failure of the entire mission depends upon his skill with the bombsight in the following all-important seconds. Unlike the football eleven the bombing team must score on "one down."

—Major Paul R. Nugent
47th Wing Bombardier
Fifteenth Air Force

Flying Combat Missions

Radar was new in World War II, and was routinely used by British bombers because they bombed at night when targets weren't visible. Their British radar equipment was referred to as the H2S "Stinky." There are conflicting stories as to how the radar equipment got its name. One story is that it came from a remark by one of Churchill's top advisors, Professor Frederick Lindemann, an English physicist, who said it "stinks" that radar equipment wasn't invented sooner. Another story is that H2S (i.e., H_2S) is the symbol for hydrogen sulfide that has a terrible odor.[23] Hydrogen sulfide is a colorless gas that smells like rotten eggs. Another story is that it came from a remark from Lord Cherwell, scientic advisor for Churchill, who supposedly said, "It stinks. Call it H2S." [24]

British scientists shared the secrets of their H2S radar with American scientists at the Massachusetts Institute of Technology (MIT) Radiation Laboratory in Cambridge, Massachusetts, which had pledged to support the Allied effort. Its scientists developed an improved version called the H2X for use on B-17 bombers. The H2X radar was enclosed in a structural, wea-therproof retractable ball on the aircraft called a randome.[25]

With this radar capability, Cowart and Rabo laid out plans for the establishment of a 482nd Pathfinder Bomb Group in the Eighth Air Force to bomb using radar. When Major Rabo, who would eventually lead the 482nd Pathfinder Bomb Group in combat, saw the randome for the first time lowered under and behind the nose turret of a B-17 at Grenier Field in New Hampshire, he said it looked like Mickey Mouse. The name stuck and planes with radar equipment were forever known as "Mickey ships." Also, since the 482nd Pathfinder Bomb Group was the first to use the H2X "Mickey" to bomb targets, missions using radar to find targets were often called "pathfinder missions."[26]

Second Lieutenant Robert "Bob" Askew was a navigator-bombardier who was trained as a radar operator and flew pathfinder missions during World War II with the 414th Bomb Squadron, 97th Bomb Group, 5th Bomb Wing of the Fifteenth Air Force.[27] He flew out of Amendola Airfield which was about twenty miles northeast of Castelluccio Airfield, John Cooney's base of operations.[28] Both flew strategic bombings missions in heavy bombers, only Bob flew with B-17 Flying Fortresses and John with B-24 Liberators.

Bob felt radar was an excellent navigation device but lacked the accuracy of the Norden bombsight as a bombing device.[29] You could not detect a small target with radar, but you could detect a large, general target. He said the radar scope would allow the operator to determine the contrast between land, water, and cities. Consequently, radar was used to bomb large area targets such as cities.[30] By flying over cloud cover to bomb targets you could not see, he noted that you may not have achieved the accuracy of a bombsight, but by flying high and behind cloud cover it was difficult for enemy anti-aircraft batteries to shoot you down.

Bob pointed out that while a formation of planes could fly over an overcast, you didn't want to take a formation of planes through an overcast. He said a formation flying wingtip to wingtip through an overcast would be like having an aerial demolition derby to create gold star mothers. If you had to fly through an overcast, he said it was best to send a single ship, a "lone wolf" if you will, not an entire formation of planes.[31] Lone wolf bombing operations typically involved high priority targets deep in enemy territory defended heavily by flak and fighters.[32]

Bob recalled two of his seventeen missions. In the first one, a mission to Prague, Czechoslovakia, he had a harrowing experience when a bomb got hung up on an "arming wire" with the warhead swinging perilously in the bomb bay and he had to walk out on the narrow catwalk to cut it loose. He never forgot it because the bomb he cut loose scored a direct hit on an anti-aircraft battery below.[33] In the second one, he remembered it because it was a historic mission in that it was the first time the Fifteenth Air Force based in Italy bombed Berlin, the German capital. The Eighth Air Force based in England usually flew missions to Berlin because it was closer. It was also the longest Fifteenth Air Force mission of the war.[34] The date was March 24, 1945, and the target was the Daimler-Benz Tank Works which assembled tanks that helped the Germans to resist Allied advances.[35]

Bob said it was a high-priority target and that the flak was accurate, intense, and heavy. Nevertheless, they hit the tank works with good results, and his bomb squadron suffered no losses. His bomb group, the 97th Bomb Group, went on a 6.5-minute bomb run with flak flying around them and dropped their bombs from between 28,000 and 29,000 feet going 150 miles per hour.[36] He said he got a good look at Berlin through the bomb bay. He also said they were escorted on the mission by the Tuskegee Airmen and that they did a good job—more on them later.[37]

Visibility was good that day, so they didn't have to use radar for their bombing.[38] Nevertheless, Bob said you had to worry about radar equipment. He remembered one pathfinder mission when he used his radar as soon as the ship was airborne to direct it to the target area. They were carrying a bomb load of two bombs fused for exploding on instant contact and the rest fused to explode after a two-hour interval. On that day, his radar equipment malfunctioned so they were unable to identify the target area to drop their bomb load. The pilot considered flying to Vienna to drop the bomb load but since Vienna was not the military objective of the mission and because the flak over Vienna was always heavy and often deadly, they nixed that idea and headed back to their base. On the way back, the bombardier came back to the bomb bay and took the fuses out of the bombs and handed them to Bob, then he released the bombs into the Adriatic Sea rather than land with a full load of bombs. Bob tossed the fuses through the open bomb bay.[39]

Bob said it was supposed to be SOP (Standard Operating Procedure) to bring back bombs you didn't drop. Bombs cost the taxpayers a lot of money. The reality, however, was that planes on bombing missions that were unable to drop their bombs were hesitant to return to their home base and land with live bombs, so they often salvoed them over a sea or an ocean. In the 2021 best selling book, *The Bomber Mafia: A Dream, A Temptation, and The Longest Night of the Second World War*, the author, Malcolm Gladwell, mentions that it was not uncommon to salvo bombs left over from a mission on the return trip.[40] Supposedly, Glenn Miller, the famous band leader, was killed on December 15, 1944 when a Royal Air Force bomber returning from a mission with live bombs on board salvoed them over the English Channel and one hit the plane Miller was flying in to Paris to make arrangements for a Christmas broadcast.[41] Collateral damage is one of the unfortunate circumstances of aerial bombardment during wartime.

In preparation for the winter of 1944, General Twining decided to add Mickey ships to the Fifteenth Air Force. In addition to B-17s, B-24s were also equipped with radar to fly pathfinder missions. The randome was adapted for use in the B-24s, but instead of being placed under the nose of the aircraft, it was placed behind the bomb bay in place of the ball-turret on the lead ship.[42] He also decided to have specialized forces to fly bombing missions in poor weather, and to call those forces Red Forces.

In October 1944, a month after Cookman's crew arrived on the spur of Italy, his bomb group, the 451st, began to fly combat missions with two forces instead of one on days when the weather was an issue. When two bomber forces were employed on a mission, one was typically called the Red Force and the other the Blue Force. The Red Force generally bombed a major industrial target with a fighter escort and with radar pathfinders to locate targets not visible due to overcast conditions, while the Blue Force bombed a less-important target closer to the home base that could be bombed visually without a fighter escort.[43] Even though each of these missions were listed as one mission, they would be bombing two different targets with two different forces and would in essence be flying two different missions.

FROM ONE WAR TO ANOTHER

The Targets

The 451st Bomb Group flew 245 combat missions during the war, but since some of them had two forces going to different targets, it really flew 259 missions. It flew combat missions to twelve countries as follows (number of times in parentheses): Austria (75), Italy (63), Germany (30), France (23), Romania (23) Yugoslavia (17), Hungary (15), Czechoslovakia (6), Albania (3), Greece (2), Bulgaria (1) and Poland (1) (Exhibits 9.3 and 9.4).[44]

Because most German troops, equipment, and supplies were transported via train, ninety-eight (38 percent) of the 259 bombing targets of the 451st Bomb Group were railroad marshalling yards, bridges, and viaducts. Because Nazi Germany depended on petroleum, oil, and lubrication products to fuel its weapons, fifty-eight targets (22 percent) were facilities that produced and stored these products. Because the Luftwaffe was a threat to Allied bombers, thirty-seven airdromes, airports and factories that produced German aircraft were key targets (14 percent). The other sixty-six targets (26 percent) included troop concentrations, factories that produced other war materiel such as ball bearings and submarines, and other targets that empowered Nazi Germany.

A Proud Unit

When John arrived at Castelluccio Airfield, the 451st Bomb Group already had a proud history, having received three Distinguished Unit Citations, the nation's highest award for a combat organization. The prestigious award was given to units that displayed extraordinary heroism against an armed enemy. The award was created in 1943 as the Distinguished Unit Citation (the name was changed to Presidential Unit Citation in 1957). It was awarded to units of the armed forces for "extraordinary heroism in action against an armed enemy."[45] Considering that every airman on a combat mission is displaying courage, a unit's being singled out for extraordinary heroism is indeed something to be proud of. While the 451st would never receive another Distinguished Unit Citation, it would be the only bomb group of the Fifteenth Air Force to receive three Distinguished Unit Citations.[46]

The 451st's first Distinguished Unit Citation was awarded for its outstanding work in fighting off enemy fighters and then bombing and destroying the Regensburg Prufening Aircraft Factory in Regensburg, Germany on February 25, 1944. The 451st unit was intercepted on the way to the target by enemy fighters, and in the ensuing air battle was credited with shooting

Exhibit 9.3
Missions Flown by 451st Bomb Group

Month	Missions With One Target	Missions With Two Targets	Total Missions
Jan. 1944	1	0	1
Feb. 1944	9	0	9
Mar. 1944	10	0	10
Apr. 1944	16	0	16
May 1944	20	0	20
Jun. 1944	16	0	16
Jul. 1944	22	0	22
Aug 1944	20	0	20
Sep. 1944	14	0	14
Oct. 1944	13	3	16
Nov. 1944	16	3	19
Dec. 1944	19	0	19
Total 1944	**176**	**6**	**182**
Jan. 1945	7	1	8
Feb. 1945	21	4	25
Mar. 1945	20	2	22
Apr. 1945	21	1	22
Total 1945	**69**	**8**	**77**
Grand Total	**245**	**14**	**259**

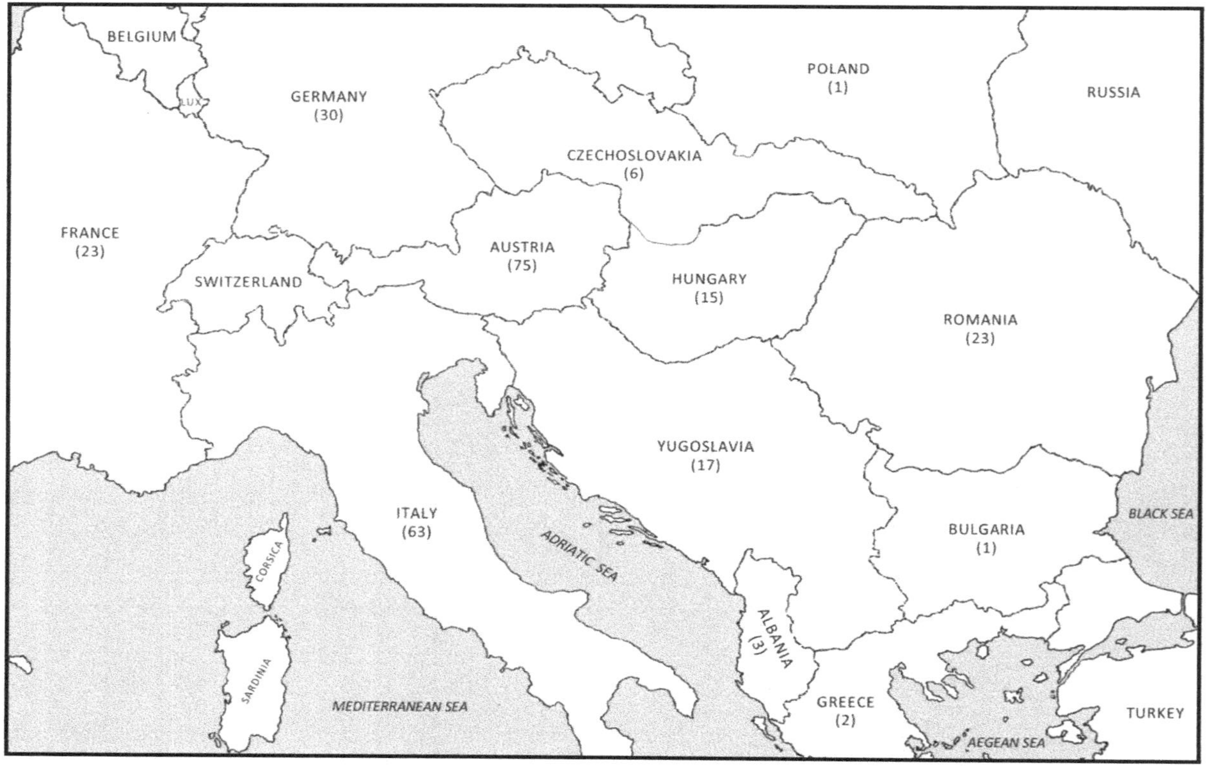
BELGIUM
LUX
GERMANY
(30)
POLAND
(1)
RUSSIA
CZECHOSLOVAKIA
(6)
FRANCE
(23)
AUSTRIA
(75)
SWITZERLAND
HUNGARY
(15)
ROMANIA
(23)
YUGOSLAVIA
(17)
ITALY
(63)
BLACK SEA
BULGARIA
(1)
CORSICA
ADRIATIC SEA
ALBANIA
(3)
SARDINIA
MEDITERRANEAN SEA
GREECE
(2)
TURKEY
AEGEAN SEA

Exhibit 9.4: Number of 451st Bomb Group Missions by Country

down sixteen enemy fighters, probably destroying three others, and damaging another six fighters.[47] The mission was effective but costly, resulting in the loss of six planes and crews.[48]

The second Distinguished Unit Citation was for its performance under fire on a mission to bomb the oil refineries and marshalling yards in Ploesti, Romania on April 5, 1944.[49] The 451st was the last bomb group over the target, and the Germans were waiting for them. German Messerschmitt Bf 109s and Foche-Wulf Fw 190s came at them from all directions, while the flak cannons pummeled them from the ground. Despite being overwhelmed by fighters and flak, they dropped seventy-one tons of bombs on the oil fields. After dumping their bomb loads, they were attacked again. For three-quarters of an hour, they fought an air battle. For the mission, they were credited with shooting down twenty enemy fighters with a dozen more they may have destroyed.[50] Again, they bombed well but the cost was high, with the loss of five planes and crews. A sixth B-24 was lost on takeoff when the plane caught fire and exploded, killing all but one crew member.[51]

The Messerschmitt Bf 109 and the Focke-Wulf Fw 190 were Germany's top two fighter planes during World War II. The Bf 109 was built by Messerschmitt AG, and was named for its chief designer, Willie Messerschmitt. The Bf stands for Bayerische Flugzeugwerke which translates to Bavarian Aircraft Factory. It went into action in 1937 and about 34,000 of them were built for the war.[52] The Focke-Wulf Fw 190 was built by Focke-Wulf Flugzeubau AG, whose chief designer was Kurt Tank. Flugzenbau translates to aircraft construction and Fw stands for Focke-Wulf. It went into action in 1941 and about 20,000 were built for the war.[53] The two fighters were the backbone of the Jagdwaffe, the Luftwaffe's fighter forces.[54]

The German Me-262 jet came too late in the war to make the impact made by the Bf 109s and Fw 190s.[55] Bad luck and lack of teamwork were reasons why. For example, Adolph Galland, a legendary fighter pilot who was the commanding general of the Luftwaffe's fighter forces, was impressed with the Me 262. He had flown the Bf 109 and Fw 190 fighters powered by piston engines and had an opportunity to fly an early model of the Me 262 powered by jet engines. He was so impressed by the potential of the Me 262 that he suggested discontinuing the development of the Me 209, a jet-engine successor to the Bf 109, because he felt the latest model of the Fw 190 was just as good as the Me 209.[56] He felt those working on the Me 209 should join the development team of Me 262 to produce them faster and in August 1973 ordered 1,000 Me 262s for his fighter forces.[57] The same month, the Messerschmitt factory in

Regensburg, where the Me-262 was being developed, was bombed and a decision was made to move the design team to the Bavarian Alps, thereby delaying the Me 262 program for months.[58] Adding to the delay was the fact that Erhard Milch, Secretary of Aviation in charge of aircraft production, was hesitant to stop development of other projects to meet Galland's order.[59]

To resolve this bottleneck, a commission was established in November 1943.[60] Ernst Udet, Chief of Procurement and Supply, also a legendary fighter pilot, was on the commission and he wanted to build more fighters.[61] When Hitler was brought into the debate, he complicated matters significantly by ordering a modification of the Me 262, designed as a fighter, to become a bomber as well. He wanted a "blitz bomber" for the invasion of Europe that everyone knew was coming sooner or later.[62] Galland, on the other hand, was focused on protecting Germany against the Allies who were strategically dropping bombs over Germany to destroy its ability to wage war.

In May 1944, when Hitler learned that they stopped the program to modify the Me 262 due to extensive design changes, he flew into a rage and said the Me 262 will enter military service exclusively as a fighter-bomber.[63] Milch tried to convince him otherwise and was relieved of his position as Secretary of Aviation.[64] Albert Speer, Minister of Armament and War Production, also tried to convince him but to no avail.[65]

It wasn't until November 1944 that Hitler came to grips with the fact that his demand was not feasible, and he allowed the Me 262 to be produced as a fighter but with a condition that it must carry at least one 550-pound bomb in case of emergency. Only 564 Me 262s were built by the end of 1944, too few and too late to make an impact as an interceptor of Allied bombers.[66] Another 740 Me 262s were produced during the first three months of 1945 but, again, too few and too late to make a difference.[67]

The third Distinguished Unit Citation awarded to the 451st was for their outstanding performance on an August 23, 1944, mission to bomb the Markersdorf Airdrome in Vienna, Austria. Before they reached the target, they were attacked by numerous fighters which were hellbent on breaking up their formation, but they hung together and destroyed or damaged thirty-eight enemy aircraft—twenty-nine in the air and twelve on the ground. In the air battles, the 451st lost nine planes and crews.[68] The three Distinguished Unit Citations are recapped in Exhibit 9.5.

While John didn't fly on the three Distinguished Unit Citation missions, he was proud to be in the unit that did, and when he was promoted to staff sergeant, the press release to his hometown carried a headline that his unit

Exhibit 9.5
Distinguished Unit Citations (DUCs) of the 451ST Bomb Group

Date	Target	Damage to Enemy	Cost to 451st BG
02/25/1944	Regensburg Prufening Aircraft Factory in Regensburg, Germany	• Attacked by about 200 enemy fighters but still scored many direct hits on the target, contributing greatly to the curtailment of aircraft production at a time of great importance. • Reported 16 enemy fighters destroyed, 3 probably destroyed, and 6 damaged.	Lost 6 B-24s
04/05/1944	Oil Installations and Marshalling Yards in Ploesti, Romania	• Attacked by about 85 enemy fighters but still caused tremendous material to the targets which curtailed oil production and shipment by the enemy. • Reported 20 enemy aircraft known to be destroyed, 12 probably destroyed, and 3 known to be damaged.	Lost 5 B-24s
08/23/1944	Markersdorf Airdrome in Vienna, Austria	• Attacked by numerous enemy fighters but still inflicted grave damage to important buildings and supplies. • Destroyed or damaged 29 enemy aircraft in the air. • Destroyed 12 enemy aircraft on the ground.	Lost 9 B-24s

was a double-citation winner for the Regensburg mission of February 25 and Ploesti mission of April 5—the 451st hadn't yet been cited for the Vienna mission of August 23.[69] The 451st Bomb Group would not be cited for that mission until October 2, 1944.[70]

During September 1944, the 451st Bomb Group flew fourteen missions—six combat missions to targets in Yugoslavia (3), Greece (2) and Italy (1) and eight supply missions to the Bron Airdrome in Lyon, France. The supply missions were to bring gas, oil, bullets, and bombs to the fighter-bombers of the Tactical Air Force that were supporting the ground troops of the U.S. Seventh Army under General Alexander Patch. His army had landed in southern France at Marseille on August 15 and depended upon air support to advance. While there was a supply of fuel and ammunition on the ships and docks at the wrecked port of Marseille, unloading and transporting these supplies over the bombed roads in a timely manner to Lyon prompted Colonel William L. Lee, the wing commander of the fighter bombers supporting the Seventh Army, to ask General Twining for help and he came through with these supply missions. It was important to keep Patch's forces advancing to the northeast toward Germany to protect the southern flank of Eisenhower's forces that had landed in France at Normandy and were advancing eastward toward Germany.[71]

The 451st Bomb Group lost only one plane during the month of September because it flew fewer combat missions, and the loss was due to an accident.[72] This was a far cry from the losses it sustained in combat operations in previous months and those it would sustain going forward. In early October, it had sixty-nine combat crews: seventeen in the 724th Bomb Squadron, seventeen in John's 725th Bomb Squadron, eighteen in the 726th, and seventeen in the 727th. It had fifty-eight B-24s of which forty-three were operational, the others under repair. The sixty-nine crews were staffed with 737 men—290 officers and 447 enlisted men. In addition, the 451st had twenty-four staff officers for the administrative work, seven PFF (Pathfinder Force) navigators for missions in poor weather when radar was needed to identify targets, and twelve aerial photographers to record the accuracy of the 451st Bomb Group's bombs.[73]

The 451st Bomb Group had inflicted a lot of damage on the Nazi war machine, but at a high cost. Large formations of American strategic bombers flying over enemy territory were targets for enemy fighter planes in the air and enemy anti-aircraft batteries on the ground. Flying combat missions was a hazardous duty and you had to have luck on your side to survive them.

Chapter 10

LUCK IN WAR

Survival in war is often a matter of luck. On combat missions, airmen were in harm's way, especially on bomb runs. A bomb run started after the lead navigator led the planes to the target area. It began at an initial point when the formation leader, the lead pilot of the lead plane, aimed his plane toward the target and turned his plane over to the lead bombardier, who had the job of sighting the target and dropping his bombs at the release point, at which time the rest of the planes in the formation would drop their bombs. The bomb run was typically from two to eight minutes but could be longer. During the bomb run, heavy bombers such as B-24 Liberators had to fly straight and narrow without taking evasive action so that the lead bombardier could sight the target.[1] Key targets were typically well-defended in the air by enemy fighters with rapid-fire machine guns and on the ground by enemy anti-aircraft batteries with powerful flak cannons. To be flying toward a well-defended enemy target without taking evasive action was a frightening experience.

Many years after the war, John Cooney said in an interview that "every mission, of course, could be the final one."[2] Danger of death was ever present on bombing missions. It took courage to fly them, and it took luck to survive them. About a month before John's crew arrived at Castelluccio Airfield, a mission took place on August 23, 1944, in which one crew of the 725th Bomb Squadron of the 451st Bomb Group (the squadron Cookman's crew would join) was lucky, and another was not. It was one of the three missions for which the 451st Bomb Group received a Distinguished Unit Citation. It inflicted a lot of damage on the enemy, but the cost was high in terms of American lives and planes lost.

FROM ONE WAR TO ANOTHER

Both Sides of Luck

On that fateful day, Captain George E. Tudor and his 725th Bomb Squadron crew were scheduled to fly in a B-24 nicknamed *Extra Joker* in the #1 position to lead a formation of twenty-four B-24s on a mission to bomb the Markersdorf Airdrome, about forty miles west of Vienna, Austria. Tudor had flown all his missions in *Extra Joker*. As luck would have it, on this mission his bombardier told him that the Sperry bombsight they were using did not have the setting capability for dropping the fragmentation bombs they were carrying that day. Consequently, Tudor switched planes with First Lieutenant Kenneth A. Whiting, who was scheduled to fly deputy lead off Tudor's right wing in the #2 position. His plane, *Sassy Lassy*, was equipped with a Norden bombsight that had the setting required for Tudor's plane to accurately sight the target. This was an unlucky development for Whiting's crew, and a lucky one for Tudor's crew.[3]

Staff Sergeant Leo Stoutsenberger, a photographer for their bomb group, was scheduled to fly with Tudor that day on *Extra Joker* in the #1 position but because of the switched planes he ended up flying with Tudor on *Sassie Lassie* in the #1 position. On the way to the target, the waist gunners asked him if he would take photos of their plane, *Extra Joker*, the one in which they had been flying their missions, which was now in the #2 position.[4] In the target area, he obliged them and while he was photographing *Extra Joker*, the aircraft he was supposed to be in, it was hit by flak that ripped a large hole in the left wing behind the left outboard motor. As the engine caught fire and started to burn profusely, Stoutsenberger kept snapping away.[5]

According to Technical Sergeant Lindley G. Miller, Tudor's right waist gunner, the formation was attacked by German Fw 190s over the initial point of their bomb run and *Extra Joker* was hit, causing its main tanks to burst into flames, after which it went into a spin. After dropping about five-thousand feet with enemy Fw 190s in pursuit, it exploded in mid-air, killing Whiting and his entire crew.[6]

While the 451st Bomb Group did not know it at that time, they were attacked by the best Luftwaffe fighter group the Germans had—the Strumme Grouppe (Storm Group). As soon as the Americans started on their bomb run, when they were most vulnerable, the Storm Group came out of the clouds and attacked from all angles.[7] The 451st Bomb Group fought back valiantly, destroying, or damaging twenty-nine enemy aircraft in the air while destroying twelve enemy aircraft on the ground in addition to inflicting considerable damage to the buildings and supplies of the airdrome.[8]

Stoutsenberger ended up with a sequence of photos of the destruction of *Extra Joker* and the tragic loss of its crew.[9] The photos were so dramatic that he was awarded the Distinguished Flying Cross for capturing the tragedy on film.[10] His emotions must have run the gamut by seeing a plane in which he was scheduled to fly get blown out of the sky, and then receiving a medal for photographing the disaster. For the families of Whiting and his crew, the news that their loved ones were killed in action was devastating, a circumstance of extraordinary bad luck (Exhibit 10.1).

The bodies of the ten members of Whiting's crew were brought to a temporary burial ground in the village of Neuville-en-Condroz, twelve miles southwest of Liège, Belgium.[11] This Belgian cemetery had been liberated from German occupation and became the Ardennes American Cemetery, one of the many American cemeteries in Europe developed by the American Battle Monuments Commission (ABMC) under the guidance of General Pershing, who headed the ABMC from its inception in 1923 until the day he died in 1948.[12] The Ardennes American Cemetery is the resting place for 5,162 Americans, two-thirds of whom are American airmen.[13]

The ten members of Whiting's crew remained temporarily buried in Belgium for the rest of the war. After the war, the temporary burial grounds were disestablished by the American Graves Registration which was responsible for overseeing the American war dead to ensure that they were handled with the dignity and respect they deserved for their sacrifices. Nine of the ten members of the crew were memorialized in a group burial at the Jefferson Barracks National Cemetery near St. Louis, Missouri.[14] A tenth member of the crew, Sergeant Harry Vaughn Bates, was laid to rest at the Swamp Church Cemetery in his hometown of Reinholds, Pennsylvania.[15] There were 560 group burials at the Jefferson Barracks National Cemetery for World War II.[16]

Six days after *Extra Joker* was destroyed, it was replaced by a new plane that came off the assembly line at the Ford Willow Run Airplane Plant on July 7, 1944. The replacement plane was given the name of *Betty Jo* and assigned to the 725th Bomb Squadron on August 27.[17] It was also given *Extra Joker*'s revetment number of 35, the number of the parking space it was assigned on the ground at Castelluccio Airfield.[18] The revetment number was painted in bold numbers on the nose and fuselage of the aircraft. Two weeks later, John Cooney and Meyer Osofsky would have the bad luck of flying in *Betty Jo* when it went down over Italy, and their pilot, Bob Cookman, would have the worst possible luck.

Exhibit 10.1
Unlucky Crew of *Extra Joker* Shot Down Over Austria
August 23, 1944

Name	Position	Next of Kin	Final Resting Place*
1st Lt. Kenneth Austin Whiting	Pilot	Mother, Salt Lake City, UT	Jefferson Barracks National Cemetery St. Louis, MO
1st Lt. Alvin Warren Moore	Co-Pilot	Mother, McMinnville, OR	Jefferson Barracks National Cemetery St. Louis, MO
2nd Lt. Francis Joseph Bednarek	Navigator	Wife, Ashley, PA	Jefferson Barracks National Cemetery St. Louis, MO (Had son Francis, Jr.)
2nd Lt. Edward Steven Waneski	Bombardier	Mother, Brooklyn, NY	Jefferson Barracks National Cemetery St. Louis, MO
S/Sgt. Peter Breda	Engineer and Top-Turret Gunner	Mother, Lima, OH	Jefferson Barracks National Cemetery St. Louis, MO (Born in Netherlands)
Aviation Cadet Harry Vaugh Bates	Ball-Turret Gunner	Mother, Reinholds, PA	Swamp Church Cemetery Reinholds, PA
Sgt. Joseph Garbacz	Right Waist Gunner	Aunt, Detroit, MI	Jefferson Barracks National Cemetery St. Louis, MO
S/Sgt. Milton Robert Nitsch	Radio Operator and Left Waist Gunner	Father, Sheboygan, WI	Jefferson Barracks National Cemetery St. Louis, MO
Sgt. Elmer James Anderson	Nose-Turret Gunner	Mother, Los Angeles, CA	Jefferson Barracks National Cemetery St. Louis, MO
Sgt. Oscar Watson Bateman	Tail-Turret Gunner	Wife, Baton Rouge, LA	Jefferson Barracks National Cemetery St. Louis, MO (Father of Three)

*The crew was buried temporarily at Neuville-en-Condroz, Belgium before each next-of-kin decided upon final resting place.

Luck In War

Friday the 13th

The officers and enlisted men in Cookman's crew were separated by rank. The four officers lived together in one tent and the six enlisted men lived together in another tent. Osofsky said the enlisted men were all close, having trained together in the States and having traveled together on a truck on the deck of a ship to Italy. He also noted that each of them flew their first mission with another crew to gain some combat experience rather than have all of them fly together on their first combat mission.[19] The enlisted men were all trained to be aerial gunners from different combat positions—the front, top, bottom, sides, and back of the aircraft. They always had to be alert to attacks by enemy fighters because a sudden attack could be quick and deadly.

Mosher was the first one in the enlisted tent to experience bad luck, the worst possible kind. On October 13, 1944, ten days before his five tent mates went down in Cookman's plane, Mosher was assigned as a replacement crew member for a mission to bomb the Oesterreichische Motor Works and marshalling yards in Vienna, Austria. Vienna was the second most heavily defended enemy target, and where *Extra Joker* was blown out of the sky. The most heavily defended target was Berlin, the capitol of Nazi Germany, and the third most heavily defended target was Ploesti, Romania, a key supplier of fuel for the Nazi war machine. Missions to these targets were dreaded because the crews could expect a pounding from anti-aircraft batteries as well as attacks from enemy fighters.[20]

Four years earlier after British bombers attacked Berlin in late August 1940, Hitler ordered the construction of colossal flak towers in Berlin (1940-43), Hamburg (1941-43), and Vienna (1942-44) to better protect those cities from Allied bombing. By the fall of 1944, Vienna was well-defended by three pairs of prodigious flak towers.[21] Each pair of these colossal cement structures had a smaller L-tower—the "lead" tower—which acted as the command center with trained personnel and equipment to spot the Allied bombers, and a larger G-tower—the "gun" tower—with trained soldiers to shoot them down with their powerful anti-aircraft cannons.[22]

The G-towers were as high as 128 feet with four anti-aircraft cannons on the top that could fire 7,000 to 8,000 rounds a minute with an average range of nine miles.[23] These blockhouses had walls as thick as eleven feet and were also used as above-ground air-raid shelters that could accommodate as many as ten thousand civilians.[24] The fact that most of them are still standing today is testimony to their durability.

FROM ONE WAR TO ANOTHER

The Todt Organization built these massive towers with hundreds of forced laborers from countries Germany occupied in Europe plus prisoners of war.[25] The Todt Organization was the engineering group of the Third Reich that had 1.4 million personnel and oversaw the construction of projects for Nazi Germany. It was named for Fritz Todt.[26] When Hitler came to power in 1933, he put Todt in charge of building a national highway system; and when he took Germany to war, he made Todt his chief architect and engineer. Todt was killed in a plane accident in February 1942 after which Albert Speer replaced him as Reich Minister of Munitions.[27] After the war, Speer was convicted at the Nuremberg Trials of war crimes and crimes against humanity and was sent to prison for twenty years.[28]

Airmen like Mosher who were assigned to bombing missions in Vienna had good reason to worry. Despite Luftwaffe fighters being of lesser concern now that Allied airpower dominated the skies, the flak batteries were of major concern because they were more powerful than ever, the result of Hitler assigning a high priority to anti-aircraft home defenses. Some felt he should have assigned a higher priority to aircraft that attacked Allied bombers rather than anti-aircraft batteries that defended against such bombing raids, but in a dictatorship, decisions are not often made by committee. Hitler regarded airpower as an offensive weapon not a defensive weapon. He put his eggs into the anti-aircraft basket instead of the interceptor-fighter basket, thereby allowing the Allies to dominate the skies and bomb German industries that supported the Nazi war machine.[29]

Osofsky said Mosher had a premonition that he would not return from his first mission. In fact, he announced to his tent mates: "I'm not coming back."[30] He knew the odds of making it home were not high, and most likely saw them go down when he heard about this mission. Vienna was known to be a hornet's nest, and they were flying into the nest on Friday the 13th. As luck would have it, he was right. Eight B-24s and their crews from the 451st Bomb Group were shot down on that mission, including his plane. According to the Missing Air Crew Reports (MACRs) of the eight planes, seventeen airmen from the 451st were fatalities on that day, including him. Forty-two airmen became prisoners of war and twenty-two evaded the enemy with help. It was another mission from hell (Exhibit 10,2).[31]

Bob Cookman and Calvin Chin were also on the Friday the 13th mission, flying in other heavy bombers. It was Cookman's first combat mission and Chin's third. Chin had already survived two of them and was less apprehensive than Kirk. Cookman would be killed in action on his third combat

Exhibit 10.2
Fate of 451st Bomb Group Crews Shot Down on Friday the 13th
October 13, 1944

Bomb Squad	Nickname of Plane Shot Down	Shot Down Over	Pilot	MACR	Crew Total	KIA	POW	Evaded Enemy
724	None	Hungary	2nd Lt. Kenneth R. Elliott	9048	10	0	10	0
724	Our Gal	Austria	1st Lt. James M. Moye	9092	10	1	9	0
724	Fickle Finger	Austria	1st Lt. William L. Goin	9134	10	10	0	0
725	Rabbit Habit	Austria	1st Lt. Robert K. Baker	9047	10	5	5	0
725	None	Hungary	2nd Lt. Ashley D. Smith	9051	9	1	7	1
726	Leading Lady	Yugoslavia	1st Lt. James H. Rowley	9066	11	0	0	11
726	None	Yugoslavia	2nd Lt. Ibar M. Spellacy	9056	10	0	0	10
727	Weesie	Austria	1st Lt. Homer T. Brewer	9088	11	0	11	0
			Fate of 81 Crew Members of 451ST Bomb Group		**81**	**17**	**42**	**22**

mission. Chin never forgot the Friday the 13th mission because he lost his tentmate in it and because he had a photograph taken from his plane of the flack-filled sky that day which he passed down to his son David.[32] He's not the only one who never forgot the mission.

First Lieutenant Harry O. Rohde, one of the B-24 pilots on the mission, wrote about the mission in his memoirs. He said that he would never forget that day because the flak was accurate, and they got "shot to hell." He "saw planes going down in flames and men jumping out with parachutes."[33] Rohde was not the only one to write about the mission. Staff Sergeant John C. Schumacher, a waist gunner on a B-24 nicknamed *Our Gal,* wrote that it was a day he will never forget, and no wonder.[34] It was a clear day and there were 620 B-24 Liberators on the mission, giving the Nazi anti-aircraft batteries plenty of targets to shoot at with their powerful cannons.[35] He said the flak was so heavy that it rattled his plane, and it must have rattled other planes as well because one of the planes flying above him dropped its bombs on a plane that was flying next to him, resulting in an explosion that knocked him off his feet.[36]

As the left waist gunner, Schumacher was on the left side of his aircraft while co-pilot, First Lieutenant Devon R. Hall, was on the right side, close to the explosion. The navigator, First Lieutenant Robert E. Zimmer, said the interphone was knocked out, but he could hear someone yell, "We've been hit badly! Looks bad!" Since the interphone wasn't working, the pilot, First Lieutenant James M. Moye, asked Hall to check on the men in the back of the plane to be sure they were okay.[37]

The nose-turret gunner, Staff Sergeant Joseph E. Roman, said he saw Hall get up, take off his flak suit, and pick up his chute.[38] Zimmer thought Hall may have had a serious head injury because he didn't seem to be himself. He said he "was a fine, brave cool man" and "was absolutely fearless," but he may have been rattled by the explosion because he was the closest to the plane that blew up. When Schumacher learned later that Moye had sent Hall to check on the four of them behind the bomb bay, he said he never arrived. Nobody knew for sure what happened to Hall, but the later consensus among the crew, when discussing the matter later in a prison camp, was that as he was walking along the narrow catwalk through the open bomb bay toward the back of the plane, he might have either fallen off or been knocked off the catwalk by the concussion of another flak burst.[39]

The bombardier, First Lieutenant Vernon V. Drower, told the engineer and top-turret gunner, Staff Sergeant John T. Scully, that he saw Hall going toward the bomb bay. Since the catwalk through the bomb bay is less than a foot wide and is held up only by narrow vertical supports, walking across it was like walking across a very narrow bridge over a canyon, only in a B-24 with the bomb bay doors open, the drop was a lot higher.[40] Walking the catwalk under good conditions was dangerous, and Hall was walking it under harrowing and violent combat conditions, and his condition was not stable. Schumacher said that when the crew was captured and brought together the next day, they surmised that Hall probably didn't have a parachute on when he was walking on the catwalk and was blown off when the plane took a hit by a shell in the bomb bay.[41]

By sheer luck, the flak that hit the bomb bay did not explode. It did, however, puncture a tank, causing high octane fuel to spray all over Schumacher and three of his crewmates in the waist of the plane—Technical Sergeant Mario DiMeo, the right waist gunner; Staff Sergeant Leonard Dumas, the tail gunner; and Staff Sergeant Joseph Galenas, the ball-turret gunner. The B-24 Liberator has fuel in its main tanks, auxiliary wing tanks, and an extra tank fitted in the bomb bay. The extra tank in the bomb bay was the one that was hit. It did not blow, and they were ready to bail.[42]

Moye gave the signal to bail, and all nine remaining crew members bailed out before *Our Gal* crashed somewhere in the vicinity of Vienna. They were all captured and brought together the next day. The three surviving officers (Moye, Zimmer, and Drowser) were imprisoned in Stalag Luft III in Zagan, Germany (now Zagan, Poland), and the six enlisted men (Scully, Galenas, DiMeo, Schumacher, Dumas, and Roman) were imprisoned in Stalag Luft IV in Gross Tychow, Pomerania (now Tychowa, Poland).[43] Three months later, David Orkin would join the six enlisted men in Stalag Luft IV. Years later, Schumacher would write about his experience in Stalag Luft IV.

While they endured hard times as prisoners of war, they all made it home after the war. Hall wasn't so lucky—he made the ultimate sacrifice. It was later confirmed that he didn't have a parachute on when his body was found. Even though Roman saw him pick up his parachute, he never put it on, probably because it is difficult to walk across a B-24 catwalk with a parachute on. Sadly, he was a casualty of war. He was laid to rest in the Lorraine American Cemetery in St. Avold, France, one of 10,489 American patriots in that cemetery who were killed during World War II.[44]

On that Friday the 13th, Mosher was flying with pilot First Lieutenant Robert K. Baker in a B-24 nicknamed *Rabbit Habit*. According to co-pilot Second Lieutenant Garfield W. Andrews, after the plane released its bombs, it received three direct hits by flak—in the nose, the forward part of the bomb bay, and between the engines on the right wing—causing the plane to immediately burst into flames. The left waist gunner, Sergeant Clenon Earnest, said Mosher, the right waist gunner, was killed immediately by the flak.[45] Sadly, Mosher's premonition that he would meet his maker on Friday the 13th came true.

Sergeant Sam A. Holquin, the tail-turret gunner, was another fatality. Andrews said Earnest told him that he saw Holquin leave his tail turret and head for the camera hatch. The hatch was located between Holquin and the two waist gunners. As Earnest bailed out though the hatch, Holquin was standing over it. Earnest surmised later that Holquin was staying in the plane to check on the ball-turret gunner, Sergeant Edwin Schoonover, because he knew they were close friends. The two friends left this world together moments later. Andrews said that after he jumped, he looked up and saw the plane blow up.[46]

Five men on *Rabbit Habit* were killed on that Friday the 13th. Mosher was killed when flak ripped through the aluminum fuselage. Staff Sergeant Harry Egnatenko, the nose-turret, was most likely killed when flak hit the nose. It is written on Schoonover's memorial website page that he and two fellow crewmen, who were attempting to free him, were killed when the plane blew up.[47] Those two were most likely Holquin and Second Lieutenant George C. Phelps. War takes a terrible toll. Mosher was only 21; Holquin, 25; Schoonover, 19; Egnatenko, 22; and Phelps, 22.[48]

In addition to *Our Gal* and *Rabbit Habit*, six other planes from the 451st Bomb Group were shot down on that Friday the 13th, and two of them experienced fatalities. The crew of First Lieutenant William L. Goin's plane, *Fickle Finger*, flew into a barrage of flak over its target, took a direct hit on the number one engine, the outboard engine on Goin's left, knocking the propeller off and catching fire. The plane started to lose altitude fast with the fire increasing because as a plane descends the oxygen in the atmosphere fuels the fire. This caused the plane to explode in the sky, killing all ten members of the crew.[49]

The crew of Second Lieutenant Ashley D. Smith's plane, with no nickname, also took a direct hit in the top turret which killed the top-turret gunner, Sergeant James J. Devlin.[50] He was eventually laid to rest in the Ardennes American Cemetery. If you were to google him today at that cemetery you would see his War Dead Certificate with this quote by General John J. Pershing: "Time will not dim the glory of their deeds."[51]

Smith flew with a crew of nine that day, not the usual ten—Second Lieutenant William G. Vorhaus was both the navigator and bombardier on the mission. The other eight bailed out over Hungary. Seven were captured and sent to prison camps. Two of the seven, co-pilot Second Lieutenant Lloyd E. Yarborough and right waist gunner Sergeant Richard E. Clark, were treated for wounds before being sent to prison camps. One crew member, Sergeant Arnold R. Silverstein, the radio operator and left waist gunner, had luck on his side and evaded capture.[52]

The Friday the 13th mission for the 451st Bomb Group was rated as "Excellent" with 12.3 percent of its bombs falling within 1,000 feet of its target.[53] It was also costly with eight planes shot down and eighty-one casualties—seventeen were killed in action and sixty-four were missing in action of which twenty-two evaded capture and forty-two were captured and became prisoners of war.[54]

There were rumors floating around that a fourth Distinguished Unit Citation for the 451st Bomb Group was in the works for this mission, but one never materialized.[55] In the three missions that received citations, six, five, and nine B-24s were lost compared with eight in the Friday the 13th mission. However, in the three cited missions, the 451st was attacked by many fighters and the response of the 451st in destroying or damaging many of them in air battles was recognized in the citations. By the time of the Friday the 13th mission, the Luftwaffe was no longer the threat it had been, but the anti-aircraft batteries were better because Hitler's focus was on defensive warfare, namely beefing up the anti-aircraft batteries around large cities such as Vienna while the Americans were focused on offensive warfare.[56] Thus, the Friday the13th mission lacked the air battles with German fighters which characterized the three cited missions.

Hiding in Hungary

Sergeant Arnold R. Silverstein was one of those shot down over Hungary on Friday the 13th and had the good fortune to evade capture. His story is an interesting one because Hungary was a country that was persecuting Jews and he was Jewish. When Hitler came into power, Hungary sought to build an alliance with Germany. In 1938, Hungary began to pass laws to identify and remove Jews from its economy. After that, things got steadily worse for Jewish residents. In 1941, Hungary allied with Germany in the war against the Soviet Union. Three years later when Germany learned that Hungary was attempting to back out of the alliance by engaging in armistice negotiations with the United States and the United Kingdom, Hitler invaded Hungary and established a new government faithful to Germany.[57] Consequently, Hungary became a target of Allied bombing during the war and Silverstein's bomb group, the 451st, flew fourteen missions with targets in Hungary.[58] Silverstein was now entering a Nazi-occupied country that was persecuting people of his faith. Not only that, but Hungary was a battleground being bombed by the Allies, a double whammy for an airman of the Jewish faith like Silverstein.

When Silverstein landed, he hit the ground hard and sprained his ankle. He landed in a forest in Pusztacsalád, a small village in Hungary about fifty-five miles southeast of Vienna, Austria. As he gathered his parachute and hobbled along, a lady approached him. Józsefné Szalay, who had been working on her family's thirty-acre farm, saw him descending, and rushed to his aid. Silverstein pulled his gun, but when he saw that she was friendly, he put it away and let her help him to her farmhouse. This was a stroke of good luck for Silverstein because Hungarian police and soldiers were soon combing the area in search of him.[59]

Józsefné lived in the farmhouse with her mother-in-law and her stepson Miklós, called Miki. Her husband, József, was away serving in the Hungarian Army. In November, Silverstein had a close call when the house was searched by the Gsendors (i.e., gendarme in English, meaning soldiers to enforce laws) looking for guns.[60] Józsefné and her family were risking their lives by helping an American airman, especially a Jewish airman. She and her family viewed Americans as friends and kept Silverstein well-hidden and well-fed for five-and-a-half months. At first, Miki would stand guard nightly when Silverstein was hiding in the farmhouse. Later, when they hid him in an air-raid shelter in the woods, Józsefné would bring him food every day.[61] Another Hungarian, Sandor Csongey, helped by bringing him cigarettes, shoes, and clothing; and by keeping him informed of the political situation.[62]

Józsefné's husband, József, spoke English because he had spent nine years in Canada and the United States before he was deported to Hungary. In late November, he was dismissed from the Army, but when Hungary issued an order in January 1945 for all men between the ages of twenty-one and forty-eight to report for military duty, he went back into the Army.[63] Csorgey also joined the Army after he was arrested by the Hungarian police and questioned for four days. Because he was under police scrutiny, he said he joined the Hungarian Army to get away from the scrutiny.[64]

In January 1945, three Hungarian Jews who had escaped from a Vienna camp arrived at the farmhouse. They planned to escape to Russia. Silverstein was tempted to join them but decided against it. Luck was again on his side—he later heard they were apprehended and hanged.[65]

In early February, when Silverstein was hiding in the woods, the farmhouse was searched by the Gsendors and the Nyilas.[66] The Gsendors, or Royal Hungarian Gendarmes, were soldiers from Army units who were trained to enforce the law in rural areas.[67] Nyilas was short for *Nyilaskeresztes Párt*, the Hungarian term for the pro-Nazi Arrow Cross Party, a national socialist party that was the Hungarian fascist party.[68] Silverstein feared both, and for good reason.

As the battlefront neared the farm, Silverstein began to hear the roar of the Russian artillery in the distance. As Hungarian soldiers were retreating, some were dropping by the farmhouse to change into civilian clothes for the purpose of deserting and waiting to be liberated by the Russians.[69]

When the Russians arrived on March 30, Silverstein approached them. They weren't convinced of his identity and sent him for interrogation. After being jockeyed around for about a month, he ended up in Budapest where he was turned over to the Swiss Embassy which linked him up with the American Embassy. On April 11, 1945, he left Hungary for America, and freedom at last.[70] Osofsky said Silverstein stopped by their home base at Castelluccio Airfield on his way home and was sporting Russian boots and had put on some weight.[71] Apparently, Józsefné fed him well.

Back on the farm, the Szalay family was still not free despite being liberated from the Nazis. Things got worse instead of better. The Russians helped themselves to their food and possessions. If they resisted, they were in danger of being shot. Miki was called upon to serve as a soldier in Budapest, where he was mistreated for harboring Silverstein. Even when not on duty, he was forced to clean the barracks and polish the boots of the officers.[72]

After the war, an Allied Control Commission for Hungary was set up in Budapest with United States representation, for the purpose of recommending either an award or compensation for Hungarians who helped Allied airmen evade capture. Its Aid Rescue Section evaluated the claims of helpers and dispensed the funds.[73] For helping Silverstein, the Szalay family received 150,000 Pengö on October 25, 1945, and on the same day Sandor Csongey received 60,000 Pengö.[74] The sums were not much help because the Pengö was on its way to becoming worthless.

On March 26, 1946, Józsefné wrote a letter to Silverstein explaining that they were in dire straits because the Russians had taken everything and they were working in vain because the Pengö had been devalued to the point that the one cigarette cost 80,000 Pengö.[75] After the Pengö became worthless, it was replaced by a new currency, the Florint on August 1, 1946.[76] The Aid Rescue Section determined that the Szalay family deserved another 400 Florint as compensation for helping Silverstein, to be dispensed as soon as a peace treaty was signed with Hungary.[77] The Treaty of Peace with Hungary was signed on February 10, 1947, allowing Hungary to resume as a sovereign state in international affairs.[78]

After the war, József said he wanted to write a book about his wartime experiences and those of American pilots shot down over Hungary, and to publish it in the United States.[79] In his wife's letter to Silverstein, she said Miki would like to go to America, and so would she because of her miserable situation in Hungary.[80] Whether or not any of them made it to America is unknown, but what is known is that Józsefné and József now rest together in peace at the Pestszenterzsébeti Cemetery in Budapest, Hungary.[81] Arnold Silverstein, the airman they risked their lives to help, rests in peace at the Baltimore Hebrew Cemetery. Inscribed on his gravestone is, "Devoted Husband, Father and Grandfather."[82] He was one of the lucky ones who made it home and had a good life thanks to his Hungarian friends.

Hiding in Yugoslavia

Four of the crews shot down on Friday the 13th were fortunate and experienced no fatalities. Two of them went down over Austria. The crew of Second Lieutenant Kenneth R. Elliott's plane, which didn't have a nickname, was captured. The four officers were imprisoned in Stalag Luft III, and the six enlisted men in Stalag Luft IV. All ten survived the war.[83] The crew of First Lieutenant Homer T. Brewer's plane, *Weesie*, was very lucky to avoid a fatality because their plane took a direct hit in the bomb bay and exploded soon after the crew bailed out. They were all captured, became prisoners of war, were liberated at war's end, and made it home.[84]

The other two crews went down over Yugoslavia and, with the help of operatives from an Air Crew Rescue Unit and the Office of Strategic Services, were able to evade capture in enemy territory and make it back to friendly territory. The crew of First Lieutenant James H. Rowsey's B-24, *Leading Lady*, was on the way home when their plane started to lose altitude and they had to bail out.[85] The crew of Second Lieutenant Ibar M. Spellacy's B-24, which didn't have a nickname, also lost altitude and they had to bail out over Yugoslavia. Both crews evaded capture and were evacuated to Italy by American operatives working with the Yugoslav resistance.[86] The Yugoslav resistance at that time consisted of two groups—one loyal to the exiled king and the other committed to communism.

Yugoslavia was, like Hungary, occupied by the Germans. When they took over the country in 1941, King Peter fled to Britain where he became the head of the Yugoslav government in exile. In his absence, two Yugoslav resistance groups—the Chetniks and the Partisans—were formed who hated each other and were engaged in a civil war. The Chetniks were led by General Draza Mihailovich and the Partisans were led by Marshal Josip Tito. Both hated Hitler, but also hated each other and were merciless in fighting against each other.[87] While they both loved their country, they had different visions for its future and were passionate about their visions.

Mihailovich was loyal to King Peter who Tito felt was a fascist. Tito favored communism which he viewed as providing a wider representation of citizens from different ethnic backgrounds. Mihailovich felt that communism posed an even greater threat to his country than the German forces now occupying it. Early on, British intelligence supported Mihailovich, but later switched its allegiance to Tito's Partisans because they were more active in fighting the Germans than Mihailovich's Chetniks.[88]

Roosevelt understood the importance of intelligence and in 1940 asked William Joseph Donovan to visit England as an unofficial envoy to learn about British intelligence. After traveling to Britain and parts of Europe during 1940 and 1941 and meeting with people in British intelligence such as Ian Fleming, who later wrote the James Bond novels, he came back with a recommendation that the United States needed a centralized means of collecting foreign intelligence.[89] Roosevelt appreciated his foresight and established the Office of the Coordination of Information (COI) in July 1941, with Donovan in charge.[90]

Even though Donovan was a Republican, Roosevelt reached across the aisle for him because he felt he was the best man for the job. He had known him since they were classmates at Columbia Law School. Before that, Donovan had been a quarterback on the Columbia football team. Roosevelt knew he was smart, had leadership skills, and had courage. He was a war hero in World War I who was wounded three times and received an impressive array of awards for bravery. He is the only American to receive the nation's four highest awards—the Congressional Medal of Honor, the Distinguished Service Cross, the Distinguished Service Medal, and the National Security Medal.[91]

After Pearl Harbor was bombed in December 1941, the United States recognized that they should have had better intelligence to see it coming. The result was an upgrade of the COI to the Office of Strategic Services (OSS) in June 1942 with Donovan still at the helm.[92] With the endorsement of Roosevelt, the OSS was formed as an undercover foreign intelligence service operating under the authority of the Joint Chiefs of Staff.[93] During World War II, Donovan and the OSS developed espionage and special operations forces that led to the eventual creation of the Central Intelligence Agency (CIA) in September 1947.[94]

Donovan is remembered as the "Father of Modern American Intelligence Gathering" and there is a statue of him in the lobby of the CIA Headquarters in Langley, Virginia.[95] While he had the nickname "Wild Bill," he was not a wild man. There is no definitive explanation of how he got the nickname but one which makes sense is that he had the same name as a famous major league pitcher of his time who was called Wild Bill Donovan because he walked a lot of batters. Donovan the quarterback, war hero, lawyer, and public servant was always an inspirational leader very much in control. When he died in 1959, President Eisenhower said, "What a man! We have lost the last hero."[96]

The OSS had over 13,000 employees during World War II, and more than half of them served overseas, including those who rescued Rowsey's and Spellacy's crews.[97] With many planes being shot down over enemy territory, Roosevelt wanted the crews rescued and so did General Twining, commander of the Fifteenth Air Force whose headquarters were in Bari, Italy. As a result, Lieutenant General Ira Eaker, the commander of the Mediterranean Allied Air Force, signed an order in July 1944 to create the Air Crew Rescue Unit (ACRU) which called for OSS agents to work with the Fifteenth Air Force to rescue and evacuate Allied airmen who went down over Nazi-occupied countries of Europe.[98] The ACRU and its OSS control agent, George Vuj-novich, set up shop near the headquarters of the Fifteenth Air Force in Bari, Italy. From this base of operations, the ACRU, working with the Fifteenth Air Force, parachuted OSS intelligence agents behind enemy lines to work with resistance groups in rescuing and evacuating downed airmen.[99]

The OSS viewed both Mihailovich's Chetniks and Tito's Partisans as valuable allies in Yugoslavia. Mihailovich led the resistance in the eastern part of Yugoslavia and Tito the resistance in the western part. At one point, Donovan, the OSS head, thought of parachuting into Yugoslavia and propos-ing a truce between the two rival resistance groups but this never happened because Churchill decided to sever ties with Mihailovich and demanded that Roosevelt do the same.[100] The OSS disagreed with Churchill because its operatives, which were working with both resistance groups, felt that they were both valuable assets in helping downed airmen to evade capture.

During the second half of 1944, Mihailovich's Chetniks participated in a rescue operation called Operation Halyard. The British were against Operation Halyard because it involved the Chetniks. As a result, the Americans went ahead with the rescue operation without British help.[101] Operation Halyard was led by OSS operative George Vujnovich, a Pittsburgh native of Yugoslav descent who had gone to study in Yugoslavia because he could not afford higher education in the States. When he was studying in Belgrade, he saw firsthand the country that his parents emigrated from go from peace to horror.[102] Later, he was recruited by the OSS because he spoke the Serbo-Croat language and knew the region. Now he had the job of sending OSS agents on missions throughout Europe.[103]

For Operation Halyard, Vujnovich selected a team of three OSS agents—Lieutenant George Musulin, Master Sergeant Michael Rajacich, and Specialist Arthur Jibilian, a radio operator. Musulin was an American of Yugoslav descent who also spoke the local language.[104] He was a big, strong man who played tackle for the University of Pittsburgh football team.[105] Rajacich was also of Yugoslavian descent and spoke the local language.[106] They needed a reliable radioman, and Jibilian had already proven himself to be an excellent radioman doing OSS intelligence work behind enemy lines in Yugoslavia for which he received the Silver Star.[107] The mission for the trio was to parachute into Yugoslavia and organize an effort to clear a landing strip for C-47s to land and rescue the downed airmen.[108]

The Douglas C-47 Skytrain was a military cargo plane that was used extensively in World War II to transport troops, equipment, and supplies. During the Normandy Invasion of June 6, 1944, over 800 C-47s dropped over 13,000 paratroopers behind enemy lines. Seventy-five years later, on June 6, 2019, a formation of restored C-47s flew over Normandy to honor the sacrifices of those who fought in the Normandy Invasion.[109]

The United States does not forget its veterans. It continues to honor their sacrifices, and the Commemorative Air Force, a nonprofit Texas corporation, does this by restoring and preserving World War II-era combat aircraft for the education and enjoyment of present and future generations of Americans. For the 2019 flyover in Normandy, its Central Texas Wing in San Marcos, Texas, restored *That's All, Brother*, the actual C-47 that led the main airborne invasion of Normandy on June 6, 1944. On June 5, 2019, it flew with eighteen re-enactor paratroopers from England over the English Channel and made a successful paratrooper drop over Normandy. On June 6, it flew with twelve other C-47s over the United States Cemetery at Normandy and then flew to Berlin for the 70th commemoration of the Berlin Airlift and back to France for the Paris Airshow.[110] Greg Young was on the Central Texas Wing team that restored and traveled with *That's All, Brother* to Normandy in 2019 and had this to say about the experience:

> *"To fly over Normandy in the very same aircraft that dropped the first load of paratroopers was both humbling and honorable. I felt as well as my fellow crew members that the flights honored the sacrifices of all the fallen soldiers. To see the graves in the cemetery we flew over is an experience few are able to share from our aerial views. God bless all those who made the ultimate sacrifice."*[111]

On August 2, 1944, the three operatives in Operation Halyard parachuted into enemy territory in Pranjane, a small village in central Yugoslavia (now Pranjani, Serbia). Six days later, a landing strip was ready for the C-47s that would transport the airmen to Bari, Italy. The rescue operation began on the night of August 9 when the first C-47 arrived and had on board another OSS operative, Nick Lalich of Serbian descent, who helped with the operation.[112] On that night and the following morning, 272 airmen were evacuated, including 241 Americans. Operation Halyard continued for five months until the last rescue mission on December 27, 1944.[113]

There were conflicting accounts of how many airmen were rescued in Operation Halyard. One source stated 417 airmen including 343 Americans.[114] Another stated 512 airmen including 432 Americans.[115] Gregory A. Freeman, the author of the book *The Forgotten 500: The Untold Story of the Men Who Risked All for the Greatest Rescue Mission of World War II*, who stated 512 airmen were rescued, feels that his total was the most reliable because it came from the Interagency Working Group's "Records of the Office of Strategic Services 1940-1941."[116] Whatever the exact figure may be, Operation Halyard was a very successful rescue mission.

During the war, the ACRU rescued 5,718 Allied airmen from fifteen European countries including Russian-occupied Hungary, Poland, Germany, and Austria. Most of the airmen, 2,350, were rescued from Yugoslavia. The rest were rescued from Romania (1,309), Hungary (651), Switzerland (332), Bulgaria (305), Northern Italy (241), Poland (215), Greece (76), Czechoslovakia (64), France (60), Turkey (50), Germany (25), Spain (18), Albania (16) and Austria (6).[117]

Both Mihailovich's Chetniks and Tito's Partisans fought the Germans and helped the Allies. They both also worked with OSS operatives in the

Air Crew Rescue Unit and provided critical aid to Allied airmen hiding in Yugoslavia. Unfortunately, they were also fighting with each other for control of their country and had diametrically opposed views of what was right for their country. Tito prevailed and his government hunted down Mihailovich and put him on trial for treason. He was found guilty and executed by a firing squad. The trial was viewed as unfair by Americans who Mihailovich helped evade capture. Unfortunately, they were not allowed by Tito to speak on his behalf at the trial.[118]

Mihailovich was the victim of bad luck. Yugoslavia was different from America where every citizen is entitled to a fair trial and where two different parties with opposing views can present them to a jury for resolution. America is not a country where the loser of a two-party battle can be put on trial for his life by the winner. A democracy is different from a dictatorship and is worth fighting for.

Mihailovich lost his life but not his legacy. Churchill and Roosevelt both realized too late that they made a serious mistake in backing Tito because he and his Partisans contributed to the postwar takeover of communism in Yugoslavia.[119] Fortunately, the threat of communism became a major concern of the Truman Administration. The Soviet Union led by Joseph Stalin was hell bent on spreading communism throughout the free world and the Truman Administration wrestled with how best to deal with it. When Britain stepped down as leader of the free world to focus on recovering from World War II, the United States with Truman's leadership stepped up to become the leader of the free world by supporting free peoples trying to prevent communist takeovers.[120]

The story of how the Truman Administration developed a policy to accomplish this is nicely told in a book entitled *Saving Freedom: Truman, the Cold War, and the Fight for Civilization*. The policy led to the Cold War between the democratic West and the communist East. During World War II, the United States was fighting against Nazism and fascism, both threats to the free world, and now it was fighting against communism, another threat to the free world.[121]

Ever since the threat of communism was recognized, American leaders have tried to make amends for their mistake by honoring Mihailovich. In 1948, President Truman presented Mihailovich with the posthumous honor of the Legion of Merit, but it was not widely known because the State Department did not want to offend communist Yugoslavia. In 1966, President Nixon paid tribute to him by calling him "a patriot ally of the United States and every nation that went to war in the early forties to destroy the tyrannies that sought to enslave the world." In 1979, Ronald Reagan, at that time a former governor and future president, sent a letter to the California Citizen's Committee to commemorate General Draja Mihailovich for leaving a "legacy of patriotism and heroism." In 2004, the Governor of Ohio, George Vujnovich, and four American veterans including Arthur Jibilian, visited the Pranjani landing strip used to rescue and evacuate Allied airmen and unveiled a commemorative plaque that read, "Airfield of Freedom and War Alliance Between the United States and the Forces of General Draza Mihailovich."[122] In 2005, two of the OSS operatives and three of the rescued airmen from Operation Halyard traveled to Serbia and presented Mihailovich's Legion of Merit to his daughter Gordana in a small ceremony. They wish this could have been done in a public ceremony by the State Department. Nevertheless, Gordana appreciated them traveling to her country to honor her father's memory.[123]

Good Luck Amidst Bad Luck

The Friday the 13th mission was a three-star mission, which meant the 451st Bomb Group and the other two bomb groups in the 49th Bomb Wing—the 461st and 484th—were all on the mission, and likewise they all had their share of bad luck. After takeoff, the 461st planes assembled into a formation and, as they headed to Vienna, two planes collided and nine of the ten crew members in one of the planes were killed when it blew up. The lone survivor, tail-turret gunner Sgt. Van V. Smith, Jr., had luck on his side. Before they boarded the plane that day, his bombardier wanted to trade his seat parachute for Smith's chest parachute, so Smith said okay. Normally, the tail gunner had a chest parachute and kept it outside his tail-turret so it wouldn't get in the way of his firing his machine guns. Luck was with Smith on this day because he was wearing a seat parachute in his tail turret. When his plane blew up and was cut in half, he was thrown out of the plane. He was knocked out by the explosion, but on his way down he woke up with his chute on, pulled the chord, and survived the disaster. If he and his bombardier had not traded parachutes, he would have been killed along with the rest of the crew.[124]

The pilot of the other plane, despite having had an engine knocked off and having sustained severe damage to the tail, was able to fly out over the Adriatic Sea to salvo his bombs and then return to his base to land safely. Sixteen of the other planes in the 461st were hit by flak on Friday the 13th, but they all made it back to their home base.[125]

Twenty planes in the 484th were also damaged by the extremely heavy flak over Vienna, but only one of them was shot down.[126] The crew of First Lieutenant James H. Oakley's plane, with no nickname, was pounded repeatedly by flak. Sergeant Alexander Bazer, the tail-turret gunner, said the plane was hit by three flak barrages. The first hit was in the nose just before bombs away. He thought Second Lieutenant George M. Duncomb, Jr., the bombardier, deserved a citation for getting the bombs off in that chaos. He also thought Second Lieutenant Raymond Clamage, the navigator, deserved a citation for the way he acted in trying to hold everything together when the plane was in distress.[127]

Four crew members in the back of the aircraft were able to bail out, but the five members of the crew in the front of the aircraft—pilot Oakley, co-pilot Second Lieutenant Junior R. Sporn, navigator Clamage, a second navigator Second Lieutenant Will H. Layton, and bombardier Duncomb—were all killed, as was ball-turret gunner Sergeant Joseph W. Burness, who was in an exposed position under the plane as its ball-turret gunner.[128]

The four who bailed out, all enlisted personnel—Bazer, Staff Sergeant Thomas E. Sainsbury, Staff Sergeant Joseph F. Murphy and Sergeant Frank E. Fishbaugh—were captured and interred in Stalag Luft IV where the enlisted men of Moye's crew were sent, and where David Orkin would join them two months later. When they were liberated, they were interviewed by military intelligence. At that time, Bazer wrote "the crew members who died on the mission are definitely due for a citation." He added: "And damn it why the hell shouldn't they get the Congressional Medal of Honor?" One could certainly understand why he felt that way.[129]

Friday the 13th was surely an unlucky day for the 451st Bomb Group, as well as the 461st and 484th Bomb Groups, but there had been other unlucky days earlier in the war when there were fewer escort fighters to protect them from more enemy fighters who were attacking them. At this point in the war, Allied airpower had come of age and dominated the skies that were once dominated by the Luftwaffe, but the 451st, 461st and 484th still had to deal with flak batteries that had become very proficient with their cannons, especially those defending Vienna.

The Harsh Reality of War

Cooney's introduction to war was harsh. One of his tentmates with whom he trained in the States was killed flying his first combat mission. The personal effects of Mosher were soon gathered and sent to his father Frank in Albuquerque, New Mexico.[130] This was the day the music died for them because Kirk used to play his mandolin in the tent. Meyer said Kirk was a chain smoker and would always have a cigarette hanging off his lips as he played his mandolin.[131] The personal effects of his crewmate Sam Holquin, who was also killed that day, were likewise gathered and sent to his mother Amanda in Los Angeles, California.[132]

The United States cares deeply about its war dead. After the war, the Graves Registration Service of the Quartermaster Corps, responsible for the care of deceased military personnel, went looking for the bodies of Mosher and Holquin. It took a while, but they found them buried next to each other in Plot 88 of the Vienna Central Cemetery. On August 7, 1946, their bodies were exhumed along with the body of another airman buried next to them, Delbert Trueman who, like Mosher, was killed on his first mission only four days after Mosher and Holquin became fatalities.[133]

Trueman's story was told by his granddaughter, Kim Clarke. In 2016, it appeared on the 450th Bomb Group's website. In a meticulously researched and beautifully written tribute to him, Clarke noted that Trueman's brother Dale was a B-24 pilot who was killed in a training exercise in the States in July 1943, prompting Delbert to join the service to finish what his brother started, even though he was married with a six-year old daughter. He trained as an aerial gunner with a B-24 crew and then headed overseas for combat duty. The crew was assigned to the 450th Bomb Group at Manduria Airfield on the heel of Italy, about 130 miles south of the where Mosher's 451st Bomb Group was based on the spur of Italy at Castelluccio Airfield. On October 17, Trueman went on his first mission to bomb an oil refinery in Vienna, the same hornet's nest that took the lives of twenty-two airmen from the 451st, 461st and 484th Bomb Groups on Friday the 13th.[134]

As they approached the oil refinery, their plane was pounded so hard by flak that it went into a spin, which is curtains because the centrifugal force of a spinning plane pins the crew against the walls of the aircraft. Four of the crew were able to pry themselves loose and bail out, but the other six went down with the plane, including Trueman.[135] His parents lost their only two children to war, and Delbert's wife lost her husband, the father of their young daughter.

Trueman's path crossed the paths of Mosher and Holquin when the Graves Registration Service exhumed their bodies together and notified their families. Trueman's family decided to bring Delbert home where he was buried next to his brother at Grant Memorial Park Cemetery in Marion, Ohio.[136] Holquin's family chose to have Sam interned at the Lorraine American Cemetery in St,

Avold, France, where Devon Hall was also laid to rest.[137] Mosher's family chose to have Kirk brought home and laid to rest at the Santa Fe National Cemetery in Santa Fe, New Mexico.[138] All these wishes were carried out with dignity and honor.

Mosher's and Holquin's crewmates who were killed in action on Friday the 13th—Engatenko, Phelps, and Schoonover—were also laid to rest with dignity and honor. Engatenko's final resting place was at the Ardennes American Cemetery in Neupré, Belgium.[139] Phelps' final resting place was at the New Albany National Cemetery in New Albany, Indiana.[140] Schoonover's final resting place was at the Orchid Hill Cemetery in Louisville, Illinois.[141]

Sergeant Joseph Leslie Goss III from Clinton, Missouri replaced Mosher as the crew's radio operator and waist gunner. However, according to Osofsky, he didn't take Mosher's place in their tent. Consequently, they didn't get to know him as well as they knew each other, having trained together in the States.[142]

Goss was called by his middle name, Leslie, and was very active at Clinton High School in Clinton, Missouri, He participated in the dramatic club as an actor in several plays and as its president in his senior year.[143] He was in the glee club.[144] He played the drums in the school band and the tympani in the school orchestra.[145] The tympani, also called the timpani, are drums that look like upside-down teakettles which is why they are called kettledrums. They help to support the rhythm, melody, and harmony of an orchestra, and the tympani player is expected to have a good ear to change the pitches of the drums during performances.[146]

While in high school Leslie was also active in his community. He played in the municipal band and acted in county plays.[147] What's more, he was a reporter and later the editor of "The Cardinal" which provided news about the Clinton Public Schools in a section of the local newspaper, *The Clinton Eye*.[148] The name "The Cardinal" came from the fact that his high school sports teams were called the "Cardinals." Even though he engaged in all these activities, he was an honor student in high school.[149]

After graduating from high school in 1941, Leslie attended the University of Missouri's College of Arts and Sciences where he was a member of the Freshman Council.[150] During his second semester, the United States went to war and as soon as his freshman year was over so did Leslie. He enlisted in the Army on June 26, 1942, and did his basic training at the Jefferson Barracks on the Mississippi River in Lemay, Missouri, just south of St. Louis. Named after Thomas Jefferson, the barracks date back to the Civil War and housed some famous military leaders such as Ulysses S. Grant and Robert E. Lee.[151]

After basic training at Jefferson Barracks, he received training as a radio operator in Sioux Falls, South Dakota, and Greenville, Mississippi.[152] Next, he was assigned to the Air Force Materiel Command in Dayton, Ohio.[153] The Materiel Command was responsible for all aircraft and equipment research, development, procurement, maintenance, supply, and flight tests.[154] This was a comparatively easy assignment with the probability that he would remain in the States during the war, but this did not suit him.[155] He wanted to see action and signed up to fly combat missions in the Army Air Forces where he would see plenty of action.

Casualties and Medical Support

Flying combat missions was hazardous duty. For example, 25,577 (39.7 percent) of the 67,441 airmen who flew for the Fifteenth Air Force from November 1, 1943, to May 25, 1945, were casualties. Of these casualties, 19,075 (74.6 percent) were missing in action, 5,008 (19.6 percent) were wounded in action, 1,157 (4.5 percent) were killed in action including operational accidents, and 337 (1.3 percent) were killed in other accidents including non-operational accidents.[156]

The causes of the 1,157 airmen killed in action were 801 (69.2 percent) from operational accidents, 160 (13.8 percent) from enemy flak, 59 (5.1 percent) from ditching, 52 (4.5 percent) from enemy bullets, 52 (4.5 percent) from parachuting, and 33 (2.9 percent) from anoxia or the lack of oxygen. These figures show that 212 (18.3 percent) of the 1,157 airmen killed in action were the victims of enemy fire.[157] The fact that most were killed in accidents reflects the inherent danger of being a crew member of a sophisticated flying machine that requires precise teamwork to operate efficiently and safely.

The causes of the 5,008 airmen wounded in action were 2,791 (55.7 percent) from enemy flak, 1,793 (35.8 percent) from operational accidents, and 424 (8.5 percent) from enemy bullets. The figures show that 3,215 (64.2 percent) of the 5,008 airmen wounded in action were the victims of enemy fire from anti-aircraft cannons on the ground and fighter aircraft machine guns in the sky.[158]

When Cooney's and Osofsky's 451st Bomb Group was activated in April 1943, its commander, Colonel Robert E. L. Eaton, recognized the need for medical support. In June 1943 a team of five medical officers joined the 451st for the purpose of providing such support—Captain Clyde L. Wagner, First Lieutenant Joe W. King, First Lieutenant Marshall Y. Kremers, First

Lieutenant Ward J. McFarland, and First Lieutenant Henry F. Quinn. They assembled with a cadre of key officers and enlisted personnel in Orlando, Florida, to attend the Army Air Force School of Applied Tactics, and then moved to Pinecastle, Florida, for practical instructions under simulated operational conditions.[159]

The five doctors and its medical support team soon joined the 451st Bomb Group and underwent further training at Wendover Field in Utah where Captain Howard C. Peterson, a dental surgeon, was assigned to the group in late July 1942. Wendover became a tent city and in August a tornado blew down or destroyed a hundred tents and most medical records were lost. In September they moved to Fairmount Army Air Base in Nebraska where they completed their training in the middle of November and began conducting physical examinations to assess the health of the men for overseas duty. In so doing, they disqualified seventy-eight for physical reasons—twenty-three aircrew fliers and fifty-five ground support personnel. Also, to provide more focused medical support, the team was divided into an air echelon to support the air crews and a ground echelon to support the ground crews. In late November 1943, each echelon went to Camp Patrick Henry, the staging area where they waited for their ship to arrive at the Hampton Roads Port of Embarkation in Newport News, Virginia, to take them overseas.[160]

In Europe, the air echelon set up camp to polish up their techniques at Teleghma, Algeria, in early January 1944 and the ground echelon did the same thing at Gioia Del Colle, Italy, where the 451st Bomb Group was stationed at the time. In January 1944, the air echelon joined the ground echelon and the rest of the 451st in Gioia Del Colle and the 451st Bomb Group began flying combat missions on January 30, 1944. On April 6, 1944, the 451st and its medical support team moved to Castelluccia di Sauri where it remained until the 451st flew its last combat mission on April 26, 1945.[161]

According to its commander, Colonel Eaton, the 451st Bomb Group sustained 1,140 battle casualties during 1944—882 (77.4%) were missing in action, 164 (14.4%) were wounded in action, and 94 (8.2%) were killed in action. As per Exhibit 10.3, most of those wounded in action received their wounds in accidents (86), not by being hit by missiles from anti-aircraft batteries or enemy fighters (78). That is how two of Cooney's crewmates—Chin and Goss—would receive their wounds. Also, most of those killed in action were killed in accidents, not by missiles from anti-aircraft batteries or enemy. However, Cooney's crewmate Mosher was killed by flak flying a combat mission with another crew.[162]

Exhibit 10.3
1944 Battle Casualties for the 451st Bomb Group

Month	WIA		MIA	KIA		Battle Casualties
	Enemy Missiles	Accidents		Enemy Missiles	Accidents	
Jan.	0	0	0	0	0	0
Feb.	5	4	60	1	7	77
Mar.	0	1	11	1	23	36
Apr.	2	1	134	0	9	146
May	13	1	51	1	0	66
Jun.	7	7	39	0	2	55
Jul.	8	4	93	3	6	114
Aug.	5	16	190	1	4	216
Sep.	0	7	0	0	0	7
Oct.	15	19	101	3	11	149
Nov.	9	8	65	1	21	104
Dec.	14	18	138	0	0	170
Year	78	86	882	11	83	1,140

Luck In War

In addition to treating patients who received battle wounds, the medical support team treated patients with intestinal, venereal, and other diseases in addition to patients with respiratory problems, malaria, infectious hepatitis, and frostbite. As preventative measures, the men received smallpox, typhus, typhoid, cholera, and tetanus immunizations in addition to physical examinations.[163]

Cooney's father was part of a medical support team during World War I. He never talked about his wartime experiences with John before he passed away when John was only sixteen, but John saw the good work of the medics in his bomb group and no doubt appreciated his father's service in World War I. John would go down over Italy with a crew that included airmen who were killed in action, wounded in action, and missing in action. He considered himself incredibly lucky to have survived the war, as did other airmen who survived combat missions and made it home. They knew, as did John, that the next mission could be their last. Yet, they continued to do their duty and fly combat missions into enemy territory. They were part of a team that fought together and relied on each other to hit their targets and get back to their home base. The thought of going down in a plane was a frightening one for John and his crewmates and for other crews flying combat missions. Those who made it home had luck on their side and were forever grateful for their good fortune.

Chapter 11

MISSIONS FROM HELL

First Lieutenant Robert "Bob" Cookman, Cooney's pilot, flew only three missions during World War II and they were all missions from hell. According to a news article, Cookman flew two missions before his fatal one.[1] Both missions had tragic results in different ways. His first was the Friday the 13th mission in which eight planes from his bomb group were shot down with seventeen men killed in action, forty-two captured and sent to prison camps, and twenty-two evading the enemy. Among those killed on Friday the 13th was Kirk Mosher who he trained with in the States. Like Mosher, he flew his first mission with another crew to get his feet wet in combat before leading his own crew into battle. His baptism by fire was rough as he saw firsthand the dangers of flying combat missions. He would soon experience those dangers in the worst possible way.

The Dark Days of War

Due to inclement weather, Cookman didn't fly his second mission until October 20, 1944. During the month, the 451st flew only thirteen missions and eight of them were washouts due to either poor weather on the way to the target or poor weather in the target area.[2] As per Exhibit 11.1, the 451st Bomb Group had a compliment of 841 men in four bomb squadrons of nineteen crews each. Of the 841 men, 316 were officers and 525 were enlisted men, an average of seventy-nine officers per squadron and 131 enlisted men per squadron. It also had fifty-six planes or fourteen per squadron. Of the fifty-six planes in the bomb group, six were fitted with radar for bombing under overcast conditions.[3]

FROM ONE WAR TO ANOTHER

The 451st Bomb Group typically flew its missions with the 461st and 484th Bomb Groups of the 49th Bomb Wing. As per Exhibit 11.2, the 451st Bomb Group was based at Castelluccio Airfield and the 461st and 484th Bomb Groups were based at Torretta Airfield. They all received their orders from the 49th Bomb Wing located in Bari. There were many Fifteenth Air Force airfields based on the Foggia plain which was called the Foggia Airfield Complex. Exhibit 11.2 also shows where Cookman's plane would go down over Italy on October 23, 1944. Crew members at that time were expected to fly thirty-five missions for a tour of duty. Cooney would fly his complement of thirty-five missions by averaging a mission every six days. Cookman would not be so fortunate.

On October 20, the weather was forecast to be good, so the Fifteenth Air Force decided to send 1,158 aircraft on bombing missions. The total included 563 B-24 Liberators and 218 B-17 Flying Fortresses to do the bombing, and 216 P-51 Mustangs and 161 P-38 Lightnings to escort the bombers to their targets and protect them from enemy fighters.[4] The P-51s and the P-38s had long-range, disposable fuel tanks allowing them to escort the heavy bombers all the way to distant targets. The German fighters—the Bf 109s and the Fw 190s—were more likely to run out of gas.[5]

The P-38 Lightning was an odd-looking fighter plane with two twin fuselages, each with an engine in the front (twin engines) extending to a rudder in the tail (twin rudders), and a shorter egg-shaped fuselage between them extending only to the back of the front wing which housed the cockpit and the plane's armament of four 50-caliber machine guns and a 75-mm cannon.[6] It was versatile and rugged and could sink a ship.[7] Joe Moser, who flew a P-38 during the war, wrote about his experiences in *A Fighter Pilot in Buchenwald*. He said that the P-38 was a large, formidable fighter that German fighter pilots were not eager to engage in a dogfight. In fact, he said that they "flat out avoided us."[8]

The P-38 was the first American fighter with two turbo supercharged engines that powered it to fly at great speed and at high altitude, and the first to be favorably compared to the German Bf 109 and the British Spitfire.[9] Two of the highest scoring aces in American history, Major Richard I. Bong (40 victories) and Major Thomas B. McGuire, Jr. (38 victories), who were both recipients of the Medal of Honor, flew P-38s during World War II.[10]

The P-51 Mustang was another American fighter which compared favorably with the British Spitfire as well as the German Bf 109 and Fw 190. The P-51 was a sleek-looking fighter plane that was a "game changer" for the Americans

Exhibit 11.1 Profile of 451st Bomb Group October 21, 1944					
Four Bomb Squadrons	724th	725th	726th	727th	Totals
Number of Crews	19	19	19	19	76
Number of Officers					
Pilots	19	22	21	20	82
Co-Pilots	21	23	20	20	84
Navigators	18	18	17	20	73
Bombardiers	20	21	17	19	77
Totals	78	84	75	79	316
Number of Enlisted Men					
Engineer Gunners	41	30	36	30	137
Radio Gunners	21	21	24	19	85
Armored Gunners	76	82	72	73	303
Totals	138	133	132	122	525
Total Crew Members	216	217	207	201	841
Number of B-24s	14	14	14	14	56*
Number Operational	9	14	12	13	48
*Included six B-24s with radar for bombing in poor weather.					

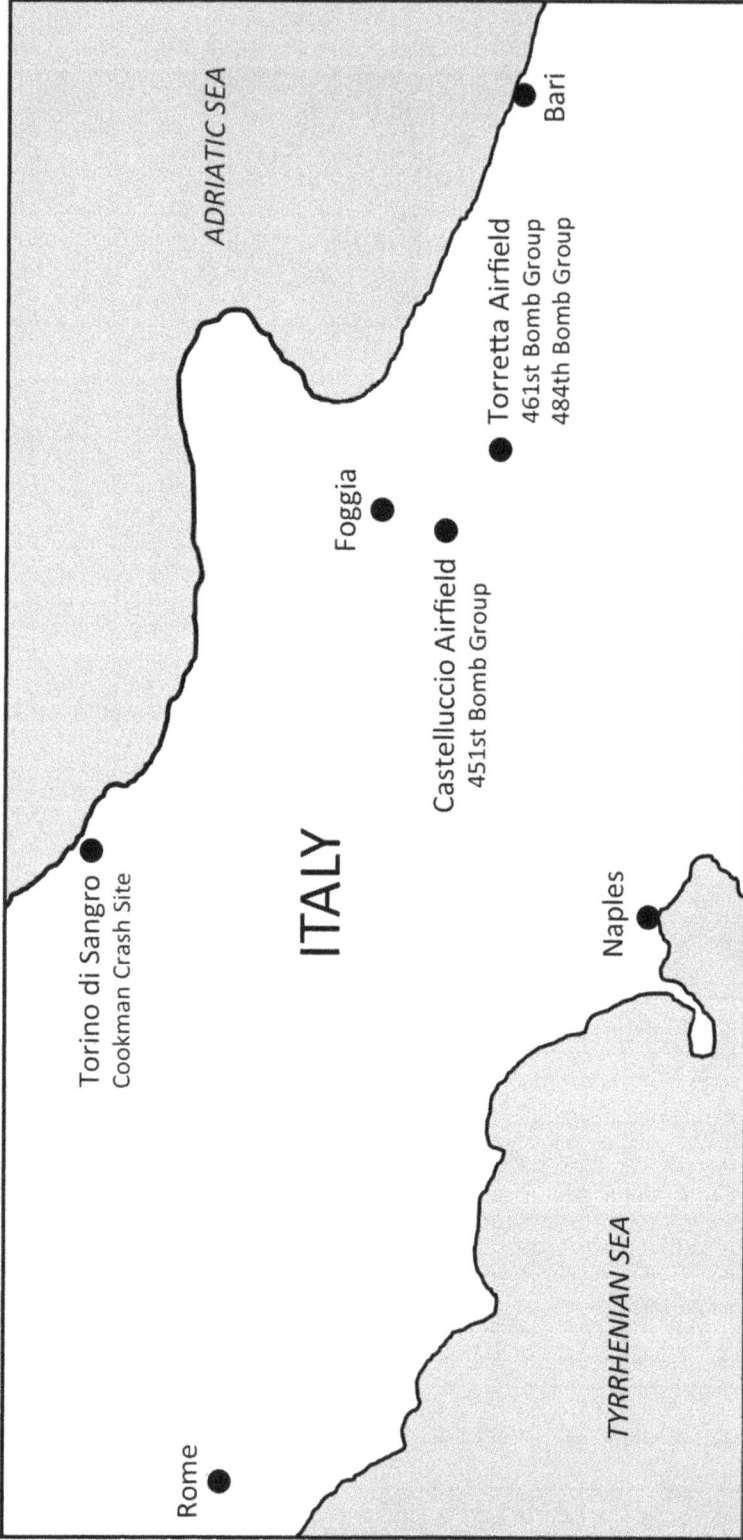

Exhibit 11.2: The 451st, 461st, and 484th Bomb Groups flew together and received their orders from the 49th Bomb Wing headquarters based in Bari. On October 23, 1944, Cookman's B-24 crashed in Torino di Sangro.

because it had an amazing range, was fast and maneuverable, and could more than hold its own against enemy aircraft in dogfights. Its range enabled it to fly as far into enemy territory as the heavy bombers to protect them.[11]

On October 20, the 451st, 461st, and 484th Bomb Groups (111 B-24s) of the 49th Bomb Wing were ordered to attack three Italian industrial targets while other bomb wings in the Fifteenth Air Force (1,047 aircraft) were ordered to attack targets such as the Brux Synthetic Oil Refinery (5th Bomb Wing), the Regensburg Oil Storage Depot (5th Bomb Wing), the Rosenheim Marshalling Yard (55th Bomb Wing), the Innsbruck Marshalling Yard (304th Bomb Wing), and the Bad Aibling Airdrome (304th Bomb Wing).[12]

The day before on October 19, the 451st, 461st, and 484th Bomb Groups received their orders from the 49th Bomb Wing Headquarters in Bari, Italy. Operations Order No. 215 directed the three bomb groups with thirty-six B-24s in each bomb group to bomb three industrial targets in Milan around 11:00 am on October 20. These targets were selected because they were believed to be manufacturing military transports and armaments and performing ordnance repair work for the German armies in Italy. The Order specified that:[13]

- The 451st Bomb Group was to bomb the Milan Breda Works.
- The 461st Bomb Group was to bomb the Milan Isotta Fraschini Works.
- The 484th Bomb Group was to bomb the Milan Alpha Romeo Works.

An Annex was attached to the Order at 1830 hours (6:30 pm) with an intelligence report that contradicted the Order. It specified that:[14]

- The target for the 451st Bomb Group was the Milan Alpha Romeo Works. This contradicted the Order that stated the target for the 451st Bomb Group was the Milan Breda Works.
- The target for the 461st Bomb Group was the Milan Isotta Fraschini Works. This was consistent with the Order.
- The target for the 484th Bomb Group was the Milan Breda Works. This contradicted the Order that stated that the target for the 484th Bomb Group was the Milan Alpha Romeo Works.

While the two contradictions may have been an issue for the 451st and 484th Bomb Groups, they both followed the Order and not the Annex. The Intelligence Operations Report dated October 20, the date of the bombings, stated that:[15]

- The 451st Bomb Group sent thirty-six B-24s to the Milan Breda Works and thirty-five of them dropped 85.5 tons of bombs on the target at 11:27 am. One B-24 returned early. It was reported that bomb strike photos showed two large assembly shops at the southeast end of the target area received several direct hits and near misses. Many hits were made on the north half of rubber factory and direct hits and near misses were scored on three assembly-type buildings. Post-raid reconnaissance photos showed minor damage to one large probable locomotive shop and more severe damage to the Pirelli Works which is probably the rubber factory alluded to above as Pirelli makes tires.
- The 461st Bomb Group sent forty-one B-24s to the Milan Isotta Fraschini Works and thirty-two of them dropped 59.75 tons of bombs on the target at 12:01 pm. Three B-24s returned early. It was reported that bomb strike photos showed concentration of hits along the northeast edge of target with direct hits on three long assembly buildings. Also, the barracks area north of target area received several direct hits on at least ten buildings." Post-raid reconnaissance photos showed severe damage on the West side of the target and scattered points of structural damage elsewhere. It was also reported that six B-25s jettisoned their bombs. There are a couple of reasons why a pilot would jettison his bombs after missing a target—to reduce the weight of the plane so it could fly higher and faster or to make sure it didn't land with live bombs which could detonate with a rough landing. In this case, no reason was given for why and where the six B-24s of the 461st Bomb Group jettisoned their bombs. Consequently, it is unknown where they landed or if they resulted in collateral damage.
- The 484th Bomb Group sent thirty-four B-24s to the Milan Alpha Romeo Works and twenty-nine B-24s dropped 65.25 tons of bombs on the target at 11:37 am. Five B-24s returned early. It was reported that bomb strike photos showed a close concentration of bombs falling on the eastern half of the target scoring many direct hits and near misses on assembly buildings and shops. Other direct hits were made on warehouses northeast of the target. Post-raid reconnaissance photos showed that six of nine major buildings were seriously damaged.

While fighters on that day were ordered to escort the bombers on the missions to Germany where enemy fighters were anticipated, no fighters were ordered to escort the bombers going to Milan because enemy fighters were not anticipated, and none were encountered.[16]

On October 21, the day after the bombings, an analysis of the bombing of the targets and the navigation to get to the targets was produced that evaluated the mission and stated that the 461st Bomb Group bombed the Milan Isotta Fraschini Works with fair results and that the 484th Bomb Group bombed the Milan Alfa Romero Works with good results. However, it also stated that the 451st Bomb Group bombed the Milan Breda Works with very poor results.[17]

Missions were typically rated in terms such as Excellent, Good, Fair, but every now and then a mission would be rated as SNAFU (Situation Normal, All Fouled Up). The rating for the 484th Bomb Group for the October 20 mission was Fair and the rating for the 461st Bomb Group was Good.[18] On the other hand, the rating for the 451st Bomb Group was SNAFU. The monthly intelligence report stated, "only two ships managed to hit the target while the other planes left their bombs all over the Po Valley" and that 49th Bomb Wing headquarters let them have it because they missed the target.[19]

On that day, the 451st Bomb Group encountered problems from the start. Despite a weather forecast of good weather, take off was delayed by about thirty minutes because of low clouds and poor visibility. When the three bomb groups were finally off the ground, they were unable to rendezvous into a wing formation because of a technical problem that prevented them from getting on the wing radio frequency required to communicate with each other. As a result, there was no wing formation for the mission. Instead of flying to the target area (Milan) together in a wing formation, each bomb group flew different routes to the target area which was not the norm.[20]

The B-24s of the 451st were flying in two combat units with three boxes of six planes in each unit (Exhibit 11.3). The first combat unit reached its Initial Point—the beginning of its bomb run—at Varese, Italy, about thirty miles northwest of the target.[21] On a bomb run, the planes in the formation release their bombs when the lead plane releases its bombs. On this bomb run, the lead plane encountered a problem with the toggle switch to release the bombs. The switch either shorted or was hit by accident, causing the plane to release its bombs too soon. The lead plane tried to warn the other planes of this mishap by firing a flare, but the flare didn't fire. As a result, most of the other planes in the lead box also released their bombs too soon. The deputy-lead plane of the box to the right of the lead's box could see they were not upon the target and did not release its bombs, but the rest of the planes in its box dropped their bombs when the lead plane dropped its bombs. The box to the left of the lead plane's box held back and did not drop its bombs until it was upon the target and hit the target in what was said to be "a beautiful job."[22]

Exhibit 11.3
Group Formation of B-24 Heavy Bombers

Combat Unit 1

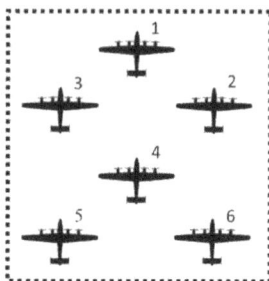

**Combat Box
With
Plane Positions**

Combat Unit 2

The second combat unit lagged far behind the first unit and went on a bomb run that was too short to give the bombardier time to cite the target. As a result, all three boxes in the combat unit missed the target. An analysis of the bombing and navigation that day concluded that because of poor judgment and teamwork, the mission was a colossal failure.[23] It was a humiliating mission for the 451st Bomb Group because it was a proud unit that had performed so well on previous missions.[24] The 451st Bomb Group would end the war as the only bomb group in the Fifteenth Air Force to receive three Distinguished Unit Citations. It would also finish with the highest bomb score in the entire Fifteenth Air Force. In addition, it would be the only bomb group in the European Theater to achieve a perfect mission.[25] In the chaos of war, even the best units make costly mistakes.

The dark days of war were many for crews flying the missions and civilians in countries they were bombing, especially civilians located near bombing targets. The objective of strategic bombing was "to destroy a country's ability to wage war by demoralizing civilians and targeting features of an enemy's infrastructure—such as factories, railways, and refineries—that are essential for the production and supply of war materials."[26] If military targets were near residential neighborhoods, civilians and their homes were at risk.

The bombing of innocent civilians is abhorrent to civilized people, but during World War II many innocent civilians were bombed to death. There were attempts to prevent this before World War II, but to no avail. In 1923, Britain, France, Italy, Japan, and the United States agreed to a set of rules which, among other things, prohibited bombing to terrorize civilians, but the rules were never ratified. In 1932, the world's powers agreed that air attacks on civilians violated the laws of war, but never finalized the agreement. The same year Japanese warplanes bombed workers in China. In 1936, Mussolini ordered bombings in Ethiopia which killed civilians. In 1939, Hitler started a war in which his Nazi regime bombed civilians in Poland and the Netherlands. In 1940 and 1941, Nazi Germany conducted bombing raids over London killing thousands of civilians.[27]

Britain responded initially to the Nazi-bombing of London with daylight bombing to hit German military targets but after being decimated by German fighters, resorted in early 1942 to night bombing which put civilians at risk.[28] Their rationale for such bombing was that they were bombing for survival unlike the Germans who were bombing for conquest.[29]

When the United States entered the war, it developed a more precise daylight bombing method using the Norden bombsight to better sight and hit military targets without hitting residential neighborhoods near these targets.

FROM ONE WAR TO ANOTHER

By entering the speed and altitude of the aircraft along with the wind conditions into the bombsight's analog computer, the bombardier would sight the target and the bombsight would do the calculations and release the bombs at the right moment to hit the target. A Dutch immigrant, Carl Norden, invented the bombsight and sold his rights to the United States government for one dollar.[30] Like Danish immigrant William Knudsen who was paid a one-dollar salary for leading the American mobilization effort, Norden also appreciated the country which provided him the freedom to pursue his dreams.

While the use of the Norden bombsight made daylight bombing more accurate and less likely to result in collateral damage, its accuracy depended upon more than its technical capability. It depended upon the conditions surrounding its use such as the weather, the training and experience of the air crews using it, the training and experience of the ground crews servicing it, the accuracy of the enemy fighter planes shooting at it from the air, and the accuracy of anti-aircraft batteries shooting at it from the ground. On October 20, while the weather and enemy guns were not a factor, the teamwork required for a successful bombing mission fell short, and technical difficulties played a part as well.

The Americans were against bombing which put civilians at risk but their bombing by radar during overcast conditions put civilians in harm's way.[31] Late in the war of Europe when Hitler was bombing cities in England with unmanned rockets from Holland and it was evident that Hitler would fight to the finish, the Allies decided to deal a devastating blow to Germany by bombing major cities such as Munich, Berlin, Leipzig, and Dresden. When it was also evident that Hirohito would fight to the finish, the same approach was taken to end the war against Japan with atomic bombs. When the war in Europe ended, the Germans were working on an unmanned rocket to cross the Atlantic and bomb New York City.[32]

Today, nine countries possess about 13,000 nuclear warheads—Russia, United States, China, France, United Kingdom, Pakistan, India, Israel, and North Korea.[33] These nuclear arsenals could cause a lot more damage than those unmanned German rockets or even the atomic bomb. Nuclear warfare would be devastating, making treaties to prevent their proliferation and use critical for the welfare of civilians around the world. Collateral damage in a nuclear war would be unfathomable.

The 451st Bomb Group did not know that errant bombs caused serious collateral damage on October 20, resulting in the deaths of 614 civilians in the Milan suburbs of Gorla and Precotto. The victims included 184 children plus teachers and others at the Francesco Crispi Elementary School in Gorla, a district of Milan, that took a direct hit while they were rushing toward an air-raid shelter.[34] A monument was constructed in 1952 in memory of the children. Its purpose was to keep the children together and remind the world of the sacrifice of these innocent victims of war.[35] What happens in a war-torn country is tragic not only to those fighting the war but to innocent civilians in harm's way such as these children.

In his effort to make his country more powerful on the world stage, Mussolini aligned with Hitler and Hirohito, two other fascist leaders, and led his country into a war that resulted in the death of many innocent civilians and the destruction of many homes, schools, churches, public works, transportation facilities, and other structures that form the infrastructure of a civilized society. Not only that, but his desire to become more powerful led to his own death when he was executed on April 28, 1945, and on the following day hung by his feet in a public square in Milan where his body was kicked and beaten by a crowd of his own people.[36] The following day, Hitler, who started the war that killed fifty million people, committed suicide with orders to burn his body so that it would not be put on display as was Mussolini's.[37] War takes a heavy toll on a wide spectrum of people, including the powerful leaders who led their countries to war and later fell from grace.[38]

Cookman's Third Mission

After flying two missions with tragic results of different sorts, Bob Cookman flew his third mission on Monday, October 23, 1944, a mission that would prove to be even more tragic for him personally. It was his second mission with his crew and a day Cooney would never forget. It looked as though the weather might be a problem on that Monday. Nevertheless, the Fifteenth Air Force decided to start the week with an "all-out effort" and dispatched 1,217 aircraft to bomb major industrial targets—the Allach BMW (BMW is Bayerische Motoren Werke in German and Bavarian Motor Works in English) aero-engine plant near Munich, Germany that produced airplane engines; the Skoda Works in Pilsen, Czechoslovakia that produced armaments such as heavy guns and tanks; a manufacturing plant in Augsburg, Germany that produced diesel engines for armored vehicles; the Winterhafen Oil Storage Depot in Regensburg, Germany, that stored up to 35,000 tons of oil for motor fuel; and smaller targets in northern Italy such as trains (including train tracks and bridges) and vehicles (including roads and bridges) used for transporting troops, equipment and supplies to the battlefront.[39]

FROM ONE WAR TO ANOTHER

The Fifteenth Air Force had all its bomb wings (5th, 47th, 49th, 55th and 304th) and fighter wings (305th and 306th) deployed on October 23, 1944. The 1,217 aircraft that took to the skies that day included 610 B-24 Liberators and 215 B-17 Flying Fortresses to do the bombing, and 237 P-51 Mustangs and 155 P-38 Lightnings to escort the bombers to their targets and protect them from enemy fighters.[40]

As a point of interest, the Tuskegee Airmen's 332nd Fighter Group, which flew P-51s, was in the 306th Fighter Wing that escorted the 304th Bomber Wing that day to bomb the Winterhafen Oil Storage Depot in Regensburg.[41] On the mission, two Tuskegee Airmen—First Lieutenants Robert C. Chandler and Shelby F. Westbrook—were shot down.[42] It is also noteworthy that, on Cookman's first mission on October 13, the Tuskegee Airmen escorted the 304th Bomb Group to bomb the Blechhammer South Oil Refinery and that three Tuskegee Airmen—First Lieutenants Walter D. Westmoreland, William W. Green, Jr., and Luther A. Smith, Jr.—were shot down.[43] On Cookman's second mission on October 20, the Tuskegee Airmen flew as escorts for the 5th Bomb Group to bomb the Brux Oil Refineries and as escorts for a PBY Catalina aircraft that was making a rescue at sea. On that day, no Tuskegee Airmen were shot down.[44]

The PBY Catalina was a U.S. Navy amphibious aircraft. The PB stands for Patrol Boat and the Y is the letter used by the Navy to identify Consolidated Aircraft Company of San Diego as the manufacturer of the aircraft. The Navy had a letter designating each of its aircraft manufacturers. The PBYs were flying boats that could land and take off on water and the British used them to rescue airmen whose planes were ditched at sea. The British purchased 700 of them during World War II. Consolidated Aircraft also built the B-24 Liberator and the man who was the principal designer for the Catalina—Isaac Machlin "Mac" Laddon—was also the principal designer for the B-24 Liberator. It is ironical that the same man who designed the flying boat that saved airmen who ditched at sea also designed the B-24 that was known to sink quickly and endanger the lives of airmen who ditched at sea. The Catalina derived its name from Catalina Island, a small island off the coast of California about eighty miles northwest of San Diego. [45]

Legacy of Tuskegee Airmen

The Tuskegee Airmen made history during the war by demonstrating that African Americans could be successful combat pilots. Their performance under fire on 1,578 combat missions for the Twelfth Air Force (1,267) and the Fifteenth Air Force (311) helped pave the way for the desegregation of the military after the war.[46] They flew their share of missions from hell just like other airmen, putting their lives on the line time after time throughout the war. Late in the war, they also demonstrated their proficiency by shooting down German Me 262 jet-powered planes which flew 100 mph faster than their P-51 propeller-driven planes.

Bob Askew, a bombardier-navigator discussed earlier in the book, flew on the longest mission of the war for the Fifteenth Air Force, and was complimentary of the Tuskegee Airmen. The mission was to bomb the Daimler-Benz Tank Works in Berlin, the German capital, on March 24, 1945. It was a high-priority mission because the factory assembled tanks that were powerful weapons for the Germans in resisting Allied advances. Because of the importance of the factory, it was heavily defended by anti-aircraft artillery as well as the best German fighters including the new Messerschmitt Me 262 jet fighters. On that day, the air battles were intense because the Germans launched thirty Me 262s, and the Americans met the challenge by shooting down eight of them, the most ever shot down in one day.[47]

Of the eight Me 262s downed that day, the Tuskegee Airmen shot down three. First Lieutenants Roscoe C. Brown and Earl R. Lane and Second Lieutenant Charles V. Brantley of the 332nd Fighter Group's 100th Fighter Squadron registered these aerial victories against the speedier jets.[48] Of the five fighter groups on this historical mission, the 332nd Fighter Group was the only one which earned a Distinguished Unit Citation.[49] To receive this award, a unit "must display such gallantry, determination, and esprit de corps in accomplishing its mission as to set it apart from and above the other units participating in the same campaign." The level of heroism is equivalent to the level of heroism an individual would warrant for a Distinguished Service Cross. In 1957, as previously noted, the name of the Distinguished Unit Citation was changed to Presidential Unit Citation.[50]

The mission was not without sacrifices by the Tuskegee Airmen as five of them were casualties of war that day. All five were initially reported as missing in action. Subsequently, it was learned that three survived and two were killed. Captain Armour G. McDaniel was shot down, captured, and sent to Stalag VIIA outside of Moosburg in Bavaria. He was only a prisoner there for a month because the prison camp was liberated on April 29, 1945, by General George S. Patton, Jr., and his Third Army. Second Lieutenants Ronald W. Reeves and Robert C. Robinson, Jr., were low on fuel on the way home and had to crash-land their planes in the Udine area of northeastern

Italy.[51] Neither of them survived and were presumed to have been killed when they crash-landed their planes.[52] Flight Officer Leon W. Spears was hit over the target by flak from a German anti-aircraft 88mm shell that caused engine trouble prompting Spears to head west to Poland where he was shot down and captured by the Germans and sent to prison for a short stay before the war ended.[53] Flight Officer James T. Mitchell is also believed to have developed some sort of mechanical failure and left his formation on the way home and landed his plane just south of Chemnitz, Germany, which is about 164 miles south of Berlin.[54] McDaniel, Spears, and Mitchell survived the war; Reeves and Robinson were not so lucky.

A couple of years after the war on July 26, 1947, the Army Air Forces became the United States Air Force, a separate military service that was no longer under the United States Army. This was the culmination of years of lobbying by airpower pioneers like Billy Mitchell, Hap Arnold, Ira Eaker, Carl Spaatz, Jimmy Doolittle, and others to put the air forces on a par with the ground forces of the Army and the sea forces of the Navy. A year later, on July 26, 1948, the first major step in ending racial discrimination in the military was taken by President Harry S. Truman with his landmark Executive Order 9981 of July 26, 1948, that stated:[55]

> *"It is hereby declared the policy of the President that there shall be equality of treatment and opportunity for all persons in the armed forces without regard to race, color, religion, or national origin. This policy shall be put into effect as rapidly as possible, having due regard to the time required to effectuate any necessary changes without impairing efficiency or morale."*

The first armed services to officially integrate was the Air Force. This happened under the guidance of the Secretary of the Air Force, W. Stuart Symington. He and General Carl A. Spaatz, first chief of staff of the new United States Air Force, believed it was the right thing to do and risked their careers for the cause of racial equality.[56] The success of the Tuskegee Airmen helped lay the groundwork for this achievement.[57] Thus, by serving their country in a commendable manner, the Tuskegee Airmen achieved a double victory in fighting against Nazism and fascism abroad and against racism at home.[58]

Many honors have been bestowed upon the Tuskegee Airmen over the years as a group and as individuals. On March 29, 2007, President George W. Bush presented the Congressional Gold Medal to the Tuskegee Airmen as a group with 300 of them present at the U.S. Capitol. President Bush praised them, saying, "The Tuskegee Airmen helped win a war, and you helped change our nation for the better. Yours is the story of the human spirit, and it ends like all great stories—with wisdom and lessons and hope for tomorrow."[59]

Dr. Roscoe Brown Jr., Director of the Center of Urban Education Policy and University Professor at the Graduate School and University Center of the City University of New York who shot down a German Me 262 and later commanded the 100th Fighter Squadron of the 332nd Fighter Group, accepted the honor on behalf of all the Tuskegee Airmen. Dr. Brown received many honors during his lifetime as a champion for civil rights and in 2012 said, "In my generation, in the generation of segregation, there were many African Americans who knew that we could do anything that whites could do, all we wanted was the opportunity."[60] They got that opportunity during World War II and served their country with honor and courage which paved the way to the desegregation of the Armed Forces and much more.

Just like Bob Cookman and his crew, the Tuskegee Airmen flew missions from hell, and some made it home and some were not so lucky. War is hell whether fought in the air, on land, or at sea. It is hell to those engaged in combat, to those in the vicinity of the fighting, and to those worrying about their loved ones at war. Cookman trained with a crew of ten in the States and flew combat missions with a crew of ten overseas. Most of those he trained with and flew combat missions with would make it home, but he would not be so lucky.

Chapter 12

GOING DOWN OVER ITALY

On October 23, Cookman's third mission, the 451st Bomb Group was flying a double mission. Because the late fall brought poor weather and because it was important to continue bombing enemy targets, the Fifteenth Air Force began flying double missions on poor weather days in which one force called a Red Force bombed using radar to identify its targets while another force called a Blue Force bombed using visual identification of its targets. Typically, the Red Force attacked major targets far away while the Blue Force attacked targets closer to its home base.[1] Cookman was flying with the Red Force on this fateful day.

The 451st Bomb Group's Blue Force was tasked with bombing the Milan Breda Works and hoping to make amends for the poor performance three days earlier. It was still unknown to them that some of their errant bombs on the October 20 mission killed a lot of civilians. The Blue Force was ordered on October 22 to send eighteen B-24s from each of the 451st, 461st, and 484th Bomb Groups of the 49th Bomb Wing, a total of fifty-four B-24s, to bomb the Milan Breda Works at 11:13 am on October 23.[2] They were determined to avenge their humiliation three days earlier when their bombs missed that target, but poor weather on October 23 ran them off the target to an alternate target, a troop concentration in Podgorica, Yugoslavia, where they also encountered poor weather, thereby ending up with a disappointing and ineffective mission in which no targets were bombed.[3]

The 451st Bomb Group's Red Force had a different experience. It was tasked with bombing the Munich Allach BMW Works, a factory that manufactured aircraft engines for the Fw 190 fighter. The Red Force re-

249

ceived orders on October 22 to send twenty-four B-24s from each of the 451st, 461st, and 484th Bomb Groups of the 49th Bomb Wing, or a total of 72 B-24s, to bomb the BMW factory at 11:55 am on October 23.[4] An Intelligence Annex "A" to the Operations Order stated that the factory was at the northern end of the Allacher Forest northwest of the center of Munich and that it was a high-priority target. It also cautioned the bombing crews that Munich was defended by 260 anti-aircraft guns with another 125 in Augsburg about twenty-five miles west of Munich. It added that the Germans could muster up seventy-five to 100 fighters from Augsburg and another seventy-five to 100 fighters from Frankfurt, about 190 miles away, and not to underestimate the ability of the Germans to bring help from distant locations quickly.[5]

On the morning of October 23, the Red Force was briefed to fly to Munich following a route mapped out for them by combat intelligence to avoid anti-aircraft batteries along the way. First, they would fly over the Adriatic Sea to Caorle (Italy), then change course to Ubersee (Germany), change course again to Velden (Germany), and change course one more time to Moosburg (Germany) which was the Initial Point of the bomb run. The bomb run would then be 29 miles to the mission target—the Allach BMW factory in Munich—which they were scheduled to bomb at 11:55 am.[6]

After the briefing, the 451st, 461st, and 484th Bomb Groups of the 49th Bomb Wing prepared for takeoff. At 8:44 am on October 23, 1944, Cookman's plane was among the twenty-four B-24s in the 451st Bomb Group that took off from their home base in Castelluccio dei Sauri, Italy. They headed to nearby Bovino to rendezvous with twenty-seven B-24s from the 461st Bomb Group and twenty-four B-24s from the 484th Bomb Group, both of which had taken off from their home base in Torretta, Italy, at 8:15 am and 8:14 am, respectively.[7]

The 451st Bomb Group, the leader of the formation, rendezvoused into position at 9,000 feet with the 484th following suit on its right at 8,000 feet and the 461st aligning into position on its left at 7,000 feet.[8] After they assembled into a tight formation, they linked up with their thirty-eight P-38 escorts. A tight formation was necessary for protection from enemy fighters who might intercept them. It prevented fighters from penetrating the formation by flying between them. Once assembled into formation with their escorts to protect them, they headed north over the Adriatic Sea toward Germany. Their target, the Munich-Allach BMW aircraft engine factory, was about 500 air miles away, and they were scheduled to bomb it around noontime.

They would fly more miles because they were ordered to fly a zig-zag route mapped out by intelligence to avoid known anti-aircraft batteries and or areas where fighters may attack them.[9]

Target of Friends

The Munich Allach BMW factory was a new modern factory built in 1939 to manufacture aircraft engines for the Luftwaffe.[10] It was the largest aircraft engine plant in the Third Reich, the term the Nazis gave to their empire from 1933 to 1945. Reich is a word that is difficult to translate into English and fully capture its meaning, but realm or empire are two English words that are used to describe it. The First Reich was from 962 to 1806, and the Second Reich was from 1871 to 1918. BMW was established just before World War I and built a reputation for engineering excellence in producing aircraft engines. The Munich Allach BMW factory made the formidable 801 twin-row radial engine for the Focke-Wulf Fw190, considered to be one of the two best German fighters, the other being the Messerschmitt Bf 109.[11] As a result, the BMW factory was a high priority target. BMW was first and foremost an engine builder, and its engines powered the Luftwaffe.[12]

The BMW factory was located about seven miles northwest of the center of Munich, at the northern end of the Allacher Forest. Normally, the forest itself and extensive railway sidings (a low-speed track section distinct from a main line) leading along the south side of the forest to the main rail line would be conspicuous landmarks that would help in locating the target. On a clear day, landmarks were geographic clues that led navigators to targets. However, this didn't turn out to be a clear day and they were ordered to bomb it even if they couldn't see it by using radar with radar operators to identify the target.[13]

John Cooney and his crewmates did not know that most workers at the BMW factory were not the enemy. The factory used forced or slave labor from other countries that were invaded by Hitler's troops and were now under Nazi-occupation. Over twenty million men, women, and children from Nazi-occupied countries of Europe, along with prisoners of war and concentration camp inmates, were forced to perform labor for the Third Reich during World War II.[14] The BMW factory utilized more than 17,000 workers, and most were forced to work there, and to live in barracks set up around the factory grounds that housed about 14,000 workers. By the end of the war, 90 percent of the workers at the BMW plant were foreign civilians, prisoners of war, and concentration camp inmates who had been working in harm's way of Allied bombs.[15]

FROM ONE WAR TO ANOTHER

Work was the only way for concentration camp inmates to avoid death. Beginning in March 1943, a Nazi sub-camp was established in Allach, about ten miles from the main camp at Dachau. It began with 3,000 Jewish prisoners and 6,000 non-Jewish prisoners. Its purpose was to provide workers for the BMW plant. In 1944, the Allach camp was expanded by the Todt Organization with the construction of another camp in neighboring Karlsfeld. The conditions in the Nazi sub-camp were awful, and inspections were carried out twice daily to determine if the inmates were fit for work. If they were not, they were taken away and shot. It was the first of seven such camps to provide workers for the BMW plant.[16] Sadly, these prisoners could be going from the frying pan into the fire if their workplace were a target of Allied bombers.

A Frightening Experience

Cookman's plane never made it to Munich. While flying over the Adriatic Sea, his plane encountered engine trouble about 150 miles from its home base. The number one engine, the outboard engine on Cookman's left, was the one in trouble. It is noteworthy that it was a new engine that was throwing off oil excessively. It would later be learned that it had only an hour and forty-five minutes of service when the plane went down compared to the other three engines which each had 154 hours and twenty-five minutes of service. The engine trouble prompted a check of the gauges which showed that the cylinder head temperature was high at 320 degrees. Then the engine exploded![17]

Co-pilot Flint believed the explosion was caused by a blown cylinder head. The engine was feathered which means the propeller blades were turned to align them with the airstream to reduce drag on the plane.[18] Unable to keep up with the formation, their plane dropped out and took a 155-degree heading (southeast) back to the base. Left waist gunner Osofsky got on the interphone and reported that the control surfaces were covered with oil and smoking. The oil pressure in the number two engine, the inboard engine on Cookman's left, was also dropping and they feathered that engine as well.[19]

Osofsky, who became an experienced multi-engine pilot after the war, surmised years later that advancing number two engine fast may have blown a cylinder in that engine too.[20] With both engines lost on the left side, the aircraft was losing altitude and threatening to go into a spin, which could be deadly.[21] Once a plane goes into a spin, the centrifugal force of the spin and the force of the downward plunge could pin the crew against the wall of the fuselage and prevent them from bailing out.[22]

Going Down Over Italy

Acting quickly and deliberately, Cookman and Flint gave their all to prevent the aircraft from going into a spin, making every effort to keep it flying. Osofsky recalled that Cookman instructed them to do everything they could to lighten the ship.[23] Flint later reported that they released their bombs into the Adriatic and started throwing guns and ammunition into the sea as well then took a west heading toward the Italian coastline.[24] Osofsky also recalled that they threw out their flak suits and looked for their parachutes.[25]

With the plane going down, it was imperative to get back to the Italian mainland. They did not want to ditch at sea—ditching a B-24 was a dangerous and risky venture because of its high wing and soft underbelly. The beast was known to sink quickly. Just a month earlier, a B-24 that was retired from service was purposely ditched in the James River near Langley Field in Virginia to study and figure out how to improve its ditching capabilities. Even though the fuselage of the test aircraft had been reinforced and its four engines were working fine, the ditching still broke its back when it hit the relatively calm water of the James River which was probably softer than the rough water of the Adriatic Sea. The only reason the test plane did not sink was because it was rigged with flotation devices to prevent it from sinking.[26]

The report of that ditching is still viewed as the definitive study on landing a distressed aircraft in water that led to further study and procedures and guidelines for commercial and military planes to save lives. A dramatic and highly publicized ditching that occurred in 2009 is a good example of these safety procedures and guidelines saving lives. On January 15, 2009, Captain Chester B. "Sully" Sullenberger III, a former Air Force pilot, relied on the fundamentals and procedures he was trained to follow in ditching his distressed U.S. Airways jumbo jet on the Hudson River and saved the lives of all 155 people on board.[27]

Going down in a plane is a frightening experience. Louis Zamperini, the hero of the best-selling book, *Unbroken,* and the movie that followed, had many frightening experiences. He went down at sea in a B-24, survived shark attacks for forty-seven days in a six-foot by three-foot rubber raft, was captured by the Japanese, and then tortured by a sadistic Japanese prison official who had it in for him. Of all these frightening experiences, he said "the most frightening experience in life is going down in a plane."[28]

Another B-24 pilot, Second Lieutenant Charles R. Rhein, who was on the same mission as Cookman, had to ditch his plane with tragic results. He developed engine trouble and had to ditch his aircraft in the Adriatic Sea. Only three members of the ten-man crew survived and all three said they were knocked out upon impact with the water. The navigator, Second Lieutenant Morris J. Nadia, said he regained consciousness and was pinned down, but wriggled free and got out through the escape hatch. The top-turret gunner, Staff Sergeant Charles W. Loudon, said when he regained consciousness, he saw no one in the waist of the plane so he climbed out of the top of the plane, where the tail assembly had broken off, jumped into the water, and swam away from the aircraft. The bombardier, Second Lieutenant Albert Jorgensen, Jr., said when he regained consciousness, "he crawled and swam under the fuselage and came up under the trailing edge of the right wing" where he saw about twenty feet away the radio operator, Staff Sergeant Robert B. Helms, with a bad cut on his head which may have been the reason he didn't survive. Then he saw Nadia about forty feet away hanging on to a piece of board. He also saw the radio operator, Staff Sergeant Mitchell M. Lindstrom, about fifty feet from the aircraft who appeared to be dead. All three survivors—Nadia, Loudon, and Jorgensen—plus the body of Lindstrom, who was floating in his life preserver, were later picked up by British air-sea rescue operations in a PBY Catalina flying boat.[29]

B-24 pilots dreaded the possibility of ditching at sea, and Cookman was facing that possibility. After unloading their bombs, guns, and ammunition, they were heading west for the coast of Italy. The B-24 was also known to fly poorly on two engines, so getting it back to the Italian mainland was a challenge but they made it. When they reached the coast, Flint said they were flying at 4,000 feet and descending at a rate of 200 to 300 feet per minute. With no fields in sight for a crash landing, they turned north to avoid the mountains and clouds ahead and continued to look for a place to land along the coast. As they went through a small cloud and emerged over a valley at about 2,500 feet, they saw hilly terrain below, unsuitable for a forced landing. This prompted Cookman to tell Flint to give the order to abandon ship at 2,000 feet, a low altitude for bailing out of a plane, especially over hilly terrain.[30]

Exhibit 12.1 shows the positions of Cookman's B-24 crew. Osofsky, the left-waist gunner, remembers the alarm bell going off, and more. In the heat of the moment, he had snapped his chute on upside down.[31] Cooney, the ball-turret gunner, bailed out through the back end of the bomb bay followed by Goss, the radio operator and right-waist gunner. When Osofsky was ready to jump, Muth, the tail gunner, was standing over the back hatch looking down. He said he wanted to make sure the men in the front got out okay. While Muth was contemplating his next move, Osofsky bailed out head over heels, and Muth followed him out.[32]

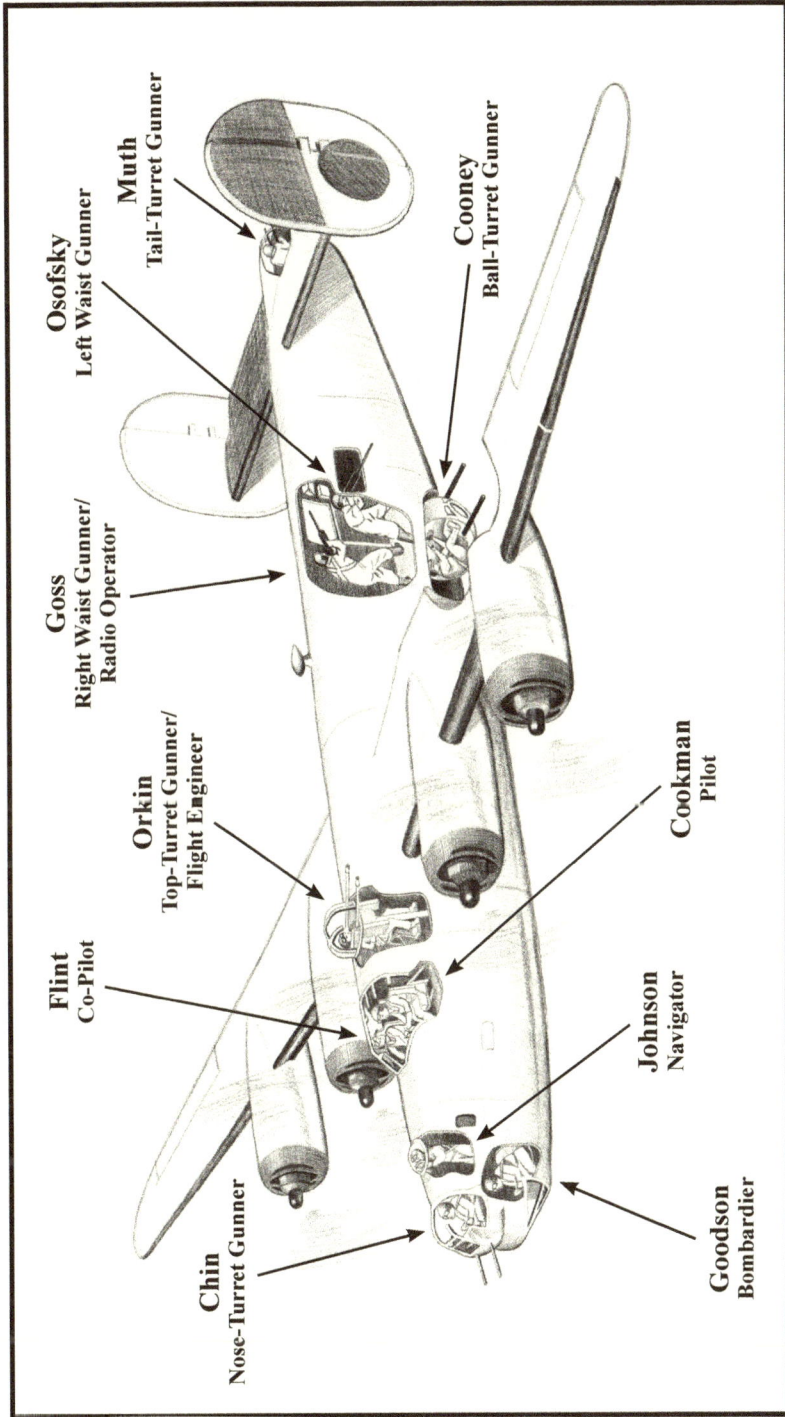

Exhibit 12.1
Positions of Cookman's Crew
Drawing by Todd Slater

FROM ONE WAR TO ANOTHER

Even though Osofsky's chute was upside down, it worked fine. He was left-handed, so pulling the rip cord on the upside-down chute was not a problem. As he was descending, his old boxing partner Goodson, the bombardier, was descending near him. He had bailed out of the front hatch as did Johnson, the navigator, and Chin, the nose-gunner. Since Goodson was within earshot, they conversed on the way down. With the ground coming up fast, Goodson tensed up and yelled "Here comes the ground!" They hit hard. Osofsky said his legs gave way as he landed, but he was okay. So was Goodson.[33] Chin and Goss hit harder and were not okay.

Cookman was still hoping to save the aircraft, and asked Flint what he thought. Flint thought it was still too hilly for a landing, so Cookman ordered him to bail out. He jumped at about 1,000 feet and landed on a hill. He saw their plane make a gentle turn to the left, crash into another hill, and explode on impact. Osofsky also saw their plane hit and blow up. They both learned later that Cookman was able to exit the aircraft before it crashed, but that he bailed at too low an altitude for his chute to open enough to save his life.[34] Exhibit 12.2 shows the last flight of Cookman's plane.

According to the Accident Report, the plane crashed at 10:26 am in Torino di Sangro, about ten miles north of Vasto, Italy.[35] Edward Ardizzone, an artist who was commissioned by the War Art Advisory Committee and who traveled with the British Eight Army during the war, kept a diary with his artwork that was published in 1974 as *Diary of a War Artist*.[36] In his diary, he refers to Torino di Sangro as a beautiful little hill town.[37] After the war, it was selected as the site of the Sangro River War Cemetery in which 2,617 soldiers of the British Commonwealth were laid to rest in a beautiful setting.[38] During the war, it was difficult to enjoy the beautiful surroundings because Italy had become a battleground.

Vasto was also a hilltop town on the Adriatic coast with a lot of history. The fascists ran a concentration camp there for anti-fascists and Slavs from 1940 to 1943. Fascism encouraged racism against Slavs—people who spoke Slavic languages and resided in Eastern European countries such as Bulgaria, Czechoslovakia, Poland, Serbia, Croatia, Slovenia, and Russian. The town and camp were liberated by the British in late 1943 and became the headquarters of the British Eighth Army in Italy. In fact, it was in Vasto that on December 30, 1943, General Bernard Montgomery turned over the command of the Eighth Army in Italy to General Oliver Leese. This freed Montgomery up to prepare to lead ground forces in the invasion of Normandy on D-Day, June 6, 1944.[39]

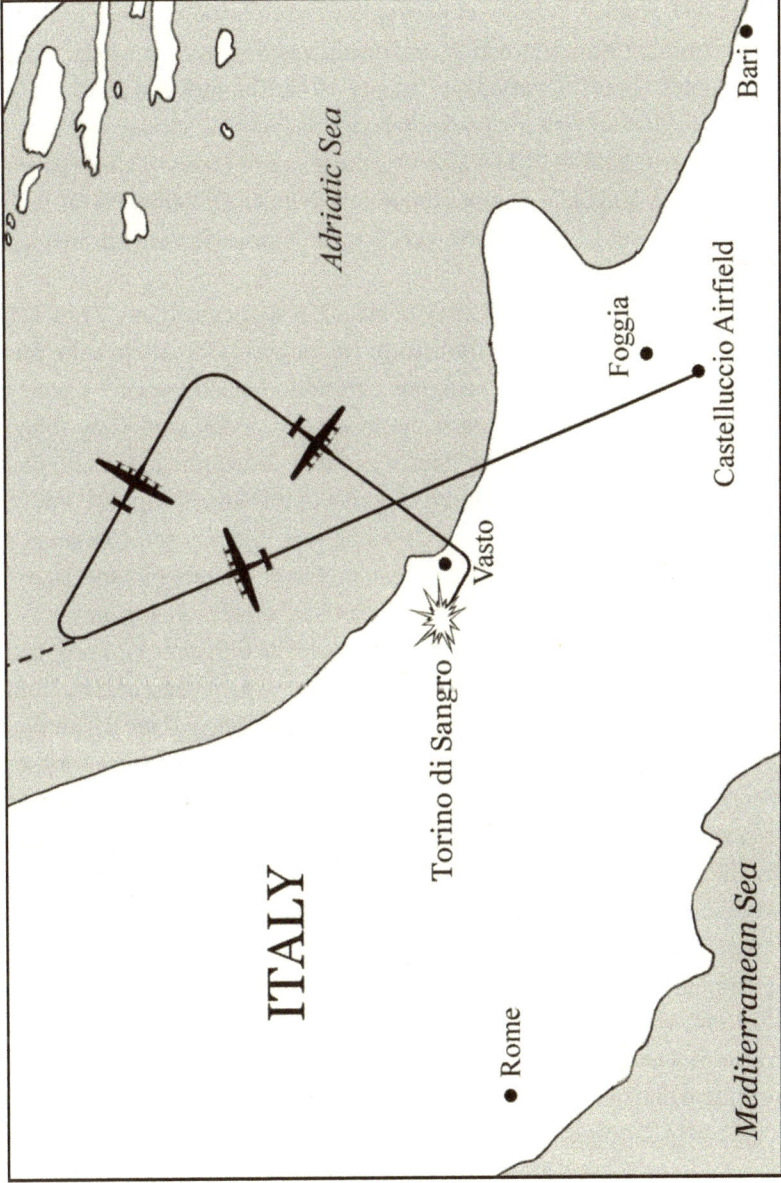

Exhibit 12.2: Last Flight of Cookman's Plane

FROM ONE WAR TO ANOTHER

Change was not new to the town of Vasto. In 1938, its name was changed to Istonio by Mussolini as this was its Latin name when it was part of the Roman Empire. This was very much in line with Mussolini's desire to build a new Roman Empire. However, instead of bringing glory to Italy, Mussolini brought war, destruction, and death. Vasto got its name back when it was liberated by British troops in January 1944. Today, it is a picturesque town—a nice place to visit for a quiet, relaxing vacation or holiday. For about eight years from 2003 to 2011 Vasto was the home of Harvard University's intensive Italian-language summer program. Elvira G. Di Fabio, Ph.D., who ran the program, said, "We all have very fond memories of Vasto, its history, the generosity of its inhabitants."[40]

The Report of Burial stated that Cookman's place of death was Vasto. His body was probably transported from Torino di Sangro to Vasto where he was declared dead with the reason being his parachute failed to open.[41] Cooney said he and Flint went to the crash site to look for Cookman. They found his plane destroyed from the fiery crash, and they found him about 500 feet from the crash. Flint said two lance corporals of the British Military Police were with them at the time. Cooney said he and Flint carried Cookman's body up a hill on a ladder to a truck which probably brought him to Vasto.[42]

Three days later, on October 26, Cookman was buried in a temporary grave at the U.S. Military Cemetery in Bari, Italy, where the Fifteenth Air Force had its headquarters.[43] Bari is about 150 miles down the eastern coast of Italy from Vasto. Cookman was interred in this temporary grave pending a later determination by his family of his final resting place. In 1945, his hometown newspaper reported that he had been posthumously awarded an Air Medal for "meritorious achievement in aerial flight while participating in sustained operational activities against the enemy."[44] What he did was more than meritorious—it was heroic. He saved the lives of his crew while sacrificing his own life.

Their aircraft, nicknamed *Betty Jo,* had a short life, as did many B-24s flying combat missions. She came off the assembly line at Willow Run on July 7, 1944, was assigned to Cookman's squadron on August 27, and was destroyed on October 23 after 154.25 hours of flying time.[45] The Accident Report stated that the weather on that day was cloudy and overcast at 8,000 feet and partly overcast at 3,000 feet. The Accident Report concluded (1) that the crash was caused by 100 percent materiel failure when it lost engines number one and two; (2) that the pilot was unable to maintain enough altitude of the disabled aircraft to return the ship to a landing strip; and (3) that it crashed into a mountain after the crew abandoned it.[46]

The Accident Report also stated that Cookman was a fatality, that two crew members (Goss and Chin) sustained major injuries, that four (Flint, Osofsky, Muth, and Cooney Jr.) sustained minor injuries, and that three (Johnson, Goodson, and Orkin) were not injured at all.[47] The 451st Bomb Group Roster of Combat Casualties for October 1944 stated that Cookman was killed in action (KIA), and that Chin and Goss were lightly injured in action (LIA).[48] Exhibit 12.3 notes the fate of each crew member.

Years later, Cooney and Osofsky said they were not injured in the accident. Osofsky did, however, recall that he, Chin, Goss, and Muth were transported to a hospital in a British lorry, which is the British name for a truck.[49] Osofsky said Goss fractured his ankle but did not recall Chin's injury. Chin had sprained his ankle when he landed and did not fly again until December 8, 1944, even though he was returned to duty on November 8.[50] Goss had fractured the lower extremity of his fibula and was not discharged from the hospital until December.[51] You can fracture your fibula by twisting your ankle, which is what happened to Goss.

Bottom line, Cookman led his crew back to land where they were lucky to survive the ordeal. If they had ditched at sea, his crew might not have been so fortunate. Some were banged up, but they were all alive, thanks to their pilot and their parachutes. Parachutes saved lives and its inventor, Leslie Irvin, initiated a program whereby anyone whose life was saved by parachuting from a disabled aircraft would automatically qualify for membership in the Caterpillar Club and be eligible to receive a tiny gold-plated Caterpillar Pin.[52] All but Cookman qualified for membership that day, but none of them would have had the opportunity to qualify if Cookman had not brought the disabled aircraft back to the Italian mainland where they could parachute to safety.

A couple of months after he got home, John wrote a letter to the Irwin Parachute Company, applying for membership into the exclusive Parachute Club. In the letter, he gave his account of going down over Italy:

"Our airplane, B-24 Liberator, was descending rapidly and gradually getting out of control, despite the heroic efforts of both pilots, Cookman and Flint. A clearing in the clouds afforded us a chance to observe the terrain below. The surrounding country was suitable for grazing, but not for a forced landing, fairly-large hills loomed everywhere. The altimeter read two thousand feet, which is mighty low in a descending airplane, with ten men, who must also bail out. Simultaneously the bail-out bell rang and the co-pilot, Russ Flint, said on the interphone to each of us,

Exhibit 12.3
Fate of Cookman's Crew Downed Over Italy
October 23, 1944

Crew Member	Position	Accident Report	451st BG Combat Casualties Report
2nd Lt. Robert G. "Bob" Cookman	Pilot	Killed in Action	Killed in Action
2nd Lt. Russell J. "Russ" Flint	Co-Pilot	Minor Injury	Returned to Duty
2nd Lt. David G. Johnson	Navigator	Not Injured	Returned to Duty
2nd Lt Ray M. Goodson	Bombardier	Not Injured	Returned to Duty
S/Sgt. Hong Sing "Calvin" Chin	Nose-Turret Gunner	Major Injury	Lightly Injured
T/Sgt. David Orkin	Engineer and Top-Turret Gunner	Not Injured	Returned to Duty
S/Sgt. Joseph "Leslie" Goss	Radio Operator and Right Waist Gunner	Major Injury	Lightly Injured
T/Sgt. Meyer "Mike" Osofsky	Left Waist Gunner	Minor Injury	Returned to Duty
S/Sgt. John J. Cooney Jr.	Ball-Turret Gunner	Minor Injury	Returned to Duty
T/Sgt. Charles J. "Chuck" Muth	Tail-Turret Gunner	Minor Injury	Returned to Duty

Going Down Over Italy

'This is it! Hit the silk, men.' We did just that, carefully and separately, four of us escaped uninjured upon hitting the ground. Five were injured.

With profound regret on behalf of my crew and myself, our very much-admired pilot, Lt. Robert G. Cookman, Mason City, Iowa, made the 'supreme sacrifice' for his fellow crew members and his country. An act of unselfishness that will remain imbedded in our memories." [53]

John appreciated and never forgot his pilot, Bob Cookman. He also appreciated his parachute and had a dress made out of it that has been a legacy for his daughter. Years later, the author obtained a Caterpillar Pin for Meyer Osofsky, and he appreciated the gesture.

Cookman's crew that went down with him over Italy on October 23, 1944—Flint, Goodson, Johnson, Chin, Orkin, Goss, Osofsky, Cooney, and Muth—all made it home after the war. They were all grateful and appreciated their commander's sacrifice. When he was interviewed by military intelligence for the Accident Report, Flint said: "The pilot tried his utmost to save the ship." [54] This was an understatement because Cookman died trying. While he was unable to save his malfunctioning ship, he did save his crew, sacrificing his life in the process. He was a true hero of the war.

The Cookman Family

The Cookman family did more than their share to serve their country. Bob Cookman had an uncle and four cousins in the military. His Uncle John, his father Harvey's youngest brother, was in the Navy. His cousins Willie, Jim and Dan, whose father was Harvey's brother Leslie, were in the Army, Navy and Army Air Forces, respectively. His cousin Harry, called Joe, who was the son of Harvey's brother Victor, was in the Army. [55]

When the family learned that Bob had been killed in action, Joe (Harry) was seventeen and had not yet enlisted in the Army. He remembers that time as one of mourning for the family. Two weeks before Bob was killed in action, his cousin, First Lieutenant William B. "Willie" Cookman of the U.S. Army's 47th Infantry Regiment, 9th Infantry Division, was wounded in action in Germany on October 15, and died the next day of his wounds. [56] While grieving for Willie, the Cookman family learned of the death of Bob. [57]

In February 1941—after six years in the National Guard—Willie was called into active service. Following his training, he shipped out for his first tour of duty overseas. After nine months, he was selected for officer training and returned to the States where he received a commission as a second lieutenant after which he was shipped overseas again in December 1943 for his second tour of duty. He was wounded twice in France and was awarded the Silver Star for gallantry of action.[58]

After recovering from his wounds, he was sent to Germany for a third tour of duty. Three months later, he sustained fatal wounds.[59] He now rests in peace as one of 7,992 Americans at the Henri-Chapelle American Cemetery in Belgium, one of the twelve American cemeteries in Europe.[60] All of them are on hallowed grounds which are meticulously cared for by the American Battle Monuments Commission in memory of American men and women who sacrificed their lives in the service of their county.[61]

War is hard on families, and it was particularly hard on the Cookman family. Bob's father, Harvey, and Willie's father, Leslie, were brothers who lost sons to war within two weeks of each other in October 1944. At the time, Willie's two brothers were also serving overseas—Staff Sergeant Daniel V. Cookman with the 306th Bomb Group of Eighth Air Force based in England, and Gunner's Mate Second Class James L. Cookman serving on a landing craft for infantry (LCI) in the Navy. The three brothers had participated in the Normandy Invasion while serving in the land, sea, and air forces. Willie was in the infantry fighting on the beaches; Jim was on a landing craft dropping infantrymen off on the beaches; and Dan was as a tail gunner on a B-17 Flying Fortress flying bombing missions over the beaches.[62]

After nineteen months overseas, Dan came home on leave after having flown thirty-two missions and having been awarded the Purple Heart for wounds received in aerial combat. He also received the Air Medal with three oak leaf clusters for meritorious achievement on combat missions. He was invited to speak to the Mason City Lions Club in early November 1944. Of the Normandy Invasion, he said, "I knew my two brothers were fighting below me, and I was plenty worried about them." While he was home mourning his brother Willie, he learned that his cousin Bob was killed in action. He returned to duty after his twenty-one-day furlough, saddened by the loss of his brother and his cousin.[63] Bob Cookman came from a patriotic family that would never forget him nor would the crew who flew with him on that fateful day.

Chapter 13

BEHIND ENEMY LINES

October 23, 1944, the day Bob Cookman made the ultimate sacrifice, was not the last time that Ray Goodson and David Orkin had to parachute from a disabled B-24. On December 2, 1944—forty days later—they were shot down over Blechhammer, Germany. During the war, Blechhammer was a part of Nazi Germany with chemical plants, prisoner of war camps, and forced labor camps. Today, it is part of Poland.[1] The Army Air Forces targeted Blechhammer during the war because it was the location of Germany's principal synthetic oil plants. Germany needed oil to fuel its war machine and because it had limited natural petroleum deposits it initiated a program to turn bituminous and brown coal into gasoline. It constructed two plants in Blechhammer to produce this synthetic oil—Blechhammer North and Blechhammer South.[2] Over the course of the war, the Fifteenth Air Force dropped 7,082 tons of bombs on Blechhammer.[3] They were important and well-defended targets, and missions to bomb them were fraught with danger.[4] Blechhammer was believed to be defended by more than a hundred anti-aircraft guns.[5]

Goodson and Orkin experienced this danger firsthand when their B-24 was pounded by flak on December 2, 1944.[6] Osofsky was on the mission in another plane and saw their plane go down with several chutes opening. As one might guess, it's a harrowing experience to see your friends shot down, and Meyer was hoping two of the chutes belonged to Goodson and Orkin.[7] It's an even worse experience to learn that your son was shot down. Sensing this, Osofsky sent a letter to Orkin's father informing him that he saw chutes open when his son's plane was shot down, giving his father hope that one belonged to his son.[8]

FROM ONE WAR TO ANOTHER

The flak was intense, heavy, and accurate that day and their plane lost the supercharger on engine number two which cut the power to that engine by about 50 percent.[9] A supercharger uses the energy of the engine's exhaust gas to drive a turbine which enables the supercharger to force more air into the cylinders. The additional air mixed with the fuel allows the engine to continue producing significant power in high altitudes where the air is thinner.[10] This loss of power made it difficult for the pilot, First Lieutenant John D. Eckersley, and the co-pilot, Second Lieutenant Michael E. Butinsky, to keep the ship in the formation on the bomb run.[11]

First Lieutenant Fred R. Capstetter, the navigator in the lead plane flying in the number one position on the bomb run, later reported that Eckersley's plane was flying in the number three position and, about thirty seconds before his plane released its bombs, he saw Eckersley's plane peel sharply to the left and disappear behind him and was lost from his view.[12] The reason Eckersley's plane dropped out of the formation was because it received an almost direct hit in its nose section, taking out their controls and knocking out a second engine—engine number one.[13]

The blast also knocked the navigator, Flight Officer Paul J. Dillon, unconscious. Both bombardier Goodson and nose gunner Sergeant Sherman B. Schapiro thought he was killed instantly. With engines one and two out, Eckersley ordered his crew to bail out, Schapiro dragged Dillon over to the nose wheel hatch, grabbed and pulled the rip cord to his parachute, and pushed him out. Whether he pulled the cord hard enough to open the parachute is anyone's guess. As soon as it was time for Eckersley to leave, he ordered co-pilot Butinsky to leave ahead of him, and the last time he saw his co-pilot was when he was getting into position to bail out of the bomb bay.[14]

Dillon and Butinsky were found dead on the ground by the Germans. Dillon's body was found in Stara Kuźnia, a small Polish village in Upper Silesia, and Butinsky's body was found in woods near Stara Kuźnia. Eckersley and Goodson surmised that Butinsky's parachute may not have opened.[15] Butinsky and Dillon were buried in a local cemetery.[16] At that time, Stara Kuźnia was occupied by the Nazis who called the village Klein-Althammer, and in 1944 established in the village the Althammer subcamp of Auschwitz where Jews from France, Poland, Hungary, and the Netherlands were put to work. Jews who were rounded up in Nazi-occupied countries were sent to Auschwitz and other concentration camps, and the only way you could avoid the gas chamber was to be fit for work, in which case you were shipped out to sub-camps to do work. Another sub-camp of Auschwitz was in Blechhammer. The prisoners in these camps were put to work and treated brutally and those who became too weak to work were shot.[17] As one might expect, Polish residents whose country was occupied by the Nazis during this reign of terror never forgot the Allies who were fighting to liberate them—people like Butinsky and Dillon—and neither did the families of Butinsky and Dillon.

After the war, Butinsky was brought home by his family and laid to rest in St. Michael Cemetery in Brattleboro, Vermont; and Dillon was likewise brought home by his family and laid to rest in Lakewood Park Cemetery in Rocky River, Ohio.[18] The rest of the crew—Eckersley, Goodson, Schapiro, Orkin, Sergeant George Bilanych, Sergeant Floyd M. Sprinkle, Staff Sergeant Morris S. Gadol, and Sergeant Edward H. Pultz—were captured and became prisoners of war. At war's end, they were liberated and, unlike their crewmates Butinsky and Dillon, made it home alive.

Unbeknownst to the families of Butinsky and Dillon, local residents in the area around Blechhammer, located only five miles from Stara Kuźnia, started to research the planes and crews that were shot down in the area during the war. Their efforts led to the formation of the Blechhammer 1944 Association. One of its members, Edward Haduch, reached out to pilot Eckersley and then connected with Michelle Sheldon, the niece of co-pilot Dillon, and Lowell R. Dillon, the nephew of navigator Butinsky. Michelle and Lowell provided him with information on their respective uncles.

The work of the Blechhammer 1944 Association led in 2019 to the opening of a small museum in the town of Kedzierzyn-Kozle, about eight miles from Stara Kuźnia.[19] The museum has a section on the fallen airmen which states: "In Memory of the Fallen Airmen of the 15th U.S.A.A.F." Among other things, the museum preserves the memory of those airmen who were killed in action and ensures that their ultimate sacrifice is not forgotten.[20] The Butinsky and Dillon families were pleased to learn that they were being remembered and honored in this way.

Prisoners of War

Captured Allied airmen who became prisoners of war were first sent to a Dulag Luft for interrogation before being assigned to a permanent prisoner of war camp. The largest Dulag Luft was at Oberursel, Germany. If prisoners needed medical care, they were sent to a nearby hospital in Hohemark, about three miles away, for treatment after which they were also sent to the interrogation center. Following interrogation, prisoners were sent to a permanent prisoner of war camp—a Stalag, which was a prisoner of war camp for noncommissioned officers and enlisted men, or a Stalag Luft, which was a prisoner of war camp for commissioned officers. However, late in the war enlisted men in the Army Air Forces who were noncommissioned officers such as sergeants, staff sergeants, and technical sergeants, were also sent to Stalag Lufts, which were expanded to accept them because so many Allied airmen were being shot down.[21]

According to the Articles (Rules) of War under the Geneva Convention of 1929, prisoners of war were required to provide only their name, rank, and serial number when interrogated, but the interrogators tried to get them to provide more information through charm, threats, bribes, and in other ways.[22] Consequently, captured prisoners had to be on their toes so that they did not unwittingly provide the enemy with useful intelligence. The Articles of War also stated that the officers and enlisted men were to be separated by rank.[23] The Luftwaffe treated Allied prisoners who were officers better than enlisted men so that Allied prison camps would treat German prisoners who were officers better than those who were enlisted men.[24] Rank has its privileges even in prison camps.

Goodson, an officer, and Orkin, an enlisted man who was a noncommissioned officer, were sent to different prisoner of war camps after they were captured. Their dog tags indicated that Goodson was an officer and that Orkin was not an officer (Exhibit 13.1).[25] The dog tag was a small rectangular-shaped aluminum tag that airmen had to always wear when on duty. It had the airman's name, serial number, years of tetanus shots, blood type, and religious preference. Some also had the name and address of next of kin.[26] Officers had an "O" before their serial number.[27]

Goodson and Orkin were interrogated at the Dulag Luft in Oberursel after which Goodson was sent to Stalag Luft I and Orkin was sent to Stalag Luft IV. Stalag is short for stammlager which means base camp and Luft means air, so a Stalag Luft camp was a prisoner of war camp for airmen who were fighting against the Luftwaffe, the German Air Force. Luftwaffe translates to air weapon in English.[28] As previously mentioned, as the war progressed, and more airmen were shot down, enlisted men who were noncommissioned officers often ended up in the same camps as officers.

Goodson was sent to Stalag Luft I located in Barth, Germany, a small village about 125 miles north of Berlin near the Baltic Sea. It was opened in 1942 for British officers and had two compounds—South and West. With American officers being shot down in increasing numbers, it was expanded in 1944 with three more compounds—North 1, North 2, and North 3.[29] It would

Exhibit 13.1

Dog Tags of Goodson and Orkin

Ray Goodson was a commissioned officer (O) who received a tetanus shot (T) in 1943 and 1944. His blood type was AB and his religious preference was P for Protestant.

David Orkin was an enlisted man (non-commissioned officer) who received a tetanus shot (T) in 1943 and 1944. His blood type was B and his religion was H for Hebrew.

grow to about 9,200 prisoners of war (7,700 American men and 1,500 British and British Commonwealth men) by the time it was liberated on May 1, 1945.[30]

Orkin was sent to Stalag Luft IV located in Gross-Tychow, Pomerania, Prussia, then part of Germany.[31] Today, the town is called Tychowo, now part of Poland. Like Stalag Luft I, Stalag Luft VI was also located near the Baltic Sea. Both sites were probably chosen because of their remote positions and high-water tables which made escape by tunneling difficult.[32] Some of the enlisted men from their bomb group, the 451st, were imprisoned there after being shot down on the Friday the 13th mission.

Osofsky said Orkin told him that he was abused as a prisoner of war because his dog tag had "H" for Hebrew.[33] During World War II, dog tags indicated the religious affiliation for only three religions, the other two being "C" for Catholic and "P" for Protestant.[34] The purpose of identifying a person's religious preference was to ensure that in the event of death his or her remains would be handled in accordance with his or her religious beliefs. On the other hand, for a Jewish serviceman fighting against Nazi Germany, as was the case with Orkin, being identified as Jewish could affect how you were treated as a prisoner of war. Being identified as Jewish in Nazi Germany could also be the difference between life and death.[35]

Staff Sergeant Bill Krebs, who was like Orkin in Stalag Luft IV, said the head prison guard was a rough character. He wanted to segregate the Jewish prisoners from the rest to give them the hard work and menial tasks.[36] Since Orkin was Jewish, he was a target for abuse. Osofsky said Goodson also told him he was abused, and he wasn't surprised because Goodson was such a feisty guy.[37]

Today, servicemen and servicewomen have more options on dog tags for specifying their religious beliefs. For example, a protestant could simply have PROTESANT or be more specific and have BAPTIST on his or her dog tag. Those with religions other than Protestant, Catholic or Jewish can also have their religion designated such as MUSLIM or whatever religion they believe in.[38]

Orkin remained in Stalag Luft IV until the Russians were approaching from the East to liberate that prison camp. Since Hitler did not want the Allied airmen back in action, he gave an order to evacuate prison camps such as Stalag Luft IV to the West. Consequently, on January 28, 1945, Orkin was among 1,500 mostly sick and wounded Americans who were evacuated westward by train to Stalag Luft I. On February 2, another 1,500 Americans were evacuated southwestward by train to Nuremberg. On February 6, the other prisoners, about 6,000 of them, were ordered to leave on foot for what became known as a "Death March" which took 86 days, covered 600 miles, and resulted in about 1,300 prisoners dying from disease, starvation, or at the hands of the German guards.[39]

Even though Ray Goodson, with whom Orkin was shot down on December 2, 1944, was in Stalag Luft I, they were not reunited with each other because they were in different compounds. Goodson was interned in the North 3 compound and Orkin was interned in the North 2 compound.[40] The compounds were separated by double barbed wire fences with coils between the fences.[41]

Orkin was in a better place in Stalag Luft I than Stalag Luft IV because living conditions were better in commissioned officer camps than in non-commissioned officer and enlisted men camps. Also, according to Second Lieutenant Irwin Stovroff, a Jewish prisoner of war in Stalag Luft I, the senior leader of that prison camp, Colonel Hubert "Hub" Zemke, warned the Germans not to harm the Jewish prisoners of war.[42]

Zemke, the Senior Allied Officer for Stalag Luft I, was a leader in combat, and he was a leader in prison. In combat, he commanded the 56th Fighter Group which had more air victory credits against the Luftwaffe than any other fighter group in Europe.[43] In prison, after he was shot down over Germany in a P-51 Mustang on October 30, 1944, he became the leader of the Allied prisoners in Stalag Luft I. He was the son of German immigrants and was fluent in German. This helped him to communicate effectively with the German camp commander, Oberst Von Warnstadt. Oberst means colonel in English.[44]

Zemke oversaw an organization of prisoners with capable leaders in each of the four compounds. The aim of the organization was to effect order and discipline in a military manner to establish a unity that allowed Zemke to speak with one voice to Colonel Von Warnstadt when acting in the best interests of the prisoners. Each compound leader, who reported to Zemke and had a title of either Senior American Officer or Senior Allied Officer, had an impressive resume.

The Senior American Officer of Goodson's North 3 compound was Colonel Francis "Gabby" Gabreski, who was shot down over Germany in a P-47 Thunderbolt on May 22, 1944. Gabreski was one of the top American fighter pilots of World War II.[45] You cannot keep a good man down, and Gabreski went on to serve honorably in the Korean War. He died in 2002 at the age of 83 and was laid to rest in the Calverton National Cemetery on Long Island, the same cemetery that Calvin Chin was laid to rest in 1987 at age 62, and that John Cooney was laid to rest in 2014 at age 91.[46]

The Senior American Officer of Orkin's North 2 compound was Colonel Cy Wilson, another fighter pilot who was shot down over the North coast of Denmark in a P-51 Mustang on August 27, 1944.[47] Wilson was the commander of the 20th Fighter Group of the Eighth Air Force during World War II and survived seventy-eight combat missions.[48] He was a leader like Jimmy Doolittle who never asked his pilots to do anything he wouldn't do. He was a tough guy who sometimes flew with a cigar in his mouth and was loved by the pilots under his command. One of his men even named his son after him.[49] After the war, he commanded the 27th Fighter Escort Group at Bergstrom Air Force Base near Austin, Texas. and was a pioneer in the long-range overwater flights of jets. His outfit won the Mackay Air Force Trophy in 1953 which is awarded for the "most meritorious flight of the year" to an Air Force person, persons, or organization.[50] He was killed in January 1955 when his F-84 jet fighter encountered an engine icing problem and he tried to land on a highway. Ironically, four-and-a-half years earlier in August 1950, one of his F-84 pilots landed on a highway and Wilson flew the F-84 jet off the highway and back to Bergstrom.[51] You don't often hear of a jet landing or taking off on a highway.

The Senior American Officer of the North 1 compound was Lieutenant Colonel Ross Greening who was shot down over Italy in a B-25 Mitchell bomber on July 17, 1943. Greening had been the pilot of one of the sixteen B-25 Mitchell bombers that attacked Tokyo in the Doolittle Raid on April 18, 1942. In fact, he designed a simple bombsight out of two pieces of aluminum for the Raid because they were flying too low for the sophisticated Norden bombsight to be of use. His ingenuity was effective because the improvised bombsight proved to be surprisingly accurate.[52] In the wake of the Japanese attack on Pearl Harbor, America and its Allies needed a morale boost and the Doolittle Raiders' attack on Tokyo, the first offensive air action against the Japanese home islands, provided that boost.[53]

Greening was a colorful and resourceful guy. When he was shot down over Italy, he was imprisoned in Italy, escaped, was captured again, and imprisoned in Germany in Stalag Luft I. He was in that prison of war camp longer than the other American camp leaders and was the type of guy that everyone wanted to be around.[54] He created an environment in which talented prisoners were able to create artwork which became part of an exhibit he took around the country after the war. One of those talented prisoners was Claire Cline who made a violin out of scavenged wood, using makeshift tools and adhesive scraped from the bottom of tables in the mess hall. On Christmas Eve 1944, he played his violin in a concert in his barracks. Today, his violin is at the National World War II Museum in New Orleans.[55]

Greening was a talented artist himself and produced many drawings of his wartime experiences. After the war, he also tape-recorded his wartime experiences with the help of his wife Dorothy, and she preserved the recordings. After he passed away, Dorothy transcribed his recordings and, with the help of their niece, Karen Morgan Driscoll, edited the material and produced a book published in 2001 entitled *Not As Briefed: From the Doolittle Raid to a German Stalag*. The book included Greening's extensive drawings of his experiences as a bomber pilot and a prisoner of war.[56]

The Senior Allied Officer of the West Compound was British Group Captain C. T. (Cecil Thomas) Weir who went down over Germany when his Avro Lancaster bomber was hit by a bomb from another aircraft in November 1944—he was the sole survivor of his crew. Weir was born in Scotland and educated in Canada and after the war he commanded a task force that carried out the first airdrop of a British nuclear weapon in Australia. He rose to the rank of Air Vice-Marshall and was deputy head of the British defense staff in Washington, D.C. when he died from a heart attack in 1965.[57]

Goodson and Orkin were fortunate to be in a prison camp with leaders like this who worked well together under Zemke for the welfare of the prisoners. With Russian troops approaching from the East, Zemke learned from Colonel Von Warnstadt on April 18, 1945, that all German personnel and prisoners of war were to be ready to evacuate from Stalag Luft I on twenty-four hours' notice. Zemke and his men decided that they did not want to evacuate because of the risk of the prisoners being attacked from the air. They confronted Von Warnstadt on April 30, 1945, which happened to be the day Hitler committed suicide. They encouraged him not to follow Hitler's order because the prisoners were organized and prepared to resist and because it was evident that the war was lost by Germany and mistreating the prisoners would not be in his best interests. Von Warnstadt heeded their warning and had his men out of Stalag Luft I by May 1, the day before the Russians arrived on May 2.[58]

The next challenge for Zemke and his organization was how to deal with the Russians who were planning to evacuate the American and British prisoners from Stalag Luft I by ship to Odessa, a Russian port on the Black Sea about 1,500 miles to the East. Since Stalag Luft I was only 150 miles from Allied territory to the West, this made no sense.[59] Zemke again was an effective representative of the prisoners because he spoke some Russian, having spent some time in Russia training Russian pilots to fly the P-40 Warhawk fighters and working for the U. S. Embassy in Moscow. The P-40 Warhawks had been given to Russia under the Lend-Lease Act of 1941 which enabled the United States to help its allies without violating its official policy of neutrality.[60] That was before the United States went from being a neutral nation to a nation at war after Pearl Harbor.

Zemke worked closely with his British counterpart, Weir, to develop and implement a plan to airlift the American prisoners to France and the British prisoners (including those from the British Commonwealth countries such as Canada) to England. Weir was instrumental in bringing the air evacuation plan to the attention of General Bernard Montgomery, who cleared it with Marshall Konstantin Rokosoffsky, one of the Red Army's top commanders in World War II.[61] The plan came to be known as Operation Revival. It called for B-17 Flying Fortresses stationed in England to be modified to fit from twenty-five to thirty prisoners on each plane from its normal crew complement of ten. In addition, some military transport planes such as the C-46 Commando and the C-47 Skytrain were also used for the airlift.[62]

When Stalag Luft I was liberated on May 1, it had about 9,200 prisoners (7,700 Americans and 1,500 British) including Goodson and Orkin. When the airlift began on May 12, it had about 8,500 prisoners which means that about 700 of them had decided to find other ways to freedom rather than wait for the airlift.[63] It took about 300 flights from April 12 to 15 to transport prisoners from Stalag Luft I to France (American prisoners) and England (British prisoners).[64] As for the missing 700 prisoners, Zemke was given the job of looking for them.[65]

Goodson and Orkin were among the Americans airlifted to France. They were transported to Camp Lucky Strike in St. Valery, France, about forty-five miles from the port of Le Havre. Camp Lucky Strike was one of several camps named for cigarettes which processed Recovered American Military Persons (RAMPs) like Goodson and Orkin. Other cigarette camps were Camp Old Gold, Camp Pall Mall, Camp Philip Morris, and Camp Chesterfield. The processing of the RAMPs included being cleaned up, getting deloused to get rid of lice, having medical examinations, and adjusting to a better diet and lifestyle. Camp Lucky Strike was the largest of the cigarette camps and processed more than 73,000 troops. It was said to be a mix of chaos and seventh heaven.[66] After being refreshed, Goodson and Orkin waited for their ship to come in to take them home.

Goodson and Orkin weren't the only members of Cookman's crew who had to bail out of a disabled plane again. Leslie Goss had to bail out again too. The first time he parachuted out of a plane, on October 23, 1944, he fractured his fibula for which he received a Purple Heart. He also appreciated his parachute for saving his life and sent it to his parents in Clinton, Missouri.[67]

On March 21, 1945, he was a replacement radio operator and waist gunner for Charlie Russell who had been badly wounded on an earlier mission and was in a hospital in Foggia.[68] Luck was not with Goss on that day.

They were on a mission to bomb the railroad marshalling yards in Bruck, Austria, when his plane was hit by flak over the target area, knocking out engine number three. The pilot and co-pilot encountered difficulty feathering the engine which became a runaway engine as they headed for home. There was concern that the propeller of the runaway engine might fly off into the flight deck or put too much stress on the wing causing it to break off.[69]

The pilot, Second Lieutenant William N. Silliman, informed the crew of the situation and said he and the co-pilot, Second Lieutenant Carl B. Roberts, were getting out of their seats, no doubt to get out of the path of the propeller should it rip off into the flight deck where they were sitting. Before they got up, they put the plane on autopilot. According to the flight engineer, Staff Sergeant Forest G. Millis, eight members of the crew bailed out, leaving only him, Silliman, and Roberts on the flight deck. The three of them went to the bomb bay to bail out, but the plane seemed to stabilize, so Millis went back to the flight deck and reported to Silliman that the instruments were on normal readings, namely that the revolutions per minute of the propeller on engine number three were no longer exceptionally high.[70]

Standing in the bomb bay with the aircraft on autopilot, Silliman saw the island of Vis, a small island in the Adriatic Sea that had an emergency landing strip for Fifteenth Air Force air crews returning from missions to Austria, Poland, Hungary, and other target areas. The island was 125 miles from their home base. Taking advantage of the situation, Silliman and Roberts returned to their seats and made an emergency landing on Vis. [71]

They learned later that one member of the crew who bailed out, the left waist gunner, Sergeant Richard F. Morton, became a fatality. It was reported that he bailed out about thirty miles southwest of Lake Balaton in Hungary, that his parachute failed to open properly causing him to break his back when he landed, and that he was taken to a hospital in Hungary where he didn't survive. The other seven members of the crew, including Goss, were captured and became prisoners of war.[72] When a crew bails out and the plane continues to fly, it does not do much for morale. In the chaos of combat, things like this happen which is why war is hell.

While Silliman, Roberts, and Millis missed the trauma of jumping out of a plane that day, they had a frightening experience only twelve days earlier. On March 9, 1945, the trio was returning from a mission with a full bomb load in a thunderstorm and faced landing on a slippery runway with a violent gusty wind. Adding to the problem was static interference from the storm making it difficult for the tower to communicate with the returning ships. As Silliman's plane came in, another plane was coming in below him. When he saw it, he pulled up quickly but got caught in the other plane's propwash which added to the turbulence he was already experiencing. As soon as he touched down, his plane pulled to the left and in trying to right the ship it went into a skid, hit the edge of the runway, and blew a tire. Silliman and Roberts were able to bring the aircraft to a stop and the crew evacuated quickly because the oil around number three engine was burning and the plane had a full bomb load. Fortunately, the engine stopped burning of its own accord. [73]

When they got a safe distance from their plane, they turned and saw another plane skidding down the runway which blew its left tire, hit the tail of their plane, and pulled off the runway. The tower closed the field for about seven minutes, but it was getting dark and returning ships were running out of gas and were anxious to land so the tower notified all ships of the situation and they started to come in. One of the planes, in which Flint was the co-plot and Goss was the radio operator, did not get the message that two planes were off to one side of the runway. Flint said he and his pilot, First Lieutenant Robert L. Worsthorn, did not even see the two planes until they touched down, whereupon they hit the brakes and started to skid toward them. To keep from colliding, he said they did a ground loop which resulted in their tail section ramming the left wing of Silliman's plane. In other words, they applied the left brake and powered up engines number three and four on the right side to spin the plane in a counterclockwise direction. Miraculously, nobody was injured in the three incidents, but they all experienced high drama. Silliman said that Worsthorn did "a very nice job" by spinning his plane around which "undoubtedly saved the life of everyone on the ship."[74] Twelve days later, Goss would have a much more frightening experience of going down in a B-24 over Italy for the second time after breaking his leg the first time.

Osofsky flew most of his missions with Worsthorn and Flint and had a high regard for their ability to handle a plane. He liked them too. He said Worsthorn was a tall, smart, wonderful guy who had been shot down over Yugoslavia on August 22, 1944, and tore his nose when a branch went up it as he landed in a tree. He had been a student at Long Island University in Brooklyn, Osofsky's hometown, before he went off to war. Osofsky said Worsthorn bent over a lot, probably to get through doorways as he was six feet four inches tall and weighed 210 pounds. As a big guy, he no doubt came crashing down hard into that tree. He was helped by partisans, evaded capture, and made it back to the base too soon to be sent home, so he kept on flying missions, and many of them were flown with Osofsky as his left waist gunner and Flint as his co-pilot.[75]

Osofsky had a good sense of humor, and so did Flint and Worsthorn. In the April 28, 1945, issue of *Ad-Lib*, the 451st Bomb Group newsletter, Flint and Worsthorn were asked if they would continue to fly after the war. Flint said, "Only for pleasure and flying without flak will be a pleasure." Worsthorn added, "I'll fly for commercial airlines, providing they use B-24s and I get the Hoboken to Mitchel Field run," alluding to Hoboken in New Jersey and Mitchel Field on Long Island. [76] Neither of them flew after the war, but Osofsky did—he became a pilot and so did his wife. They flew for business and pleasure.

Flying combat missions was dangerous, and flying in general could also be dangerous. Silliman, Roberts, and Millis flew and survived many combat missions during the war, but their luck ran out on their flight home. About a month after the war in Europe ended with V-E Day (Victory in Europe Day—May 8, 1945), they took off on June 3 with twelve men on board, two of whom were passengers from another bomb group, for a flight across the Atlantic Ocean from Mallad Field in Dakar, Senegal, to Hunter Field in Savannah, Georgia. They never made it. It was said later that someone smelled gas before they took off, but they were anxious to get home and took off anyway.[77] Their plane failed to gain altitude, banked to the left, and exploded on impact when it crashed into the ocean only two miles off the coast. Nobody survived.[78] The unlucky twelve are listed in Exhibit 13.2.

All twelve had gone to war overseas and survived the ordeal, but their luck ran out on the way home. The bodies of ten of them were never recovered but were commemorated in the North Africa American Cemetery in Tunisia. Their names are engraved on the Wall of the Missing, which honors 3,724 Americans, with this inscription: "HERE ARE RECORDED THE NAMES OF AMERICANS WHO GAVE THEIR LIVES IN THE SERVICE OF THEIR COUNTRY AND WHO SLEEP IN UNKNOWN GRAVES."[79] The bodies of the two others—Staff Sergeant William Geller and Corporal Edwin B. Wiggins—were recovered, and both were buried in temporary graves during the war. After the war, they were brought home with military escorts. Geller was laid to rest in Mount Hebron Cemetery in his hometown of Bronx, New York; and Wiggins was laid to rest in Memorial Park Cemetery in his

Exhibit 13.2
Crew Lost at Sea on the Way Home
June 3, 1945

Airmen	Crew Member/Passenger	Hometown	Commemorated
1st Lt. William M. Silliman	Pilot	Quincy, IL	Wall of the Missing North African American Cemetery
1st Lt. Carl B. Roberts	Co-Pilot	Yazoo City, MS	Wall of the Missing
1st Lt. Clarence L. Wellman	Navigator	Silverton, OR	Wall of the Missing
1st Lt. Martin E. Walsh	Bombardier	Astoria, Queens, NY	Wall of the Missing
T/Sgt. Forrest G. Millis	Flight Engineer	Martinsville, IL	Wall of the Missing
S/Sgt. Malcolm R. Smith	Radio Operator	Manor, TX	Wall of the Missing
S/Sgt. John P. Chylek	Gunner	Chicago, IL	Wall of the Missing
Pvt. John E. Preiskorn	Gunner	Wayne, MI	Wall of the Missing
PFC Curtis L. Kline	Passenger	Attalla, AL	Wall of the Missing
S/Sgt. Eugene Dye	Gunner	Ardmore, OK	Wall of the Missing
Cpl. Edward B. Wiggins	Passenger	Bartlesville, OK	Memorial Park Cemetery Bartlesville, OK
S/Sgt. William Geller	Gunner	Bronx, NY	Mount Hebron Cemetery Bronx, NY

hometown of Bartlesville, Oklahoma.[80] In addition to the 3,724 Americans commemorated on the Wall of the Missing, there are 2,841 Americans buried at that cemetery.[81] War takes an awful toll.

The Rest of Cookman's Crew

Kirk Mosher flew his first and last combat mission on Friday, October 13, 1944, when his plane was shot down over Vienna, Austria. Bob Cookman flew his third and last combat mission on October 23, 1944, when his plane developed engine trouble and went down over Italy. Ray Goodson and David Orkin flew their last mission on December 2, 1944, when they were shot down over Germany and became prisoners of war. Leslie Goss flew his last mission on March 21, 1945, when he was shot down over Yugoslavia and became a prisoner of war. The rest of the crew that went down with Cookman on October 23—Russ Flint, David Johnson, Calvin Chin, John Cooney, Meyer Osofsky, and Charles Muth—flew combat missions until the end of the war. Because their 451st Bomb Group did not pass down their loading lists with the names of all crew members on each mission flown, one cannot pinpoint every combat mission flown by every member of the crew.[82]

We do know that Cooney flew thirty-five missions, Osofsky flew thirty-one missions, Flint flew twenty-five missions, and Chin flew twenty-five missions. As we will see later, there is reason to believe that Flint flew twenty-seven missions, and that Chin flew twenty-six missions. We can conclude that Johnson flew at least thirty-five missions because he like Cooney received an Air Medal with three Oak Leaf Clusters—an Air Medal was typically awarded in their bomb group after five combat missions and an Oak Leaf Cluster was added for each additional ten combat missions. We are reasonably sure that Orkin flew ten missions because this was stated in a news article about him.[83] However, since he received an Air Medal with one Oak Leaf Cluster, he may have flown at least fifteen missions. Cookman flew three missions and was killed on the third one.[84] Mosher was killed on his first combat mission.[85] Both of them received an Air Medal.[86]

The Air Medal was authorized on May 11, 1942. It was awarded, retroactive to September 8, 1939, to airmen who distinguished themselves by meritorious achievement while serving with the Army Air Forces in aerial flight.[87] It was an award that provided combat aircrews with a visible sign that their devotion to duty was appreciated by their country.[88] Bottom line, it took courage to fly combat missions and being rewarded for meritorious service with an Air Medal was a morale booster. Furthermore, we know that Chin, Goss, and Goodson received the Purple Heart for being injured in the line of duty, and that Goodson, Orkin, and Goss were prisoners of war eligible for the Prisoner of War Medal. We also know that Johnson received the Distinguished Flying Cross.

There are medals of valor and medals of service. Medals of valor include the Distinguished Flying Cross, the Air Medal, and the Purple Heart. Medals of service include the EAME (European, African, and Middle Eastern) Campaign Medal with a Bronze Service Star for each battle campaign. For example, Cooney served in six Battle Campaigns—the Air Combat Balkans, Northern Apennines, Po Valley, Rhineland, Central Europe, and Rome-Arno Campaigns—and earned six Bronze Service Stars which were attached to his EAME ribbon bar. The Prisoner of War Medal is also classified as a service award. Other medals for service are the World War II Victory Medal for service during the war and the American Campaign Medal for service in the United States.[89] Calvin Chin also earned the Good Conduct Medal awarded for exemplary conduct over three years of active service."[90] Also, any airmen who successfully parachuted out of a disabled airplane qualified for a Caterpillar Pin which means that all members of Cookman's crew who successfully bailed out qualified for a Caterpillar Pin.

Chin kept track of his missions and passed the list down to his son David. He flew eleven missions to targets in Austria, eleven to targets in Italy, two to targets in Czechoslovakia, and one to a target in Poland. His list, however, did not include the October 23, 1944, mission on which his pilot Cookman was killed. We know from the accident report that he flew the mission, sprained his ankle when he landed, and did not fly again until December 4, forty-three days later. A likely assumption is that he did not record it as a mission because they never reached the target. They developed engine trouble on the way to the target, reversed course, and crashed in friendly territory on the way back.

John saw plenty of action on his thirty-five missions. When he received his first Air Medal, the press release noted that he participated in attacks against such strategic targets as the Pilsen Skoda Works in Czechoslovakia, the Blechhammer Synthetic Oil Refinery in Germany, and other important strategic targets in Austria, Italy, and Hungary.[91] Of the thirty-five missions he flew, the one he most remembered was the October 23 mission when they went down over Italy.

Meyer Osofsky also saw plenty of action flying thirty-one missions. Like John, his most memorable mission was the one on which they went down over

Italy. Meyer thought the service shaped him. Flying combat missions was tough duty but he knew what he was fighting for because his grandparents and parents had been the victims of persecution. He loved the camaraderie of being part of a crew serving his country and was always proud of his service. He had never seen a dead person before he went to war, and when he did, it was a rude awakening for him.[92]

The incident occurred on a mission when the tail gunner was hit by flak. He was wearing the body armor called a "flak suit" or "flak vest." It hung like an apron over his shoulders and flight suit. The front part protected his abdomen, groin and private parts and the rear part protected his backside. It had fasteners on the sides holding the front and rear together, but the tail gunner had not fastened them. The flak hit him through the open space and dealt him a lethal blow. Meyer gave him morphine to help relieve the pain, but he did not make it. Meyer never forgot that tragic experience.[93]

Meyer never forgot another experience that could have been tragic when the waist gunner opposite him collapsed during a mission. They were flying at a high altitude where temperatures were as low as forty or fifty degrees below zero. Airmen were trained in the proper use of equipment but very often the real-life experience was different from the training experience. The proper use of an oxygen mask was critical because lack of oxygen at 30,000 feet could result in unconsciousness, sometimes leading to death. Because most anoxia (lack of oxygen) deaths occurred among new crew members, rookies were assigned to fly early missions with experienced crew members.[94] At high altitudes, since oxygen equipment and its proper use prevented a flyer from death by anoxia, it was important to know how to use it on combat missions because even the best equipment is only as efficient as the person using it.[95]

On this mission, Meyer was the experienced waist gunner flying with a rookie who collapsed when his oxygen mask froze up cutting off his oxygen supply. Meyer acted quickly, lifted him up, and kept squeezing the ice in the tube leading to his mask until he could breathe again. He said his crewmate was light—he weighed 130 pounds.[96] He never forgot the incident nor the name of the airman, Jackson Dube, who like him was from New York City.[97] He saved his life. Dube went on to form an international film distribution company (J.E.D. Production Corporation), marry actress Patricia Lavelle, and father journalist Deirdre Mendoza.[98]

Meyer had fond memories of the crew he went down with—the officers he flew with, and the enlisted men he not only flew with but also lived with. Of the officers, he remembered Cookman as a responsible leader with premature gray hair who liked to kid him and Orkin about their respective Brooklyn and Queens accents. He thinks Cookman was a courageous man who should have received the Medal of Honor for sacrificing his life to save his crew. He remembered Flint as a good-natured fellow, as nice as could be, and thought he was a good co-pilot. He was afraid of mice, so they put one in his sleeping bag. When he woke up and took off, Cookman quipped, "There goes our hero!"[99] Flint was also thoughtful and considerate—when Cookman was killed, he led an effort to collect $50 from each crew member and sent the money to his wife Marianne back in Mason City.[100]

Meyer flew most of his missions with Flint as co-pilot and Bob Worsthorn as pilot. However, he wasn't on the mission when Worsthorn was shot down over Yugoslavia on August 22, 1944, nor was he with Worsthorn when he had an accident on March 9, 1945, in which he spun his plane to avert disaster for his crew. Flint was on that mission helping him spin the plane.[101] Meyer had a high regard for Worsthorn and Flint personally and professionally. After the war, the three of them got together on Long Island and no doubt told war stories.[102]

Meyer remembered his boxing partner, Ray Goodson, as a skinny, feisty guy who didn't take crap from anyone, which is probably why he was beat up in a German prison camp. His memory was good because Goodson, who ran track in high school, was five feet eleven inches, the same height as him, but weighed only 132 pounds. Meyer said he was game to box and could take a punch—Meyer was almost forty pounds heavier than him. He was the guy Meyer was chatting with when they were descending in their parachutes on October 23 and had far more on their minds than a boxing match. Goodson was the recipient of an Air Medal and a Purple Heart. He was shot down and imprisoned before he had an opportunity to obtain Oak Leaf Clusters to supplement his Air Medal, but he qualified for the Prisoner of War Medal.

Meyer did not remember much about the fourth officer, David Johnson, who replaced Cylkowski as navigator when Cylkowski was grounded for air sickness. He only flew one mission with him. Johnson ended up as the most decorated member of the crew, earning an Air Medal with three Oak Leaf Clusters along with a Distinguished Flying Cross which was awarded for heroism or extraordinary achievement in flight.[103]

Unbeknownst to Meyer, Johnson was born and brought up in Long Beach, California. He was the second of four children—Gloria, David, Sylvia, and Daniel—born to Frank and Florence Johnson.[104] He was eighteen when he registered for the draft on December 18, 1942. At that time, he was a civilian doing work for the military in Alaska.[105] In 1939, when it was discovered that

Hitler's goal was global domination, the United States began to focus on its coastal defenses and Alaska was one of those places of concern.

Billy Mitchell was a visionary who saw and promoted air power and came to be regarded as the "Father of the United States Air Force." He also saw the importance of Alaska and said, "I believe in the future he who holds Alaska will hold the world." At the urging of him and others, Congress appropriated funds in 1939 for the construction of naval bases in Sitka, Dutch Harbor, and Kodiak, Alaska and the Navy employed civilian contractor Siems Drake Puget Sound to build all three naval bases.[106] Johnson was employed by Siems Drake.[107]

When Pearl Harbor was attacked on December 7, 1941, concern over coastal defenses intensified. In March 1942, construction of the naval base at Sitka was completed and it was the only defensive base in Southeast Alaska. Its PBY Catalinas, the same plane used by the British for their air-sea rescue operations, patrolled the coast while work on the Dutch Harbor and Kodiak bases was stepped up.[108] Johnson saw firsthand the mobilization for war that took place in Alaska and understood why he was called upon to serve his country.

Osofsky also never knew that Johnson, like Goodson, Orkin and Goss, had to bail out of a disabled B-24 again. After going down in Cookman's plane, Johnson was assigned to a new crew and ran into trouble on November 11, 1944, his third mission flying with the new crew. The primary target that day for Mission 148 of the 451st Bomb Group was the Herman Goering Benzol Fuel Plant in Linz, Austria and of the twenty-seven B-24s that flew the mission, Johnson had the bad luck of being on the only one that did not return. Due to poor weather, they aborted the primary target and went after targets of opportunity and some of them bombed the Aviano Airdrome in Italy with fair results. Consequently, the Aviano Airdrome was listed as the target on November 11, 1944, even though the Herman Goering Benzol Fuel Plant was the primary target. Johnson's plane ran into trouble on the way to the primary target.[109]

Johnson's pilot was First Lieutenant Hubert C. Fones from Aurora, New York. Fones displayed leadership skills early. He played high school football, basketball, baseball, and golf while serving as class vice president in his junior and senior years and was a member of the National Honor Society. He went on to the University of Michigan where he was class president his freshman year, majored in engineering, and was president of an engineering honor society.[110] Now he was the commander of a B-24 crew and flying into trouble and would need his leadership skills on this day. After the war, Johnson wrote about the trouble in a letter to his wife's brother-in-law, Wendell Dodge.[111]

On the way to the target, Johnson's plane encountered engine trouble. They lost engine number two and the strain of increasing power in the other three engines led to an oil leak in engine number three which they feathered to reduce drag. Unable to keep up with the formation, they dropped out and headed home, crossing the Alps, and releasing their bombs over the Brenner Pass, a mountain pass through the Alps which formed the border between Italy and Austria.[112]

They came upon five B-24s from the 461st Bomb Group which he thought looked upon them suspiciously because there had been instances of Germans flying a captured solo B-24. It was a nerve-racking situation to be in, but they survived that threat before running into more trouble. As they flew over Venice, they sustained five direct hits by flak from German anti-aircraft batteries which cut three main control cables.[113] What next?

As Fones and his co-pilot, First Lieutenant William H. Lang, guided the plane south over the Adriatic Sea toward the Italian coastline, they flew into a hailstorm which iced the windshield and wings, forcing them to fly the plane on instruments. Johnson said Fones did a beautiful job in getting them through the storm. He felt that he saved their lives. When they reached the Italian coast, they flew down the coast to friendly territory and then bailed out. The nose gunner, Sergeant Joseph H. Tweedie, broke his leg when he landed, and Johnson said they never saw him again.[114] He was later reported as SIA, or Seriously Injured in Action.[115] Johnson said the tail gunner, Staff Sergeant Odis R. Gadberry, also hurt his back and legs and had to be hospitalized. He tried to fly again with their crew, but his injuries prevented it. Johnson said they missed him a lot because he was always so upbeat and full of hell.[116]

Johnson and the rest of the crew had a far different experience when they landed because they landed on the estate of a wealthy Italian. With their ball-turret gunner Staff Sergeant Ray A. Marchetto translating, they were treated like kings for a couple of days and had a wonderful time—eating, drinking, and hunting before the British picked them up and drove them back to their home base in Castelluccio dei Sauri. Johnson said that their crew was closer than ever after that mission and felt as though they could survive anything.[117] Three months later they would be recognized for superior performance on one of the most effective and destructive missions ever flown by the 451st Bomb Group.[118]

On March 25, 1945, David Johnson was flying again with pilot Hubert Fones and his crew. His 451st Bomb Group, along with the 461st and 484th Bomb Groups of the 49th Bomb Wing, were ordered to participate in a mission with the 5th, 47th, 55th, and 304th Bomb Wings and with fighter escorts from the 15th Fighter Command. The targets for the 49th Bomb Wing were enemy fighter aircraft parked at the Kbely Airdrome located five miles northeast of Prague, Czechoslovakia.[119]

According to their military intelligence, 203 fighters were parked at the Airdrome on March 23 and included Me 262 jet fighters. The German Me 262 was the first operational fighter jet in history and was significantly faster than American propeller-driven P-47 and P-51 fighters and the British propeller-driven Spitfires. Intelligence also warned that it was possible that twenty to twenty-five Me 262s in the target area could attack them and that forty to fifty Fw 190 and Bf 109 fighters could intercept them on the way to the target and on the way back from the target. It was a dangerous, challenging, and strategically important mission because there had been a sharp increase in the number of aircraft at the Airdrome.[120]

At 7:40 am on March 25, thirty-six B-24s from the 451st Bomb Groups started their engines, then taxied into position and took off at 8:00 am. The thirty-six planes rendezvoused into a formation of six combat boxes with six B-24s in each box and each box had a flight name—Able, Baker, Charlie, Dog, Baby, and Fox. Fones was the leader of the six planes in Charlie Flight flying to the left of Able Flight where the leader of the flight was also the leader of the entire formation of thirty-six aircraft for the 451st Bomb Group. They met up with the 461st and 484th Bomb Groups in Bovino, Italy, and headed for their target at 9:26 am, flying a route outlined for them by military intelligence to avoid areas known to have anti-aircraft batteries and fighter aircraft ready to intercept Allied bombers. The plan was for them to arrive at the Initial Point at Kabel, Czechoslovakia, at 11:57 am, and then go on a seven-minute bomb run to drop clusters of fragmentation bombs on the German fighter planes parked at the Kbely Airdrome at 12:04 pm.[121]

On the bomb run, the 461st Bomb Group ran into trouble. The interphone system on the lead plane went out making it impossible for the bombardier and pilot to achieve the coordination necessary for an effective bomb run for their twenty-nine B-24s and had to turn away from the target even though crew members saw many aircraft parked on the airfield. The 484th Bomb Group also ran into trouble and were unable to identify the target due to surrounding terrain, smoke, and haze, but nevertheless dropped forty-five tons of fragmentation bombs in the target area.[122]

The 451st Bomb Group had a far different experience. Only twenty-eight of its planes were able to make it to the target and dropped fifty-four tons of bombs on the Kbely Airdrome with "superior" results. It was the only bomb group in the 49th Bomb Wing to hit the target. It was reported that they did a magnificent job. The results from the strike photos that were borne out by reconnaissance showed that at least twenty-five enemy planes were destroyed and eight were damaged. These results were said to be equal to the efforts of an entire wing of six groups and that it was one of the most effective and destructive missions ever flown by the 451st Bomb Group. General Twining himself commended the 451st Bomb Group for the mission.[123]

For their performance on the mission, First Lieutenant Hubert C. Fones as pilot, First Lieutenant David G. Johnson as navigator, and First Lieutenant Myron L. Carl as bombardier, each received a Distinguished Flying Cross for heroism and extraordinary achievement while participating in aerial flight in the Mediterranean Theater of Operations. The citation went on to say:[124]

> *"By their heroism, skill and airmanship, as shown throughout their combat careers, together with intense devotion to duty during this period of intense combat operations against the enemy, these men have upheld the highest traditions of the Military Service, thereby reflecting great credit upon themselves and the Armed Forces of the United States of America."*

Meyer never knew that David Johnson received the Distinguished Flying Cross. He knew a lot about most of his enlisted crewmates because he trained and lived with them. One crewmate was David Orkin who like him grew up in New York City. Meyer said David was a pleasant guy but not one of the boys. He was also thin (145 pounds to Meyer's 170) and fit into the top-turret which was tight fit for Meyer. While Meyer qualified to fly as an engineer and top-turret gunner, he was more comfortable in the waist gunner position which wasn't as cramped and allowed him to move around.[125]

He remembered Calvin Chin, a year younger than him, as a good kid who was a lot of fun to be around. He used to kid Calvin about his accent, same as he was kidded by Cookman about his accent.[126] With the tension of flying combat missions, kidding around helped reduce the tension. Calvin was a very upbeat person, very sociable, a personality he put to good use later in his life's work. Meyer appreciated and liked Calvin and connected with him after the war.[127] The crew kept a Browning camera on board and passed it around. Since Calvin had a good view from his nose turret, he took many pictures with that camera and passed them down to his son David.[128]

Meyer remembered that Cooney had nightmares after they went down over Italy, and no wonder. Going down in a plane is a traumatic experience and carrying the body of his pilot, someone he had great respect for, up a hill after the crash was not something you easily forget. Meyer said John used to volunteer for missions to complete his tour of duty as soon as possible. He thought John was a wonderful guy.[129] He recalled that he was an ardent Catholic and had a friend, Staff Sergeant Jack Holcomb, that he palled around with. They invited him to attend mass with them once, so he was a good sport and went with them, but he did not kneel when they knelt.[130] John was the guy who said many years later in an interview that the reason he went to war was because he objected to all the Jewish people being killed.[131]

Meyer also invited John to box, but he said he only wrestled, probably, Meyer thought, because he was a handsome guy who didn't want to mess up his face.[132] Since Meyer was not a fan of tight spaces, he marveled at how Cooney, not a small man, squeezed into the ball-turret on missions. In fact, it was so tight that Cooney couldn't fit into it with his flak suit or his parachute. He let Meyer stand on his flak suit to protect his private parts from bullets or flak from below, and on one combat mission it did just that for which Meyer was always grateful.[133]

Meyer palled around with Charles Muth, who he always called Chuck. Both had been welders—Meyer at the Brooklyn Navy Yard and Chuck at the International Harvester Company—so they had that in common and enjoyed each other's company. Every now and then they would get a pass and visit Foggia where they would barter with native Italians, trading items like toothpaste and soap for wine and bread. The Red Cross ladies served ice cream in Foggia, and they took advantage of that perk as well. Foggia was also where Meyer had his parachute made into scarves and handkerchiefs that were later stolen except for one handkerchief that he gave his wife after the war.[134]

Once, they bought a radio in Foggia. Meyer said they used to listen to Axis Sally who made propaganda broadcasts.[135] She was an American named Mildred Gillars who had an affair with a German professor—Otto Max Koischwitz—in New York City and followed him to Berlin where he became the head of propaganda broadcasts for Radio Berlin. She was also called the Berlin Bitch. A lot of airmen listened to her because she played popular American music between her propaganda rants against America. After the war, she was tried for treason, spent twelve years in a federal prison, and thereafter lived a quiet and reclusive life until she died in 1988 at the age of eighty-seven.[136]

The members of Cookman's crew who were lucky enough to survive the war had different experiences during the war and different experiences after the war. They returned home as veterans and brought many wartime memories with them. Some shared their memories with other veterans, some shared them with family and friends, and some preferred to not talk about them. It has been difficult to write about those who preferred not to talk about them. All of them, however, were grateful for having survived the war, and our nation was grateful for their service.

Chapter 14

AFTER THE WAR

After the war, John Cooney, Meyer Osofsky, and eight of the ten men they trained with in the States or went down with over Italy on October 23, 1944, were lucky to make it home and get on with their lives. Unfortunately, Bob Cookman and Kirk Mosher never had an opportunity to get on with their lives. Their lives were sacrificed in a war to protect our way of life which was threatened by dictators who represented a different way of life. They could never take advantage of the GI Bill to get a college education, receive training to enhance a skill, or buy a home to help close the gap between the haves and the have nots and build a strong middle class that contributed to a strong postwar America.

In his book, *The Greatest Generation*, Tom Brokaw said their generation "was united not only by a common purpose, but also by common values—duty, honor, economy, courage, service, love of family and country, and, above all, responsibility for oneself."[1] He tells the stories of a dozen veterans who the GI Bill helped prepare for careers they could never have imagined before the war.[2] It made education, training, and home ownership accessible and affordable to veterans and 7.8 million veterans took advantage of the benefits to enhance their education and skills and to purchase homes.[3]

There are so many success stories of veterans who were educated through the GI Bill and here is one of them. Like John Cooney's father, Livingston Boone was a World War I veteran who died young with a wife and five children but had sons the GI Bill impacted in a positive way. Livington served with the African American 369th Infantry Regiment known as the Harlem Hellfighters.[4] He died in 1942 at fifty-one leaving his wife Beatrice, who was sick with tuberculosis, to care for five children—Livington Jr. (16), Nathaniel called Nate (14), Sylvia (12), Janette (7) and David called Dave (5).[5]

Dave said his father was exposed to poison gas during the war which contributed to his untimely death. He also said his oldest brother, Livingston Jr., who was sixteen, dropped out of high school to help keep the family afloat.[6] Two years later Livingston Jr. was drafted into the Army and served with the African American 784th Tank Battalion during World War II.[7] He returned home after the war. When his mother died of tuberculosis in 1951, he joined the Air Force and served during the Korean and Vietnam Wars as a Technical Sergeant.[8] Dave said Livingston Jr. was always viewed as a hero for managing to support the family during hard times.[9]

Nate, who had been working before and after school to help, decided he wanted to go to college and joined the Marines with a goal of subsequently using the GI Bill to get a college education.[10] It was not an easy way to get to college. He did his basic training with the Montfort Point Marines who were segregated and trained in a snake-infested section of Camp Lejune in North Carolina.[11] They were not treated well, a wrong that was recognized many years later in 2011 when the Montford Point Marines were awarded a Congressional Gold Medal for helping to break the racial barrier in the Marines.[12]

After the Marines, Nate used the GI Bill to get an education at Bates College. He went on to Boston University Law School, practiced law for over forty years, and did well.[13] On June 21, 2014, he was featured on the CBS Morning Show commemorating the 70th anniversary of the GI Bill of Rights.[14] On February 17, 2017, he was honored for his military and community service with a proclamation signed by the Governor of Vermont declaring that day as "Nathaniel Boone Day" in the State of Vermont.[15]

Dave was only fourteen when his mother died. After high school, he also joined the Marines to get to college like his brother but while he was in the Marines the original GI Bill ended on July 25, 1956.[16] Nevertheless, after fulfilling his military obligation, he also went to Bates College encouraged by his brother's performance at Bates, helped by financial aid, and supported by good summer jobs.[17] His brother Nate was called "The Englewood Express" at Bates because he was from Englewood, New Jersey, and was good at football and track in addition to being a good student, and so was Dave.[18]

After college, Dave pursued a business career. In 1968, he founded Boone, Young & Associates, a minority-owned management consulting company which helped minority businesses to succeed.[19] In 1976, his company acquired three manufacturing subsidiaries—LaGrange Screw Products,

Miller Gear Company, and Judd Industries, Inc. Dave retired as chairman of his companies in 1998.[20] Dr. Benjamin Mays, also a Bates graduate and the President of Morehouse College, was his mentor and served on his board. Dr. Mays was also the mentor of Dr. Martin Luther King, Jr. and delivered the eulogy at Dr. King's funeral.[21]

The GI Bill made it possible for Nate to go to college and pave the way for Dave to follow in his footsteps but without the aid of the GI Bill. Both brothers did well, appreciated Bates, and served as trustees of the college, just like Dave's mentor, Dr. Mays. In 2002, Dave and his wife Carol were the recipients of the college's Distinguished Alumni Service Award.[22] Nate said in an interview on the CBS Morning Show, "I attribute everything which I've done and what I am today to the GI Bill of Rights."[23]

Because of the GI Bill many veterans like Nate Boone and John Cooney were able to afford a college education. In 1946, the presence of veterans was seen on the Boston University football team as thirty-five of the thirty-seven players on the roster were World War II veterans (Exhibit 14.1). Their game program also listed the branch each served with—Army, Navy, Air Force, Marines, or Coast Guard.[24] Veterans had a strong presence in colleges after the war. In 1947 for example, 49 percent of all college students nationwide were veterans.[25] They had defended the nation in what many viewed as the last "good war," and their nation responded to their needs and concerns after the war with the GI Bill.[26] It was a life-changing experience for many veterans who became good, productive citizens in peacetime after being good, productive soldiers during wartime.[27]

This chapter provides a brief recap of what each member of Cookman's crew did after the war and starts with a discussion of Cookman and Mosher who did not have after-the-war experiences. The recaps are arranged in chronological order from Kirk Mosher's death on October 13, 1944, at the age of 21 to Meyer Osofsky's death on October 13, 2019, at the age of 95, exactly seventy-five years after Mosher was a casualty of war. The crew came from different parts of the country, and returned to different parts of the country, but during the war they came together to serve their country honorably for which they and their families were proud, and for which their country was grateful. Those who made it home were Americans citizens who had survived the horror of war.

Exhibit 14.1
Veteran Presence in College Football After World War II
1946 Boston University Football Roster

No.	Name	Service	Class	Pos.	Wgt.	Prep School	Home
48—Anderson, Jim	AAC	4	B	205	Belfast H. S.	Portland, Me.
31—Anderson, Walter	Navy	1	B	175	Waltham H. S.	Waltham, Mass.
44—Bevins, Ralph	Navy	1	C	170	Arlington H. S.	Arlington, Mass.
51—Botsford, Harry	Marines	2	E	226	Winthrop H. S.	Winthrop, Mass.
46—Boyle, Arthur	Army	1	T	200	Cathedral H. S.	Boston, Mass.
49—Cella, Silvio	Marines	2	B	200	Revere H. S.	Revere, Mass.
29—Chruniak, Gregory	Marines	2	G	170	Lynn English H. S.	Lynn, Mass.
23—Creteau, Paul	Navy	3	E	170	Spaulding H. S.	Rochester, N. H.
55—Crisafi, William	Marines	1	G	210	Revere H. S.	Dorchester, Mass.
35—Dobiecki, Edward	Marines	1	B	180	Springfield Tech	Springfield, Mass.
Dorr, Everett	Marines	2	B	170	Scituate H. S.	North Scituate, Mass.
20—Figueira, Ed	AAF	2	B	163	Hudson H. S.	Hudson, Mass.
52—Fitzpatrick, Cliff	Marines	4	E	195	Brookline H. S.	Brookline, Mass.
33—Giles, Don	C.G.	3	B	188	Milton H. S.	Milton, Mass.
25—Hanlon, Robert	Marines	2	B	170	Winthrop H. S.	Winthrop, Mass.
30—Hatch, Bob	Marines	2	B	183	Melrose H. S.	Melrose, Mass.
43—Heller, Irving	Navy	1	T	203	Revere H. S	Revere, Mass.
53—Jillson, Merton	Army	1	T	215	Lexington H. S.	Lexington, Mass.
45—Keusch, Dave	Army	1	C	190	Durfee H. S.	Fall River, Mass.
32—Landry, Norman	C.G.	1	E	180	Lynn Classical	Lynn, Mass.
28—Martin, Paul	Navy	1	G	177	North Quincy H. S.	Squantum, Mass.
39—McCarthy, Daniel	Army	4	G	185	Cathedral H. S.	Springfield, Mass.
27—Parsons, Bill	Navy	4	G	170	Melrose H. S.	Stoneham, Mass.
34—Perry, Robert	AAF	1	B	175	Attleboro H. S.	Attleboro, Mass.
40—Powers, Robert	Navy	1	E	180	Attleboro H. S.	Attleboro, Mass.
38—Quinn, David	AAF	2	E	190	Hudson H. S.	Hudson, Mass.
41—Ruggieri, Carmen		1	B	200	Peck H. S.	Barrington, R. I.
26—Sicuso, Joseph	Navy	1	B	165	St. Clements H. S.	Medford, Mass.
47—Ramacorti, George	AAF	1	T	230	Dorchester H. S.	Dorchester, Mass.
36—Stewart, Alvin	Navy	1	G	200	Revere H. S.	Revere, Mass.
24—Sarno, Peter	Marines	1	B	160	Revere H. S.	Revere, Mass.
42—Simpson, John	Marines	1	C	190	Brookline H. S.	Brookline, Mass.
37—Souza, Manuel	Marines	1	E	193	Bridgewater H. S.	Bridgewater, Mass.
21—Tighe, William	AAF	2	B	160	Ashland H. S.	Framingham, Mass.
22—Winograd, Gerald	Navy	2	E	175	Mt. Pleasant H. S.	Providence, R. I.
54—Wister, Al	Marines	1	T	225	Carl Schurz H. S.	Chicago, Ill.
50—Zeno, Ernie		1	B	200	Waltham H. S.	Waltham, Mass.

Sergeant Kirk Gaylord Mosher
January 14, 1923 - October 13, 1944

Courtesy of Kathy Krajewski

Kirk Mosher did not make it home alive. At the age of twenty-one, he was killed in action flying his first combat mission on October 13, 1944. On that day, according to his brother Dan's daughter Kathy, his mother Ruth, who was sewing at home in Albuquerque, New Mexico, had a vision of Kirk being in trouble but telling her he was alright.[1] He was not alright.

Most of Kirk's time in the service was spent training in Texas, South Dakota, Arizona, Nebraska, Idaho, and Kansas, where he got married to his high school sweetheart Carmelita "Carmie" Smallridge. Worried that he might not return from the war, he purchased an insurance policy before he shipped out, naming Carmie as beneficiary. He arrived in Italy on September 27, 1944, as a highly trained member of a B-24 combat crew, then sixteen days later lost his life on his first mission when he was shot down over Vienna, Austria, on Friday the 13th.

When Kirk was reported as missing in action, his two brothers—Dan and Jerry—were, like him, serving in World War II, but as Marines. Dan was based in Edenton, North Carolina and Jerry was based in Paris Island, South Carolina, where he was hospitalized with pneumonia.[2] Dan was as an aviation machinist overhauling engines during the war and, like his older brother Kirk, was a good musician.[3] They were two years apart in age and had played music together before they went into the service.[4] Jerry was four years younger than Kirk and played the banjo. Their father Frank, a World War I veteran, was a musician by trade and passed down his love of music to his sons.[5]

Kirk was reported as missing in action until February 11, 1945, when the Secretary of War received sufficient evidence from the German Government through the International Red Cross that established the fact of his death.[6] When his parents Frank and Ruth and his wife Carmie received this news, they requested a memorial mass at the Sacred Heart Church in Albuquerque where family and friends congregated on February 23, 1945, to grieve together and pay tribute to Kirk.[7]

On May 3, 1945, Kirk's personal effects were sent to his father and included four wallets, three wings, a bracelet, a mandolin, a picture album, a picture folder, and a train ticket.[8] Kirk's mother Ruth still could not resign herself to the fact that her son had been killed and on September 22, 1945, sent a letter to the Adjutant General's Office asking for more tangible evidence such as a record of his burial site.[9]

The Adjutant General's Office and the Quartermaster General's Office of the War Department handled inquiries involving deceased military personnel, and the Graves Administration Service of the Quartermaster General's Office was responsible for the care of deceased military personnel.[10] The Quartermaster General waited until Kirk was moved from the Central Cemetery of Vienna, Austria, where the Germans had buried him, to the U.S. Military Cemetery in St. Avold, France, before getting back to the Mosher family.

On January 7, 1947, the Quartermaster General, Major General T.B. Larkin, sent a letter to Kirk's father informing him that the identification and interment of Kirk was handled with fitting dignity and solemnity, and that he was buried in the U.S. Military Cemetery at St. Avold, France, under the constant care and supervision of United States military personnel. He also informed him that, at some later date, Kirk's next of kin could determine his final resting place.[11]

Today, that cemetery is called the Lorraine American Cemetery and Memorial. It is located just outside the town of St. Avold in the Lorraine region of northeastern France near the border of Germany. It is the largest American cemetery in Europe with 10,481 American servicemen and women who gave their lives in the cause of liberty.[12]

After the War

Kirk's widow Carmie married again on March 7, 1948, and transferred to Kirk's father Frank her right as next of kin to determine Kirk's final resting place.[13] Frank and his wife Ruth chose to bring Kirk home from his temporary resting place in St. Avold to his final resting place at the Santa Fe National Cemetery in Santa Fe, New Mexico. Consequently, Kirk was disinterred on April 23, 1948, and prepared for the trip home. With the dignity afforded the war dead, he was transported by train on the first leg of his trip home from St. Avold to Antwerp, Belgium, the second biggest port in Europe, arriving on June 14. He was one of 4,300 Americans who were killed during the war and who were being moved from military cemeteries in Europe to the United States on the USS *Oglethorpe.*[14]

As a bit of maritime history, a shipbuilding program was launched in the United States with the passage of the Merchant Marine Act of 1936 that led to the mass-production of 2,710 merchant cargo ships—called Liberty ships—for the U.S. Maritime Commission. When World War II broke out, the Maritime Commission realized it needed faster and bigger cargo ships and that some needed to be equipped as attack transport ships because German U-boats were sinking ships. As a result, 531 Victory ships were built during the war—414 Victory merchant cargo ships and 117 Victory attack transport ships.[15] The USS *Oglethorpe* was one of the Victory attack transport ships.[16]

The 117 Victory attack transport ships were named for counties in the United States and the USS *Oglethorpe* was named for Oglethorpe County, Georgia, which was named for James Oglethorpe, the founder of the State of Georgia.[17] By coincidence, the ship was built in Kearny, New Jersey, where John Cooney worked before going to war, and it was commissioned at the Brooklyn Navy Yard, where Meyer Osofsky worked before going to war.[18] Not only that, but the USS *Oglethorpe* was headed for Brooklyn where Meyer grew up. It arrived at the Brooklyn Army Base on July 9, 1948, with 4,300 bodies on board, bringing to 60,000 the war dead returned to this country since October 1947.[19] A memorial service was held at the base located at 58th Street and First Avenue in Brooklyn. If Cooney, Osofsky, Chin, Orkin, and Cylkowski—all of whom trained and lived with Kirk in the States and who traveled with him to Italy—knew of the service, they no doubt would have been in attendance because they all lived in the area and aircrews support one another.

Six days later, on July 15, Sergeant Kirk G. Mosher and three other soldiers—Private First Class Jesse D. Renner, Private First Class Atoche Romero, and Private Roy A. Shaul—were transported by train to Santa Fe,

New Mexico for their final resting place at the Santa Fe National Cemetery.[20] They arrived in Santa Fe on August 13. On Saturday, August 14, 1948, the Mosher family held a funeral service in Santa Fe for Kirk, after which he was laid to rest in the Santa Fe National Cemetery.[21]

It's a shame that the music stopped for Kirk during the war because he was such a good musician. Dan's wife Genie, who plays piano by ear, said Kirk played lead guitar and Dan played steel guitar and that both were talented musicians.[22] Dan's daughter Kathy added that their brother Jerry was a talented banjo player and that their father Frank was a terrific drummer in addition to leading his orchestra. She also mentioned that one of her cousins had a recording of Kirk singing and that he sounded like Willie Nelson.[23]

The music didn't stop for Dan after the war. He went on to play guitar with his father and elsewhere. Kathy said he used to jam with Glen Campbell during the 1950s when Campbell lived in Albuquerque. Glen played with his uncle's band—Dick Bills' Sandia Mountain Boys—and viewed those years as his apprenticeship before he left for the bright lights of Los Angeles and became a recording and television star, ending up in the Country Music Hall of Fame.[24]

Kathy also recalled that her father had a music engagement every week. She said he loved music and even made a guitar once. At one point, he formed his own band and called it Dan Mosher and the Hatchmen.[25] At that time, Dan lived in Hatch, almost 170 miles southeast of Albuquerque as the crow flies. If Kirk had survived the war, he no doubt would also have been part of the music scene along with his musical family.

The music stopped for Dan as he aged and contracted an eye disease called macular degeneration that resulted in vision loss.[26] The disease affects people with a family history of smoking, and he and his brother Kirk were smokers. Meyer said Kirk always had a cigarette hanging out of his mouth when he played the mandolin in their tent.[27] A lot of people smoked back then. The first half of the 20th century was said to be the golden age of cigarettes and in 1950 about half the population in industrialized countries smoked. It wasn't until the Surgeon General's Committee on Smoking and Health came out with a report in 1964 on the dangers of smoking that the trend began to reverse itself in the United States.[28]

Kirk's father Frank passed away in 1990 at ninety-seven and his mother Ruth passed away in 1998 at ninety-five. They were laid to rest at the Sunset Memorial Park Cemetery in Albuquerque along with their son Jerry (Gerald), who died of cancer in 1985 at fifty-eight, and his wife Marion, who died in 2008 at eighty-nine.

After the War

Kirk's brother Dan chose to leave this world in a different way. He requested that his ashes be sprinkled on the Pecos River. He enjoyed its beautiful scenery and fishing for its brown, rainbow, and Rio Grande cutthroat trout. The Pecos River originates in the Sangre de Cristo Mountains at the southernmost part of the Rocky Mountains and flows through valleys, forests, canyons, and desert lands.[29] J. Robert Oppenheimer, the "father of the atomic bomb," loved the area and had a cabin with a magnificent view of the Sangre de Cristo Mountains and the Pecos River. He thought it was the most beautiful place on earth.[30]

The Pecos River is part of the National Wild and Scenic Rivers System and is managed under the U.S. Forest Service by the Santa Fe National Forest. Santa Fe is where Kirk was laid to rest in a national cemetery which is a shrine that serves as a reminder of veterans like him whose sacrifices helped to preserve our precious freedoms.[31]

FROM ONE WAR TO ANOTHER

Second Lieutenant Robert "Bob" Grant Cookman
January 1, 1920 - October 23, 1944

Courtesy of David Chin

Bob Cookman also did not make it home alive. Ten days after Kirk was killed in action, Bob was killed in action on October 23, 1944, at the age of twenty-four, and buried three days later in a temporary grave at the U.S. Military Cemetery in Bari, Italy. A wooden cross was placed on his grave. His personal effects were sent to his wife Marianne and included his wings, ring, wallet, short snorter, field jacket, and other personal effects.[1] She was also sent some money from his crew—each crew member had chipped in $50 to send her along with their condolences.[2]

Bob's short snorter was a string of paper money kept by airmen with signatures of crew members or others who were with them when they were part of a notable event such as crossing the Equator or traveling to another country. Some short snorters included signatures of famous people like Bob Hope. It was a status symbol of each airman's travels and helped to strike up a conversation whenever airmen got together for a drink. The word "snort" was slang for a stiff drink. The airman with the shortest string usually picked up the tab. One of the longest short snorters belonged to Hank Myers, the pilot of President Roosevelt's personal plane, the *Sacred Cow*, as well as President Truman's personal plane, the *Independence*. In addition to the signatures of Roosevelt and Truman, he had the signatures of Churchill, Stalin, Eisenhower, and other dignitaries on his short snorter which was thirty-five feet long.[3] Needless to say, he probably never had to pick up a tab.

While Bob did not make it home alive, he was never forgotten by his patriotic family. For the next three years on the anniversary of this death, his family posted in the local paper the following poems in his memory:

1945
The depth of sorrow we cannot tell,
Of the loss of one we love so well.
And while he lies in peaceful sleep
His memory we shall always keep.[4]

1946
We little thought when leaving home,
He would no more return.
That he in death so soon should sleep,
And leave us here to mourn.
We do not know the pain he bore,
We did not see him die.
We only know he passed away,
And never said "good-by."[5]

1947
Friends may think we have forgotten,
They think time, the wound will heal.
Little do they know the anguish,
That our suffering hearts conceal.[6]

On June 6, 1947, Bob's father Harvey sent a letter to the Quartermaster General in the Memorial Division of the War Department to start the process of bringing his son home to be laid to rest in the hometown cemetery.[7] While Bob's wife Marianne as next of kin had the right to determine the final resting place of her husband, she relinquished that right to Bob's mother Pearl.[8] Consequently, Pearl and her husband Harvey decided that the final resting place of their son should be in Memorial Park Cemetery in Mason City, Iowa. It took a while, but on September 2, 1948, Bob's remains were brought by truck from Bari, Italy, to Naples, Italy, then by ship to the United States, and finally by train to Mason City, Iowa.[9]

Bob's body arrived in Mason City with a military escort on Thursday morning, September 23, almost four years after he went down in a plane over Italy on October 23, 1944.[10] The commander of the local American Legion oversaw the military honors at the train station, and the American Legion color guard did the honors with representatives of the Amvets (American Veterans) and Veterans of Foreign Wars participating in the ceremony.[11]

The following Monday, September 27, 1948, a funeral service was held at the Paterson-James Chapel followed by a burial at Veterans Field of Honor in Memorial Park Cemetery in Mason City, Iowa. Three days later, the local paper published this "Card of Thanks" from the Cookman family:[12]

> *We wish to express our gratitude to our friends, and all others for their kindness and for the beautiful floral tribute for military rites of our departed Lt. Robert G. Cookman. We especially desire to mention those who helped with the service: the Amvets, the Clausen Warden Post 101 of the American Legion, San Juan Marne Post 733, and Veterans of Foreign Wars.*
>
> *Mr. and Mrs. Harvey Cookman Family*

In 1959, a notice appeared in the Mason City newspaper that the flag that was flying over Memorial Park Cemetery that week was in memory of veteran Robert G. Cookman.[13] His hometown still remembered him, and his crewmates like John Cooney and Meyer Osofsky never forgot him. He was a true hero of World War II.

Second Lieutenant Thaddeus "Ted" Cylkowski
September 8, 1917 - October 12, 1977

Courtesy of David Cylkowski

Meyer Osofsky said Ted Cylkowski was brilliant and had a special talent for holding the attention of an audience.[1] He never lost that special talent. After the war, he went on to compose and teach music. For the rest of his life, he organized and conducted concerts in the metropolitan New York City area. He and his wife Doris also raised a family of four children in Rye, New York—David (1948), Madeline (1949), Steven (1951), and Jeffrey (1957). In the early 1960s, he formed a musical ensemble called Canticum Musicum, a Latin term that means poetry is music and music is poetry. The ensemble put on musical programs at Carnegie Recital Hall with Ted as composer and conductor and Doris as one of the performers.[2]

Carnegie Recital Hall was one of the three auditoriums that made up Carnegie Hall, one of the most prestigious venues for classical music in the world. It still is. The Main Hall, the Stern Auditorium named after Isaac Stern, has 2,804 seats.[3] Zankel Hall, named after Judy and Arthur Zankel, has 599 seats.[4] Weill Recital Hall, named after Stanford I. Weill and his wife Joan, has

268 seats.[5] Weill Recital Hall was called Carnegie Recital Hall when Ted's Canticum Musicum featured programs there during the 1960s.[6]

Their son David said his mother was more of a performer than his father who usually composed music and conducted concerts.[7] Ted also researched medieval and renaissance music, taught piano, and inspired scores of children to love music. He was always good at organizing events around the music he loved. According to David, his favorite composers were Bach and Beethoven. He also had a strong interest in literature, art, and architecture.[8] As Meyer remembered, he also knew a lot about the stars.

David said he learned more at home than at school. His father would have students over to the house on weekends and he would often sit in. His father would also invite talented musicians to their house to perform for the family. As a result, David grew up in a stimulating environment surrounded by talented and interesting people, brought together by his father. He mentioned that his father gave Mark Ginsburg his first paying job out of Juilliard, noting that Ginsburg went on to become the concert master for the Metropolitan Opera House. He remembers him playing Bach's Chaconne at his house.[9]

Over the years, Ted taught classical music and organized classical musical programs in Westchester County, New York. David said he presented children's shows at the Chrysler Building in Rye in which he would have someone write lyrics for the music of composers such as Bach to give children an appreciation of classical music.[10] In 1974, he organized and presented a children's concert celebrating Beethoven's birthday at the historic Wildcliff Center for the Arts in New Rochelle. In 1975, he organized and presented another children's concert celebrating Mozart's birthday. David said his father also wrote musical compositions for well-known Rudyard Kipling stories such as "The Elephant's Child," "The Cat That Walked by Himself," and "How the Camel Got His Hump."[11]

We all know that life is not perfect, and the music Ted and Doris made together stopped when they divorced in 1967 after twenty-three years of marriage. They both continued to make music but with different people. David remembers Doris becoming friends with Garrick Ohlsson, a Juilliard graduate who was the only American to have won the prestigious Chopin International Piano Competition. He used to come over to her house in Rye and play for hours.[12] Ted married again—to Muriel "Mitzi" Hass who was a soloist in his Canticum Musicum ensemble when Doris was the harpsichordist. He moved to nearby Mamaroneck to live with Mitzi, who was like him a music teacher who touched many lives through music and who shared his interests in music, art, and literature.[13] He also got involved with that town's Emelin Theater for the Performing Arts.

In 1975, Ted arranged for Doris's friend Garrick Ohlsson to give a concert at the Emelin Theater. David remembers that he played "Pictures at an Exhibition" that was composed for piano by Modest Petrovich Mussorsky. After the concert, they went to a reception at the home of Eugene and Emily Grant, well-known philanthropists in Westchester County.[14] Eugene was a P-47 pilot during World War II who built a successful real-estate business after the war. He was also pianist and a patron of the arts.[15] David said their daughter, Terry Grant, was a devoted student of his father and spent two decades as a classical radio announcer at WTJU-FM in Charlottesville, Virginia, where she was also an executive board member of the Charlottesville Chamber Music Festival.[16]

In 1977, Ted died at the age of sixty and was laid to rest in Mt. Hope Cemetery in Hastings-on-the-Hudson.[17] He was not forgotten by his students nor others for his influence as a music educator in Westchester County. In 1978, Doris's friend Garrick Ohlsson gave a recital at White Plains High School in his memory.[18] The Emelin Theater for the Performing Arts also established the Thaddeus Cylkowski Music Fund in appreciation of his contributions to music. In 1981, the Y String Ensemble of the Mid-Western YM-YWHA Music School presented a concert to benefit the Fund.[19]

As a youngster, Ted was greatly influenced by R. Augustus Lawson, a leading music educator in the Hartford area where he grew up. One wonders if he ever thought then that he would one day become a leading music educator in Westchester County where his children grew up and where he would influence so many other children to love music.

Doris lived until 101. Her sister, Irma Glaser, said Doris was frail in her twilight years and was living in a nursing home in New York City, but music was her companion. The facility had a baby grand piano on which she played songs from classical artists such as Chopin which were a treat for many of the residents. She loved performing and did so until the end of her life—a long one filled with music.[20]

FROM ONE WAR TO ANOTHER

Technical Sergeant Joseph "Leslie" Goss III
August 20, 1923 - February 8, 1985

Source: The Clinton Eye

Leslie wanted to go overseas and see action and he saw plenty of action. In one of his first combat missions with Cookman's crew, he fractured his lower leg when he went down over Italy on October 23, 1944. When he recovered from the injury, he was discharged from the hospital in December, returned to duty, and continued to fly combat missions. On March 9, 1945, he had another frightening experience when his plane blew a tire landing in a rainstorm, skidded along the slippery runway with one engine catching fire. He came away from the accident shaken but okay. Two weeks later, on March 21, he had to bail out of a disabled plane for the second time when it was shot down over Yugoslavia, resulting in one of his crewmates being killed and him going to a prison camp for the rest of the war. Fortunately, he was one of the lucky ones who made it home after the war.

While Leslie had his share of harrowing experiences, he did not complain to his parents about his war service. His letters to them expressed his liking for the branch of service he chose and his satisfaction with the job he was doing.[1] However, when he was shot down over Yugoslavia on March 21, 1945, and was reported missing in action, it was his parents' turn to deal with a harrowing experience, namely the possibility of losing a loved one. War is tough on families as well as those in harm's way.

Fortunately, the story has a good ending. While Leslie spent the rest of the war in a prisoner of war camp, he was liberated by a combination of American and Russian troops. Just before he arrived home in October 1945, he sent a telegram to his folks, saying: "Get a box of moth balls and reserve a bottom drawer for excess army equipment, 'cause MISTER Joe L. Goss will be home this weekend. All my 'civie' love."[2] While most people called him Leslie, he was always Joe to his parents.

When Leslie was discharged from the service in October 1945, he did not return to college for a while.[3] He spent a year working on the U.S. Coast and Geodetic Survey of 1946.[4] During World War II, the U.S. Army conducted many accurate geodetic surveys.[5] Geodetic comes from geodesy which is the science of accurately measuring and understanding the Earth's geometric shape, its orientation in space, and its gravity field.[6] Among other things, these wartime surveys resulted in to the production of forty-three aeronautical chart maps covering the entire world for the U.S. Army Air Forces. The maps showed geographic features such as elevations, seaplane and landplane bases, military and civilian airfields, limited landing strips, large cities, towns, villages, international boundaries, state boundaries, main roads, important trails, railroads, canals, and other geographic features.[7] After the war, the United States decided to conduct a geodetic survey of the United States to provide control for mapping to the Corps of Engineers, the U.S. Army, the U.S. Bureau of Reclamation, and the U.S. Forest Service. Manpower was needed for this project.[8] Many young men found the work to understand the country's interior, coast, and borders interesting and Leslie was one of them.[9]

The Goss family was well-known in Leslie's hometown Clinton, Missouri. His grandfather, Joseph Leslie Goss Sr., started J. L. Goss Clothing Company in Clinton around the turn of the century and his father's oldest brother, William Dodson Goss, and his father, Joseph Leslie Goss, Jr., carried on the business. Leslie chose not to get into the family business which was one of the leading businesses of Clinton for four decades.[10]

When he enlisted, Leslie stated that he was an actor. He became an experienced amateur actor in high school.[11] He may have done some acting when he returned home from the war because he did not return to the University of Missouri until the fall of 1948. And when he did, he changed from the College of Arts and Science to the Business School and graduated with a Bachelor of Science in Business Administration degree on February 1, 1950.[12]

In 1951, Leslie moved to Scottsdale, Arizona, where he lived for the rest of his life. He was an only child and his parents also moved to Scottsdale where they lived for the rest of their lives. In 1954, he married Glendora Murdock, another Midwesterner who was from Anderson, Indiana.[13] He retired as an inspector for the State Department of Public Safety, and she retired as a bank trust officer.[14] He survived a terrible war, but he could not survive cancer. In 1985, he died of that awful disease at the age of sixty-one.[15] Both his parents—Joseph, Jr., and Grace—died the following year.[16] Glendora lived until 1998 when she died at the age of eighty-one.[17]

Leslie (Joseph III), his father (Joseph Jr.), and his grandfather (Joseph Sr.) were all laid to rest at the Englewood Cemetery in Clinton, Missouri, along with the wives of Joseph Jr. (Grace) and Joseph Sr. (Chloe).[18] When Leslie's wife Glendora died in Scottsdale, thirteen years after Leslie's passing, her ashes were sent to her sister Martha Styers in Michigan. Leslie's uncle, William Dodson Goss, his father's brother, who was a captain in the Adjutant General Department in World Wars I and II, was also laid to rest in the Englewood Cemetery as was his wife Carmen, who was 101 years old when she passed away in 2005 as a member of the Henry County Historical Society and the American Legion Post No. 14 in Clinton.[19] The Goss family made Clinton proud, and Leslie did his part by serving his country well during World War II.

Staff Sergeant Hong Sing "Calvin" Chin
October 18, 1925 – November 27, 1987

Courtesy of David Chin

Calvin Chin returned to the States on June 6, 1945, then received his honorable discharge on November 6, 1945.[1] He flew 530 hours during the war, and when he got home, he used the GI Bill to finish his schooling at the Roosevelt Aviation School.[2] However, instead of pursuing a career in aviation, he worked various jobs, married, started a family, and did what many other veterans on Long Island did after the war—he purchased a house in Levittown with a government guaranteed loan under the GI Bill. Levittown began in 1946 as a housing project for World War II veterans and grew to a town of 60,000 by the late 1950s.[3]

The Chin family bought their house in 1958, around the time Calvin decided to get into the restaurant business. He started out as the manager and host of a Chinese restaurant in Hempstead called Chun King Royal that was owned by his close friend and mentor, Arthur Lem.[4] Lem was probably the best-known Chinese American on Long Island.[5] He came to America in 1926 at the age of twelve when it was difficult for Chinese Americans to get ahead. He labored in laundries for years with little pay while attending school. He graduated from Hempstead High School and went on to own his own restaurant.[6]

When China became an ally of the United States during World War II, the attitude toward Chinese Americans started to change. This led to a repeal of the 1882 Chinese Exclusion Act that prohibited all immigration by Chinese laborers and excluded all Chinese residents from citizenship.[7] Lem took advantage of these changing times and became the sole owner of Chun King Royal restaurant in 1945.

A newspaper that served Long Island, *Newsday*, was located down the block from Lem's restaurant. Its reporters and editors frequented his restaurant and often wrote about him, making him a well-known Chinese American on Long Island.[8] Because he had a successful business, he was able to help relatives and others immigrate to America from China. In 1958, the year he hired Calvin, he was presented with "The Brotherhood Award" in Hempstead by the Lions, Kiwanis, and Rotary Clubs for "outstanding services rendered throughout 1957 to improve brotherhood, goodwill, understanding and co-operation among the various faiths and races in the village of Hempstead."[9] The following year, his world fell apart.

In 1959, he was indicted on charges of helping Chinese nationals to enter the United States in an illegal manner and spent time and money defending himself in a highly publicized court case. He was deported but returned five years later and became a U.S. citizen.[10] He eventually returned to the restaurant business, became successful again, and left a legacy at the Chinese Center of Long Island in the form of a scholarship that bears his name. Children of members can apply for the scholarship which encourages them to pursue higher education, promote their Chinese heritage, participate in community service, and follow their dreams.[11]

Calvin entered the work force after the attitude toward Chinese Americans changed and after becoming a decorated veteran who served his country honorably. One of his service awards was a Certificate of Valor that stated: "Major General Nathan F. Twining, the commander of the Fifteenth Air Force, directed this certificate to be presented to Hong S. Chin in recognition of courage and service in aerial combat."[12] He had indeed served his country well.

Calvin and his wife Mary raised two sons, David and Jeffrey, and a daughter, Patricia. Interestingly, David got his name from the nurse who delivered him. She was Jewish and he was born under the Star of David on Yom Kippur.[13] David said his parents were a sociable young couple who enjoyed life and frequented nightclubs in New York City such as the Latin Quarter that featured top stars and was owned by Lou Walters, the father of Barbara Walters.[14]

Calvin was indeed sociable and had a long career in the restaurant business. After Chun King Royal, he managed the Mah Jong Restaurant in Syosset and the Gam Wah Restaurant in Carle Place. The first restaurant he owned (with a partner) was the Dragon Sky in Plainview and the second was the Golden Fan in Carle Place, which became the Golden Kai. These restaurants were frequented by local politicians and *Newsday* reporters due in large part to Calvin's personality.[15]

He was proud of his military service and never forgot the crew he trained with in the States, lived with in Italy, and went down in a plane with over Italy. And they never forgot him. When he opened his first restaurant, Meyer Osofsky threw a big party for him. Meyer lived in nearby East Meadow and David remembered his parents getting together with Meyer and his wife Aileen during the 1960s and that they were talking about Aileen, Inc., the business Meyer started in his wife's name.[16]

He also remembered visiting David Orkin and his family in Queens. He recalled that David had a plaque with his medals displayed on the wall over a staircase, and that David's son took him and his brother Jeffrey to an ice cream parlor for a treat.[17] Those were the days when they called the person who worked at the counter at an ice cream parlor a soda jerk, and Meyer was a soda jerk when he was in high school. When he became a successful businessman, his mother would keep him grounded by teasing him, "Meyer, remember when you were a jerk!"[18]

David even remembered visiting the Orkin family in Houston when they moved there from Queens. He said before his sister was born in 1965 his father bought a new 1963 Pontiac Bonneville and drove the family to Florida for a vacation where they visited with Orkin's parents and then to Houston where they visited with Orkin and his family.[19] He still has photos of him and his brother frolicking in a hotel swimming pool with Orkin's sons Paul and Rick.[20]

David said his earliest inspiration was his father who flew in combat and kept many of the books and paperwork on aircraft engines from his days studying at the Roosevelt Aviation School.[21] He grew up loving aviation. He liked to watch the television show Sky King and he liked to go to the end of the runway at the Grumman plant in Bethpage to watch the planes take off and land. His interest in planes led him to a degree in aeronautical engineering and a career in aviation at Grumman. It also inspired him to get a private pilot's license.[22]

One interesting assignment that David drew at Grumman took place when *Top Gun* starring Tom Cruise was being filmed at the Naval Air Station in Miramar, California. The Grumman F-14s they were flying in the movie had a structural issue and David was among those sent to Miramar to resolve the issue.[23] He said it was exciting being around the filming of that classic film. He remembered that he ran into Tom twice. The first time was in a hallway of Hanger 1 where he didn't recognize him at first in his crew cut wearing Navy khakis and looking like a Naval aviator. The second time was a night scene in which Tom was checking out one of the F-14s. David and a colleague didn't know Paramount was doing a preliminary staging. They were immediately scooted off the set.[24] Before they left Miramar, however, David and his colleagues resolved the issue and were commended for it.[25]

David always appreciated his father. In the late 1980s, Calvin started growing different types of vegetables from cherry tomatoes and string beans to several types of oriental vegetables. David entered a few of his father's vegetables in the 1987 Grumman Garden Forum Fall Garden Show and won an honorable-mention ribbon. His father also liked to fish, and David would take him out in his power boat to Great South Bay to fish for fluke and seabass.[26]

Calvin died on November 27, 1987, at the age of sixty-two. His longtime friend, Arthur Lem, delivered the eulogy.[27] He was laid to rest at the Calverton National Cemetery where his crewmate and tentmate John Cooney would also be laid to rest twenty-seven years later and where the author would deliver a eulogy on that sad occasion. Calvin's wife Mary would also be laid to rest with him thirty-six years later in 2023.[28]

David treasures his father's wartime memorabilia and has a deep respect for his father and his wartime friends, which has deepened over the years. On November 27, 2020, the anniversary of his father's passing, he visited and placed potted flowers by his father's gravesite. He did the same for John Cooney. He took photographs and sent them to the Cooney family.[29] On the anniversary of his father's passing in 2021 and 2022, he again paid his respects to his father and Cooney with potted flowers in 2021 and due to inclement weather with poinsettias in 2022.[30] His parents raised a respectful and considerate son.

First Lieutenant Russell "Russ" John Flint
July 25, 1922 - May 24, 1988

Courtesy of Russell Flint, Jr.

In appreciation of his service, Russ Flint received a "Certificate of Valor in Recognition of Courageous Service in Aerial Combat" that stated he flew twenty-five combat missions.[1] However, his monthly Individual Flight Record reports for the seven months he flew from October 1944 to April 1945 stated that he flew twenty-seven combat missions. He flew his combat missions in three different models of the B-24 (12 in a B-24H, 12 in a B-24J, and 3 in a B-24M).[2] Of his 553 hours of flying time during the war, 207 hours, or 37 percent, were flown in combat. In other words, he flew into harm's way the equivalent of 8.6 days. His longest mission was 8.5 hours on December 26, 1944, when his bomb group dropped 156 bombs on the Oświecim Synthetic Oil Refinery & Rubber Works in Oświecim, Poland, with good results.[3]

After flying twenty-seven combat missions, Russ returned home as a first lieutenant with an Air Medal and two Oak Leaf Clusters having flown in four battle campaigns.[4] He had his share of harrowing experiences in overseas combat duty and was ready to settle down and did not waste any time. Fifteen days after returning to the United States on July 10, 1945, he married Marie Ruth Schuttler on July 25 at the Trinity Lutheran Church in Chicago.[5] He was still in the service when they married—a month later, he received his honorable discharge on August 29, 1945.[6]

Russ and Marie had a lot in common. Both had grown up in Chicago, went to the same high school (Austin High School), and had fathers who served in World War I and owned their own businesses. Russ's father had a chiropractic business and later a retail liquor establishment, and Marie's father had a laundry business.[7] Marie's brother Robert Sr. also attended Austin High School and was an entrepreneur like his father, starting a construction company that grew into a family business.[8]

Meyer Osofsky said Russ visited him after the war when he was living in East Meadow on Long Island. He thought Russ's father owned a saloon in Chicago and years later Russ's oldest son, Russ Jr., said that was correct. When Russ visited Meyer, they went to see Bob Worsthorn, the pilot with whom they flew most of their combat missions.[9] Worsthorn lived in nearby Levittown and like Meyer and other crewmates had purchased his house under the GI Bill. Years later, Meyer's daughter Randy tried to locate Russ because Meyer wanted to connect with him again, but to no avail. Meyer always had fond memories of Russ.[10]

Russ and Marie had two sons—Russ Jr. in 1947 and Greg in 1949. When Russ's parents retired, they moved to Hollywood, Florida. Russ, who became an only child when his sister died at the age of four, was close to his parents and decided to move his family to Hollywood as well. He got a job as a salesman for Ford Motors in 1957 and then became an insurance agent for the New York Life Insurance Company from 1958 to 1960.[11] Russ also enjoyed golf and was good at it. In 1960, he qualified for the 25th Annual Hollywood Men's Golf Tournament at Orange Brook Golf Course and made it to the championship round before losing 5-4.[12] He would one day become a part of that golf course.

While selling insurance for New York Life, Russ was offered a position selling insurance to GIs in Germany. According to Russ Jr., his father viewed the offer as a great opportunity and took advantage of it. He moved his family to Germany and enrolled his sons in the American School in Frankfurt, a city bombed many times during World War II. Russ Jr. said he spent his junior year of high school at that school. He also said his parents separated at that time, and Marie returned to the States with the two boys. Her brother Robert had a big house in Park Ridge, Illinois, and they stayed with him and his family until things settled down for Marie.[13]

Robert and his wife Marge dreamed of owning their own business and in December 1954 acted on their dreams by launching Victor Construction which was named for his father Victor. Robert had been a salesman for a home remodeling company. In their new venture, he and his wife were a team—he found the clients and Marge kept the books—while they raised a family of five. They built a large home in Park Ridge, Illinois, which is where Marie and the two boys lived when they returned to the States.

Russ Jr. finished high school at Maine East High School in Park Ridge, graduating in 1965, the year his parents divorced. His brother Greg graduated from Maine East in 1967. Harrison Ford, the movie star, grew up in Park Ridge and graduated from Maine East High School in 1960. Hillary Rodham Clinton, the politician, also grew up in Park Ridge and attended Maine East High School until her senior year when she moved across town to a new Maine South High School from which she graduated in 1965.[14]

The year 1970 was a sad year for the family because Marie died in August at the age of 46, Russ's father John died in September at the age of 76, and Marie's father Victor died in December at the age of 76.[15] Marie had rheumatic fever as a child which tends to weaken the heart, as it did in Marie's case.[16] Marie and her father were both laid to rest at Mount Cemetery in Elmhurst, Illinois. Ruth joined them ten years later.[17] Before then, Ruth had the good fortune of seeing her son Robert Jr. and his wife Margaret develop the business named for her husband into a successful family business with her son Jeff and her daughters Pam, Peggy, and Kathy all chipping in to help the business grow. When Robert Jr. retired, he turned the business over to his brother Jeff, and when Jeff retired, he turned it over to his son Zak.[18] Russ's father was laid to rest at Fred Hunter's Hollywood Memorial Gardens East in Hollywood, Florida, where his mother Selma would join him in 1981.[19] Russ would choose a different course when he passed away.

Russ's yearbook said he was "Lucky, Loose, Happy-Go-Lucky."[20] Russ Jr. agreed with that assessment.[21] He appreciated his father's tongue and cheek humor that was reflected in his yearbook when his stated ambition was to be as handsome as his pal McNellis while his pal McNellis's stated ambition was to be as handsome as Flint. This camaraderie among friends exhibited in high school carried over to his crew. Russ was responsible for the safety and discipline of an aircrew of ten men and his ability to keep the crew loose when flying into harm's way was an asset.[22] This is one reason why Meyer liked him in addition to respecting his ability as a co-pilot.

Russ took this out-of-the-box attitude to the grave. He did not want a funeral service and he loved golf. Consequently, his wish was to be cremated and have three of his golf buddies spread his ashes on the Orange Brook Golf Course. His wish was fulfilled when he died in 1988 at the age of sixty-five.[23] His high school pal McNellis no doubt would have appreciated the way Russ chose to leave this world. Because Russ Jr. knew how much his father loved golf, he also appreciated how he chose to leave this world. While his father never talked about his wartime experiences with him, he left him his war records from which Russ Jr. grew to appreciate his father's service that made him a proud son.

Technical Sergeant Charles "Chuck" Joseph Muth
May 27, 1917 - January 24, 2005

Courtesy of David Chin

Chuck Muth's 451st Bomb Group flew its last mission on April 26, 1945. Twelve days later the war in Europe ended on May 8, 1945—Victory in Europe Day, also known as V-E Day. It ended with Germany signing two surrenders. On May 7, German Colonel General Alfred Jodl signed Germany's surrender in Reims, France; and on May 8, German Field Marshall Wilhelm Keitel signed a second surrender, insisted upon by Soviet Premier Joseph Stalin, in Berlin. V-E Day was wonderful news for those fighting in Europe, but not for Jodl and Keitel. Both were later tried and convicted of war crimes by the International Military Tribunal in Nuremberg, Germany, and were executed for their crimes.[1]

When the war in Europe ended, there was still important work to be done such as delivering medical supplies and food packages to sustain Allied prisoners in two prison camps in southern Austria until they could be reached by land. The 461st Bomb Group, which typically flew missions with Chuck's 451st Bomb Group, was assigned the task of flying all-volunteer missions to deliver these supplies, and Chuck was one of the volunteers. He transferred from the 451st Bomb Group to the 461st Bomb Group on May 7, 1945, where he became part of the volunteer force that flew six missions from May 9 to May 15 to drop medical supplies and food packages over two prisoner of war camps—Stalag VIIIA 18A at Wolfsberg, Austria, and Stalag 18B at Spittal an der Drau, Austria.[2] These missions were called "Mercy Missions."[3]

Chuck cared about his fellow airmen. Even when his plane was going down on October 23, 1944, a terrifying experience, Meyer said Chuck was standing by the escape hatch worried about his crewmates instead of himself, and here again we see him volunteering for missions after completing his tour of duty. When the war ended, many Allied prisoners of war needed medical supplies and food which had become scarce because it was such a chaotic time, and Chuck was one of the volunteers who stayed around to help them rather than simply go home. His actions were in sync with the long-standing military tradition of "leave no soldier behind" as evidenced by efforts like this to help soldiers, sailors, marines, and airmen with efforts above and beyond the call of duty.

Chuck may not have been anxious to get home after the war. He did not have strong roots to return to. His last name had been changed three times from Shea, his birthfather's name, to Kershaw, his mother's stepfather's name, and finally to Muth, his stepfather's name. He had moved around from Illinois to Tennessee to Indiana. His mother Victoria married young and had him as a teenager, and he married young and had his son James when his wife Mildred was a teenager.[4] He was not returning to a stable lifestyle. Thus, it is not surprising that Chuck and Mildred went their separate ways after the war. Their son grew up close to his mother.

Chuck married again a couple of years later to Margaret Elle Sears from Barrington, Illinois, the town where he had lived with his mother and stepfather and where Margaret's father, Walter M. Sears, taught music to three generations of students for over fifty years. This quote reflects how much he was appreciated in the community: "The number of persons musically influenced by the tall, dignified maestro, are countless."[5] Among those he influenced was Margaret's sister Beth who was an accomplished oboist, having been first oboist with the North Carolina Symphony Orchestra and the Kalamazoo Symphony Orchestra.[6] Walter also played the violin which he considered "the master of all musical instruments."[7]

Margaret was also involved in her community. When Chuck was overseas flying bombing missions during World War II, she was working in the office of Arthur Lueder, the Illinois State Auditor. Two days after Chuck went down in a plane over Italy, Margaret marched in a parade on October 25, 1944, with ladies from her office to welcome Republican Presidential nominee Thomas Dewey to Chicago.[8] Dewey was scheduled to give a campaign speech that evening at Chicago Stadium which was preceded by entertainment involving celebrities Barbara Stanwyck, Adolph Menjou, and Eddie Bracken.[9] While this festive affair was taking place, Chuck and his crew were recovering from a frightening wartime experience. Chuck and Margaret were miles apart and worlds apart.

Chuck and Margaret connected after the war, married in 1947, and had a son, Charles Joseph Muth II, in 1948. A year later, they had a daughter Victoria, named after his mother. Chuck, Margaret, and Charles II moved to Phoenix where they put down roots for the rest of their lives. Chuck's daughter Victoria ended up in the Phoenix area as well. Chuck's mother Victoria moved there too after her husband, Henry R. Muth, passed away.[10]

Victoria died in 1985 at eighty-four, and four years later Charles II died young at forty-one.[11] Margaret died fourteen years later in 2003 at eighty-two, and Chuck died in 2005 at eighty-seven. Chuck, Margaret, and Charles II were laid to rest at the National Memorial Cemetery of Arizona in Phoenix. Like his father, Charles II was a veteran, having served as a Specialist 4th Class in the U.S. Army during the Vietnam War. On the gravestone of Chuck and Margaret are inscribed the words, "Together Forever."[12]

Chuck's first wife Mildred and their son James put down roots in Las Cruces, New Mexico, where James married and raised a family. When his stepsister Victoria got married in 1970, James and his wife were both in the wedding party.[13] James died in 2014 after eleven years of battling cancer. Many nice things were said about him such as he was "a true gentleman," and "a sweet man," who fought cancer "with the strength and courage of a strong faith-based family."[14] Mildred did a nice job in bringing him up and lived to be over a hundred.

FROM ONE WAR TO ANOTHER

Second Lieutenant David Gordon Johnson
September 8, 1924 – January 25, 2006

1961 Tourist Card for Brazil
Source: Amnestry.com

David Johnson was always adventuresome. Growing up in Long Beach, California, he had many year-round adventures as a kid sailing on the vast Pacific Ocean. As soon as he graduated from high school, the adventure bug led him to the Alaskan wilderness where he worked on construction until his country went to war. Like many young men at that time, he signed up for the more dangerous adventures of war, experienced some hair-raising times flying combat missions, survived them, and came home with a Distinguished Flying Cross for heroism and extraordinary achievement while participating in aerial flight.[1]

After flying thirty-five combat missions and going down in a plane twice, David made it home without a serious injury. However, when on leave back in the States, his luck ran out. While helping his father around the house, he cut off all four fingers on his left hand with a power saw, leaving him with only a thumb.[2] While feeling down and recuperating at a military hospital, he made a positive out of a negative. He met a nurse who cheered him up and became his wife.[3]

Mary Esther Ladd had grown up on a farm in Loudon, New Hampshire. She was the oldest of four and had two sisters, Betty and Pauline, and a brother, Levi, Jr.[4] She also had an appreciation for veterans. Her father, Levi, served in the Army during World War I and her brother Levi Jr. was currently serving in the Navy and had a hair-raising experience on April 7, 1945.[5] He was on the aircraft carrier, USS *Hancock,* when it was attacked by a Japanese kamikaze plane whose 500-pound bomb went through the fight deck and exploded, setting planes on fire on both the flight deck and the hanger deck, killing sixty-two sailors and wounding another seventy-one.[6]

Mary was serving her country as a nurse in the United States Cadet Nurse Corps.[7] After America entered World War II, the demand for nurses increased dramatically and the Nurse Training Act was unanimously passed by Congress and signed into law by President Roosevelt on June 15, 1943. The Cadet Nurse Corps Program was supervised by the United States Public Health Service and its purpose was to address the critical shortage of nurses. By the end of the war, 1,125 of the 1,300 nursing schools in the United States participated in the program.[8] Mary was in one of those nursing schools at Elliot Hospital in Manchester, New Hampshire and was admitted to the program when it started on July 1, 1943.[9] About 120,000 nurses served honorably in the United States Cadet Nurse Corps during World War II, and Mary was one of them.[10]

Mary met David in a hospital when he was recovering from his injury and fell in love with him. They were married on November 4, 1946, in Tacoma, Washington by an Army chaplain while David was still in the service.[11] Her sisters married military men as well. Betty married a Navy aviation cadet, Elliot Winsor Burbank, Jr., three years earlier in September 1943.[12] Elliot became a flight instructor during World War II, retired from the Navy as a lieutenant commander, and went on to fly for Trans World Airlines for twenty-nine years.[13] Her sister Pauline, a nurse like Mary, married Dr. Wendell Dodge, a supervisory research biologist for the U.S. Fish and Wildlife Services who, like David, served in the Army Air Forces during World War II.[14]

Mary's nephew Daniel Ladd, her brother's son, remembers that David was a lot of fun. Daniel was a private pilot who owned a Beechcraft Model H18 known as a Twin Beech. It has two engines and seats from six to eleven passengers. The Model H18 was introduced in 1963 and featured an optional tricycle undercarriage. Only109 of them were built by the Beech Aviation Corporation of Wichita, Kansas. He bought the plane from an officer at West

FROM ONE WAR TO ANOTHER

Point.[15] Daniel's father Levi, Jr. was also a private pilot, having received pilot training in the Navy, so the apple didn't fall far from the tree.[16]

Daniel remembers the first time Mary brought David to the farm in New Hampshire. He said they gave him a chore to pick up some hay. They directed him to drive their 1929 Chevy pickup to a spot on a hill next to the hay. The wooden floorboards of the vehicle had rotted away over the years, leaving a gaping hole in the floor of the vehicle, and the spot they directed him to park was over a nest of yellow jackets. He had flown over many hornets' nests in Europe and now he was driving over a yellow jackets' nest back in the States. As expected, he riled up the yellow jackets. As he exited the vehicle at great speed, they were all laughing their heads off over the prank. He took it well and made a hit with the family. Daniel said David was a good egg.[17]

Daniel also said David didn't talk much about the war but once sent a letter about one of his wartime experiences to Pauline's husband Wendell who had also served in the Army Air Forces and was interested in David's wartime experiences. The letter detailed a mission in which David had to bail out of a disabled plane for the second time.[18] Wendell's daughter Karen said her father always held David in very high regard and that she and her sister Carole always looked forward to visits from Uncle Dave and Aunt Mary.[19] Carole remembered as a little girl being amazed at Uncle Dave peeling an apple or an orange with his missing fingers. She also thought her Uncle David and Aunt Mary were a great team.[20]

After serving his country honorably, David, like many World War II veterans, went to college on the GI Bill. He attended Washington University in St. Louis, Missouri, graduated with an accounting degree, and went to work for Arthur Andersen in South America helping to increase its international business.[21] Along the way, he and Mary raised four children—Betty, twins David Jr. and Dan, and John.

Carole Dodge remembered that her Uncle Dave had a sailboat and did a lot of sailing when the family lived in South America.[22] His son John said his father loved to sail and could do celestial navigation. He added that he once sailed around Cape Horn, the most southerly part of South America, with his twin sons, David Jr. and Dan.[23] Sailing around Cape Horn is still considered risky due to its rough and unpredictable weather. It is the sailor's equivalent of climbing Mount Everest.[24] Being adventuresome, David relished the challenge and was confident enough in his sailing ability to bring his kids along.

The twins survived that venture but ran into trouble later. Daniel said David Jr. broke his neck in a diving accident when he was a teenager that confined him to a wheelchair as a paraplegic for the rest of his life. His twin brother Dan took it very hard. Both twins have since passed away. David Jr. died when he fell from his wheelchair and struck his head on a rock, and Dan died of cancer.[25] David and Mary had their share of heartache.

Their daughter Betty lives in Nevada now while his son John lives in California. John said he had a wonderful childhood. He was only five when they moved to South America in the early 1960s and lived for about a decade in Bogota, Colombia, and Caracas, Venezuela. He remembers sailing to America from South America on a couple of occasions with his father. He said his father was a good sailor and had a strong work ethic.[26]

When David retired from Arthur Andersen, the family moved to Crestline, California, and had hopes of building a house in New Hampshire, even bought some land, but never got around to building one. Daniel said their son John still owns the land.[27]

David and Mary eventually sold their sailboat and bought a motor home and a Saturn to pull behind it and did a lot of traveling, including trips to New Hampshire to visit Mary's family.[28] Abby Ladd, the wife of Daniel's brother David Ladd, remembered her Uncle David fondly, saying he had quite a life.[29] David Johnson died in 2006.[30] Mary died eight years later in 2014.[31] John has his father's ashes and Betty has her mother's ashes.[32] Betty also has her father's wartime medals for which the family made a shadow box as they were very proud of his service.[33] David and Mary had many adventures together and left the family with many fond memories.

.

FROM ONE WAR TO ANOTHER

Second Lieutenant Ray Martin Goodson
February 19, 1924 - November 12, 2013

Source: FindAGrave.com

After Ray Goodson was shot down with David Orkin on December 2, 1944, the second time he and David went down in a plane, they spent the last five months of the war in Europe as prisoners of war. Ray was sent to Stalag Luft I because he was a commissioned officer and David was sent to Stalag Luft IV because he was an enlisted non-commissioned officer. Stalag Luft IV was further east and when the Russians were approaching, its prisoners were evacuated westward, and David landed in Stalag Luft I where Ray was interred. They were two of about 9,200 prisoners of war in Stalag Luft I where Colonel Hubert Zemke was the highly regarded senior Allied officer.[1] Oscar G. Richard III, a B-17 bombardier who had been shot down about a year and a half earlier and was also a prisoner in Stalag Luft I, wrote an article fifty years later telling how Zemke helped the prisoners of Stalag Luft I. He wanted Zemke to be remembered as a skilled negotiator and a "class act."[2]

Ray and David were two of the prisoners in Stalag Luft I who benefitted from the negotiation skills of Colonel Zemke. More on David later. As regards

Ray, after flying combat missions, going down in a plane twice, and surviving a German prisoner of war camp, he made it home to Joliet, Illinois, where he spent the rest of his life. He loved the outdoors and met a young lady, Doris Dodge, who also loved the outdoors. Doris grew up near him in Lockport, only five miles away. They married on January 1, 1947, and raised four children—Ray Jr., Tom, Susan Goodson Cowger, and Laurie Goodson Fahrmer.[3]

After the war, Ray worked as a chemist for Blockson Chemical, which was taken over by Olin Chemical in 1955, whereupon he spent the rest of his career at Olin, retiring from the company. Blockson produced uranium from phosphoric acid and was involved with weapons production.[4] Olin manufactured and distributed chemicals and ammunition. It grew to employ 7,780 employees on six continents with customers in nearly 100 countries. In 2017, it celebrated 100 years of continuous listing on the New York Stock Exchange.[5]

Doris worked at different times for Texaco Oil, Mechling Barge Lines, and the First National Bank in Joliet, retiring from that bank. She and her husband loved camping together with the family and Ray loved to fish and golf. They belonged to the St. Patrick Catholic Church, and Ray was a member of the Cantigny Post #364 Veterans of Foreign Wars in Joliet, the Disabled American Veterans Will County Chapter 103, and the Fox River Valley chapter of the American Ex-POWs.[6] He was proud of his service.

The Joliet Army Ammunition Plant, where Ray worked after high school and before he went to war, operated until it was decommissioned in 1976 and production stopped in 1977. The land was subsequently determined to be contaminated and over a period of years the land was cleaned up and reused in different ways—by the State of Illinois to build several business parks to create jobs lost by the shutdown of the ammunitions plant, by Will County to build a recycling center called the Prairie View Recycling and Disposal Facility, and by the Department of Veterans Affairs to develop the Abraham Lincoln National Cemetery, the resting place of Ray and Doris.[7]

Ray's son Tom said his father was reticent when it came to talking about the war. Perhaps he saw many things during the war he just did not want to talk about.[8] In any case, his crewmate Meyer Osofsky, who boxed with him and conversed with him when they bailed out of a disabled plane, never forgot him. Once, when he was in Chicago on business, Meyer invited Ray and his wife Doris to dinner in the Pump Room at the Ambassador East Hotel in Chicago, which was frequented by celebrities.[9] While they weren't celebrities, they were more than that as veteran airmen who were called upon to fly combat missions during a war and served their country honorably.

FROM ONE WAR TO ANOTHER

It was Ray's wish not to a have a service when he passed away and his wish was honored by his family—he still had an edge to him.[10] Ray died in 2013 at the age of eighty-nine and was laid to rest in the Abraham Lincoln National Cemetery.[11] His wife of sixty-six years, Doris, died four years later in 2017 and joined him in the Abraham Lincoln National Cemetery.[12]

Staff Sergeant John Joseph Cooney
May 4, 1923 - September 21, 2014

Courtesy of Cooney Family

Thanks to the heroics of Bob Cookman, to his parachute, and to good luck, John Cooney survived the war. When he came home, he got a job at a law firm and took night accounting courses at Rutgers while he thought about his future. Meyer sought him out to help him with his fledgling sweater business in Brooklyn and John did some work for him. Meyer said he got to know John's mother Anna during this time and found her to be a wonderful lady. Her son Peter also thought she was an extraordinary woman and gave a couple of reasons why. When her mother died, Anna was only seventeen years old yet cared for her brothers and her younger sister. When her husband died at age thirty-nine, leaving her with five children, ages one to sixteen, she again cared for her family in a commendable manner under difficult circumstances.[1]

After the war, when her position as a driver for the Newark Signal Corps ended, Anna got a job at Stern's Department Stores. She was a buyer and worked there for over twenty years, retiring in 1964, then got a job at

FROM ONE WAR TO ANOTHER

Chase Manhattan Bank and worked there for fourteen years, retiring again in 1979.[2] Anna lived for fifty-seven fruitful years after her husband passed away. When she died in 1996 at the age of 97, she was laid to rest in the Holy Cross Cemetery in North Arlington, New Jersey, with her husband, who served in the Army Medical Department in World War I, and her brother, Joseph Millon, who served in the Navy during World War II.[3]

College was never an option for Anna, but she knew the value of a good education. So did her son John who as a teenager went to high school at night after working all day to help support the family. After the war, the GI Bill made college affordable for John and many other veterans. Its purpose was to help veterans by granting them stipends covering tuition and expenses for attending college or trade schools, and John was a beneficary. John's brother, Peter, said it best: "My brother's experience is a model for the GI Bill, which gave the middle-class entry into colleges, probably one of the most important social changes in U.S. history."[4]

In 1947, John enrolled in Haverford College, a Quaker college just outside of Philadelphia. Peter said his brother was a handful. The Quakers believe in peace, but the warrior mentality was still with John. On his first day, he encountered a senior who told him to wear a beanie. He responded that he could kill with either hand and the senior backed off. He did not think much of hazing and was elected freshman class vice president for his stand on eliminating it.[5]

Meyer said John was a stand-up guy and he was surely that, and sometimes it didn't work in his favor. For example, late in the war he got into an altercation with an officer regarding the use of a gym by the fliers versus the ground crew. In the military, enlisted men do not win arguments with officers, and so when John received his honorable discharge it stated that he was a Private despite his having flown thirty-five combat missions at the higher rank of Staff Sergeant.[6] He would be a stand-up guy until the day he died. It was in his DNA.

The war toughened him up and Haverford calmed him down and helped prepare him for a successful business career, but it was a process. His Haverford yearbook described him as "a playmaker with haymakers" in playing intramural basketball. He was also a handsome young man, described in the yearbook as "a debonair cover boy."[7] This was a reference to the fact that he took advantage of his good looks and did some modeling to help pay for his college expenses. Having been a breadwinner for his family at a young age and having a mother like Anna, he learned to be resourceful.

At a memorial service for John years later, his niece, Nancy Leo, said: "John definitely was a handsome man with movie-star looks. I remember seeing the photographs of him modeling and proudly remember the comical one where he was dressed as a husband in his suit, shirt, and tie with a frilly apron around his waist washing pots and pans while the 'wife' was smiling."[8] The wife was Grace Kelly, the movie star who married the Prince of Monaco. While Prince Rainer was born in the same month as John, he was born under different circumstances. He was born to privilege while John was not, yet both had to serve in World War II.

John's college yearbook also said he was a "professional debutante charmer until he met Phyllis."[9] Phyllis Dalton was a student at nearby Rosemont College. Rosemont was a Catholic women's college. Patricia Kennedy Lawford, the sister of President John F. Kennedy, and Rosalind Russell, an actress known for her roles as a witty independent woman, were graduates. Both found their way to Hollywood where Pat married actor Peter Lawford and where Rosalind was nominated four times for an Oscar as Best Actress. She never won one, but she won a Tony for Best Actress in a Broadway musical.[10]

John married Phyllis on February 18, 1950, during his junior year and they moved into a makeshift apartment in an office space owned by her family near the Paoli train station, not far from Haverford.[11] Phyllis's father Thomas and his brother Vincent were developers in the area. Two streets were named for them—Thomas Road and Vincent Road (Thomas Road was later changed to Dalton Road because there were so many Thomas Roads).[12] The couple had their first child before John graduated from Haverford in 1951.[13] They named him Thomas after Phyllis's father who, unbeknownst to them in their lifetimes, had served in the same area of France as John's father during World War I.

Years later, Thomas would, like his father John and both his grandfathers—John J. Cooney Sr. and Thomas Dalton—serve his country well. During the Vietnam War, Thomas was a Private First Class in the United States Army (Company C, 1st Infantry Battalion [Airmobile], 7th Calvary) and was awarded the Bronze Star Medal with a "V" for valor for his actions on January 28, 1972. His citation read:[14]

> *With complete disregard for his own safety, he courageously took actions which were an inspiration to the other members of his unit and were instrumental in the successful completion of the mission. His display of personal bravery and devotion to duty is in keeping with the highest traditions of the military service, and reflects great credit upon himself, his unit, and the United States Army.*

John was always thinking ahead, sometimes way ahead. For example, when he was in Italy, he had some ladies in a tailor shop in Foggia, Italy, make his parachute into a silk wedding dress. He said, "I worked in a tailor shop when I was a kid and knew the value of silk. I wasn't going to let it go to waste."[15] He also appreciated the workmanship of the seamstresses who made the dress, and they appreciated him. Whenever he came into their shop, they would sing, "Oh Johnny, Oh Johnny, how you can love!"[16] There was a bullet hole in the silk. Years later, when asked where it came from, he simply said, "things happened."[17] While he already had a wedding gown for Phyllis—a special one at that, with some history behind it—the story did not play out according to plan. Phyllis opted for a traditional Irish wedding with a traditional Irish wedding gown.[18]

After graduating from Haverford, John and his family moved to Tenafly, New Jersey. Meyer remembers taking his young son, Larry, and young daughter, Randy, to visit John and Phyllis and their son Thomas. He knew John came from good stock in addition to being a hard-working, industrious person like himself, so he expressed an interest in having John join him in the business he had been developing while John was going to college. He said John's wife was not receptive to the idea, so they went in different directions.[19] Meyer went on to a successful career in the knitwear business and John went on to a successful career in corporate finance. Eventually, John and Phyllis also went in different directions.

John and Phyllis had five children—Thomas, Jack, Carol, Mary, and Kevin. When their family lived in Tenafly, John's mother Anna bought a house in Teaneck, less than five miles away, where she lived with three of John's siblings. Her brothers, Bill and Emil Millon, lived nearby and helped her maintain her home. Bill had been a good baseball player who was inducted into the St. Peter's University Athletic Hall of Fame and signed with the New York Yankees out of college. He played in the Yankee organization for a couple of years before going on to a successful career with IBM.[20]

Like his mother, John knew the value of a good education and went on to study economics and statistics at the University of California and Columbia University.[21] He set a good example for his daughter Mary who has degrees from Smith and Columbia and is a teacher at a Catholic school; and for his son Kevin who has degrees from Berkeley and Columbia and is a teacher at a Quaker school.[22] John's brother Peter, who was fourteen years younger than him, also went to Columbia.[23] The mission of the high school John attended in New York City was to prepare young men for careers in business, and so it should come as no surprise that John pursued a business career.[24]

John's brother Robert also knew the value of a good education. After serving with the Army and the Marine Corps in the Pacific during World War II, he also took advantage of the GI Bill and enrolled at Antioch College in Yellow Springs, Ohio. He was a good student and won a Fulbright Scholarship to study at Oxford University in England, after which he had a successful career as a journalist and eventually became a member of the National Press Club. He met and married his wife Bente, who was from Denmark, in Washington, D.C. They married in 1951 and raised two children—Annelise and Brendan. Annelise went to John's alma mater, Haverford.[25]

Like Robert, John also had a successful career. Early in his career, he spent seven years doing research with Johnson & Johnson and Sterling Drug, after which he came to Wall Street and worked with firms in the areas of personal investments with an emphasis on mergers and acquisitions involving clients such as WR Grace, Pepsi, Teledyne, and General Foods. He was also a consultant to blue chip companies on divestments and acquisitions, and later a financial consultant with Shearson/American Express, one of the most dynamic retail and investment banking firms on Wall Street.[26]

After many years raising five children together in Tenafly, New Jersey, and Washington, Connecticut, John and Phyllis parted ways in 1975 and John was awarded full custody of the children.[27] His daughter Mary remembered her father meeting a lady on the tennis courts in Washington who became his life partner. Her name was Elisabeth "Betsy" Bing and she worked for The Metropolitan Museum of Art. She was her father's date at her high school graduation from The Wykeham Rise School, a private girls' school. Many of its graduates went to the "Seven Sister" colleges and so did she—to Smith College. Betsy and her daughter Virginia became part of John's extended family.[28]

Mary has fond memories of Betsy who became a guardian for her younger brother Kevin. She said, "Betsy was an angel," and remembers tagging along with her and her father to holiday parties and other social events at "The Met." She said Betsy spoiled them but also taught them kindness, thoughtfulness, and respect and sees these qualities in Virginia and Kevin. She has fond memories of fun times spent with her father and Betsy.[29]

John and Betsy lived in an apartment on Park Avenue in New York City where his two youngest children attended Columbia and where he had also studied. He became an active member of the University Club, one of the most prestigious private social clubs in New York City. It was an all-male club since its organization in 1865 but a century and a quarter later in 1987 the city's Human Rights Commission filed gender-discrimination charges against it and two other all-male private social clubs. Being the stand-up guy that he always was, John led the opposition group which challenged the antidiscrimination law, but to no avail. The University Club had to open its doors to women members in 1987.[30]

John's niece Nancy Leo remembers John inviting her to the University Club to discuss her career path or simply to have lunch. At a memorial celebration of John's life at the University Club in 2014, she fondly remembered his "helping others get ahead in life, whether it was in his encouragement for higher education, or helping someone find a job." She said, "he definitely had an unyielding devotion to mentoring others" and added that he was "a larger-than-life personality, a creator of everything that was 'FUN' and the patriarch of the Clooney clan."[31]

She thought he set a good example. The Great Depression hit his family hard as did the loss of his father when he was sixteen years old. He handled the adversity by stepping up to get a day job to help support the family while going to high school at night. When more adversity came his way—World War II—he went to war and survived thirty-five combat missions, came home, continued his education, started what became a successful business career, and raised a family. She said he was a good uncle who made her life richer because he was always interested in what she was doing, cared about her, and was always there for her.[32]

John never stopped caring. In his twilight years at the Long Island State Veterans Home, he represented residents, employees and volunteers who initiated a "Butterfly Project" to plant bushes with flowers that attracted butterflies. He knew that butterflies produce silk, and a parachute made of silk saved his life during the war. He also spoke on behalf of veterans in state veterans' homes on the importance of having the Senior Crimestoppers Program to protect 30,000 veterans in 160 state veterans' homes in the United States. When the television show *Heroes of the Island* was looking for a veteran who had done extraordinary things to make the world a better place, John was selected to appear on the show. When they were looking for a veteran to grace the cover of the brochure for the Long Island State Veterans Home, John got the call. And when the author of this book visited his veterans' home, John sought him out and planted the seed that grew into this book before he died in 2014 at the age of ninety-one.

John served his country well. He objected to the Jewish people being killed, and then did something about it. He returned from the war with a dress made from the parachute that saved his life, and the significance of the silk dress has always been appreciated by his daughter, Mary. She has

Exhibit 14.2
Mary Cooney in Parachute Dress

Courtesy of Cooney Family

worn it to school on many Veterans Days to honor her father, and to help educate her students about the veterans like her father who are celebrated on that day. On Veterans Day 2010, she wore it to a dedication ceremony for the Veterans Memorial Plaza outside the Brevard Veterans Memorial Center in Merritt Island, Florida (Exhibit 14.2). The Plaza and Center help to keep alive the memory of veterans whose service and sacrifices helped to preserve our precious freedoms.[33]

On Veterans Day 2015, Mary wore the parachute dress to the Veterans Day Parade in New York City, where her father lived and worked. She stood with Army dignitaries on the Fifth Avenue viewing stand. After the parade, she attended a reception where she was interviewed with tears in her eyes as she talked about her father.[34] On Veterans Day 2016, she let one of her students wear the dress to school so she and her classmates could get into the spirit of the day.[35] The dress has been a wonderful legacy for Mary who is very proud of her father.

Technical Sergeant David Orkin
February 7, 1925 - December 17, 2014

Courtesy of Rick Orkin

David Orkin was in two different prison of war camps—Stalag Luft IV from December 1944 to January 1945 and Stalag Luft I from February 1945 to April 1945. He was liberated and made it home to the United States on June 21, 1945.[1] He survived two hellholes in Nazi Germany as a Jewish prisoner of war, no small task. When he got home, he learned that Meyer Osofsky had written to his father Adolph after he was shot down encouraging him not to give up hope because he was on the same mission and saw several parachutes open when David's plane was shot down over Yugoslavia.[2] As it turned out, Meyer was right, and Adolph's only son made it home.

David connected with Meyer when he got home and was an usher in Meyer's wedding to Aileen Bryant in Brooklyn on July 28. 1945.[3] David told Meyer that he was mistreated as a prisoner of war because he was Jewish, and that confinement in two prison camps took its toll on him.[4] He was hospitalized with jaundice back in the States, a condition which was common to men confined in prison camps. When David's father notified Meyer that David was at a hospital in Brooklyn, Meyer and Aileen visited him to cheer him up.[5]

David recovered and, almost a year after Meyer got married, he tied the knot with Adrienne Friedman in Queens on July 11, 1946.[6] They had two sons—Paul was born in 1948 and Rick was born in 1952. They lived in Queens and connected with the family of Calvin Chin who like Meyer lived nearby on Long Island. Comrades in arms tend to form strong bonds of respect and that was the case with David, Meyer, Calvin and so many other veterans of World War II.

According to his Honorable Discharge, David Orkin was awarded an Air Medal with one Oak Leaf Cluster, a World War II Victory Medal, an American Campaign Medal, and an EMEA (European-African-Middle Eastern) Service Medal.[7] He also qualified for a Prisoner of War Medal.[8] Calvin Chin's son David remembered when his family visited Orkin's family in Queens and he saw a display of David's wartime medals on the wall over the staircase.[9] He also remembered his parents getting together with Meyer and Aileen Osofsky and them talking about the company Meyer started in his wife's name—Aileen, Inc.[10]

Calvin's family also got to know Orkin's parents Adolph and Elsie. In 1963, Calvin and his family took a long trip south to visit Orkin's parents in Hallandale Beach, Florida, and Orkin's family in Houston, Texas.[11] David Chin has photos with Orkin's parents in Hallandale Beach as well as photos of him and his brother Jeffrey in a swimming pool in Houston with Orkin's sons Paul and Rick. The Chin's daughter Patricia wasn't born yet. She came later in 1965.[12]

Rick said his father bounced around in different jobs over the years.[13] The family left Queens in the late 1950s for Rock Island, Illinois, where David was a foreman for Alcoa (The Aluminum Company of America) which makes one wonder if he knew that 85 percent of his twenty-ton B-24 was made of aluminum.[14] Adrienne was an assistant in at Scott Studio which produced fine photography. In the early 1960s they moved to Houston where the Chin family visited them in 1963. David and Adrienne Orkin brought their kids up in the Houston area where Rick graduated from Westbury High School in 1970 and where he still lives.[15]

His parents lived there for years as well and when David retired, he kept active by serving his community. At the age of sixty-nine in 1994, he ran for and was elected to a three-year term on the Jamaica Beach City Board of

Aldermen in Galveston, Texas. Galveston is one of the nine counties in the greater Houston area.[16] Adrienne died in 1995 at the age of sixty-six after being married to David for almost fifty years.[17]

The following year David's term as an alderman ended and he met a lady who became his wife, Cora Jean Bransford.[18] He continued to stay active in his community, but his community changed. He and Cora Jean moved to San Marcos in San Diego County, California, where he served with the San Marcos Senior Volunteer Patrol as assistant administrator for three years. The Senior Volunteer Program was sponsored by the San Diego Sheriff's Department and consisted of citizens over fifty years of age who wanted to serve their community in promoting safety and service programs. David retired from the Senior Volunteer Program in 2001 so he could spend some time with his grandkids. When he retired, the Sheriff's Department recognized him for "his ongoing leadership and support to the volunteers in the field."[19]

David never spoke of his wartime experiences with his wives or his sons Paul or Rick. This was not unusual. Many veterans chose not to talk about their combat or prisoner of war experiences except maybe with veterans who shared the same experiences. David was one of many veterans who passed away without much fanfare despite having served his country honorably and with courage. According to Rick, his brother Paul has his father's ashes.[20]

FROM ONE WAR TO ANOTHER

Technical Sergeant Meyer "Mike" Osofsky
July 23, 1924 - October 30, 2019

Courtesy of David Chin

Meyer Osofsky picked up the nickname "Mike" when he went to work in the Brooklyn Navy Yard after high school to save money for college. Meyer was not a familiar name, so the workers dubbed him "Mike."[1] His B-24 crew-mates also called him "Mike," just as they called some other members of the crew by their nicknames—Hong Sing Chin was called "Calvin," Russell Flint was called "Russ," Charles Muth was called "Chuck," Thaddeus Cylkowski was called "Ted," and Joseph Goss was called by his middle name "Leslie." Meyer was referred to by his birth name throughout this book because the author knew him only as Meyer.

Immigrants often changed their unfamiliar last names to sound less ethnic, making it easier for them to assimilate in the land of opportunity. When Meyer's father immigrated to the United States his name was quickly changed from Herschel Osowski to Harry Osofsky.[2] Meyer's brother Abe went a step further and changed his name again from Osofsky to Oberlin.[3] Meyer's wife's father changed the family name from Brodsky to Bryant, and the father of one of his crewmates, Russ Flint, changed the family name from Kravesky to Flint even though he had been awarded a Purple Heart for being wounded in World War I as Kravesky.[4] People of color were at a distinct disadvantage in the assimilation process because a name change did not change the color of their skin.

When Meyer came home from war, he flew the North Atlantic Route which took him from Italy to Oran in Tehran (about 1,000 miles); to Marrakesh in Morrocco (about 1,400 miles); to the Azores Islands in the Atlantic Ocean west of Gibraltar (about 1,100 miles); to Gander in Newfoundland (over 1,600 miles); to Grenier Army Airfield near Manchester, New Hampshire (about 900 miles); and finally, to Bradley Field in Windsor Locks, Connecticut (almost 100 miles). He said the 6,100-mile trip took about ten days because they encountered engine trouble on the longest leg from the Azores to Newfoundland and had to get a new engine.[5]

The South Atlantic Route was longer and the preferred flying route during winter, but Meyer flew home during summer. The South Atlantic Route was about 10,000 miles and went south from Morrocco to Senegal and Liberia in Africa, to Ascension Island in the South Atlantic Ocean, to South America with stops in Brazil and Guyana, then to Puerto Rico, and finally to Florida.[6] If he had sailed home, the trip would have been much longer. For example, when he and his crew traveled to Italy, they went by ship and the trip took twenty six days.[7]

When Meyer got home, he went to work at his father's knitting shop and reunited with his high school sweetheart, Aileen Bryant. On July 28, 1945, he and Aileen got married in Brooklyn. David Orkin, who grew up in nearby Queens, was one of the ushers.[8] On the morning of the Saturday evening wedding, Meyer and David were not far from a disaster. A B-25 Mitchell medium bomber crashed into the Empire State Building. The plane with two pilots and one passenger was flying from Bedford, Massachusetts, to LaGuardia Airport but was redirected to Newark Airport because of a thick fog. While flying slow and low over Manhattan, the pilot saw the Chrysler Building ahead, swerved left to avoid it, and flew into the Empire State Building, killing eleven people in the building along with the three on the plane. If it had been a weekday, the death toll would most likely have been significantly higher.[9]

One can only imagine what was running through the minds of Meyer and David that day. They had returned from flying combat missions over foreign lands in a heavy bomber and a medium bomber crashed in their hometown New York City on Meyer's wedding day. The war in Europe was over and they were home, but the war in Japan was still raging. They had to have been relieved to be home among loved ones but saddened by this local tragedy.

Meyer's father Harry had been in the knitting business since he came to America. In a 1915 Census, when he was only twenty-years old, he reported that he was a sweater knitter.[10] On his World War I draft registration card, he reported that his trade was knitting.[11] In the 1940 Census he reported that he was in the knitting business and on his World War II registration card, he reported that he was the owner of a knitting company in Brooklyn.[12] Harry came to America by himself, and Meyer saw how hard his father worked to support his family and how hard his mother worked in raising him and his seven brothers and sisters. He grew up to appreciate the value of hard work.[13]

Meyer started in the business by cleaning sweaters and recruited his crewmate John Cooney to help him. John had use of his mother's car to drive to Brooklyn to help him. Meyer said John earned a couple of thousand dollars helping him.[14] When John decided to go to college on the GI Bill, Meyer decided to forgo college. He said being in the service was his higher education.[15] He went to work learning the knitwear business from the bottom up. He had a father who had been in the knitting business since the time knitting machines were operated by hand.[16]

While John was going to college, Meyer was developing his business and starting a family. Son Larry was born in 1947 and daughter Randy in 1950. Even though Meyer did not use the GI Bill to go to college, he did use it to buy a house in East Meadow on Long Island and said it was a lifesaver for him. It was a small house with only one bedroom for his two children but was affordable when he was putting a lot of his time and money into his business.[17]

In 1948, Meyer started his own women's wear company and named it Aileen, Inc. after his wife. He brought his brother Abe into the business and with $4,000 in capital they opened a shop in Brooklyn to make women's cotton-knitted sport shirts.[18] Abe, three years older, had gone to college and came into the business with an accounting degree from City College of New York and a new last name, Oberlin, which was more Americanized than Osofsky.[19] Meyer said they took a gamble by putting money into an advertising campaign when their volume was only a million dollars but they believed in their product—women's and girl's knitwear—and it paid off because they became millionaires before they reached the age of forty.[20]

After John Cooney graduated from college in 1951 and moved to Tenafly, New Jersey, Meyer brought his son Larry and daughter Randy to visit him and his family. At that time, he invited John to join his business. Meyer said

John's wife was against it, so it never happened.[21] Nevertheless, they both had successful careers.

Meyer loved the camaraderie of the crews he trained and flew with, and he kept in touch with some of them after the war. When he lived in East Meadow, Russ Flint visited him, and they both drove to nearby Levittown to visit Bob Worsthorn. Meyer had flown most of his missions with Worsthorn as his pilot and Flint as his co-pilot, so they had a lot to talk about.[22] Around that time, he also connected with Calvin Chin who he always enjoyed being around and who also lived in Levittown. When Calvin opened a Chinese restaurant in 1965 Meyer threw a party for him.[23]

In 1955, Meyer and Aileen had their third child, Alan. The business was growing fast, and he and his brother decided to move operations to the South. They built operating plants in Strasburg and New Market, Virginia and by the end of the 1950s were employing over 600 people.[24] Things were going well, so Meyer bought a bigger house in Roslyn, a small village on Long Island not far from East Meadow.[25]

Aileen, Inc. continued to build plants in Virginia into the 1960s to keep up with sales. In 1961, Aileen, Inc. went public, and sales reached $15 million in 1962.[26] By 1963, the company was trading on the American Stock Exchange.[27] By owning and controlling the plants that made the clothes and by styling the clothes themselves they were able to be sticklers for quality. The clothes were designed by a staff of fifteen in the firm's executive offices in New York. They also had showrooms in New York, Chicago, Los Angeles, Atlanta, Dallas, and Minneapolis.[28]

Meyer did a lot of business traveling and once when he was in Chicago, he invited Ray Goodson, with whom he boxed and parachuted out of a plane, to the Pump Room along with his wife.[29] The Pump Room was a highly acclaimed and iconic Chicago restaurant that was a magnet for celebrities from the 1930s to the 1980s. It was where Humphrey Bogart and Lauren Bacall celebrated their wedding and was a favorite gathering place for other famous movie stars such as Frank Sinatra, Marilyn Monroe, Clark Gable, Bette Davis, and many others whose pictures appeared in its gallery of celebrity photographs.[30]

The late 1960s was the heyday of the knit business and Aileen, Inc. capitalized on it. By 1968, the company had operations in ten plants in Virginia with more than 1,800 employees, and sales of $37 million. In 1969, they built another plant in Abilene, Texas to serve states west of the Mississippi which composed a third of its business.[31] The Abilene plant eventually had more than 1,000 employees.[32]

FROM ONE WAR TO ANOTHER

By 1970, Aileen operated thirteen plants in Virginia with executive headquarters in New York and was manufacturing 6,000 dresses and matching coordinates a day. It produced summer, fall, and holiday clothing lines with between 200 and 350 styles of women's and girl's clothes in each line.[33] It became a leader in the cotton-knit field and eventually got listed on the New York Stock Exchange.[34]

Meyer retired from the business in 1978 and devoted the rest of his life to his wife, his family, and his philanthropic efforts. He was proud to have brought his family from humble beginnings to prosperity by founding a company, naming it after the love of his life, and developing it with his brother to become a $70 million dollar business. When the author contacted him, he said, "How did you find me?" The author replied. "…through your wife who gives away your money."

The adage "Behind every great man is a great woman" applied here. Aileen was a smart lady from the get-go, skipping a couple of grades to catch up with Meyer in high school, and very much in-step with him as he grew his business. Because his business required a lot of travel, he learned to fly a twin-engine plane, and so did she in case he ever got incapacitated during a flight.[35] She was always there for him, and vice versa.

The couple had homes in New York City, Shelter Island, New York, and Phoenix, Arizona; and their home on Shelter Island was considered the signature work of Norman Jaffe, an American architect widely noted for his contemporary residential architecture.[36] Aileen served on the boards of many secular and Jewish philanthropic organizations in New York and Phoenix.[37] She was also a fine bridge player and as chair of the Goodwill Committee of the American Contract Bridge League (ACBL) became one of the most influential voices of friendly behavior at the bridge table.[38] When she died in 2010, the accolades were many. The Goodwill Committee was renamed the Aileen Osofsky ACBL Goodwill Committee in her honor.[39] The past president of the ACBL, Jerry Fleming, said: "Aileen was a powerful force for civility and friendliness at the bridge table and elsewhere." One tournament bridge player, Zeke Jabour, said: "She was an angel long before she got to heaven."[40]

In 1991, she and Meyer co-funded with two other families an airplane transfer of Russian Jewish refugees from Russian barracks in Budapest, Hungary, to Israel.[41] Russia had occupied Hungary since 1944 and it wasn't until 1991 that the Russians left Hungary in the wake of the fall of communism in Central and Eastern Europe.[42] The property rights of Russian barracks were now shared by the Hungarian state and the local government. In Budapest, an agreement had been reached to provide transit accommodation for Jews emigrating from Russia to Israel.[43]

Meyer was shocked at the condition of the barracks, but the reality was that the Soviet army had occupied Hungary for five decades and many of the properties they occupied were in a very dilapidated condition. He said a Russian lady who spoke English, Russian, and Hungarian served as a translator when they were making arrangements for the refugees to fly to Tel Aviv, Israel. All went well, and he was very proud of having helped these refugees.[44] His father had once been a Russian Jewish refugee.

Meyer always appreciated those he served with during World War II. After all, his military service was his higher education, and it served him well. In his twilight years, he made donations to the 451st Bomb Group in memory of Bob Cookman and Calvin Chin, and he visited John Cooney when John was on his last legs at the Long Island State Veterans Home. Meyer lived longer than any other member of the crew he trained and went down with over Italy. He passed away on October 30, 2019, at the age of ninety-five. One family said, "Mike (Meyer) was known for his work ethic, intelligence, storytelling, infectious sense of humor and meticulous attention to detail."[45]

This book contains many of his stories, and his life itself makes for a good story. His son Alan Osofsky said his father's story was a Horatio Alger story except that he vaulted over the middle class.[46] Horatio Alger was an American author who wrote inspirational stories about young people who came from limited means and became successful through hard work.[47] Meyer inspired Alan who said he thinks of his father every day because to him he was larger than life.[48] Twelve days after Meyer died, his grandson Ryder Kessler posted on Facebook on Veterans Day this tribute to his grandfather which was later posted on the website of his bomb group:

"Though he lived a full and exciting life in the nearly 75 years after his service—starting the womenswear business named for my grandmother, Aileen, that brought his family out of poverty and into prosperity; traveling the world; raising three children; showering boundless love and opportunity on seven grandchildren—he always spoke with the most vivid and vital recollection about his army service. My grandfather was grateful to the army for shaping him, and we are grateful to him for shaping us."[49]

Meyer appreciated his parents, his children, and his grandchildren, and they all appreciated him. Meyer learned from his parents the value of hard work. He felt his time in the service was his higher education where he learned the value of working with others to accomplish a goal. He saw what happened when the government, industry, civilians, and the military of his country worked together with a common purpose. He felt that serving was the great honor of his life.[50] He learned his lessons well, applied them, and got to live the American dream of going from rags (well, not quite rags) to riches.

Epilogue

Since I retired in 2006, I have come to appreciate our veterans of war more than ever. It all started that year when I asked my uncle what happened to him in World War II. I ended up bonding with him for a book about his wartime experiences and those he flew with in combat. In the process of so doing, I attended the annual reunions of his 57th Bomb Wing Association, the last five Doolittle Raiders reunions, and three of the last four Stalag Luft III reunions. In my retirement years, I have been around many veterans including some I have read about in books and seen portrayed in movies. I felt fortunate and privileged to be around them, and I may be a member of the last generation to fully appreciate them.

My first book, *Shot Down Over Italy*, took four years to write and was published in 2010. In giving a talk at the Long Island State Veterans Home in 2011, veteran John Cooney approached me to tell me about his wartime experiences which led me to start writing this book in 2014. It took me ten years to write it, more than twice as long as my first book. Through it all, I have become acutely aware of the horrors of war. World War I was so destructive that it was tabbed as "the war to end all wars," but it did not stop the development of more powerful weapons of destruction which made World War II even more destructive. This makes me worry about how inconceivably horrible a third world war would be with the proliferation of nuclear weapons.

History has shown that leaders should never underestimate the length and severity of a war. Regarding World War I, Henry Kissinger said: "Not one of the leaders who entered that war would have done so if he had known what the outcome would be like."[1] Also, none of the autocratic leaders of the belligerent empires in World War I (the German, Austro-Hungarian, Russian, and Ottoman Empires) benefitted from the war—none were in power after the war.

In like fashion, none of the dictatorial leaders of the belligerent nations of World War II (Germany, Japan, and Italy) benefitted from the war. Instead of helping their countries, they brought great harm to them. War resulted in a tremendous loss of life, the loss of homes and businesses, the destruction of cities, and the collapse of their economies.

The intensity of the arms race in World War II led to the creation of the atomic bomb. The use of uranium and plutonium to produce powerful nuclear energy made this possible and the United States wanted to create one before the Germans did and they were successful.[2] Ironically, it was not used against Germany. It was used against Japan and its use ended the war and changed the nature of war forever because of the ongoing fear of war fought with nuclear weapons.

At that time—almost eighty years ago—leading scientists like Neils Bohr believed that such bombs could put an end to civilization because they gave humans the power to destroy themselves.[3] Bohr was a Danish physicist who received the Nobel Prize in 1922 for his work on the structure of atoms.[4] When the Nazis occupied Denmark during World War II, he escaped and worked on the project to build the atom bomb.[5]

President Roosevelt said we were fighting to protect and preserve America's four precious freedoms—freedom of speech, freedom of religion, freedom from want, and freedom from fear, and, to him, freedom from fear meant "a world-wide reduction in armaments to such a point and in such a thorough fashion that no nation anywhere will be in a position to commit an act of physical aggression against any neighbor."[6] This did not happen after World War II.

After the war, instead of reducing armaments, security concerns led to an even more destructive thermonuclear bomb which was called the hydrogen bomb because it added the hydrogen isotopes deuterium or tritium to fuel the bomb in the way uranium and plutonium fueled an atomic bomb. The concern was that the Soviets might create one and the United States wanted to beat them to it and were successful.[7] They created a bomb that had the power of 700 Hiroshima bombs and it was thought that it would be a deterrent to war or a retaliatory weapon in case of a war started with a nuclear weapon.[8]

In 1960, American journalist and historian William L. Shirer wrote the following in the foreword of his bestselling book *The Rise and Fall of the Third Reich: A History of Nazi Germany*:

> *"In our new age of terrifying, lethal gadgets, which supplanted so swiftly the old one, the first great aggressive war, if it should come, will be launched by a suicidal little madman pressing an electronic button. Such a war will not last long and none will ever follow it. There will be no conquerors and no conquests, but only the charred bones of the dead on an uninhabited planet."[9]*

Epilogue

It is noteworthy that those who were designing and manufacturing the atomic bomb during World War II referred to the military weapon as a "gadget" and not a "bomb" for security reasons.[10] In any case, Shirer's concern was expressed over sixty years ago when weapons were nowhere near as destructive as they are today. Nuclear weapons have proliferated to the point where nine countries now have arsenals of them.[11] Two of those countries, the United States and Russia, possess about 90 percent of them.[12] History has shown that leaders who seek power through force pose a serious threat to world peace. This is cause for concern. Countries rationalize their nuclear arsenals by saying they want to be prepared in case some country decides to use nuclear weapons against them. This was the same rationale that led to the buildup of arsenals for World Wars I and II.

If there is any lesson to be learned from this book, it is that war is started by few and fought by many, and the few who start a war bring great harm to their countries and to themselves while creating a living hell for those who are called upon to fight the war. With so many countries possessing weapons of mass destruction, it is critical for countries to find common ground through understanding and compromise to enable them to co-exist peacefully and prevent the possibility of a nuclear war in which everybody loses.

These concerns are not new. President Franklin Delano Roosevelt had similar concerns. After serving in World War I, and presiding over World War II, he knew all too well about the horror of war. On the day before he died, he said, "…if civilization is to survive, we must cultivate the science of human relationships—the ability of all peoples, of all kinds, to live together and work together, in the same world, in peace." He was hoping the United Nations would be a step in the direction of stopping the "impractical, unrealistic settlement of the differences between governments by the mass killing of peoples."[13] Albert Einstein, considered by many to be the greatest scientist of the twentieth century, shared Roosevelt's concerns. He said to Roosevelt's successor, President Harry S. Truman: "I know not with what weapons World War III will be fought, but World War IV will be fought with sticks and stones."[14]

Despite the concerns of Roosevelt and Einstein, countries kept on building more destructive weapons to the point that a World War III has the potential to destroy our civilization.[15] The United States, Russia, and China have led the charge in building these weapons. Let us hope more and more people become concerned with this reality and learn from World Wars I and II before history repeats itself again and we all suffer the consequences.

Acknowledgements

The best part of writing this book has been meeting so many wonderful and interesting people. The most rewarding experiences I had during the ten years it took me to write this book were my conversations with John Cooney and Meyer Osofsky.

First, let me thank John posthumously for planting the seed that grew into this book. He was very proud of his service. I would also like to thank his daughter Mary, son Kevin, and brother Peter who provided me with information for the book. John's sister Joan Cooney Stern, his brother Robert's son Brendan, and his sister Kathleen's daughter Nancy Leo were also helpful for which I am grateful. I appreciated Mary's support and encouragement throughout the process.

Second, let me thank Meyer Osofsky posthumously who was also proud of his service and was so generous in providing me with so much information on the men he served with during the war. He had many nice things to say about his crewmates and his footprint is all over what I wrote about them. I would also like to thank his son Alan for his help and encouragement. He viewed his father as being larger than life and I could see why.

I never had an opportunity to speak with other members of the crew, but I did have the good fortune to speak with some of their relatives. David Chin, the son of Calvin Chin, was especially helpful. He appreciated his father's service, saved his wartime records and photographs, was very generous in sharing them with me, and cheered me on, which I appreciated more than he knows. David also shared his remembrances of his family's visits with Meyer's family and with David Orkin's family. I was also fortunate to connect with David Orkin's sons Rick and Paul, who also were very helpful, as was Paul's daughter Jaime Nicole Brown. For their help, I am grateful, and special thanks to Rick for sharing a photo of his father for the book.

Bob Cookman gave his life saving his crew, a true hero of the war. He came from a close-knit and patriotic family, but I was only able to speak with one member of his family. Joe Cookman, his cousin, was a teenager when Bob was killed around the same time as his cousin Willie, and he remembered how devastating these losses were for the family. I appreciated his sharing that and more with me.

Like Bob, Kirk Mosher never made it home. I learned from Genie Mosher, the wife of Kirk's brother Dan, and their daughter, Kathy Krajewski, how much Kirk loved music and how good he was at it. It was a shame the music stopped for him during the war. I appreciated my conversations with Genie and Kathy and the information they shared with me about Kirk and his musical family.

Music was also important to Ted Cylkowski. I learned from his son David that his father used his musical talent to teach a generation of students to appreciate classical music. His mother's sister, Irma Glaser, also shared information on how his mother Doris was still playing classical music on piano when she was over a hundred years old. It was nice to hear how much David appreciated his parents, and how much Irma appreciated her sister, and for that experience I am thankful.

I connected with Russ Flint's son Russ Jr. who had his father's military records which he shared with me along with his father's official Army Air Forces portrait photograph. He still appreciates his father's service. The same with John Johnson, the son of David Johnson. I not only spoke with John but with his sister's husband, Greg Marsella, and several relatives of his mother—Daniel and Abby Ladd and Carole and Karin Dodge. All of them were generous in sharing information with me, for which I am grateful.

Ray Goodson's son Tom said his father never talked about the war, so I shared with him some of the nice things Meyer said about his father and some of what I knew about his father's wartime experiences. I never connected with a family member of Chuck Muth's family, but I felt I knew him from conversations with Meyer who spent time with him when they were off duty and enjoying rest and relaxation away from the stress of flying combat missions. Regarding my research on Chuck, I would like to thank Jo Stately, an archivist and historian of Monroe County, Tennessee, for helping me connect with Peggy Bebb and Lynn Fox who knew the history of the Tennessee Military Institute in Sweetwater, Tennessee. Chuck was a student there and Lynn sent me information and photographs of Chuck on the basketball and track teams. I appreciated my time corresponding with each and am thankful for the experience.

I had the darndest time trying to find information on Joseph Goss, but when I connected with the registrar of his high school, Melissa Willings, things changed. Melissa found news clips of him for me, including one with his photograph for this book. I also learned from her that Joseph went by his middle name, Leslie, and this enabled me to find more news clips of him during high school and beyond. I appreciated her going the extra mile to help me. I would also like to thank Tonia Bobay, the deputy clerk of Watervliet, Michigan, for helping me locate the daughter of Leslie's wife's sister even though it was just after she had passed away. I appreciated her help.

Researching a book about Army Air Force veterans who flew combat missions eighty years ago is challenging, but I am lucky to live in a country that cares deeply about its veterans and preserves their history through the United States Air Force History and Museums Program. The Program has dedicated personnel at the Air Force Historical Research Agency at Maxwell Air Force Base in Alabama and the Air Force Historical Support Division at Joint Base Anacostia Bolling in Washington, D.C. who help researchers like me.[1]

The Air Force Historical Research Agency is an archive and repository for Air Force historical documents.[2] Its archivists, historians, and others were very helpful. Archangel "Archie" Difante, an archivist, helped me obtain documents about the crew I was researching such its general orders for its missions, reports of its missions, and awards received for flying them. Lynn Gamma, a chief archivist, helped me obtain CDs with information about the Fifteenth Air Force operations. Pamela Ives, a historian, helped me obtain a CD with information about a crew member who received a Distinguished Flying Cross. Tammy Horton helped me obtain CDs with documents that included general orders, mission summaries, and other information on airmen who escaped and evaded capture. They were wonderful resources for me, providing useful information in a courteous manner for which I am thankful.

The Air Force Historical Support Division is the keeper of Headquarters Air Force history.[3] Before she retired in 2019, Yvonne Kincaid, a research historian, helped me obtain the general orders for John Cooney's air medals and referred me to someone at the Air Force Historical Research Agency for help with other matters. Helen "Terry" Kiss, a librarian at the Air Force Historical Research Agency, was also helpful. They were wonderful resources, and I am grateful for their help.

Through the Freedom of Information and Privacy Office, I was able to obtain the Individual Deceased Personnel Files of some of the airmen I was researching. The Office is part of the U.S. Army Human Resources Command in the Department of the Army at Fort Knox, Kentucky. Personnel of that Office who were a great help to me included Patricia Dugdale, Alan Alton,

FROM ONE WAR TO ANOTHER

Tifanie Cropper, and Ron Hoggard. Through them, I was able to learn a lot about valiant airmen such as Bob Cookman and Kirk Mosher who gave their lives in the service of their country. For their help, I am thankful.

David Hardin, an archivist at the National Archives at St. Louis, Missouri, helped me obtain the Individual Personnel File of another airman, Arnold Silverstein, and I am grateful for his help. Also helpful were Theresa Fitzgerald and Corey Stewart and I appreciated their help as well.

I received help from the National Personnel Records Center which is the central repository of personnel-related records for military services of the United States Government.[4] I would like to thank Alexandra Courtney, Diane Turnquist, and Nicholas Wintjen who responded to my requests for information despite the issues they had to deal with due to the pandemic. I appreciated their responsiveness.

Jonathan Tudor manages a terrific website on the 451st Bombardment Group (https://451st.org/). The airmen of the 451st flew B-24 heavy bombers during World War II and included the crew members I wrote about in the book. Jonathan does this in memory of his father, George E. Tudor, a B-24 pilot who flew thirty-seven combat missions for the 451st and was the recipient of the Purple Heart, Distinguished Flying Cross, and Silver Star.[5] Jonathan's website was my "go to" source for information about the 451st Bomb Group. I am impressed with what Jonathan has done to honor his father and appreciate the information I obtained from his website for the book.

I am so thankful for four online services I subscribe to which were valuable resources for me—*Ancestry.com*, *Newspapers.com*, *Fold3.com*, and *E-Yearbook.com*. They led me to so much information about the people and events I was writing about as evidenced in my endnotes. Through *Fold3.com*, I was able to obtain Missing Air Crew Reports with information on crews who were shot down during the war. Through both *Fold3.com* and *Ancestry.com*, I was able to obtain the Draft Registration Cards of the World War I and World War II veterans I was writing about. Through *Newspapers.com*, I found many articles on people and events I was researching and through *E-Yearbook.com*, I was able to learn about the interests of those I was writing about when they were in high school and college. I have the utmost respect for and appreciation of those who conceived, developed, and maintain these online services.

I would like to thank Mike Stowe of *Accident Report.com* for providing me with Reports of Aircraft Accidents such as the B-24 heavy bomber, *Betty Jo*, that I was writing about that went down over Italy due to engine trouble. I would also like to thank Craig Fuller of Aviation Investigation and

Acknowledgements

Research for helping me obtain a Missing Air Crew Report that was helpful in my research. In addition, a special thanks to Phojoe, a small, family run company, for its fine work in restoring and enhancing many of the photographs in this book. Speaking of fine work, I wish to add my sincere thanks to John Hetland who built websites for both my books.

I was very fortunate to have very talented people help me prepare this book for publication. Foremost was Todd Slater who, as he did for my first book, laid it out and enhanced it for publication. He also added some fine artwork. The Force was with me in having Todd in my corner. I was also fortunate to have Lisa Weaver do the Index. Her skills, like those of Todd, are greatly appreciated by me and no doubt by readers like you. As regards the book cover, I have been blessed with the artwork of Jim Ryan, a military artist who is the recipient of the Association of the United States Army's Citation for Exceptional Service in Support of National Defense in recognition of his contributions as an artist specializing in American military history. I am thankful to have his skill grace the cover of this book. To have Todd, Lisa, and Jim be part of this book make me think of the quote "my cup runneth over."

I have saved the best for last, and that is my wife, Diana. When I decided to write this book in 2014, I figured it would take less time to write than my first book which took four years. Well, I was wrong. It took ten years. Throughout the process, Diana was my patient, encouraging, and loving partner. She saw how important this book was to me and helped me stay the course. She even proofread my work. I am lucky—my cup does runneth over!

About the Author

John Lanza grew up in Revere, Massachusetts. After graduating from Bates College in 1967, he was a banker in New York City for almost forty years, retiring from JPMorgan Chase in 2006. He has an MBA from Baruch College and taught undergraduate and graduate courses on payments systems for over twenty-five years.

John has five grown children and eight grandchildren, and lives with his wife, Diana, in Caldwell, New Jersey. He is an avid reader and has always been involved with team sports as a player, coach, booster, writer, and photographer. He was once a Red Sox prospect and later a Yankee bird dog scout, at which time his father accused him of treason.

He has spent his retirement years reading, researching, and writing about veteran airmen and the history around them. He spent the first four years of his retirement writing *Shot Down Over Italy* after falling upon a story about a crew that included his uncle, Willam Lanza. In giving a talk on the book at a veterans' home, he met another veteran airman, John Cooney, who sparked his interest in spending another ten years researching and writing this book.

Notes

Preface

[1] Jessica Fragoso, "Interview of John Cooney," *Heroes on Our Island* at Verizon FiOS 1 News, Greater New York City Area, Broadcast Media, August 31, 2010, https://www.youtube.com/watch?v=aQQgTuNxjiA. This video isn't available anymore.

[2] *Caring for America's Heroes*, Long Island State Veterans Home, 100 Patriots Road, Stony Brook, NY, 2010.

[3] John J. Cooney, letter to Fred S. Sganga, September 20, 2010.

[4] John J. Cooney, "Protect Our Nation's Elderly Veterans," Speech, Senior Housing Crime Prevention Foundation, 2013. This video isn't available anymore.

[5] Long Island State Veterans Home, "A Resident's Story by John Lanza," *Veteran Times Newsletter*, 2014.

[6] Yvonne Kinkaid, Reference Historian, *Air Force Historical Research Agency*, Maxwell Air Force Base, Montgomery, Alabama, email to author, January 30, 2015.

[7] John J. Pershing, *My Experiences in the World War, Volumes 1 & 2*, (Originally published in New York: Frederick A. Stokes Company, 1931; republished in Middletown, DE, 2019), 8.

Chapter 1: THE ROAD TO WORLD WAR I

[1] "WWI Service Record of John J. Cooney (WWI)," State of New Jersey, Department of State, (Trenton, NJ: New Jersey State Archives, PO Box 307, Trenton, NJ 08625-0307), Form ORM No. 42, A.G.O. (For National Army).

[2] "Participants in World War I," The United States World War I Centennial Commission, *WorldWar1Centennial.org*, accessed February 15, 2022, https://www.worldwar1centennial.org/index.php/edu-home/edu-topics/583-world-at-war/5048.

[3] Michael Showalter, *Encyclopedia Britannica Online*, s.v. "World War I," (See section entitled Armed Forces Mobilized and Casualties in World War I), accessed February 8, 2022, britannica.com/event/World-War-I/killed-wounded-missing.

[4] Nadège Mougel, "World War I Casualties," The Robert Schuman European Center, *Centre-Robert-Schuman.org*, accessed February 15, 2022, http://www.centre-robert-schuman.org/userfiles/files/REPERES%20%E2%80%93%20module%201-1-1%20-%20explanatory%20notes%20%E2%80%93%20World%20War%20I%20casualties%20%E2%80%93%20EN.pdf.

[5] Showalter, "World War I."

[6] Susanne Mettler, "How the GI Bill Built the Middle Class and Enhanced Democracy," The Scholars Strategy Network, *Scholars.org*, accessed February 8, 2022, scholars.org/contribution/how-gi-bill-built-middle-class-and-enhanced-democracy.

FROM ONE WAR TO ANOTHER

[7] Charles L. Mee, Jr., *The End of Order: Versailles 1919* (New York: E.P. Dutton, 1980), 247-248.

[8] Mee, Jr., *The End of Order*, 260.

[9] "Beer Hall Putsch," last updated August 21, 2018, *History.com*, https://www.history.com/topics/Germany/beer-hall-putsch.

[10] Joan Stern, email to Peter Cooney, January 15, 2015.

[11] Peter Cooney, "Family History of the Cooney-Millon Family," sent to author, August 24, 2015.

[12] U.S. Census Bureau, *Thirteenth Census of the United States Taken in the Year 1910: Volume I, Population, General Report and Analysis* (Chapter VII, "Country of Birth of the Foreign-Born Population," 781), prepared by William C. Hunt, accessed February 13, 2022, census.gov/library/publications/1913/dec/vol-1-population.

[13] Roger Matuz, revised and updated by Bill Harris and Thomas J. Craughwell, *The President's Fact Book: The Achievements, Campaigns, Events, Triumphs, and Legacies of Every President* (New York: Black Dog & Leventhal Publishers, Inc., 2021), 61.

[14] Editors of Encyclopedia Britannica, *Encyclopedia Britannica Online*, s.v. "The French Revolution of Marquis de Lafayette," accessed February 15, 2022, britannica.com/biography/Marquis-de-Lafayette/The-French-Revolution.

[15] "FDR and the Four Freedoms Speech," Franklin D. Roosevelt Presidential Library and Museum, *FDRLibrary.org*, accessed February 11, 2022, https://www.fdr library.org/four-freedoms.

[16] Mary J. Manning, "Being German, Being American: In World War I They Faced Suspicion, Discrimination Here are Home," *Archives.gov*, accessed February 11, 2022, archives.gov/files/publications/prologue/2014/summer/germans.pdf.

[17] Richard Rubin, "Why Don't Americans Remember the War," *The Atlantic.com*, accessed February 11, 2022, theatlantic.com/magazine/archive/2014/08/why-don't-americans-remember-the-war/373469/.

[18] Willis Mason West, *The War and The New Age* (Boston: Allyn and Bacon, 1919), 38-39.

[19] *The World Book Encyclopedia* (Chicago, IL: Field Enterprises Educational Corporation, 1968), s.v. "Prussia," Volume 15, 744-745.

[20] West, *The War and New Age*, 22.

[21] West, *The War and New Age*, 26.

[22] West, *The War and New Age*, 22-23.

[23] The World Book Encyclopedia (1968), s.v. "Bismarck," Volume 2, 300-301.

[24] William Stearns Davis in collaboration with William Anderson and Mason W. Tyler, *The Roots of War: A Non-technical History of Europe 1870-1914* (New York: The Century Co., 1919), 6.

[25] Davis, Anderson, and Tyler, *Roots of War*, 15.

Notes

[26] Davis, Anderson, and Tyler, *Roots of War*, 21-22.

[27] Davis, Anderson, and Tyler, *Roots of War*, 205-207.

[28] "Kaiser Wilhelm," *Biography.com*, accessed February 16, 2022, biography.com/political-figure/kaiser-wilhelm.

[29] "World War I & Its Aftermath," The American Yawp, *AmericanYawp.com*, accessed February 16, 2022, https://www,americanyawp.com/text/21-world-war-i.

[30] West, *The War and New Age*, 5.

[31] *The World Book Encyclopedia* (1968), s.v. "Bismarck," Volume 2, 300-301.

[32] *The World Book Encyclopedia* (1968), s.v. "Wilhelm II," Volume 20, 255.

[33] West, *The War and New Age*, 6

[34] West, *The War and New Age*, 9-11.

[35] Niall Ferguson, *The Pity of War* (New York: Basic Books, 1999), 82.

[36] West, *The War and New Age*, 9-12.

[37] Ferguson, *Pity of War*, 150.

[38] Ferguson, *Pity of War*, 153.

[39] West, *The War and New Age*, 19.

[40] West, *The War and New Age*, 15.

[41] "The Balkans," *AlphaHistory.com*, accessed February 16, 2022, http://alphahistory.com/worldwar1/balkans/.

[42] "The Balkans," *AlphaHistory.com*.

[43] Editors of Encyclopedia Britannica, *Encyclopedia Britannica Online*, s.v. "Slav," accessed February 16, 2022, http://www.britannica.com/topic/Slav.

[44] West, *The War and New Age*, 20.

[45] West, *The War and New Age*, 20-21.

[46] West, *The War and New Age*, 18.

[47] Christopher Clark, *The Sleepwalkers: How Europe Went to War in 1914* (New York: HarperCollins Publishing, 2012), 48-49.

[48] G. J. Meyer, *A World Undone: The Story of the Great War 1914-1918* (New York: Delacorte Press, 2006), 8.

[49] Micheal Shackelford, "The Assassination of Archduke Franz Ferdinand," *Net.Lib.BYU.edu*, accessed February 17, 2022, net lib byu.edu/~rdh7/wwi/comment/sarajevo.html.

FROM ONE WAR TO ANOTHER

[50] Andrew Carroll, *My Fellow Soldiers: General John Pershing and the Americans Who Helped Win the Great War* (New York: Penguin Books, 2018), page xxi.

[51] Hew Strachan, *The First World War* (New York: Viking, 2004), 9.

[52] Clark, *The Sleepwalkers*, 368.

[53] Clark, *The Sleepwalkers*, 370.

[54] Jesse Greenspan, "The Assassination of Archduke Franz Ferdinand," *History.com*, updated February 12, 2020, https://www.history.com/news/the-assassination-of-archduke-franz-ferdinand.

[55] Ed Backhouse and Others, *Encylopedia Britannica Online*, s.v. "Franz Ferdinand, Archduke of Austria-Este," accessed February 17, 2022, https://www.britannica.com/biography/Franz-Ferdinand-Archduke-of-Austria-Este.

[56] Clark, *The Sleepwalkers*, 370.

[57] Meyer, *A World Undone*, 7.

[58] Meyer, *A World Undone*, 177 and 254.

[59] Meyer, *A World Undone*, 254.

[60] Carroll, *My Fellow Soldiers*, page xxii.

[61] John Gilbert Thompson and Inez Bigwood, *Lest We Forget: World War Stories* (Boston, New York, and Chicago: Silver, Burdett, and Company, 1918), p. 68.

[62] West, *The War and New Age*, 30.

[63] Meyer, *A World Undone*, 46.

[64] Family Tree Editors, "Timeline of Major War Declarations in World War I," *FamilyTreeMagazine.com*, accessed February 19, 2022, https://www.familytreemagazine.com/history/ww1-war-declarations-timeline/.

[65] Family Tree Editors, "Timeline of Major War Declarations."

[66] "The Ottoman Empire Enters WWI on the Side of the Central Powers," *ThenAgain.info*, accessed February 28, 2022, http://www.thenagain.info/WebChron/EastEurope/TurkeyCentral.html.

[67] "Italy Declares War on Austria-Hungary," *History.com*, accessed February 28, 2020, https://www.history.com/this-day-in-history/italy-declares-war-on-austria-hungary.

[68] Family Tree Editors, "Timeline of Major War Declarations."

[69] Family Tree Editors, "Timeline of Major War Declarations."

[70] Matuz, *The President's Fact Book*, 442.

[71] Erik Larson, *Dead Wake: The Last Crossing of the Lusitania* (New York: Crown Publishing Group, 2015), 331.

Notes

[72] Larson, *Dead Wake*, 3.

[73] "Unrestricted U-Boat Warfare: The German Naval Tactic of WWI," The National WWI Museum and Memorial, *TheWorldWar.org*, accessed February 19, 2022, theworldwar.org/learn/wwi/unrestricted-u-boat-warfare.

[74] Editors of Encyclopedia Britannica, *Encyclopedia Britannica Online*, s.v. "Lusitania," accessed February 20, 2022, http://www.britannica.com/topic/Lusitania-British-ship.

[75] Larson, *Dead Wake*, 331.

[76] Carroll, *My Fellow Soldiers*, 41; West, *The War and New Age*, 53.

[77] "Wilson Notes," The Lusitania Resource, *RMSLusitania.info*, accessed February 21, 2022, https://rmslusitania.info/primary-docs/wilson-notes/.

[78] "Wilson Notes," The Lusitania Resource.

[79] "SS Arabic," The Lusitania Resource, *RMSLusitania.info*, accessed August 11, 2022, https://www.rmslusitania.info/related-ships/arabic/; "SS *Arabic* Sunk, Feared Many Lost," *Boston Evening Globe*, August 19, 1915, accessed August 10, 2022, as subscriber to *Newspapers. com*, https://www.newspapers.com/image/430917711/?terms=ss%20arabic%20sunk%2C%20feared%20many%20lost&match=1; "SS *Arabic* (1902)," *Wikipedia*, accessed August 11, 2022, https://en.wikipedia.org/wiki/SS_Arabic_(1902).

[80] Annette McDermott, "How the Sinking of the Lusitania Changed World War I," *History.com*, April 17, 2018, updated February 9, 2021, accessed August 10, 2022, https://www.history.com/news/how-the-sinking-of-lusitania-changed-wwi.

[81] "SS *Arabic* (1902)," Wikipedia.

[82] Larson, *Dead Wake*, 333; Jennifer D. Keene, *World War I: The American Soldier Experience* (Lincoln, NB: University of Nebraska Press, 2011), 8.

[83] Keene, *World War I*, 8.

[84] "April 19, 1916: Message Regarding German Actions," Miller Center/University of Virginia, *MillerCenter.org*, accessed February 21, 2022, millercenter.org/the-presidency/presidential speeches/ April-19-1916-message-regarding-german-actions.

[85] "Definition and Summary of the Sussex Pledge," United States History for Kids, *American-Historama.org*, accessed February 21, 2022, https://www.american-historama.org/1913-1928-ww1-prohibition-era/sussex-pledge.htm.

[86] "Germany Resumes Unrestricted Warfare," *History.com*, accessed February 28, 2022, https://www.history.com/this-day-in-history/germany-resumes-unrestricted-submarine-warfare.

[87] "U.S. Entry into World War I, 1917," Office of the Historian, *History.State.gov*, accessed February 21, 2022, history.state.gov/milestones/1914-1920/wwi#:~:text=.

[88] Margaret MacMillan. *Paris 1919: Six Months That Changed the World* (New York: Random House, 2001), 315; Keene, World War I, 10.

[89] Woodrow Wilson, "Joint Address to Congress Leading to a Declaration of War Against

Germany (1917)," National Archives, *Archives.gov*, accessed May 6, 2023, https://www.archives.gov/milestone-documents/address-to-congress-declaration-of-war-against-germany.

[90] Woodrow Wilson, "Joint Address to Congress Leading to a Declaration of War."

[91] "U.S. Entry into World War I," *History.com*, accessed February 22, 2022, https://www.history.com/topics/world-war-i/i-s-emtru-into-world-war-i-1.

[92] Philip Stevens, *The Great War Explained* (Barnsley, UK: Pen & Sword, 2014), 99.

Chapter 2: AMERICA MOBILIZES FOR WORLD WAR I

[1] John J. Pershing, *My Experiences in the World War, Volumes 1 & 2* (Originally published in New York: Frederick A. Stokes Company, 1931; republished in Middleton, DE, 2019), 63.

[2] "This Day History: April 22, 1915, Germans Introduce Poison Gas," History Channel, *History.com*. accessed May 16, 2023, https://www.history.com/this-day-in-history/germans-introduce-poison-gas.

[3] American Battle Monuments Commission, *American Armies and Battlefields in Europe: A History, Guide, and Reference Book* (Washington, D.C.: Government Printing Office, 1938) (reprinted in Delaware MD: Center for Military History, United States Army, 2019), 501.

[4] American Battle Monuments Commission, *A Guide to the American Battle Fields in Europe* (originally printed in 1927 by the Government Printing Office in Washington, D.C. but reprinted here in 2018 by Forgotten Books in London, England), 12.

[5] Jonathan H. Jaffin, "Medical Support for the American Expeditionary Forces in France During the First World War," (Thesis for Master of Military Art and Science, U.S. Army Command and General Staff College, Fort Leavenworth, KS, 1990), 185, AMEED Center of History & Heritage, *ACHH.Army.mil*, accessed May 7, 2023, https://achh.army.mil/history/book-wwi-jaffin-default.

[6] Patrick K. O'Donnell, *The Unknowns: The Untold Story of America's Unknown Soldier and WWI's Most Decorated Heroes Who Brought Him Home* (New York: Atlantic Monthly Press, 2018), 45.

[7] O'Donnell, *The Unknowns*, 45.

[8] Troy Fedderson, "Huskers Restart Nebraska's Pershing Rifles Drill Team," *Nebraska Today* (University of Nebraska-Lincoln), May 15, 2018), *news.unl.edu*, accessed August 17, 2023, https://news.unl.edu/newsrooms/today/article/huskers-restart-nebraska-s-pershing-rifles-drill-team/.

[9] "Pershing at UNL," Archives of the University of Nebraska-Lincoln, *UNLHistory.inl.edu*, accessed March 2, 2022, unlhistory.inl.edu/exhibits/show/generalpershing/pershingteaching.

[10] O'Donnell, *The Unknowns*, 45.

[11] O'Donnell, *The Unknowns*, 45.

[12] "Theodore Roosevelt," Congressional Medal of Honor Society, *CMOHS.org*, accessed March 2, 2022, cmohs.org/recipients/theodore-roosevelt.

[13] Everett T. Tomlinson, *The Story of General Pershing* (New York and London: D. Appleton and Company, 1919), 77.

Notes

[14] "The Spanish-American War," *The Volume Library, Volume 2* (Nashville, TN: The Southwestern Company, 1988), 2211-2212.

[15] "The Philippines," *The Volume Library, Volume 2*, 186.

[16] O'Donnell, *The Unknowns*, 44-46.

[17] Andrew Carroll, *My Fellow Americans: General Pershing and the Americans Who Helped to Win the Great War* (New York: Penguin Books, 2017), 8

[18] O'Donnell, *The Unknowns*, 47.

[19] "The Highest Ranked Officer Buried at Arlington National Cemetery: John J. Pershing," Arlington National Cemetery Tours, *Arlington.Tours.com*, accessed March 2, 2022, arlingtontours.com/john-j-pershing.

[20] O'Donnell, *The Unknowns*, 46.

[21] Associated Press, "Senator's Daughter Weds an Officer of the Army," *Pittsburgh Gazette*, January 27, 1905, 10, accessed on March 2, 2022, as subscriber to *Newspapers.com*.

[22] "Mrs. Boswell is in the Hospital," *The San Francisco Examiner*, August 29, 1915, 10, accessed on March 2, 2022, as subscriber to *Newspapers.com*; Wellesley College yearbook, *Legenda* (Wellesley, MA: 1903 and 1904), Frances Warren in 1903 *Legenda*, 6, and Anne D. Orr in 1904 *Legenda*, 57, accessed on March 2, 2022, as subscriber to *e-Yearbook.com*.

[23] "John Pershing-World War I," National Park Service, *NPS.gov*, accessed March 2, 2022, https://www.nps.gov/prsf/learn/historyculture/john-pershing.htm; "1915 Panama-Pacific International Exposition," *National Park Service, NPS.gov*, accessed March 2, 2022, https://www.nps.gov/prsf/learn/historyculture/1915-panama-pacific-international-exposition.htm.

[24] Plaque with an inscription at the Presidio of San Francisco, California Registered Historical Landmark No. 79, California State Park Commission in Cooperation with the California History Commission and the United States Army, September 18, 1965.

[25] Gravestone of Anne Pershing and her three children who were laid to rest at Lakeview Cemetery in Cheyenne, Wyoming, *FindaGrave.com*, accessed April 29, 2022, https://www.findagrave.com/memorial/80818195/anne-orr-pershing.

[26] Associated Press Night Wire, "Wife of General Victim in Fire at Army Post," *Los Angeles Times*, August 28, 1915, 1, accessed on March 2, 2022, as subscriber to *Newspapers.com*.

[27] "Pershing Tragedy to Start Presidio Inquiry," *San Francisco Examiner*, August 28, 1915, 3, accessed on March 3, 2022, as subscriber to *Newspapers.com*.

[28] Associated Press, "Wife of General Victim," 5.

[29] "Frederick Funston Letters," Kansas Historical Society, *KsHS.org*, accessed March 3. 2022, kshs.org/p/Frederick-funston-papers13027.

[30] "Pershing Tragedy," *The San Francisco Examiner*.

[31] "Mansion is Death Trap," *Oakland Tribune*, 1, accessed on March 3, 2022, as subscriber to *Newspapers.com*.

32 Associated Press, "Wife of General Victim," 1 and 5.

33 Associated Press, "Wife of General Victim," 1 and 5.

34 Carroll, *My Fellow Soldiers*, 11.

35 Carroll, *My Fellow Soldiers*, 58.

36 Carroll, *My Fellow Soldiers*, 1

37 Carroll, *My Fellow Soldiers*, 61.

38 Carroll, *My Fellow Soldiers*, 10.

39 Carroll. *My Fellow Soldiers*, 36; Editors of Encyclopedia Britannica, s.v. "Mexican Revolution," *Encyclopedia Britannica Online*, accessed March 3, 2022, https://www.britannica,com/event/ Mexican-Revolution.

40 Carroll, *My Fellow Soldiers*, 61.

41 "Punitive Expedition in Mexico, 1916-1917," U.S. Department of State Archive, *State.gov*, accessed March 3, 2022, 2001-2009.state.gov/r/pa/ho/time/wwi/108653.htm.

42 Pershing, *My Experiences*, 11-12.

43 Carroll, *My Fellow Soldiers*, 105-107.

44 "World War I Draft Registration Cards," National Archives Military Records, *Archives.gov*, accessed March 3, 2022, archives.gov/research/military/ww1/draft-registration.

45 World War I Registration Cards of the fathers of the crew John Cooney trained with for World War I were obtained from the National Archives through the author's subscription with *Ancestry.com.*

46 "Registration (for Draft)," *Annual Report of the Secretary of War, 1918* (Washington, D.C.: Government Printing Office, 1918), 14. The figures for all three World War I draft registrations were taken from page 14 of this report.

47 David Vergun, "First Peacetime Draft Enacted Just Before World War II," Department of Defense News, *Defense.com*, April 7, 2020, defense.gov/News/Feature-Stories/story/article/214942/first-peacetime-draft-enacted-before-world-war-ii/.

48 Newton D. Baker, *Annual Report of the Secretary of War, 1918* (Washington, D.C.: Government Printing Office, 2018), 5.

49 John O'Brien, "Army Forts, Camps, and Cantonments: Where Adapting to Peace, Preparing for War, and Responding to Crisis Meet," U.S. Army Center of Military History, *History.Army. mil*, accessed March 3, 2022, https://history.army.mil/events/ahts2015/presentations/seminar1/ sem1_JohnOBrien_text.pdf.

50 John O'Brien, "Army Forts, Camps, and Cantonments."

51 "World War I Training Camps," *Encyclopedia,com*, accessed March 4, 2022, encyclopedia.com/ history/dictionaries-thesauruses-pictures-and-press-releases/world-war-i-training-camps.

Notes

[52] Carroll, *My Fellow Soldiers*, 67.

[53] John Gilbert Thompson and Inez Bigwood, *Lest We Forget: World War I Stories* (Boston, New York: Silver, Burdett and Company, 1918), 251.

[54] Mary Stockwell, "Marquis de Lafayette," The George Washington Presidential Library at Mount Vernon, *Mount Vernon.org*, accessed March 4, 2022, https://www.mountvernon.org/library/digitalhistory/digital-encyclopedia/article/marquis-de-lafayette/.

[55] John J. Pershing, "Report of General Pershing," *Annual Report of the Secretary of War, 1918* (Washington, D.C.: Government Printing Office, 1918), 67.

[56] Pershing, "Report of General Pershing," 67-68.

[57] Pershing, "Report of General Pershing," 70.

[58] Baker, *Annual Report of the Secretary of War*, 5.

[59] "Basic Fighting Unit of the AEF: The Square Division," *WorldWar1.com*, accessed March 4, 2022, http://www.worldwar1.com/dbc/squarediv.htm.

[60] American Battle Monuments Commission, *American Armies and Battlefields*, 501.

[61] American Battle Monuments Commission, *American Armies and Battlefields*, 17.

[62] "Basic Fighting Unit of the AEF," *Worldwar1.com*.

[63] "World War I Divisions: Then and Now," U.S. Army Center of Military History, *History.Army. mil*, accessed March 7, 2022, https://history.army.mil/html/bookshelves/resmat/wwi/wwi_bomad/index.html.

[64] Philip Stevens, *The Great War Explained* (South Yorkshire, England: Pen and Sword Ltd., 2014), 158.

[65] Pershing, "Report of General Pershing," 68-69.

[66] American Battle Monuments Commission, *American Armies and Battlefields*, 502.

[67] American Battle Monuments Commission, *American Armies and Battlefields*, 501 and 515.

[68] American Battle Monuments Commission, *American Armies and Battlefields*, 515.

[69] "POWs and MIAs: Status and Accounting Issues," Congressional Research Service, *EveryCRSReport.com*, accessed 6-3-2020, https://www.everycrsreport.com/reports/RL33452.html#_Toc225931061.

[70] American Battle Monuments Commission, *American Armies and Battlefields*, 515.

[71] "America's Wars," Department of Veterans Affairs, Office of Public Affairs, *VA.gov*, accessed May 11, 2023, https://www.va.gov/opa/publications/factsheets/fs_americas_wars.pdf.

[72] History.com Editors, "U.S. President Woodrow Wilson Signs National Defense Act," *History. com*, accessed March 6, 2022, https://www.history.com/this-day-in-history/u-s-president-woodrow-wilson-signs-national-defense-act.

FROM ONE WAR TO ANOTHER

73 Bernard M. Baruch, *American Industry in the War: A Report of the War Industries Board* (New York: Prentice-Hall, 1941), 17.

74 "Efficiency Board of Advisors Named/Seven to Aid in Planning for National Defense/President Wilson Outlines Aim of Continuous Preparedness," *Boston Globe*, October 12, 1916, 10, accessed March 6, 2022, as subscriber to *Newspapers.com*.

75 "Wilson Names 7 Advisers for the U.S. Defense Council: Daniel Willard, Samuel Gompers and Bernard Baruch Are in List—President Says Selections Are Made Without Regard to Party," *New York Herald*, October 12, 1916, 1, accessed March 6. 2022 as subscriber to *Newspapers. com*, https://www.newspapers.com/image/207217691/?terms=Wilson%20Names%207%20 Advisers&match=1.

76 "Efficiency Board of Advisers," *Boston Globe*, 10.

77 Robert Longley, "War Industries Board: History and Purpose," *ThoughtCo.com*, accessed March 11, 2022, https://www.thoughtco.com/war-industries-board-history-and-purpose-5181082.

78 Bernard M. Baruch, "Final Report of the United States War Industries Board as Submitted to President Wilson by its Chairman Bernard M. Baruch," December 24, 1919, 2, Internet Archive, *Archive.org*, accessed May 7, 2023, https://archive.org/details/UnitedStatesWarIndustriesBoard.

79 Arthur Herman, *Freedom's Forge* (New York: Random House Trade Paperbacks, 2012), 77; Margaret L. Coit, *Mr. Baruch* (Boston: Houghton Mifflin Company, 1957), 166.

80 Herman, *Freedom's Forge*, 12.

81 Coit, *Mr. Baruch*, 167-170.

82 Coit, *Mr. Baruch*, 170-171.

83 Coit, *Mr. Baruch*, 171.

84 Coit, *Mr. Baruch*, 171.

85 Herman, *Freedom's Forge*, 77.

86 Coit, *Mr. Baruch*, 220.

87 Benjamin R. Beede, "War Industries Board," 1914-1918 *Online International Encyclopedia of the First World War*, accessed March 7, 2022, https://encyclopedia.1914-1918-online.net/article/war_industries_board.

88 American Battle Monuments Commission, *A Guide to the American Battle Fields*, 10.

89 American Battle Monuments Commission, *American Armies and Battlefields*, 515.

90 American Battle Monuments Commission, *A Guide to the American Battlefields*, 11.

91 American Battle Monuments Commission, *American Armies and Battlefields*, 515.

92 Carroll, *My Fellow Soldiers*, 153-154.

93 American Battle Monuments Commission, *American Armies and Battlefields*, 515.

Notes

[94] American Battle Monuments Commission, *A Guide to the American Battle Fields*, 16.

[95] American Battle Monuments Commission, *American Armies and Battlefields*, 17.

[96] American Battle Monuments Commission, *American Armies and Battlefields*, 17.

[97] Michael S. Nieberg and Harold K. Johnson (respectively chairman and professor at U.S. Army War College), "Pershing's Decision: How the United States Fought Its First Modern Coalition War," December 10, 2010, U.S. Army, *Army.mil*, accessed June 3, 2020, https://www.army.mil/article/49291/pershings_decision_how_the_united_states_fought_its_first_modern_coalition_war.

[98] American Battle Monuments Commission, *American Armies and Battlefields*, 17-18.

[99] American Battle Monuments Commission, *American Armies and Battlefields*, 17-18.

[100] American Battle Monuments Commission, *A Guide to the American Battle Fields*, 16.

[101] "1st Division (RA) Record of Events," U.S, Army Center of Military History, *History.Army. mil*, accessed June 30, 2020, https://history.army.mil/books/wwi/ob/1-ROE-OB.htm.

[102] American Battle Monuments Commission, *American Armies and Battlefields*, 17-18.

[103] Carroll, *My Fellow Soldiers*, 183.

[104] Carroll, *My Fellow Soldiers*, 213.

[105] Carroll, *My Fellow Soldiers*, 219.

Chapter 3: THE IMPORTANCE OF MEDICAL SUPPORT

[1] Department of Foreign Affairs, *America's Wars*, Department of Veterans' Affairs, *Va.gov.* accessed May 7, 2023, www.va.gov/opa/publications/factsheets/fs_americas_wars.pdf.

[2] Andrew Carroll, *My Fellow Soldiers: General John Pershing and the Americans Who Helped Win the Great War* (New York: Penguin Books, 2017), 110.

[3] American Battle Monuments Commission, *American Armies and Battlefields in Europe: A History, Guide, and Reference Book* (Washington, D.C.: Government Printing Office, 1938) (Reprinted in Delaware, MD: Center of Military History, United States Army, 2019), 437-438.

[4] Isaac F. Marcosson, *S.O.S.: America's Miracle in France* (New York: John Lane Company, 1919), 21.

[5] Major F. W. Nichol, "Logistics—Before and After Victory," *Think: Think Magazine's Diary of U.S. Participation in World War II* (New York, NY: International Business Machines Corporation, 1950), 322.

[6] Stan Moore, *Seasaw: How November '42 Shaped the Future* (Scotts Valley, CA: CreateSpace Publishing Company, 2012) (Reprinted in 2021 in Middletown, DE), purchased from Stan Moore by author in 2021), 43.

[7] Marcosson, *S.O.S.*, 23.

FROM ONE WAR TO ANOTHER

[8] Marcosson, *S.O.S.*, 28-29.

[9] R. Elberton Smith, *The Army and Economic Mobilization* (Washington, D.C.: Center of Military History, U.S. Army, 1991), 39.

[10] Brief Overview of the Medical Department," WW2 US Medical Research Centre, *Med-Dept. com*, accessed March 12, 2022, https://www.med-dept.com/articles/brief-overview-of-the-medical-department/.

[11] Charles Lynch, Frank W. Weed, and Loy McAfee, *The Medical Department of the United States in the World War, Volume I: The Surgeon General's Office* (Washington, D.C.: Government Printing Office, 1923), 117-118, National Library of Medicine Digital Collections, https://collections.nlm.nih.gov/bookviewer?PID=nlm:nlmuid-14120390RX1-mvpart.

[12] Brief Overview of the Medical Department," *Med-Dept.com.*

[13] Major General Merritte W. Ireland, Surgeon General (directed the publishing of fifteen volumes from 1921 to 1929), *The Medical Department of the United States Army in the World War*, Volumes 1-15 (Washington, 1921-1929), https://www.kumc.edu/school-of-medicine/academics/departments/history-and-philosophy-of-medicine/archives/wwi/essays/further-study/medical-department.html.

[14] Jonathan H. Jaffin, "Medical Support for the American Expeditionary Forces in France During the First World War," (Thesis for Master of Military Art and Science, U.S. Army Command and General Staff College, Fort Leavenworth, KS, 1990), 17, AMEED Center of History & Heritage, *ACHH.Army.mil*, accessed May 7, 2023, https://achh.army.mil/history/book-wwi-jaffin-default.

[15] Jaffin, "Medical Support," 22.

[16] Jaffin, "Medical Support," 18-21.

[17] Wallis Landes Craddock, "The Achievements of William Crawford Gorgas," *Military Medicine, Vol. 162*, May 1967, 325-327, accessed August 25, 2018, https://academic.oup.com/milmed/article-abstract/162/5/325/4831513.

[18] Merritte W. Ireland, "Memoir of Major General Merritte W. Ireland," *AMEDD Center of History & Heritage*, accessed March 13, 2022, https://ckapfwstor001.blob.core.usgovcloudapi.net/achh/MGMerritteIreland.pdf.

[19] John Campbell, "Medicine on the Battlefield," *Tar Heel Junior Historian*, reprinted on *NCPedia.org* with permission of *Tar Heels Junior Historian*, Spring 1993, accessed March 13, 2022, https://www.ncpedia.org/wwi-medicine-battlefield.

[20] Hew Strachan, *The First World War* (New York: Viking, 2004), 163.

[21] Joseph F. Ahern (Adjudication Officer, Veterans Administration, Lyons, NJ), "Letter to Mrs. Anna Cooney," December 6, 1939 (courtesy of her son Peter Clooney).

[22] Eduardo Faerstein and Warren Winkelstein Jr., "William Gorgas, Yellow Fever Meets Its Nemesis," *Epidemiology, Volume 22, Number 6*, November 2011, 872, accessed March 13, 2022, https://journals.lww.com/epidem/Fulltext/2011/11000/William_Gorgas__Yellow_Fever_Meets_Its_Nemesis.18.aspx.

[23] Nancy Bristow, "Pandemic Then and Now: Lessons from the 1918 Influenza," The National WWI Museum and Memorial, *TheWorldWar.org*, accessed March 13, 2022, https://www.theworldwar.org/learn/wwi/influenza.

Notes

[24] Albert G. Love, *Volume XV, Statistics, Part Two, Medical and Casualty Statistics, The Medical Department of the United States in the World War* (Washington, D.C.: Government Printing Office, 1925), Table 122: Admissions, Deaths. Discharges, and Days Lost, 1183, *Collections. NLM.NIH.gov*, accessed via National Library of Medicine Digital Collections on March 5, 2024, https://collections.nlm.nih.gov/bookviewer?PID=nlm:nlmuid-14120390RX17-mvpart.

[25] Robert Gaynes, "The Discovery of Penicillin—New Insights After More Than 75 Years of Clinical Use," U.S. National Center for Biotechnology Information, National Library of Medicine, National Institute of Health, *NCBI.NLM.NIH.gov*, accessed March 13 2022, https://www.ncbi.nlm.nih.gov/pmc/articles/PMC5403050/.

[26] "America's Wars," Department of Veterans Affairs, Office of Public Affairs, *VA.gov*, accessed May 11, 2023, https://www.va.gov/opa/publications/factsheets/fs_americas_wars.pdf.

[27] Sanders Marble (Borden Institute, U.S. Army Medical Department, Fort Sam Houston, Texas), *Skilled and Resolute: A History of the 12th Evacuation Hospital and the 212th Mash, 1917-2006* (Falls Church, Virginia: Office of the Surgeon General, United States Army, 2013), 5.

[28] Charles Lynch, Joseph H. Ford, and Frank W. Weed, *The Medical Department of the United States in the World War, Volume VIII: Field Operations* (Washington, D.C.: Government Printing Office,1925), 19, accessed via National Library of Medicine Digital Collections, https://collections.nlm.nih.gov/bookviewer?PID=nlm:nlmuid-14120390RX8-mvpart.

[29] Jaffin, "Medical Support," 55.

[30] Lisa M. Budreau and Richard M. Prior (Editors), *Answering the Call: The U.S. Army Nurse Corps, 1917-1919, A Commemorative Tribute to Military Nursing in World War I* (Washington, D.C.: Office of The Surgeon General, Department of the Army, 2008), 97.

[31] Jaffin, "Medical Support," 2.

[32] American Battle Monuments Commission, *American Armies and Battlefields in Europe*, 501; Lynch, Ford, and Weed, *Field Operations*, 157.

[33] American Battle Monuments Commission, *American Armies and Battlefields in Europe*, 158.

[34] Newton D. Baker, *Annual Report of the Secretary of War 1918* (Washington, D.C.: Government Printing Office, 1918), 23.

[35] Robert U. Patterson (produced by his directive as the Surgeon General from 1931 to 1935), *In Memoriam, The Medical Department of the United States Army in the World War, Volume 1, Supplement, Army Medical Bulletin No 27*, produced in memory of and lists the Commissioned Officers of the Medical Department and the members of the Army Nurse Corps who died in active service between April 1, 1917, and June 30, 1920 (Carlisle Barracks, PA: Medical Field Service School, publication date unknown), 1.

[36] Baker, *Annual Report of the Secretary of War*, 21.

[37] Patterson, *In Memoriam*, 7.

[38] Jaffin, "Medical Support," 166.

[39] Jaffin, "Medical Support," 166.

[40] "WWI Service Record of John J. Cooney (WWI)," State of New Jersey, Department of State, (Trenton, NJ: New Jersey State Archives, PO Box 307, Trenton, NJ 08625-0307), Form ORM No. 42, A.G.O. (For National Army).

[41] "U.S. World War I Draft Registration Cards, 1917-1918," s.v. "John Cooney," accessed on August 4, 2022, as subscriber to *Ancestry.com*, https://www.ancestry.com/discoveryui-content/view /33472940:6482?tid=&pid=&queryId=00e253dbd055030da5bab3ec082e381a&_phsrc=zsS283&_ phstart=successSource.

[42] "World War I Draft Registration Cards," s.v. "John Cooney."

[43] Stephen G. Melly, "Camp Dix: 95 Years of Army Heritage," Joint Base McGuire-Dix-Lakehurst, NJ: Army Support Activity, July 18, 2014, *JBMDL.JB.mil*, accessed March 18, 2022, https://www.jbmdl.jb.mil/News/Article-Display/Article/826576/camp-dix-95-years-of-army-heritage/#:~:text=Camp%20Dix%20served%20as%20a,Camp%20Dix%20to%20Fort%20Dix; Phil Gast, "The Civil War Picket," *Civil-War-Picket.Blogspot.com*, March 8 2018, accessed March 18, 2022, http://civil-war-picket.blogspot.com/2018/03/shoot-him-on-spot-letter-that-made.html.

[44] "Women in Uniform," *Encyclopedia.com*, accessed March 18, 2022, https://www.encyclopedia.com/ social-sciences-and-law/political science-and-government/military-affairs-nonnaval/women-military.

[45] "A Pictorial History of a National Army Cantonment," *Camp Dix Pictorial Review*, November 1917, 21, accessed March 18, 2022, http://www.afhmus.org/wp-content/uploads/1917.pdf.

[46] "Fort Dix," *en.wikipedia.org*, accessed March 18, 2022, https://en.wikipedia.org/wiki/Fort_Dix.

[47] "WWI Service Record of John J. Cooney," State of New Jersey.

[48] Jaffin, "Medical Support," 1-2.

[49] Jaffin, "Medical Support," 82-87.

[50] Marble, *Skilled and Resolute*, 1-2.

[51] Marble, *Skilled and Resolute*, 2-4

[52] Marcosson, *S.O.S.*, 81.

[53] Marcosson, *S.O.S.*, 82.

[54] "Atterbury, William Wallace, BG," Together We Served Roll of Honor, U.S. Army, *Army. TogetherWeServed.com*, accessed February 5, 2024, https://army.togetherweserved.com/army/ servlet/tws.webapp.WebApp?cmd=ShadowBoxProfile&type=Person&ID=338503.

[55] E. M. Foxwell, "The U.S. Female Doctors Who Served in WWI," American Women in World War I, March 9, 2017, *AmericanWomeninWWI.WordPress.com*. accessed March 20, 2022, https:// americanwomeninwwi.wordpress.com/2017/03/09/the-u-s-female-doctors-who-served-in-wwi/.

[56] Foxwell, "The U.S. Female Doctors."

[57] "Dr. Margaret D. Craighill," Changing the Face of Medicine, U.S. National Library of Medicine, *CFMedicine.nlm.nih.gov*, accessed March 20, 2022, https://cfmedicine.nlm.nih.gov/physicians/ biography_72.html.

Notes

[58] "The Evacuation Hospital," Appendix, *AMEDD Center of History & Heritage*, 854-858, accessed March 20, 2022, https://achh.army.mil/history/book-wwi-adminamerexp-apend1report.

[59] *Lexico.com*, s.v. "quartermaster," accessed March 20, 2022, lexico,com/en/definition/quartermaster.

[60] Harry B. Rodcay, "Soldier's Letter," *The Fulton County News*, July 18, 1918, 1, digital image, accessed March 20, 2022, as subscriber to *Newspapers.com*, https://www.newspapers.com/image/194147246/?terms=Harry%20B.%20Rodcay%2C%20%22Soldier%27s%20Letter%2C%22%20&match=1.

[61] "WWI Service Record of John J. Cooney," State of New Jersey.

[62] "Evacuation Hospital No. 12," United States War Department, *Report of the Surgeon General, U. S. Army, to the Secretary of War, 1919, Volume II* (Washington, D.C.: Government Printing Office, 1919), 1713, *US.Archive.org*, https://ia600706.us.archive.org/6/items/reportofsurgeong19192unit/reportofsurgeong19192unit_bw.pdf. (Note: Different sections of this report are cited in this chapter as "*Surgeon General*," along with the page numbers.)

[63] "City of Exeter," *Passengers in History*, South Australian Maritime Museum, accessed March 20, 2022, https://passengers.history.sa.gov.au/node/923022.

[64] "SS *Archangel*," *WreckSite.edu*, accessed March 20, 2022, https://www.wrecksite.eu/wreck.aspx?61940.

[65] "Evacuation Hospital No. 12," *Surgeon General*, 1713.

[66] "Evacuation Hospital No. 12," *Surgeon General*, 1713.

[67] "Evacuation Hospital No. 12," *Surgeon General*, 1713-1714.

[68] Alexander Macomber and Meade Brunet (Editors), *The 56th Engineers in the World War* (Albany, NY: The Brandow Printing Company, 1920), 66. (Published by Scholar Select, Andesite Press, an imprint of Creative Media Partners.)

[69] Charles Hendricks, "Combat and Construction: U.S. Army Engineers in World War I," (Fort Belvoir, Virginia: Office of History, U.S. Army Corps of Engineers, 1993), 66.

[70] Macomber and Brunet (Editors), *The 56th Engineers in the World War*, 9-10.

[71] "Evacuation Hospital No. 12," *Surgeon General*, 1714.

[72] William N. Bispham, *The Medical Department of the United States in the World War, Volume VII, Training* (Washington, D.C.: Government Printing Office, 1927), 183, accessed via National Library of Medicine Digital Collections, https://collections.nlm.nih.gov/bookviewer?PID=nlm:nlmuid-14120390RX7-mvpart.

[73] "Evacuation Hospital No. 1," *Surgeon General*, 1677.

[74] "Evacuation Hospital No. 1," *Surgeon General*, 1677.

[75] "Evacuation Hospital No. 1," *Surgeon General*, 1677.

[76] "Reports of Chief Surgeons of Armies," *Surgeon General*, 1508.

FROM ONE WAR TO ANOTHER

[77] "Evacuation Hospital No. 1," *Surgeon General*, 1677-1678.

[78] Lynch, Ford, and Weed, *Field Operations*, 507-508.

[79] "Evacuation Hospital No. 1," *Surgeon General*, 1677.

[80] Stephen Scarpa, "Wallingford Honors WWI Fighter Pilot," *Myrecordjournal.com*, May 5, 2018, accessed March 21, 2022, https://www.myrecordjournal.com/News/Wallingford/Wallingford-News/World-War-I-flying-ace-Raoul-Lufbery-honored-in-Wallingford-on-centennial-of-his-death.html.

[81] "Lufbery, Gervais Raoul, Military Combat/Military Strategist, Enshrined 1998," The National Aviation Hall of Fame, *NationalAviation.com*, accessed March 21, 2022, https://www.nationalaviation.org/our-enshrinees/lufbery-gervais-raoul/#:~:text=For%20the%20courage%20and%20valor,National%20Aviation%20Hall%20of%20Fame.

[82] T.B. Murphy, *Kiffin Rockwell, the Lafayette Escadrille and the Birth of the United States Air Force* (Jefferson, NC: McFarland & Company, 2016), 159.

[83] David Drury, "World War I Flying Ace Raoul Lufbery," April 6, 2020, *Connecticuthistory.org*, accessed March 21, 2022, https://www.connecticuthistory.org/world-war-i-flying-ace-raoul-lufbery.

[84] Eddie V. Rickenbacker, *Fighting the Flying Circus* (Garden City, NY: Doubleday & Company, 1965), 193.

[85] Eddie Rickenbacker, "How Lufbery, America's Greatest Ace, Was Killed," Sunday Globe Editorial and News Feature Section, *Boston Globe*, May 25,1919, 2, accessed May 11, 2023, as subscriber of *Newspapers.com*, https://www.newspapers.com/.image/430801251/?terms=Lufbery.

[86] American Battle Monuments Commission, "Lafayette Escadrille Memorial Cemetery," *ABMC.gov*, accessed March 21, 2022, https://www.abmc.gov/Lafayette-Escadrille.

[87] "History," American Battle Monuments Commission, *ABMC.gov*, accessed March 21, 2022, https://www.abmc.gov/about-us/history#:~:text=On%20March%204%2C%201923%2C%20President,honoring%20the%20American%20Expeditionary%20Forces.

[88] "Evacuation Hospital No. 1," *Surgeon General*, 1677.

[89] "WWI Service Record of John J. Cooney," State of New Jersey.

[90] "WWI Service Record of John J. Cooney," State of New Jersey.

[91] "Evacuation Hospital No. 37," *Surgeon General*, 1739.

[92] "Evacuation Hospital No. 37," *Surgeon General*, 1740.

[93] Lynch, Ford, and Weed, *Field Operations*, 23.

[94] *The World Book Encyclopedia* (Chicago, IL: Field Enterprises Educational Corporation, 1968), s.v. "Joan of Arc, Saint," Volume 11, 106-107.

[95] Lynch, Ford, and Weed, *Field Operations*, 23.

Notes

[96] "Evacuation Hospital No. 37," *Surgeon General*, 1740.

[97] Frederick M. Dearborn, "Forty-Eight, A History of U.S. Army Base Hospital No. 48, Mars Hospital Center 1919," *American Homeopathy in the World War*, accessed March 22, 2022, http://homeoint.org/books2/ww1/48mars19.htm.

[98] "Base Hospital No. 48," AMEDD Center of History & Heritage, Chapter XXIV, Base Hospitals, 674, *ACHH.Army.mil*, accessed March 22, 2022, https://achh.army.mil/history/book-wwi-adminamerexp-chapter24.

[99] Frederick M, Dearborn, "Forty-Eight, A History of U.S. Army Base Hospital No. 48, Our Nurses," *American Homeopathy in the World War*, accessed March 22, 2022, http://homeoint.org/books2/ww1/48nurses.htm.

[100] "Base Hospital No. 48," *ACHH.Army.mil*.

[101] "Hospital Centers," *Surgeon General*, 1340.

[102] "Mars Hospital Center," *Surgeon General*, 1849.

[103] Merritte W. Ireland, "Hospital Center, Mars-Sur-Allier," *The Medical Department of the United States in the World War, Volume II, Administration American Expeditionary Forces* (Washington, D.C.: Government Printing Office, 1927), 575, National Library of Medicine Digital Collections, accessed May 11, 2023, https://collections.nlm.nih.gov/bookviewer?PID=nlm:nlmuid-14120390RX2-mvpart.

[104] Rebecca Goethe DeVries, "The Fiftieth Anniversary of the Armistice, A Testimony from Beyond the Atlantic by Rebecca Goethe DeVries about the Former American Hospital Installed at Mars-sur Allier," *Stories of World War I in France/La Grande Guerre*, March 12, 2010, accessed March 25, 2022, https://franceworldwarone.blogspot.com/2010/03/fiftieth-anniversary-of-armistice.html.

[105] "Mars Hospital Center," *Surgeon General*, 1849-1850.

[106] Dearborn, "Base Hospital No. 48."

[107] "The Yesterday and Today of Mars Hospital Center," *The Martian* (Camp Newspaper, U.S. Base Hospital No. 48, A.E.F., France WWI), April 27, 1919, 3, accessed March 23, 2022, http://freepages.rootsweb.com/~gregkrenzelok/genealogy/martinnewspaperbhno48.html.

[108] Dearborn, "Base Hospital No. 48."

[109] "Base Hospital No. 80," *Surgeon General*, 1988.

[110] Lucy DeVries Duffy "Rebecca and Charles: A Testimony from Beyond the Atlantic," Special to The United States World War I Centennial Commission, accessed March 27, 2022, https://www.worldwar1centennial.org/index.php/communicate/press-media/wwi-centennial-news/2388-rebecca-and-charles-a-testimony-from-beyond-the-atlantic.html.

[111] Lucy DeVries Duffy, "A Brewster-French Armistice Day Connection," *The Patriot Ledger*, posted November 11, 2015, accessed March 27, 2022, https://www.patriotledger.com/article/20151111/news/151119724.

[112] Abe Cohen, "Yanks at Bordeaux Put Through Mill," *The Tacoma Daily Ledger* (Tacoma, Washington), February 26, 1919, 6, accessed March 26, 2022, as subscriber of *Newspapers.com*.

[113] "John J. Cooney," Evacuation Hospital No. 37, Passenger List of USS *Virginia* leaving Brest, France, on June 23, 1919, and arriving in Boston, MA, on July 5, 1919, accessed on March 26, 2022, as subscriber to *Fold3.com*, https://www.fold3.com/image/604475731?rec=628006347.

[114] "Championship to Dempsey: Willard Quits After Third," *Boston Globe*, July 5, 1919, 1, accessed March 27, 2022, as subscriber to *Newspapers.com*, https://www.newspapers.com/image/430818813/?terms=Championship%20to%20Dempsey%3A%20Willard%20Quits%20After%20Third.

[115] Jerry Schmidt (volunteer, Edward Jones Research Center Attendant, World War I Museum and Memorial, Kansas City, MO) email to author, August 8, 1915.

Chapter 4: DECISIVE BATTLES

[1] Andrew Carroll, *My Fellow Soldiers: General Pershing and the Americans Who Helped to Win the Great War* (New York: Penguin Books, 2017), 262-263.

[2] American Battle Monuments Commission, "The Founding of the Supreme War Council in World War I," November 7, 2017, *ABMC.gov*, accessed May 11, 2022, https://www.abmc.gov/news-events/news/founding-supreme-war-council-world-war-i.

[3] Ferdinand Foch, translated by T. Bentley Mott, *The Memoirs of Marshall Foch* (New York: Doubleday, Doran and Company, 1931), 257-258.

[4] Foch, *Memoirs*, 265.

[5] Foch, *Memoirs*, 306; "African Americans in the Military during World War I," National Archives, *Archives.gov*, accessed June 9, 2022, https://www.archives.gov/research/african-americans/wwi/war.

[6] Michael Ray, *Encyclopedia Britannica Online*, s.v. "Harlem Hellfighters," accessed Jun 15, 2022, https://www.britannica.com/topic/Harlem-Hellfighters.

[7] Foch, *Memoirs*, 303-308.

[8] Foch, *Memoirs*, 278.

[9] Joseph J. DiDomenico, "The Rise and Fall of a Coalition: The Supreme War Council and Marshal Foch," (Monograph, School for Advanced Military Studies, United States Army Command and General Support College, Fort Leavenworth, Kansas, 2027), 17-18, *Academia.edu*, https://www.academia.edu/32463685/The_Rise_and_Fall_of_a_Coalition_The_Supreme_War_Council_and_Marshal_Foch_1917_1919.

[10] Joseph C. Greaney and Spencer C. Tucker, "Calias Conference (26 February 1917)," Spencer C. Tucker and Priscilla Roberts, editors, *World War I: Encyclopedia, Volume I: A-D* (Santa Barbara, CA: ABC-CLIO, 2005), 249.

[11] David L. Roll, *George Marshall: Defender of the Republic* (New York: Dutton Caliber, 2019), 22.

[12] DiDomenico, "The Rise and Fall of a Coalition," 18.

[13] DiDomenico, "The Rise and Fall of a Coalition," 23.

[14] DiDomenico, "The Rise and Fall of a Coalition," 30-33.

Notes

[15] Foch, *Memoirs*, 403-404.

[16] Foch, *Memoirs*, 370.

[17] Foch, *Memoirs*, 372-373.

[18] Foch, *Memoirs*, 371.

[19] Foch, *Memoirs*, 373.

[20] "The Hundred Days Offensive," The National WWI Museum and Memorial, *TheWorldWar.org*, accessed May 11, 2022, https://www.theworldwar.org/learn/about-wwi/hundred-days-offensive.

[21] Foch, *Memoirs*, 393.

[22] Foch, *Memoirs*, 393-394.

[23] John J. Pershing, *My Experiences in the World War, Volumes 1 & 2* (Originally published in New York: Frederick A. Stokes Company, 1931; republished in Middletown, DE, 2019), 557-558.

[24] Pershing, *My Experiences*, 562.

[25] Carroll, *My Fellow Soldiers*, 265-266; Pershing, *My Experiences*, 566-567.

[26] Carroll, *My Fellow Soldiers*, 267-268, 278; Pershing, *My Experiences*, 575.

[27] Carroll, *My Fellow Soldiers*, 353.

[28] Jonathan Boff, "Foch's Grand Offensive: The Biggest Battle You've Never Heard Of," *HistoryExtra.com*, accessed May 11, 2022, https://www.historyextra.com/period/first-world-war/ww1-fochs-grand-hundred-days-offensive-battle-allies-germany-france-armistice/.

[29] Pershing, *My Experiences*, 566.

[30] American Battle Monuments Commission, *American Armies and Battlefields in Europe* (Washington, D.C.: Government Printing Office, 1938), 106-107.

[31] Pershing, *My Experiences*, 565.

[32] American Battle Monuments Commission, *American Armies and Battlefields*, 106.

[33] Pershing, *My Experiences*, 566.

[34] Carroll, *My Fellow Soldiers*, 342.

[35] David Zabecki, "Mentor to the Stars: The WW1 Officer Who Molded America's Top WW2 Generals," World War II Magazine, *WorldWar1Centennial.org*, accessed May 2, 2022, https://www.worldwar1centennial.org/index.php/communicate/press-media/wwi-centennial-news/1336-mentor-to-the-stars-the-man-behind-eisenhower-and-patton.html.

[36] Pershing, *My Experiences*, 572 and 575; American Battle Monuments Commission, *American Armies and Battlefields*, 110.

[37] "The American Expeditionary Forces, " Stars and Stripes Collection: The American Soldiers' Newspaper of World War I, 1918 to 1919, Library of Congress, *LoC.gov*, accessed May 2,

2022, https://www.loc.gov/collections/stars-and-stripes/articles-and-essays/a-world-at-war/american-expeditionary-forces/; American Battle Monuments Commission, *American Armies and Battlefields*, 110.

[38] Carroll, *My Fellow Soldiers*, 279.

[39] Pershing, *My Experiences*, 574-575.

[40] William Mitchell, *Memoirs of World War I: "From Start to Finish of Our Greatest War"* (New York: Random House, 1960), 238-239.

[41] Pershing, *My Experiences*, 575; American Battle Monuments Commission, *American Armies and Battlefields*, 109.

[42] American Battle Monuments Commission, *American Armies and Battlefields*, 112.

[43] Carroll, *My Fellow Soldiers*, 269.

[44] Newton D. Baker, *Annual Report of the Secretary of War* (Washington, D.C.: Government Printing Office, 1918), 76.

[45] "German Comments of the Attack," The Project Gutenberg eBook (Michelin & Cie, *The Americans in the Great War, Volume II, The Battle of St. Mihiel (St. Mihiel, Pont-à-Mousson, Metz)*, 1920), *Gutenberg.org*, https://www.gutenberg.org/files/50412/50412-h/50412-h.htm.

[46] Baker, *Annual Report*, 76.

[47] John Gilbert Thompson and Inez Bigwood, *Lest We Forget: World War Stories* (Boston, New York, and Chicago: Silver, Burdett, and Company, 1918), 335.

[48] Thompson and Bigwood, *Lest We Forget*, 335; Pershing, *My Experiences*, 581.

[49] Pershing, *My Experiences*, 581.

[50] Pershing, *My Experiences*, 581-582.

[51] Minnie L. Jones (Installation Management Command, U.S. Army), "William 'Billy' Mitchell—'The Father of the United States Air Force'," October 17, 2009, *Army.mil*, https://www.army.mil/article/33680/william_billy_mitchell_the_father_of_the_united_states_air_force.

[52] Booth Mooney, *General Billy Mitchell* (Chicago: Follett Publishing Company, 1968), 8.

[53] Ruth Mitchell, *My Brother Bill: A Biography of General Mitchell* (New York: Harcourt, Brace and Company, 1953), 24-25

[54] Mitchell, *My Brother Bill*, 25-28.

[55] Mitchell, *My Brother Bill*, 28-31.

[56] Mooney, *General Billy Mitchell*, 12-13.

[57] C.V. Glines, "William 'Billy' Mitchell: Air Power Visionary," *Historynet.com*, June 12, 2006, accessed May 5, 2022, https://www.historynet.com/william-billy-mitchell-an-air-power-visionary/.

[58] Mooney, *General Billy Mitchell*, 33-34.

Notes

[59] Mitchell, *My Brother Bill*, 52-53.

[60] Mooney, *General Billy Mitchell*, 42.

[61] Mitchell, *My Brother Bill*, 63-64.

[62] Mitchell, *My Brother Bill*, 60.

[63] Mitchell, *My Brother Bill*, 77.

[64] Mitchell. *My Brother Bill*, 108.

[65] Mitchell, *My Brother Bill*, 107-111.

[66] Mitchell, *My Brother Bill*, 112.

[67] Mitchell, *My Brother Bill*, 161.

[68] Jason Wenger, "WAMCATS: The Washington-Alaska Military Cable and Telegraph System," *LitsiteAlaska.org*, accessed May 5, 2022, http://www.litsitealaska.org/index.cfm?section=digital-archives&page=Industry&cat=Media-and-Communications&viewpost=2&ContentId=2613.

[69] Mitchell, *My Brother Bill*, 159.

[70] William M. Higginbotham (Air Force Network Integration Center), "The Birth of Powered Flight and Air-to-Ground Communications," accessed May 5, 2021, https://www.cyberspacecapabilitiescenter.af.mil/News/Article-Display/Article/1507182/the-birth-of-powered-flight-and-air-to-ground-communications/.

[71] Stephen L. McFarland, *A Concise History of the U.S. Air Force* (Washington, D.C.: Air Force History and Museums Program, Air Force Fiftieth Anniversary Commemorative Edition, 1997), 2.

[72] Wisconsin Historical Society, "First to Fly—Army Demonstration," accessed May 5, 2022, https://www.wisconsinhistory.org/Records/Image/IM10400.

[73] McFarland, *A Concise History*, 2.

[74] McFarland, *A Concise History*, 3.

[75] David Langley, "The Life and Times of Glenn Hammond Curtiss," The Aviation History On-Line Museum, *Aviation-History.com*, November 18, 2009, http://aviation-history.com/early/curtiss.htm.

[76] McFarland, *A Concise History*, 3.

[77] Jones, "William 'Billy' Mitchell."

[78] Bert Frandsen, "Learning and Adapting: Billy Mitchell in World War I," *Joint Force Quarterly Online*, Issue 72, First Quarter 2014, National Defense University Press, accessed May 5, 2022, https://ndupress.ndu.edu/JFQ/Joint-Force-Quarterly-72/Article/577489/learning-and-adapting-billy-mitchell-in-world-war-i/.

[79] McFarland, *A Concise History*, 3-4; Gary Glynn, "1st Aero Squadron in Pursuit of Pancho Villa," *Historynet.com*, accessed May 6, 2022, https://www.historynet.com/mexican-expedition-1st-aero-squadron-in-pursuit-of-pancho-villa/.

[80] Barret Tillman, *Forgotten Fifteenth: The Daring Airmen Who Crippled Hitler's War Machine* (Washington, D.C.: Regnery History, 2014), 28.

[81] Brian Hutchins, "General Nathan Twining and the Fifteenth Air Force in World War II," (Master's Thesis, University of North Texas, May 2008), 5, accessed August 17, 2023, https://digital.library.unt.edu/ark:/67531/metadc6094/m2/1/high_res_d/thesis.pdf.

[82] Edward A. Guiérrez, "Lafayette Escadrille," *1914-1918 Online, International Encyclopedia of the First World War*, accessed May 6, 2022, https://encyclopedia.1914-1918-online.net/article/lafayette_escadrille.

[83] McFarland, *A Concise History*, 3-7.

[84] McFarland, *A Concise History*, 5.

[85] McFarland, *A Concise History*, 5.

[86] "de Havilland DH-4", Smithsonian National Air and Space Museum, *AirandSpace.si.edu*, accessed May 7, 2022, https://airandspace.si.edu/collection-objects/de-havilland-dh-4/nasm_A19190051000.

[87] Edgar S. Gorrell, *The Measure of America's World War Aeronautical Effort* (Burlington, VT: The Lane Press, 1940), 70.

[88] American Battle Monuments Commission, *American Armies and Battlefields*, 110.

[89] Gorrell, *Measure of America's World War*, 53.

[90] Mitchell, *Memoirs*, 238.

[91] Mitchell, *Memoirs*, 240.

[92] Hew Strachan, *The First World War* (New York: Viking, 2004), 168.

[93] Erik Larson, *Dead Wake: The Last Crossing of the Lusitania* (New York: Crown Publishing Group, 2015), 189-190.

[94] Larson, *Dead Wake*, 337-343.

[95] Pershing, *My Experiences*, 181.

[96] Mitchell, *Memoirs*, 276.

[97] Pershing, *My Experiences*, 581-582.

[98] Carroll, *My Fellow Soldiers*, 265-266.

[99] Roll, *George Marshall*, 36 and 44.

[100] Roll, *George Marshall*, 42.

[101] Roll, *George Marshall*, 38.

[102] Pershing, *My Experiences*, 568.

Notes

[103] American Battle Monuments Commission, *American Armies and Battlefields*, 189.

[104] American Battle Monuments Commission, *American Armies and Battlefields*, 167.

[105] Roll, *George Marshall*, 44-45.

[106] Pershing, *My Experiences*, 602.

[107] Forrest C. Pogue, with the editorial assistance of Gordon Harrison, *George C. Marshall: Education of a General* (New York: Viking Press, 1963), 182.

[108] Dan Simonsen, "Book Review of Robert H. Ferrell's *America's Deadliest Battle:Meuse-Argonne, 1918*," November 17, 2010, Air University, *AirUniversity.af.edu*, accessed May 13, 2023, https://www.airuniversity.af.edu/SSQ/Book-Reviews/Article/1293339/americas-deadliest-battle-meuse-argonne-1918/.

[109] Carroll, *My Fellow Soldiers*, 316.

[110] "The Hundred Days Offensive," National WWI Museum.

[111] "The Hundred Days Offensive," National WWI Museum.

[112] Arthur Herman, *Freedom's Forge: How American Business Produced Victory in World War II* (New York: Random House, 2012), 77.

[113] Pershing, *My Experiences*, 680-681.

[114] "Medal of Honor Citation for Charles White Whittlesey," Military Times Hall of Valor (Doug Sterner, Contributing Editor and Curator), *Valor.MilitaryTimes.com*, accessed June 3, 2022, https://valor.militarytimes.com/hero/478.

[115] "Medal of Honor for Charles White Whittlesey," Military Times Hall of Valor.

[116] "Medal of Honor Citation for Alvin Cullium York," Military Times Hall of Valor (Doug Sterner, Contributing Editor and Curator), *Valor.MilitaryTimes.com*, accessed June 5, 2022, https://valor.militarytimes.com/hero/134.

[117] "Medal of Honor Citation for Samuel Woodfill," Military Times Hall of Valor (Doug Sterner, Contributing Editor and Curator), *Valor.MilitaryTimes.com*, accessed June 5, 2022, https://valor.militarytimes.com/hero/2842.

[118] Allen Mikaelian, with commentary by Mike Wallace, *Medal of Honor: Profiles of America's Military Heroes from the Civil War to the Present* (New York: Hyperion, 2002), 77.

[119] DiDomenico, "The Rise and Fall of a Coalition," 34.

[120] "The Fourteen Points: Woodrow Wilson and the U.S. Rejection of the Treaty of Versailles," The National WWI Museum and Memorial, *TheWorldWar.org*, accessed June 5, 2022, https://www.theworldwar.org/learn/peace/fourteen-points.

[121] DiDomenico, "The Rise and Fall of a Coalition," 35.

[122] Margaret MacMillan, *Paris 1919: Six Months That Changed the World* (New York: Random House, 2001), 19.

[123] MacMillan, *Paris 1919*, 18-19.

[124] "History of Veterans Day," U.S. Department of Veterans Affairs, *VA.gov*, accessed June 5, 2022, https://www.va.gov/opa/vetsday/vetdayhistory.asp.

[125] Blake Stilwell, "How Armistice Day Became Veterans Day," August 1, 2022, *Military.com*, accessed August 24, 2023, https://www.military.com/off-duty/2020/10/30/how-armistice-day-became-veterans-day.html.

Chapter 5: BETWEEN WORLD WARS

[1] Jonathan H. Jaffin, "Medical Support for the American Expeditionary Forces in France During the First World War," (Thesis for Master of Military Art and Science, U.S. Army Command and General Staff College, Fort Leavenworth, KS, 1990), 166, AMEED Center of History & Heritage, *ACHH.Army.mil*, accessed May 7, 2023, https://achh.army.mil/history/book-wwi-jaffin-default.

[2] "John J. Cooney," Evacuation Hospital No. 37, Passenger List of USS *Virginia* leaving Brest, France, on June 23, 1919, and arriving in Boston, MA, on July 5, 1919, accessed on March 26, 2022, as subscriber to *Fold3.com*, https://www.fold3.com/image/604475731?rec=628006347.

[3] Peter Cooney, email to author, September 4, 1914; Joan Stern, email to Peter Cooney, June 1, 2015.

[4] Stephen L. McFarland, *A Concise History of the U.S. Air Force* (Washington, D.C.: Air Force History and Museums Program, Air Force Fiftieth Anniversary Commemorative Edition, 1997), 29.

[5] *The World Book Encyclopedia* (Chicago, IL: Field Enterprises Educational Corporation, 1968), s.v. "World War I," Volume 20, 378-379.

[6] Margaret MacMillan, *Paris 1919: Six Months That Changed the World* (New York, Random House, 2001), vii.

[7] *The World Book Encyclopedia* (1968), s.v. "Versailles, Treaty of," Volume 19, 272-273.

[8] John D. Clare, "The Aims of 'the Big Three'," *JohnDClare.net*, accessed June 22, 2022, https://www.johndclare.net/peace_treaties3.htm.

[9] Clare, "Big Three."

[10] Clare, "Big Three."

[11] Clare, "Big Three."

[12] August Heckscher, *Woodrow Wilson* (Norwalk, CT: Easton Press, Collector's Edition, 1997), 513.

[13] Heckscher, *Woodrow Wilson*, 531.

[14] Heckscher, *Woodrow Wilson*, 534.

[15] Heckscher, *Woodrow Wilson*, 513.

[16] Patrick J, Kiger, "How World War I Fueled the Russian Revolution," *History.com*, accessed August 28, 2023, https://www.history.com/news/world-war-i-russian-revolution.

Notes

[17] "U.S. World War I Draft Registration Cards, 1917-1918," s.v. "Harry Osofsky," accessed on August 4, 2022, as subscriber to *Ancestry.com*, https://www.ancestry.com/discoveryui-content/view/16108370:6482?tid=&pid=&queryId=015756fee5978828b855ced5b271d6bf&_phsrc=zsS285&_phstart=successSource.

[18] Heckscher, *Woodrow Wilson*, 473.

[19] S.L.A. Marshall, *The American Heritage History of World War I* (New York: American Heritage Publishing Company, 1964), 228.

[20] History.com Editors," Treaties of Brest-Litovsk," August 21, 2018, updated November 9, 2009, *History.com*, accessed August 8, 2023, https://www.history.com/topics/world-war-i/treaties-of-brest-litovsk.

[21] John H, Wheeler-Bennett, *Brest-Litovsk: The Forgotten Peace, March 1918* (London: Macmillan and Co., 1939), xi.

[22] Wheeler-Bennett, *Brest-Litovsk*, 370-371.

[23] Heckscher, *Woodrow Wilson*, 534-535.

[24] Heckscher, *Woodrow Wilson*, 545.

[25] Heckscher, *Woodrow Wilson*, 545.

[26] Francis Perkins, *The Roosevelt I Knew* (New York: Penguin Books, reprint edition 2011), 16-19.

[27] MacMillan, *Paris 1919*, 492; Jennifer D. Keene, *World War I: The American Soldier Experience* (Lincoln, NB, and London: University of Nebraska Press, 2011), 28-29.

[28] Keene, *World War I*, 27-28.

[29] Keene, *World War I*, 28-29

[30] Keene, *World War I*, 29

[31] Heckscher, *Woodrow Wilson*, 616.

[32] Keene, *World War I*, 28-29; Nancy J, Skarmeas, *First Ladies of the White House* (Nashville, TN: Ideals Publications, 2004), 52; Margaret Brown Klapthor, *The First Ladies* (Washington, D.C.: White House Historical Association in cooperation with National Geographic Society, 1981), 65; Howard Markel, "When a Secret President Ran the Country," PBS NewsHour, October 2, 2015, *PBS.org*, https://www.pbs.org/newshour/health/woodrow-wilson-stroke.

[33] Klapthor, *The First Ladies*, 65.

[34] "Treaty of Versailles, 1919: Summary of the Principal Items," The Heritage of the Great War, *GreatWar.nl*, accessed July 9, 2022, https://greatwar.nl/versailles/versail-summary.html.

[35] "Treaty of Versailles," Heritage of the Great War.

[36] MacMillan, *Paris 1919*, 480.

[37] Office of the Historian, Foreign Service Institute, United States Department of State, "The Dawes Plan, the Young Plan, German Reparations, and Inter-allied War Debts," *History.State.gov*, accessed June 26, 2022, https://history.state.gov/milestones/1921-1936/dawes.

[38] Niall Ferguson, *The Pity of War: Explaining World War I* (New York: Basic Books, 1999), 397

[39] Erin Blakemore, "Germany's World War I Debt Was So Crushing It Took 92 Years to Pay Off," June 17, 2019, *History.com*, 27, 2019, https://www.history.com/news/germany-world-war-i-debt-treaty-versailles.

[40] Office of the Historian, "The Dawes Plan."

[41] David Crossland, "Germany Set to Make Final World War I Reparation Payment," September 29, 2010, *ABCnews.go.com*, https://abcnews.go.com/International/germany-makes-final-reparation-payments-world-war/story?id=11755920.

[42] Crossland, "Reparation Payment."

[43] MacMillan, *Paris 1919*, 180.

[44] "World War I, Versailles Settlement," *The Volume Library 1* (Nashville, TN: The Southwestern Company, 1988), 652.

[45] MacMillan, *Paris 1919*, 185.

[46] Clare, "Big Three."

[47] History.Com Editors, "Marshall Plan," updated June 5, 2020, *History.com*, https://www.history.com/topics/world-war-ii/marshall-plan-1.

[48] Office of the Historian, Foreign Services Institute, United States Department of State, "Occupation and Reconstruction of Japan, 1945-1952," *History.State.gov*, accessed June 27, 2022, https://history.state.gov/milestones/1945-1952/japan-reconstruction.

[49] Lindsay Maizland and Nathanael Cheng, "The U.S.-Japan Security Alliance," accessed June 26, 2022, https://www.cfr.org/backgrounder/us-japan-security-alliance; "Germany and the United States: Reliable Allies," Pew Research Center, *PewResearch.org*, accessed June 26, 2022, https://www.pewresearch.org/global/2015/05/07/germany-and-the-united-states-reliable-allies/.

[50] "WWI Service Record of John J. Cooney (WWI)," State of New Jersey, Department of State, (Trenton, NJ: New Jersey State Archives, PO Box 307, Trenton, NJ 08625-0307), Form ORM No. 42, A.G.O. (For National Army).

[51] Nancy Leo, "Uncle John," Speech at Remembrance Celebration for John J. Cooney, University Club in Manhattan, November 29, 2014.

[52] Peter Cooney (grandson of Peter Cooney), "A Short Genealogical History of the Cooney-Millon Family," (Written on March 1, 2011, and shared with the author on August 24, 2014).

[53] "Automatic Sewerage Ejector," *Municipal Journal and Engineer*, Volume 27, July-December 1909 (New York: Swetland Publishing Company, 1909), 375, University Library, Princeton, NJ, accessed June 29, 2022, https://books.google.com/books?id=2pVMAAAAYAAJ&pg=PA575&lpg=PA575&dq=municipal+journal+and+engineer,+Automatic+Sewerage+Ejection,+John+W.+Cooney&source=bl&ots=aXpGU5C8LO&sig=ACfU3U1M5xBNeGeJV1ACTZu2eMgjxUjHkw&hl=en&sa=X&ved=2ahUKEwjL19fEj9T4AhWKIEQIHchiBHIQ6AF6BAgCEAM#v=onepage&q=municipal%20journal%20and%20engineer%2C%20Automatic%20Sewerage%20Ejection%2C%20John%20W.%20Cooney&f=false.

Notes

[54] "Blair Building Sold to Stock Exchange: Purchase Is Step in Move to Provide for Market Expansion," *New York Times*, November 1, 1928, 31, accessed as subscriber to *New York Times*, https://www.nytimes.com/1928/11/01/archives/blair-building-sold-to-stock-exchange-purchase-is-step-in-move-to.html.

[55] Nancy Leo, "Uncle John."

[56] Paul J, Mateyunas, *Long Island's Gold Coast: Images of America* (Charleston, SC: Arcadia Publishing, 2012), 8-9 and back cover.

[57] Peter Cooney, "A Short Genealogical History."

[58] Peter Cooney, "A Short Genealogical History."

[59] "The Advantages of Family-Based Immigration," American Immigration Council, *American ImmigrationCouncil.org*, March 14, 2013, https://www.americanimmigrationcouncil.org/research/advantages-family-based-immigration.

[60] Jessica Fragoso, "Interview of John Cooney," *Heroes on Our Island* at Verizon FiOS 1 News, Greater New York City Area, Broadcast Media, August 31, 2010, https://www.youtube.com/watch?v=aQQgTuNxjiA. This video isn't available anymore.

[61] Kathleen Cooney Leo, phone conversation with author soon after her daughter, Nancy Leo, said in an email to author on June 1, 2015, that her mother would welcome a call from author to discuss her father John Sr. and her brother John. Author did not put a date on his notes but for this cite will put June 1, 2015.

[62] Peter Cooney, email message to author, September 4, 2014.

[63] "North Bergen Brothers Complete Year in Army," news clip from the now defunct *Hudson Dispatch* of Union City, NJ, sent to author by Peter Cooney. It states John Cooney entered the Army on May 15, 1943, and his brother Robert Cooney entered the Army two days later. John would serve with the Army Air Forces and Bob would transfer and serve with the Marine Corps during World War II.

[64] Joan Cooney Stern, email message to Peter Cooney, June 1, 2015, that Peter forwarded to the author on the same date.

[65] Nancy Leo, email message to author and family members, June 1, 2015.

[66] Kathleen Cooney Leo, telephone conversation with author after her daughter, Nancy Leo, sent author her mother's telephone number in an email dated June 1, 2015.

[67] Annelise Cooney Mora, email message to Peter Cooney dated May 31, 2015, that Peter forwarded to the author on June 1, 2015.

[68] Peter Cooney, email message to author and some family members, June 1, 2015.

[69] Joan Cooney Stern, email message to Peter Cooney, June 1, 2015, that Peter forwarded to the author on the same date.

[70] Neil Clark, "Cause of Death—Trench Nephritis," The Great War (1914-1918) Forum, *GreatWarForum.org*, accessed July 4, 2022, https://www.greatwarforum.org/topic/111290-cause-of-death-trench-nephritis/.

[71] Clark, "Cause of Death."

[72] Joan Cooney Stern, email message to Peter Cooney, June 1, 2015, which Peter forwarded to the author on the same date.

[73] William L. Shirer, *The Rise and Fall of the Third Reich: A History of Nazi Germany* (New York: Simon and Schuster, 1960), 61; Edward Taylor, *The Fall of the Dynasties: The Collapse of the Old Order 1905-1922* (Garden City, NY: Doubleday & Company, Inc., 1963), 393.

[74] Shirer, *Third Reich*, 61.

[75] Shirer, *Third Reich*, 61-62.

[76] Shirer, *Third Reich*, 63.

[77] John Keegan, *The Second World War* (New York: Penguin Books, 2005), 31-33.

[78] Shirer, *Third Reich*, 62.

[79] Keegan, *The Second World War*, 33.

[80] Shirer, *Third Reich*, 281.

[81] Peter Cooney, package of mail sent to author on February 5, 2015, with two news clips "John Cooney, 45, War Veteran, in Woodcliff, Ill Short Time," and "John J. Cooney." Presumably, they came from the now defunct *Hudson Dispatch* of Union County, NJ.

[82] Jon Meacham, *Destiny and Power: The American Odyssey of George Herbert Walker Bush* (New York: Random House, 2015), 74.

[83] Jonathan Eig, *Luckiest Man: The Life and Death of Lou Gehrig* (New York: Simon & Shuster, 2005), 233.

[84] Eig, *Luckiest Man*, 248.

[85] Eig, *Luckiest Man*, 316-317.

[86] Eig, *Luckiest Man*, 287-288, 291, 297, 308, 310, 321, 353-356.

[87] Eig, *Luckiest Man*, 3-4.

[88] Eig, *Luckiest Man*, 3-5.

[89] Eig, *Luckiest Man*, 7.

[90] Eig, *Luckiest Man*, 7.

[91] Eig, *Luckiest Man*, 10.

[92] Eig, *Luckiest Man*, 10.

[93] "The Lost High School of Commerce—155 West 65th Street," Daytonian in Manhattan: The stories behind the buildings, statues and other points of interest that make Manhattan fascinating, May 30, 2022, *DaytonianinManhattan.blogspot.com*, http://daytoninmanhattan.blogspot.com/2022/05/the-lost-high-school-of-commerce-155.html.

Notes

[94] Eig, *Luckiest Man*, 317-319.

[95] Mary Cooney, phone conversation with author on July 3, 2014, during which Mary said she went to Smith undergraduate and Columbia graduate, and her brother Kevin went to Berkeley undergraduate and Columbia graduate; Mary Cooney, email to author on July 7, 2014, which included as an attachment announcement that her father joined Shearson/American Express as a financial consultant and had attended Haverford undergraduate and subsequently studied at the University of California and Columbia emphasizing economics and statistics.

[96] Jim Hague, *Braddock: The Rise of the Cinderella Man* (New York: Chamberlain Bros., 2005), back cover.

[97] Hague, *Braddock*, 106, 123.

[98] Hague, *Braddock*, 118.

[99] John Cooney, discussion with author on June 28, 2014, at the Long Island State Veterans Home in Stony Brook, NY.

[100] Sam Carliner, "An Honor Fit for a World Champion," *The Star-Ledger*, August 15, 2018, A17.

[101] "Cinderella Man Plot," Internet Movie Database, *IMDb.com*, accessed July 8, 2022, https://www.imdb.com/title/tt0352248/plotsummary.

[102] Kathleen Cooney Leo, telephone conversation with author after her daughter, Nancy Leo, said in an email dated June 1, 2015 that her mother would welcome author's call.

[103] John Cooney, discussion with author on March 12, 2014, at the Long Island State Veterans Home in Stony Brook, NY.

[104] Kurt Orzeck, "Global 20: Shearman & Sterling," accessed July 8, 2022, Law360, *Law360.com*, http://www.law360.com/articles/460278/global-20-shearman-sterling.

[105] George H. Locke, "The High School of Commerce, New York City," *The School Review*, September 1, 1903, Vol. 11, No. 7, 555-562, *Archive.org*, accessed July 8, 2022, https://archive.org/details/jstor-1075231/mode/2up.

[106] Joseph F. O'Hern (Adjudication Officer, Veterans Administration) letter to Mrs. Anna Cooney regarding veteran benefits from her husband's passing, December 6, 1939. Provided to author by Peter Cooney.

[107] "FDR and Housing Legislation: 75th Anniversary of the Wagner-Steagall Housing Act of 1937," Franklin D. Roosevelt Presidential Library and Museum, *FDRlibrary.org*, accessed July 8, 2022, https://www.fdrlibrary.org/housing.

[108] "Public Housing," Rockefeller University, *Roosevelt.edu*, accessed July 8, 2022, https://www.roosevelt.edu/centers/new-deal-studies/history-fair/public-housing.

[109] "Moore Terms Meadow View Village Monument to FDR," *Hudson Dispatch* (now defunct newspaper), October 14, 1940, acquired at Jersey City Public Library.

[110] "Widow First Person to Occupy Home in Meadow View Village," *Hudson Dispatch* (now defunct newspaper), June 28, 1940, acquired at Jersey City Public Library.

[111] "Widow First Person," *Hudson Dispatch.*

[112] Kathleen Cooney Leo, telephone conversation with author following June 1, 2015 email from her daughter, Nancy Leo.

[113] Peter Cooney, email message to author, September 4, 2014.

[114] "History of Aluminum in the Aerospace Industry," *MetalSupermarkets.com,* posted February 8, 2016, accessed July 9, 2022, https://www.metalsupermarkets.com/history-of-aluminum-in-the-aerospace-industry/.

[115] McFarland, *A Concise History,* 14-15.

[116] "History of Aluminum in the Aerospace Industry," *MetalSupermarkets.com*; Willis Frazier (Operations Officer, 601st Squadron, 398th Bomb Group), "Eighth Air Force Operations in England During World War II," 389th.org, accessed July 9, 2022, https://www.398th.org/Research/8th_AF_Operations.html.

[117] Bill Yenne, *The American Aircraft Factory in WWII* (Grand Rapids, MI: Zenith, 2010), 28.

[118] Yenne, *American Aircraft Factory,* 31.

Chapter 6: AMERICA MOBILIZES FOR WORLD WAR II

[1] Arthur Herman, *Freedom's Forge: How American Business Produced Victory in World War II* (New York: Random House, 2012), 7.

[2] Herman, *Freedom's Forge,* 12-13.

[3] James MacGregor Burns, *Roosevelt: The Soldier of Freedom: 1940-1945* (New York: Francis Parkman Prize Edition, History Book Club, 2006), 51.

[4] Frank N. Schubert, *Mobilization: The U.S. Army in World War II: The 50th Anniversary* (Washington, D.C.: Center of Military History, United States Army, 1994), 3, *History.Army.mil,* accessed August 15, 2022, https://history.army.mil/html/books/072/72-32/CMH_Pub_72-32.pdf.

[5] History.com Editors, "Otto von Bismarck," *History.com,* original December 16, 2009, updated June 7, 2019, accessed August 18, 2022, https://www.history.com/topics/germany/otto-von-bismarck.

[6] David L. Roll, *George Marshall: Defender of the Republic* (New York: Dutton Caliber, 2019), 146.

[7] R. Elberton Smith, *The Army and Economic Mobilization* (Washington, D.C.: Center of Military History, United State Army, 1991), 133, *History.Army.mil,* accessed May 14, 2023, https://history.army.mil/html/books/001/1-7/CMH_Pub_1-7.pdf.

[8] Schubert, *Mobilization,* 5.

[9] Alan L. Gropman, *Mobilizing U.S. Industry in World War II* (Washington, D.C.: Institute for National Strategic Studies, National Defense University, McNair Paper 50, August 1996), 9-10.

[10] John W. Maenhardt, "The Effectiveness of the Army and Navy Munitions Board during the Interwar Period" (Thesis for Master of Military Art and Science, U.S. Army Command and General

Notes

Staff College, Fort Leavenworth, Kansas, 2008), 26 and 29, accessed May 14, 2023, via the Defense Technical Information Center, *DTIC.mil*, //apps.dtic.mil/sti/pdfs/ADA483049.pdf,

[11] Gropman, *Mobilizing U.S. Industry*, 20-22.

[12] Gropman, *Mobilizing U.S. Industry*, 24.

[13] Schubert, *Mobilization*, 10.

[14] Gropman, *Mobilizing U.S. Industry*, 26.

[15] Norman Beasley, *Knudsen: A Biography* (New York: Whittlesey House, 1947), 234-241; Donald M. Nelson, *Arsenal of Democracy: The Story of American War Production* (New York: Harcourt, Brace and Company, 1946), 80-83.

[16] Nelson, *Arsenal of Democracy*, 81-82.

[17] Charles Rappleye, "When the President's Best and Brightest Were Also the Richest," What It Means to be American: A National Conversation Hosted by Smithsonian and Arizona State University, *WhatItMeanstobeAmerican.org*, accessed October 15, 2022, https://www.whatitmeanstobeamerican. org/encounters/when-the-presidents-best-and-brightest-were-also-the-richest/#:~:text=Bernard%20 Baruch%2C%20a%20financier%20and,appointed%20by%20President%20Woodrow%20Wilson.

[18] Herman, *Freedom's Forge*, 15.

[19] Beasley, *Knudsen*, 4.

[20] Herman, *Freedom's Forge*, 29.

[21] Herman, *Freedom's Forge*, 16.

[22] David McCullough, *The Wright Brothers* (New York: Simon & Schuster, 2015), 22, 37, 39.

[23] Herman, *Freedom's Forge*, 30, 67.

[24] Herman, *Freedom's Forge*, 76.

[25] Herman, *Freedom's Forge*, 67.

[26] Doris Kearns Goodwin, *Team of Rivals: The Political Genius of Abraham Lincoln* (New York: Simon & Shuster, 2005), xvi.

[27] Beasley, *Knudsen*, 234-235.

[28] Herman, *Freedom's Forge*, 67.

[29] A. J. Baime, *The Arsenal of Democracy: FDR, Detroit, and an Epic Quest to Arm an America at War* (Boston/New York: Houghton Mifflin Harcourt, 2015), 72-73.

[30] Herman, *Freedom's Forge*, 76.

[31] Arthur Herman, "The Arsenal of Democracy: How Detroit turned industrial might into military power during World War II," January 13, 2013, *DetroitNews.com*, http://www.detroitnews.com/ article/20130103/OPINION01/301030336.

[32] Baime, *Arsenal of Democracy*, xiii-xiv, xvii.

[33] H.H. Arnold, *Global Mission* (New York: Harper & Brothers, 1949), 175.

[34] Arnold, *Global Mission*, 175-180.

[35] Herman, *Freedom's Forge*, 222; Wesley Frank Craven and James Lea Cate, editors, *The Army Air Forces in World War II, Vol. 6, Men and Planes* (Chicago: The University of Chicago Press, 1955), 206.

[36] John T. Correll, "The Third Musketeer," *Air Force Magazine*, December 2014, 58, *AirandSpaceForces.com*, https://www.airandspaceforces.com/PDF/MagazineArchive/ Magazine%20Documents/2014/December%202014/1214musketeer.pdf.

[37] Donald L. Miller, *The Story of World War II* (New York: Simon & Shuster Paperbacks, 2006), 32; Margaret E. Wagner, Linda Barrett Osborne, Susan Reyburn, and Staff of the Library of Congress, *The Library of Congress World War II Companion* (New York: Simon & Schuster, 2007), 447.

[38] Miller, *Story of World War II*, 35-36.

[39] Baime, *Arsenal of Democracy*, 69.

[40] "Morgenthau is Boss of Defense: Names George J. Mead to Standardize Production of Plane Engines," *The Buffalo Evening News*, May 14, 1940, Page 10, accessed July 12, 2022 as subscriber to *Newspapers.com*, https://www.newspapers.com/image/840788406/?terms=Morgent hau%20is%20Boss%20of%20Defense&match=1.

[41] Cary Hoge Mead, *Wings Over the World: The Life of George Jackson Mead* (Wauwatosa, WI: The Swannet Press, 1971), 216.

[42] Mead, *Wings Over the World*, 210.

[43] Mead, *Wings Over the World*, 216.

[44] "Co-Founder of Aircraft Firm is Dead," *The Hartford Courant*, January 21, 1949, 4, accessed on July 12, 2022, as a subscriber to *Newspapers.com*, https://www.newspapers.com/ image/370469312/?terms=co-founder%20of%20aircraft%20firm%20is%20dead&match=1.

[45] Mead, *Wings Over the World*, 205.

[46] Beasley, *Knudsen*: 234-241; Nelson, *Arsenal of Democracy*, 92.

[47] Joseph L. Weiner, "The New Deal and the Corporation," *The University of Chicago Law Review*, Vol. 19, Issue 4, Article 6, 1951, accessed August 20, 2022, 724, https://chicagounbound. uchicago.edu/cgi/viewcontent.cgi?article=2759&context=uclrev.

[48] Weiner, "The New Deal and the Corporation," 728.

[49] Beasley, *Knudsen*, 326.

[50] Beasley, *Knudsen*, 326.

[51] Goodwin, *No Ordinary Time*, 56-57.

Notes

[52] Beasley, *Knudsen*, 142-143.

[53] Mead, *Wings Over the World*, 210, 240-241.

[54] Mead, *Wings Over the World*, one of the photos between page 156 and 157 shows a Treasury check to George J. Mead for $0.05, his federal annual salary as Special Advisor to the Office of Production Management during 1940-41.

[55] Mead, *Wings Over the World*, 169.

[56] Smith, *The Army and Economic Mobilization*, 130-133.

[57] Abe Greenberg, "Knudsen and Doolittle Led Auto Men to War," *Sunday Daily News*, October 25, 1942, accessed May 19, 2023, 296, as subscriber to *Newspapers.com*, https://www.newspapers.com/image/433099651/?terms=Knudsen%20and%20doolittle&match=1

[58] Craven and Cate, *Men and Planes*, 312.

[59] James H, "Jimmy" Doolittle with Carroll V. Glines, *I Could Never Be So Lucky Again* (New York: Bantam Books, 1991), 149-151.

[60] Doolittle and Glines, *I Could Never Be So Lucky*, 197-201.

[61] Doolittle and Glines, *I Could Never Be So Lucky*, back cover of book.

[62] Greenberg, "Knudsen and Doolittle," *Daily News Sunday*, 296; The J.L. Hudson Company, "A Salute to Detroit's Council for War Production: Through Which Detroit's 'Know-How' Has Proven Itself America's Greatest Secret Weapon," *Detroit Free Press*, September 18, 1944, accessed on August 18, 2022, as a subscriber to *Newspapers.com*, https://www.newspapers.com/image/98282535/?terms=A%20salute%20to%20detroit%27s%20council%20of%20war%20production&match=1.

[63] Herman, *Freedom's Forge*, 66-67.

[64] Beasley, *Knudsen*, 344.

[65] Gropman, *Mobilizing U.S. Industry*, 136-137; Beasley, *Knudsen*, 324.

[66] "Office of Emergency Management," *Victory: Official Weekly Bulletin of the Agencies in the Office of Emergency Management*, Volume 3, Number 3, January 20, 1942 (Washington, D.C.: United States Government Printing Office, 1942), 32, accessed September 5, 2022, http://www.idaillinois.org/digital/collection/isl3/id/18570/rec/107.

[67] David McCullough, *Truman* (New York: Simon & Schuster, 1992), 258-259; "Special Committee to Investigate the National Defense Program, Notable Senate Investigations, U.S. Senate Historical Office, Washington, D.C.," *Senate.gov*, accessed August 15, 2022, https://www.senate.gov/about/resources/pdf/truman-committee-full-citations.pdf.

[68] McCullough, *Truman*, 260.

[69] McCullough, *Truman*, 231-232 and 272.

[70] "Special Committee," Senate Historical Office.

[71] McCullough, *Truman*, 255 and 268)

[72] Bease, *Knudsen*, 310.

[73] McCullough, *Truman*, 288.

[74] "Lend-Lease Act (1941)," National Archives, *Archives.gov*, accessed August 14, 2023, https://www.archives.gov/milestone-documents/lend-lease-act#:~:text=Passed%20on%20March%2011%2C%201941,defense%20of%20the%20United%20States.%22.

[75] Mark Skinner Watson, *Chief of Staff: Prewar Plans and Preparations* (Washington, D.C.: Center of Military History, United States Army, U.S. Government Printing Office, 1991) 331 and 337, accessed August 23, 2012, https://history.army.mil/books/wwii/csppp/index.htm#contents.

[76] Watson, *Chief of Staff*, 331-333.

[77] Gropman, *Mobilizing U.S. Industry*, 41.

[78] Watson, *Chief of Staff*, 338-339.

[79] James G. Lacey, "World War II's Real Victory Program," 11, accessed September 19, 2022, file:///C:/Users/Archie/Downloads/Victory%20Program%20-%20Article%20Version%20(3).pdf.

[80] Smith, *The Army and Economic Mobilization*, 133.

[81] Charles E. Kirkpatrick, *An Unknown Future and a Doubtful Present: Writing the Victory Plan of 1943* (Washington, D.C.: Center of Military History, United States Army, 1992), History.Army.mil, 133, accessed September 14, 2022, https://history.army.mil/html/books/093/93-10/CMH_Pub_93-10.pdf.

[82] Kirkpatrick, *An Unknown Future*, 101; Gropman, *Mobilizing U.S. Industry*, 42.

[83] Lacey, "World War II's Real Victory Program," 13.

[84] James C. Gaston, *Planning the American Air War: Four Men and Nine Days in 1941* (Washington, DC: National Defense University, Fort Lesley J. McNair, 1982), 1-3, Defense Technical Information Center, accessed August 18, 2023, https://apps.dtic.mil/sti/citations/ADA123505.

[85] Gaston, *Planning the American Air War*, 6.

[86] Richard Overy, *Why the Allies Won* (New York: W. W. Norton & Company, 1996), 323.

[87] Kirkpatrick, *An Unknown Future*, 104

[88] Roll, *George Marshall*, 264.

[89] Roll, *George Marshall*, 265.

[90] Roll, *George Marshall*, 266.

[91] Gropman, *Mobilizing U.S. Industry*, 55.

[92] McCullough, *Truman*, 266-268

Notes

[93] James MacGregor Burns, *Roosevelt: The Soldier of Freedom: 1940-1945* (New York: Francis Parkman Prize Edition, History Book Club, 2006), 53.

[94] McCullough, *Truman*, 269.

[95] James Preston, "Washington Snapshots," *Neligh News* (Neligh, Nebraska), February 26, 1942, 2, accessed October 13, 2022, as subscriber to *Newspapers.com*, https://www.newspapers.com/image/729879825/?terms=Washington%20Snapshots&match=1.

[96] "Dollar-a-Year Men Needed, Nelson Says: Tells Truman Committee He'll Be a 'Goat' If War Production Fails," *The St. Louis Star and Times* (St. Louis, Missouri), accessed on October 14, 2022, as subscriber to *Newspapers.com*, https://www.newspapers.com/image/205864988/?terms=Dollar-a-year%20men%20needed%2C%20nelson%20says%2C%22&match=1.

[97] McCullough, *Truman*, 279.

[98] "Special Committee, Senate Historical Office.

[99] "Special Committee, Senate Historical Office.

[100] Burns, *Roosevelt: The Soldier of Freedom*, 88.

[101] "Any Necessary Changes Will Be Made," *Victory: Official Weekly Bulletin of the Agencies in the Office of Emergency Management*, Volume 3, Number 3, January 20, 1942 (Washington, D.C.: United States Government Printing Office, 1942), 5, accessed August 22, 2022, http://www.idaillinois.org/digital/collection/isl3/id/18570/rec/107.

[102] Nelson, *Arsenal of Democracy*, 93.

[103] Bill McKern, "Memorial to William Signius Knudsen," *FindaGrave.com*, accessed August 24, 2022, https://www.findagrave.com/memorial/44779961/william-signius-knudsen.

[104] "Nelson Revamps Whole Setup of War Industry Organization," *Richmond Times Dispatch*, January 22, 1942, 1 and 21, accessed August 18, 2022, as subscriber to *Newspapers.com*, https://www.newspapers.com/image/828037872/?terms=Nelson%20revamps&match=1; "President Appoints Knudsen Director of Production for War Department and a Lieutenant General," *Victory: Official Weekly Bulletin of the Agencies in the Office of Emergency Management*, Volume 3, Number 3, January 20, 1942 (Washington, D.C.: United States Government Printing Office, 1942), 3, accessed August 22, 2022, http://www.idaillinois.org/digital/collection/isl3/id/18570/rec/107.

[105] Beasley, *Knudsen*, 351

[106] Beasley, *Knudsen*, 379.

[107] "War Production Board," *The Columbia Electronic Encyclopedia*, 6th ed., 2012, Columbia University Press, accessed August 18, 2012, https://www.infoplease.com/encyclopedia/history/north-america/us/war-production-board#:~:text=War%20Production%20Board%20(WPB)%2C,over%20the%20nation's%20economic%20life; Nelson, *Arsenal of Democracy*, 228.

[108] J. F. Knowlson, "The Conclusion of a Dollar-a-Year Man," *TheAtlantic.com*, May 1943 Issue, accessed October 11, 2022, https://www.theatlantic.com/magazine/archive/1943/05/the-conclusions-of-a-dollar-a-year-man/656027/.

[109] David J. A. Stone, Writer (plus Contributing Writers and Consultants), *World War II Chronicle* (Lincolnwood, IL: Legacy Publishing, 2007), 182.

[110] Arnold, *Global Mission*, 291.

[111] Arnold, *Global Mission*, 292.

[112] Craven and Cate, *Men and Planes*, 350.

[113] Craven and Cate, *Men and Planes*, 352; "Official Munitions Production of the United States," (Initiated and Prepared by the War Production Board chaired by J.A. Krug), Civilian Production Administration, May 1, 1947, 339, accessed September 20, 2022, file:///C:/Users/John/Downloads/p4013coll8_3332.pdf.

[114] Franklin D. Roosevelt, "Message to Congress on the Progress of the War," September 17, 1943, *The American Presidency Project*, accessed July 14, 2022, https://www.presidency.ucsb.edu/documents/message-congress-the-progress-the-war.

[115] Herman, *Freedom's Forge*, 219.

[116] "A Bomber an Hour: Charlie Sorensen's Story," Strategos, *StrategosInc.com*, accessed July 12, 2022, https://strategosinc.com/RESOURCES/04-Lean_History/willow_run.htm.

[117] Herman, *Freedom's Forge*, 226.

[118] Beasley, *Knudsen*, 379.

[119] Beasley, *Knudsen*, 217

[120] Herman, *Freedom's Forge*, 220-221.

[121] Craven and Cate, *Men and Planes*, 312.

[122] Craven and Cate, *Men and Planes*, 313.

[123] Stephen L. McFarland, *A Concise History of the U.S. Air Force* (Washington, DC: Air Force History and Museums Program, Air Force Fiftieth Anniversary Commemorative Edition, 1997), 20.

[124] Herman S. Wok, *Planning and Organizing the Postwar Air Force* (Washington, D.C.: Office of Air Force History, United States Air Force, 1984), 21, accessed July 12, 2022, https://media.defense.gov/2010/Sep/28/2001329803/-1/-1/0/planning_and_organizing_the_postwar_af.pdf.

[125] Bill Yenne, *The American Aircraft Factory in WWII* (Grand Rapids, MI: Zenith Press, 2010), 144-148.

[126] History.com Editors, "Rosie the Riveter," *History.com*, April 23, 2010, updated October 12, 2021, accessed July 13, 2022, https://www.history.com/topics/world-war-ii/rosie-the-riveter.

[127] "Will the Real 'Rosie the Riveter' Please Flex," Gillian Brockell (*Washington Post*), *The Star-Ledger Affiliated with NJ.com*, March 22, 2023, A8.

[128] Jeannette Gutierrez, "Little People at the Willow Run Bomber Plant," September 25, 2013, Diary of a Rosie, *DiaryofRosie,com*, accessed July 13, 2022, https://diaryofarosie.com/2013/09/25/little-people-at-the-willow-run-bomber-plant/.

[129] Christopher Cook, "The Warriors of Willow Run," *Detroit Free Press Magazine*, December 4, 1988, Issue No. 25, 117-121, accessed July 13, 2022, as subscriber to *Newspapers.com*;

"Memories of the 801st/492nd Bombardment Group as Told to Col. Robert W. Fish," page 363, *Scribd.com*, accessed July 13, 2022, https://www.scribd.com/document/49646248/Memories-of-the-801st-492nd-Bombardment-Group-Carpetbaggers.

[130] Michael R. Majerczyk, "Overcoming Fear: Realizing Production at the Willow Run Bomber Plant," *Saber and Scroll*, Volume 5, Issue 2, September 1, 2016, 60-61, accessed July 13, 2022, https://saberandscroll.scholasticahq.com/article/28627-overcoming-fear-realizing-production-at-the-willow-run-bomber-plant.

[131] Richard Rothstein, "Race and Public Housing: Revisiting the Federal Role," December 17, 2012, Economic Policy Institute, *Epi.org*, accessed July 13, 2022, https://www.epi.org/publication/race-public-housing-revisiting-federal-role/.

[132] "B-24 Liberator Models, Production, and Assembly Plants," *Airplanes-Online.com*, accessed July 13, 2022, https://www.airplanes-online.com/b24-liberator-production-assembly-plants.htm.

[133] Allan G. Blue, *The B-24 Liberator: A Pictorial History* (New York: Charles Scribner's Sons, 1976), 191-192.

[134] "B-24 Liberator Models," *Airplanes-Online.com*.

[135] "Individual Flight Record of Russell F. Flint for the Eight Months of October 1944 to April 1945," sent to author by Russell F. Flint, Jr. and received by author on June 30. 2021.

[136] Yenne, *American Aircraft Factory*, 151.

[137] Robert Grant Cookman (Born September 8, 1920), "U.S., WWII Draft Cards Young Men, 1940-1947," Serial No. 363, Mason City, Cerro Gordo, IA, Local Board No. 2 (Registered February 16, 1942), accessed July 15, 2022. as subscriber to *Ancestry.com*, accessed January 28, 2024, https://www.ancestry.com/discoveryui-content/view/38178117:2238?tid=&pid=&queryId=867101d0-5004-4024-89b8-8ba52bf6eae6&_phsrc=KOP107& phstart=successSource.

[138] "Servicemen's Readjustment Act (1944), National Archives, *Archives.com*, accessed July 17, 2022, https://www.archives.gov/milestone-documents/servicemens-readjustment-act.

[139] "Western Electric—A Brief History," Bell System Memorial, *BellSystemMemorial.com*, accessed July 17, 2022, https://www.bellsystemmemorial.com/westernelectric_history.html#Western%20Electric%20-%20A%20Brief%20History.

[140] "Western Electric," Bell System Memorial.

[141] "Air Medal for Sergeant Clooney," newspaper clipping sent to author by Peter Clooney, presumably from the now defunct *Hudson Dispatch* of Jersey City, NJ; "Enlisted Record and Report of Separation: Honorable Discharge," s.v. "John J. Cooney (born May 6, 1923)," copy mailed to author by Peter Cooney, brother of John J. Cooney, on September 15, 2014.

[142] *Collins Online English Dictionary*, s.v. "Job Setter," accessed July 17, 2022, https://www.collinsdictionary.com/us/dictionary/english/job-setter#:~:text=job%20setter%20in%20American%20English,tooling%20on%20the%20production%20line.

[143] Editors of Encyclopedia Britannica, *Encyclopedia Britannica Online*, s.v. "Joseph Heller," accessed July 18, 2022, https://www.britannica.com/biography/Joseph-Heller; "Biography (of James Arness)," James Arness Official Website, accessed July 18, 2022, http://www.jamesarness.com/biography.html; Editors of Encyclopedia Britannica, *Encyclopedia Britannica Online*, s.v.

"Rainier III, prince de Monaco," accessed July 18, 2022, https://www.britannica.com/biography/Rainier-III-prince-de-Monaco.

[144] *Encyclopedia Britannica Online,* "Heller,"

[145] Arness Website, "Biography."

[146] *Encyclopedia Britannica Online,* "Rainier III."

[147] Nancy Leo, "Uncle John," Speech at Remembrance Celebration of John J. Cooney Jr., University Club in Manhattan, November 29, 2014.

[148] "Famous B-24/PB4Y Crew Members," *B24BestWeb.com,* last modified July 8, 2021, accessed July 18, 2022, http://www.b24bestweb.com/b24bestweb-famous.htm.

[149] Brendan Cooney, email message to author, July 16, 2015.

[150] Brendan Cooney, email message to author, December 1, 2018.

[151] Peter Cooney, email message to author, July 8, 2018, followed up by a mail package with a copy of his mother's identification card as a chauffeurette in the Newark Signal Corps.

[152] "Women in Uniform," American Home Front in World War II, *Encyclopedia.com,* updated June 21, 2022, accessed July 18, 2022, https://www.encyclopedia.com/history/news-and-education-magazines/women-uniform.

[153] "Women in Uniform," *Encyclopedia.com.*

[154] Peter Cooney, sent author copy of document dated April 21, 1943, certifying Anna Cooney as a chauffeurette who has demonstrated proficiency in driving along with a copy of her identification card as a driver for the Newark Signal Corps.

[155] Peter Cooney, sent a photo to author of his mother in the Army staff car she drove for the Newark Signal Corps.

[156] Peter Cooney, email message to author, July 8, 2015.

[157] Richard J. Thompson, *Crystal Clear: The Struggle for Reliable Communications Technology in World War II* (Hoboken, NJ: John Wiley & Sons, 2012), 5.

[158] Thompson, *Crystal Clear,* 6.

[159] Susan Thompson (Command Historian), "Signal Corps in World War II," *Army.mil,* June 26, 2020, accessed July 18, 2022, https://www.army.mil/article/236799/signal_corps_in_world_war_ii#:~:text=The%20Signal%20Corps%20Laboratories%20were,the%20first%20FM%20backpack%20radio.

[160] Rebecca Robbins Raines, *Getting the Message Through: A Branch History of the U.S. Army Signal Corps* (Washington, D.C.: Army Historical Series, Center of Military History, United States Army, 2011), 136, accessed January 28, 2024, https://history.army.mil/html/books/030/30-17-1/CMH_Pub_30-17-1.pdf.

[161] Merrill I. Skolnik, *Encyclopedia Britannica Online,* s.v. "radar," accessed July 20, 2022, https://www.britannica.com/technology/radar.

[162] "Radar During World War II," Engineering and Technical History Wiki, *Ethw,org*, accessed July 20, 2022, https://ethw.org/Radar_during_World_War_II.

[163] Steven O'Connor, "Western Electric Manufactured RADAR Equipment" (Mr. Connor quotes information from page 104 of the book *Illinois in the Second World War, Volume 2: The Production Front*, edited by Mary Watters and published by the State of Illinois on January 1, 1951), *Industrial History* (blog), accessed July 21, 2022, http://industrialscenery.blogspot.com/2015/11/western-electric-manufactured-radar.html.

[164] George Raynor Thompson and Dixie R. Harris, *The Signal Corps: The Outcome (Mid-1943 Through 1945)* (Washington, D.C.: Center of Military History, United States Army, 1991), 374, Army.mil, https://history.army.mil/html/books/010/10-18/index.html.

[165] George Raynor Thompson, Dixie R. Harris, Pauline M, Oakes, and Dulany Terrett, *The Signal Corps: The Test (December 1941 to July 1943)* (Washington, D.C.: Office of the Chief of Military History, Department of the Army, 1957), 324, *Army.mil*, https://history.army.mil/html/books/010/10-17/index.html.

[166] Peter Cooney, sent author copy of card in which the War Department, Army Service Forces, certifies an "Efficiency Award" to "Anna Cooney, Chauffeurette" that was approved by her commander, Frank Prina, Lt. Col., Signal Corps, January 15, 1944.

[167] Thompson, *The Signal Corps: The Test*, 177.

[168] Thompson, *The Signal Corps: The Test*, 180.

[169] John Cooney, interview by Jessica Fragosa, Reporter & Host of *Heroes On Our Island* at Verizon FiOS 1 News, Greater New York City Area, Broadcast Media, August 31, 2010, https://www.youtube.com/watch?v=aQQgTuNxjiA. This video isn't available anymore.

[170] Stephen G. Melly, "Camp Dix: 95 Years of Army Heritage," July 18, 2014, Joint Base McGuire-Dix-Lakehurst, NJ (website), accessed July 22, 2022, https://www.jbmdl.jb.mil/News/Article-Display/Article/826576/camp-dix-95-years-of-army-heritage/#:~:text=Camp%20Dix%20served%20as%20a,Camp%20Dix%20to%20Fort%20Dix.

[171] "Air Medal for Sergeant Clooney," newspaper clipping sent to author by Peter Clooney, presumably from the now defunct *Hudson Dispatch* of Jersey City, NJ.

[172] John J. Cooney, letter to Chairman, Irwin Parachute Company, dated August 1, 1945, that was given to author by John J. Cooney; "Obituary of John J. Cooney, Jr.," *New York Times*, November 27, 2014, https://www.legacy.com/us/obituaries/nytimes/name/john-cooney-obituary?id=22635249.

Chapter 7: TRAINING FOR COMBAT MISSIONS

[1] "The Home Front: How Rivets and Ration Cards Won WWII," American History for Travelers, January 18, 2012, accessed July 24, 2022, https://americanhistory4travelers.com/2012/01/18/the-home-front-how-rivets-and-ration-cards-won-wwii/#:~:text=What%20made%20production%20of%20that,production%20of%20just%20one%20Liberator.

[2] Tom Faulkner, *Flying with the Fifteenth Air Force: A B-24 Pilot's Missions from Italy During World War II* (Denton, TX: University of North Texas Press, 2018), 130.

[3] Robert F. Dorr, *B-24 Liberator Units of the Fifteenth Air Force* (Oxford, UK: Osprey Aviation, 2000), 13.

[4] Dorr, *B-24 Liberator Units*, 8.

[5] Stephen E. Ambrose, *The Wild Blue: The Men and Boys Who Flew B-24s Over Germany* (New York: Simon & Schuster, 2001), 21.

[6] Martin W. Bowman, *B-24 Combat Missions: First-Hand Accounts of Liberator Operations Over Nazi Europe* (New York, Metro Books, 2009), 121.

[7] Dorr, *B-24 Liberator Units*, 7.

[8] Bowman, *B-24 Combat Missions*, 14.

[9] Larry Dwyer, "Consolidated B-24 Liberator: Specifications," The Aviation History Online Museum, *Aviation-History.com*, accessed July 22, 2022, http://www.aviation-history.com/consolidated/b24.html.

[10] Bowman, *B-24 Combat Missions*, 11.

[11] "Pilot, B-24 (1092)," *TM 12-405 War Department Technical Manual: Officer Classification— Commissioned and Warrant: Classification and Coding of Civilian Occupations* (Washington, D.C.: United States Government Printing Office, 1943), 57, accessed July 26, 2022, http://www.coulthart.com/134/mos-officer.pdf.

[12] "Navigator (1034)," *TM 12-405*, 53.

[13] "Bombardier (1035)," *TM 12-405*, 54-55.

[14] "Aerial Gunner (611)," *TM 12-427 War Department Technical Manual: Military Occupational Classification of Enlisted Personnel* (Washing, D.C.: United States Government Printing Office. 1944), 79, accessed July 26, 2022, http://www.coulthart.com/134/mos-em.pdf.

[15] "Airplane Mechanic-Gunner (748)," *TM 12-427*, 94-95.

[16] "Radio Operator-Mechanic-Gunner (757)," *TM 12-427*, 95-96.

[17] "Airplane Armorer-Gunner (612)," *TM 12-427*, 79.

[18] The Signal Corps in Collaboration with the Chief of the Air Corps, *Aerial Bombs: Method of Loading Bombs*, Official Training Film of the War Department, 1941, *Youtube.com*, accessed July 31, 2022, https://www.youtube.com/watch?v=vYQp0TxsOMg; *Aircraft Bombs, Fuzes and Associated Components* (Published under the Direction of The Chief of the Bureau of Naval Weapons, August 1, 1960), 1-3, 1-4, 1-5, 1-6, 1-7, 1-8, 1-9, 1-11,1-12, accessed August 1, 2012, https://bulletpicker.com/pdf/OP%202216,%20Aircraft%20Bombs,%20Fuzes,%20and%20Associated%20Components%20(1960).pdf.

[19] Signal Corps and Air Corps, *Aerial Bombs*.

[20] Dale J. Satterthwaite, *Truth Flies with Fiction* (Bloomington, IN: Archway Publishing, 2014), 140-141.

[21] "MACR 2070 (Pilot Pickard)," digital images, accessed on August 3, 2022, as a subscriber to *Fold3.com* (Missing Air Crew Reports [MACRs] of the U.S. Army Air Forces, 1942-1947), https://www.fold3.com/image/28713652?terms=2070,macr.

Notes

[22] "MACR 2070," *Fold3.com*.

[23] "Appendix A: The B-24 Liberator & Its Crew," revised January 12, 2021 (Michael Weber, "The Story of The White L for Love," revised May 3, 2023), *Freepages.Rootsweb.com*. accessed May 20, 2023, http://freepages.rootsweb.com/~webermd1/family/Liberator-Info.html.

[24] Adam Higginbotham, "There Are Still Thousands of Tons of Unexploded Bombs in Germany, Left Over from World War II, *SmithsonianMag.com*, January 2016, accessed September 21, 2022, https://www.smithsonianmag.com/history/seventy-years-world-war-two-thousands-tons-unexploded-bombs-germany-180957680/.

[25] Higginbotham, "Unexploded Bombs in Germany."

[26] J. Weston Phippen, "50,000 Evacuate Hanover While Unexploded Bombs Are Disabled," *TheAtlantic.com*, accessed September 21, 2022, https://www.theatlantic.com/news/archive/2017/05/hanover-bombs-world-war-ii/525735/.

[27] Phippen, "50,000 Evacuate Hanover."

[28] "50,000 Evacuated in Hanover, Germany, Over World War II Bombs," Deutsche Welle (DW) Global Media Forum, *Dw.com*, accessed September 21, 2022, http://www.dw.com/en/50000-evacuated-in-hanover-germany-over-world-war-ii-bombs/a-38734208.

[29] "50,000 Evacuated in Hanover, Germany," *Dw.com*.

[30] Erik Kirschbaum, "A 500-Pound Bomb is Detonated in Germany—More Than Seven Decades Later," *LAtimes.com*, April 14, 2019, accessed September 22, 2022, https://www.latimes.com/world/la-fg-germany-world-war-ii-bomb-20190414-story.html.

[31] Peter Cooney, email message to author, January 4, 2022; Ambrose, *The Wild Blue*, 230; Interview of John Cooney by Jessica Fragosa, Reporter & *Host of Heroes On Our Island* at Verizon FiOS 1 News, Greater New York City Area, Broadcast Media, August 31, 2010, https://www.youtube.com/watch?v=aQQgTuNxjiA. This video isn't available anymore.

[32] Martin W. Bowman, *B-24 Combat Missions: First-Hand Accounts of Liberator Operations Over Nazi Europe* (New York, Metro Books, 2009), 113-125; "U.S. World War I Draft Registration Cards, 1917-1918," s.v. "John Cooney," accessed on August 4, 2022, as subscriber to *Ancestry.com*, https://www.ancestry.com/discoveryui-content/view/33472940:6482?tid=&pid=&queryId=00e253dbd055030da5bab3ec082e381a&_phsrc=zsS283&_phstart=successSource.

[33] Bowman, *B-24 Combat Missions*, 113-125; Jesse N. Bradley, "The Ball Turret on a B-24," http://home.comcast.net/~ralph608/ballturret.htm (it was accessed through a link on another website at https://cassidiesscheme.weebly.com/from-family-to-facts.html to Bradley's website, but the link does not work now, probably because Bradley passed away. The author copied the article. Bradley like John J. Cooney, flew 35 combat missions as a ball-turret gunner in a B-24.)

[34] Meyer Osofsky, telephone conversation with author, July 15, 2017.

[35] Gregory A. Freeman, *The Forgotten 500: The Untold Story of the Men Who Risked All for the Greatest Rescue Mission of World War II* (New York: New American Library Caliber, 2007), 20.

[36] "Anatomy of a Bombing Mission (Ball Turret Gunners: An Elite Group)," 392nd Bomb Group, *B24.net*, accessed August 19, 2023, https://www.b24.net/MissionAnatomy.htm.

[37] Ambrose, *The Wild Blue*, 95-96.

[38] Paul M. Stevens, "A Chaplain's Story," *450thbg.com*, Official Website of the 450th Bomb Group Memorial Association, accessed September 22, 2022, https://www.450thbg.com/real/stories/chaplain.shtml.

[39] Meyer Osofsky, telephone conversation with author, June 2, 2017.

[40] Mason City High School, *Masonian* (Mason City, Iowa, 1938), 63, accessed September 23, 2022, as subscriber to *E-yearbook.com*, https://www.e-yearbook.com/sp/eybb?school=48028&year=1938.

[41] "Mason City Athletes Pass in Review During 1936," *Mason City Globe-Gazette* (Mason City, Iowa), December 31, 1936, 87, accessed on September 23, 2022, as subscriber to *Newspapers.com*, https://www.newspapers.com/image/1914221/?terms=Cookman%2C%20Globe-Gazette&match=1.

[42] "Legion Ballplayers Visit Tom Mix," *Mason City Globe-Gazette* (Mason City, Iowa), July 10, 1935, 36, accessed September 23, 2022, as subscriber to *Newspapers.com*, https://www.newspapers.com/image/2544067.

[43] "Mason City Athletes," Globe-Gazette, 87; "Mason City Jaysees Win," *The Des Moines Register* (Des Moines, Iowa), September 16, 1938, 10, accessed September 23, 2022, as subscriber to *Newspapers.com*, https://www.newspapers.com/image/128414019/?terms=Mason%20City%20Jaysees%20Win&match=1.

[44] "Packers Defeat Electrics 1 to 0 to Finish Race," *Mason City Globe-Gazette* (Mason City, Iowa), August 2, 1940, 9, accessed September 23, 2022, as subscriber to *Newspapers,com*, https://www.newspapers.com/image/38215521/?terms=Packers%20defeat%20electrics%2C%20mason%20city%20globe-gazette&match=1.

[45] Joe (Harry) Cookman, telephone conversation with author, March 23, 1917.

[46] "Flyers Speak at Lions Club," *Mason City Globe-Gazette* (Mason City, Iowa), November 2, 1944, 15, accessed September 23, 2022, as subscriber to *Newspapers.com*, https://www.newspapers.com/image/391309385/?terms=Cookman%2C%20Mason%20city%20globe-gazette&match=1.

[47] "Veteran's Compensation Application 210819, Commonwealth of Pennsylvania," s.v. "John Kravesky," applied February 10, 1934, accessed September 23, 2022, as subscriber to *Ancestry.com*, https://www.ancestry.com/discoveryui-content/view/1157406:60884?tid=&pid=&queryId=0c46a76b48fd7d6618fa288912bdb4bd&_phsrc=zsS275&_phstart=successSource.

[48] Jennifer Stratman of Palmer College of Chiropractic, email message to author, April 19, 2021.

[49] Stratman, email message to author, April 19, 2021; "Biography–Daniel David (D.D.) Palmer," Palmer College of Chiropractic, accessed September 27, 2022, https://www.palmer.edu/wp-content/uploads/2022/02/biography-palmer-daniel-david.pdf.

[50] "Find A Grave," s.v. "Geraldine Krivesky (1923-1928)," *FindaGrave.com*, accessed September 27, 2022, https://www.findagrave.com/memorial/77983761/geraldine-krivesky.

[51] Austin High School, *Maroon and White* (Chicago, Illinois, 1940), 61 and 73, accessed September 27, 2022, as subscriber to *E-yearbook.com*, https://www.e-yearbook.com/sp/eybb?school=20104&year=1940.

[52] Colonel Woolf Gross, "The Army Officers' Training Corps, A Hundred Years Old and Still Going Strong," The Army Historical Foundation, *ArmyHistory.org*, accessed September 27, 2022, https://armyhistory.org/army-reserve-officers-training-corps-hundred-years-old-still-going-strong/.

Notes

[53] Russell J. Flint, "Army Separation Qualification Record," sent to author by Russell J. Flint, Jr. and received by author on June 3, 2021.

[54] "A Rich History," The Aviation Lofts, *Aviationlofts.com*, accessed September 27, 2022, https://www.aviationlofts.com/building-history/index.html.

[55] "Lieutenant Willa Brown – Aviatrix, Maker of Pilots," The National WWII Museum, *Nationalww2museum.org*, accessed September 27, 2022, https://www.nationalww2museum.org/war/articles/lieutenant-willa-brown.

[56] "U.S. World War II Draft Cards Young Men, 1940-1947," s.v. "Russell John Flint," accessed on August 4, 2022, as subscriber to *Ancestry.com*, https://www.ancestry.com/discoveryui-content/view/300481954:2238?tid=&pid=&queryId=504f3f0f30ac0fed5efe0e7a48d0d7e9&_phsrc=zsS88&_phstart=successSource.

[57] "Spence Air Base During World War 2," Spence Air Base, *Spenceairbase.com*, accessed September 27, 2022, https://spenceairbase.com/WW2.html.

[58] "Final 44-C Aviation Cadets Payroll of Aviation Cadet Attachment, Air Forces, Spence Field, Georgia, February and March 1944," *National Personnel Records Center*, nprc.digitaldelivery@nara.gov, email message to author with information on Russell Flint, April 22, 2022.

[59] "Spence Air Base During World War 2," *Spenceairbase.com*; "With America's Fighters, Russell J. Flint," Chicago Tribune, March 26, 1944, 9, accessed October 2, 2022, as subscriber to Newspapers.com, https://www.newspapers.com/image/370873078/?terms=Russell%20J.%20Flint&match=1.

[60] "Obituary: Mrs. Caroline Cylkowski," *Hartford Courant* (Connecticut), March 27, 1961, accessed October 2, 2022, as a subscriber to *Newspapers.com*, https://www.newspapers.com/image/371222392/?terms=Mrs.%20Caroline%20Cylkowski&match=1.

[61] Martin M. Masters, "He's Dean of Hartford's Music Teachers," *The Hartford Courant Magazine*, May 11, 1952, 85, accessed October 2, 2022, as subscriber to *Newspapers.com*, https://www.newspapers.com/image/370422704/?terms=He%27s%20Dean%20of%20Hartford%27s%20Music%20Teachers&match=1; "Lawson's Pupils Give Third Piano Recital," *Hartford Courant* (Hartford, CT), accessed October 2, 2022, as subscriber to *Newspapers.com*, https://www.newspapers.com/image/370431723/?terms=Lawson%20Pupils%20Give%20Third%20Piano%20Recital&match=1.

[62] "Lawson's Pupils," *Hartford Courant*, 85.

[63] Rebecca Vaccarelli (Director of Alumni Relations, The Julliard School), email message to author, April 1, 2021.

[64] Vaccarelli, email to author, April 6, 2021.

[65] Irma Glaser (sister of Doris Markus), telephone conversation with author, April 2, 2021.

[66] Post Card sent from Ted Cylkowski to his mother, Mrs. B. Cylkowski, dated June 9, 1944, which was sent to author via email message with Dropbox link by David Cylkowski, son of Ted, on March 17, 2021.

[67] "Obituary: Henry Cylkowski," *Hartford Courant*, May 29, 1991, 70, accessed October 3, 2022, as subscriber to *Newspapers.com*, https://www.newspapers.com/image/241961071/?terms=Henry%20

Cylkowski&match=1; "Obituary: Edward Cylkowski," *Hartford Courant*, August 15, 2011, B02, accessed October 3, 2022, as subscriber to *Newspapers.com*, https://www.newspapers.com/image/247564051/?article=da527bc3-1435-4175-a028-ce6bba2dd9f5; "Conrad Cylkowski," Veterans Affairs BIRLS Death File, accessed October 3, 2022, as subscriber to *Fold3.com*, https://www.fold3.com/record/619355561/conrad-cylkowski-1930-veterans-affairs-birls-death-file.

[68] "1930 United States Federal Census," Joliet Township, Will County, Illinois, s.v. "Ray Goodson," accessed October 9, 2022, as subscriber to *Ancestry.com*, https://www.ancestry.com/discoveryui-content/view/88202739:6224.

[69] Joliet Township High School, *The J* (Joliet Township, Illinois, 1942), 167, accessed October 3, 2022, as subscriber to E-yearbook.com, https://www.e-yearbook.com/sp/eybb?school=20648&year=1942.

[70] Mary R. McCorvie and Patricia M, Welch, "The Homefront: The Joliet Arsenal During WW II," Shawnee National Forest, Forest Service, U.S. Department of Agriculture, *FS.USDA.gov*, 5-6, accessed October 3, 2022, https://www.fs.usda.gov/Internet/FSE_DOCUMENTS/stelprdb5269917.pdf.

[71] Peter Rathbun, "Joliet Army Ammunition Plant: Written Historical and Descriptive Data," (Washington, D.C.: Historic American Engineering Record, National Park Service, Department of the Interior for the Department of the Army, 1984), 21, accessed October 3, 2022, http://lcweb2.loc.gov/master/pnp/habshaer/il/il0400/il0463/data/il0463data.pdf.

[72] "The Joliet Army Ammunition Plant," Forest Service: U.S. Department of Agriculture, *FS.USDA.gov*, accessed October 3, 2022, https://www.fs.usda.gov/detail/midewin/learning/history-culture/?cid=stelprdb5155180.

[73] "The Joliet Army Ammunition Plant," Forest Service.

[74] Rathbun, "Joliet Army Ammunition Plant," 23, accessed October 3, 2022.

[75] "The Joliet Army Ammunition Plant," Forest Service.

[76] Phil Angelo, "Wartime Explosion Rocks Area," *Daily Journal* (Kankakee, IL), June 2, 2017, accessed October 3, 2022, https://www.daily-journal.com/news/local/wartime-explosion-rocked-area/article_22c33c59-0481-5f48-9d07-6394dc7397ec.htm.

[77] McCorvie and Welch, "The Homefront," 2, accessed October 3, 2022.

[78] "With America's Fighters, Staff Sgt. Glenn A. Goodson," *Chicago Tribune*, January 21, 1945, 115, accessed October 3, 2022, as subscriber to *Newspapers.com*, https://www.newspapers.com/image/370470263/?terms=Glenn%20Goodson&match=1.

[79] "U.S. World War II Draft Cards Young Men, 1940-1947," s.v. "Hong Suey Chin," accessed as subscriber to *Ancestry.com* on August 4, 2022, https://www.ancestry.com/discoveryui-content/view/302841306:2238?tid=&pid=&queryId=b73694015738fd45700f63cfbc2d0420&_phsrc=zsS96&_phstart=successSource.

[80] Ray Dalio, *Principles for Dealing with The Changing World Order: Why Nations Succeed and Fail* (New York: Simon & Shuster, 2021), 1.

[81] Joshua Stoff (Curator), "The Aviation History of Long Island," Cradle of Aviation Museum, *CradleofAviation.org*, accessed October 3, 2022, https://www.cradleofaviation.org/history/history/heritage.html.

[82] A. Scott Berg, *Lindbergh* (New York: Berkley Books, 1999), 114.

[83] Stoff, "The Aviation History of Long Island."

[84] David Chin, email message to author, May 20, 2020.

[85] "Aileen Bryant Wed to Meyer Osofsky," *Harrisburg Telegraph*, August 3, 1945, 6, accessed October 4, 2022, as subscriber to *Newspapers.com*, https://www.newspapers.com/ image/43019336/?terms=Harrisburg%20Telegraph%2C%20Osofsky&match=1.

[86] "1930 United States Federal Census," 3rd Assembly District, Queens County, New York City, New York, s.v. "Adolf Orkin," accessed October 9, 2022, as subscriber to *Ancestry.com*, https:// www.ancestry.com/discoveryui-content/view/44821990:6224?tid=&pid=&queryId=716b375a 2032297426832dc6363d54f2&_phsrc=zsS294&_phstart=successSource; "1940 United States Federal Census," Brooklyn, Kings County, New York City, New York, s.v. "Adolf Orkin," accessed October 9, 2022, as subscriber to Ancestry.com, https://www.ancestry.com/discoveryui-content/view/3765922:2442?tid=&pid=&queryId=716b375a2032297426832dc6363d54f2&_phsrc=zsS293&_phstart=successSource.

[87] "U.S. World War II Draft Cards Young Men, 1940-1947," s.v. "David Orkin," accessed as subscriber to *Ancestry.com* on August 4, 2022, https://www.ancestry.com/discoveryui-content/view/195368363:2238?tid=&pid=&queryId=9804f284c92f515697da03308b4de28c&_phsrc=zsS98&_phstart=successSource; "Enlisted Record and Report of Separation: Honorable Discharge," s.v. "David Orkin (born February 7, 1925)," copy emailed to author on August 30, 2021 by Rick Orkin, son of David Orkin.

[88] Richard Johnson, "Hudson Hotel, New York City," *Flickr.com*, accessed October 4, 2022, https://www.flickr.com/photos/dickjohnson/6022271904.

[89] Johnson, "Hudson Hotel."

[90] Christine Lehner, "The Fate of the Henry Hudson Hotel," Sort Quench & Dump, *SortQuenchDump.blogspot.com*, March 25, 2009, accessed October 4, 2022, https:// sortquenchdump.blogspot.com/2009/03/fate-of-henry-hudson-hotel.html.

[91] "U.S. World War II Draft Cards," David Orkin.

[92] "1930 United States Federal Census," Dewitt Township, Clinton County, Michigan, s.v. "Frank Mosher," accessed October 9, 2022, as subscriber to *Ancestry.com*, https://www.ancestry.com/ discoveryui-content/view/13390122:6224.

[93] "Musician Frank Mosher Dies," *Albuquerque Journal* (Albuquerque, New Mexico), November 7, 1990, 41, accessed August 20, 2023, as subscriber to *Newspapers.com*, https://www. newspapers.com/image/158639106/?terms=Frank%20Mosher&match=1.

[94] "Stronghurst P.T.A. Friday at School," *Albuquerque Journal*, March 3, 1936, 7, accessed October 4, 2022, as subscriber to *Newspapers.com*, https://www.newspapers.com/ image/156324357/?terms=Kirk%20mosher&match=1.

[95] "Children Will Give Musical, Dance Review," *The Albuquerque Tribune* (Albuquerque, NM), May 7, 1937, 7, accessed March 21, 2023, as subscriber to *Newspapers.com*, https://www. newspapers.com/image/782479823/?terms=Children%20will%20give%20musical&match=1.

[96] "Society Flashes," *Albuquerque Journal*, December 1, 1938, 10, accessed October 4, 2022, as subscriber to *Newspapers.com*, https://www.newspapers.com/ image/157469861/?terms=society%20flashes&match=1.

97 "Completes Training," *Albuquerque Journal*, August 10, 1944, 7, accessed October 4, 2022, as subscriber to *Newspapers.com*, https://www.newspapers.com/image/156169430/?terms=Completes%20Training&match=1.

98 "U.S. World War II Draft Cards Young Men, 1940-1947," s.v. "Kirk Gaylord Mosher," accessed as subscriber to *Ancestry.com* on August 4, 2022, https://www.ancestry.com/discoveryui-content/view/6264183:2238?tid=&pid=&queryId=b005426d48ac8676c1d8308963b997d8&_phsrc=zsS100&_phstart=successSource.

99 U.S. Army Corps of Engineers, Albuquerque District, "History of the Albuquerque District," accessed March 23, 2023, https://www.spa.usace.army.mil/About/History/.

100 "Kirkland AFB, NM History," *Kirklandhousing.com*, accessed March 23, 2023, https://www.kirtlandhousing.com/history.

101 Ray Monk, *Robert Oppenheimer: A Life Inside the Center* (New York: Anchor Books, 2014), 338.

102 Monk, *Oppenheimer*, 335-336.

103 Monk, *Oppenheimer*, 338; Jennie Rothenberg Gritz, "An Exclusive Behind-the-Scenes Look at the Los Alamos Lab Where Robert Oppenheimer Created the Atomic Bomb," July/August 2023, *SmithsonianMagazine.com*, accessed August 17, 2023, https://www.smithsonianmag.com/history/exclusive-behind-scenes-look-los-alamos-lab-where-robert-oppenheimer-created-atomic-bomb-180982336/.

104 "History of the Albuquerque District," US Army Corps of Engineers, Albuquerque District Website, accessed August 15, 20223, https://www.spa.usace.army.mil/About/History/.

105 "Completes Training," *Albuquerque Journal*.

106 "Sgt. Kirk Mosher Missing," *Albuquerque Journal*, 3, December 29, 1944, 9, accessed October 4, 2022, as subscriber to *Newspapers.com*, https://www.newspapers.com/image/156237450/?terms=Sgt%20Kirk%20Mosher%20missing%20in%20action&match=1.

107 Kathleen Krajewski (daughter of Dan Mosher), telephone conversation with author, March 16, 2023.

108 "Michigan, Census of World War I Veterans with Card Index, 1917-1919," s.v. "Frank Mosher," accessed August 14, 2023, as subscriber to *FamilySearch.org*, https://www.familysearch.org/search/record/results?f.collectionId=3007553&q.anyDate.from=1893&q.anyPlace=Dundar%2C+Canada&q.givenName=Frank&q.surname=Mosher

109 "1940 United States Federal Census," Brooklyn, Kings County, New York City, New York, s.v. "Harry Osofsky," accessed October 9, 2022, as subscriber to *Ancestry.com*, https://www.ancestry.com/discoveryui-content/view/14296579:2442?tid=&pid=&queryId=7ae8359cfde1d3b2a4c0121ff02732fd&_phsrc=zsS313&_phstart=successSource.

110 *The World Book Encyclopedia* (Chicago, IL: Field Enterprises Educational Corporation, 1968), s.v. "Ellis Island," Volume 6, 192.

111 Meyer Osofsky, telephone conversation with author, December 17, 2016; "Declaration of Intention and Petition for Naturalization," s.v. "Harry Osofsky," New York, U.S., State and Federal Naturalization Records, 1794-1943, June 7, 1920, accessed July 23, 2023, as subscriber to *Ancestry.com*, https://www.ancestry.com/discoveryui-content/view/3367720:2280?tid=&pid=&queryId=8d5f96736723be68b48ff02ae4f845bd&_phsrc=bgd479&_phstart=successSource.

[112] "U.S. World War I Draft Registration Cards, 1917-1918," s.v. "Harry Osofsky," accessed on August 4, 2022, as subscriber to *Fold3.com*, https://www.fold3.com/image/567992512?terms=war,i,harry,world,united,america,osofsky,states.

[113] Meyer Osofsky, telephone conversation with author, June 2, 2017,

[114] History.Com Editors," Treaties of Brest-Litovsk," August 21, 2018, updated November 9, 2009, *History.com*, accessed August 8, 2023, https://www.history.com/topics/world-war-i/treaties-of-brest-litovsk.

[115] "New York, U.S., Abstracts of World War I for Military Service," s.v. "Harry Osofsky," accessed October 5, 2022 as subscriber to *Ancestry.com*, https://www.ancestry.com/discoveryui-content/view/290246:3030?tid=&pid=&queryId=1f26713f916957d9c6da258e8ff9166b&_phsrc=zsS281&_phstart=successSource.

[116] Meyer Osofsky, telephone conversation with author, May 16, 1916.

[117] Carl Edward Glock, *History of the 316th Regiment of Infantry in the World War 1918*, Gift to the Congressional Library War Records by Carl Edward Glock, Captain, 316th Infantry, who was from Pittsburgh, on April 9, 1920, 103, accessed on October 5, 2022, http://www.314th.org/books/History-of-the-316th-Infantry.pdf.

[118] Glock, *History of the 316th Regiment*, 8.

[119] Glock, *History of the 316th Regiment*, 103.

[120] Glock, *History of the 316th Regiment*, 100-101.

[121] Glock, *History of the 316th Regiment*, 103-104.

[122] Glock, *History of the 316th Regiment*, 105-106.

[123] Glock, *History of the 316th Regiment*, 106; "New York, U.S., Abstracts of World War I for Military Service," s.v. "Harry Osofsky.".

[124] "1940 United States Federal Census," Brooklyn, Kings County, New York City, New York, s.v. "Harry Osofsky," accessed October 9, 2022, as subscriber to *Ancestry.com*, https://www.ancestry.com/discoveryui-content/view/14296579:2442?tid=&pid=&queryId=7ae8359cfde1d3b2a4c0121ff02732fd&_phsrc=zsS313&_phstart=successSource.

[125] Meyer Osofsky, telephone conversation with author, December 19, 2016,

[126] James Madison High School, *The Log* (Brooklyn, New York, 1942), 21 and 25, accessed October 5, 2022, https://www.e-yearbook.com/sp/eybb?school=82004&year=1942.

[127] "Aileen Osofsky Obituary," *The New York Times*, June 26, 2010, accessed October 5, 2022, https://archive.nytimes.com/query.nytimes.com/gst/fullpage-9D0CE5DD123AF935A15755C0A9669D8B63.html.

[128] "Aileen Osofsky, Infobridge: Bridge for all the world, *Infobridge.it*, accessed October 5, 2022, http://www.infobridge.it/Campioni_OsofskyA.htm.

[129] Meyer Osofsky, telephone conversation with author, August 20, 2014.

[130] James Madison High School, *The Log*, 47.

[131] "Abe Oberlin," *Mailtribune.com*, February 7, 1012, accessed October 5, 2022, https://www.mailtribune.com/obituaries/2012/02/07/abe-oberlin/.

[132] "Aileen Osofsky, *Infobridge.it*.

[133] "Al Bryant, Past JCC President, Community Leader Passes Away," *Community Review* (Published by The Jewish Federation of Greater Harrisburg/Greater Harrisburg's Jewish Newspaper, Vol. 87, No. 25, December 13, 2013), 6, accessed October 5, 2022, https://cdn.fedweb.org/102/197/12-13-13.pdf?v=1396013818.

[134] "Indiana, U.S., Birth Certificates, 1907-1944," s.v. "James Robert Muth," accessed October 9, 2022, as subscriber to *Ancestry.com*, https://www.ancestry.com/imageviewer/collections/60871/images/40474_357669-01628?treeid=&personid=&hintid=&queryId=3a0e2771aed4bc856585b1cf3b5ee7f8&usePUB=true&_phsrc=zsS316&_phstart=successSource&usePUBJs=true&pId=2012226.

[135] "U.S. World War II Draft Cards Young Men, 1940-1947," s.v. "Charles Joseph Muth," accessed as subscriber to *Ancestry.com* on August 4, 2022, https://www.ancestry.com/discoveryui-content/view/41217489:2238?tid=&pid=&queryId=6387c15ece4c684f79cba2033f78872e&_phsrc=zsS286&_phstart=successSource; "U.S., Social Security Death Index, 1935-2014," s.v. "Victoria Muth," (born March 30, 1901), accessed October 10, 2022, as subscriber to *Ancestry.com*, https://search.ancestry.com/cgi-bin/sse.dll?dbid=3693&h=44554145&indiv=try&o_vc=Record:OtherRecord&rhSource=61370&_gl=1*rf6zky*_ga*ODE2MTI1Mjk4LjE2NjQyODA0OTY.*_ga_4QT8FMEX30*MTY2NTQ0MDM3OS40LjEuMTY2NTQ0MTA4OS4wLjAuMA; "Illinois, County Marriage Records, 1800-1940," s.v. "Victoria Boudreau" (married Charles J. Shea on August 3, 1916), accessed October 10, 2022, as subscriber to *Ancestry.com*, https://www.ancestry.com/discoveryui-content/view/901317122:61370?tid=&pid=&queryId=4f66fd7642ad94b04fbbc6643cb095a3&_phsrc=bgd76&_phstart=successSource.

[136] "U.S., Army Transport Service, Passenger Lists, 1910-1939," s.v. "Charles J. Shea," (USS *Calamares* from St. Nazaire, France, to Hoboken, New Jersey), accessed October 10, 2022, as subscriber to *Fold3.com*, https://www.fold3.com/image/604224429?rec=624609708&terms=war,shea,j,i,world,charles.

[137] "1930 United States Federal Census," Barrington Township, Cook County, Illinois, s.v. "Charles J. Kershaw," accessed October 10, 2022, as subscriber to *Ancestry.com*, https://www.ancestry.com/discoveryui-content/view/83534350:6224.

[138] "U.S., City Directories, 1822-1995, Indianapolis, Indiana, 1936," s.v. "Charles J. Muth," accessed October 19, 2022, as subscriber to *Ancestry.com*, https://www.ancestry.com/discoveryui-content/view/657500750:2469?tid=&pid=&queryId=63eb47107dd2459318f7a58d8e4459fb&_phsrc=zsS323&_phstart=successSource.

[139] Lynn Fox, telephone conversation with author, November 8, 2020. On November 15, 2020, he texted to the author two photographs of Charles J. Muth on the 1935 track and basketball teams at TMI.

[140] "Birth Certificates," James Robert Muth.

[141] "1940 United States Federal Census," Indianapolis, Marion County, Indiana, s.v. "Charles J. Muth," accessed October 10, 2022, as subscriber to *Ancestry.com*, https://www.ancestry.com/discoveryui-content/view/53180660:2442?tid=&pid=&queryId=63eb47107dd2459318f7a58d8e4459fb&_phsrc=zsS324&_phstart=successSource.

[142] David D. Jackson, "International Harvester in World War II," accessed October 10, 2022, *USAutoIndustryWorldWarTwo.com*, http://usautoindustryworldwartwo.com/internationalharvester.htm.

Notes

[143] "U.S. World War II Draft Cards," Charles Joseph Muth.

[144] "Army-Navy E Award," Naval History and Heritage Command, *History.Navy.mil*, accessed October 10, 2022, https://www.history.navy.mil/research/library/online-reading-room/title-list-alphabetically/a/army-navy-e-award.html.

[145] "Local Bombardier, Gunner, Navigator Win Medals for Fighting Over Italy," *The Indianapolis Star*, November 4, 1944. 16, accessed October 10, 2022, as subscriber to *Newspapers.com*, https://www.newspapers.com/image/104958756/?terms=Local%20Bombardier%2C%20Gunner%2C%20Navigator&match=1.

[146] Drew Middleton, "Gelsenkirchen Hit in Daylight Blows," *The New York Times*, November 6, 1943, 1, accessed October 10, 2022, as subscriber to *TimesMachine.NYTimes.com*, https://timesmachine.nytimes.com/timesmachine/1943/11/06/85130318.pdf?pdf_redirect=true&ip=0

Chapter 8: THE COMBAT TEAM

[1] Tom Faulkner, *Flying with the Fifteenth Air Force: A B-24 Pilot's Missions from Italy During World War II* (Denton, TX: University of North Texas Press, 2018), 130; Martin W. Bowman, *B-24 Combat Missions: First-Hand Accounts of Liberator Operations Over Nazi Europe* (New York, Metro Books, 2009), 76.

[2] Paul R. Nugent (Major, Air Corps, 47th Wing Bombardier), "Fundamentals," Fifteenth Air Force Weekly Summary of Bombing, October 7 to October 13, 1944, *Air Force Historical Research Agency*, Microfilm Reel A6384, 542.

[3] Yancy D. Mailes, *Mountain Home Air Force Base* (Charleston, SC: Arcadia Publishing, 2007), 7.

[4] "Crew Coordination," *Radio Operators' Information File*, War Department, AAF Form No. 24R, Section 1, 1-2-1, November 1944, Revised June 1945, accessed August 7, 2022, http://www.radiomanual.info/schemi/Surplus_Handbooks/Radio_operators_information_file_1944.pdf.

[5] Stephen E. Ambrose, *The Wild Blue: The Men and Boys Who Flew B-24s Over Germany* (New York: Simon & Schuster, 2001), 99-100; Mailes, Mountain Home, 22-23.

[6] Meyer Osofsky, telephone conversation with author, August 26, 2016.

[7] Meyer Osofsky, telephone conversation with author, September 16, 1916.

[8] Joseph F. Baugher, "Martin AT-23/TB-26 Marauder," March 14, 2000, Joseph F. Baugher (Blog), *JoeBaugher.com*, accessed October 27, 2022, http://www.joebaugher.com/usaf_bombers/b26_16.html.

[9] Office of Statistical Control, *Army Air Forces Statistical Digest: World War II* (Washington, D.C.: Department of the Air Force, Headquarters United States Air Force, December, 1945), 310, accessed October 28, 2022, https://apps.dtic.mil/sti/pdfs/ADA542518.pdf.

[10] Ambrose, *Wild Blue*, 100.

[11] David Chin, son of Calvin, sent copy to author in email dated May 22, 2020.

[12] Meyer Osofsky, telephone conversation with author, June 24, 1916; Tech/Sgt. Chuck Blaney, "World War II – Prisoners of War – Stalag Luft I: A collection of stories, photos, art, and

information on Stalag Luft I," Stalag Luft I Online, accessed October 30, 2022, http://www. merkki.com/blaneychuck.htm.

[13] Meyer Osofsky, telephone conversation with author, March 7, 2017.

[14] "Cpl. and Mrs. Mosher," *Albuquerque Journal* (Albuquerque, New Mexico), August 30, 1944, 7, accessed October 31, 2022, as subscriber to *Newspapers.com*, https://www.newspapers.com/ image/156182905/?terms=Kirk%20Mosher&match=1.

[15] Alison Skaggs, "A Look Inside Camp Patrick Henry," July 30, 2015, The Mariners Museum and Park, *MarinersMuseum.org*, accessed October 31, 2012, https://www.marinersmuseum. org/2015/07/inside-look-at-camp-patrick-henry/.

[16] "Hampton Roads History: Pictures: Hampton Roads Port of Embarkation provided non-stop pipeline to World War II," June 16, 2017, *Dailypress.com*, accessed May 23, 2022, https://www. dailypress.com/history/dp-hampton-roads-port-of-embarkation-provided-nonstop-pipeline-to-world-war-ii-20170616-photogallery.html.

[17] "Kilpatrick Predicts Post-War Sports Boom," *Daily News* (Newport News, Virginia), September 17, 1944, 8B, accessed October 31, 2022, as a subscriber to *Newspapers.com*, https://www. newspapers.com/image/231226404/?terms=Army%20to%20Stress%20Games%20during%20 Demobilization&match=1.

[18] Honorable Discharge of John J. Cooney sent to author by Peter Cooney, John's brother, in September 2014.

[19] Ambrose, *Wild Blue*, 99 and 103-104.

[20] Ambrose, *Wild Blue*, 100.

[21] Meyer Osofsky, telephone conversation with author, June 24, 2016.

[22] Meyer Osofsky, telephone conversation with author, June 24, 2016.

[23] David Cylkowski, telephone conversation with author, March 16, 2021.

[24] Meyer Osofsky, telephone conversation with author, January 17, 2017.

[25] "450th Bombardment Group (H) Narrative January 1945," 450th Bomb Group Memorial Association, *450thBG.com*, accessed October 31, 2022, https://www.450thbg.com/real/ history/1945/january.shtml.

[26] "450th Bombardment Group (H)," *450thBG.com*.

[27] "Thaddeus Cylkowski," 450th Bomb Group Memorial Association, *450thBG.org*, accessed October 31, 2022, https://www.450thbg.com/real/biographies/cylkowski/cylkowski.shtml.

[28] Morale Services Division, Army Service Forces, War Department and Educational Services Section, Bureau of Naval Personnel, Navy Department, *Catalog of the United States Armed Forces Institute*, Second Edition (Washington, D.C.: U. S. Government Printing Office, Second Edition, March 1944), 1-2.

[29] History.com Editors, "G.I. Bill," originally published May 27, 2010, updated June 7, 2019, *History.com*, accessed October 31, 2022, https://www.history.com/topics/world-war-ii/gi-bill.

Notes

[30] "76th Anniversary of the G.I. Bill," FDR Presidential Library and Museum of the National Archives and Records Administration, *FDRLibrary.tumblr.com*, June 25, 2020, accessed November 1, 2022, https://fdrlibrary.tumblr.com/post/621638819686514688/76th-anniversary-of-the-gi-bill.

[31] "Servicemen's Readjustment Act (1944)," National Archives, Milestone Documents, *Archives.gov*, accessed November 1, 2022, https://www.archives.gov/milestone-documents/servicemens-readjustment-act.

[32] "Servicemen's Readjustment Act (1944)," National Archives.

[33] "Bonus Expeditionary Forces March on Washington," National Park Service, *NPS.gov*, accessed November 1, 2022, https://www.nps.gov/articles/bonus-expeditionary-forces-march-on-washington.htm#:~:text=In%20May%201932%2C%20jobless%20WWI,they%20really%20needed%20the%20money.

[34] Paul Dickson and Thomas B. Allen, "Marching on History: When a 'Bonus Army' of World War I veterans converged on Washington, MacArthur, Eisenhower and Patton were there to greet them," Smithsonian Magazine, *SmithsonianMag.com*, February 2003, accessed November 1, 2022, https://www.smithsonianmag.com/history/marching-on-history-75797769/.

[35] Dickson and Allen, "Bonus Army," *SmithsonianMag.com*.

[36] Editors of Encyclopedia Britannica, s.v. "Bonus Army," *Encyclopedia Britannica Online*, December 4, 2019, accessed November 1, 2022, https://www.britannica.com/event/Bonus-Army.

[37] Dickson and Allen, "Bonus Army," *SmithsonianMag.com*.

[38] Dickson and Allen, "Bonus Army," *SmithsonianMag.com*.

[39] Dickson and Allen, "Bonus Army," *SmithsonianMag.com*.

[40] Dickson and Allen, "Bonus Army," *SmithsonianMag.com*.

[41] Dickson and Allen, "Bonus Army," *SmithsonianMag.com*.

[42] Dickson and Allen, "Bonus Army," *SmithsonianMag.com*.

[43] "World War and Veterans: Struggle for Compensation," History, Art & Archives, United States House of Representatives, *History.House.gov*, accessed November 1, 2022, https://history.house.gov/the-first-women-in-congress-struggle-for-compensation/#:~:text=The%20World%20War%20Adjusted%20Compensation,to%20be%20issued%20until%201945.

[44] GI Bill: How Transformative It's Been," United States Department of Defense, *Defense.gov*, January 9, 2019, accessed November 1, 2022, https://www.defense.gov/News/Feature-Stories/story/Article/1727086/75-years-of-the-gi-bill-how-transformative-its-been/.

[45] Meyer Osofsky, telephone conversation with author, June 24, 2016.

[46] Meyer Osofsky, telephone conversations with author, August 26, 2016, and January 27, 2017.

[47] "American War Memorial by Gibraltar Rock Tours," August 12, 2017, Gibraltar Rock Tours, *Gibraltar-Rock-Tours.com*, accessed November 1, 2022, https://www.gibraltar-rock-tours.com/american-war-memorial-by-gibraltar-rock-tours/.

[48] Richard G. Davis, *HAP: Henry H. Arnold Military Aviator* (Washington, D.C.: Air Force History and Museums Program, 1997), 30.

[49] James Parton, *"Air Force Spoken Here": General Ira Eaker and the Command of the Air* (Bethesda, MD: Adler & Adler, Publishers, Inc., 1985), 114.

[50] Carroll V. Glines, *The Doolittle Raid: America's daring first strike against Japan* (Atglen, PA: Schiffer Publishing Ltd., 1991), 206.

[51] Craig Nelson, *The First Heroes: The Extraordinary Story of the Doolittle Raid—America's First World War II Victory* (New York: Penguin Books, 2003), xi.

[52] Harold Faber, editor, *Luftwaffe: A History* (New York: New York Times Books, 1977), 179.

[53] Raymond Limbach, *Encyclopedia Britannica Online*, s.v. "Blitzkrieg," August 22, 2023, accessed August 31, 2023, https://www.britannica.com/topic/blitzkrieg.

[54] Faber, *Luftwaffe*, 175, 203-207, and 250.

[55] Faber, *Luftwaffe*, 139.

[56] Faber, *Luftwaffe*, 24.

[57] Faber, *Luftwaffe*, 61.

[58] James MacGregor Burns, *Roosevelt: The Soldier of Freedom: 1940-1945* (New York: Francis Parkman Prize Edition, History Book Club, 2006), 496.

[59] Faber, *Luftwaffe*, 124.

[60] Faber, *Luftwaffe*, 27-34.

[61] Faber, *Luftwaffe*, 10.

[62] Sven Felix Kellerhoff, *The Fuhrer Bunker: Hitler's Last Refuge* (Berlin, Germany: Berlin Story Verlag, 2014), 90.

[63] David J.A. Stone, Writer (plus Contributing Writers and Consultants), *World War II Chronicle* (Lincolnwood, IL: Legacy Publishing, 2007), 471.

[64] "Erhard Milch," *Spartacus-educational.com*, accessed November 1, 2022, https://spartacus-educational.com/GERmiltch.htm.

[65] Richard Overy, *Why the Allies Won* (New York: W. W. Norton & Company, 1996), 219.

[66] Meyer Osofsky, telephone conversation with author, March 23, 2017.

[67] Ambrose, *Wild Blue*, 128.

[68] "See Naples and Die," Margie in Italy, *MargieinItaly.com*, accessed November 6, 2022, https://margieinitaly.com/2014/10/see-naples-die/.

[69] Jeff Mathews, "Air Raids on Naples in WWII," June 2006, *Around Naples Encyclopedia*, University of Maryland University College, Italian Studies (Naples), accessed November 6,

Notes

2022, https://web.archive.org/web/20110611112050/http://faculty.ed.umuc.edu/~jmatthew/naples/Naples%20bombing.htm.

[70] Michael Korda, *Ike: An American Hero* (New York: Harper Collins, 2007), 412; Thomas R. Brooks, *The War North of Rome: June 1944-May 1945* (New York: Sarpedon, 1966), 1-3.

[71] Matthew Parker, *Monte Cassino: The Hardest-Fought Battle of World War II* (New York: Anchor Books, 2005), 31.

[72] John W. Lanza, *Shot Down Over Italy: A true story of courage and survival in Nazi-occupied Italy during World War II* (Caldwell, NJ: Bright Spot Books, 2010), 202-205

[73] Korda, *Ike*, 564.

[74] Parker, *Monte Cassino*, 31-32.

[75] Parker, *Monte Cassino*, 32.

[76] Meyer Osofsky, telephone conversation with author, December 17, 2016.

[77] Mae Mills Link and Hubert A. Coleman, *Medical Support of the Army Air Forces in World War II* (Washington, D.C.: Office of the Surgeon General, USAF, 1955), 686.

[78] Meyer Osofsky, telephone conversation with author, December 17, 2016.

[79] Meyer Osofsky, telephone conversation with author, March 23, 2017.

[80] Meyer Osofsky, telephone conversation with author, January 27, 2017.

[81] Ambrose, *Wild Blue*, 137.

[82] "The European Union and Countries in the EU," Schengen Visa Information, *SchengenVisaInfo.com*, accessed November 7, 2022, https://www.schengenvisainfo.com/countries-in-europe/eu-countries/; "What is the currency in Italy?" Think in Italian, *ThinkinItalian.com*, accessed November 7, 2022, https://www.thinkinitalian.com/italian-currency/.

[83] Booth Mooney, *General Billy Mitchell* (Chicago: Follett Publishing Company, 1968), 14-16.

[84] "European Union," Schengen Visa.

[85] Mikaela Gavas and Svea Koch, "Germany's Role in EU Development Policy: From Broker to Agenda-Setter," September 9, 2021, Center for Global Development, *CGDev.org*, accessed November 7, 2022, https://www.cgdev.org/blog/germanys-role-eu-development-policy-broker-agenda-setter.

[86] Meyer Osofsky, telephone conversation with author, August 8, 2014; Honorable Discharge of John J. Cooney sent to author by Peter Cooney, John's brother, in September 2014.

[87] 446th Historian, "Castelluccio: Military Site: Airfield," American Air Museum in Britain, *AmericanAirMuseum.com*, November 5, 2016, accessed November 8, 2022, https://www.americanairmuseum.com/place/167829.

[88] "Foggia Airfield Complex," written December 20, 2010, updated September 26, 2018, Forgotten Airfields in Europe, *ForgottenAirfields.com*, accessed November 8, 2022, https://www.forgottenairfields.com/airfield-foggia-airfield-complex-561.html.

[89] Ambrose, *Wild Blue*, 124.

[90] Faulkner, *Flying with the Fifteenth*, xvii and 105; James H. "Jimmy" Doolittle with Carroll V. Glines, *I Could Never Be So Lucky Again* (New York: Bantam Books, 1991), 359-360.

Chapter 9: FLYING COMBAT MISSIONS

[1] Mae Mills Link and Hubert A. Coleman, *Medical Support of the Army Air Forces in World War II* (Washington, D.C.: Office of the Surgeon General, USAF, 1955), 438.\

2 Headquarters, Mediterranean Allied Air Forces, "The Mediterranean Allied Strategic Air Force—Trends of Activity, October to December 1944," *R.A.F. Mediterranean Review No. 9, October to December 1944*, 41-53.

[3] "Foggia Airfield Complex: Abandoned Forgotten & Little Known Airfields in Europe," written December 20, 2010, updated September 26, 2018, *ForgottenAirfields.com*, accessed November 8, 2022, https://www.forgottenairfields.com/airfield-foggia-airfield-complex-561.html.

[4] "Foggia Airfield Complex," *ForgottenAirfields.com*.

[5] "General Ira C. Eaker," Biographies, United States Air Force, *AF.mil*, accessed November 10, 2022, https://www.af.mil/About-Us/Biographies/Display/Article/107172/general-ira-c-eaker/.

[6] James Parton, *"Air Force Spoken Here": General Ira Eaker and the Command of the Air* (Bethesda, MD: Adler & Adler, Publishers, Inc., 1985), 355; "Caserta Royal Palace and Park, Italy," Royal Europe, World Heritage, National Geographic, *WorldHeritage.com*, accessed November 10, 2022, https://visitworldheritage.com/en/eu/caserta-royal-palace-and-park-italy/73cf1988-9d13-4658-99f5-2f23a706bc00.

[7] Brian Hutchins, "General Nathan Twining and the Fifteenth Air Force in World War II," (Master's Thesis, University of North Texas, May 2008), 5, https://digital.library.unt.edu/ark:/67531/metadc6094/m2/1/high_res_d/thesis.pdf.

[8] Link and Coleman, *Medical Support*, 440.

[9] Hutchins, "General Nathan Twining," 20.

[10] Hutchins, "General Nathan Twining," 15.

[11] Hutchins, "General Nathan Twining," 25.

[12] Hutchins, "General Nathan Twining," 34 and 35.

[13] Steve Blank, "Hidden in Plain Sight: The Secret History of Silicon Valley" (Slide Presentation), Computer History Museum, *Internet-Salmagundi.com*, accessed November 10, 2022, https://internet-salmagundi.com/2019/02/hiding-in-plain-sight-the-secret-history-of-silicon-valley/.

[14] Hutchins, "General Nathan Twining," 35.

[15] Hutchins, "General Nathan Twining," 20.

[16] "Twining, Nathan: Military Strategist," Enshrined in National Aviation Hall of Fame, *NationalAviation.com*, 1976, accessed November 10, 2022, https://www.nationalaviation.org/our-enshrinees/twining-nathan/.

Notes

[17] Michael E. Haskew, *West Point 1915: Eisenhower, Bradley and the Class the Stars Fell On* (Minneapolis, MN: Zenith Press, 2014), fourth photo caption after page 128.

[18] Paul R. Nugent (Major, Air Corps, 47th Wing Bombardier), "Fundamentals," Fifteenth Air Force Weekly Summary of Bombing, October 7 to October 13, 1944, *Air Force Historical Research Agency*, Microfilm Reel A6384, 542.

[19] "How H2X 'Mickey' – Got its name," 482nd Bombardment Group (P), The 8th Army Air Force Pathfinders, *482nd.org*, accessed November 11, 2022, http://www.482nd.org/h2x-mickey.

[20] "H2X 'Mickey'," 482nd Bombardment Group (P).

[21] "Radar," 482nd Bombardment Group (P), The 8th Army Air Force Pathfinders, *482nd.org*, accessed November 11, 2022, https://www.482nd.org/radar.

[22] *The World Book Encyclopedia* (Chicago, IL: Field Enterprises Educational Corporation, 1968), s.v. "Radar," Volume 16, 64.

[23] Neil Hunter Raiford, *Shadow: A Cottontail Bomber Crew in World War II* (McFarland & Company, Jefferson, NC, 1969), 139.

[24] "H2S & the Pathfinders," RAF Pathfinders Archive, *RAFPathfinders.com*, accessed November 12, 2022, https://rafpathfinders.com/h2s-the-pathfinders/.

[25] "H2X 'Mickey'," 482nd Bombardment Group (P).

[26] "H2X 'Mickey'," 482nd Bombardment Group (P).

[27] Bob Askew had discussions with author about his wartime experiences when he resided at Twin Lakes, a retirement community in Cincinnati, Ohio. He also exchanged emails with author.

[28] Bob Askew, email message to author, July 7, 2013.

[29] Bob Askew, email message to author, April 22, 2021.

[30] Donald L. Miller, *Masters of the Air: America's Bomber Boys Who Fought the Air War Against Nazi Germany* (New York: Simon & Shuster, 2006), 236.

[31] Bob Askew, email message to author, April 22, 2021.

[32] "Operational Employment of Lone Wolf Tactics," Monograph in which a discussion of sixteen lone wolf missions is presented, Fifteenth Air Force (Foreword by its commander, Nathan F. Twining), accessed November 12, 2022, https://15thaf.org/PDFs/LONE%20WOLF%20OPERATIONS.pdf.

[33] Robert Newton Askew (Obituary), Geo. J. Rohde & Son Funeral Home, *RohdeFuneral.com*, accessed November 12, 2022, https://www.rohdefuneral.com/obituary/robert-newton-askew; Bob Askew, email message to author, May 8, 2021.

[34] Daniel L. Haulman, "A Tale of Two Missions: Memmingen, July 18, 1944 & Berlin, March 24, 1945," *Air Power History*, Winter 2010, 34 and 39.

[35] Daniel L. Haulman, "Target: Berlin," Air Force Historical Research Agency, May 25, 2012, accessed November 13, 2022, https://tuskegeeairmen.org/wp-content/uploads/2020/11/TAI_Resources_Target-Berlin.pdf.

[36] Haulman, "Tale of Two Missions," 35.

[37] Bob Askew, email message to author, December 11, 2012. Attached to email was an article from *Stars and Stripes* by Sgt, I. Federgreen, "Returnees Tell Own Story Of 15th's 'Famous First'."

[38] Haulman, "Tale of Two Missions," 37.

[39] Bob Askew, email message to author, April 22, 2021.

[40] Malcolm Gladwell, *The Bomber Mafia: A Dream, A Temptation, and the Longest Night of the Second World War* (New York: Little, Brown and Company, 2021), x.

[41] John W. Lanza, *Shot Down Over Italy: A true story of courage and survival in Nazi-occupied Italy during World War II* (Caldwell, NJ: Bright Spot Books, 2010), 13.

[42] "H2X 'Mickey'," 482nd Bombardment Group (P).

[43] Barret Tillman, *Forgotten Fifteenth: The Daring Airmen Who Crippled Hitler's War Machine* (Washington, D.C.: Regnery History, 2014), 197-198.

[44] Mike Hill, *The 451st Bomb Group in World War II: A Pictorial History* (Atglen, PA: Schiffer Publishing, 2001), 111-113.

[45] "Presidential Unit Citation," Air Force Personnel Center, *AFPC.AF.mil,* https://www.afpc.af.mil/Fact-Sheets/Display/Article/421897/presidential-unit-citation/.

[46] Michael D. Hill and John R. Beitling, *B-24 Liberators of the 15th Air Force/49th Bomb Wing in World War II* (Atglen, PA: Schiffer Publishing, 2006), 10.

[47] Roger McCollester, "Raid on Regensburg," *Flight Journal,* December 2001 (On page 50 is copy of General Order No. 1481 dated July 1, 1944, for "Distinguished Unit Citation" to 451st Bombardment Group for Mission to Regensburg Prufening Aircraft Factory, Regensburg, Germany, on February 25, 1944), accessed November 14, 2022, https://www.flightjournal.com/wp-content/uploads/2011/10/RAID-ON-REGENSBURG2.pdf.

[48] "History of the 451st Bombardment Group (H)," 451st Bombardment Group (H), *451st. org,* accessed November 15, 2022, 10, https://451st.org/History/pdf's/History-of-the-451st-Bombardment-Group%20_H_.pdf.

[49] "History of the 451st," 451st Bombardment Group (H), 11.

[50] Hill, *The 451st Bomb Group,* 27-28.

[51] "History of the 451st," 451st Bombardment Group (H), 11.

[52] John F. Guilmartin, *Encyclopedia Britannica Online,* s.v. "Bf 109," accessed November 17, 2022, https://www.britannica.com/technology/Bf-109; "Fw-190 vs Bf-109," *Aviatia.net,* accessed November 17, 2022, https://aviatia.net/fw-190-vs-bf-109/.

[53] John F. Guilmartin, *Encyclopedia Britannica Online,* s.v. "Fw 190," accessed November 17, 2022, https://www.britannica.com/technology/Fw-190; "Fw-190 vs Bf-109," *Aviatia.net,* accessed November 17, 2022, https://aviatia.net/fw-190-vs-bf-109/.

[54] "Focke-Wulf Fw 190," Steel Division Wiki, accessed November 18, 2022, https://steeldivision.fandom.com/wiki/Focke-Wulf_Fw_190.

Notes

55 Harold Faber, editor, *Luftwaffe: A History* (New York: New York Times Books, 1977), 195.

56 Faber, *Luftwaffe*, 190; Richard Pearson, "Famed German Flying Ace Adolph Galland Dies at 83," *Washington Post*, accessed November 23, 2022, https://www.washingtonpost.com/archive/local/1996/02/17/famed-german-flying-ace-adolf-galland-dies-at-83/faf8376d-0fec-47a8-bf6a-51b36d96b1fb/.

57 Faber, *Luftwaffe*, 190.

58 Marek J. Murawski, *Messerschmitt Me 262: In Defense of the Third Reich* (Casemate Publishers, 2010), 10-11.

59 Faber, *Luftwaffe*, 190; Murawski, *Messerschmitt Me 262*, 9.

60 Faber, *Luftwaffe*, 192.

61 Faber, *Luftwaffe*, 213.

62 Faber, *Luftwaffe*, 193.

63 Murawski, *Messerschmitt Me 262*, 11.

64 Faber, *Luftwaffe*, 66 and 194; Murawski, *Messerschmitt Me 262*, 11.

65 William L. Shirer, *The Rise and Fall of the Third Reich: A History of Nazi Germany* (New York: Simon and Schuster, 1960), 927: Faber, Luftwaffe, 194; Murawski, Messerschmitt Me 262, 11.

66 Faber, *Luftwaffe*, 194-195.

67 Faber, *Luftwaffe*, 195.

68 R. K. Taylor (By command of Major General Twining), "Distinguished Unit Citation to 451st Bombardment Group," Mission to Markersdorf Airdrome, Vienna, Austria, on August 23, 1944, General Order No. 3757, October 2, 1944, *Air Force Historical Research Agency*, Microfilm Reel B0595, Frame 1365.

69 "North Bergen Man's Unit Double Citation Winner," *Hudson Dispatch* (Union City, NJ), Peter Cooney, brother of John Cooney, sent me a copy of this news clip, along with four other news clips, in an envelope post-dated September 15, 1914, but none of them had a date.

70 Taylor (Twining), General Order No. 3757.

71 "Liberators Run Supply Missions to France," Thursday, October 15, 1944, Narrative History from October 1 to October 31, 1944, Headquarters, 451st Bombardment Group (H), Office of the Intelligence Officer, November 3, 1944, *Air Force Historical Research Agency*, Microfilm Reel B0595, Frame 1338.

72 Robert B. N. Peck, "Narrative History, September 1944," Headquarters, 451st Bombardment Group (H), Office of the Intelligence Officer, *Air Force Historical Research Agency*, Microfilm Reel B0595, Frame 1248.

73 Henry D. Richardson, "Statistical Summary, Week Ended October 7, 1944," Headquarters, 451st Bombardment Group (H), Office of the Intelligence Officer, *Air Force Historical Research Agency*, Microfilm Reel B0595, Frames 1341 and 1342.

FROM ONE WAR TO ANOTHER

Chapter 10: LUCK IN WAR

[1] Daniel L. Haulman, "A Tale of Two Missions: Memmingen, July 18, 1944 & Berlin, March 24, 1945," *Air Power History*, Winter 2010, 35; Martin W. Bowman, *B-24 Combat Missions: First-Hand Accounts of Liberator Operations Over Nazi Europe* (New York, Metro Books, 2009),78; Harry O. Rohde, "The Evolution of a WWII Army Air Corps Bomber Pilot; The Memoirs of 1st Lieutenant Harry O. Rohde, 1942-1945," 451st Bombardment Group (H), *451st.org*, 30, accessed November 23, 2022, https://www.451st.org/Stories/Pdfs/Memoirs-of-Harry-O-Rohde-FINAL-1.pdf.

[2] Interview of John Cooney by Jessica Fragosa, Reporter & Host of *Heroes on Our Island* at Verizon FiOS 1 News, Greater New York City Area, Broadcast Media, August 31, 2010, https://www.youtube.com/watch?v=aQQgTuNxjiA. This video isn't available anymore.

[3] George Tudor, "The Saga of the *Extra Joker*," 451st Bombardment Group (H), accessed November 23, 2022, https://451st.org/Stories/Pdfs/Saga%20of%20the%20Extra%20Joker.pdf; Michael D. Hill and John R. Beitling, *B-24 Liberators of the 15th Air Force/49th Bomb Wing in World War II* (Atglen, PA: Schiffer Publishing, 2006), 64.

[4] Tudor, "Sage of *Extra Joker*; Joy Wallace Dickinson, "After decades, Orlando family learns truth about WWII Death," *Orlando Sentinel*, November 9, 2014, accessed November 23, 2022, https://www.orlandosentinel.com/features/os-joy-wallace-dickinson-1109-20141109-column.html.

[5] Nicky U. Fox (pseudonym for Nathan U. Firestone), *Extra Joker* (Bloomington, IN: Xlibris Corporation, 2002), 165-167.

[6] "MACR 7956 (Pilot Whiting)," digital images, accessed on August 3, 2022, as a subscriber to *Fold3.com* (Missing Air Crew Reports [MACRs] of the U.S. Army Air Forces, 1942-1947), https://www.fold3.com/image/28666209?terms=macr,7956; Hill and Beitling, *B-24 Liberators*, 60; Fox, *Extra Joker*, 167.

[7] Mike Hill, *The 451st Bomb Group in World War II: A Pictorial History* (Atglen, PA: Schiffer Publishing, 2001), 54.

[8] R. K. Taylor (By command of Major General Twining), "Distinguished Unit Citation to 451st Bombardment Group," Mission to Markersdorf Airdrome, Vienna, Austria, on August 23, 1944, General Order No. 3757, October 2, 1944, *Air Force Historical Research Agency*, Microfilm Reel B0595, Frame 1365.

[9] Hill and Beitling, *B-24 Liberators*, 60.

[10] Jayna Legg, "WWII former prisoner of war recounts harrowing story," *The Apollo* (Official Newsletter of the Captain James A. Lovell Federal Health Care Center), Aug-Sept-Oct 2016, Volume 9, Issue 10, 6.

[11] "Lt. Francis Bednarek To Be Buried May 16," *The Times Leader* (Wilkes-Barre, PA), May 3, 1950, 20, accessed November 24, 2022, as subscriber to *Newspapers.com*, https://www.newspapers.com/image/396241754/?terms=Lt.%20Francis%20Bednarek&match=1; "Overview," Ardennes American Cemetery, American Battle Monuments Commission, accessed November 24, 2022, https://www.abmc.gov/Ardennes.

[12] "History," American Battle Monuments Commission, *ABMC.gov*, accessed November 25, 2022, https://www.abmc.gov/about-us/history.

[13] "Overview," Ardennes American Cemetery.

Notes

[14] "Lt. Francis Bednarek," *The Times Leader*, 20.

[15] "Find A Grave," s.v. "Harry Vaughn Bates," *Findagrave.com*, accessed November 25, 2022, https://www.findagrave.com/memorial/57687994/harry-v-bates.

[16] "Historical Information," Jefferson Barracks National Cemetery, National Cemetery Administration, United States Department of Veterans Affairs, *Cem.VA.gov*, accessed November 25, 2022, https://www.cem.va.gov/cems/nchp/jeffersonbarracks.asp.

[17] "Report of Aircraft Accident (Model B-25J, Serial Number 42-51632, Accident October 23, 1944)," *Air Force Historical Research Agency*, Maxwell Air Force Base (AL), Department of the Air Force, sent to author by Craig A. Mackey, Archives Technician/USAFR Historian, February 14, 2018.

[18] Hill, *451st Bomb Group*, 126.

[19] Meyer Osofsky, telephone conversation with author, June 26, 2016.

[20] Stephen E. Ambrose, *The Wild Blue: The Men and Boys Who Flew B-24s Over Germany* (New York: Simon & Schuster, 2001), 120-121.

[21] "The flak towers," *Airpower.at*, Austria's virtual military journal, accessed June 16, 2020, http://www.airpower.at/news03/0813_luftkrieg_ostmark/flaktuerme.htm.

[22] "The flak towers," *Airpower.at*.

[23] Brad Smithfield, "Flak towers: massive reinforced concrete buildings built by the Nazis during World War II to protect cities from aerial attacks," The Vintage News, *TheVintageNews.com*, January 17, 2018, accessed June 16, 2020, https://www.thevintagenews.com/2018/01/17/flak-towers/.

[24] Smithfield, "Flak towers."

[25] Smithfield, "Flak towers."

[26] John W. Lanza, *Shot Down Over Italy: A true story of courage and survival in Nazi-occupied Italy during World War II* (Caldwell, NJ: Bright Spot Books, 2010), 167-168.

[27] John Simkin, "Fritz Todt," Spartacus Educational, *Spartacus-Educational.com*, September 1977, updated January 2020, accessed November 26, 2022, https://spartacus-educational.com/GERtodt.htm.

[28] Editors of Encyclopedia Britannica (revised and updated by Amy Tikkanen), s.v. "Albert Speer," *Encyclopedia Britannica Online*, accessed November 26, 2022, https://www.britannica.com/biography/Albert-Speer.

[29] R. J. Overy, *The Air War 1939-1945* (New York: Stein and Day, 1981), 121-122.

[30] Meyer Osofsky, telephone conversation with author, August 11, 2014.

[31] "MACRs 9048 (Pilot Elliott), 9092 (Pilot Moore), 9134 (Pilot Goin), 9047 (Pilot Baker), 9051 (Pilot Smith), 9066 (Pilot Rowsey), 9056 (Pilot Spellacy), and 9088 (Pilot Brewer)," accessed on August 3, 2022, as a subscriber to *Fold3.com*.

[32] David Chin sent email message to author on April 28, 2020, with attachments of a list his father kept of his missions in addition to some photographs.

[33] Rohde, "Memoirs," 32.

[34] John C. Schumacher, "POW Memoirs of Stalag Luft IV," *451 Ad-Lib*, Issue 40, Summer 2005, 16, *451st.org*, accessed November 26, 2022, https://www.451st.org/Ad%20Lib/Pdfs/Issue%2040.pdf.

[35] Barret Tillman, *Forgotten Fifteenth: The Daring Airmen Who Crippled Hitler's War Machine* (Washington, D.C.: Regnery History, 2014), 190.

[36] Schumacher, "POW Memoirs," 16.

[37] "MACR 9092 (Pilot Moore)," digital images, accessed on August 3, 2022, as a subscriber to *Fold3.com* (Missing Air Crew Reports [MACRs] of the U.S. Army Air Forces, 1942-1947), https://www.fold3.com/image/28691604.

[38] MACR 9092, *Fold3.com*.

[39] MACR 9092, *Fold3.com*.

[40] William C. Atkinson, *The Jolly Roger: An Airman's Tale of Survival in World War II* (Indianapolis, IN: Dog Ear Publishing, 2015), 278; Ambrose, *The Wild Blue*, 230.

[41] Schumacher, "POW Memoirs," 18; MACR 9092 (Some members of the crew thought Hall was hurt by the explosion and was in a semi-conscious state and may have slipped out of the plane when walking on the narrow catwalk in the open bomb bay.)

[42] "MACR 9092," *Fold3.com*.

[43] Schumacher, "POW Memoirs," 19; MACR 9092, *Fold3.com*.

[44] Schumacher, "POW Memoirs," 18; MACR 9092, *Fold3.com*.

[45] "MACR 9047 (Pilot Baker)," digital images, accessed on August 3, 2022, as a subscriber to *Fold3.com* (Missing Air Crew Reports [MACRs] of the U.S. Army Air Forces, 1942-1947), https://www.fold3.com/image/28677366.

[46] "MACR 9047," *Fold3.com*.

[47] "MACR 9047," *Fold3.com*.

[48] "U.S. World War II Draft Cards Young Men, 1940-1947," obtained the age of each crew member by accessing their draft registration cards as a subscriber to *Ancestry.com*.

[49] "Last Flight of Fickle Finger," 451st Bombardment Group (H) Stories (Letter from Peter A. Massare, who witnessed Fickle Finger being shot down, to Jay Auten, brother of Frank M. Auten, who was a crew member of Fickle Finger), 451st Bombardment Group (H), *451st.org*, accessed November 27, 2022, https://451st.org/Stories/Pdfs/Last%20Flight%20of%20the%20Fickle%20 Finger.pdf; MACR 9134, Fold3.com.

[50] "MACR 9051 (Pilot Smith)," digital images, accessed on August 3, 2022, as a subscriber to *Fold3.com* (Missing Air Crew Reports [MACRs] of the U.S. Army Air Forces, 1942-1947), https://www.fold3.com/image/28679462.

[51] "James J. Devlin," interred at Ardennes American Cemetery (Neupré, Belgium), American Battle Monuments Commission, *ABMC.gov*, accessed November 27, 2022, https://www.abmc.gov/decedent-search/devlin=james-3.

Notes

[52] "MACR 9051," *Fold3.com.*

[53] "Table 6, Summary of Missions (Mission 134, October 13, 1944)," Statistical Summary, Week Ending October 14, 1944," Headquarters, 451st Bomb Group (H), *Air Force Historical Research Agency*, Microfilm Reel B0595, Frame 1346.

[54] See Table 10.2: Fate of 451st Bomb Crews Shot Down on Friday the 13th, the statistics of which were obtained from the eight Missing Air Crew Reports of the eight crews and planes shot down.

[55] Hill, *451st Bomb Group*, 61.

[56] Donald L. Miller, *Masters of the Air: America's Bomber Boys Who Fought the Air War Against Nazi Germany* (New York: Simon & Shuster, 2006), 202-203.

[57] "Hungary," Life in Nazi-controlled Europe, The Holocaust Explained, The Wiener Holocaust Library, *TheHolocaustExplained.org*, accessed November 27, 2022, http://www.theholocaustexplained.org/ks3/life-in-nazi-occupied-europe/jews-in-occupied-countries/hungary/#.WJR7S1MrLcs.

[58] Hill, *451st Bomb Group*, 111-113.

[59] "Statement by Sandor Csongey," Case Files of Hungarian Helpers, Case File of József Szalay, National Archives Identifier 26311031), Container Identifier 1202, *National Archives Catalog*, 23-24, accessed February 3, 2024, https://catalog.archives.gov/id/26311031?objectPage=23.

[60] "Escape Statement by Arnold R. Silverstein," Headquarters of the Fifteenth Air Force, United States Army, *Air Force Historical Research Agency*, Microfilm Reel #806534, Frames 1255-1260 (CD received by author on December 15, 2021, from Pam Ives, Historian, AFHRA).

[61] "Statement by Sandor Csongey," Case File of József Szalay.

[62] "Statement by Sandor Csongey," Case File of József Szalay.

[63] "Escape Statement by Silverstein," *Air Force Historical Research Agency.*

[64] "Statement by Sandor Csongey," Case File of József Szalay.

[65] "Escape Statement by Silverstein," *Air Force Historical Research Agency.*

[66] "Escape Statement by Silverstein," *Air Force Historical Research Agency.*

[67] "Gendarmerie, Hungarian," Vad Vashem: The World Holocaust Remembrance Center, *YadVashem.org*, accessed February 3, 2024, www.yadvashem.org/odot_pdf/Microsoft%20Word%20-%206245.pdf.

[68] "Arrow Cross Party," Jewish Virtual Library, *JewishVirtualLibrary.org*, https://www.jewishvirtuallibrary.org/arrow-cross-party.

[69] "Escape Statement by Silverstein," *Air Force Historical Research Agency.*

[70] "Escape Statement by Silverstein," *Air Force Historical Research Agency.*

[71] Meyer Osofsky, telephone conversation with author, August 26, 2016.

[72] "Letter from Józsefné Szalay to Arnold Silverstein," Case File of József Szala, 25.

[73] "Letter from Kaarel R. Pusta to Arnold R. Silverstein on Szalay Claim," Case File of József Szalay, 9.

[74] "József Szalay Given 150,000 Pengos," Case File of József Szalay, 6; "Sandor Csorsey Given 60,000 Pengos," Case File of József Szalay, 18.

[75] "Letter from Józsefné Szalay to Arnold Silverstein," Case File of József Szalay, 25.

[76] Bryan Taylor, "The Worst Hyperinflations in History: Hungary," *Global Financial Data*, accessed December 1, 2022, https://www.globalfinancialdata.com/gfdblog/?p=2382.

[77] "Handwritten Note Stating Mr. and Mrs. Szalay Promised 4,000 Florint," Case File of József Szalay, 3.

[78] "Treaty of Peace with Hungary, 1947," *Treaties of Peace with Italy, Bulgaria, Hungary, Roumania and Finland*, (Washington, D.C.: Department of State, Publication 2743, European Series 21, U.S. Government Printing Office, 1947), 151-188, accessed December 1, 2022, https://babel.hathitrust.org/cgi/pt?id=osu.32435066406612&view=1up&seq=151.

[79] "József Szalay Helped Arnold Silverstein," Case File of József Szalay, 5.

[80] "Letter from Józsefné Szalay to Arnold Silverstein," Case File of József Szalay, 25.

[81] "Gravestone of József and Józsefné Szalay," Pestszenterzsébeti Cemetery, Budapest, Hungary, *Billion Graves*, accessed December 2, 2022, https://billiongraves.com/grave/J%C3%B3zsef-Szalay/9001342.

[82] "Arnold Robert Silverstein," Baltimore Hebrew Cemetery, *Findagrave.com*, accessed December 2, 2022, https://www.findagrave.com/memorial/171926193/arnold-robert-silverstein.

[83] "MACR 9048 (Pilot Elliott)," digital images, accessed on August 3, 2022, as a subscriber to *Fold3.com* (Missing Air Crew Reports [MACRs] of the U.S. Army Air Forces, 1942-1947), https://www.fold3.com/image/28678124.

[84] "MACR 9088 (Pilot Brewer)," digital images, accessed on August 3, 2022, as a subscriber to *Fold3.com* (Missing Air Crew Reports [MACRs] of the U.S. Army Air Forces, 1942-1947), https://www.fold3.com/image/28690300?terms=war,macr,united,world,9088,america,ii,states.

[85] "MACR 9066 (Pilot Rowsey)," digital images, accessed on August 3, 2022, as a subscriber to *Fold3.com* (Missing Air Crew Reports [MACRs] of the U.S. Army Air Forces, 1942-1947), https://www.fold3.com/image/28685246.

[86] "MACR 9056 (Pilot Spellacy)," digital images, accessed on August 3, 2022, as a subscriber to *Fold3.com* (Missing Air Crew Reports [MACRs] of the U.S. Army Air Forces, 1942-1947), https://www.fold3.com/image/28681432.

[87] Gregory A. Freeman, *The Forgotten 500: The Untold Story of the Men Who Risked All for the Greatest Rescue Mission of World War II* (New York: New American Library Caliber, 2007), 128.

[88] Freeman, *Forgotten 500*, 133 and 135-137.

[89] Freeman, *Forgotten 500*, 152-153.

[90] Daniel Dancis (an Archivist at the National Archives in College Park, MD), "Establishment of the Office of the Coordinator of Information, July 1940-July 1941," posted on the text-message

blog of the National Archives under "Crime, Justice, and Intelligence, World War II," by Dr. Greg Bradsher, Senior Archivist at the National Archives at College Park, MD, accessed December 2, 2022, https://text-message.blogs.archives.gov/2021/07/08/william-j-donovan-and-the-establishment-of-the-office-of-the-coordinator-of-information-july-1940-july-1941/.

[91] Michael Robert Patterson, "William Joseph Donovan – Major General United States Army," Arlington National Cemetery, *ArlingtonCemetery.net*, accessed December 3, 2022, https://www.arlingtoncemetery.net/wjodonov.htm.

[92] "The Office of Strategic Services," History of CIA, Central Intelligence Agency, *CIA.gov*, accessed December 3, 2022, https://www.cia.gov/legacy/cia-history/.

[93] Patrick K. O'Donnell, *Operatives, Spies and Saboteurs: The Unknown Story of WWII's OSS* (New York, Citadel Press, 2004), xiv and xv.

[94] "Office of Strategic Services," History of CIA.

[95] "About Donovan's Statue," Donovan's Statue, Central Intelligence Agency, *CIA.gov*, accessed December 3, 2022, https://www.cia.gov/legacy/headquarters/donovans-statue/#:~:text=The%20Donovan%20statue%20was%20dedicated,the%20Office%20of%20Strategic%20Services.

[96] Patterson, "William Joseph Donovan."

[97] O'Donnell, *Operatives*, 313.

[98] Freeman, *Forgotten 500*, 166.

[99] O'Donnell, *Operatives*, xv to xviii.

[100] O'Donnell, *Operatives*, 83.

[101] Freeman, *Forgotten 500*, 166.

[102] Freeman, *Forgotten 500*, 91.

[103] Freeman, *Forgotten 500*, 8.

[104] Freeman, *Forgotten 500*, 173-175.

[105] Freeman, *Forgotten 500*, 139.

[106] Freeman, *Forgotten 500*, 173-174.

[107] Freeman, *Forgotten 500*, 174 and 182.

[108] Freeman, *Forgotten 500*, 170-172.

[109] Commemorative Air Force, "Mission: Normandy," That's All Brother, *ThatsAllBrother.org*, accessed January 13, 2023, https://thatsallbrother.org.

[110] Commemorative Air Force, "That's All, Brother," accessed June 2, 2023, https://thatsallbrother.org/.

[111] Greg Young, email message to author, June 2, 2023.

[112] Freeman, *Forgotten 500*, 201-203 and 212-213.

[113] Freeman, *Forgotten 500*, 238.

[114] Thomas T. Matteson, "An Analysis of the Circumstances Surrounding the Rescue and Evacuation of Allied Aircrewmen from Yugoslavia, 1941-1945," Research Report No. 128 (A Research Paper Submitted to the Faculty, Air War College, Air University, United States Air Force, Maxwell Air Force Base, Alabama, April 1977), 31, accessed February 3, 2024, https://znaci.org/00002/406.pdf.

[115] Freeman, *Forgotten 500*, 238-239.

[116] Gregory A. Freeman, email message to author, July 7, 2016.

[117] Matteson, "Rescue and Evacuation of Allied Aircrewmen," 36.

[118] Matteson, "Rescue and Evacuation of Allied Aircrewmen," 37-42.

[119] Freeman, *Forgotten 500*, 250.

[120] Joe Scarborough, *Saving Freedom: Truman, the Cold War, and the Fight for Western Civilization* (New York: HarperCollins Publishers, 2020), xvii-xix and 60-63.

[121] Scarborough, *Saving Freedom*, 189-194.

[122] "Operation Halyard—Serbs Rescued 500 American Pilots in WWII," Tesla Society, *TeslaSociety.com*, accessed January 14, 2023, https://www.teslasociety.com/500_2.htm.

[123] Freeman, *Forgotten 500*, 279-280.

[124] Van Vernett Smith, Jr. (Tail Gunner in Fifteenth Air Force, 49th Wing, 461st Bomb Group, 765th Squadron), 461st Bombardment Group (H), *461st.org*, accessed January 14, 2023, https://461st.org/Crews/765th%20Crews/King.html.

[125] "Mission #115: Target: Vienna North Marshalling Yard, Austria," 461st Bombardment Group (H), *461st.org*, accessed January 14. 2023, https://461st.org/Missions/October1944.htm.

[126] "Mission #97: Target: Vienna, Austria," 484th Bombardment Group (H), *484th.org*, accessed January 14, 2023, https://484th.org/Missions/October_1944.html.

[127] "MACR 9064 (Pilot Oakley)," digital images, accessed on August 3, 2022, as a subscriber to *Fold3.com* (Missing Air Crew Reports [MACRs] of the U.S. Army Air Forces, 1942-1947), https://www.fold3.com/image/28684466.

[128] "MACR 9064," *Fold3.com*.

[129] "MACR 9064," *Fold3.com*.

[130] "Kirk G. Mosher," *Individual Deceased Personnel File*, emailed to author on December 13, 2016, by Tifanie L. Cropper, Government Information Specialist, US Army Human Resources Command, Freedom of Information and Privacy Act Office.

[131] "Meyer Osofsky, telephone conversation with author, June 2, 2017.

Notes

[132] "Sam A. Holquin," *Individual Deceased Personnel File*, emailed to author on November 23, 2016, by Tifanie L. Cropper, Government Information Specialist, US Army Human Resources Command, Freedom of Information and Privacy Act Office.

[133] "Mosher," *Individual Deceased Personnel File* ("List of American Deceased Military Personnel in Vienna Central Cemetery, Vienna, Austria.")

[134] "Cpl. Delbert W. Trueman, 721st Squadron," 450th Bomb Group Memorial Association, *450thBG. com*, accessed on February 10, 2016, accessed again on January 17, 2023 at which time the story on Delbert Trueman had been significantly reduced from 2016 to 2023, https://www.450thbg.com/real/ biographies/trueman/trueman.shtml; Kim Clarke, "Tell Mother that Daddy is OK," *Kim-Clarke.com*, accessed January 17, 2023, https://kim-clarke.com/category/world-war-ii-history/.

[135] "1st Lt. Leonard T. Mojica Crew, 721st Squadron," 450th Bomb Group Memorial Association, *450thBG.com*, accessed January 17, 2023, https://www.450thbg.com/real/crews/mojica.shtml.

[136] "Trueman," *450thBG.com*; "Find A Grave," s.v. "Delbert Wayne Trueman" (1917-1944), *Findagrave.com*, accessed January 17, 2023, https://www.findagrave.com/memorial/102882436/ delbert-wayne-trueman; "Find A Grave," s.v. "Dale J. Trueman" (1919-1943), *Findagrave.com*, accessed January 17, 2023, https://www.findagrave.com/memorial/99993691/dale-j-trueman.

[137] Sam A. Holquin, Lorraine American Cemetery, Decedent Search Results, American Battle Monuments Commission, *ABMC.gov*, accessed January 17, 2023, https://www.abmc.gov/database-search-results?field_first_name=Sam&field_last_name=Holquin&service_number=&field_abmc_ burial_unit=&field_place_of_entry=All&field_cemetery=All&field_cemetery2=All&field_branch_ of_service=All&search_api_fulltext=&field_dod_day=All&field_dod_month=All&field_dod_ year=&field_missing_status=All&items_per_page=10&sort_bef_combine=field_last_name_ASC.

[138] "Find A Grave," s.v. "Kirk G. Mosher (1923-1944)," *Findagrave.com*, accessed January 17, 2023, https://www.findagrave.com/memorial/17574167/kirk-g-mosher.

[139] Harry Egnatenko, Ardennes American Cemetery, Decadent Search Results, American Battle Monuments Commission, *ABMC.gov*, accessed January 17, 2023, https://www.abmc.gov/database-search-results?field_first_name=Harry&field_last_name=Egnatenko&service_number=&field_abmc_ burial_unit=&field_place_of_entry=All&field_cemetery=All&field_cemetery2=All&field_branch_ of_service=All&search_api_fulltext=&field_dod_day=All&field_dod_month=All&field_dod_ year=&field_missing_status=All&items_per_page=10&sort_bef_combine=field_last_name_ASC.

[140] U.S. Veterans' Gravesites, ca. 1775-2019, s.v. "George C. Phelps, Jr. (1922-1944)," accessed on January 17, 2023, as subscriber to *Fold3.com*, https://www.fold3.com/record/708467748/phelps-george-c-us-veterans-gravesites-ca1775-2019.

[141] "Find A Grave," s.v. "Edwin Lee Schoonover (1925-1944)," *Findagrave.com*, accessed January 17, 2023, https://www.findagrave.com/memorial/24630403/edwin-lee-schoonover.

[142] Meyer Osofsky, telephone conversation with author, June 24, 2016.

[143] "The Cardinal: High School Clubs Elected Officers and Sponsors," *The Clinton Eye*, October 10, 1940, 4-B, accessed October 20, 2023, as subscriber to *Newspapers.com*, https://www.newspapers. com/image/335201359/?terms=Leslie%20Goss&match=1.

[144] "Working Hard: Miss Lobaugh's Class Rehearsing Operetta," *Henry County Democrat*, December 8, 1938, 5, accessed October 23, 2023, as subscriber to *Newspapers.com*, https://www. newspapers.com/image/493568487/?terms=Working%20Hard&match=1.

145 "The Cardinal: Band and Orchestra," *The Clinton Eye*, September 14, 1939, 5-A, accessed October 20, 2023, as subscriber to *Newspapers.com,* https://www.newspapers.com/image/335181961/?terms=Leslie%20Goss&match=1.

146 "The Percussion Family," Oregon Symphony, *Orsymphony.org*, accessed October 23, 2023, https://www.orsymphony.org/learning-community/instruments/percussion/#:~:text=Timpani%20are%20a%20central%20part,tipped%20mallets%20or%20wooden%20sticks.

147 "The Cardinal: The County Play Festival," *The Clinton Eye*, March 14, 1940, 5-C, accessed October 20, 2023, as subscriber to *Newspapers.com,* https://www.newspapers.com/image/335190406/?terms=Leslie%20Goss&match=1; "J. Leslie Goss, III: Class of 105 Graduates," *The Clinton Eye*, April 24, 4B, accessed October 24, 2023, as subscriber to *Newspapers.com,* https://www.newspapers.com/image/335189000.

148 "The Cardinal: Staff," *The Clinton Eye*, September 5, 1940, 3-A, https://www.newspapers.com/image/335199772/?terms=Leslie%20Goss&match=1, accessed October 20, 2023, as subscriber to *Newspapers.com*; "The Cardinal: Staff," *The Clinton Eye* (Clinton, MO), October 24, 1940, 5-A, accessed October 20, 2023, as subscriber to *Newspapers.com,* https://www.newspapers.com/image/335201790/?terms=Leslie%20Goss&match=1.

149 "School Standings: Scholastic Records of High School Pupils: Honor Students in Band," *Henry County Democrat*, May 29, 1941, 6, accessed October 20, 2023, as subscriber to *Newspapers.com,* https://www.newspapers.com/image/494065089/?terms=School%20Standings&match=1.

150 "City Schools: Items of Interest to Parents and Pupils," *Henry County Democrat*, October 30, 1941, 6, accessed October 23, 2023, as subscriber to *Newspapers.com,* https://www.newspapers.com/image/494066558/?terms=City%20Schools&match=1.

151 "Jefferson Barracks National Cemetery, Saint Louis, Missouri," National Park Service, *NPS.gov*, accessed July 2, 2023, https://www.nps.gov/nr/travel/national_cemeteries/Missouri/Jefferson_Barracks_National_Cemetery.html#:~:text=In%20March%201863%2C%20the%20U.S.,officer%20stationed%20at%20the%20barracks.

152 "In Radio School," *Henry County Democrat*, August 6, 1942, 3, accessed October 20, 2023, as subscriber to *Newspapers.com,* https://www.newspapers.com/image/494072029/?terms=Leslie%20Goss&match=1; "Our Boys in Service," *Henry County Democrat*, February 18, 1943, 6, accessed October 20, 2023, as subscriber to *Newspapers.com* https://www.newspapers.com/image/494064509/?terms=Leslie%20Goss&match=1

153 "Personal: in the Armed Forces," *The Clinton Eye*, September 16, 1943, accessed October 21, 2023, as a subscriber to *Newspapers.com,* https://www.newspapers.com/image/335156092/?terms=In%20the%20Armed%20Forces&match=1.

154 "Air Force Materiel Command History in Brief," Air Force Materiel Command Office of History, *AFMC.AF.mil*, accessed October 21, 2023, https://www.afmc.af.mil/History/?Page=3.

155 "Missing in Action: J.L. Goss Jr., Last Reported Over Yugoslavia, *The Henry County Democrat* (Clinton, MO), April 12, 1945, 1, accessed March 7, 2023, as subscriber to *Newspapers.com*, https://www.newspapers.com/image/493918321/?terms=J.L.%20Goss&match=1.

156 Mae Mills Link and Hubert A. Coleman, *Medical Support of the Army Air Forces in World War II* (Washington, D.C.: Office of the Surgeon General, USAF, 1955), 516.

157 Link and Coleman, *Medical Support*, 517.

Notes

[158] Link and Coleman, *Medical Support*, 517.

[159] Colonel Robert E. L. Eaton (Commanding Officer), "Medical History: Four Hundred and Fifty First Bombardment Group (H)," 451st Bombardment Group (H), *451st.org*, accessed January 18, 2023, https://www.451st.org/History/pdf's/Medical%201.pdf.

[160] Eaton, "Medical History."

[161] Eaton, "Medical History."

[162] Eaton, "Medical History."

[163] Eaton, "Medical History."

Chapter 11: MISSIONS FROM HELL

[1] "Posthumous Award to Lt. Cookman," *Mason City Globe-Gazette*, January 29, 1945, 10, accessed January 19, 2023, as subscriber to *Newspapers.com*, https://www.newspapers.com/image/391359273/?terms=Robert%20G.%20Cookman.

[2] "Narrative History from October 1 to October 31, 1944," Headquarters, Office of the Intelligence Officer, 451st Bombardment Group (H), *451st.org*, November 3, 1944, accessed January 19, 1945, https://www.451st.org/History/pdf's/October_1944.pdf.

[3] "Table 3, Statistical Summary for Week Ending October 21, 1944," Headquarters, 451st Bomb Group (H), *Air Force Historical Research Agency*, Microfilm Reel B5095, 1349-1350.

[4] "Intops (Intelligence Operations) Summary No. 456, October 20, 1944," Office of Assistant Chief of Staff A-2, Headquarters, Mediterranean Allied Strategic Air Force, *Air Force Historical Research Agency*, Microfilm Reel A6384, 821-823.

[5] Tom Faulkner, *Flying with the Fifteenth Air Force: A B-24 Pilot's Missions from Italy During World War II* (Denton, TX: University of North Texas Press, 2018), 121-122.

[6] Walter J. Boyne, *Silver Wings: A History of the United States Air Force* (New York: Simon & Shuster, 1993), 148; Tony Holmes, *Warbird Legends* (St. Paul, MN: Zenith Press [an imprint of MBI Publishing Company], 2000), 207.

[7] "The P-38: When Lightning Strikes," *LockheedMartin.com*, accessed September 4, 2023, https://www.lockheedmartin.com/en-us/news/features/history/p-38.html#:~:text=First%20conceived%20in%201937%20by,and%20a%2020%2Dmm%20can.

[8] Joseph F. Mosher with Gerald A. Baron, *A Fighter Pilot in Buchenwald: Joe Mosher's journey from farm boy to fighter pilot to near starvation in a Nazi concentration camp* (Bellingham, WA: All Clear Publishing [Edens Veil Media], 2009), 2.

[9] Wesley Frank Craven and James Lea Cate, editors, *The Army Air Forces in World War II, Vol. 6, Men and Planes* (Chicago: The University of Chicago Press, 1955), 214-215.

[10] Tony Holmes, *Warbird Legends*, 207.

[11] "P-51D Mustang Baby Duck," Dayton Air Show, *DaytonAirshow.com*, accessed February 5, 2023, https://daytonairshow.com/p51d-mustang-baby-duck/.

[12] "Intops Summary No. 456, Microfilm Reel A6384, 821-823.

[13] "Operations Order No. 215, 19 October 1944," Headquarters, 49th Bombardment Wing (H), *Air Force Historical Research Agency*, Microfilm Reel B0595, 1414-1415.

[14] "Intelligence Annex "A" for Operations Order No. 215, 19 October 1944," Headquarters, 49th Bombardment Wing (H), A*ir Force Historical Research Agency*, Microfilm Reel B0595, 1416-1417.

[15] "Intops Summary No. 456," Microfilm Reel A6384. 822; "Operations Order 215 for Mission 121," 49th Bombardment Wing (H), *15thAF.org*, accessed January 21, 2023, https://15thaf. org/49th_BW/Missions/October%201944/PDFs/Op_Rpt_215.pdf.

[16] "Intops Summary No. 456," Microfilm Reel A6384. 822.

[17] "Bombing-Navigation Analysis for 20 October 1944," Headquarters, 49th Bomb Wing (H), *15thAF.org*, accessed January 31, 2023, https://15thaf.org/49th_BW/Missions/October%201944/ PDFs/Analysis_215.pdf.

[18] "Bombing-Navigation Analysis," 49th Bomb Wing.

[19] "Summary of Missions (Table 8)," Headquarters, 451st Bomb Group (H), Statistical Summary, Week Ended October 21, 1944, Mission 138, *Air Force Historical Research Agency*, Microfilm Reel B0595, 1351; "Narrative History from October 1 to October 31," 451st Bomb Group.

[20] "Bombing-Navigation Analysis," 49th Bomb Wing.

[21] "Bombing-Navigation Analysis," 49th Bomb Wing.

[22] "Bombing-Navigation Analysis," 49th Bomb Wing.

[23] "Bombing-Navigation Analysis," 49th Bomb Wing.

[24] "Narrative History from October 1 to October 31, 1944," 451st Bomb Group.

[25] Mike Hill, *The 451st Bomb Group in World War II: A Pictorial History* (Atglen, PA: Schiffer Publishing, 2001), 73-74.

[26] Editors of Encyclopedia Britannica (revised and updated by Kathleen Sheetz), *Encyclopedia Britannica Online*, s.v. "strategic bombing," accessed February 6, 2023, https://www.britannica. com/topic/strategic-bombing.

[27] "Firestorms: The Bombing of Civilians in World War II," Constitutional Rights Foundation (Member of Civics Renewal Network), *CRF-USA.org*, accessed February 6, 2023, https://www.crf-usa.org/bill-of-rights-in-action/bria-15-3-a-firestorms-the-bombing-of-civilians-in-world-war-ii.

[28] Boyne, *Silver Wings*, 150.

[29] Donald L. Miller, *Masters of the Air: America's Bomber Boys Who Fought the Air War Against Nazi Germany* (New York: Simon & Shuster, 2006), 53.

[30] "Firestorms," Constitutional Rights Foundation; John W. Lanza, *Shot Down Over Italy: A true history of courage and survival in Nazi-occupied Italy during World War II* (Caldwell, NJ: Bright Spot Books. 2010), 46.

Notes

31 Miller, *Masters of the Air*, 412-413.

32 Miller, *Masters of the Air*, 418.

33 "Nuclear Weapons: Who Has What at a Glance," Arms Control Association, *ArmsControl.org*, accessed February 6, 2023, https://www.armscontrol.org/factsheets/Nuclearweaponswhohaswhat.

34 "That Autumn Morning," Ecco La Guerra (Here is the War), *PiccoliMartiri.it*, accessed February 6, 2023, http://www.piccolimartiri.it/02-PAGINE-IN-INGLESE/E-p03.htm.

35 "The Massacre of Gorla and the Sad Story of the Little Martyrs," Random Times, *Random-Times.com*, accessed February 6, 2023, https://random-times.com/2019/10/20/the-massacre-of-gorla-and-the-sad-story-of-its-little-martyrs/.

36 Lanza, *Shot Down Over Italy*, 203.

37 Sven Felix Kellerhoff, *The Fuhrer Bunker: Hitler's Last Refuge* (Berlin, Germany: Berlin Story Verlag, 2014), 92.

38 C.L. Sulzberger, *The American Heritage Picture History of World War II* (Avenel, NJ: Wing Books, 1966), 556.

39 "Intops (i.e., Intelligence Operations) Summary No. 459," Office of Assistant Chief of Staff A-2, Headquarters, Mediterranean Allied Strategic Air Force, *Air Force Historical Research Agency*, Microfilm Reel A6384. 978-980; "Operations - 23 to 27 October 1944" and "Attacks Against German Industrial Plants and Communications in North Italy, 23 October 1944," Fifteenth Air Force Summary of Operations, Historical Section, October 23 to 29, 1944, *Air Force Historical Research Agency*, Microfilm Reel A6384, 973-977.

40 "Intops Summary No. 459," Microfilm Reel A6384, 978-980.

41 "Intops Summary No. 459," Microfilm Reel A6384, 979.

42 Daniel L. Haulman, "Tuskegee Airmen Chronology," Organizational History Branch, *Air Force Historical Research Agency*, July 5, 2012, 44, https://www.tuskegee.edu/Content/Uploads/Tuskegee/files/TUSKEGEE_AIRMEN_CHRONOLOGY12.2011.pdf.

43 Haulman, "Tuskegee Airmen Chronology," 42-43.

44 Haulman, "Tuskegee Airmen Chronology," 43.

45 "Consolidated Catalina in British Service," History of War, *HistoryofWar.org*, accessed February 7, 2023, , http://www.historyofwar.org/articles/weapons_PBY_catalina_RAF_service.html; "Find A Grave," s.v. "Isaac Machlin 'Mac' Laddon," *Findagrave.com*, accessed February 7, 2023, https://www.findagrave.com/memorial/194758152/isaac-machlin-laddon.

46 Lynn M. Homan and Thomas Reilly: *Black Knights: The Story of the Tuskegee Airmen* (Gretna, LA: Pelican Publishing Company, 2012), 235; "Tuskegee Airmen War Accomplishments," Our World War II Veterans, *OurWWIIVeterans.com*, accessed February 7, 2023, http://www.ourwwiiveterans.com/gallery/tuskegee-airman-photo-album/tuskegee-airmen-war-accomplishments.

47 Daniel L. Hallman, "Target: Berlin," *Air Force Historical Research Agency*, May 25, 2012, 6, *TuskegeeAirmen.org*, accessed February 7, 2023, https://tuskegeeairmen.org/wp-content/uploads/2020/11/TAI_Resources_Target-Berlin.pdf.

48 Hallman, "Target: Berlin," 6-7.

49 Hallman, "Target: Berlin," 8.

50 "Presidential Unit Citation," Air Force Personnel Center, accessed February 7, 2023, https://www.afpc.af.mil/Fact-Sheets/Display/Article/421897/presidential-unit-citation/.

51 "MACR 13269 (Pilot Reeves)," digital images, accessed on August 3, 2022, as a subscriber to *Fold3.com* (Missing Air Crew Reports [MACRs] of the U.S. Army Air Forces, 1942-1947), https://www.fold3.com/image/712857150; "MACR 13270 (Pilot Robinson)," digital images, accessed on August 3, 2022, as a subscriber to *Fold3.com* (Missing Air Crew Reports [MACRs] of the U.S. Army Air Forces, 1942-1947), https://www.fold3.com/image/29425793.

52 "Ronald W. Reeves," CAF Rise Above, *CAFRiseAbove.org*, October 28, 2021, accessed February 8, 2023, https://cafriseabove.org/ronald-w-reeves/; "Robert C. Robinson, Jr.," CAF Rise Above, *CAFRiseAbove.org*, March 21, 2019, accessed February 8, 2023, https://cafriseabove.org/robert-c-robinson-jr/.

53 "Leon 'Woodie' Spears," CAF Rise Above, *CAFRiseAbove.org*, August 11, 2021, accessed February 8, 2023, https://cafriseabove.org/leon-woodie-spears/; "MACR 13266 (Pilot Spears)," digital images, accessed on August 3, 2022, as a subscriber to *Fold3.com* (Missing Air Crew Reports [MACRs] of the U.S. Army Air Forces, 1942-1947), https://www.fold3.com/image/29425734?terms=13266,macr,war,world,united,america,ii,states.

54 "MACR 13268 (Pilot Mitchell)," digital images, accessed on August 3, 2022, as a subscriber to *Fold3.com* (Missing Air Crew Reports [MACRs] of the U.S. Army Air Forces, 1942-1947), https://www.fold3.com/image/29425771; Hallman, "Target: Berlin," 8.

55 "Executive Order 9981: Desegregation of the Armed Forces (1948)," Milestone Documents, National Archives, *Archives.gov*, accessed February 8, 2023, https://www.archives.gov/milestone-documents/executive-order-9981.

56 Benjamin O. Davis, Jr., *Benjamin O. Davis, Jr.: American: An Autobiography* (Washington, D.C.: Smithsonian Institution Press, 1991), 158-159 and 165.

57 Davis, Jr., *Benjamin O. Davis*, 165.

58 Homan and Reilly, *Black Knights*, 17-18.

59 "Tuskegee Airmen Congressional Gold Medal Ceremony," The White House/President George W. Bush, Honoring Our Veterans, *GeorgeWBush-WhiteHouse.archives.gov*, accessed February 8, 2023, https://georgewbush-whitehouse.archives.gov/infocus/veterans/tuskegee/index.html.

60 CNN Wire, "Roscoe C. Brown, Jr., Tuskegee Airman, Civil Rights Champion, Dies at 94," FOX61, *FOX 61.com*, (Hartford, CT), accessed February 8, 2023, https://www.fox61.com/article/news/local/outreach/awareness-months/roscoe-c-brown-jr-tuskegee-airman-civil-rights-champion-dies-at-94/520-8b67acbb-d1bf-4542-8527-5896cb596d6c.

Chapter 12: GOING DOWN OVER ITALY

1 Barret Tillman, *Forgotten Fifteenth: The Daring Airmen Who Crippled Hitler's War Machine* (Washington, D.C.: Regnery History, 2014), 197.

Notes

2 "Operations Order No. 221, 22 October 1944," Headquarters, 49th Bombardment Wing (H), *Air Force Historical Research Agency*, Microfilm Reel B0575, 1404-1405.

3 "Chapter X: Period Covered: October 1944," History of the 451st Bombardment Group (H), 20, *451st.org*, accessed February 8, 2023, https://www.451st.org/History/pdf's/History-of-the-451st-Bombardment-Group%20_H_.pdf; "Narrative History from October 1 to October 31, 1944," Headquarters, 451st Bombardment Group (H), Office of the Intelligence Officer, November 3, 1944, *451st.org*, accessed January 19, 1945, https://www.451st.org/History/pdf's/October_1944.pdf.

4 "Operations Order No. 220, Headquarters, 49th Bombardment Wing (H), *Air Force Historical Research Agency*, Microfilm Reel B0575, 1406-1407.

5 "Intelligence Annex 'A' for Operations Order 220, 22 October 1944" and "Briefing Notes for Operations Order No. 220, Plan A, Red Force, October 23, 1944," A-2 Section, Headquarters, 49th Bomb Wing, *Air Force Historical Research Agency*, Microfilm Reel B0575, 1408-1410.

6 "Briefing Notes for Operations Order No. 220," Microfilm Reel B0595, 1410.

7 "Operations Report for Operations Order No. 220, 49th Bombardment Wing (H), accessed February 9, 2023, https://15thaf.org/49th_BW/Missions/October%201944/PDFs/Op_Rpt_220.pdf.

8 "Operations Order No. 220," Microfilm Reel B0595, 1406.

9 "Briefing Notes for Operations Order No. 220," Microfilm Reel B0595, 1410.

10 Jan P. Norbye, *BMW: Bavaria's Driving Machines* (Skokie, IL: Publications International, Ltd., 1984), 72.

11 "The BMW 801 Radial Engine," TIGHAR Historic Preservation, *Tighar.org*, accessed February 11, 2023, https://tighar.org/Projects/Histpres/Corrosion_Report/bmw801.html.

12 Norbye, *BMW: Bavaria's Driving Machines*, 14.

13 "Intelligence Annex 'A' for Operations Order 220, 22 October 1944," Microfilm Reel B0575, 1408.

14 "Nazi Forced Labor - Background Information," Interview Archive, Forced Labor: 1939-1945 Memory and History, *Zwangsarbeit-Archiv.de*, accessed February 11, 2023, https://www.zwangsarbeit-archiv.de/en/zwangsarbeit/zwangsarbeit/zwangsarbeit-hintergrund/index.html.

15 "Munich-Allach: Working for BMW," Art Blart Art and Cultural Memory Archive, *ArtBlart.com*, accessed February 12, 2021, https://artblart.com/tag/munich-allach-working-for-bmw/.

16 "Forgotten Horrors: The Nazi Sub-Camp System: Allach-Kharsfeld," *RobinWhitlock1966.wixsite.com*, accessed February 12, 2023, http://robinwhitlock1966.wixsite.com/forgotten-horrors/allach-karsfeld.

17 "Statement of Russell J. Flint," Report of Aircraft Accident of B-24J (42-51682) Piloted by Robert G. Cookman on October 23, 1944, War Department, Army Air Forces, obtained from Craig A. Mackey, Historian, *Air Force Historical Research Agency*, February 18, 2014.

18 "Statement of Russell J. Flint," Report of Aircraft Accident.

19 "Statement of Russell J. Flint," Report of Aircraft Accident.

[20] Meyer Osofsky, telephone conversations with author, August 8, 2014, and June 26, 2016.

[21] "Statement of Russell J. Flint," Report of Aircraft Accident.

[22] John W. Lanza, *Shot Down Over Italy: A true story of courage and survival in Nazi-occupied Italy during World War II* (Caldwell, NJ: Bright Spot Books, 2010), 125.

[23] Meyer Osofsky, telephone conversation with author, August 8, 2014.

[24] "Statement of Russell J. Flint," Report of Aircraft Accident.

[25] Meyer Osofsky, telephone conversation with author, August 8, 2014.

[26] J. Raymond Long, "B-24 'Ditched' to Experiment on Structures: James River Test Designed to Save Lives in Future," *Daily Press* (Newport News, VA), September 21, 1944, 1, accessed on February 14, 2023, as subscriber to *Newspapers.com,* https://www.newspapers.com/image/231226955/?terms=raymond%20long%20ditching%20b-24&match=1.

[27] Peter Frost, "A Plane Crash in1944 is Saving Lives Today," *Daily Press*, February 22, 2009, A1, accessed May 25, 2023, as subscriber to *Newspapers.com*, https://www.newspapers.com/image/270813619/?terms=Peter%20Frost&match=1.

[28] Louis Zamperini with David Rensen, *Devil at My Heels: A Heroic Olympian's Story of Survival as a Japanese POW in World War II* (New York, NY: Perennial [An imprint of HaperCollins Publishers], 2004), 84-85, 89, 116-118, 157, 180-181.

[29] "MACR 9512," digital images, accessed on August 3, 2022, as a subscriber to *Fold3.com* (Missing Air Crew Reports [MACRs] of the U.S. Army Air Forces, 1942-1947), https://www.fold3.com/image/28722639.

[30] "Statement of Russell J. Flint," Report of Aircraft Accident.

[31] Meyer Osofsky, telephone conversation with author, June 24, 2016.

[32] Meyer Osofsky, telephone conversation with author, August 26, 2016.

[33] Meyer Osofsky, telephone conversation with author, August 26, 2016

[34] "Statement of Russell J. Flint," Report of Aircraft Accident.

[35] "Report of Aircraft Accident of B-24J (42-51682) Piloted by Robert G. Cookman on October 23, 1944, War Department, U.S. Army Air Forces," received from Craig A. Mackey, Historian, *Air Force Historical Research Agency*, February 18, 2014.

[36] Julie LeBlanc, "Edward Ardizzone's Multimedial Play with Format in his War Diaries," Open Edition Journals, *Journals.OpenEdition.org*, accessed February 18, 2023, https://journals.openedition.org/interfaces/2358?lang=en.

[37] "With the 8th Army on the Sangro, November 1943: the Road to Casalbordino in the Rain," Imperial War Museum, *iwm.org.uk*, accessed May 25, 2023, https://www.iwm.org.uk/collections/item/object/639.

[38] "Sangro River War Cemetery," Commonwealth War Graves Commission, *cwgc.org*, accessed February 18, 2023, https://www.cwgc.org/visit-us/find-cemeteries-memorials/cemetery-details/2021204/sangro-river-war-cemetery/.

Notes

[39] "The Campaign in Italy, September-December 1943: The Allied Advance to the Gustav Line: Personalities," Imperial War Museum, *iwm.org.uk*, accessed February 18, 2023, https://www.iwm.org.uk/collections/item/object/205125165.

[40] Dr. Elvira G. DiFabio, "Vasto," email message to author, March 12, 2021.

[41] "Report of Burial: Robert G. Cookman," October 26, 1944, *Individual Personnel Records File: Robert G. Cookman*, emailed to author by Patricia A. Dugdale, Freedom of Information and Privacy Office, February 20, 2014.

[42] Jessica Fragosa, "Interview of John Cooney," *Heroes on Our Island* at Verizon FiOS 1 News, Greater New York City Area, Broadcast Media, August 31, 2010, https://www.youtube.com/watch?v=aQQgTuNxjiA. This video isn't available anymore.

[43] "Report of Burial: Robert G. Cookman," *Individual Personnel Records File*.

[44] "Posthumous Award to Lt. Cookman," *Mason City Globe-Gazette* (Mason City, IA), January 29, 1945, 10, accessed February 19. 2023 as subscriber to *Newspapers.com*, https://www.newspapers.com/image/391359273/?terms=Cookman&match=1.

[45] "Individual Aircraft Record Card, B-24, 42-51682, Ford, Willow Run," emailed to author by USAF Pentagon, Air Force Historical Support Division, AFHSO Research, July 18, 2014; "Unsatisfactory Report, War Department, Army Air Forces," Report of Aircraft Accident of B-24J, *Air Force Historical Research Agency*.

[46] "Report of Aircraft Accident of B-24J," *Air Force Historical Research Agency*.

[47] "Report of Aircraft Accident of B-24J," *Air Force Historical Research Agency*.

[48] "Roster of Combat Casualties, 725th Bomb Squadron (H)," Headquarters, 451st Bombardment Group (H) for Month of October 1944, *Air Force Historical Research Agency*, Microfilm Reel B0595, 1358.

[49] Meyer Osofsky, telephone conversation with author, August 26, 1916.

[50] "Hong S. Chin, Military Record and Report of Separation, Certificate of Service" and "Hong S. Chin's Personal Record of His Missions," both shared with author by his son David Chin; "Report of Battle Casualties for Month of November 1944, 725th Bombardment Squadron (H)," Headquarters, 451st Bombardment Group (H), *Air Force Historical Research Agency*, Microfilm Reel B0595, 1562.

[51] "Joseph L. Goss in the U.S., World War II Hospital Admission Card Files, 1942-1954," accessed February 19, 2023, as a subscriber to *Ancestry.com*, https://www.ancestry.com/discoveryui-content/view/15234752:61817?tid=&pid=&queryId=d0adc8f12b1bb1c2b78f6bca89bf9464&_phsrc=bgd153&_phstart=successSource.

[52] Lanza, *Shot Down Over Italy*, 149-150.

[53] John J. Cooney gave the letter to author on February 27, 2011. Author gave talk on his book, *Shot Down Over Italy*, at the Long Island State Veterans Home on February 27, 2011. Cooney sought out author to say he also went down in a plane over Italy.

[54] "Statement of Russell J. Flint," Report of Aircraft Accident.

55 "Directory of Names," Mason City Area Veteran's Monument (Mason City, IA), updated August 2022, 11, *MasonCity.net*, accessed February 19, 2023, https://www.masoncity.net/files/documents/VeteransMonumentDirectoryofNamesThru820221178043838102622PM.pdf.

56 "Cookman, William B.," Field of Honor Foundation, *FieldsofHonor-database.com*, accessed February 19, 2023, https://www.fieldsofhonor-database.com/index.php/en/american-war-cemetery-henri-chapelle-c/52946-cookman-william-b.

57 Harry J. "Joe" Cookman, telephone conversation with author, June 29, 2014; "Lt. Cookman Died of Wounds Received in Action, Germany, Was Serving Second Time Overseas, Twice Wounded Previously," *Mason City Globe-Gazette*, November 8, 1944, 13, accessed July 11, 2016, as a subscriber to *Newspapers.com*, https://www.newspapers.com/image/391310848/?terms=Lt.%20Cookman%20Died%20of%20Wounds&match=1.

58 "Cookman, William B.," Field of Honor Foundation.

59 "Lt. Cookman Died of Wounds," *Globe-Gazette*, 13.

60 "Cookman, William B.," Field of Honor Foundation.

61 "Cemeteries & Memorials," American Battle Fields Commission, *ABMC.gov*, accessed February 19, 2023, https://www.abmc.gov/cemeteries-memorials#.WDj9SrIrLcs.

62 "Flyers Speak at Lions Club," *Mason City Globe-Gazette*, November 2, 1944, 15, accessed on November 25, 2016, as subscriber to *Newspapers.com*, https://www.newspapers.com/image/391309385/?terms=Flyers%20Speak%20at%20Lions%20Club&match=1.

63 "Flyers Speak at Lions Club," *Globe-Gazette*, 15.

Chapter 13: BEHIND ENEMY LINES

1 Barret Tillman, *Forgotten Fifteenth: The Daring Airmen Who Crippled Hitler's War Machine* (Washington, D.C.: Regnery History, 2014), 119.

2 Duane L. "Sparky" Bohnstedt, "Bleckhammer," 460th Bomb Group (H) Stories, *15thAF.org*, accessed February 20, 2023, http://15thaf.org/55th_BW/460th_BG/Stories/PDFs/Blechhammer.pdf.

3 "Blechhammer," *Wikipedia*, accessed February 25, 2023, https://en.wikipedia.org/wiki/Blechhammer.

4 Duane L. "Sparky" Bohnstedt, "A Brief History of the 460th Bomb Group (H): 760th, 761st, 762nd & 763rd Squadrons," 460th Bomb Group (H) Stories, *15thAF.org*, accessed February 20, 2023, http://15thaf.org/55th_BW/460th_BG/Stories/PDFs/Brief%20History%20of%20the%20460th.pdf.

5 Tillman, *Forgotten Fifteenth*, 187.

6 "MACR 10034 (Pilot Eckersley)," digital images, accessed on August 3, 2022, as a subscriber to *Fold3.com* (Missing Air Crew Reports [MACRs] of the U.S. Army Air Forces, 1942-1947), https://www.fold3.com/image/139285598.

7 Meyer Osofsky, telephone conversation with author, January 27, 2017.

[8] Meyer Osofsky, telephone conversation with author, June 24, 2016.

[9] "Table 6, Summary of Missions (Mission 158, December 2, 1944)," Statistical Summary, Week Ending December 2, 1944, Headquarters, 451st Bomb Group (H), *Air Force Historical Research Agency,* Microfilm Reel B0595, 1560; Lowell R. Dillon, Nephew of Paul J. Dillon, responded to request for information on his uncle's plane in a thread on *ArmyAirForces.com,* accessed by author before it was shut down on December 1, 2017, http://forum.armyairforces.com/Dec-2-1944-crash-near-Blechhammer-ml56628.aspx.

[10] Ian Abbott, "B-24: GE Turbosupercharger," *Flicker.com,* accessed February 22, 2023, https://www.flickr.com/photos/ian_e_abbott/17760961020.

[11] Dillon, *ArmyAirForces.com.*

[12] "MACR 10034 (Eckersley)," *Fold3.com.*

[13] Dillon, *ArmyAirForces.com.*

[14] "MACR 10034 (Eckersley)," *Fold3.com.*

[15] MACR 10034 (Eckersley), *Fold3.com;* "Find A Grave," s.v. "2LT Michael E Butinsky (1922-1944)," see comment posted on April 22, 2012, by Michelle Sheldon, niece of Michael Butinsky, accessed February 25, 2023, https://www.findagrave.com/memorial/11249429/michael-e-butinsky?_gl=1*1fbua3p*_gcl_aw*R0NMLjE2NzY4Mjc2MzIuRUFJYUlRb2J DaE1Jbk12TnlveWlfUUlWaWNpVUNSM2plZ2llRUFBWUFTQUFFZ0xBU1BEX0J3RQ..*_gcl_dc*R0NMLjE2NzY4Mjc2MzIuRUFJYUlRb2JDaE1Jbk12TnlveWlfUUlWaWNpVUNSM2plZ2llRUFBWUFTQUFFZ0xBU1BEX0J3RQ..*_ga*ODE2MTI1Mjk4LjE2NjQyODA0OTY.*_ga_4QT8FMEX30*MTY3NzIwNzkxMy4yNi4xLjE2NzcyMDgxNjAuNTYuMC4w*_ga_B2YGR3SSMB*NTkxZmY5NWQtYTRmOC00OBjLTg3NDAtOTAyZDRjNDAzY2MzLjI1LjEuMTY3NzIwODE2MS41NS4wLjA.

[16] "MACR 10034 (Eckersley)," *Fold3.com;* "Find A Grave," Butinsky.

[17] Franciszek Piper and Gerard Majka, "Althammer," Holocaust Encyclopedia, United States Holocaust Memorial Museum, *Encyclopedia.USHMM.org,* accessed March 11, 2023, https://encyclopedia.ushmm.org/content/en/article/althammer-subcamp-of-auschwitz.

[18] "Find A Grave," Butinsky.; Find A Grave, s.v. "Paul J Dillon," accessed February 25, 2023, https://www.findagrave.com/memorial/161686094/paul-j-dillon?_gl=1*qs2hze*_gcl_aw*R0NMLjE2NzY4Mjc2MzIuRUFJYUlRb2JDaE1Jbk12TnlveWlfUUlWaWNpVUNSM2plZ2llRUFBWUFTQUFFZ0xBU1BEX0J3RQ..*_gcl_dc*R0NMLjE2NzY4Mjc2MzIuRUFJYUlRb2JDaE1Jbk12TnlveWlfUUlWaWNpVUNSM2plZ2llRUFBWUFTQUFFZ0xBU1BEX0J3RQ..*_ga*ODE2MTI1Mjk4LjE2NjQyODA0OTY.*_ga_4QT8FMEX30*MTY3NzA0NTEyNS4yNC4xLjE2NzcwNDUxNjkuMTYuMC4w*_ga_B2YGR3SSMB*YWIyNGEzMzYtNzA1NS00OTI1LWEwMmYtYTViMmRjNjUzNThlLjIzLjEuMTY3NzA0NTE3MC4xNy4wLjA.

[19] Mel Laytner, "From a Number to a Name: Tracking down the identity of an anonymous Auschwitz prisoner," April 19, 2020, Tablet Magazine, *TabletMag.com,* accessed March 4, 2024, https://www.tabletmag.com/sections/community/articles/from-a-number-to-a-name.

[20] Dillon, *ArmyAirForces.com;* "Find A Grave," Butinsky.

[21] "Kriegsgefangenen Lagers: Home of the 'Kriegie' Airmen," 392nd Bomb Group, *B24.net,* accessed February 26, 2023, https://b24.net/powCamps.htm.

[22] "The Luftwaffe Interrogators at Dulag Luft - Oberursel," *Stalag Luft I Online,* accessed February 26, 2023, http://www.merkki.com/new_page_2.htm; Hubert Zemke and Roger A. Freeman, *Zemke's Stalag: The Final Days of World War II* (Washington, D.C.: Smithsonian Institution Press, 1991), 6; "Convention Relative to the Treatment of Prisoners of War, Geneva, July 27, 1929," International Humanitarian Law - Geneva Convention Prisoners of War 1929 (printed from the International Committee of the Red Cross website on October 31, 2005), Article 5, 1, accessed March 2, 2023, https://www.legal-tools.org/doc/1d2cfc/pdf/.

[23] "Convention Relative to the Treatment of Prisoners of War," International Humanitarian Law.

[24] John W. Lanza, *Shot Down Over Italy: A true story of courage and survival in Nazi-occupied Italy during World War II* (Caldwell, NJ: Bright Spot Books, 2010), 224.

[25] "David Orkin Dog Tag," File Unit ME-2490, Series Downed Allied Reports, Record Group 242: National Archives Collection of Foreign Records Seized, National Archives Catalog, accessed March 21, 2023, https://catalog.archives.gov/id/143487528?objectPage=26; "Ray M Goodson Dog Tag," File Unit ME-2490, Series Downed Allied Reports, Record Group 242: National Archives Collection of Foreign Records Seized, National Archives Catalog, accessed March 21, 2023, https://catalog.archives.gov/id/143487528?objectPage=30.

[26] Lanza, *Shot Down Over Italy,* 107.

[27] "U.S. Army WW2 Dog Tags," WW2 US Medical Research Center, *Med-Dept.com,* accessed April 26, 2020, https://www.med-dept.com/articles/u-s-army-ww2-dog-tags/.

[28] Michael Ray, *Encyclopedia Britannica Online,* s.v. "Luftwaffe," updated January 13, 2023, accessed March 5, 2023, https://www.britannica.com/topic/Luftwaffe.

[29] Greg Hatton, "Stalag Luft I: American Prisoners of War," Military Intelligence Service War Department, 1 November 1945," 392nd Bomb Group, *b24.net,* accessed January 5, 2023, https://www.b24.net/powStalag1.htm.

[30] Zemke and Freeman, *Zemke's Stalag,* 110.

[31] Greg Hatton, "Stalag Luft 4: American Prisoners of War: Prepared by Military Intelligence Service War Department, 1 November 1945," 392nd Bomb Group, *b24.net,* accessed January 5, 2023, https://www.b24.net/powStalag4.htm.

[32] Zemke and Freeman, *Zemke's Stalag,* 18.

[33] Meyer Osofsky, telephone conversation with author, December 17, 2016.

[34] Lt. Col. David S. Bowerman (Chaplain, U.S. Army Public Health Command), "What's on Your Dog Tag?" April 1, 2014, *Army.mil,* accessed March 5, 2023, https://www.army.mil/article/123034/whats_on_your_dog_tag.

[35] Akiva Males, "Jewish GIs and Their Dog Tags," *Hakirah.org,* accessed April 26, 2020, https://hakirah.org/Vol15Males.pdf.

[36] "Excerpt from S/Sgt. Bill Krebs Deposition for the Judge Advocate War Crimes Investigation," Stalag Luft IV: American Prisoners of War in Germany, 392nd Bomb Group, *b-24.net,* accessed March 5, 2023, https://www.b24.net/powStalag4.htm.

[37] Meyer Osofsky, telephone conversation with author, December 17, 2016.

Notes

[38] Bowerman, "What's on Your Dog Tag?"

[39] "Stalag Luft IV," German POW Camps with 303rd BG(H) Prisoners, 303rd Bomb Group (H), *303rdBG.com,* accessed March 6, 2023, http://www.303rdbg.com/pow-camps.html; Greg Hatton, "The Death March," 392nd Bomb Group, *b24.net,* accessed March 6, 2023, https://www.b24.net/powMarch.htm.

[40] "Listing by Rooms of the POWs at Stalag Luft I, North 3," *Stalag Luft I Online,* Ray M Goodson in North 3, Barracks 6 (Block 306), Room 6, accessed March 6, 2023, http://www.merkki.com/north3.htm; "Listing by Rooms of the POWs at Stalag Luft I, North 2, *Stalag Luft I Online,* David Orkin in North 2, Barrack 3, Room 5, accessed March 6, 2023, http://www.merkki.com/north2.htm.

[41] Zemke and Freeman, *Zemke's Stalag,* photograph of the double barbed wire fence separating the compounds of Stalag Luft I which is among the photographs between pages 52 and 53.

[42] Irwin Stovroff, "Life as a POW," The Digital Collections of the National WWII Museum, *WWII-Online.org,* accessed March 6, 2023, https://www.ww2online.org/view/Irwin-stovroff#life-as-a-pow.

[43] Zemke and Freeman, Zemke's Stalag, ix.

[44] Oscar G. Richard III, "Hubert Zemke – A Man to Remember," *Stalag Luft I Online,* accessed March 7, 2023, http://www.merkki.com/zemkehubert.htm.

[45] "Listing by Rooms of the POWs at Stalag Luft I, North 3," *Stalag I Online,* accessed March 6, 2023, http://www.merkki.com/north3.htm.

[46] Calverton National Cemetery, *U.S. Department of Veterans Affairs,* National Cemetery Administration, Nationwide Gravesite Locator, s.v. "Francis S. Gabreski (1919-2002)," "John J. Cooney (1923-2014)," "Calvin Chin (1925-1987)," accessed March 6, 2023, U.S. Department of Veterans Affairs, https://gravelocator.cem.va.gov/ngl/.

[47] "MACR 8304 (Pilot Wilson)," digital images, accessed on August 3, 2022, as a subscriber to *Fold3.com* (Missing Air Crew Reports [MACRs] of the U.S. Army Air Forces, 1942-1947), https://www.fold3.com/image/28688853.

[48] "Col, Cy Wilson Receives French Croix de Guerre," *Kearney Daily Hub,* July 17, 1948, 1, accessed March 6, 2023, as a subscriber to *Newspapers.com,* https://www.newspapers.com/image/708648931/?terms=Cy%20Wilson&match=1.

[49] Col. Jack Ilfrey (79FS, 20th FG), "Col. Ilfrey Remembers Cy Wilson," accessed March 6, 2023, https://www.geocities.ws/jackilfrey/wilson.html; Capt. Art Heiden (79th FS, 20th FG), "Col. Cy Wilson Remembered," accessed March 6, 2023, https://www.geocities.ws/jackilfrey/wilson.html.

[50] "Mackay Trophy," *National Aeronautical Association,* accessed March 5, 2023, https://naa.aero/awards/awards-and-trophies/mackay-trophy/; "Military Rites Set Today For Col. Cy Wilson, *The Austin Statesman* (Austin, TX), December 30, 1954, 1, accessed March 7, 2023 as subscriber to *Newspapers.com,* https://www.newspapers.com/image/359864267/?terms=Cy%20Wilson.

[51] "Military Rites," *The Austin Statesman,* 1; "Bergstrom Jet Uses Road As Flight Strip," *The Austin Statesman* (Austin, TX), August 11, 1950, 11, accessed March 7, 2023, as subscriber to *Newspapers.com,* https://www.newspapers.com/image/357865659/?terms=Like%20a%20Fish%20out%20of%20water&match=1.

[52] Carroll V. Glines, *The Doolittle Raid: America's daring first strike against Japan* (Atglen, PA: Schiffer Publishing Ltd., 1991), 33-34.

[53] Glines, *The Doolittle Raid,* xi-x.

[54] C. Ross Greening, Dorothy Greening and Karen Morgan Driscoll, *Not As Briefed: From the Doolittle Raid to a German Stalag* (Pullman, WA: Washington State University Press, 2001), ix.

[55] Kim Guise, "From the Collection of Stalag Symphony: Clair Cline," July 21, 2017, *NationalWW2Museum.org,* accessed Jun 13, 2023, https://www.nationalww2museum.org/war/articles/stalag-symphony-clair-cline.

[56] Greening, *Not As Briefed,* x-xiii.

[57] "Air Vice-Marshall C.T. Weir," Obituary, *The Brandon Sun* (Brandon, Manitoba, Canada), August 7, 1965, 13, accessed March 7, 2023, as subscriber to *Ancestry.com*, https://www.newspapers.com/image/68569048/?clipping_id=1753758&fcfToken=eyJhbGciOiJIUzI1NiIsInR5cCI6IkpXVCJ9.eyJmcmVlLXZpZXctaWQiOiY4NTY5MDQ4LCJpYXQiOjE2Nzgy MTAxOTMsImV4cCI6MTY3ODI5NjU5M30.FVri7wrOPMH RaN8tUbboeFXkUvVWNFd6ssVAlfNL0N0.

[58] Zemke and Freeman, *Zemke's Stalag,* 75-79.

[59] Zemke and Freeman, *Zemke's Stalag,* 106.

[60] John Florea and Eugene A. Valencia, "Interview with Humber Zemke (Part 3 of 9)," *The Museum of Flight Digital Collections,* July 1965, accessed March 7, 2023, https://digitalcollections.museumofflight.org/items/show/49914; Oscar G. Richard III, "Hubert Zemke – A Man to Remember," *Stalag Luft I Online,* accessed March 7, 2023, http://www.merkki.com/zemkehubert.htm.

[61] Zemke and Freeman, *Zemke's Stalag,* 111; "Konstantin Rokossovsky, December 21, 1896-August 3, 1968," *GlobalSecurity.org,* accessed March 7, 2023, https://www.globalsecurity.org/military/world/russia/rokossovsky.htm.

[62] Zemke and Freeman, *Zemke's Stalag,* 111-113; "Operation Revival: Rescue from Stalag Luft I," May 20, 2020, *NationalWW2Museum.org,* accessed March 7, 2023, https://www.nationalww2museum.org/war/articles/operation-revival-stalag-luft-i; "The Liberation of Stalag Luft I," April 30, 2020, *NationalWW2Museum.org,* accessed March 7, 2023, https://www.nationalww2museum.org/liberation-stalag-luft.

[63] Zemke and Freeman, *Zemke's Stalag,* 110; "The Liberation of Stalag Luft I," *National WWII Museum.*

[64] Oscar G. Richard III, "Hubert Zemke."

[65] Zemke and Freeman, *Zemke's Stalag,* 116.

[66] "Camp Lucky Strike: RAMP Camp No. 1," June 26, 2020, *NationalWW2Museum.org,* accessed March 7, 2023, https://www.nationalww2museum.org/war/articles/camp-lucky-strike.

[67] "Missing in Action: J.L. Goss Jr., Last Reported Over Yugoslavia," *The Henry County Democrat* (Clinton, MO), April 12, 1945, 1, accessed March 7, 2023, as subscriber to *Newspapers.com,* https://www.newspapers.com/image/493918321/?terms=J.L.%20Goss&match=1.

[68] "More on the 1LT William Silliman Incident (Crash Off the Coast of North Africa on Way Home)," *Ad-Lib* (the newsletter of the 451st Bomb Group), Issue 34, Fall 2001, *451st.org,* 11, accessed March 7, 2023, https://www.451st.org/Ad%20Lib/Pdfs/Issue%2034%20Fall%202001.pdf.

[69] "MACR 13217 (Pilot Silliman)," digital images, accessed on August 3, 2022, as a subscriber to Fold3.com (Missing Air Crew Reports [MACRs] of the U.S. Army Air Forces, 1942-1947), https://www.fold3.com/image/29423273.

[70] "Victor Melnick, 726th [AEG: LEW MORSE'S CREW]," *Ad-Lib* (the newsletter of the 451st Bomb Group), Issue 33, Spring 2001, 21, *451st.org,* accessed March 7, 2023, https://www.451st.org/Ad%20 Lib/Pdfs/Issue%2033%20Spring%202001.pdf.

[71] "More on Silliman Incident," *Ad-Lib,* 11-12.

[72] "MACR 13217 (Silliman)," *Fold3.com;* "More on Silliman Incident," *Ad-Lib,* 11-12.

[73] "Report of Aircraft Accident of B-24J (42-51372) Piloted by William M. Silliman on March 9, 1945, War Department, U.S. Army Air Forces," accessed under Aircraft Accidents via the 451st Bombardment Group (H) website, *45st.org,* on March 8, 2023, https://www.451st.org/Accident%20 Reports/Accident%20Reports/42-51372/42-51372%20Combined.pdf.

[74] "Report of Aircraft Accident of B-24J (42-94908), Piloted by Robert L. Worsthorn on March 9, 1945, War Department, U.S. Army Air Forces," accessed under Aircraft Accidents via the 451st Bombardment Group (H) website, *451st.org,* on March 8, 2023, https://www.451st.org/Accident%20 Reports/Accident%20Reports/42-94908/42-94908%20Combined.pdf.

[75] "MACR 8005 (Pilot Worsthorn)," digital images, accessed on August 3, 2022, as a subscriber to *Fold3.com,* (Missing Air Crew Reports [MACRs] of the U.S. Army Air Forces, 1942-1947), https://www.fold3.com/image/28674129; Meyer Osofsky, telephone conversation with author, June 24, 2016.

[76] "Squadron Life Is What You Make It - 725," *Ad-Lib* (the newsletter of the 451st Bomb Group). Vol. 1, No. 12, April 28, 1945, *Air Force Historical Research Agency,* Microfilm Reel B0596, 436.

[77] "Victor Melnick," *Ad-Lib.*

[78] "MACR 15868 (Pilot Silliman)," *Fold3.com.*

[79] "North African American Cemetery," American Battle Monuments Commission, *abmc.gov,* accessed March 9, 2023, https://www.abmc.gov/North-Africa; "American Cemetery North Africa (TU)," accessed March 9, 2023, https://www.bensavelkoul.nl/North_Africa_Cemetery.htm.

[80] "Find A Grave," s.v. "Edward B. Wiggins (1923-1945)," accessed March 10, 2023, https://www.findagrave.com/memorial/48929064/edward-benson-wiggins; "Request for Reimbursement of Internment Expenses of William Geller," May 30, 1948, *Individual Deceased Personnel File: William Geller,* emailed to author on May 24, 2022, by David Hardin, Archivist, National Archives at St. Louis.

[81] "North Africa America Cemetery and Memorial (Brochure)," American Battle Monuments Commission, December 2018, *abmc.gov,* accessed March 8, 2023, https://www.abmc.gov/sites/default/files/2021-03/North%20Africa%20American%20Cemetery%20and%20Memorial%20 %282019%20brochure%29.pdf.

[82] Yvonne Kinkaid (reference historian at the Air Force History Office at Bolling Air Force Base in Washington, D.C.), email to author, January 30, 2015.

[83] "Local Man Retires from San Marcos Volunteer Patrol," *North County Times,* September 14, 2001, 22, accessed March 13, 2023, as subscriber to *Newspapers.com,* https://www.newspapers.com/image/577909141/?terms=David%20Orkin%20Retires&match=1.

84 "Posthumous Award to Lt. Cookman," *Mason City Globe-Gazette,* January 29, 1945, 10, accessed June 5, 2023 as subscriber to *Newspapers.com,* https://www.newspapers.com/image/391 359273/?terms=Posthumous%20Award%20to%20Lt.%20Cookman&match=1.

85 Meyer Osofsky, telephone conversation with author, August 11, 2014.

86 "Posthumous Award to Lt. Cookman," *Mason City Globe-Gazette,* January 19, 1945, 10, accessed August 5, 2023, as subscriber to *Newspapers.com,* https://www.newspapers.com/image/ 391359273/?terms=Posthumous%20Award%20to%20Lt.%20Cookman&match=1; "Sgt. Mosher Killed in Action Over Austria, Oct. 13," *Albuquerque Journal* (Albuquerque, NM), February 13, 1945, 3, accessed August 5, 2023, as subscriber to *Newspapers.com,* https://www.newspapers. com/image/391359273/?terms=Posthumous%20Award%20to%20Lt.%20Cookman&match=1.

87 "Air Medal Criteria," *USAMM.com,* accessed March 14, 2023, https://www.usamm.com/ products/air-medal.

88 Yvonne Kinkaid, email to author, January 30, 2015.

89 Stephen Sherman, "Medals of World War II," August 2022, updated July 8, 2013, *Acepilots. com,* accessed March 14, 2023, http://acepilots.com/medals/main.html.

90 "Medal, Good Conduct Medal, United States Army," Air and Space Museum, Smithsonian Institution, *AirandSpace.si.edu,* accessed September 12, 2023, https://airandspace.si.edu/collection-objects/medal-good-conduct-medal-united-states-army/nasm_A19630423000#:~:text=The%20 Good%20Conduct%20Medal%20was,three%20years%20of%20active%20service.

91 "Air Medal for Sergeant Cooney," news clip (date unknown) presumably from the now defunct *Hudson Dispatch* of Union City, NJ, which was mailed to author by Peter Cooney on February 5, 2015.

92 Meyer Osofsky, telephone conversations with author on August 26, 2016, December 17, 2016, and March 7, 2017.

93 Meyer Osofsky, telephone conversations with author on June 24, 2016, and August 26, 2016.

94 Meyer Osofsky, telephone conversations with author on August 26, 2016, and September 16, 2016; Air Force Medical Service History Office, "Creation of the first Central Medical Establishment in World War II," August 31, 2017, *AirForceMedicine.af.mil,* accessed April 22, 2023, https://www.airforcemedicine.af.mil/News/Display/Article/1317434/creation-of-the-first-central-medical-establishment-in-world-war-ii/.

95 C.G. Sweeting, *Combat Flying Equipment: U.S. Army Aviators' Personal Equipment,* 1917-1945 (Washington and London: Smithsonian Institution Press, 1989), 21.

96 U.S., World War II Draft Cards Young Men, 1940-1947, s.v. "Jackson Elliott Dube," accessed as subscriber to *Ancestry.com* on April 22, 2023, https://www.ancestry.com/discoveryui-content/view/195220516:2238?tid=&pid=&queryId=c7480aead4b997e91d61540fe3df39ba&_ phsrc=bgd307&_phstart=successSource.

97 Meyer Osofsky, telephone conversations with author on August 26, 2016, September 16, 2016, and March 23, 2017.

98 Variety Staff, "Jackson E. Dube," June 11, 2002, *Variety.com,* accessed April 24, 2023, https:// variety.com/2002/scene/people-news/jackson-e-dube-1117868364/.

Notes

[99] Meyer Osofsky, telephone conversation with author, June 24, 2016.

[100] Meyer Osofsky, telephone conversation with author, January 27, 2017.

[101] "MACR 8005 (Worsthorn)," *Fold3.com;* "Report of Aircraft Accident of B-24J (42-94908), Piloted by Worsthorn.

[102] Meyer Osofsky, telephone conversation with author, June 24, 2016.

[103] "Military Record and Report of Separation, Certificate of Service," s.v. "David G. Johnson (born September 8, 1924)," copy mailed to author on November 25, 2022, by Diane Turnquist, Expert Archives Technician, National Personnel Records Center in St. Louis, MO; James W, Peterson, *The World Book Encyclopedia* (Chicago, IL: Field Enterprises Educational Corporation, 1968), s.v. "Decorations and Medals." Volume 5, D, 71.

[104] "1940 United States Federal Census," Long Beach, Los Angeles, California, s.v. "David Johnson," accessed April 24, 2023, as subscriber to *Ancestry.com,* https://www.ancestry.com/discoveryui-content/view/74435977:2442?tid=&pid=&queryId=e4539cd6ccb8cd0f3132a9105348 97fa&_phsrc=mRc1&_phstart=successSource.

[105] "U.S. World War II Draft Cards Young Men, 1940-1947," s.v. "David Gordon Johnson," accessed August 4, 2022, as subscriber to *Ancestry.com,* https://www.ancestry.com/discoveryui-content/view/18938466:2238?tid=&pid=&queryId=17902e6f83bc76ec3735461819df4e25&_phsrc=zsS92&_phstart=successSource.

[106] Anne Pollnow with assistance from Matt Hunter and Kitty Sopow, "World War II Base End and Searchlight Stations of Sitka Sound: Harbor Defenses of Sitka, U.S. Army Coast Artillery, Sitka, Alaska," U.S. Army Corps of Engineers, Anchorage, AK, December 2014, accessed April 24, 2023, https://www.sealevelsitka.com/wp-content/uploads/2018/10/Lisianski-Searchlight-Stations-Booklet.pdf.

[107] U.S. World War II Draft Cards Young Men, "David Gordon Johnson."

[108] Pollnow, Hunter, and Sopow, "World War II Base End and Searchlight Stations of Sitka Sound."

[109] "Combat Operations and Summary of Operations for Mission 148," Headquarters, 451st Bombardment Group (H), Statistical Summary, Week Ending 11 November 11, 1944, *Air Force Historical Research Agency,* Microfilm Reel B0595, 1548.

[110] "Class of 1938 (Herbert C. Fones)," *The Michigan Technic,* Volume XLVII, Number 4, January 1935, 70, accessed July 29, 2023, https://www.google.com/books/edition/The_Michigan_Technic/mVHiAAAAMAAJ?hl=en&gbpv=1&dq=The+Michigan+Technical,+University+of+Michigan+College+of+Engineering,+January+1935&pg=RA1-PA61&printsec=frontcover; "Elect Triangles President," *The Michigan Daily,* May 22, 1936, 2, https://digital.bentley.umich.edu/midaily/mdp.39015071755990/494.

[111] Daniel Ladd, email to author on September 6, 2021, with a copy of a "Letter to Wendell Dodge" by David Johnson recapping his November 11, 1944, mission to bomb the Herman Goering Benzol Plant in Linz, Austria, for which he received the Distinguished Flying Cross.

[112] Daniel Ladd, email to author, "Letter to Wendell Dodge."

[113] Daniel Ladd, email to author, "Letter to Wendell Dodge."

[114] Daniel Ladd, email to author, "Letter to Wendell Dodge."

[115] "Report of Battle Casualties for the Month of November 1944," Headquarters, 451st Bombardment Group (H), *Air Force Historical Research Agency,* Microfilm Reel B0595, 1561.

[116] Daniel Ladd, email to author, "Letter to Wendell Dodge."

[117] Daniel Ladd, email to author, "Letter to Wendell Dodge."

[118] "Narrative Statement, 1 March to 31 March 1945," Headquarters, 451st Bombardment Group (H), Office of the Intelligence Officer, *Air Force Historical Research Agency,* Microfilm Reel "Lanza Request #80653," 218, received by author on December 14, 2021, via mail from Pam Ives, Historian at AFHRA.

[119] "Operations Order Number 149 and Intelligence Annex 'A'," Headquarters, 49th Bombardment Wing (H), March 24, 1945, *Air Force Historical Research Agency,* Microfilm Reel "Lanza Request #80653," 369-371, received by author on December 14, 2021, via mail from Pam Ives, Historian at AFHRA.

[120] "Operations Order Number 149 and Intelligence Annex 'A'," *Air Force Historical Research Agency.*

[121] "Plan Able, Mission 148, March 25, 1945," 451st Bombardment Group (H), *451st.org,* accessed April 26, 2023, https://451st.org/Missions/Mission%20Flimsies/451st%20BG%20Pilot%20Flimsies/450325.JPG.

[122] "Mission No. 212, March 25, 1945, Target: Wels Airdrome, Austria (Abandoned primary target of Kbely Airdrome due to mechanical failures), 461st Bombardment Group (H), *461st.org,* accessed April 26, 2023, https://461st.org/Missions/March1945.htm; "Mission No. 168, 25 March 1945, Prague, Czechoslovakia", History of the 484th Bombardment Group (Heavy) 1 March 1945 to 31 March 1945, 484th Bombardment Group (H), *484th.org,* accessed April 26, 2023, https://484th.org/History/PDFs/484th%20History,%20450301.pdf.

[123] "Narrative Statement, 1 March to 31 March 1945," *Air Force Historical Research Agency;* Mike Hill, *The 451st Bomb Group in World War II: A Pictorial History* (Atglen, PA: Schiffer Publishing, 2001), 70.

[124] "General Orders Number 2024: Awards of the Distinguished Flying Cross, April 16, 1945," Headquarters, Fifteenth Air Force, *Air Force Historical Research Agency*, Microfilm Reel "Lanza Request #80653," 369-371, received by author on December 14, 2021, via mail from Pam Ives, Historian at AFHRA.

[125] Meyer Osofsky, telephone conversation with author, March 23, 2017.

[126] Meyer Osofsky, telephone conversation with author, December 17, 2016.

[127] Meyer Osofsky, telephone conversation with author, March 7, 2017.

[128] David Chin, email message to author, April 30, 2020.

[129] Meyer Osofsky, telephone conversations with author on May 16, 2016, and August 16, 2016.

[130] Meyer Osofsky, telephone conversation with author, August 26, 2016.

[131] Jessica Fragoso, "Interview of John Cooney," *Heroes On Our Island* at Verizon FiOS 1 News, Greater New York City Area, Broadcast Media, August 31, 2010, https://www.youtube.com/watch?v=aQQgTuNxjiA. This video isn't available anymore.

[132] Meyer Osofsky, telephone conversations with author on August 26, 2016, and December 19, 2016.

[133] Meyer Osofsky, telephone conversation with author, August 26, 2016,

[134] Meyer Osofsky, telephone conversations with author on March 7, 2017, and March 23, 2017.

[135] Meyer, telephone conversation with author, January 7, 2017.

[136] Lanza, *Shot Down Over Italy,* 92-93.

Chapter 14: AFTER THE WAR

[1] Tom Brokaw, *The Greatest Generation* (New York: Random House, 1998), book cover jacket.

[2] Brokaw, *Greatest Generation*, 56, 65, 80, 130, 142, 190, 288, 312, 324, 345, 354, and 372.

[3] "Born of Controversy: The GI Bill of Rights," Celebrating America's Freedoms, U.S. Department of Veterans Affairs, *VA.gov*, accessed January 19, 2024, https://www.va.gov/opa/publications/celebrate/gi-bill.pdf.

[4] David Boone, email message to author, June 8, 2023.

[5] "Find A Grave," s.v. "Livingston Boone (1891-1942)" accessed January 15, 2024, https://www.findagrave.com/memorial/187041876/livingston-boone; "1940 United States Federal Census," Englewood, Bergen County, New Jersey, s.v. "Livingston Boone," accessed January 19, 2024, as subscriber to *Ancestry.com*, https://www.ancestry.com/discoveryui-content/view/13442119 2:2442?tid=&pid=&queryId=bb3edd3c-afae-4048-be5d-44783f18e107&_phsrc=KOP101&_phstart=successSource; James Brown and Alvin Patrick, "GI Bill, a game changer for veterans, turns 70" CBS News, June 21, 2014, *CBSNews.com*, accessed January 18, 2024, https://www.cbsnews.com/news/gi-bill-turns-70-bill-of-opportunity-was-a-game-changer for veterans/.

[6] David Boone, email message to author, January 8, 2024.

[7] David Boone, email message to author, January 18, 2024.

[8] "Find A Grave," s.v. "Livingston Boone (1926-2019)," accessed January 15, 2024, https://www.findagrave.com/memorial/198468002/livingston-boone.

[9] David Boone, email message to author, January 8, 2024.

[10] Brown and Patrick, "GI Bill;" Tony Rich, "A hard working Renaissance man: Northshire says goodbye to Nathaniel Boone," *ManchesterJournal.com*, accessed January 15, 2025, https://www.manchesterjournal.com/local-news/a-hard-working-renaissance-man-northshire-says-goodbye-to-nathaniel-boone/article_26fa8fc2-45e8-11ee-be24-1b0f00891490.html.

[11] Tory Rich, "Today is Nathaniel Boone Day in Vermont," February 16, 2023, updated August 28, 2023, accessed January 18, 2024, https://www.manchesterjournal.com/opinion/columnists/today-is-nathaniel-boone-day-in-vermont/article_8e986868-ae29-11ed-ad3b-7bd668315d2f.html.

[12] Drew F. Lawrence, "2 Black Marines who Broke Racial Barriers During WWII Die Within Days of Each Other, *Military.com*, August 24, 2023, accessed January 15, 2024, https://www.military.com/daily-news/2023/08/24/2-black-marines-who-broke-racial-barriers-during-wwii-die-within-days-of-each-other.html.

[13] "Nathaniel A Boone Obituary (1927-2023)," Mahar Funeral Home and Cremation Services, accessed January 15, 2024, https://www.maharandsonfuneralhome.net/obituary/nathaniel-boone.

[14] Brown and Patrick, "GI Bill."

[15] "Nathaniel A Boone Obituary (1927-2023)," Mahar Funeral Home.

[16] "Born of Controversy: The GI Bill of Rights," *VA.gov.*.

[17] David Boone, telephone conversation with author, January 9, 2024.

[18] "'Englewood Express' Recovering at CMG," *The Lewiston Daily Sun*, May 15, 1950, 12, accessed on January 18, 2024, as a subscriber to *Newspapers.com*, https://www.newspapers.com/image/829285567/?terms=Englewood%20Express&match=1.

[19] "David O. Boone '62," Induction into Bates Scholar Athlete Society, Bates College, *GoBatesBobcats.edu*, accessed January 19, 2024, https://gobatesbobcats.com/sports/2020/6/4/scholar-athlete-society-2010-David-O-Boone-E2-80-9962.aspx.

[20] "David O. Boone," *GoBatesBobcats.edu*; David Boone, email to author, January 28, 2024.

[21] "Benjamin E. Mays," Bates Greats, Bates Celebrates 150 Years, *Bates.edu*, accessed January 15, 2024, https://www.bates.edu/150-years/bates-greats/benjamin-e-mays/.

[22] "David O. Boone," *GoBatesBobcats.edu*.

[23] Brown and Patrick, "GI Bill."

[24] "Boston University Varsity Football Roster," Syracuse vs. Boston University, *The Stadium Review*, Official Football Magazine, September 28, 1946, copy sent to author by Peter Slovenski, son of Walter Slovenski, a player on the Syracuse team.

[25] Suzanne Mettler, *Soldiers to Citizens: The G.I. Bill and the Making of the Greatest Generation* (New York: Oxford University Press, 2005), caption on one of the photographs between pages 126 and 127 which cited the Indiana University Archives, PS 47-1254.

[26] Mettler, *Soldiers to Citizens*, 119.

[27] Mettler, *Soldiers to Citizens*, 126-128.

Sergeant Kirk Gaylord Mosher

[1] Kathleen Mosher Krajewski, telephone conversation with author, May 3, 2023.

[2] "News of New Mexicans in Service: On All Fronts: Mosher," *The Albuquerque Tribune*, November 2, 1944, 2, accessed April 30, 2023, as subscriber to *Newspapers.com*, https://www.newspapers.com/image/782775282/?terms=On%20All%20Fronts&match=1.

[3] "U.S. Marine Corps Report of Separation for Daniel Alfred Mosher," New Mexico, U.S. World War II Records. 1941-1945 for Daniel Alfred Mosher, accessed April 30, 2023, as subscriber to *Ancestry.com*, https://www.ancestry.com/discoveryui-content/view/103481:8867.

[4] "News of New Mexicans in Service," *The Albuquerque Tribune*, 2.

Notes

[5] "Frank Mosher Obituary," *Albuquerque Journal*, November 3, 1990, 75, accessed May 1, 2023, as subscriber to *Newspapers.com*, https://www.newspapers.com/image/158601951/?terms=Dan%20Mosher&match=1.

[6] "Report of Death of Kirk G, Mosher," War Department, The Adjutant General's Office, February 16, 1945, *Individual Deceased Personnel File (IDPF): Kirk G. Mosher*, Freedom of Information Office, Department of the Army, U.A. Army Human Resources Command, Fort Knox, KY, IDPF was attached to email to author from Tifanie L. Cropper, Government Information Specialist, December 12, 2016.

[7] "Memorial Mass," *Albuquerque Journal*, February 21, 1945, 2, accessed March 21, 2023, as subscriber to *Newspapers.com*, https://www.newspapers.com/image/782627579/?terms=Frank%20Mosher&match=1.

[8] A.G. Schumacher (1st Lt., Q.M.C., Asst. Chief, Admin, Division), "Letter to Mr. Frank Mosher" with "Inventory of Effects for Kirk G. Mosher," *Individual Deceased Personnel File: Kirk G. Mosher.*

[9] "Letter from Mrs. Frank Mosher to the Adjutant General's Office," September 22, 1945, *Individual Deceased Personnel File: Kirk G. Mosher.*

[10] John W. Lanza, *Shot Down Over Italy: A true story of courage and survival in Nazi-occupied Italy during World War II* (Caldwell, NJ: Bright Spot Books, 2010), 236-237.

[11] T.B. Larkin, "Letter to Mr. Frank Mosher," January 7, 1947, *Individual Deceased Personnel File: Kirk G. Mosher*; "Report of Internment of Kirk R. Mosher," War Department, September 4, 1946, *Individual Deceased Personnel File: Kirk G. Mosher.*

[12] "Overview," Lorraine American Cemetery, American Battle Monuments Commission, *abmc. gov*, accessed June 21, 2023, https://www.abmc.gov/Lorraine; "Lorraine American Cemetery," American Battle Monuments Commission, *abmc gov*, accessed June 21, 2023, https://www.abmc.gov/multimedia/videos/lorraine-american-cemetery#:~:text=Lorraine%20American%20Cemetery%20is%20located,rolling%20woodlands%20of%20eastern%20Lorraine.

[13] "Letter to Frank Mosher from Major F.E. Hyll of the American Graves Administration Division confirming him as next-of-kin to son Kirk Mosher," July 20, 1948, *Individual Deceased Personnel File: Kirk G. Mosher.*

[14] "Disinterment Directive and Record of Custodial Transfer of Kirk G. Mosher," started April 29, 1948, and completed August 19, 1948, *Individual Deceased Personnel File: Kirk G. Mosher.*

[15] "Liberty Ships and Victory Ships, America's Lifeline in War (Teaching with Historic Places)," *National Park Service.gov*, accessed May 2, 2013, https://www.nps.gov/articles/liberty-ships-and-victory-ships-america-s-lifeline-in-war-teaching-with-historic-places.htm/.

[16] "687 Oglethorpe Victory, VC2-S-AP3," Victory Ships Built by the United States Maritime Commission During World War, Oregon Shipbuilding Corporation, Portland, OR, *USMM.org*, accessed May 1, 2023, http://www.usmm.org/victoryard.html.

[17] "Liberty Ships and Victory Ships," *National Park Service.gov*.

[18] United States Navy, "Log of USS Oglethorpe," 1946, *World War Regimental Histories*, 147, accessed May 2, 2023, http://digicom.bpl.lib.me.us/ww_reg_his/147?utm_source=digicom.bpl.lib.me.us%2Fww_reg_his%2F147&utm_medium=PDF&utm_campaign=PDFCoverPages.

[19] "4,300 War Dead to Arrive Today," *Daily News* (New York, NY), July 9, 1948, 200, accessed May 2, 2023, as subscriber to *Newspapers.com*, https://www.newspapers.com/image/447303281/?terms=Oglethorpe&match=1.

[20] "Record of Custodial Transfer of Kirk G. Mosher," *Individual Deceased Personnel File: Kirk G. Mosher*; "Funeral Services Today for Four War Heroes," *Albuquerque Journal*, August 13, 1948, 16, accessed March 21, 2023, as subscriber to *Newspapers.com*, https://www.newspapers.com/image/158243748/?terms=Frank%20Mosher&match=1.

[21] "Funeral Services Today for Four War Heroes," *Albuquerque Journal.*

[22] Genie Mosher, telephone conversation with author (cannot recall date).

[23] Kathleen Mosher Krajewski, telephone conversation with author, March 15, 2023.

[24] Hugh Gallagher, "Glen Campbell Riding the Trail Back to Albuquerque," *Albuquerque Journal*, July 2, 1979, 19, accessed May 4, 2023, as subscriber to *Newspapers.com*, https://www.newspapers.com/image/262738171/?terms=glen%20campbell%20riding%20the%20trail%20back%20to%20albuquerque&match=1; Kathleen Mosher Krajewski, telephone conversation with author, March 15, 2023.

[25] "Dan Mosher and the Hatchmen," Advertisement in the *Las Cruces Sun-News* (Las Cruces, New Mexico), July 18, 1975, 7, accessed May 4, 2023, as subscriber to *Newspapers.com*, https://www.newspapers.com/image/35309777/?terms=We%20Can%20Help&match=1; Kathleen Mosher Krajewski, telephone conversation with author, June 13, 2023.

[26] Kathleen Mosher Krajewski, telephone conversation with author, June 13, 2023.

[27] "Meyer Osofsky, telephone conversation with author, June 2, 2017.

[28] Matthew J. Hilton, "A social and cultural history of smoking," *Encyclopedia Britannica Online*, accessed June 19, 2023, https://www.britannica.com/topic/smoking-tobacco/A-social-and-cultural-history-of-smoking.

[29] Nicole Cordan, "In New Mexico, Pecos River Sustains Communities, Traditions, and Wildlife," July 22, 2020, accessed August 22, 2023, The Pew Charitable Trusts, *PewTrusts.org*, https://www.pewtrusts.org/en/research-and-analysis/articles/2020/07/22/in-new-mexico-pecos-river-sustains-communities-traditions-and-wildlife.

[30] Ray Monk, *Robert Oppenheimer: A Life Inside the Center* (New York: Anchor Books, 2014), 154,

[31] "Santa Fe National Cemetery," U.S. Department of Veterans Affairs, National Cemetery Administration, accessed August 22, 2023, https://www.cem.va.gov/cems/nchp/santafe.asp.

Second Lieutenant Robert "Bob" Grant Cookman

[1] "Report of Burial: Robert G. Cookman," October 26, 1944, and "Inventory of Effects: Robert G. Cookman," October 23, 1944, *Individual Personnel Records File: Robert G. Cookman*, emailed to author by Patricia A. Dugdale, Freedom of Information and Privacy Office, February 20, 2014.

[2] Meyer Osofsky, telephone conversation with author, January 17, 2017.

Notes

[3] John W. Lanza, *Shot Down Over Italy: A true story of courage and survival in Nazi-occupied Italy during World War II* (Caldwell, NJ: Bright Spot Books, 2010), 39.

[4] "In Memory of Lt. Robert G. Cookman, 15th Air Force," In Memoriam A2, *Mason City Globe-Gazette*, October 23, 1945, 16, accessed June 27, 2023, as subscriber to *Newspapers.com*, https://www.newspapers.com/image/391176980/?terms=card%20of%20thanks&match=1.

[5] "Lt. Robert Cookman, killed in action, Oct. 23, 1944," In Memoriam A2, *Mason City Globe-Gazette*, October 23, 1946, 22, accessed June 27, 2023, as subscriber to *Newspapers.com*, https://www.newspapers.com/image/391319767/?terms=In%20Memoriam&match=1.

[6] "In Memory of Lt. Robert G. Cookman, 15th A.A.F., killed in action, Oct. 23, 1944," Memoriam A2, *Mason City Globe-Gazette*, October 23, 1947, 33, accessed June 27, 2023, as subscriber to *Newspapers.com*, https://www.newspapers.com/image/391417016/?terms=In%20Memory%20of&match=1.

[7] "Letter from Harvey A. Cookman to the Quartermaster General, Memorial Division," *Individual Personnel Records File: Robert G. Cookman*, emailed to author by Patricia A. Dugdale, Freedom of Information and Privacy Office, February 20, 2014.

[8] "Relinquishment of Disposition Authority," *Individual Personnel Records File: Robert G. Cookman*, emailed to author by Patricia A. Dugdale, Freedom of Information and Privacy Office, February 20, 2014.

[9] "Record of Custodial Transfer," *Individual Personnel Records File: Robert G. Cookman*, emailed to author by Patricia A. Dugdale, Freedom of Information and Privacy Office, February 20, 2014.

[10] "Certificate of Interment in a Civil or Private Cemetery," *Individual Personnel Records File: Robert G. Cookman*, emailed to author by Patricia A. Dugdale, Freedom of Information and Privacy Office, February 20, 2014.

[11] "Lt. R. Cookman Rites Monday: Services to Be Held at Funeral Chapter," *Mason City Globe-Gazette*, September 24, 1948, 17, accessed June 27, 2023, as subscriber to *Newspapers.com*, https://www.newspapers.com/image/2220876/?terms=Cookman&match=1.

[12] "Card of Thanks," *Mason City Globe-Gazette*, September 30, 1948, 5, accessed June 27, 2023, as subscriber to *Newspapers.com*, https://www.newspapers.com/image/2220024/?terms=Card%20of%20Thanks&match=1.

[13] "The Flag that is flying over Memorial Park Cemetery this week is In Memory of Veteran Robert G. Cookman," *Mason City Globe-Gazette*, October 5, 1959, 9, accessed June 27, 2023, as subscriber to *Newspapers.com*, https://www.newspapers.com/image/8383517/?terms=flag%20cookman&match=1.

Second Lieutenant Thaddeus "Ted" Cylkowski

[1] Meyer Osofsky, telephone conversation with author, June 24, 2016.

[2] "Concert Program Covers 400 Years: Canticum Musicum Presents Machaut Mass With Old and Odd Instruments," *New York Times*, March 15, 1961, 42.

[3] "Isaac Stern Auditorium/Ronald O. Perelman Stage," *Carnegie Hall.org*, accessed June 28, 2023, https://www.carnegiehall.org/About/Building-Overview/Stern-Auditorium-Perelman-Stage; "Performance Halls: Three Great Stages," *CarnegieHall.org*, accessed June 28, 2023, https://www.carnegiehall.org/About/Rentals/Performance-Halls.

[4] "Judy and Arthur Zankel Hall, *CarnegieHall.org*, accessed June 28, 2023, https://www.carnegiehall.org/About/Building-Overview/Zankel-Hall.

[5] "Joan and Sanford I. Weill Recital Hall," *CarnegieHall.org*, accessed June 28, 2023, https://www.carnegiehall.org/About/Building-Overview/Weill-Recital-Hall.

[6] "Concert Program Covers 400 Years," *New York Times*.

[7] David Cylkowski, telephone conversation with author, April 1, 2021.

[8] "Thaddeus Cylkowski, Headquarters," Biographies (Information courtesy of David Cylkowski, son of Thaddeus Cylkowski), 450th Bomb Group Memorial Association, *450thBG.com*, https://www.450thbg.com/real/biographies/cylkowski/cylkowski.shtml.

[9] David Cylkowski, email message to author, April 7, 2021.

[10] David Cylkowski, telephone conversation with author, April 1, 2021.

[11] David Cylkowski, email message to author, April 7, 2021.

[12] David Cylkowski, email message to author, April 7, 2021.

[13] "Obituary of Muriel Cylkowski," Published by *New York Times* on Jul. 7, 2021, accessed June 29, 2023, via *Legacy.com*, https://www.legacy.com/us/obituaries/nytimes/name/muriel-cylkowski-obituary?id=11921147.

[14] David Cylkowski, email message to author, April 7, 2021.

[15] "Eugene Grant Obituary," *The Journal News* (White Plains, NY), April 5, 2018. A11, accessed June 29, 2023, as subscriber to *Newspapers.com*, https://www.newspapers.com/image/414742118/?match=1.

[16] David Cylkowski, email message to author, April 7, 2021; "Terry Grant," *StauntonMusicFestival.org*, accessed June 29, 2023, https://www.stauntonmusicfestival.org/leadership.

[17] David Cylkowski, email message to author, July 7, 2021.

[18] "Pianist Garrick Ohlsson back in his ol' backyard," *The Reporter Dispatch* (White Plains, NY), January 5, 1979, 39, accessed June 29, 2023, as subscriber to *Newspaper.com*, https://www.newspapers.com/image/910761243/?terms=Pianist%20Garrick%20Ohlsson&match=1.

[19] "News Briefs: Three Events at the Emelin," *The Daily News* (Westchester County, NY, and Fairfield County, CT), March 31, 1981, 505, accessed June 29, 2023, as subscriber to *Newspapers.com*, https://www.newspapers.com/image/484179225/?terms=Three%20Events%20at%20the%20Emelin&match=1.

[20] Irma Glaser, telephone conversation with author, April 2, 2021.

Technical Sergeant Joseph "Leslie" Goss III

[1] "Missing in Action: J.L. Goss Jr., Last Reported Over Yugoslavia," *The Henry County Democrat* (Clinton, MO), April 12, 1945, 1, accessed March 7, 2023, as subscriber to *Newspapers.com*, https://www.newspapers.com/image/493918321/?terms=J.L.%20Goss&match=1.

Notes

[2] "Leslie Goss a Civilian," *The Henry County Democrat* (Clinton, MO), October 18, 1945, 2, accessed March 7, 2023, as subscriber to Newspapers.com, https://www.newspapers.com/image/493920053/?terms=Leslie%20Goss&match=1.

[3] "Joseph L. Goss," U.S., Department of Veterans Affairs BIRLS Death File, 1850-2010, accessed March 4, 2024, as a subscriber to *Ancestry.com*, https://www.ancestry.com/discoveryui-content/view/11093358:2441?tid=&pid=&queryId=fd0bef774e6c86dac0d1ae6231b3229b&_phsrc=KOP15&_phstart=successSource.

[4] "Personal," *The Clinton Eye*, March 28, 1946, 2B, accessed October 20, 2023, as subscriber to *Newspapers.com*, https://www.newspapers.com/image/335116197/?terms=Leslie%20Goss&match=1.

[5] "Peacetime Victories of the U.S. Army," *Waxahachie Daily Light* (Waxahachie, TX), April 13, 1946, 4, accessed October 31, 2023, as subscriber to *Newspapers.com*, https://www.newspapers.com/image/87320421/?terms=Peacetime%20victories&match=1.

[6] "What is geodesy?" National Ocean Service: National Oceanic and Atmospheric Administration, *OceanService.NOAA.gov*, accessed October 24, 2023, https://oceanservice.noaa.gov/facts/geodesy.html.

[7] "Summary," U.S. Coast and Geodetic Survey, 1946," Wikipedia Commons, *Commons.Wikipedia.com*, accessed October 24, 2023, as subscriber to *Newspapers.com*, https://commons.wikimedia.org/wiki/File:U.S._Coast_and_Geodetic_Survey,_1946_(15328042).jpg.

[8] J.H. Brittain, "Progress in Geodetic Surveys by the United States Coast and Geodetic Survey, July 1946 to June 1947," Advancing and Earth and Space Sciences, Wiley Online Library, accessed October 31, 2023, as subscriber to *Newspapers.com*, https://agupub.onlinelibrary.wiley.com/doi/abs/10.1029/TR029i002p00254.

[9] "Geodetic Control Survey Work Appeals to Young Men," *The Canyon News*, October 24, 1946, 14, accessed October 24, 2023, as subscriber to *Newspapers.com*, https://www.newspapers.com/image/42469838/?terms=Geodetic%20Control&match=1.

[10] "J.L. Goss is Dead: Veteran Clothier Succumbs to Heart Malady," *The Henry County Democrat*, January 30, 1941, 1, accessed July 2, 2023, as subscriber to *Newspapers.com*, https://www.newspapers.com/image/494064002/?terms=J.L.%20Goss&match=1.

[11] "Big Event Is Tonight: The Senior Play, 'Cross My Heart,' Will Be Presented at the H.S. Auditorium," *The Clinton Eye*, May 1, 1941, 1, accessed October 18, 2023, as a subscriber to *Newspapers.com*, https://www.newspapers.com/image/335189771/?terms=cross%20my%20heart&match=1..

[12] Office of the University Registrar, University of Missouri, email message to author, July 7, 2020.

[13] "Joseph Leslie Goss, III," Cemetery Index, Englewood Cemetery, Clinton, Henry County, Missouri, accessed July 2, 2023, http://www.henrycomo.us/Cemeteries/engG.html.

[14] "Obituaries: Joseph L. Goss," *Arizona Republic* (Phoenix, AZ), February 10, 1985, 11, accessed July 2, 2023, as subscriber to Newspapers.com, https://www.newspapers.com/image/117948901/?article=a043d3fb-40a4-4895-a2a7-83f81aee407f&terms=Joseph%20L.%20Goss; "Obituaries: Glendora J. Goss," *Arizona Republic* (Phoenix, AZ), May 18, 1998, 16, accessed July 2, 2023, as subscriber to *Newspapers.com*, https://www.newspapers.com/image/124179748/?terms=Glendora%20J.%20Goss&match=1.

[15] "Obituaries: Joseph L. Goss," *Arizona Republic.*

[16] "Grace M. Freeman Goss and Joseph Leslie Goss, Jr.," Cemetery Index, Englewood Cemetery, accessed March 4, 2024, http://www.henrycomo.us/Cemeteries/engG.html.

[17] "Obituaries: Glendora J. Goss," *Arizona Republic.*

[18] "Chloe M. Goodman Goss; Grace M. Freeman Goss; Joseph Leslie Goss, III; Joseph Leslie Goss, Jr.; Joseph Leslie Goss, Sr., Cemetery Index, Englewood Cemetery, accessed March 4, 2024, http://www.henrycomo.us/Cemeteries/engG.html.

[19] "Carmen Josephene Goss, March 27, 1904 - December 26, 2005," Vansant-Mills Funeral Home, accessed July 3, 2023, https://www.vansant-millsfuneralhome.com/obituaries/print?o_id=26594; Goss, Carmen J. Blake, Cemetery Index, Englewood Cemetery.

Staff Sergeant Hong Sing "Calvin" Chin

[1] "Honorable Discharge: Hong S. Chin," Army of the United States, November 6, 1945, emailed to author by David Chin on May 24, 2020.

[2] "Separation Qualification Record: Hong S. Chin," Army of the United States, November 6, 1945, emailed to author by David Chin on May 22, 2020; "Certificate of Completion: Hong S. Chin," Roosevelt Aviation School at Roosevelt Field, Mineola, NY, September 28, 1946, emailed to author by David Chin on May 22, 2020.

[3] William E. Young, *The World Book Encyclopedia* (Chicago, IL: Field Enterprises Educational Corporation, 1968), s.v. "Levittown," Volume 12, L, 196.

[4] David Chin, email message to author, May 12, 2020.

[5] Aileen Jacobson, "Chinese Americans on Long Island," Long Island Pulse, *LIPulse.com*, January 23, 2015, accessed June 29, 2023, http://lipulse.com/2015/01/23/chinese-americans-on-long-island/.

[6] "The Arthur Lem Story," Chinese Center on Long Island, *CCLI.yolasite.com*, accessed June 29, 2023, http://ccli.yolasite.com/arthur-lem-memorial-scholarship.php.

[7] Jacobsen, "Chinese Americans on Long Island."

[8] Dick Kraus, "Through a Lens Dimly: The Chinaman," The Digital Journalist, *DigitalJournalist.org*, accessed June 29, 2023, http://digitaljournalist.org/issue0505/assign/dk_tald14_0505.htm.

[9] "Arthur Lem Given Brotherhood Award," *Newsday* (Nassau County Edition), February 21, 1958, 20, accessed June 29, 2923, as subscriber to *Newspapers.com*, https://www.newspapers.com/image/711847974/?match=1.

[10] Jacobsen, "Chinese Americans on Long Island."

[11] "The Arthur Lem Story," Chinese Center on Long Island.

[12] Major General Nathan F. Twining, "Certificate of Valor to Hong S. Chin in Recognition of Courageous Service in Aerial Combat," emailed to author by David Chin on April 28, 2020; David Chin, email message to author, May 30, 2020.

Notes

[13] David Chin, email message to author, May 3, 2020.

[14] David Chin, email message to author, May 8, 2020.

[15] "Calvin Chin, Restaurateur," *Newsday* (Nassau Edition, November 30, 1987, 31, accessed June 30, 2023, as subscriber to *Newspapers.com*, https://www.newspapers.com/image/710751058/?match=1.

[16] David Chin, email message to author, April 30, 2020.

[17] David Chin, email message to author, May 3, 2020.

[18] "Meyer Osofsky Obituary," *New York Times*, November 2, 2019, accessed via *Legacy.com* on June 30, 2023, https://www.legacy.com/us/obituaries/nytimes/name/meyer-osofsky-obituary?id=14818709.

[19] David Chin, email message to author, May 3, 2020.

[20] David Chin, email message to author, May 20, 2020.

[21] David Chin, email message to author, May 12, 2020.

[22] "David C. Chin: Why Do We Fly?" The Texas Pilots Association, *TexasPilots.org*, United States of American, accessed July 1, 2023, http://www.texaspilots.org/Why_We_Fly.html.

[23] David Chin, email message to author, May 28, 2020.

[24] David Chin, email message to author, April 29, 2020.

[25] "Commendation Letter from Bill Dengler (Quality Operations, Grumman Aerospace Corporation) to Inspection Team (which resolved structural issue with the F-14s), November 25, 1985, emailed to author by David Chin on May 28, 2020.

[26] David Chin, email message to author, May 8, 2020.

[27] David Chin, email message to author, May 12, 2020.

[28] David Chin, email message to author, June 27, 2023.

[29] David Chin, email message to author, December 3, 2020.

[30] David Chin, email messages to author, December 1, 2021, and November 28, 2022.

First Lieutenant Russell "Russ" John Flint

[1] Major General Nathan F. Twining, "Certificate of Valor to Russell J. Flint in Recognition of Courageous Service in Aerial Combat," emailed to author by Russell J. Flint, Jr., on June 2, 2021.

[2] "Individual Flight Record of 2nd Lt. Russell J. Flint," Russell J. Flint, Jr., emailed to author on June 2, 2012, his father's Individual Flight Records for the seven months from October 1944 to April 1945.

[3] Headquarters, 451st Bombardment Group (H), "Narrative History: 1 Dec. to 31 Dec. 1944," accessed July 5, 2023, https://451st.org/History/pdf's/December%201944.pdf; Henry D.

Richardson, Group Commander, "Daily Operations Report: December 26, 1944," 451st Bomb Group (H), 451st.org, Daily Operations Reports, 441206.1 and 441206.2, accessed July 5, 2023, https://451st.org/Daily%20Ops%20Reports/Daily%20Operations%20Reports.html.

[4] "Military Record and Report of Separation, Certificate of Service for Russell J. Flint," emailed to author by Russell J. Flint, Jr., on June 2, 2021.

[5] "Marriage Record: Russell J. Flint to Marie R. Schuttler, July 27, 1945," U.S., Evangelical Lutheran Church in America Church Records, 1781-1969, accessed July 5, 2023, as subscriber to *Ancestry.com*, https://www.ancestry.com/discoveryui-content/view/4333305:60722?tid=&pid=&queryId=6610ef0e524e9d667f40ff6bcde449b4&_phsrc=bgd373&_phstart=successSource.

[6] "Military Record and Report of Separation, Certificate of Service (Russell J. Flint)," emailed to author by Russell J. Flint, Jr., on June 2, 2021.

[7] "1940 United States Federal Census," Chicago, Cook County, Illinois, s.v. "Victor Schuttler," accessed July 6, 2023, as subscriber to *Ancestry.com*, https://www.ancestry.com/discoveryui-content/view/147513582:2442?tid=&pid=&queryId=c73b5a3db31e3c3dbd08e17e0c698c56&_phsrc=mRc141&_phstart=successSource; "1930 United States Federal Census," Chicago, Cook County, Illinois, s.v. "John S. Flint," accessed July 6, 2023, as subscriber to *Ancestry.com*, https://www.ancestry.com/discoveryui-content/view/84119844:6224?tid=&pid=&queryId=13be38c0a545ea8d680728a03c09e98e&_phsrc=mRc142&_phstart=successSource; "1940 United States Federal Census, Chicago, Cook County, Illinois, s.v. "John S. Flint," accessed July 6, 2023, as subscriber to *Ancestry.com*, https://www.ancestry.com/discoveryui-content/view/146529957:2442?tid=&pid=&queryId=13be38c0a545ea8d680728a03c09e98e&_phsrc=mRc143&_phstart=successSource.

[8] U.S., World War II Draft Cards Young Men, 1940-1947, s.v. Robert Victor Schuttler, accessed on July 6, 2023, as subscriber to *Ancestry.com*, https://www.ancestry.com/discoveryui-content/view/40478410:2238?tid=&pid=&queryId=fbd244c21268e110052160f77692ba6a&_phsrc=mRc145&_phstart=successSource.

[9] Meyer Osofsky, telephone conversation with author, July 24, 2016.

[10] Meyer Osofsky, telephone conversation with author, August 26, 2016.

[11] "Hollywood, Florida, City Directory, 1957," U.S., City Directories, 1822-1995, s.v. "Russell J Flint (Salesman, Ford Motors)," accessed July 6, 2023, as subscriber to *Ancestry.com*, https://www.ancestry.com/discoveryui-content/view/669132224:2469?tid=&pid=&queryId=9d2101e6aeff6971fef40a5eabd45d4c&_phsrc=mRc150&_phstart=successSource; "Hollywood, Florida, City Directory, 1958," U.S., City Directories, 1822-1995, s.v. "Russell J Flint (Agent, New York Life)," accessed July 6, 2023. as subscriber to *Ancestry.com*, https://www.ancestry.com/discoveryui-content/view/927262254:2469?tid=&pid=&queryId=9d2101e6aeff6971fef40a5eabd45d4c&_phsrc=mRc153&_phstart=successSource; "Hollywood, Florida, City Directory, 1959," U.S., City Directories, 1822-1995, s.v. "Russell J Flint (Agent, New York Life)," accessed July 6, 2023. as subscriber to *Ancestry.com*, https://www.ancestry.com/discoveryui-content/view/667264723:2469?tid=&pid=&queryId=f2b5efabe27ce2ce575c771fd44cb989&_phsrc=bgd376&_phstart=successSource; "Hollywood, Florida, City Directory, 1960," U.S., City Directories, 1822-1995, s.v. "Russell J Flint (Agent, New York Life)," accessed July 6, 2023, as subscriber to *Ancestry.com*, https://www.ancestry.com/discoveryui-content/view/674436940:2469?tid=&pid=&queryId=9d2101e6aeff6971fef40a5eabd45d4c&_phsrc=mRc151&_phstart=successSource.

[12] "Reigning City King Pegs Win," *Fort Lauderdale News*, April 25, 1960, 43, accessed July 6, 2023, as subscriber to *Newspapers.com*, https://www.newspapers.com/image/229792351/?match=1.

[13] Russell J. Flint, Jr., telephone conversation with author, May 13, 2021.

Notes

[14] Jennifer Johnson, "Hillary Clinton and Park Ridge," *Chicago Tribune*, Twitter: @Jen_Tribune, jjohnson@pioneerlocal.com, https://www.chicagotribune.com/suburbs/park-ridge/ct-prh-hillary-clinton-hometown-facts-tl-1110-20161108-story.html.

[15] "Death Notices: Flint (Marie R. Flint), *Chicago Tribune*, August 21, 1970, 20, accessed July 7, 2023, as subscriber to *Newspapers.com*, https://www.newspapers.com/image/377116913/?terms=Marie%20R.%20Flint&match=1; "Death Notices: Schuttler (Victor C. Schuttler)," *Chicago Tribune*, December 12, 1970, 14, accessed July 7, 2023, as subscriber to *Newspapers.com*, https://www.newspapers.com/image/377375877/?terms=Victor%20 Schuttler&match=1; "Find A Grave," s.v. "John S. Flint (1893-1970), accessed July 7, 2023, https://www.findagrave.com/memorial/71548178/john-s-flint.

[16] Russell J. Flint, Jr., telephone conversation with author, May 24, 2021.

[17] "Find A Grave," s.v. "Ruth Schuttler (1904-1980)," accessed July 7, 2023, https://www.findagrave.com/memorial/181372330/ruth-schuttler.

[18] "Victor Construction's History is Family History," *VictoryConstruction.com*, accessed July 7, 2023, https://www.victorconstruction.com/our-history/#:~:text=In%20December%20of%201954%2C%20Robert,their%20family%20to%20five%20children.

[19] "Find A Grave," s.v. "John S. Flint (1893-1970), accessed July 7, 2023, https://www.findagrave.com/memorial/71548178/john-s-flint; "Find A Grave, s.v. "Selma E. Flint (1899-1981)," accessed July 7, 2023, https://www.findagrave.com/memorial/71548490/selma-e-flint.

[20] Austin High School, *Maroon and White* (Chicago, Illinois, 1940), 61 and 73, accessed September 27, 2022, as subscriber to *E-yearbook.com*, https://www.e-yearbook.com/sp/eybb?school=20104&year=1940.

[21] Russell J. Flint, Jr., telephone conversation with author, May 13, 2021.

[22] "Army Separation Qualification Record (Russell J. Flint)," emailed to author by Russell J. Flint, Jr., on June 2, 2021.

[23] Russell J. Flint, Jr., telephone conversation with author, May 13, 2021.

Technical Sergeant Charles "Chuck" Joseph Muth

[1] "Victory in Europe Day: Time of Celebration, Reflection," U.S. Department of Defense, *Defense.com*, accessed October 21, 2020, https://www.defense.gov/Multimedia/Experience/VE-Day/#:~:text=On%20May%208%2C%201945%20%2D%20known,World%20War%20II%20in%20Europe.&text=The%20first%20was%20on%20May,all%20fronts%20in%20Reims%-2C%20France.

[2] "Charles J. Muth," 765th Roster, 461st Bombardment Group (H), *461st.org*, accessed July 8, 2023, https://461st.org/Roster/Roster%20765th.htm; "Supply Missions from May 6, 1945, to May 15, 1945," 461st Bombardment Group (H), *461st.org*, accessed December 21, 2022, https://461st.org/Missions/May1945.htm.

[3] Sean Sims (Army Heritage and Education Center), "Mercy Missions," *The 461st Liberaider*, Vol. 29, No. 1, 14, June 2012, 461st Bombardment Group (H), *461st.org*, accessed July 8, 2023, https://461st.org/Liberaider/PDFs/June%202012.pdf.

[4] "Indiana, U.S., Birth Certificates, 1907-1944," s.v. "James Robert Muth," accessed October 9, 2022, as subscriber to *Ancestry.com*, https://www.ancestry.com/imageviewer/collections/60871/images/40474_357669-01628?treeid=&personid=&hintid=&queryId=3a0e2771aed4bc85658 5b1cf3b5ee7f8&usePUB=true&_phsrc=zsS316&_phstart=successSource&usePUBJs=true& pId=2012226; "U.S. World War II Draft Cards Young Men, 1940-1947," s.v. "Charles Joseph Muth," accessed as subscriber to *Ancestry.com* on August 4, 2022, https://www.ancestry.com/discoveryui-content/view/41217489:2238?tid=&pid=&queryId=6387c15ece4c684f79cba2033 f78872e&_phsrc=zsS286&_phstart=successSource; "U.S., Social Security Death Index, 1935-2014," s.v. "Victoria Muth," (born March 30, 1901, accessed October 10, 2022, as subscriber to *Ancestry.com*, https://search.ancestry.com/cgi-bin/sse.dll?dbid=3693&h=44554145&indiv=try &o_vc=Record:OtherRecord&rhSource=61370&_gl=1*rf6zky*_ga*ODE2MTI1Mjk4LjE2NjQy ODA0OTY.*_ga_4QT8FMEX30*MTY2NTQ0MDM3OS40LjEuMTY2NTQ0MTA4OS4wLjAu MA; "Illinois, County Marriage Records, 1800-1940," s.v. "Victoria Boudreau" (married Charles J. Shea on August 3, 1916), accessed October 10, 2022, as subscriber to *Ancestry.com*, https://www.ancestry.com/discoveryui-content/view/901317122:61370?tid=&pid=&queryId=4f66fd7 642ad94b04fbbc6643cb095a3&_phsrc=bgd76&_phstart=successSource; "1930 United States Federal Census," Barrington Township, Cook County, Illinois, s.v. "Charles J. Kershaw," accessed October 10, 2022, as subscriber to *Ancestry.com*, https://www.ancestry.com/discoveryui-content/view/83534350:6224.

[5] "Now in 50th Year of Music Instruction," *Arlington Heights Herald* (Arlington Heights, IL), September 3, 1953, 18, accessed July 9, 2023, as subscriber of *Newspaper.com*, https://www.newspapers.com/image/75834404/?match=1.

[6] "Musin' and Meanderin'," *The McHenry Plaindealer* (McHenry, IL), September 10, 1953, 1, accessed July 9, 2023, as subscriber to *Newspapers.com*, https://www.newspapers.com/image/167278007/?match=1; "Miss Beth Sears First Oboist with Symphony Orchestra," *The McHenry Plaindealer* (McHenry, IL), October 26, 1950, 6, accessed July 9, 2023, as subscriber to *Newspapers.com*, https://www.newspapers.com/image/172830809/?terms=Miss%20Beth%20 Sears%20&match=1.

[7] "Now in 50th Year of Music Instruction," *Arlington Heights Herald*.

[8] "Girls to Aid Dewey Welcome," *Chicago Tribune*, October 25, 1944, 3, accessed July 9, 2023, as subscriber to *Newspapers.com*, https://www.newspapers.com/image/372623940/?terms=Girls%20 to%20Aid%20Dewey&match=1.

[9] "Musin' and Meanderin'," *The McHenry Plaindealer*, 1.

[10] "Henry Muth," Obituary, *The Tampa Tribune*, May 14, 1966, 33, accessed July 8, 2023, as subscriber to *Newspapers.com*, https://www.newspapers.com/image/330440827/?terms=Henry%20Muth&match=1.

[11] "Victoria Mary Muth," *The Arizona Republic* (Phoenix, AZ), August 7, 1985, 58, accessed July 8, 2023, as subscriber to Newspapers.com, https://www.newspapers.com/image/120201549/?terms=Victoria%20Mary%20Muth&match=1; "Find A Grave," s.v. Charles J. Muth II (1948-1989)," accessed July 8, 2023, https://www.findagrave.com/memorial/1022858/charles-joseph-muth.

[12] "Find A Grave," s.v. "Charles Joseph Muth (1917-2005)," accessed July 8, 2023, https://www.findagrave.com/memorial/36506422/charles-joseph-muth; "Find A Grave," s.v. Charles J. Muth II (1948-1989)," accessed July 8, 2023, https://www.findagrave.com/memorial/1022858/charles-joseph-muth.

[13] "Tisdale-Muth," *Arizona Republic* (Phoenix, AZ), August 2, 1970, 124, accessed July 9, 2023, as subscriber to *Newspapers.com*, https://www.newspapers.com/image/11754 7622/?article=5c85ea95-2d63-4e83-8e29-f671cd053350&focus=0.38782853,0.15760 6,0.5063392,0.3067133&xid=3398&_gl=1*19ixigk*_gcl_aw*R0NMLjE2ODI0ODAy MjEuRUFJYUlRb2JDaE1JcmItbm1zX0dfZ0lWSHNfakJ4M0VTUVk1RUFBWUFp QUFFZ0lOUHZEX0J3RQ..**_gcl_dc*R0NMLjE2ODI0ODAyMjEuRUFJYUlRb2JDa E1JcmItbm1zX0dfZ0lWSHNfakJ4M0VTUVk1RUFBWUFpQUFFZ0lOUHZDX0J3RQ..*_ gcl_au*MTA4NTM1MTEwNC4xNjgxMzMyMTQ3*_ga*ODE2MTI1Mjk4L jE2NjQyODA0OTY.*_ga_4QT8FMEX30*ZGU1YzZkMGUtY2E3ZC00Y2JjLTg5NGUtNGMx ODQ4ZWMwYTIxLjY3LjEuMTY4ODkyNzY5Ny4yOC4wLjA.&_ga=2.179097126.368832953 .1688834835-816125298.1664280496.

[14] "James Muth Obituary" and "Memories and Condolences for James Muth," *Las Cruces Sun-News*, March 19, 2014, *Legacy.com*, accessed March 31, 2021, https://www.legacy.com/us/obituaries/lcsun-news/name/james-muth-obituary?id=19290196&fhid=7145.

Second Lieutenant David Gordon Johnson

[1] "Military Record and Report of Separation, Certificate of Service for David G. Johnson," mailed to author by Diane Turnquist, Expert Archives Technician, National Personnel Records Center, November 25, 2022; "The Distinguished Flying Cross…'for heroism or extraordinary achievement while participating in aerial flight'," The Distinguished Flying Cross Society, *DFCSociety.org*, accessed July 10, 2023, https://www.dfcsociety.org/; "General Orders Number 2024: Awards of the Distinguished Flying Cross, April 16, 1945," Headquarters, Fifteenth Air Force, *Air Force Historical Research Agency*, Microfilm Reel "Lanza Request #80653," 369-371, received by author on December 14, 2021, via mail from Pam Ives, Historian at AFHRA.

[2] "Military Record and Report of Separation for David G. Johnson," National Personnel Records Center.

[3] "Marriage Certificate," Pierce County, WA, Certificate #80653, David Gordon Johnson to Mary Esther Ladd, November 4, 1946, accessed July 10, 2023, as subscriber to *Ancestry.com*, https://www.ancestry.com/discoveryui-content/view/1391510:2378?tid=&pid=&queryId=9165534d24b4 52319e6e1a77cde21246&_phsrc=bgd406&_phstart=successSource.

[4] "1940 United States Federal Census," Loudon, Merrimack, New Hampshire, s.v. Mary Esther Ladd, accessed July 10, 2023, as subscriber to *Ancestry.com*, https://www.ancestry.com/discoveryui-content/view/83342448:2442?tid=&pid=&queryId=c3f5f8af684d87c37fbcb4b8b01a 1eae&_phsrc=mRc168&_phstart=successSource.

[5] "Find A Grave," s.v. "Levi Kimball Ladd Sr. (1900-1953)," accessed July 10, 2023, https://www.findagrave.com/memorial/116117808/levi-kimball-ladd.

[6] "Find A Grave," s.v. "Levi Kimball Ladd (1926-2009)," accessed July 10, 2023, https://www.findagrave.com/memorial/50062806/levi-kimball-ladd; David Stubblebine, "Hancock," World War II Database, *WW2db.com*, accessed July 10, 2023, https://ww2db.com/ship_spec.php?ship_id=538.

[7] "U.S. World War II Cadet Nursing Corps Card Files, 1942-1948," s.v. "Mary Ladd," accessed July 29,2023, as subscriber to *Ancestry.com*, https://www.ancestry.com/discoveryui-content/view /942433:2251?tid=&pid=&queryId=00ac15e12847cb4067be2049cb37cb6a&_phsrc=bgd518&_ phstart=successSource.

[8] Ruth Schubert, "The Push to Recognize the U.S. Cadet Nurse Corps as Veterans," November 27, 2019, Washington State Nursing Association, *WSNA.org*, accessed July 30, 2023, https://www.wsna.org/news/2019/the-push-to-recognize-the-u-s-cadet-nurse-corps-as-veterans.

[9] "U.S. World War II Cadet Nursing Corps Card Files, 1942-1948," s.v. "Mary Ladd."

[10] "U.S. Cadet Nurse Corps," American Organization for Nursing Leadership, *AONL.org*, accessed July 29, 2023, https://www.aonl.org/advocacy/key-issues/us-cadet-nurse-corps.

[11] "Marriage Certificate," David Gordon Johnson to Mary Esther Ladd.

[12] "Engagement Announced (Elliott Burbank, Jr., to Betty Ladd)" *The Landmark* (White River Junction VT), September 23, 1943, accessed July 11, 2023, as subscriber to *Newspapers.com*, https://www.newspapers.com/image/660940769/?terms=Elliott%20Burbank&match=1.

[13] "Find A Grave," s.v. "Elliott Winsor Burbank Jr. (1923-1982)," accessed July 11, 2023, https://www.findagrave.com/memorial/85973404/elliot-winsor-burbank.

[14] "Obituaries: Wendell Dodge," *Concord Monitor* (Concord, NH), April 10, 2003, 12, accessed July 11, 2023, as subscriber to *Ancestry.com*, https://www.ancestry.com/discoveryui-content/view/899222029:61843.

[15] Daniel Ladd, telephone conversation with author, November 26, 2021.

[16] "Levi K. Ladd, Jr. Obituary," *Legacy.com* (Published by Union Leader [Manchester, NH] on Feb. 1, 2009), accessed July 11, 2023, https://www.legacy.com/obituaries/unionleader/obituary.aspx?n=levi-k-ladd&pid=123542711&fhid=4796.

[17] Daniel Ladd, telephone conversation with author, November 26, 2021.

[18] Daniel Ladd, telephone conversation with author, September 6, 2021.

[19] Karen Dodge, email message to author, September 28, 2021.

[20] Karen Dodge, email message to author, September 30, 2021.

[21] John Johnson, telephone conversation with author, October 12, 2021.

[22] Carole Dodge, email message to author, September 30, 2021.

[23] John Johnson, telephone conversation with author, October 12, 2021.

[24] Daniel Ladd, telephone conversation with author, November 26, 2021; "Joe Harris: Cape Horn, With Gratitude," Scuttlebutt Sailing News, *SailingScuttlebut.com*, March 10, 2016, accessed July 11, 2023, https://www.sailingscuttlebutt.com/2016/03/10/joe-harris-cape-horn-with-gratitude/.

[25] Carole Dodge, email message to author, September 30, 2021: Daniel Ladd, telephone conversation with author, November 26, 2021.

[26] John Johnson, telephone conversation with author, October 12, 2021.

[27] John Johnson, telephone conversation with author, October 12, 2021; Daniel Ladd, telephone conversation with author, November 26, 2021.

[28] Carole Dodge, email message to author, September 30, 2021.

Notes

[29] Abby Ladd, telephone conversation with author, May 19, 2021.

[30] "David G. Johnson," U.S. Social Security Death Index, 1935-2014, accessed July 11, 2023, as subscriber to *Ancestry.com*, https://www.ancestry.com/discoveryui-content/view/77005706:3693.

[31] "Mary Esther Johnson (1922-2014)," *WikiTree.com*, accessed July 30, 2023, https://www.wikitree.com/wiki/Ladd-1783.

[32] John Johnson, telephone conversation with author, October 12, 2021; Gregory Marsella (husband of Betty Johnson Marsella), email message to author, July 30, 2023.

[33] John Johnson, telephone conversation with author, October 12, 2021.

Second Lieutenant Ray Martin Goodson

[1] Hubert Zemke and Roger A. Freeman, *Zemke's Stalag: The Final Days of World War II* (Washington, DC: Smithsonian Institution Press, 1991), 111-113; "Operation Revival: Rescue from Stalag Luft I," May 20, 2020, National WWII Museum, accessed March 7, 2023, https://www.nationalww2museum.org/war/articles/operation-revival-stalag-luft-i; "The Liberation of Stalag Luft I," April 30, 2020, National WWII Museum, accessed March 7, 2023, https://www.nationalww2museum.org/liberation-stalag-luft.

[2] Oscar G. Richard III, "Hubert Zemke – A Man to Remember," *Stalag Luft I Online*, accessed March 7, 2023, http://www.merkki.com/zemkehubert.htm.

[3] "Matrimonial Register," No. 234, Ray Martin Goodson to Doris Mae Dodge, January 19, 1947, Diocese of Joliet; Joliet, IL; Sacramental Records 1935-1968; Church: St Dennis, Lockport; Description: Marriage Register, 1935-1968; Volume: 1, accessed July 12, 2023, as subscriber of *Ancestry.com*, https://www.ancestry.com/discoveryui-content/view/143982:62097?tid=&pid=&quseryId=5e6f0b8ea6bc46d62584a6a66e0916e8&_phsrc=bgd427&_phstart=successSource; "Find A Grave," s.v. "Ray M . Goodson (1924-2013)," accessed July 12, 2023, https://www.findagrave.com/memorial/120337570/ray-m-goodson.

[4] "Waste Lands: America's Forgotten Nuclear Legacy: Blockson Chemical Company," *The Wall Street Journal, WSJ.com*, updated October 29, 2013, accessed July 12, 2023, https://www.wsj.com/graphics/waste-lands/site/71-blockson-chemical-co/.

[5] "A Historical Look at Olin, a Globally Recognized Corporation," Olin: Building a Legacy of Integrity, *Olin.com*, accessed July 13, 2023, https://olin.com/about-olin/history/; "Olin's History," accessed July 12, 2023, http://www.b2i.us/profiles/investor/fullpage.asp?BzID=1548&to=cp&Nav=0&LangID=1&s=0&ID=6661; "Olin Corp: Overview," *Global Data.com*, accessed July 13, 2023, https://www.globaldata.com/company-profile/olin-corp/#:~:text=Olin%20Corp%20(Olin)%20is%20a,organics%2C%20hydrochloric%20acid%20and%20bleach.

[6] "Find A Grave," s.v. "Ray M. Goodson (1924-2013)," accessed July 12, 2023, https://www.findagrave.com/memorial/120337570/ray-m-goodson; "Find A Grave," s.v. "Doris M. Dodge Goodson (1924-2017)," accessed July 12, 2023, https://www.findagrave.com/memorial/184007029/doris-mae-goodson.

[7] "Collaboration Leads to Early Cleanup Completion, Joliet Army Ammunition Plant," Federal Facilities Restoration and Reuse Office, U.S. Environmental Protection Agency, *EPA.gov*, accessed July 12, 2023, https://www.epa.gov/sites/default/files/documents/success_story_joliet_0.pdf.

[8] Tom Goodson, telephone conversation on October 8. 2010.

[9] Meyer Osofsky, telephone conversation with author, January 27, 2017.

[10] "Ray M. Goodson Obituary," *Legacy.com* (Published by the *Herald-News* [Elmhurst, IL] on November 15, 2013), accessed July 12, 2023, http://www.legacy.com/obituaries/theherald-news/obituary.aspx?n=ray-m-goodson&pid=168002241&fhid=16037.

[11] "Find A Grave," s.v. "Ray M. Goodson.

[12] "Find A Grave," s.v. "Doris M. Dodge Goodson.

Technical Sergeant John Joseph Cooney

[1] Peter Cooney, "Our Family History," September 1, 2015, originally dated March 1, 2011, and mailed to author by Peter Cooney in July 2015.

[2] "Obituaries: Anna M. Cooney," *Asbury Park Press*, December 29, 1996, 15, accessed July 15, 2023, as subscriber of *Newspapers.com*, https://www.newspapers.com/image/147702606/?terms=Anna%20M%20Cooney&match=1.

[3] "Find A Grave," s.v. "John J. Cooney (Died 1939)," accessed July 15, 2023, https://www.findagrave.com/memorial/131116160/john-j-cooney#view-photo=103303059.

[4] Peter Cooney, email message to author, September 4, 2014.

[5] Peter Cooney, email message to author, September 4, 2014; "John J. Cooney," *The Record* (Haverford College Yearbook), 1951, 36, accessed July 15, 2023, as subscriber to *E-Yearbook.com*, https://www.e-yearbook.com/sp/eybb.

[6] Peter Cooney, email message to author, September 4, 2014; "John J. Cooney," Military Record and Report of Separation: Certificate of Service and Honorable Discharge: Army of the United States, both documents mailed to author by Peter Cooney in September 2014.

[7] "John J. Cooney," *The Record*, 36.

[8] Nancy Leo, Speech and Handout, Remembrance Celebration for John J. Cooney at the University Club in New York City on November 29, 2014.

[9] "John J. Cooney," *The Record*, 36.

[10] "Patricia Kennedy Lawford," John F. Kennedy Presidential Library & Museum, *JFKLibrary. org*, accessed July 16, 2023, https://www.jfklibrary.org/learn/about-jfk/the-kennedy-family/patricia-kennedy-lawford; "Rosalind Russell (1907-1976)," Hollywood's Golden Age, *HollywoodsGoldenAge. com*, accessed July 16, 2023, http://www.hollywoodsgoldenage.com/actors/rosalind_russell.html.

[11] John J. Cooney, discussion with author at Long Island State Veterans Home, March 12, 2014.

[12] Eleanor Chworowsky, Mary R. Ives, and Bob Goshorn, "Paoli," History on a Sign Post II, Tredyffrin Easttown Historical Society History Quarterly Digital Archives, *TEHistory.org*, October 1990, Volume 28, Number 4, 155-159, accessed July 16, 2023, https://tehistory.org/hqda/html/v28/v28n4p155.html.

Notes

[13] "John J. Cooney," *The Record*, 36.

[14] Lieutenant Commander Herbert E. Moody, "Award of the Bronze Star Medal for Heroism to Thomas A. Cooney," General Orders No. 353, Department of the Army, Headquarters of the 3rd Brigade, 1st Calvary Division, February 9, 1972, mailed to author by Peter Cooney in September 2014.

[15] "Brevard, News/Events," *Perimeter Report: Vietnam and All Veterans of Brevard, Inc.*, Volume 30, Issue 12, December 2010, mailed to author by Mary Cooney, July 1914.

[16] John J. Cooney, discussion with author at Long Island State Veterans Home, March 12, 2014.

[17] "Brevard, News/Events," *Perimeter Report*.

[18] Mary Cooney, telephone conversation with author, July 3, 2014.

[19] Meyer Osofsky, telephone conversation with author, June 24, 2016.

[20] Peter Cooney, "Our Family History."

[21] John J. Cooney, Shearson/American Express," emailed to author by Mary Cooney, July 7, 1914.

[22] Mary Cooney, telephone conversation with author, July 3, 2014.

[23] Peter Cooney, "Our Family History."

[24] "The High School of Commerce, 1902-1968," WritLargeNYC: New York City's Educational Past from the Ground Up, Columbia's Teachers College for Teaching and Learning, *WritLarge.CTL.Columbia.edu*, accessed July 17, 2023, https://writlarge.ctl.columbia.edu/view/82/.

[25] "Obituaries: Robert Brendan Cooney," *WashingtonPost.com*, accessed July 17, 2023, https://www.washingtonpost.com/archive/local/1999/02/16/obituaries/f65305de-c1f1-4b1d-8e65-2907696b6589/?utm_term=.2f73c4768109; Peter Cooney, "Our Family History."

[26] John J. Cooney, Shearson/American Express," emailed to author by Mary Cooney, July 7, 1914.

[27] Peter Cooney, "Our Family History"; "Phyllis Dalton Cooney," Connecticut, U.S., Divorce Index, 1968-1997, accessed July 17, 2023, as a subscriber to *Ancestry.com*, https://www.ancestry.com/discoveryui-content/view/381274:1706.

[28] Mary P. Cooney, "Eulogy of Elisabeth Githens-Bing (1/7/1932-6/1/2013)," June 14, 2013, copy of eulogy given to author by Mary P. Cooney.

[29] Mary P. Cooney, "Eulogy of Elisabeth Githens-Bing."

[30] Susan Heller Anderson, "University Club Votes To Keep Women Out," *New York Times*, January 20, 1987, B1, accessed July 17, 2023, as subscriber to the *New York Times*, https://www.nytimes.com/1987/01/20/nyregion/university-club-votes-to-keep-women-out.html; E. R. Shipp, "The University Club Votes to Take Women As Members," *New York Times*, June 6, 1987, 31, accessed on July 17, 2023, as a subscriber to the *New York Times*, https://www.nytimes.com/1987/06/06/nyregion/the-university-club-votes-to-take-women-as-members.html.

[31] Nancy Leo, Speech at the University Club.

[32] Nancy Leo, Speech ay the University Club.

[33] "Brevard, News/Events," *Perimeter Report*.

[34] Kristal Hart, "Veterans Day Parade New York City 2015, November 11, 2015, YouTube, 28 minutes (Mary Cooney is featured at 23:04 minutes wearing a dress made out of the silk parachute that saved the life of her father, John J. Cooney, during World War II), accessed July 17, 2023, https://www.youtube.com/watch?app=desktop&v=3zuzzuW-otk; Mary Cooney, email message to author, November 13, 2016.

[35] Mary Cooney, email message to author, November 11, 2016.

Technical Sergeant David Orkin

[1] "David Orkin: Enlisted Record and Report of Separation, Honorable Discharge," emailed to author by Rick Orkin, August 30, 2021.

[2] Meyer Osofsky, telephone conversation with author, June 2, 2017.

[3] "Aileen Bryant Wed to Meyer Osofsky," *Harrisburg Telegraph*, August 3, 1945, 6, accessed July 19, 2023, as subscriber to *Newspapers.com*, https://www.newspapers.com/image/43019336/?match=1.

[4] Meyer Osofsky, telephone conversation with author, December 17, 2016.

[5] Meyer Osofsky, telephone conversation with author, June 2, 2017; Dr. Morris Fishbein, "Your Health: Hepatitis or Jaundice," *The Fresno Bee*, August 12, 1948, accessed July 20, 2023, as subscriber to *Newspapers.com*, https://www.newspapers.com/image/701704536/?terms=Hepititus%20or%20Jaundice&match=1.

[6] "Adrienne Friedman Marriage to David Orkin, Queens, New York City, July 11, 1946," New York, New York, U.S., Marriage License Indexes, 1907-2-18, accessed July 20, 2023, as subscriber to *Ancestry.com*, https://www.ancestry.com/discoveryui-content/view/2074104:61406.

[7] "David Orkin, Honorable Discharge."

[8] "David Orkin: Prisoner of War," U.S., World War II Prisoners of War, 1941-1946, accessed July 20, 2023, as subscriber to *Ancestry.com*, https://www.ancestry.com/discoveryui-content/view/88121:8919?tid=&pid=&queryId=115400e5751fdce63455a43b8fb25981&_phsrc=bgd455&_phstart=successSource.

[9] David Chin, email message to author, May 3, 2020.

[10] David Chin, email message to author, April 30, 2020.

[11] David Chin, email message to author, May 3, 2020.

[12] David Chin, email message to Jamie Nicole Brown (granddaughter of David Orkin) copying author, May 20, 2020.

[13] Rick Orkin, telephone conversation with author, August 26, 2021.

[14] "Building the B-24 Bomber during WWII 'The Story of Willow Run'," Ford Motor Company, *www.PeriscopeFilm.com*, PF #74182 00:07:12:00, accessed March 17, 2024, https://www.youtube.com/watch?v=p2zukteYbGQ&t=18s.

Notes

[15] "Rick Orkin," Westbury High School, Class of 1970, U.S., School Yearbooks, 1900-2016, accessed July 20, 2023, as subscriber to *Ancestry.*com, https://www.ancestry.com/discoveryui-content/view/580090554:1265?tid=&pid=&queryId=2d62ceea333cdf07b9950f57cf606213&_phsrc=bgd458&_phstart=successSource.

[16] Maggie Sieger, "Quiet Campaign for this Council," *Daily News* (Galveston, TX), April 27, 1994, 7, accessed July 20, 2023, as subscriber to *Newspapers.com*, https://www.newspapers.com/image/36375993/?match=1.

[17] "Adrienne P. Orkin: Death Date: September 21, 1995," U.S., Social Security Death Index, 1935-2014, accessed July 20, 2023, as subscriber to *Ancestry.com*, https://www.ancestry.com/discoveryui-content/view/46536493:3693.

[18] "Cora Bransford Marriage to David Orkin. Fort Bend, Texas, April 15, 1996," Texas, U.S., Marriage Index, 1824-2019, accessed July 20, 2023, as subscriber to *Ancestry.com*, https://www.ancestry.com/discoveryui-content/view/2805910:8795.

[19] "Local Man Retires from San Marcos Volunteer Patrol," *North Country Times* (Oceanside, CA), September 14, 2001, 22, accessed July 21, 2023, as subscriber to *Newspapers.com*, https://www.newspapers.com/image/577909141/?match=1.

[20] Rick Orkin, telephone conversation with author, August 26, 2021.

Technical Sergeant Meyer "Mike" Osofsky

[1] Meyer Osofsky, telephone conversation with author, August 20, 2014.

[2] "Declaration of Intention and Petition for Naturalization," s.v. "Harry Osofsky," New York, U.S., State and Federal Naturalization Records, 1794-1943, June 7, 1920, accessed July 23, 2023, as subscriber to *Ancestry.com*, https://www.ancestry.com/discoveryui-content/view/3367720:2280?tid=&pid=&queryId=8d5f96736723be68b48ff02ae4f845bd&_phsrc=bgd479&_phstart=successSource.

[3] Helen Hennessy, "A Sportsman's Approach to Knits," *The Central Jersey News* (New Brunswick, NJ), March 28, 1966, 8, accessed July 23, 2023, as subscriber to *Newspapers.com*, https://www.newspapers.com/image/315895351/?terms=Aileen&match=1.

[4] "Find A Grave," s.v. "Harry Bryant (1900-1954)," accessed July 25, 2023, as subscriber to *Ancestry.com*, https://www.findagrave.com/memorial/153069165/harry-bryant; "Veteran's Compensation Application 210819, Commonwealth of Pennsylvania," s.v. "John Kravesky," applied February 10, 1934, accessed September 23, 2022, as subscriber to *Ancestry.com*, https://www.ancestry.com/discoveryui-content/view/1157406:60884?tid=&pid=&queryId=0c46a76b48fd7d6618fa288912bdb4bd&_phsrc=zsS275&_phstart=successSource.

[5] Meyer Osofsky, telephone conversation with author, June 24, 2016.

[6] John W. Lanza, *Shot Down Over Italy: A true story of courage and survival in Nazi-occupied Italy during World War II* (Caldwell, NJ: Bright Spot Books, 2010), 37-38.

[7] "John J. Cooney," Military Record and Report of Separation: Certificate of Service and Honorable Discharge: Army of the United States, both documents mailed to author by Peter Cooney in September 2014.

[8] "Aileen Bryant Wed to Meyer Osofsky," *Harrisburg Telegraph*, August 3, 1945, 6, accessed July 19, 2023, as subscriber to *Newspapers.com*, https://www.newspapers.com/image/43019336/?match=1.

[9] "Plane Crashes into Empire State Building," *History.com*, July 28, 1945, accessed July 22, 2023, https://www.history.com/this-day-in-history/plane-crashes-into-empire-state-building#:~:text=A%20United%20States%20military%20plane,Airport%20in%20New%20York%20City; Lanza, *Shot Down Over Italy*, 221.

[10] "New York, U.S. State Census, 1915," New York, Kings County, New York, s.v. "Harry Osofsky," accessed July 23, 2023, as subscriber of *Ancestry.com*, https://www.ancestry.com/discoveryui-content/view/5673476:2703.

[11] "U.S. World War I Draft Registration Cards, 1917-1918," s.v. "Harry Osofsky," accessed on August 4, 2022, as subscriber to *Ancestry.com*, https://www.ancestry.com/discoveryui-content/view/16108370:6482?tid=&pid=&queryId=015756fee5978828b855ced5b271d6bf&_phsrc=zsS285&_phstart=successSource.

[12] "1940 United States Federal Census," Brooklyn, Kings County, New York City, New York, s.v. "Harry Osofsky," accessed October 9, 2022, as subscriber to *Ancestry.com*, https://www.ancestry.com/discoveryui-content/view/14296579:2442?tid=&pid=&queryId=7ae8359cfde1d3b2a4c01 21ff02732fd&_phsrc=zsS313&_phstart=successSource; U.S., World War II Draft Cards Young Men, 1940-1947, s.v. "Harry Osofsky," accessed as subscriber to *Ancestry.com* on July 23, 2023, https://www.ancestry.com/discoveryui-content/view/1324079:1002?tid=&pid=&queryId=bc6fea8 75d7aa60e9defc2d2d2059706&_phsrc=mRc172&_phstart=successSource.

[13] Meyer Osofsky, telephone conversation with author, December 19, 2016.

[14] Meyer Osofsky, telephone conversation with author, August 26, 2016.

[15] Meyer Osofsky, telephone conversation with author, December 17, 2016.

[16] Hennessy, "A Sportsman's Approach to Knits.".

[17] Meyer Osofsky, telephone conversation with author, March 23, 2017.

[18] Betty Parker Ashton, "Aileen, Inc., Shows Significant Growth," *Richmond Times-Dispatch* (Richmond, VA), May 26, 1963, 117, accessed July 23, 2023, as subscriber to *Newspapers.com*, https://www.newspapers.com/image/829079109/?terms=Aileen&match=1.

[19] "Abe Oberlin," *MailTribune.com*, February 7, 2012, accessed October 5, 2022, https://www.mailtribune.com/obituaries/2012/02/07/abe-oberlin/.

[20] Hennessy, "A Sportsman's Approach to Knits."

[21] Meyer Osofsky, telephone conversation with author, June 24, 2016.

[22] Meyer Osofsky, telephone conversation with author, June 2, 2017.

[23] Meyer Osofsky, telephone conversation with author, March 7, 2017; "Calvin Chin, Restaurateur," *Newsday* (Nassau Edition), November 30, 1987, 31, accessed June 30, 2023, as subscriber to *Newspapers.com*, https://www.newspapers.com/image/710751058/?match=1.

[24] Ashton, "Aileen, Inc."

Notes

[25] Meyer Osofsky, telephone conversation with author, March 23, 2017.

[26] Ashton, "Aileen, Inc."

[27] Hennessy, "A Sportsman's Approach to Knits."

[28] Ashton, "Aileen, Inc."

[29] Meyer Osofsky, telephone conversation with author, January 1, 1917.

[30] Michael L. Grace, "The Pump Room at Chicago's Former Ambassador East Hotel," *CruiseLineHistory.com*, accessed July 26, 2023, https://www.cruiselinehistory.com/the-pump-room-at-chicagos-former-ambassador-east-hotel/.

[31] Merle Willson, "Competency Cited by Aileen Chief, *The Abilene Reporter-News*, May 28, 1969, accessed July 25, 2023, as subscriber to *Newspaper.com*, https://www.newspapers.com/image/762447937/?match=1.

[32] Eric Hertz, "Aileen Ups Sales by Moving 'Upstairs'," *The Abilene Reporter-News* (Abilene, TX), March 18, 1976, 8-A, accessed July 26, 2023, as subscriber to *Newspapers.com*, https://www.newspapers.com/image/762553265/?terms=Aileen&match=1.

[33] Preston Lewis, "Aileen's Keeps Growing; 350 Work at Plant Now," *The Abilene Reporter-News* (Abilene, TX), August 18, 1970, 13, accessed July 26, 2023, as subscriber to *Newspapers.com*, https://www.newspapers.com/image/762502025/?match=1.

[34] "Company Earnings: Aileen Inc. (Listed on New York Stock Exchange)," *TimeMachine. NYTimes.com*, June 10, 1987, D23, accessed July 25, 2023, as subscriber to the *New York Times*, https://timesmachine.nytimes.com/timesmachine/1987/06/10/issue.html.

[35] Brent Manley and Paul Linxwller, editors, "Aileen Osofsky Stands Tall as Goodwill Committee Chair," *Daily Bulletin* (Pittsburgh, PA), Volume 48, Number 4, March 14, 2005, 2, *ACBL.org* (American Contract Bridge League), accessed July 26, 2023, http://web2.acbl.org/nabcbulletins/2005spring/db4.pdf.

[36] "Meyer Osofsky Obituary (1924-2019)," *Legacy.com* (published in the *New York Times* on November 2, 2019), accessed July 26, 2023, https://www.legacy.com/obituaries/nytimes/obituary.aspx?pid=194329673.

[37] Linda Helser, "Pair Honored for Community Work," *Arizona Republic* (Phoenix, AZ), January 13, 2007, 308, accessed July 26, 2023, as subscriber to *Newspapers.com*, https://www.newspapers.com/image/125908130/?terms=Pair%20Honored&match=1.

[38] Manley and Linxwiler, "Aileen Osofsky Stands Tall."

[39] "Goodwill Reception Honoring Aileen Osofsky (Goodwill Day, August 11, 2010)," *Desert Empire Regional Daily Bulletin*, Phoenix, August 9-15, 2010, accessed July 27, 2023, https://silo.tips/download/d17-goodwill-day-today-we-honor-aileen-osofsky-of-top-10-goodwill-gestures-from.

[40] Ken Barbour, "Reflections and Memories of Aileen," Contract Bridge *Forum*, September 2010, 11, author has a copy.

[41] Meyer Osofsky, telephone conversation with author, February 7, 2017; "Aileen Osofsky Obituary," *New York Times*, June 26, 2010, *Archive.NYTimes.com*, accessed October 5, 2022, as

subscriber to the *New York Times*, https://archive.nytimes.com/query.nytimes.com/gst/fullpage-9D0CE5DD123AF935A15755C0A9669D8B63.html.

[42] Tamás Székely, "On This Day—In 1991 Soviet Troops Finally Left Hungary After Four Decades of Occupation," *HungaryToday.hu*, June 19, 2016, accessed July 27, 2023, https://hungarytoday.hu/day-1991-soviet-troops-finally-left-hungary-four-decades-occupation-video-59830/.

[43] Gergely Flier, "Thirty years ago, the Soviet army withdrew from Hungary – What happened to the former barracks in Budapest?" July 9. 2021, *PestBuda.hu*, accessed July 27, 2023, https://pestbuda.hu/en/cikk/20210709_thirty_years_ago_the_soviet_army_withdrew_from_hungary_what_happened_to_the_former_barracks_in_budapest.

[44] Meyer Osofsky, telephone conversation with author, February 7, 2017.

[45] Irving, Stuart, Anne, and Lori Russo, "Memories and Condolences for Meyer Osofsky," Meyer Osofsky Obituary (Published in *New York Times* on November 2, 2019), *Legacy.com*, accessed July 28, 2023, https://www.legacy.com/us/obituaries/nytimes/name/meyer-osofsky-obituary?id=14818709.

[46] Alan Osofsky, email message to author, October 2, 2020.

[47] George E. Butler, *The World Book Encyclopedia* (Chicago, IL: Field Enterprises Educational Corporation, 1968), s.v. "Horatio Alger," Volume 1, A, 343.

[48] Alan Osofsky, email message to author, November 11, 2020.

[49] Ryder Kessler, "Tribute to Meyer Osofsky," 451st Bomb Group Newsletter, No. 16, May 2020, 451st Bombardment Group (H), *451st.org*, accessed July 27, 2023, https://451st.org/Newsletters/PDFs/451st%20Bomb%20Group%20Newsletter%20No.%2016%20-%20May%202020.pdf.

[50] "Meyer 'Mike' Osofsky Obituary," Shelter Island Reporter, November 8, 2019, accessed July 28, 2023, https://obituaries709.rssing.com/chan-29872832/latest.php.

Epilogue

[1] Henry Kissinger, Conversation with J. Stapleton Roy, "'The Key Problem of Our Time': A Conversation with Henry Kissinger on Sino-U.S. Relations," Woodrow Wilson Center, September 20, 2018, *WilsonCenter.org*, accessed April 22, 2023, https://www.wilsoncenter.org/article/the-key-problem-our-time-conversation-henry-kissinger-sino-us-relations.

[2] Ray Monk, *Robert Oppenheimer: A Life Inside the Center* (New York: Anchor Books, 2014), 270 and 315-318.

[3] Melissa Chan, "What Is the Difference Between a Hydrogen Bomb and an Atomic Bomb," *Time.com*, September 22, 2017, accessed September 19, 2023, https://time.com/4954082/hydrogen-bomb-atomic-bomb/.

[4] "Niels Bohr Biographical," *NobelPrize.org*, Nobel Prize Outreach AB 2023, accessed September 21, 2023, https://www.nobelprize.org/prizes/physics/1922/bohr/biographical/.

Notes

[5] Monk, *Robert Oppenheimer*, 413-414.

[6] "FDR and the Four Freedoms Speech," Franklin D. Roosevelt Presidential Library and Museum, *FDRLibrary.org*, accessed February 11, 2022, https://www.fdr library.org/four-freedoms.

[7] Monk, *Robert Oppenheimer*, 565.

[8] Monk, *Robert Oppenheimer*, 592.

[9] William L. Shirer, *The Rise and Fall of the Third Reich: A History of Nazi Germany* (New York: Simon and Schuster, 1960), xii.

[10] Monk, *Robert Oppenheimer*, 362

[11] Union of Concerned Scientists, "Nuclear Weapons Worldwide: Nuclear weapons are still here—and they're still an existential risk," *UCSUSA.org*, accessed July 28, 2023, https://www.ucsusa.org/nuclear-weapons/worldwide?utm_source=googlegrants&utm_medium=search&utm_campaign=GSP&gclid=EAIaIQobChMI4rzv7IXt-AIVOvfjBx3-BQMYEAAYASAAEgIn_vD_BwE.

[12] Daryl G. Kimball, "'Oppenheimer,' the Bomb and Arms Control, Then and Now," Bulletin of the Atomic Scientists, *TheBulletin.org*, July 29, 2023, accessed August 14, 2023, https://thebulletin.org/2023/07/oppenheimer-the-bomb-and-arms-control-then-and-now/#post-heading.

[13] James MacGregor Burns, *Roosevelt: The Soldier of Freedom: 1940-1945* (New York: Francis Parkman Prize Edition, History Book Club, 2006), 597.

[14] "Albert Einstein, Institute of Advanced Study, March 14, 1879 - April 18, 1955," National Academy of Sciences, *NASonline.org*, accessed August 25, 2023, https://www.nasonline.org/member-directory/deceased-members/20001817.html; M. Alex Johnson, The Culture of Einstein, April 12, 2005, *NBCNews.com*, accessed August 25, 2023, https://www.nbcnews.com/id/wbna7406337.

[15] George Soros, "Vladimir Putin and the Risk of World War III," *Project-Syndicate.org*, March 11, 2022, accessed August 14, 2023, https://www.project-syndicate.org/commentary/putin-ukraine-world-war-3-risk-by-george-soros-2022-03.

Acknowledgements

[1] "About Us—USAF History and Museums Program," *AFHistoryandMuseums.AF.mil*, https://www.afhistoryandmuseums.af.mil, accessed October 25, 2023.

[2] "About Us," *AFHistoryandMuseums.AF.mil*.

[3] "About Us," *AFHistoryandMuseums.AF.mil*.

[4] "The National Personnel Records Center – A History," National Archives, *Archives.gov*, https://www.archives.gov/personnel-records-center/history, accessed October 25, 2023.

[5] "George E. Tudor," Obituary, April 30, 2010, *LCNme.com*, https://lcnme.com/obituaries/george-e-tudor/, accessed October 25, 2023.

Index

Page numbers in **bold** refer to exhibits (articles, charts, illustrations, important points, maps, and tables.)

Index

Index

Index

Index

Index

Index

Index

Index

Index

485

www.ingramcontent.com/pod-product-compliance
Lightning Source LLC
Chambersburg PA
CBHW030532100426

42813CB00001B/230